Game Theory and
Mechanism Design

IISc Lecture Notes Series

ISSN: 2010-2402

Published:

IISc Lecture Notes Series

Game Theory and Mechanism Design

Y Narahari

Indian Institute of Science, India

IISc
Press

World Scientific

NEW JERSEY · LONDON · SINGAPORE · BEIJING · SHANGHAI · HONG KONG · TAIPEI · CHENNAI

Published by

World Scientific Publishing Co. Pte. Ltd.

5 Toh Tuck Link, Singapore 596224

USA office: 27 Warren Street, Suite 401-402, Hackensack, NJ 07601

UK office: 57 Shelton Street, Covent Garden, London WC2H 9HE

British Library Cataloguing-in-Publication Data
A catalogue record for this book is available from the British Library.

IISc Lecture Notes Series — Vol. 4
GAME THEORY AND MECHANISM DESIGN

Copyright © 2014 by World Scientific Publishing Co. Pte. Ltd.

ISBN 978-981-4525-04-6

Printed in Singapore

Series Preface

World Scientific Publishing Company - Indian Institute of Science Collaboration

IISc Press and WSPC are co-publishing books authored by world renowned scientists and engineers. This collaboration, started in 2008 during IISc's centenary year under a Memorandum of Understanding between IISc and WSPC, has resulted in the establishment of three Series: IISc Centenary Lectures Series (ICLS), IISc Research Monographs Series (IRMS), and IISc Lecture Notes Series (ILNS).

This pioneering collaboration will contribute significantly in disseminating current Indian scientific advancement worldwide.

The **"IISc Centenary Lectures Series"** will comprise lectures by designated Centenary Lecturers - eminent teachers and researchers from all over the world.

The **"IISc Research Monographs Series"** will comprise state-of-the-art monographs written by experts in specific areas. They will include, but not limited to, the authors' own research work.

The **"IISc Lecture Notes Series"** will consist of books that are reasonably self-contained and can be used either as textbooks or for self-study at the postgraduate level in science and engineering. The books will be based on material that has been class-tested for most part.

Dedication

To My Beloved Parents
for giving me this wonderful life,
for teaching me the fundamentals of the game of life,
and for continuously inspiring me in this life
through their exemplary mechanisms,

and

To the 2007 Economic Sciences Nobel Laureates
Leonid Hurwicz, Eric S. Maskin, and Roger B. Myerson
for creating the wonderful edifice of mechanism design
using game theory building blocks.

Foreword

Game theory and mechanism design have come a long way. Thirty-five years ago, they were fringe subjects, taught – if at all – in specialty courses. Today they are at the center of economic theory and have become an important part of engineering disciplines such as computer science and electronic commerce.

I am very pleased that Y. Narahari has written this lovely text, which presents the fundamentals of game theory and mechanism design clearly and concisely. In doing so, Dr. Narahari has performed a great service to students and researchers interested in the lively interface between engineering sciences and economics.

Eric Maskin

Nobel Laureate in Economic Sciences - 2007

Adams University Professor

Department of Economics

Faculty of Arts and Sciences

Harvard University

Cambridge, MA, USA

16 July 2013

Opinions on the Book

The theory of *Games and Mechanism Design* find today wide applications in Economics, Engineering, and Operations Research. This is one of the few books which present a detailed account of both Non-Cooperative and Cooperative Games as well as Mechanism Design, all under one cover. Proofs of important theorems are given in a clear and succinct manner and the bibliographical and biographical references are particularly valuable. The book can serve both as a graduate text as well as a reference volume. I highly recommend it.

   – **Sanjoy K. Mitter**, Massachusetts Institute of Technology, Cambridge, MA, USA

This is a splendid book for engineers by an engineer. It has the ideal choice of topics and emphasis that reflects the driving themes in game theory, such as mechanism design, that have lead the revival of game theory in recent times and its multifarious applications in cybercommerce and allied areas. The lucidly written byte-sized chapters rich with examples and historical details make it an exciting read. This is the *right book at the right time*.

   – **Vivek Borkar**, Indian Institute of Technology-Bombay, Mumbai, India

This book covers a subject which now straddles at least three subjects – Economics, Mathematics and Computer Science. It is a comprehensive presentation for a wide range of readers from the novice to experts in related areas who want to inform themselves of Game Theory and Mechanism Design. The book has a very readable from-first-principles approach to topics which commendably illuminates while not sacrificing rigor.

   – **Ravi Kannan**, Microsoft Research and Indian Institute of Science, Bangalore, India

Narahari's book is a beautifully written text that handles both introductory material and advanced topics well.

> – **Preston McAfee**, Google, Mountain View, CA, USA

This marvelous book on *Game Theory and Mechanism Design* is an essential reference for beginners and practitioners alike. The book covers the basic concepts needed to understand game theory and powerful practical implications of the theory embodied in mechanism design. Narahari excels at elucidating the essentials of game theory, while motivating the reader with a number of illustrative examples and real-world applications from engineering, economics and networks. It is fun to read and should be on the shelf of any student or practitioner interested in the practical applications of game theory.

> – **Krishna Pattipati**, University of Connecticut, Storrs, CT, USA

Game Theory is the formal analysis of strategic behavior. It originated with the classic book of von Neumann and Morgenstern in the 1940's and over the last 70 years, has become a vital ingredient in both the social and engineering sciences. Professor Narahari is a leading expert in the burgeoning area of game theoretic applications to computer science. His lucid and elegant book, packed with examples and historical background, is a wonderful introduction to modern Game Theory. It clearly lays out the central concepts and results of the theory while conveying its potential for providing insights to a range of interesting practical problems. The book will be invaluable to students from diverse backgrounds such as economics, mathematics, and engineering.

> – **Arunava Sen**, Indian Statistical Institute, New Delhi, India

Game Theory and Mechanism Design is impressive in its broad coverage of cooperative games, non-cooperative games and mechanism design from an engineering perspective. The book is rich in examples and exercises, and couples historical appraisals of the evolution of the field with careful mathematical proofs. It should be valuable both as a graduate text and for reference.

> – **Chris Dance**, Xerox Research Centre Europe, Grenoble, France

About the Author

Professor Y. Narahari is currently teaching at the Department of Computer Science and Automation, Indian Institute of Science, Bangalore, India. The focus of his research in the last decade has been to explore problems at the interface of computer science and microeconomics. In particular, he is interested in applications of game theory and mechanism design to design of auctions and electronic markets, multiagent systems, and social network research. He has coauthored a large number of influential research papers in these and other areas. Many of his doctoral and master's students have bagged best thesis prizes for their dissertations.

He is the lead author of a research monograph *Game Theoretic Problems in Network Economics and Mechanism Design Solutions* published by Springer, London, in 2009. He coauthored an acclaimed book earlier, *Performance Modeling of Automated Manufacturing Systems* (Prentice Hall, USA, 1992). He has also created a web-based teaching resource on *Data Structures and Algorithms*.

His work has been recognized through many fellowships and awards. He is an elected Fellow of the following Institutions and Academies: IEEE, New York; Indian National Science Academy; Indian Academy of Sciences; Indian National Academy of Engineering; and the National Academy of Sciences. He has been a Senior Editor of the IEEE Transactions on Automation Science and Engineering and an Associate Editor of several reputed journals. He is currently a J.C. Bose National Fellow, a recognition awarded to distinguished scientists by the Department of Science and Technology, Government of India. In 2010, he received the Institute Award for Research Excellence in Engineering at the Indian Institute of Science.

During the past 15 years, he has been an active scientific collaborator with a host of global R & D companies and research labs including General Motors R & D, IBM Research, Infosys Technologies, Intel, and Xerox Research.

The current book represents a culmination of his teaching and research efforts in game theory and mechanism design during the past decade.

Preface

The project of writing this book was conceived and conceptualized in December 2008 during the *Centenary Conference* of the *Indian Institute of Science*, my Alma mater that has shaped my career, and life as well, for the past three and half decades. On December 16, 2008, Professor Eric Maskin who had received the 2007 Sveriges Riksbank prize (aka Nobel Prize in Economic Sciences) (jointly with Professors Leonid Hurwicz and Roger Myerson) gave a lively, lucid, enthralling, and inspirational talk entitled *Mechanism Design: How to Implement Social Goals* to an audience comprising more than 1500 scientists, engineers, and graduate students. Soon after this talk, it occurred to me that a book on game theory emphasizing not only non-cooperative games and cooperative games but also mechanism design would be valuable for engineering audience (in general) and computer science audience (in particular). I had been teaching a game theory and mechanism design course to our master's and doctoral students in computer science since 2004. This coupled with the brief but breathtakingly stimulating interaction with Professor Maskin sowed the seeds for undertaking this ambitious project of writing the book. It is therefore befitting that the book is dedicated to Professor Eric Maskin and his co-laureates Professors Leonid Hurwicz and Roger Myerson. This triumvirate, through their path-breaking work on mechanism design, have opened up this discipline to numerous powerful applications cutting across boundaries of disciplines.

Studying the rational behavior of entities interacting with each other in the context of a variety of contemporary applications such as Internet advertising, electronic marketplaces, social network monetization, crowdsourcing, and even carbon footprint optimization, has been the bread and butter of our research group here at the Game Theory Lab at the Department of Computer Science and Automation, Indian Institute of Science. Specifically, the application of game theoretic modeling and mechanism design principles to the area of Internet and network economics has been an area of special interest to the group for a decade now.

More than eight decades ago, the legendary John von Neumann played a significant role in the creation of two different exciting disciplines: *Game Theory* and *Computer Science*. Astonishingly, in the past fifteen years (1998-2013), There has been a spectacular convergence of the above two intellectual currents. The applications of game theory and mechanism design to problem solving in engineering and computer science applications have exploded in these fifteen years. This phenomenon certainly spurred us to dive into this area in the last decade.

Further, during this period, there were other developments that made sure we got locked into this area. Intel India, Bangalore, funded a collaborative project in 2000 that required the development of a multi-attribute combinatorial procurement auction for their indirect materials procurement. General Motors R & D, Warren, Michigan, next collaborated with our group to develop procurement auction mechanisms during 2002-2007. Meanwhile, Infosys Technologies, Bangalore, collaborated with us in 2006-07 on applying game theory and mechanism design to an interesting web services composition problem. The current collaboration with the Infosys team is focused on using game theory and mechanism design techniques to carbon footprint optimization. IBM India and IBM India Research Labs provided us with funding and a faculty award to make further explorations into this area. All this work culminated in a 2009 research monograph entitled *Game Theoretic Problems in Network Economics and Mechanism Design Solutions* (co-authored with my graduate students Dinesh Garg, Ramasuri Narayanam, and Hastagiri Prakash) and a string of research papers. We are also currently engaged with Xerox Research on fusing mechanism design with machine learning to extract superior performance from service markets. These projects have helped us to investigate deep practical problems, providing a perfect complement to our theoretical work in the area.

We have also been fortunate to be working in this area during an eventful period when game theorists and mechanism designers have been awarded the Nobel Prize in Economic Sciences. We were excited when Professors Robert Aumann and Thomas Schelling were awarded the Prize 2005. In fact, we had an illuminating visit by Robert Aumann in January 2007 to the Indian Institute of Science. We were delighted when, just two years later, Professors Leonid Hurwicz, Eric Maskin, and Roger Myerson were awarded the Prize in 2007 for their fundamental contributions to mechanism design theory. Finally, our excitement knew no bounds in October 2012 when Professors Lloyd Shapley and Professor Al Roth were announced as the winners of the prize for 2012.

Objectives of the Book

Set in the above backdrop, this book strives to distill the key results in game theory and mechanism design and present them in a way that can be appreciated by students at senior undergraduate engineering level and above. The book includes a number of illustrative examples, carefully chosen from different domains including computer science, networks, engineering, and microeconomics; however they are fairly generic.

There are numerous excellent textbooks and monographs available on game theory. This book has drawn inspiration from the following reference texts: Mas-Colell,

Whinston, and Green [1]; Myerson [2]; Nisan, Roughgarden, Tardos, and Vazirani [3]; Shoham and Leyton Brown [4]; Straffin [5]; Osborne [6]; and the very recent book by Maschler, Solan, and Zamir [7]. The dominating theme in many of the above texts is social sciences, particularly microeconomics. Our book is different in two ways. First, it has the primary objective of presenting the essentials of game theory and mechanism design to an engineering audience. Since I happen to be from a computer science department, there is also an inevitable emphasis on computer science based applications. Second, the book has a detailed coverage of mechanism design unlike most books on game theory. A precursor to this current book is an earlier monograph by Narahari, Garg, Narayanam, and Prakash [8].

Outline and Organization of the Book

The book is structured into three parts: *Non-cooperative game theory* (Chapters 2 to 13); *Mechanism design* (Chapters 14 to 24); and *Cooperative game theory* (Chapters 25 to 31). Chapter 1 is an introduction to the book and Chapter 32 is an epilogue while Chapter 33 attempts to provide a succinct discussion of mathematical preliminaries required for understanding the contents of the book.

Each chapter commences with a motivation and central purpose of the chapter, and concludes with a crisp summary of key concepts and results in the chapter and a set of references to probe further. At the end of each chapter, a set of exercise problems is also included. In relevant chapters, programming assignments are also suggested. The book has a table of acronyms and notations at the beginning of the book. The book further contains, at relevant places, informative biographical sketches of legendary researchers in game theory and mechanism design. We now present a chapter-by-chapter outline of the book.

Chapter Reading Sequence

The picture appearing overleaf depicts the sequential dependency among the main chapters of the book. The rectangles corresponding to Part 1, Part 2, and Part 3 are shaded differently in the picture. The diagram is self-explanatory. Since Chapter 32 (Epilogue) and Chapter 33 (Mathematical Preliminaries) have a special purpose, they are not depicted in the diagram.

Part 1: Non-cooperative Game Theory

We first introduce, in Chapter 2, key notions in game theory such as *preferences*, *utilities*, *rationality*, *intelligence*, and *common knowledge*. We then study two representations for non-cooperative games: *extensive form representation* (Chapter 3) and *strategic form representation* (Chapter 4).

In Chapters 5, 6, and 7, we describe different solution concepts which are fundamental to the analysis of strategic form games: dominant strategies and *dominant*

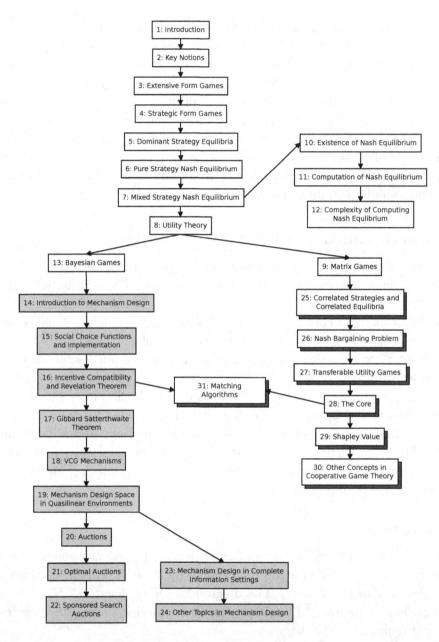

Reading sequence of chapters in the book

strategy equilibria (Chapter 5); *pure strategy Nash equilibrium* (Chapter 6); and *mixed strategy Nash equilibrium* (Chapter 7). In Chapter 8, we introduce the *utility theory* of von Neumann and Morgenstern which forms the foundation for game theory.

Chapters 9, 10, 11, and 12 are devoted to studies on existence and computation of Nash equilibria. In Chapter 9, we focus on two player zero-sum games. In

Chapter 10, we provide a detailed treatment of the Nash theorem that establishes the existence of a mixed strategy Nash equilibrium in finite strategic form games. Chapter 11 is concerned with algorithmic computation of Nash equilibria while Chapter 12 deals with computational complexity of finding Nash equilibria.

In Chapter 13, we introduce *Bayesian games* which are games with *incomplete information*. These games play a central role in mechanism design which is the subject of Part 2 of the book.

Part 2: Mechanism Design

Mechanism design is the art of designing games so that they exhibit desirable equilibrium behavior. In this part (Chapters 14-24), we study fundamental principles and key issues in mechanism design.

In Chapter 14, we introduce mechanisms with simple, illustrative examples and discuss the key notions of *social choice functions*, *direct mechanisms*, and *indirect mechanisms*. In Chapter 15, we bring out the principles underlying implementation of social choice functions by mechanisms. In Chapter 16, we define the important notion of incentive compatibility and bring out the difference between dominant strategy incentive compatibility (DSIC) and Bayesian incentive compatibility (BIC). We prove the *revelation theorem*, an important fundamental result. Chapter 17 is devoted to two key impossibility results: the Gibbard-Satterwaite theorem and the Arrow theorem.

Chapters 18-22 are devoted to different classes of quasilinear mechanisms which are either DSIC or BIC. In Chapter 18, we study VCG (Vickrey-Clarke-Groves) mechanisms, by far the most extensively investigated class of mechanisms. Chapter 19 is devoted to an exploration of mechanism design space in quasilinear environment, including Bayesian mechanisms. In Chapter 20, we discuss auctions which are a popular example of mechanisms. In Chapter 21, we study optimal mechanisms, in particular the Myerson auction. In Chapter 22, we study the sponsored search auction problem in detail to illustrate a compelling application of mechanism design.

In Chapter 23, we discuss *implementation in Nash equilibrium* which assumes a complete information setting. Finally, Chapter 24 provides a brief description of important advanced topics in mechanism design.

Part 3: Cooperative Game Theory

We commence our study of cooperative game theory in Chapter 25 with a discussion on *correlated strategies* and *correlated equilibrium*. The *Nash bargaining problem* represents one of the earliest and most influential results in cooperative game theory. Chapter 26 describes the problem and proves the Nash bargaining result. We introduce in Chapter 27, *multiplayer coalitional games* or *characteristic form games*. In particular, we introduce *transferable utility games* (TU games) with several illustrative examples.

Chapters 28-30 are devoted to solution concepts in cooperative game theory. In Chapter 28, we study *the core*, a central notion in cooperative game theory. The *Shapley value* is a popular solution concept that provides a unique allocation to a set of players in a cooperative game. In Chapter 29, we present the Shapley axioms and prove the existence and uniqueness of the Shapley value. In Chapter 30, we briefly study five other important solution concepts in cooperative game theory: *Stable sets*, *Bargaining sets*, *Kernel*, *Nucleolus*, and *Gately point*. Chapter 31 is devoted to the interesting topic of matching algorithms.

We conclude the book in Chapter 32 with some thoughts on how best to utilize the insights from the book. We have included, in Chapter 33, an appendix that contains key notions and results from probability theory, linear algebra, linear programming, mathematical analysis, and computational complexity, which are used in a crucial way at various points in this textbook.

Intended Audience

The primary audience for the book include: senior undergraduate, first year master's, and first year research students studying computer science, networks, communications, electrical engineering, industrial engineering and operations research, microeconomics, and management science. Researchers and industry professionals who wish to explore game theory and mechanism design in Internet and network economics applications will find the book useful. After a thorough reading of this book, we expect that readers would be able to apply game theory and mechanism design in a principled and mature way to solve relevant problems. It is our sincere hope that the book will whet the appetite of the intended audience and arouse curiosity in this exciting subject. To provide an idea of how different types of audience could potentially benefit from this book, here are several examples:

- Computer science students will be able to make forays into topical areas such as algorithmic game theory, algorithmic mechanism design, computational social choice, auctions and market design, electronic commerce, Internet monetization, social network research, and mechanism design for multiagent systems.
- Computer science, electronics, and electrical engineering students would be able to explore research areas like network protocol design, dynamic resource allocation in networked systems, design of multiagent smart grid networks, and network science.
- Industrial engineering or management science students would be in a position to undertake research in supply chain network design, logistics engineering, dynamic pricing in e-business, etc.
- Researchers on inter-disciplinary topics such as cyberphysical systems, intelligent transportation, service science, green supply chains, and human

computation systems (such as crowdsourcing networks) would be able to formulate and solve topical problems using the tools covered in this book.

Possible Course Offerings

I have taught for several years a course on game theory to master's and doctoral students at the Indian Institute of Science, Bangalore. About 80 percent of the students have been from a computer science background with the rest of the students drawn from communications, electrical engineering, and management. In fact the book can be considered as a culmination of my lovely experience with this course spread over a number of years. The lecture notes of the course have survived the scrutiny of the talented students and in fact many of the students have contributed to this book by providing critical comments and suggestions. The course taught by me typically covers about 60 percent each of the contents in Part 1 (Non-cooperative game theory); Part 2 (Mechanism design); and Part 3 (Cooperative game theory).

With a judicious selection of topics, it is possible to design several courses based on this book. We provide three possibilities below.

Undergraduate Level Course on Game Theory

To an audience consisting of third year or fourth year undergraduate students, the following collection of topics would make an interesting course.

- *Non-cooperative game theory*: Chapter 1, Chapter 2, Chapter 3, Chapter 4, Chapter 5, Chapter 6, Chapter 7, Chapter 9.
- *Cooperative game theory*: Parts of Chapter 25, Chapter 26, Chapter 27, Chapter 28, Chapter 29, Chapter 31.
- *Mechanism design* (optional): Parts of Chapter 13, Chapter 14, Chapter 15, Chapter 16, Chapter 20

Master's Level Course on Game Theory

To an audience consisting of final year undergraduate students, master's students, and first year graduate students, the entire book would be relevant. To cover the entire book as a one semester course would be challenging, so a judicious choice of topics will be the key.

Graduate Level Course on Game Theory

About 40 percent material of a graduate level course could be covered from this book. If the students have already gone through an undergraduate level course on game theory (as explained above), then the remaining chapters of this book (especially Chapter 10, Chapter 11, Chapter 12, Chapter 13, all chapters in mechanism design (Chapters 14-24), and all chapters in cooperative game theory (Chapters 25-31) would provide the initial content. Appropriate material from advanced books and from the current literature should complement and complete such a course offering.

Convention in Usage of Certain Common Words and Phrases

We wish to draw the attention of the readers regarding use of certain words and phrases. We use the words *players* and *agents* interchangeably throughout the text. The words *bidders*, *buyers*, and *sellers* are often used to refer to players in an auction or a market. The words *he* and *his* are used symbolically to refer to both the genders. This is not to be mistaken as gender bias. Occasionally we have also used the words *she* and *her*. We have also sporadically used the words *it* and *its* while referring to players or agents.

Supplementary Resources

The URL http://lcm.csa.iisc.ernet.in/hari/book.html will take the interested readers to supplementary material which would be continuously updated. The material includes additional references, additional problems, solutions to selected exercises, and viewgraphs for selected chapters.

Feedback is Welcome!

No book is flawless. We invite you to report any flaws and provide your valuable comments and suggestions by sending email to me at hari@csa.iisc.ernet.in. We would be delighted to post the clarifications on the website at the URL mentioned above.

References

[1] Andreu Mas-Colell, Michael D. Whinston, and Jerry R. Green. *Microeconomic Theory*. Oxford University Press, 1995.

[2] Roger B. Myerson. *Game Theory: Analysis of Conflict*. Harvard University Press, Cambridge, Massachusetts, USA, 1997.

[3] Noam Nisan, Tim Roughgarden, Eva Tardos, and Vijay Vazirani (Editors). *Algorithmic Game Theory*. Cambridge University Press, 2007.

[4] Yoam Shoham and Kevin Leyton-Brown. *Multiagent Systems: Algorithmic, Game-Theoretic, and Logical Foundations*. Cambridge University Press, New York, USA, 2009, 2009.

[5] Philip D. Straffin Jr. *Game Theory and Strategy*. The Mathematical Association of America, 1993.

[6] Martin J. Osborne. *An Introduction to Game Theory*. The MIT Press, 2003.

[7] Michael Maschler, Eilon Solan, and Shmuel Zamir. *Game Theory*. Cambridge University Press, 2013.

[8] Y. Narahari, Dinesh Garg, Ramasuri Narayanam, and Hastagiri Prakash. *Game Theoretic Problems in Network Economics and Mechanism Design Solutions*. Springer, London, 2009.

Acknowledgments

It is my pleasant duty to recall the exemplary support I have received from numerous individuals and organizations. It is a true privilege and pleasure to be associated with the Indian Institute of Science, Bangalore. I salute this magnificent temple of learning with all devotion and humility. I would like to thank the Institute Director Professor P. Balaram and the Associate Director Professor N. Balakrishnan for their fabulous support and encouragement. Professor Balaram encouraged me to bring out a special section on game theory in *Current Science*, a journal that he edited with great distinction for more than a decade. The special section appeared in November 2012 and had a foreword by Professor Eric Maskin. Professor Balakrishnan has been wonderfully supportive all these years.

Similarly, the Department of Computer Science and Automation (CSA) has been a paradise for me. Professor Viswanadham (currently a senior distinguished professor at the department) who was my master's and doctoral adviser during 1983-88 in CSA has been my friend, philosopher, and guide at all times ever since 1983. He has provided rock solid support to me in all my academic endeavors and struggles. He is directly responsible for imbibing in me the culture of writing books with contemporary content and his positive influence can be seen in many parts of this book.

I would like to remember the support and encouragement of all colleagues and staff at the Department of Computer Science and Automation. I like to specially mention Professors V.V.S. Sarma, V. Rajaraman, U.R. Prasad, C.E. Veni Madhavan, M. Narasimha Murty, and Y.N. Srikant who all provided encouragement to me whenever I needed it most.

My forays into and explorations in game theory and mechanism design have been largely due to a string of collaborative projects starting with Intel India in 2000. I thank General Motors R & D, Warren, Michigan, and the General Motors India Science Lab, Bangalore for their wonderful support during the past eight years. I must thank, for their splendid support, Intel India, Bangalore, during 2000-2003; Infosys Technologies, Bangalore, during 2007-13; the Office of Naval Research, Arlington, Virginia, during 2007-08; IBM India and IBM India Research Labs during 2009-11; and Xerox Research (2009-2013). I also would like to thank the Homi Bhabha Fellowships Council, Mumbai, for awarding me a fellowship during 2006-07. My special thanks to the Department of Science and Technology for awarding me me the prestigious J.C. Bose Fellowship for the duration 2010-15. Such fellowships go a long way in lifting the spirits of academics.

I have been fortunate to have received feedback about drafts of this book from several leading researchers: Professors Sanjoy Mitter (MIT), Ravi Kannan (MSRI), Peter Luh (University of Connecticut), Krishna Pattipati (University of Connecticut), Avrim Blum (CMU), David Parkes (Harvard University), Preston McAfee (Google), Ram Sriram (National Institute of Standards and Technology), Vivek Borkar (IIT-Bombay), Arunava Sen (ISI-New Delhi), R. Vittal Rao (IISc), Bangalore), and U.R. Prasad (IISc, Bangalore). I would like to express my profound gratitude to them. The following faculty colleagues and researchers have systematically gone through a draft version of this book and provided valuable inputs: Rajesh Sundaresan (IISc), Manoj Tiwari (IIT-Kharagpur), Vanamala Sundar (IIT-Kanpur), K. Gopinath (IISc), Shivani Agarwal (IISc), Balakrishnan Narayanaswamy (IBM IRL), Shashi Mittal (Amazon), Nagarajan Krishnamurthy (IIM-Indore), Indrajit Bhattacharya (IBM IRL), Ujjwal Maulik (Jadavpur University), Madhav Marathe (Virginia), Jugal Garg (Georgia Tech), Chris Dance (Xerox Research), Matthew Jacob (IISc), and Ambedkar Dukkipati (IISc). My sincere thanks to all of them, especially Prof. Manoj Tiwari and his army of students, Prof. Rajesh Sundaresan, and Prof. U.R. Prasad.

The typesetting of parts of this book was done by Mrs. Ashalata, who also created many of the pictures appearing in the book. The pictures appearing in the book have been contributed by Ratul Ray, Swaprava Nath, Swapnil Dhamal, Rohith Vallam, Chetan Yadati, Ramasuri Narayanam, Satyanath Bhat, and Sujit Gujar. In addition, they have also gone through drafts of the book and provided their comments at various points. Special thanks to Ratul Ray for drawing the pictures of all the game theory legends which embellish the pages of this book.

All members of the Game Theory Laboratory have been directly or indirectly involved with this monograph project over the years. I wish to thank all of them: L.M. Khan, N. Hemachandra, K. Ravikumar, Venkatapathi Raju, S. Kameshwaran, Shantanu Biswas, Dinesh Garg, T.S. Chandrashekar, Sujit Gujar, Hastagiri Prakash, Ramasuri Narayanam, Rohith Vallam, Swaprava Nath, Moon Chetry, Chetan Yadati, Gujar, Pankaj Dayama, Satyanath Bhat, Swapnil Dhamal, Shweta Jain, Praphul Chandra, Palash Dey, Debmalya Mandal, Shourya Roy, Priyanka Bhatt, Akanksha

Meghlan, Arpita Biswas, and Arupratan Ray. They have gone through various drafts of the book and provided excellent inputs.

Special thanks to Dinesh Garg, Ramasuri Narayanam, and Hastagiri Prakash who collaborated with me on the 2009 Springer monograph – *Game Theoretic Problems in Network Economics and Mechanism Design Solutions*. A couple of chapters in this book are based on the doctoral work of Dinesh Garg. Special thanks must be given to Rohith and Swaprava who not only proof-read many chapters of the book and contributed many figures but also set up the computer environment for typesetting of the book. Rohith was there to bail me out whenever I struggled with Latex or the computer environment. Thanks also to Ratul Ray, Sourav Medya, Ashutosh, Dilpreet Kaur, Gaurav, A. Rajagopal, K. Rajanikanth, Sourav Sen, Karthik Subbian, Ramakrishnan Kannan, Sunil Shelke, Nagaraj, Ashwin, Sriram, Prashanth, Raghav Gautam, Megha, Santosh Srinivas, Nikesh Srivastava, Kalyan Chakravarty, Radhanikanth, Siva Sankar, Soujanya, Durgesh, Mukti Jain, M.D. Srinivasulu, Kalyan, Madhuri, Y. Ravi Shankar, Maria Praveen Kumar, Sharvani, Devansh, Chaitanya, Ananth, Rajesh, Lavanya, Kumar, and P.N. Ravi.

Successive generations of the Game Theory course at the Indian Institute of Science have provided inputs to me at various stages. In particular, I wish to mention the following students who have also gone through drafts of the book: Thirumulanathan, Abhijeet, Suprovot, Aadirupa saha, Rohit Vaish, Kundan Kandhway, Bhushan Kotnis, Shiv Ganesh, Surabhi Punjabi, Disha Makhija, Aritra Ghosh, Ankur Gupta, Prabhu Chandran, Chandrashekhar, Aruna, and Divya Padmanabhan.

I have received excellent support from the IISc press personnel and the editorial team at World Scientific. I thank Ms. Ranjana Rajan and Mr. Steven Patt for their incredible support. They were there to address all my queries at various points in time and Steven was continuously tracking the progress of the project.

Behind any effort of this kind, there are two immortal personalities whose blessings provide the inspirational force. They are my divine parents, Brahmasri Y. Simhadri Sastry and Matrusri Y. Nagavenamma. They may not be here anymore in mortal form but their magnificent personalities continue to be a beacon and a driving force. With humility, I sincerely dedicate this work at their lotus feet. I would like to lovingly thank my *much better* half, Padmashri, who has made numerous sacrifices during the past two decades because of her husband's continuous struggle with his research. The same applies to my son Naganand, who has put up with his father during very crucial and formative years. I have to place on record the wonderful love and affection of my brothers, Y. Sadguru Murthy, Y. Santharam, Y. Rajaram, Y. Raghuram, and Y. Ekantharam, and my sisters-in-law Y. Niramalamma, Y. Vijaya Lakshmi, Y. Rajeshwari, Y. Paramjyothi, and Y. Lalithamma; my loving sister A.T. Lavanya and my affectionate brother-in-law A.T. Subrahmanyam; and two other loving sisters Gunamma and Sujathamma. My nephews, nieces, and their children have been a wonderful source of support and joy.

Acronyms

AE	Allocatively efficient (or allocative efficiency)
BB	Budget balance
dAGVA	d'Aspremont, Gérard-Varet, and Arrow (mechanism)
DSE	Dominant strategy equilibrium
DSIC	Dominant strategy incentive compatible
EFG	Extensive form game
EPE	Ex-Post efficient
EPIC	Ex-Post incentive compatible
EPIR	Ex-Post individually rational
GSP	Generalized second price (mechanism)
GST	Gibbard - Satterthwaite Theorem
GVA	Generalized Vickrey auction
IC	Incentive compatible
IIR	Interim individually rational
IR	Individually rational
LP	Linear program
MSNE	Mixed strategy Nash equilibrium
NBS	Nash bargaining solution
ND	Non-dictatorial (social choice function)
NE	Nash equilibrium
NTU	Non-transferable utility (game)
PSNE	Pure strategy Nash equilibrium
SBB	Strong budget balance
SCF	Social choice function
SDSE	Strongly dominant strategy equilibrium
SFG	Strategic form game
SGPE	Subgame perfect equilibrium
SSA	Sponsored search auction
TU	Transferable utility (game)
VWDSE	Very weakly dominant strategy equilibrium
WBB	Weak budget balance
WDSE	Weakly dominant strategy equilibrium
VCG	Vickrey-Clarke-Groves (mechanism)

Symbols and Notations

General Notation

$\mathbb{R}$	Set of all real numbers
$\mathbb{R}_+$	Set of all non-negative real numbers
$\mathbb{N}$	Set of all non-negative integers
$\emptyset$	Empty set
$|A|$	Cardinality of set A
2^A	Power set of a set A
$d(x,y)$	Euclidean distance between vectors x and y

Strategic Form Games

Γ (strategic form game)	$\langle N, (S_i)_{i \in N}, (u_i)_{i \in N} \rangle$ or $\langle N, (S_i), (u_i) \rangle$
n	Number of players in the game
N	A set of players, $\{1, 2, \ldots, n\}$
S_i	Set of actions or pure strategies of player i
$(S_i)_{i \in N}$	Short form for $(S_1, \ldots, S_n)$
(S_i)	Short form for $(S_i)_{i \in N}$ (when context is clear)
S	Set of all pure strategy profiles $= S_1 \times \ldots \times S_n$
s	A strategy profile, $s = (s_1, \ldots, s_n) \in S$
$-i$	All players other than i
s_{-i}	A profile of strategies of agents except i
(s_i, s_{-i})	Another representation for profile $(s_1, \ldots, s_n)$
S_{-i}	Set of all strategy profiles of all agents except i
u_i (strategic form game)	Utility function of player i; $u_i : S \to \mathbb{R}$
$(u_i)_{i \in N}$	Short form for $(u_1, \ldots, u_n)$
(u_i)	Short form for $(u_i)_{i \in N}$ (when context is clear)
s_i^*	An equilibrium strategy of player i
$s^* = (s_1^*, \ldots, s_n^*)$	An equilibrium strategy profile
b_i (pure strategies)	Best response correspondence of player i $b_i : S_{-i} \to 2^{S_i}$

Extensive Form Games

Γ (extensive form game)	$\langle N, (A_i)_{i \in N}, \mathbb{H}, P, (\mathbb{I}_i)_{i \in N}, (u_i)_{i \in N} \rangle$
A_i (extensive form game)	Set of actions of players i
$\mathbb{H}$	Set of all terminal histories
$S_{\mathbb{H}}$	Set of proper subhistories of terminal histories
$P : S_{\mathbb{H}} \to N$	Mapping of proper subhistories to players
$\mathbb{I}_i$	Set of all information sets of player i
u_i (extensive form game)	Utility function of player i; $u_i : \mathbb{H} \to \mathbb{R}$
$s_i(\cdot)$ (Extensive form game)	A strategy of player i; $s_i : \mathbb{I}_i \to A_i$

Mixed Strategy Games

$\Delta(S_i)$	Set of all probability distributions on the set S_i
σ_i	A mixed strategy of player i; $\sigma_i \in \Delta(S_i)$
$\sigma = (\sigma_1, \ldots, \sigma_n)$	A mixed strategy profile
σ_{-i}	A mixed strategy profile of agents except i
(σ_i, σ_{-i})	Another representation for profile $(\sigma_1, \ldots, \sigma_n)$
σ_i^*	An equilibrium mixed strategy of player i
$\sigma^* = (\sigma_1^*, \ldots, \sigma_n^*)$	A mixed strategy Nash equilibrium
u_i (mixed strategies)	Utility of player i; $u_i : \Delta(S_1) \times \ldots \times \Delta(S_n) \to \mathbb{R}$
b_i (mixed strategies)	Best response correspondence of player i
$\delta(\sigma_i)$	Support of mixed strategy σ_i
$\delta(\sigma)$; $\sigma = (\sigma_1, \ldots, \sigma_n)$	$\delta(\sigma_1) \times \ldots \times \delta(\sigma_n)$; Support of strategy profile σ

Bayesian Games

Γ (Bayesian Game)	$\langle N, (\Theta_i), (S_i), (p_i), (u_i) \rangle$
Θ_i	Set of types of player i
Θ	Set of all type profiles $= \Theta_1 \times \Theta_2 \times \ldots \times \Theta_n$
S	Set of all action profiles $= S_1 \times S_2 \times \ldots \times S_n$
θ	$\theta = (\theta_1, \ldots, \theta_n) \in \Theta$; a type profile
Θ_{-i}	Set of type profiles of agents except i $= \Theta_1 \times \ldots \Theta_{i-1} \times \Theta_{i+1} \times \ldots \times \Theta_n$
θ_{-i}	$\theta_{-i} \in \Theta_{-i}$; type profile of agents except i
p_i	Belief function of player i; $p_i : \Theta_i \to \Delta(\Theta_{-i})$
$\mathbb{P}$ (Bayesian game)	A common prior; $\mathbb{P} \in \Delta(\Theta)$
u_i (Bayesian game)	Utility function of player i; $u_i : \Theta \times S \to \mathbb{R}$
$s_i(\cdot)$ (Bayesian game)	A strategy of player i; $s_i : \Theta_i \to S_i$
$s(\cdot) = (s_1(\cdot), \ldots, s_n(\cdot))$	A strategy profile in a Bayesian game
$s^*(\cdot) = (s_1^*(\cdot), \ldots, s_n^*(\cdot))$	A pure strategy Bayesian Nash equilibrium

Matrix Games

Γ	$\langle\{1,2\}, S_1, S_2, u_1, -u_1\rangle$
1	Player 1 (row player)
2	Player 2 (column player)
S_1	$\{s_{11}, s_{12}, \ldots, s_{1m}\} = \{1, 2, \ldots, m\}$
S_2	$\{s_{21}, s_{22}, \ldots, s_{2n}\} = \{1, 2, \ldots, n\}$
a_{ij}	$u_1(i, j)$ where $i \in S_1$; $j \in S_2$
A	Matrix of payoff values of player 1; $A = [a_{ij}]$
$x = (x_1, \ldots, x_m)$	A mixed strategy of row player (player 1)
$y = (y_1, \ldots, y_n)$	A mixed strategy of column player (player 2)
$\underline{v}$	Maxmin value or lower value
$\overline{v}$	Minmax value or upper value
v	Value of a matrix game when $\underline{v} = \overline{v} = v$

Mechanism Design

X	A set of alternatives or outcomes
θ_i	A preference or type of player i
$\hat{\theta}_i$	Type announced by player i
Θ_i	Set of all types of player i
Θ	$\Theta_1 \times \ldots \times \Theta_n$ (set of all type profiles)
$\Delta(\Theta)$	Set of all probability distributions on Θ
$\mathbb{P} \in \Delta(\Theta)$	A common prior distribution on type profiles
$p_i : \Theta_i \to \Delta(\Theta_{-i})$	Belief distribution of player i
$u_i : X \times \Theta_i \to \mathbb{R}$	Utility function of player i
$f : \Theta_1 \times \ldots \times \Theta_n \to X$	A social choice function
$\mathscr{D} = (\Theta_1, \Theta_2, \ldots, \Theta_n, f(.))$	A direct mechanism
$g : S_1 \times S_2 \times \ldots \times S_n \to X$	A mapping from action profiles to outcomes
$\mathscr{M} = (S_1, S_2, \ldots, S_n, g(.))$	An indirect mechanism
$\succsim$	A preference relation on a set of outcomes
$\mathscr{R}$	Set of all rational preference relations on X
$\mathscr{P}$	Set of all strict rational preference relations on X
$\succsim_i (\theta_i)$	A rational preference relation induced by u_i and θ_i
$\mathscr{R}_i$	Set of all $\succsim_i (\theta_i)$ where $\theta_i \in \Theta_i$
K	A set of project allocations (or project choices)
$k \in K$	A project choice
$k(\theta)$	Project choice when type profile is θ
t_i	Monetary transfer to player i
$t_i(\theta)$	Monetary transfer to player i when type profile is θ
$x = (k, t_1, \ldots, t_n)$	A typical outcome in quasilinear environment
$x(\theta) = (k(\theta), t_1(\theta), \ldots, t_n(\theta))$	Outcome in quasilinear setting with type profile θ
$v_i(k, \theta_i)$	Value of allocation k for player i when type is θ_i
$h_i : \Theta_{-i} \to \mathbb{R}$	Mapping used in Groves payment rule
b_i	Bid of player i in an auction

Cooperative Game Theory

$C \subseteq N$	A coalition (subset) of players
$S_C = \times_{i \in C} S_i$	Set of strategy profiles of players in coalition C
$S = S_N = \times_{i \in N} S_i$	Set of strategy profiles of all players in N
$\Delta(S_C)$	Set of all probability distributions on S_C
$\tau_C \in \Delta(S_C)$	A correlated strategy of players in coalition C
$\tau = (\tau_C)_{C \subseteq N}$	A contract signed by all players in N
$\alpha \in \Delta(S)$	A correlated equilibrium
$F \subseteq \mathbb{R}^2$	Set of feasible allocations in bargaining problem
$v = (v_1, v_2) \in \mathbb{R}^2$	Disagreement point (default point) (de facto point)
(F, v) (Nash bargaining)	Instance with feasible set F; default point v
$f(F, v)$	Nash bargaining solution $= (f_1(F, v), f_2(F, v))$
$v : 2^N \to \mathbb{R}$	Value function in a transferable utility game
(N, v)	A transferable utility game
$\Pi(N)$	Set of all permutations of $N = \{1, 2, \ldots, n\}$
$\pi \in \Pi(N)$	A typical permutation of $N = \{1, 2, \ldots, n\}$
$P(\pi, i)$	Set of all predecessors of player i in permutation π
$S(\pi, i)$	Set of all successors of player i in permutation π
$x = (x_1, \ldots, x_n) \in \mathbb{R}^n$	A payoff allocation
$\mathbb{C}(N, v)$	The core of the transferable utility game (N, v)
$(\phi_1(N, v), \ldots, \phi_n(N, v))$	Shapley value of a transferable utility game (N, v)
$(\phi_1(v), \ldots, \phi_n(v))$	Another notation for Shapley value (N implied)
$e(C, x)$	Excess of coalition C with respect to allocation x

Contents

COOPERATIVE GAME THEORY　　　　　　　　363

Chapter 1

Introduction and Overview

In this chapter, we bring out the importance and current relevance of game theory and mechanism design. The modern era, marked by magnificent advances in information and communication technologies, has created possibilities for fascinating new applications. In many of these applications, the research challenges can be effectively addressed using game theory and mechanism design. In this chapter, we describe a few motivational examples and present several modern research trends that have brought game theory and mechanism design to the forefront.

Game theory and mechanism design deal with interactions among *strategic agents*. While game theory is concerned with *analysis of games*, mechanism design involves *designing games* with desirable outcomes. Currently these are lively and active areas of research for inter-disciplinary problem solving. The central objective of this book is to gain a sound understanding of the science behind the use of game theory and mechanism design in solving modern problems in the Internet era. This book deals with three broad areas: *non-cooperative game theory*, *cooperative game theory*, and *mechanism design*.

Disciplines where game theory and mechanism design have traditionally been used include economics, business science, sociology, political science, biology, philosophy, and engineering. In engineering, it has been most widely used in industrial engineering, inventory management, supply chain management, electronic commerce, and multiagent systems. More recently, game theory has been embraced by computer science and electrical engineering disciplines in the context of many emerging applications.

1.1   Game Theory: The Science of Strategic Interactions

The term *game* used in the phrase *game theory* corresponds to an interaction involving decision makers or players who are rational and intelligent. Informally, *rationality* of a player implies that the player chooses his strategies so as to maximize a well defined individualistic payoff while *intelligence* means that players are capable enough to compute their best strategies. Game theory is a tool for logical

1	2	
	IISc	MG Road
IISc	100, 100	0, 0
MG Road	0, 0	10, 10

Table 1.1: Payoffs for the students in different situations

and mathematical analysis that models conflict as well as cooperation between the decision makers and provides a principled way of predicting the result of the interactions among the players using equilibrium analysis. Traditional games such as chess and bridge represent games of a fairly straightforward nature. Games that game theory deals with are much more general and could be viewed as abstractions and extensions of the traditional games. The abstractions and extensions are powerful enough to include all complexities and characteristics of social interactions. For this reason, game theory has proved to be an extremely valuable tool in social sciences in general and economics in particular. While *game theory* focuses on analysis of games, *mechanism design* is concerned with design of games to obtain desirable outcomes - mechanism design could be described as reverse engineering of games. In the sequel, whenever there is no need for emphasis, we use the single phrase *game theory* instead of the phrases *game theory* and *mechanism design*.

Value of Game Theory and Mechanism Design

We provide four simple, stylized examples which bring out the value of game theory and mechanism design in modeling situations of conflict and cooperation among strategic agents. These examples are abstractions of representative real-world situations and applications.

Student Coordination Problem

Imagine two typical students (call them 1 and 2), say belonging to the Indian Institute of Science (IISc), Bangalore, who are close friends. The students derive utility by spending time together either studying (in IISc) or going to the MG Road (Mahatma Gandhi Road, a location in Bangalore, frequented by young students seeking entertainment). Thus to spend time together, they have two options (or strategies): IISc and MG Road. If both of them are in IISc, each one gets a payoff of 100. If both of them go to MG Road, each gets a payoff of only 10. If one of them remains in IISc and the other goes to MG Road, the payoff is 0 for each. The payoffs are shown in Table 1.1 and are self-explanatory. Suppose the two friends have to choose their strategies simultaneously and independently of each other. Being rational and intelligent, each one would like to select the best possible strategy. It is clear that both opting for IISc is the best possible outcome and both opting for MG Road is also fine though clearly worse than both opting for IISc. The worst happens when they choose different options since each ends up with zero utility.

Game theory helps us with a principled way of predicting the options that would be chosen by the two students. In this case, the outcome of both opting for IISc and the outcome of both opting for MG Road can be shown to be what are called *Nash equilibria* which are strategy profiles in which no player is better off by unilaterally deviating from her equilibrium strategy. Game theory also provides one more prediction for this game which on the face of it is counter-intuitive but represents an equilibrium outcome that the students will not be averse to playing. This outcome which is technically called a *mixed strategy Nash equilibrium* corresponds to the situation where each student chooses IISc with probability $\frac{1}{11}$ and MG Road with probability $\frac{10}{11}$. This perhaps explains why some students are found mostly in MG Road and rarely in IISc!

The above game which is often called the *coordination game* is an abstraction of many social and technical situations in the real world. We will not get into details here but only leave the comment that game theory enables a scientific way of predicting the outcome of such interactions among decision makers.

Braess Paradox

We now illustrate the Braess paradox which is named after the German mathematician Dietrich Braess. This paradox is usually associated with transportation networks and brings out the counter-intuitive fact that a transportation network with extra capacity added may actually perform worse for commuters (in terms of time delays) than without the extra capacity. The game that we describe here is developed on the lines presented in the book by Easley and Kleinberg [1].

Figure 1.1 shows a network that consists of a source S and a destination T, and two intermediate hubs A and B. All vehicles traveling from S can go via hub A or hub B. Suppose, regardless of the number of vehicles on the route, it takes 25 minutes to travel from S to B or from A to T. On the other hand, the travel time from S to A is $\frac{m}{50}$ minutes where m is the number of vehicles traveling on that link. Similarly, the travel time from B to T is $\frac{m}{50}$ minutes where m is the number of vehicles on that link.

Suppose we now introduce an additional fast link from A to B to ease the congestion in the network (as a degenerate case, we will assume the travel time from A to B to be zero). Figure 1.2 depicts this new network with an extra link added from A to B. Now a vehicle can go from S to T in three different ways: (1) S to A to T; (2) S to B to T; and (3) S to A to B to T. The users of this network would be happier if the time to travel from S to T is lower. Intuition tells us that the second configuration where we have an additional link should make the users happier. However, game theoretic analysis proves, using equilibrium analysis, that the first configuration is in fact better for the users.

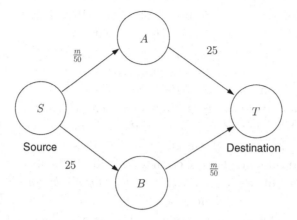

Fig. 1.1: A transportation network with four nodes

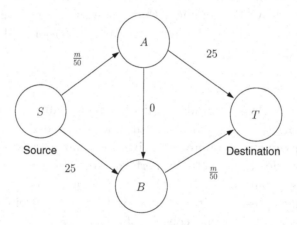

Fig. 1.2: Transportation network with an additional high speed link from A to B

There is considerable evidence for the Braess paradox. For example, in Seoul, South Korea, traffic congestion around the city dramatically reduced when a particular high speed arterial link was closed for traffic as a part of the Cheonggyecheon restoration project. In Stuttgart, Germany, a huge investment was made in decongesting the traffic on the roads by building additional roads but the traffic situation improved only when some of the newly-built roads were closed for traffic. Game theory could be used to obtain scientific predictions of what is likely to happen, by modeling the situation as a game involving the users of the transportation network and capturing their interactions. In chapters 4, 5, and 6, we study this example in some detail.

Vickrey Auction

Consider a seller who wishes to allocate an indivisible item to one of n prospective buyers in exchange for a payment. An example would be the sale of a spectrum license by the Government to one of several telecom service providers seeking to buy the license (See Figure 1.3). Each player has a certain valuation for the item on sale. For example, in the spectrum license case, imagine that there are four service providers 1, 2, 3, 4 who value the license at Rs. 400 million, Rs. 500 million, Rs. 700 million, and Rs. 1000 million. In a spectrum auction, the Government invites bids from prospective buyers and allocates the license based on an auction protocol. Two simple and common auction methods are *first price sealed bid auction* and *second price sealed bid auction*. In the first price auction, the one who bids highest will be allocated the item and the winning bidder will pay an amount equal to the bid. In the second price auction, the one who bids highest will be allocated the item but the winning bidder will pay an amount equal to the second highest bid.

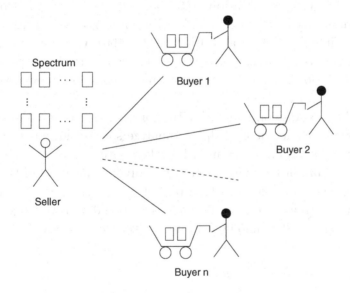

Fig. 1.3: A spectrum auction

Each auction above can be modeled as a game involving the seller and the buyers. In the first price auction, the bidders will bid amounts which are less than their valuations. In the second price auction, the bidding will be more aggressive since the bidders know that they would be paying less than what they bid in case they win. William Vickrey, in his Nobel prize winning work, proved the remarkable result that the bids in the second price auction will be exactly equal to the respective valuations. In fact, Vickrey showed that it is best for every bidder to bid her true valuation irrespective of whatever is bid by the other players. In the example above, if second price auction is employed, then the players will bid their valuations and the license will be awarded to player 4. This player will pay an amount equal to Rs. 700 million which is the second highest bid. Thus the seller who does not know the valuations of the bidders is able to extract these valuations in the form of their bids. Game theory and mechanism design constitute the science behind the design of a whole gamut of auction protocols which are ubiquitous and extensively used these days.

Divide the Dollar Game

Suppose there are three individuals who wish to divide a total wealth of 300 among themselves. Each player can propose an allocation such that no player's payoff is negative and the sum of all the payoffs does not exceed 300. Assume that if two or more players propose the same allocation, then that allocation will be implemented. For example, if players 1 and 2 propose an allocation $(150, 150, 0)$ and player 3 proposes $(100, 100, 100)$, the allocation $(150, 150, 0)$ will be implemented. However, player 3 may tempt player 2 with the allocation $(0, 225, 75)$ and if players 2 and 3 propose this, the original allocation $(150, 150, 0)$ gets overturned. Note that this allocation is strictly better for both 2 and 3. Player 1 may now entice player 3 and jointly propose with player 3 an allocation $(200, 0, 100)$ which is better for both 1 and 3. Bargaining of this kind can be never ending leading to the perpetual breaking and making of coalitions. This is a situation that is common in the real world (for example in politics and business).

Predicting the final outcome in such situations is hard using conventional techniques. Cooperative game theory helps us analyze such situations in a systematic and scientific way. For example, by modeling the above as a cooperative game, one can show that the *core* of this game is empty implying that none of the allocations is stable and can always by derailed by a pair of players coming together. One can also show that the *Shapley value* of this game is $(100, 100, 100)$ which provides a fair way of allocating the wealth among the three players in this case.

Game Theory: A Rich History

Game theory, as a mathematical discipline and modeling tool, has a rich history and its foundations and advances have been the contributions of some of the most brilliant minds of the twentieth century. Figure 1.4 shows the legends who have made path breaking contributions to game theory and mechanism design. John von Neumann and Oskar Morgenstern were the principal architects of game theory in the late 1920s, 1930s, and early 1940s. Their marvelous collaboration built the foundations of game theory and yielded a monumental book entitled *The Theory of Games and Economic Behavior* [2]. This book continues to be an authentic source of early pioneering results in game theory. Following their work, several celebrated game theorists have contributed to developing game theory as the science of economics. The importance of the discipline of game theory and their contributions have been recognized through a number of Sveriges Riksbank prizes (Nobel Prize in Economic Sciences) being awarded to game theorists, including the 1994, 1996, 2005, 2007, and 2012 prizes. In fact, between 1994 and 2012, as many as 11 game theorists have been awarded the prize.

Fig. 1.4: Legends of game theory and mechanism design

John Nash, John Harsanyi, and Reinhard Selten received the prize in 1994 for their path breaking work in equilibrium analysis of games. William Vickrey won the prize in 1996 for his influential work in auction theory. In 2005, Robert Aumann and Thomas Schelling received the prize for having enhanced the understanding of conflict and cooperation through game theory analysis. In 2007, the prize was awarded to Leonid Hurwicz, Eric Maskin, and Roger Myerson for their fundamental contributions to mechanism design theory. More recently, in 2012, Lloyd Shapley and Alvin Roth have been awarded the prize for advancing the theory of stable allocations and the practice of market design. Before all these contributions, Kenneth Arrow had been awarded the prize in 1972 for his masterly work on social choice theory which had been carried out as early as 1950s. Clearly, game theory and mechanism design have held the center-stage for several decades now in the area of social sciences. The development of game theory can be truly described as one of the most significant achievements of the twentieth century since it has shown that mathematical reasoning can be applied to studying complex human interactions.

1.2   Current Trends and Modern Applications

Since the 1990s, two related threads have catapulted game theory to the centerstage of problem solving in modern times. The first thread is the emergence of theoretical research areas at the interface of game theory and varied subjects like computer science, network science, and other engineering sciences. The second thread is the natural and often compelling use of game theory in breathtaking new applications in the Internet era. In the modern era, game theory has become a key ingredient for solving problems in areas as diverse as electronic commerce and business, Internet advertising, social network analysis and monetization, wireless networks, intelligent transportation, smart grids, and carbon footprint optimization. We touch upon a few relevant current trends and modern applications.

Current Trends

To illustrate the first thread above, we allude to a lively new theoretical research area, algorithmic game theory, at the interface of game theory and computer science. The importance and limelight can be appreciated by the fact that the 2012 Gödel Prize which recognizes outstanding papers in theoretical computer science has been awarded to six researchers (Elias Koutsoupias, Christos Papadimitriou, Tim Roughgarden, Eva Tardos, Noam Nisan, and Amir Ronen) in algorithmic game theory. The award has cited three papers [3, 4, 5] which have laid the foundations in this area. Here is a brief overview of the three papers to get a quick idea of the central themes in this area.

Koutsoupias and Papadimitriou [3] introduced the key notion of *price of anarchy* in their paper entitled *Worst-case Equilibria*. The price of anarchy measures the extent to which selfish behavior by decentralized agents affects the achievement of a social optimum. In particular, the paper quantifies how much efficiency is lost due to selfish behavior on the Internet which does not have a central monitor or authority to coordinate or control the actions of its users. Their study is based on a game theoretic model of the Internet and they use the notion of Nash equilibrium to formalize the concept of price of anarchy.

The concept of price of anarchy is used by Roughgarden and Tardos [4] to study the specific problem of routing traffic in large scale transportation networks or communication networks. Their beautiful analysis explains the well known Braess's paradox (see Chapters 4 and 5) in transportation science using a game theoretic model and establishes the relationship between centrally optimized routing and selfish routing in congested networks. Through such studies, game theory becomes a valuable tool for design of routing policies and traffic networks.

The third Gödel prize winning paper by Nisan and Ronen [5] proposes a fascinating new problem domain which they call *algorithmic mechanism design*. In this paper, the authors show how game theory and mechanism design could be used to solve algorithmic problems where the inputs to the problem constitute the private information of rational and intelligent agents. Traditional computer science assumes that algorithms once designed will work as per design when executed. The computing systems that execute the algorithms will follow the rules written for them faithfully. However if self-interested participants are required to provide inputs to the computing system during the execution of the algorithm, the inputs provided to the algorithm may or may not be truthful. Making algorithms robust to manipulation by strategic agents is the central theme of algorithmic mechanism design. Algorithmic game theory is now an active research area in many leading computer science departments in the world. It represents one of many such recent research trends in which game theory is a key ingredient.

We now take a look at the second thread which has pushed game theory to the forefront of problem solving. This thread is inspired by a natural relevance of game theory to many emerging applications in the Internet era.

Some Modern Applications

Modern applications often involve the Internet which often encourages strategic behavior by the users due to its decentralized nature. Also, modern applications in the social, economic, or business domain invariably involve individuals and organizations which have their own self-interests and act strategically. To make these modern applications perform as intended in spite of the presence of strategic users in the system, one could use creative techniques offered by game theory and mechanism design as a part of system design. This explains the second trend that has pushed game theory and mechanism design to the forefront. To drive home the point that game theory has proved crucial for advancing the current art in modern day problem solving, we provide four examples below.

Matching Markets

This is a traditional problem setting that continues to throw up exciting new applications in modern times as well. Matching is the process of allocating one set of resources or individuals to another set of resources or individuals. Examples include matching buyers to sellers in a market; matching resources to tasks; matching new doctors to hospitals; matching job-seeking engineers to companies; and matching students to schools (see Figure 1.5). There are also examples with deep societal impact such as matching kidneys to patients (or in general organ donors to organ recipients). Such matching problems are broadly categorized into marriage problems and house allocation problems. In a marriage problem, the resources on each side of the market have preferences over the resources on the other side. In house allocation, only resources on one of the sides have preferences over the resources on the other side. In either case, the matching has to be accomplished so that the individual preferences are honored and performance is optimized.

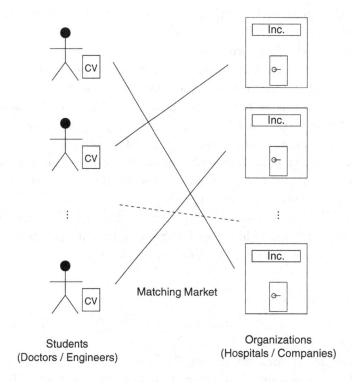

Fig. 1.5: A matching market

Two key requirements of any solution to the matching problem are *stability* and *incentive compatibility*. Informally, a solution is said to be stable if the solution cannot become strictly better through a reallocation. A solution is called incentive compatible if the preferences are reported truthfully by all the agents. Game theory has been used to analyze in a rigorous manner both stability and incentive compatibility. Since the 1960s, game theory and game theorists have contributed immensely to the development of a comprehensive theory of matching markets. The existence of a large number of successful matching markets in real world applications is one of the significant successes of game theory. In fact, the Nobel Prize in Economic Sciences for the year 2012 has been awarded to Lloyd Shapley and Alvin Roth for their pioneering work on matching theory and matching markets [6].

Matching markets have many socially important applications such as competitive matching of colleges with students and hospitals with interns, leading to maximization of social welfare. They have also saved precious human lives through better and faster matching of kidneys and human organs. Game theory and mechanism design have played a significant role in ensuring the success of these markets.

Sponsored Search Auctions

Sponsored search is by now a well known example of an extremely successful business model in Internet advertising. When a user searches a keyword, the search engine delivers a page with numerous results containing the links that are relevant to the keyword and also sponsored links that correspond to advertisements of selected advertisers. Figure 1.6 depicts a typical scenario.

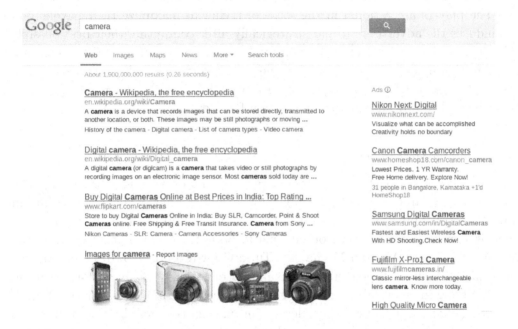

Fig. 1.6: Keyword auction on a search engine

When a sponsored link is clicked, the user is directed to the corresponding advertiser's web page. In the commonly used pay-per-click model, the advertiser makes a certain payment to the search engine for directing the user to its web page. Against every search performed by any user on any keyword, the search engine faces the problem of matching a set of advertisers to the (limited number of) sponsored slots. In addition, the search engine also needs to decide on a payment to be made by the advertiser against each click. Most search engines currently use an auction mechanism for this purpose, known as sponsored search auction. A significant percentage of the revenue of Internet giants such as Google, Microsoft, Yahoo!, etc., accrues from sponsored search auctions. In a typical sponsored search auction, advertisers are invited to specify their willingness to pay for their preferred keywords, that is, the maximum amount they would be willing to pay when an Internet user clicks on the respective sponsored slots. This willingness to pay is typically referred to as *cost-per-click*. Based on the bids submitted by the advertisers for a particular keyword, the search engine determines (1) a subset of advertisements to display; (2) the order in which the selected advertisements are displayed; and (3) the payments to be made by the selected advertisers when their respective slots are clicked by a user. The actual payment to be made depends on the bids submitted by the advertisers. The decisions (1), (2), and (3) constitute the sponsored search auction mechanism.

The search engine would typically like to maximize its revenue whereas the advertisers would wish to achieve maximum payoffs within a given budget. This leads to a classic game situation where the search engine and the advertisers are the players. The players are rational in the sense of trying to maximize their payoffs and this induces the advertisers to bid strategically after computing their best possible bids. The problem of designing a sponsored search auction mechanism becomes a problem of designing a game involving the search engine and the advertisers. The rules of the game have to be designed in a way that a well defined set of criteria would be realized by an equilibrium solution for the game.

Crowdsourcing Mechanisms

In the recent years, crowdsourcing has emerged as a major paradigm for getting work done through a large group of human resources. It can be described as distribution of work to a possibly unknown group of human resources in the form of an open call. There is a proliferation of crowdsourcing platforms in the past few years. Some of the prominent ones are Amazon Mechanical Turk, CrowdCloud, CrowdFlower, Elance, Innocentive, Taskcn, Topcoder, etc. Examples of tasks typically performed using crowdsourcing include: labeling of images, graphical design of logos, preparation of marketing plans, design of websites, developing efficient code for algorithmic business problems, classification of documents (legal documents, patents, etc.), translation services from one language to another, eliciting answers for questions, search and rescue missions in a wide geographical area, etc.

A well known crowdsourcing experiment in the recent times is the DARPA red balloon challenge which involved discovering, in as short a time as possible, 10 red balloons that were launched at ten undisclosed locations in the United States (locations shown in Figure 1.7). The total prize money was US\$ 40000. The winning team from the Massachusetts Institute of Technology (MIT) employed the following mechanism. First a team of volunteers was recruited (first level volunteers) and each member of this team recruited second level volunteers. The second level volunteers recruited third level volunteers, and so on. The volunteer (say X) who first discovers a red balloon and reports it will get an incentive of US\$ 2000 while the volunteer (say Y) who recruited X will get an incentive of US\$ 1000, the volunteer who recruited Y will get US\$ 500, and so on. The above mechanism proved highly successful and the MIT team was able to discover all ten red balloons in less than 10 hours time. The winning mechanism is an excellent example of application of game theory and mechanism design to this fascinating challenge.

In general, there are many research questions involved in deriving success out of

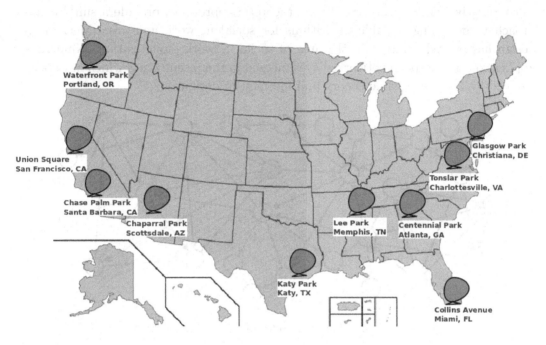

Fig. 1.7: Location of ten red balloons in the DARPA challenge

crowdsourcing. These issues include: attracting participation in required numbers, deciding on the nature and extent of incentives (cash or kind), eliciting truthful reports from the participants, and ensuring quality, timeliness, and cost-effectiveness of task execution. Game theory and mechanism design prove to be critical ingredients in designing such crowdsourcing campaigns.

Social Network Analysis

Social networks are now ubiquitous and are useful for many applications including information diffusion, electronic business, and search. Social network analysis is central to numerous Internet-based applications, for example, viral marketing, influence maximization, and influence limitation, that are based on social networks. Existing methods and tools for social network analysis have a lacuna: they do not capture the behavior (such as rationality and intelligence) of individual nodes nor do they model the strategic interactions that occur among these nodes. Game theory is a natural tool to overcome this inadequacy since it provides rigorous mathematical models of strategic interaction among autonomous, intelligent, and rational agents which form the nodes of a social network. The books by Jackson [7] and Easley and Kleinberg [1] emphasize the use of game theory in studying several social network analysis problems such as predicting topologies of social networks, modeling information diffusion, etc. For example, Figure 1.8 shows a social network in which the four most influential nodes have been identified using Shapley value, a solution concept in cooperative game theory [8]. Game theoretic approaches provide a suitable approach to designing scalable algorithms for social network analysis. Mechanism design has proved valuable in the area of social network monetization. Numerous applications using social networks have emerged in the recent times which have been enabled by the use of game theory and mechanism design.

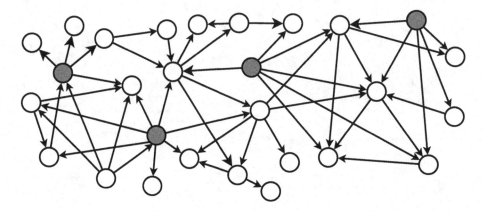

Fig. 1.8: Influential nodes in a social network

1.3 Outline of this Book

In the foregoing discussion, we have seen the increasingly influential and useful role game theory and mechanism design have come to play in inter-disciplinary research and modern applications. There is thus a heightened need to digest the foundations of game theory and mechanism design to gain a deeper understanding and appreciation of the value of game theory in the emerging applications. This textbook strives to fulfill this need.

After a thorough reading of the book, we expect that the reader will be able to use game theory and mechanism design to model, analyze, and solve centralized as well as decentralized design problems involving multiple autonomous agents that interact strategically in a rational and intelligent way. The book only assumes familiarity with an elementary course on calculus and probability. Familiarity with foundational aspects of linear algebra, real analysis, and optimization will be useful. The mathematical appendix included in Chapter 33 presents the key mathematical concepts and results that are used in the book.

There are numerous excellent textbooks and monographs available on game theory. Many of these textbooks are inspired by social sciences in general and microeconomics in particular. Our book has the primary objective of presenting the essentials of game theory and mechanism design to senior undergraduate students and above from various branches of engineering.

The book is structured into three parts:

(1) Non-cooperative game theory (Chapters 2 to 13)
(2) Mechanism design (Chapters 14 to 24)
(3) Cooperative game theory (Chapters 25 to 31)

In Part 1 (non-cooperative game theory), the chapters are devoted to key notions (such as utilities, rationality, intelligence, and common knowledge); extensive form games; strategic form games; dominant strategy equilibria; pure strategy Nash equilibria; mixed strategy Nash equilibria; utility theory; two person zero-sum games; existence theorems for Nash equilibrium (including the Nash theorem); computation of Nash equilibria; complexity of computing Nash equilibria; and Bayesian games,

Part 2 (mechanism design) is concerned with design of games. The chapters cover the following topics: building blocks of mechanisms; social choice functions and their implementation using mechanisms; notion of incentive compatibility and the equivalence of direct mechanisms and indirect mechanisms; the Gibbard-Satterthwaite theorem and the Arrow impossibility theorem; Vickrey-Clarke-Groves mechanisms; possibility and impossibility results in mechanism design; auctions and revenue equivalence theorem; optimal auctions; case study of sponsored search auctions; and mechanism implementation in ex-post Nash equilibrium.

Cooperative game theory is covered in Part 3. The chapters are devoted to correlated strategies and correlated equilibrium; Nash bargaining theory; coalitional games in characteristic form; the core of coalitional games; Shapley value; other solution concepts; and matching algorithms.

Chapter 32 (*Epilogue*) brings out the value game theory and mechanism design provide to a researcher in engineering sciences. Chapter 33 consists of a mathematical appendix that includes key concepts and results in probability, linear algebra, linear programming, mathematical analysis, and computational complexity which are often used in the textbook.

Each of the chapters commences with a motivating introduction to the chapter and concludes with a crisp summary of the chapter and a list of references to probe further. A set of problems is included in every chapter. Concepts and results are illustrated using a number of examples. These examples are carefully chosen from different domains including computer science, networks, and microeconomics; however they are fairly generic. The chapters also contain, at relevant places, informative biographical sketches of game theorists and mechanism designers who have made

We need to emphasize that our book is inspired by, and, indeed, has immensely benefited from the superb expositions available in the following books and monographs: Mas-Colell, Whinston, and Green [9]; Myerson [10]; Maschler, Solan, and Zamir [11]; Nisan, Roughgarden, Tardos, and Vazirani [12]; Shoham and Leyton-Brown [13]; Straffin [14]; and Osborne [15]. The monograph by Narahari, Garg, Narayanam, and Prakash [16] can be considered as a precursor to the current effort.

A superb collection of classic papers in game theory brought out in 1997 [17] is a must read for passionate students and researchers. We also refer the readers to a recent, very comprehensive book by Maschler, Solan, and Zamir [11].

References

[1]   David Easley and Jon Kleinberg. *Networks, Crowds, and Markets: Reasoning About a Highly Connected World*. Cambridge University Press, 2010.

[2]   John von Neumann and Oskar Morgenstern. *Theory of Games and Economic Behavior*. Princeton University Press, 1944.

[3]   E. Koutsoupias and C. Papadimitriou. "Worst-case equilibria". In: *Computer Science Review* **3**(2) (2009), pp. 65–69.

[4]   T. Roughgarden and E. Tardos. "How bad is selfish routing?" In: *Journal of ACM* **49**(2) (2002), pp. 236–259.

[5]   N. Nisan and A. Ronen. "Algorithmic mechanism design". In: *Games and Economic Behavior* **35**(1-2) (2001), pp. 166–196.

[6]   The Economic Sciences Prize Committee. *Stable matching: Theory, Evidence, and Practical Design - The Sveriges Riksbank Prize in Economic Sciences in Memory of Alfred Nobel 2012: Scientific Background*. Tech. rep. The Nobel Foundation, Stockholm, Sweden, 2012.

[7]   Mathew O. Jackson. *Social and Economic Networks*. Princeton University Press, Princeton, NJ, USA, 2007.

[8]   Ramasuri Narayanam and Y. Narahari. "A Shapley value approach to discovering influential nodes in social networks". In: *IEEE Transactions on Automation Science and Engineering* **8**(1) (2011), pp. 130–147.

[9]   Andreu Mas-Colell, Michael D. Whinston, and Jerry R. Green. *Microeconomic Theory*. Oxford University Press, 1995.

[10] Roger B. Myerson. *Game Theory: Analysis of Conflict*. Harvard University Press, Cambridge, Massachusetts, USA, 1997.

[11] Michael Maschler, Eilon Solan, and Shmuel Zamir. *Game Theory*. Cambridge University Press, 2013.

[12] Noam Nisan, Tim Roughgarden, Eva Tardos, and Vijay Vazirani (Editors). *Algorithmic Game Theory*. Cambridge University Press, 2007.

[13] Yoam Shoham and Kevin Leyton-Brown. *Multiagent Systems: Algorithmic, Game-Theoretic, and Logical Foundations*. Cambridge University Press, New York, USA, 2009, 2009.

[14] Philip D. Straffin Jr. *Game Theory and Strategy*. The Mathematical Association of America, 1993.

[15] Martin J. Osborne. *An Introduction to Game Theory*. The MIT Press, 2003.

[16] Y. Narahari, Dinesh Garg, Ramasuri Narayanam, and Hastagiri Prakash. *Game Theoretic Problems in Network Economics and Mechanism Design Solutions*. Springer, London, 2009.

[17] Harold W. Kuhn (Editor). *Classics in Game Theory*. Princeton University Press, 1997.

PART 1

NON-COOPERATIVE GAME THEORY

Informally, non-cooperative games are those in which the actions of individual players form the primitives while in cooperative games, joint actions of groups of players form the primitives. In this part, we study non-cooperative games spread over 12 chapters (Chapters 2-13).

- We first introduce, in Chapter 2, key notions in game theory such as *preferences*, *utilities*, *rationality*, *intelligence*, and *common knowledge*. We then study two representations for non-cooperative games: *extensive form representation* (Chapter 3) and *strategic form representation* (Chapter 4).

- In Chapters 5, 6, and 7, we describe different solution concepts which are fundamental to the analysis of strategic form games: dominant strategies and *dominant strategy equilibria* (Chapter 5); *pure strategy Nash equilibrium* (Chapter 6); and *mixed strategy Nash equilibrium* (Chapter 7). In Chapter 8, we introduce the *utility theory* of von Neumann and Morgenstern which forms the foundation for game theory.

- Chapters 9, 10, 11, and 12 are devoted to studies on existence and computation of Nash equilibria. In Chapter 9, we focus on two player zero-sum games. In Chapter 10, we provide a detailed treatment of the Nash theorem that establishes the existence of a mixed strategy Nash equilibrium in finite strategic form games. Chapter 11 is concerned with algorithmic computation of Nash equilibria while Chapter 12 deals with computational complexity of finding Nash equilibria.

- In Chapter 13, we introduce *Bayesian games* which are games with *incomplete information*. These games play a central role in mechanism design which is the subject of Part 2 of the book.

Chapter 2

Key Notions in Game Theory

We commence this chapter with a discussion of a simple coordination game to illustrate the building blocks of a strategic form game. Next we introduce the readers to key notions which are fundamental to game theory. These notions include *preferences*, *utilities* or *payoffs*, *rationality*, *intelligence*, and *common knowledge*. We also include a brief discussion on different types of games.

Game theory may be defined as the study of mathematical models of interaction between rational, intelligent decision makers [1]. The decision makers are usually referred to as players or agents. The interaction may involve *conflict* as well as *cooperation*. Game theory provides general mathematical techniques for analyzing situations in which two or more players make decisions that influence one another's welfare. A game could be considered as a mathematical model of a situation where every player strives to obtain her best possible outcome, knowing fully well that all other players are also striving to obtain their respective best possible outcomes [2].

2.1 Strategic Form Games

Before we describe key notions in game theory, we first introduce a representation of games called *strategic form games* or *normal form games*, a very commonly used representation for games. In fact, this book mostly deals with this representation of games.

Example 2.1. Consider the example of the student coordination problem discussed in Section 1.1 of the previous chapter. For the sake of convenience, let us rename IISc as A and MG Road as B. We have two players, namely, students 1 and 2. Each of them can choose any action or strategy from the set $\{A, B\}$. They choose their individual actions simultaneously, independent of each other. Depending on the strategies chosen, the two players obtain payoffs as shown in Table 2.1. This situation motivates the following definition. □

Definition 2.1. (Strategic Form Game). A strategic form game Γ is a tuple $\langle N, (S_i)_{i \in N}, (u_i)_{i \in N} \rangle$, where

- $N = \{1, 2, \ldots, n\}$ is a set of players;

1	2	
	A	B
A	$10, 10$	$0, 0$
B	$0, 0$	$1, 1$

Table 2.1: Payoffs for the students in different outcomes

- $S_1, S_2, \ldots, S_n$ are sets called the strategy sets of the players $1, \ldots, n$, respectively; and
- $u_i : S_1 \times S_2 \times \cdots \times S_n \to \mathbb{R}$ for $i = 1, 2, \ldots, n$ are mappings called the utility functions or payoff functions.

Example 2.2. For the example being discussed, it is clear that

$$N = \{1, 2\}; \ S_1 = S_2 = \{A, B\};$$

$$u_1(A, A) = 10; \ u_1(A, B) = 0; u_1(B, A) = 0; \ u_1(B, B) = 1;$$

$$u_2(A, A) = 10; \ u_2(A, B) = 0; u_2(B, A) = 0; \ u_2(B, B) = 1.$$

Note that the utilities of a player depend not only on his strategies but also on the strategies played by the other players.   □

The strategies are also called *actions* or more specifically *pure strategies*. We denote by S, the Cartesian product $S_1 \times S_2 \times \cdots \times S_n$. The set S is the collection of all strategy profiles or strategy vectors (we use the phrase strategy profiles in the rest of the book) of the players. Every profile of strategies corresponds to an *outcome* in the game. We use the phrases *strategy profile* and *outcome* synonymously. Also, we use the terms *players, individuals, persons, decision makers,* and *agents* synonymously.

A strategic form game is a simultaneous move game that captures each agent's decision problem of choosing a strategy that will counter the strategies adopted by the other agents. Each player is faced with this problem and therefore the players can be thought of as simultaneously choosing their strategies from the respective sets $S_1, S_2, \ldots, S_n$. We can view the play of a strategic form game as follows: each player simultaneously selects a strategy and informs this to a neutral observer who then computes the outcome and the utilities. We will be presenting several examples of strategic form games in Chapter 4.

There are certain key notions which are fundamental to game theory. We now discuss these notions and a few related issues.

2.2   Preferences

The student coordination game has four outcomes, namely (A, A), (A, B), (B, A), and (B, B) which are also the four strategy profiles. Each student has certain preferences over these outcomes. Clearly, in this case, each student prefers outcome (A, A) over (B, B); prefers outcome (B, B) over outcomes (A, B) and (B, A); and has no preference between (A, B) and (B, A). The preferences that a player has over outcomes can be formalized as a *preference relation* over the set of outcomes S. We will be studying this relation formally in Chapter 8. In the current context, it is useful to know that the preference relation of each player will be reflexive, transitive, and complete (that is, every pair of outcomes is covered by the relation). Obviously, in a general situation, the preference relations of different players will be different (though in the current example, both players have the same preference relation).

2.3 Utilities

The utility function or payoff function of a player is a real valued function defined on the set of all outcomes or strategy profiles. The utility function of each player maps multi-dimensional information (strategy profiles) into real numbers to capture preferences. It is important to note that the utility of a player in an outcome depends not only on his own strategy but also on the strategies of the rest of the players. One can ask the question whether it is possible at all to map preference profiles to real numbers without losing any preference information. The utility theory of von Neumann and Morgenstern [3] deals with this problem in a systematic and scientific way. In fact, von Neumann and Morgenstern stated and proved in [3] a significant result that establishes that there must exist a way of assigning real numbers to different strategy profiles in a way that the decision maker would always choose the option that maximizes her expected utility. This theorem holds under quite weak assumptions about how a rational decision maker behaves. We will defer a detailed discussion of this topic to Chapter 8.

2.4 Rationality

One of the key assumptions in game theory is that the players are rational. An agent is said to be rational if the agent always makes decisions in pursuit of her own objectives. In particular, it is assumed that each agent's objective is to maximize the expected value of her own payoff measured in some utility scale. The above notion of rationality (maximization of expected utility) was initially proposed by Bernoulli (1738) and later formalized by von Neumann and Morgenstern (1944) [3].

A key observation would be that rationality implies selfishness of the agent if her utility function captures her *self-interest*. It is important to note that self-interest does not mean that each player wants to harm the other players. It also does not necessarily mean that the players only care about themselves. Self-interest only means that each player has certain individual preferences over the outcomes and the player consistently seeks to obtain these preferred outcomes. A player's preferred outcomes could include outcomes which are preferred by some other players as well. For example, if the utility function of a player captures the altruistic nature of that player, then rationality would imply altruism.

 **John von Neumann** (1903 - 1957) is respected as one of the foremost mathematicians of the 20th century. He is regarded as the founding father of game theory. He was born in Budapest, Hungary on December 28, 1903. He was a mathematical genius from early childhood. Ironically and interestingly, however, his first major degree was in chemical engineering from the Swiss Federal Institute of Technology in Zurich. In 1926, he earned a Doctorate in Mathematics from the University of Budapest, working with Professor Leopold Fezer.

During 1926 to 1930, he taught in Berlin and Hamburg, and from 1930 to 1933, he taught at the Princeton University. In 1933, he was appointed as one of the six professors of the School of Mathematics at the Institute for Advanced Study in Princeton and he was the youngest among them. Albert Einstein and Kurt Godël were two of his distinguished colleagues at the center. During his glittering scientific career, von Neumann created several intellectual currents, two of the major ones being game theory and computer science. The fact that these two disciplines have converged during the 1990s and 2000s, almost sixty years after von Neumann brilliantly created them, is a true example of his visionary genius. In addition to game theory and computer science, he made stunning contributions to a wide array of disciplines including set theory, functional analysis, quantum mechanics, ergodic theory, continuous geometry, numerical analysis, hydrodynamics, and statistics. He is best known for his minimax theorem, utility theory, von Neumann algebras, von Neumann architecture, and cellular automata.   In game theory, von Neumann's first significant contribution was the minimax theorem, which proves the existence of a *randomized saddle point* in two player zero sum games. His collaboration with Oskar Morgenstern at the Institute for Advanced Study resulted in the classic book *The Theory of Games and Economic Behavior*, which to this day continues to be an authentic source of early game theory results. This book contains a deep discussion of many fundamental notions of game theory such as utilities, saddle points, coalitional games, bargaining sets, etc. von Neumann was associated with the development of the first electronic computer in the 1940s. He wrote a widely circulated paper entitled the *First Draft of a Report on the EDVAC* in which he described a computer architecture (which is now famously called the von Neumann architecture). He is also credited with the development of the notions of a computer algorithm and algorithm complexity.

Maximizing expected utility is not necessarily the same as maximizing expected monetary returns. In general, utility and money are nonlinearly related. For example, a certain amount of money may provide different utilities to different players depending on how endowed or desperate they are.

When there are two or more players, it would be the case that the solution to each player's decision problem depends on the others' individual problems and vice-versa. When such rational decision makers interact, their decision problems have to be analyzed together, like a system of simultaneous equations [1]. Game theory provides an apt and natural mathematical framework to deal with such analysis.

 **Oskar Morgenstern** (1902-1977) is widely known for his famous collaboration with John von Neumann which led to the celebrated book *The Theory of Games and Economic Behavior* in 1944. Their collaboration at the Institute for Advanced Study is quite legendary and was spread over 1928 - 44. The utility theory which is fundamental to game theory is rightly named after von Neumann and Morgenstern. Prior to this book, Morgenstern had authored another pioneering book *Economic Prediction*.

He also wrote a scholarly book in 1950, *On the Accuracy of Economic Observations*. In this book, he came down heavily on what he described as unscientific use of data on national income to deduce far-reaching conclusions about the state of the economy and to formulate major government policies. He is well known for applying game theory to business problems. Morgenstern was born in Germany in 1902 and studied economics in Vienna. When Adolf Hitler invaded Vienna, he was fortunately at Princeton where he continued to work until retirement. He was initially in the Princeton University and later moved to the Institute for Advanced Study at Princeton to collaborate with von Neumann. Morgenstern passed away in 1977.

2.5 Intelligence

Another key notion in game theory is that of intelligence of the players. This notion means that each player in the game knows everything about the game that a game theorist knows, and the player is competent enough to make any inferences about the game that a game theorist can make. In particular, an intelligent player is *strategic*, that is, would fully take into account his knowledge or expectation of behavior of other agents in determining what his optimal response should be. We call such a strategy a *best response strategy*. Each player is assumed to have enough resources to carry out the required computations involved in determining a best response strategy.

Myerson [1] provides a convincing explanation to show that the two assumptions of rationality and intelligence are indeed logical and reasonable. The assumption that all individuals are rational and intelligent may not exactly be satisfied in a typical real-world situation. However, any theory that is not consistent with the assumptions of rationality and intelligence loses credibility on the following count:

"If a theory predicts that some individuals will be systematically fooled into making mistakes, then this theory will lose validity when individuals learn to better understand the situations." On the other hand, a theory based on rationality and intelligence assumptions would be sustainable.

 **Robert Aumann** is a celebrated game theorist who has made path-breaking contributions to a wide spectrum of topics in game theory such as repeated games, correlated equilibria, bargaining theory, cooperative game theory, etc. Aumann provided in 1976 [4] a convincing explanation of the notion of common knowledge in game theory, in a classic paper entitled *Agreeing to disagree* (which appeared in the Annals of Statistics). Aumann's work in the 1960s on repeated games clarified the difference between infinitely and finitely repeated games.

With Bezalel Peleg in 1960, Aumann formalized the notion of a coalitional game with non-transferable utility (NTU), a significant advance in cooperative game theory. With Michael Maschler (1963), he introduced the concept of a *bargaining set*, an important solution concept in cooperative game theory. In 1974, Aumann went on to define and formalize the notion of *correlated equilibrium* in Bayesian games. In 1975, he proved a convergence theorem for the Shapley value. In 1976, in an unpublished paper with Lloyd Shapley, Aumann provided the perfect folk theorem using the limit of means criterion. All of these contributions have advanced game theory in significant ways. His book *Values of Non-Atomic Games* (1984) co-authored with Lloyd Shapley and the book *Repeated Games with Incomplete Information* (1995) co-authored with Michael Maschler are widely regarded as game theory classics.

Aumann was born in Frankfurt am Main, Germany on June 8, 1930. He earned an M.Sc. Degree in Mathematics in 1952 from the Massachusetts Institute of Technology where he also received his Ph.D. Degree in 1955. His doctoral adviser at MIT was Professor George Whitehead Jr. and his doctoral thesis was on knot theory. He has been a professor at the Center for Rationality in the Hebrew University of Jerusalem, Israel, since 1956 and he also holds a visiting appointment with Stonybrook University, USA. Robert Aumann and Thomas Schelling received the 2005 Nobel Prize in Economic Sciences for their contributions toward a clear understanding of conflict and cooperation through game theory analysis.

Common Knowledge

The notion of common knowledge is an important implication of *intelligence*. Aumann [4] defines *common knowledge* as follows: A fact is common knowledge among the players if every player knows it, every player knows that every player knows it, and so on. That is, every statement of the form "every player knows that every player knows that $\cdots$ every player knows it" is true forever. If it happens that a fact is known to all the players, without the requirement of all players knowing that all players know it, etc., then such a fact is called *mutual knowledge*. In game theory, analysis often requires the assumption of common knowledge to be true; however, sometimes, the assumption of mutual knowledge suffices for the analysis. A player's *private information* is any information that the player has that is not common knowledge or mutual knowledge among any of the players.

The intelligence assumption means that whatever a game theorist knows about the game must be known to or understood by the players of the game. Thus the model of the game is also known to the players. Since all the players know the model and they are intelligent, they also know that they all know the model; they all know that they all know that they all know the model, etc. Thus the model is common knowledge.

In a strategic form game with complete information, $\langle N, (S_i), (u_i) \rangle$, the set N, the strategy sets $S_1, \ldots, S_n$, and the utility functions $u_1, \ldots, u_n$ are common knowledge, that is every player knows them, every player knows that every player knows them, and so on. We will be studying strategic form games with complete information in this and the next few chapters. We will study games with incomplete information in Chapter 13.

Example 2.3 (Common Knowledge). This example is a variant of the one presented by Myerson [1]. Assume that there are five rational and intelligent mothers A, B, C, D, and E and let a, b, c, d, and e be their daughters (or sons), respectively. The kids go to the school every day, escorted by their respective mothers and the mothers get an opportunity everyday to indulge in some conservation. The conversation invariably centers around the performance and behavior of the kids. Everyday when the five mothers meet, the conversation protocol is the following. If a mother thinks her kid is *well behaved*, she will praise the virtues of her kid. On the other hand, if a mother knows that her kid is *not well behaved*, she will cry. All mothers follow this protocol.

The fact is that none of the kids is well behaved but their behaviors are unknown to their respective mothers. However, whenever a mother finds that the kid of another mother is not well behaved, she would immediately report it to all mothers except the kid's mother. For example, if A finds b was not well behaved, then A would report it to C, D, and E, but not to B. This protocol is also known to all the mothers. Let us therefore take as fact that the knowledge that kid a is not well behaved is known to all the mothers except A (who believes that a is well behaved). Similar is the knowledge and belief about other kids' well behavedness or lack thereof.

Since each mother does not know that her kid is not well behaved, it turns out that every mother keeps praising her kid everyday. On a fine day, the class teacher meets all the mothers and makes the following statement: "at least one of the kids is not well behaved." Thus the fact that one of the kids is not well behaved is now common knowledge among all the mothers. Subsequently, when the five mothers meet the next day, all of them praise their respective kids; the same happens on the 2nd day, 3rd day, and the 4th day. On the 5th day, however, all the mothers cry together because all of them realize that their respective kids are not well behaved. The readers are urged to convince themselves why the above two statements are true.

Note that the announcement made by the class teacher is common knowledge and that is what makes all the mothers cry on the fifth day. $\qquad\square$

2.6   Classification of Games

Any well developed subject like game theory which has been extensively explored
for more than eight decades will abound in numerous kinds of games being defined
and studied. We only provide a listing of some of the well known ones here.

Non-cooperative Games and Cooperative Games

Non-cooperative games are those in which the actions of individual players are the
primitives; in cooperative games, joint actions of groups of players are the primitives. John Harsanyi (1966) [5] explained that a game is cooperative if commitments
(agreements, promises, threats) among players are enforceable and that a game becomes non-cooperative if the commitments are not enforceable.

It would be false to say that non-cooperative game theory applies only to situations in which there is a conflict or non-cooperation among the players. It is just
that each individual player and the preferences of the player provide the basic modeling unit. In contrast, in cooperative games, the basic modeling unit is a group of
players. If all groups are singletons, then we have a non-cooperative game.

Static Games and Dynamic Games

In static games, players choose their actions simultaneously and no information
is received during the play. An immediate example is the situation in Example
2.1 where two students simultaneously decide their strategies and receive a certain
amount of reward based on the outcomes obtained. These are often called single-
stage games. In a dynamic game which is often called a multi-stage game, there
is a temporal order in which actions are played by the players. Typically, in a
multi-stage game, a certain player chooses an action before other players do and the
player knows that the choice of actions by other players will be influenced by her
action. Players who choose their actions subsequently make their choices dependent
on their knowledge of the actions that others have chosen. An immediate example
of a dynamic game is Chess. In dynamic games, information is received and could
be used by the players to plan their actions during the play of the game.

Different Representational Forms

A strategic form game (also called simultaneous move game or normal form game),
which was introduced in this chapter, is a model or a situation where each player
chooses the plan of action once and for all, and all players exercise their decisions
simultaneously. Strategic form representation does not capture sequence of moves
by the players and does not capture any information accrual to the players during
the play of a game. This representation is therefore very convenient for static games.
If used for dynamic games, it is to be noted that the strategic form representation
could suppress the dynamics of the game.

An extensive form game specifies a possible order of events and each player can consider his plan of action whenever a decision has to be made by him. The extensive form representation can capture the sequence of moves by the players and can also capture the information accrual to the players during the play of a game. It is therefore a suitable form of representation for dynamic games. Strategic form can be considered as a static equivalent of extensive form.

A *coalitional form game* or *characteristic form game* is one where every subset of players is represented with an associated value. This form is appropriate for cooperative games.

Games with Perfect Information and Games with Imperfect Information

When the players are fully informed about the entire past history (each player, before making a move, knows the past moves of all other players as well as his own past moves), the game is said to be of perfect information. Otherwise it is called a game with imperfect information.

Complete Information and Incomplete Information Games

A game with incomplete information is one in which, at the first point in time when the players can begin to plan their moves, some players have private information about the game that other players do not know. In a game with complete information, every aspect of the game is common knowledge.

Other Categories

There are many other categories of games, such as repeated games, evolutionary games, stochastic games, multi-level games (Stackelberg games), differential games, etc. We do not get into the details of these games in this book. We refer the reader to the books by Osborne [6] and by Maschler, Solan, and Zamir [2] for a discussion of other categories of games.

2.7 Summary and References

In this chapter, we have introduced several fundamental notions and assumptions which are key to game theory. These include: preferences, utilities or payoffs, rationality, intelligence, and common knowledge.

- Preferences of a player specify qualitatively the player's ranking of the different outcomes of the game.
- Utilities are real valued payoffs that players receive when they play different actions. The utility of a player depends not only on the action played by that player but also on the actions played by the rest of the players.
- Rationality intuitively means that players always choose their actions so as to

maximize their expected utilities. Depending on how the utility function is defined, rationality could mean self-interest, altruism, indifference, etc.

- Intelligence means that the players are as knowledgeable as game theorists and have enough computational power to compute their best response actions.
- Common knowledge is an implication of intelligence and means that all players know the entire structure of the game, all players know that all players know the game, all players know that all players know that all players know the game, etc.

Game theory is founded on the above notions. Some of the above assumptions may or may not be valid in real world situations, however the abstractions provided by game theory under the above assumptions will provide a perfect starting point for a scientific investigation into strategic situations.

The material discussed in this chapter draws mainly upon the following sources, namely the books by Myerson [1], Mas-Colell, Whinston, and Green [7], Osborne [6], Osborne and Rubinstein [8], and Maschler, Solan, and Zamir [2].

A detailed discussion of the notion of common knowledge can be found in the original paper by Aumann [4]. The book by Maschler, Solan, and Zamir [2] discusses this notion extensively with several illustrative examples.

For an undergraduate level treatment of game theory, we recommend the books by Osborne [6], Straffin [9], and Binmore [10]. For a graduate level treatment, we recommend the books by Myerson [1], Maschler, Solan, and Zamir [2], and Osborne and Rubinstein [8].

We also refer the readers to books by Rasmussen [11], Gibbons [12], Basar and Olsder [13], and Fudenberg and Tirole [14] for a scholarly treatment of game theory.

The classic treatise by John von Neumann and Oskar Morgenstern [3], published in 1944, provides a comprehensive foundation for game theory. To this day, even after many decades of its first appearance, the book continues to be a valuable reference.

References

[1]   Roger B. Myerson. *Game Theory: Analysis of Conflict.* Harvard University Press, Cambridge, Massachusetts, USA, 1997.
[2]   Michael Maschler, Eilon Solan, and Shmuel Zamir. *Game Theory.* Cambridge University Press, 2013.
[3]   John von Neumann and Oskar Morgenstern. *Theory of Games and Economic Behavior.* Princeton University Press, 1944.
[4]   Robert J. Aumann. "Agreeing to disagree". In: *The Annals of Statistics* **4**(6) (1976), pp. 1236–1239.
[5]   John C. Harsanyi. "Games with incomplete information played by Bayesian players. Part I: The basic model". In: *Management Science* **14** (1967), pp. 159–182.
[6]   Martin J. Osborne. *An Introduction to Game Theory.* The MIT Press, 2003.
[7]   Andreu Mas-Colell, Michael D. Whinston, and Jerry R. Green. *Microeconomic Theory.* Oxford University Press, 1995.

[8]   Martin J. Osborne and Ariel Rubinstein. *A Course in Game Theory*. Oxford University Press, 1994.

[9]   Philip D. Straffin Jr. *Game Theory and Strategy*. The Mathematical Association of America, 1993.

[10] Ken Binmore. *Fun and Games : A Text On Game Theory*. D. C. Heath & Company, 1992.

[11] Eric Rasmussen. *Games and Information*. Blackwell Publishing, Fourth Edition, 2007.

[12] Robert Gibbons. *Game Theory for Applied Economists*. Princeton University Press, Princeton, NJ, USA, 1992.

[13] Tamer Basar and Geert Jan Olsder. *Dynamic Non-cooperative Game Theory*. SIAM, Second Edition, Philadelphia, PA, USA, 1999.

[14] Drew Fudenberg and Jean Tirole. *Game Theory*. MIT Press, Cambridge and London, 1991.

Chapter 3

Extensive Form Games

In this chapter, we study *extensive form representation* of a game, which provides a detailed representation of a game, including the sequence of moves and information accrual to players. We explain the important notions underlying extensive form representation. In this book, we mostly deal with strategic form representation; in this chapter, we bring out the connection between extensive form and strategic form representations. We show how any extensive form game can be transformed into a strategic form game.

The extensive form representation of a game provides a detailed and richly structured way to describe a game. This form was first proposed by von Neumann and Morgenstern [1] and was later refined by Kuhn [2]. The extensive form captures complete sequential play of a game. Specifically it captures (1) who makes a move at any given time (2) what actions each player may play (3) what the players know before playing at each stage (4) what the outcomes are as a function of the actions, and (5) payoffs that players obtain from each outcome. Extensive form games with a finite number of players and with a finite number of actions available to each player are depicted graphically using game trees.

3.1 Illustrative Examples

We first present several examples before we formally define an extensive form game.

Example 3.1 (Matching Pennies with Observation). In the matching pennies game, there are two players, 1 and 2, each of whom has a rupee coin. One of the players puts down his rupee coin heads or tails up. The other player sees the outcome and puts down her coin heads up or tails up. If both the coins show heads or both the coins show tails, player 2 gives one rupee to player 1 who thus becomes richer by one rupee. If one of the coins shows heads and the other coin shows tails, then player 1 pays one rupee to player 2 who becomes richer by one rupee. Depending on whether player 1 or player 2 moves first, there are two versions of this game. Figure 3.1 shows the game tree when player 1 moves first while Figure 3.2 shows the game tree when player 2 moves first. In the game tree representation, the nodes are of three types: (1) *root node* (initial decision node); (2)

internal nodes (which are decision nodes); and (3) *leaf nodes* or *terminal nodes* (which are outcome nodes). Each possible sequence of events that could occur in the game is captured by a path of links from the root node to one of the terminal nodes. When the game is played, the path that represents the sequence of events is called the *path of play*. Each decision node is labeled with the player who takes a decision at that node. Also note that each decision node can be uniquely identified by a sequence of actions leading to that decision node from the root node. The links that are outgoing at the decision node are labeled with the actions the player may select at that node. Note that each node represents not only the current position in the game but also how it was reached. The terminal nodes are labeled with the payoffs that the players would get in the outcomes corresponding to those nodes.   □

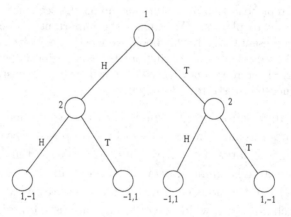

Fig. 3.1: Matching pennies game with observation when player 1 moves first

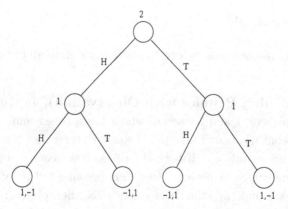

Fig. 3.2: Matching pennies game with observation when player 2 moves first

Example 3.2 (Matching Pennies without Observation). In this case, one of the players places his rupee coin heads up or tails up. The other player *does not observe the outcome* and only puts down her rupee coin heads up or tails up. Depending on whether player 1 moves first or player 2 moves first, we obtain the game tree of Figure 3.3 or Figure 3.4, respectively. Note that the game trees of Figures 3.1 and 3.3 are virtually the same except that the two decision nodes corresponding to player 2 in Figure 3.3 are connected with dotted lines. Similarly the game trees of Figures 3.2 and 3.4 are the same except that the two decision nodes corresponding to player 1 in Figure 3.4 are connected with dotted lines. A set of nodes that are connected with dotted lines is called an *information set*. When the game reaches a decision node in an information set, the player involved at that node does not know the node in the information set she is in. The reason for this is that the player cannot observe the previous moves in the game. □

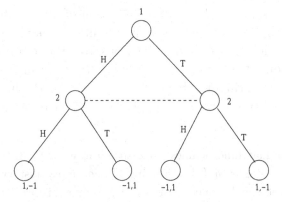

Fig. 3.3: Matching pennies game without observation when player 1 moves first

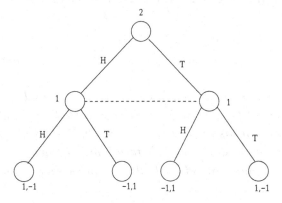

Fig. 3.4: Matching pennies game without observation when player 2 moves first

Example 3.3 (Matching Pennies with Simultaneous Play). In this version of
the game, the two players put down their rupee coins simultaneously. Clearly, each player
has no opportunity to observe the outcome of the move of the other player. The order
of play is obviously irrelevant here. Thus both the game trees depicted in Figure 3.3 and
Figure 3.4 provide a valid representation of this version of the game.   □

3.2 Extensive Form Games: Definitions

We now formally define an extensive form game. This definition follows closely the
one given by Osborne [3]. First we define an information set.

Definition 3.1 (Information Set). *An information set of a player is a set of that*
player's decision nodes that are indistinguishable to her.

An information set of a player describes a collection of all possible distinguishable
circumstances in which the player is called upon to make a move. Since each decision
node corresponds uniquely to a sequence of actions from the root node to the decision
node, each information set of a player consists of all proper subhistories relevant to
that player which are indistinguishable to that player. Clearly, in every node within
a given information set, the corresponding player must have the same set of possible
actions.

Example 3.4. In the matching pennies game shown in Figure 3.3, the only information
set of a player 1 is the singleton $\{\varepsilon\}$ consisting of the empty history. The information
set of player 2 is the set $\{H, T\}$ that consists of the proper histories H and T which are
indistinguishable to player 2. On the other hand, in the game shown in Figure 3.1, player
1 has only one information set namely $\{\varepsilon\}$ whereas player 2 has two information sets $\{H\}$
and $\{T\}$ because these two proper subhistories are distinguishable to player 2.   □

Definition 3.2 (Extensive Form Game). *An extensive form game* Γ *consists of*
a tuple $\Gamma = \langle N, (A_i)_{i \in N}, \mathbb{H}, P, (\mathbb{I}_i)_{i \in N}, (u_i)_{i \in N} \rangle$ *where*

- $N = \{1, 2, \ldots, n\}$ *is a finite set of players*
- A_i *for* $i = 1, 2, \ldots, n$ *is the set of actions available to player* i *(action set of*
  player i*)*
- $\mathbb{H}$ *is the set of all* terminal histories *where a terminal history is a path of*
  actions from the root to a terminal node such that it is not a proper subhistory
  of any other terminal history. Denote by $S_\mathbb{H}$ *the set of all proper subhistories*
  (including the empty history ε*) of all terminal histories.*
- $P : S_\mathbb{H} \to N$ *is a player function that associates each proper subhistory to a*
  certain player
- $\mathbb{I}_i$ *for* $i = 1, 2, \ldots, n$ *is the set of all information sets of player* i
- $u_i : \mathbb{H} \to \mathbb{R}$ *for* $i = 1, 2, \ldots, n$ *gives the utility of player* i *corresponding to each*
  terminal history.

Example 3.5. We illustrate the above definition for the matching pennies game shown in Figure 3.1.

$$N = \{1, 2\}$$

$$A_1 = A_2 = \{H, T\}$$

$$\mathbb{H} = \{(H, H), (H, T), (T, H), (T, T)\}$$

$$S_{\mathbb{H}} = \{\varepsilon, H, T\}$$

$$P(\varepsilon) = 1; \ P(H) = 2; \ P(T) = 2$$

$$\mathbb{I}_1 = \{\{\varepsilon\}\}; \ \mathbb{I}_2 = \{\{H\}, \{T\}\}$$

$$u_1(HH) = 1; \ u_1(HT) = -1; \ u_1(TH) = -1; \ u_1(TT) = 1$$

$$u_2(HH) = -1; \ u_2(HT) = 1; \ u_2(TH) = 1; \ u_2(TT) = -1$$

It is clear that action sets of different players can be deduced from the terminal histories and the player function. □

Note. Though the action sets of players can be deduced from terminal histories and the player function, we explicitly include action sets as a part of definition of an extensive form game for ease of understanding.

Example 3.6 (Entry Game). In this game, there are two players, 1 and 2. Player 1 is called *challenger* and player 2 is called *incumbent*. Figure 3.5 shows the game tree. Player

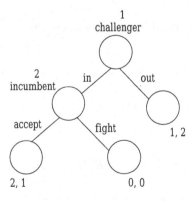

Fig. 3.5: Game tree for entry game

1 (challenger) either decides to challenge the incumbent (action: in) or drops out (action: out). Player 2 (incumbent) either decides to fight or accommodate the challenger in case the challenger decides to confront the incumbent. The respective payoffs are shown in the

game tree. For this game, we have

$$N = \{1, 2\}; \quad A_1 = \{\text{in, out}\}; \quad A_2 = \{\text{accept, fight}\}$$
$$\mathbb{H} = \{(\text{in, accept}), (\text{in, fight}), (\text{out})\}$$
$$S_{\mathbb{H}} = \{\epsilon, (\text{in})\}$$
$$P(\epsilon) = 1$$
$$P(\text{in}) = 2$$
$$\mathbb{I}_1 = \{\{\varepsilon\}\}; \quad \mathbb{I}_2 = \{\{\text{in}\}\}$$
$$u_1(\text{in, accept}) = 2; \quad u_1(\text{in, fight}) = 0; \quad u_1(\text{out}) = 1$$
$$u_2(\text{in, accept}) = 1; \quad u_2(\text{in, fight}) = 0; \quad u_2(\text{out}) = 2$$

Note again that the action sets A_1 and A_2 can be deduced from the terminal histories and the player function. $\square$

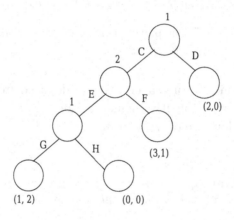

Fig. 3.6: Another game tree

Example 3.7. Consider the game tree shown in Figure 3.6. For this game, it is easy to see that

$$N = \{1, 2\}; \quad A_1 = \{C, D, G, H\}; \quad A_2 = \{E, F\}$$

The terminal histories are given by

$$\mathbb{H} = \{(C, E, G), (C, E, H), (C, F), (D)\}$$

The proper subhistories of terminal histories are given by

$$S_{\mathbb{H}} = \{\epsilon, (C), (C, E)\}$$

The player function is given by

$$P(\epsilon) = 1; \quad P(C) = 2; \quad P(C, E) = 1$$

The information sets are given by

$$\mathbb{I}_1 = \{\{\varepsilon\}, \{(C, E)\}\}; \quad \mathbb{I}_2 = \{\{(C)\}\}$$

The utility functions are given by

$$u_1(C, E, G) = 1; \quad u_1(C, E, H) = 0;$$
$$u_1(C, F) = 3; \quad u_1(D) = 2;$$
$$u_2(C, E, G) = 2; \quad u_2(C, E, H) = 0;$$
$$u_2(C, F) = 1; \quad u_2(D) = 0.$$

This completes the description of the game shown in Figure 3.6. $\square$

Definition 3.3 (Perfect Information and Imperfect Information Games).
An extensive form game with perfect information is one in which all the informa-
tion sets are singletons. If at least one information set of at least one player has
two or more elements, the game is said to be of imperfect information.

In a game with perfect information, each player is able to observe all previous moves
or the entire history thus far. Each player knows precisely where she is currently
and also knows precisely how she has reached that node.

Example 3.8. As immediate examples, the games depicted in Figures 3.1, 3.2, 3.5, and
3.6 are games with perfect information while the games shown in Figures 3.3 and 3.4 are
games with imperfect information. The matching pennies game with simultaneous play is
obviously a game with imperfect information. $\square$

3.3 Transforming Extensive Form to Strategic Form

The notion of a strategy is one of the most important notions in game theory. A
strategy can be described as a complete action plan that specifies what a player will
do at each of the information sets where he is called upon to play.

Recall that $\mathbb{I}_i$ denotes the set of all information sets of player i in the given game.
Let A_i as usual denote the actions available to player i. Given an information set
$J \in \mathbb{I}_i$, let $C(J) \subseteq A_i$ be the set of all actions possible to player i in the information
set J. Then we define a strategy of a player formally as follows.

Definition 3.4 (Strategy). *A strategy s_i of player i is a mapping $s_i : \mathbb{I}_i \to A_i$*
such that $s_i(J) \in C(J) \ \forall J \in \mathbb{I}_i$.

The strategy s_i for player i is a complete contingent plan that specifies an action
for every information set of the player. A strategy thus determines the action the
player will choose in every stage or history of the game the player is called upon
to play. In fact, the player can prepare a look-up table with two columns, one

for her information sets and the other for corresponding actions; the player or a representative of the player can then take over and play the game using table look-up. Different strategies of the player correspond to different contingent plans of actions. We illustrate the notion of strategy through an example.

Example 3.9 (Strategies in Matching Pennies with Observation).
Consider the game shown in Figure 3.1. We have $\mathbb{I}_1 = \{\{\varepsilon\}\}$; $\mathbb{I}_2 = \{\{H\}, \{T\}\}$. Player 1 has two strategies:

$$s_{11} : \{\varepsilon\} \to H$$
$$s_{12} : \{\varepsilon\} \to T$$

Player 2 has the following four strategies:

$$s_{21} : \{H\} \to H; \quad \{T\} \to H$$
$$s_{22} : \{H\} \to H; \quad \{T\} \to T$$
$$s_{23} : \{H\} \to T; \quad \{T\} \to H$$
$$s_{24} : \{H\} \to T; \quad \{T\} \to T$$

The payoffs obtained by the players 1 and 2 can now be described by Table 3.1. Note, for example, that when the strategy of player 1 is s_{11}, the player plays H and when the strategy of player 2 is s_{21}, the player 2 plays H, leading to the payoffs 1, -1.

1	2			
	s_{21}	s_{22}	s_{23}	s_{24}
s_{11}	1, -1	1, -1	$-1, 1$	$-1, 1$
s_{12}	$-1, 1$	1, -1	$-1, 1$	1, -1

Table 3.1: Payoffs obtained in matching pennies with observation

The above game is a *strategic form game* equivalent of the original extensive form game. For the game shown in Figure 3.2, player 2 will have two strategies and player 1 will have four strategies and a payoff matrix such as above can be easily derived. □

Example 3.10 (Strategies in Matching Pennies without Observation).
Consider the game shown in Figure 3.3. It is easy to see that $\mathbb{I}_1 = \{\{\varepsilon\}\}$ and $\mathbb{I}_2 = \{\{H, T\}\}$. Here player 1 has two strategies and player 2 has two strategies as shown below.

$$s_{11} : \{\varepsilon\} \to H$$
$$s_{12} : \{\varepsilon\} \to T$$
$$s_{21} : \{H, T\} \to H$$
$$s_{22} : \{H, T\} \to T$$

The payoff matrix corresponding to all possible strategies that can be played by the players is shown in Table 3.2.

	2	
1	s_{21}	s_{22}
s_{11}	$1, -1$	$-1, 1$
s_{12}	$-1, 1$	$1, -1$

Table 3.2: Payoffs obtained in matching pennies without observation

Clearly, the matching pennies game with simultaneous moves also will have the same strategies and payoff matrix as above. □

Example 3.11. Consider the game in Figure 3.6. Player 1 has four strategies given by

$$s_{11} : \{\varepsilon\} \to C; \quad \{(C, E)\} \to G$$

$$s_{12} : \{\varepsilon\} \to C; \quad \{(C, E)\} \to H$$

$$s_{13} : \{\varepsilon\} \to D; \quad \{(C, E)\} \to G$$

$$s_{14} : \{\varepsilon\} \to D; \quad \{(C, E)\} \to H$$

For the sake of convenience, let us denote the above strategies by CG, CH, DG, and DH, respectively. Player 2 has two strategies given by

$$s_{21} : \{C\} \to E$$

$$s_{21} : \{C\} \to F$$

For the sake of convenience, let us denote the above strategies by E and F, respectively. If S_1 and S_2 are the sets of strategies of players 1 and 2 respectively, it can be seen that

$$S_1 = \{CG, CH, DG, DH\}$$
$$S_2 = \{E, F\}$$

The set of strategy profiles, $S_1 \times S_2$, is given by

$$S_1 \times S_2 = \{(CG, E), (CG, F), (CH, E), (CH, F), (DG, E), (DG, F), (DH, E), (DH, F)\}$$

Note that a strategy profile uniquely determines a terminal history. For example, the profile (CG, E) corresponds to the terminal history (C, E, G); the profile (CG, F) corresponds to the terminal history (C, F); the profiles (DH, E) as well as (DH, F) correspond to the terminal history (D), etc. This example motivates the following definition. □

Definition 3.5 (Outcome). *Given an extensive form game Γ and a strategy profile $s = (s_1, \ldots, s_n)$ in the game, the outcome resulting out of the terminal history corresponding to the strategy profile s is called the outcome of s and is denoted by $O(s)$.*

Note. It is to be noted that every extensive form game has a unique strategic form representation. The uniqueness is up to renaming or renumbering of strategies. We can also immediately observe that a given strategic form game may correspond to multiple extensive form games.

Note. We have seen that any given extensive form game has an equivalent strategic form game. However, the equivalent strategic form representation may or may not contain all of the strategically relevant information present in the extensive form representation. In fact, the strategic form representation suppresses the dynamics of the game because of simultaneous play. In this book, we mostly focus on the strategic form representation. It is to be noted that dynamic games where there is sequential play as well as information accrual to the players during the play of the game warrant extensive form representation.

3.4   Summary and References

Following is a summary of salient points that we have covered in this chapter.

- Extensive form games provide a detailed representation of sequence of play and information accrual by players in a game. Finite extensive form games can be represented using game trees which consist of decision nodes and terminal nodes. Each decision node corresponds to a certain player and the player is required to choose an action in the decision node.
- An important notion in an extensive form games is that of an *information set* of a player. An information set of a player is a set of decision nodes of the player that are indistinguishable to the player (the player does not know in which of these decision nodes she is in).
- An extensive form game with perfect information is one in which all information sets of all players are singletons. This implies that at every decision node, the corresponding player has knowledge of the entire history until reaching that decision node. An extensive form game with imperfect information is one where at least one information set of at least one player is not a singleton.
- An extensive form game can be transformed into an equivalent strategic form game using the notion of a strategy. A strategy of a player is a complete action plan that specifies which action the player will choose in each of her information sets.
- A strategic form game often suppresses the dynamics of the game. However, it simplifies the analysis of games and it suffices to work with the strategic form representation for finding answers to many useful analysis questions.
- A given strategic form game could correspond to multiple extensive form games while a given extensive form game when transformed into strategic form yields a representation that is unique in structure.

Much of the material in this chapter is based on relevant discussions in the books by Osborne [3] and by Mas-Colell, Whinston, and Green [4]. In this book, we will be dealing mostly with strategic form games. In Chapter 6, we briefly return to extensive form games to introduce the notion of subgame perfect equilibrium. For a detailed treatment of extensive form games, we refer the reader to the books by Osborne [3], Myerson [5], and Maschler, Solan, and Zamir [6].

References

[1]   John von Neumann and Oskar Morgenstern. *Theory of Games and Economic Behavior*. Princeton University Press, 1944.

[2]   H.W. Kuhn. "Extensive form games and the problem of information". In: *Contributions to the Theory of Games II*. Princeton University Press, 1953, pp. 193–216.

[3]   Martin J. Osborne. *An Introduction to Game Theory*. The MIT Press, 2003.

[4]   Andreu Mas-Colell, Michael D. Whinston, and Jerry R. Green. *Microeconomic Theory*. Oxford University Press, 1995.

[5]   Roger B. Myerson. *Game Theory: Analysis of Conflict*. Harvard University Press, Cambridge, Massachusetts, USA, 1997.

[6]   Michael Maschler, Eilon Solan, and Shmuel Zamir. *Game Theory*. Cambridge University Press, 2013.

3.5   Exercises

(1) You might know the tic-tac-toe game. Sketch a game tree for this game.

(2) In a game, a certain player has m information sets indexed by $j = 1, 2, \ldots, m$. There are k_j possible actions for information set j. How many strategies does the player have?

(3) For game shown in Figure 3.7, write down the terminal histories, proper sub-histories, information sets, and the strategic form representation.

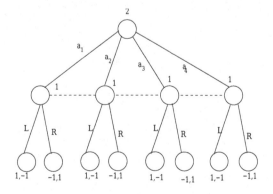

Fig. 3.7: An extensive form game

Chapter 4

Strategic Form Games

Strategic form representation is the most extensively discussed representation for games in this book. In this chapter, we provide a number of illustrative examples to help gain an intuitive understanding of strategic form games. The examples involve finite games as well as infinite games. The games discussed include matching pennies, rock-paper-scissors, Bach or Stravinsky, student's co-ordination, prisoner's dilemma, company's dilemma, duopoly pricing, tragedy of the commons, bandwidth sharing, sealed bid auction, Pigou network routing game, and Braess paradox. The examples are fairly representative of the wide canvas of applications where game theoretic modeling is relevant.

4.1 Preliminaries

We have seen in Chapter 2 (Definition 2.1) that a strategic form game Γ is a tuple $\Gamma = \langle N, (S_i)_{i \in N}, (u_i)_{i \in N} \rangle$ where $N = \{1, 2, \ldots, n\}$ is a finite set of players; $S_1, S_2, \ldots, S_n$ are the strategy sets of the players; and $u_i : S_1 \times S_2 \times \cdots \times S_n \to \mathbb{R}$ for $i = 1, 2, \ldots, n$ are utility functions. We have seen in Chapter 3 that games in extensive form can be transformed into strategic form games by mapping contingent action plans into strategies. The phrases *strategic form games*, *strategic games*, and *normal form games* are synonymous. When there is no confusion, we use the notation $\Gamma = \langle N, (S_i), (u_i) \rangle$ for a strategic form game.

We denote by S, the set of all strategy profiles or strategy vectors, which is the Cartesian product $S_1 \times \cdots \times S_n$. A typical strategy profile is represented by $(s_1, \ldots, s_n)$ where s_i is the strategy of player i $(i = 1, \ldots, n)$. We denote by S_{-i} the Cartesian product $S_1 \times \cdots \times S_{i-1} \times S_{i+1} \times \cdots S_n$ of strategy sets of all players other than player i. We denote by s_{-i} a typical strategy profile in S_{-i}. When we are focusing on a particular player i, a convenient way of representing a strategy profile is (s_i, s_{-i}) where $s_i \in S_i$ and $s_{-i} \in S_{-i}$.

The idea behind the strategic form representation is that a player's decision problem is to essentially choose a strategy that will counter most effectively the strategies adopted by the other players. Such a strategy is called a *best response strategy* which is formally defined as follows.

Definition 4.1 (Best Response Strategy). *Given a strategic form game* $\Gamma = \langle N, (S_i), (u_i) \rangle$ *and a strategy profile* $s_{-i} \in S_{-i}$, *we say* $s_i \in S_i$ *is a best response strategy of player* i *with respect to* s_{-i} *if* $u_i(s_i, s_{-i}) \geq u_i(s_i', s_{-i}) \, \forall s_i' \in S_i$.

Given a strategy profile $s_{-i} \in S_{-i}$ of all players except player i, there could exist multiple best response strategies for player i.

In a strategic form game, each player is faced with the problem of choosing his best response strategy and the players can be thought of as simultaneously choosing their strategies from the respective sets $S_1, \ldots, S_n$.

Many interpretations have been provided in the game theory literature for strategic form games. We present here two interpretations provided by Osborne and Rubinstein [1].

In the first interpretation, a strategic form game is a model of an event that occurs only once. Each player knows the details of the game and the fact that all players are rational. The players choose their strategies simultaneously and independently. Each player is unaware of the choices being made by the other players.

In the second interpretation, a player is assumed to form an expectation of the other players' behavior on the basis of information about the way the game or a similar game was played in the past. A strategic form game models a sequence of plays of the game under the condition that there is no strategic link between the plays of the game. That is, a player who plays the game many times should only worry about his own instantaneous payoff and ignore the effects of his current action on the future behavior of the other players. A class of games called *repeated games* is relevant if there is a strategic link between plays of a game.

The extensive form representation, discussed in Chapter 3, is a more detailed representation than the strategic form representation. A given strategic form game could correspond to multiple extensive form games. The strategic form game suppresses the dynamics of the game but is more convenient for certain kinds of analysis of games. It is enough to work with strategic form for finding answers to many useful analysis questions.

4.2 Matching Pennies with Simultaneous Moves

We have already studied this game in Chapter 3. Recall that in this game, two players 1 and 2 put down their respective rupee coins, heads or tails up. If both the coins match (both heads or both tails), then player 2 pays one rupee to player 1. Otherwise, player 1 pays one rupee to player 2. Let us say A denotes *heads* and B denotes *tails*. It is easy to see that:

$$N = \{1, 2\}$$
$$S_1 = S_2 = \{A, B\}$$
$$S = S_1 \times S_2 = \{(A, A), (A, B), (B, A), (B, B)\}$$

The payoff matrix is given by

1	2	
	A	B
A	$1, -1$	$-1, 1$
B	$-1, 1$	$1, -1$

This is perhaps the simplest example of a two player game. This belongs to a class of games called two player zero-sum games (so called because the sum of utilities in every outcome is equal to zero). In the above game, it is easy to see that the best response strategy of player 1 is A (B) when player 2 plays A (B). On the other hand, the best response strategy of player 2 is A (B) when player 1 plays B (A).

To understand why a simple game such as the above is important to study, let us consider the following situation. There are two companies, call them 1 and 2. Each company is capable of producing two products A and B, but at any given time, a company can only produce one product, due to high setup and switchover costs. Company 1 is known to produce superior quality products but company 2 scores over company 1 in terms of marketing and advertising. If both the companies produce the same product (A or B), it turns out that company 1 makes all the profits and company 2 loses out, because of the superior quality of products produced by company 1. This is reflected in our model with a payoff of $+1$ for company 1 and a payoff of -1 for company 2, corresponding to the strategy profiles (A, A) and (B, B).

On the other hand, if one company produces product A and the other produces product B, it may turn out that because of aggressive marketing by company 2 in differentiating the product offerings A and B, company 2 captures all the market, resulting in a payoff of $+1$ for company 2 and a payoff of -1 for company 1.

The two companies have to simultaneously decide (each one does not know the decision of the other) which product to produce. This is the strategic decision facing the two companies. This situation is captured by a strategic form game $\Gamma = \langle N, S_1, S_2, u_1, u_2 \rangle$, where $N = \{1, 2\}$; $S_1 = S_2 = \{A, B\}$, and the utility functions are as described in the above table.

4.3 Rock-Paper-Scissors Game

This is an example of another two player zero-sum game where each player has three strategies, called *rock*, *paper*, and *scissors*. Actually, this is a popular hand game played by two persons. Another name for this game is *roshambo*. Two players simultaneously display one of three symbols: a *rock*, a *paper*, or *scissors*. The *rock* symbol beats *scissors* symbol; *scissors* symbol beats *paper* symbol; *paper* symbol beats *rock* symbol (symbolically, rock can break scissors; scissors can cut paper; and paper can cover rock). The payoff matrix for this game is given as follows.

1	2 Rock	Paper	Scissors
Rock	0, 0	−1, 1	1, −1
Paper	1, −1	0, 0	−1, 1
Scissors	−1, 1	1, −1	0, 0

4.4   BOS (Bach or Stravinsky) Game

This game is named after the famous musicians Bach and Stravinsky. This is also called the *Battle of Sexes* game. This is a game where the players want to coordinate with each other; however, they have a disagreement about which of the outcomes is better. Let us say two players 1 and 2 wish to go out together to an event A or to an alternative event B. Player 1 prefers to go to event A and player 2 prefers to go to event B. The payoff matrix is as shown.

1	2 A	B
A	2, 1	0, 0
B	0, 0	1, 2

Clearly, this game captures a situation where the players want to coordinate but they have conflicting interests. The outcomes (A, B) and (B, A) are unfavorable to either player. The choice is essentially between (A, A) and (B, B). Recalling the company analogy, suppose we have two companies, 1 and 2. Each company can produce only one of two competing products A and B, but at any given time, a company can only produce one type of product. Assume product A is a niche product of company 1 while product B is a niche product of company 2. If both the companies produce product A, the consumers are compelled to buy product A and would naturally prefer to buy it from company 1 rather than from 2. Assume that company 1 captures two thirds of the market. We can reflect this fact by making the payoff to company 1 twice that of company 2. If both the companies produce product B, the reverse situation will prevail and company 2 will make twice as much payoff as company 1.

On the other hand, if the two companies decide to produce different products, then the market gets segmented and each company tries to outwit the other through increased spending on advertising. In fact, their competition may actually benefit a third company and, effectively, neither company 1 nor company 2 makes any payoff. The above table depicts the payoff structure for this game.

4.5 A Coordination Game

We have already presented this game in Chapter 1 (student's coordination game). This game is similar to the BOS game but the two players now have a preference for the same option, namely event A. The payoff matrix is as shown below; note that the outcomes (A, A) and (B, B) in that order are preferred.

		2	
1	A	B	
A	10, 10	0, 0	
B	0, 0	1, 1	

Continuing our analogy of companies, the above game corresponds to a situation wherein the two companies produce the same product, and they have equal market share. This market share is ten times as much for product A as for product B. On the other hand, if the two companies produce different products, a third company may capture all the market share leaving nothing for companies 1 and 2.

Since the payoffs are the same for both the players in all outcomes, such games are also called *common payoff games*.

4.6 Prisoner's Dilemma Game

This is one of the most extensively studied problems in game theory, with many interesting interpretations in a wide variety of situations. Two individuals are arrested for allegedly committing a crime and are lodged in separate cells. The interrogator questions them separately. The interrogator privately tells each prisoner that if he is the only one to confess, he will get a light sentence of 1 year in jail while the other would be sentenced to 10 years in jail. If both players confess, they would get 5 years each in jail. If neither confesses, then each would get 2 years in jail. The interrogator also informs each prisoner what has been told to the other prisoner. Thus the payoff matrix is common knowledge.

		2	
1	NC	C	
NC	$-2, -2$	$-10, -1$	
C	$-1, -10$	$-5, -5$	

How would the prisoners behave in such a situation? They would like to play a strategy that offers a best response to a best response strategy that the other player may adopt, the latter player also would like to play a strategy that offers a best response to the other player's best response strategy, and so on. First observe that

C is each player's best response strategy regardless of what the other player plays:

$$u_1(C,C) = -5 > u_1(NC,C) = -10; \quad u_1(C,NC) = -1 > u_1(NC,NC) = -2.$$
$$u_2(C,C) = -5 > u_2(C,NC) = -10; \quad u_2(NC,C) = -1 > u_2(NC,NC) = -2.$$

Thus (C,C) is a natural prediction for this game. However, the outcome (NC,NC) is the best outcome jointly for the players. Prisoner's dilemma is a classic example of a game where rational, intelligent behavior does not lead to an outcome where the sum of utilities of the players is maximal. Also, each prisoner has a negative effect or externality on the other. When a prisoner moves away from (NC,NC) to reduce his jail term by 1 year, the jail term of the other prisoner increases by 8 years.

An alternate way of interpreting the strategies of the prisoners is also popular. In this interpretation, each prisoner has two strategies, *cooperate* and *defect*. The strategy *cooperate* corresponds to cooperating with the other player by not confessing and therefore is equivalent to the strategy NC. The strategy *defect* corresponds to betraying the other player by confessing to the crime and therefore is equivalent to the strategy C. In the rest of the book, we will consistently use the C and NC strategies and not the *defect* and *cooperate* nomenclature.

4.7   Company's Dilemma Game

On the lines of the prisoner's dilemma problem, we present an analogous game involving two companies. Consider two companies 1 and 2, each of which can produce two competing products A and B, but only one at a time. The companies are known better for product A than for product B. However, environmentalists have launched a negative campaign on product A branding it as eco-unfriendly.

If both the companies produce product A, then, in spite of the negative campaign, their payoff is quite high since product A happens to be a niche product of both the companies. On the other hand, if both the companies produce product B, they still make some profit, but not as much as they would if they both produced product A.

On the other hand, if one company produces product A and the other company produces product B, then because of the negative campaign about product A, the company producing product A makes zero payoff while the other company captures all the market and makes a high payoff. The table below depicts the payoff structure for this game.

1	2 A	B
A	6, 6	0, 8
B	8, 0	3, 3

4.8   A Non-Symmetric Company's Dilemma Game

The examples we have provided so far, namely, matching pennies; rock-paper-scissors; BOS; coordination; prisoner's dilemma; and company's dilemma are instances of *symmetric games*. A two player strategic form game is called symmetric if $S_1 = S_2$ and $u_1(s_1, s_2) = u_2(s_2, s_1)$ $\forall s_1 \in S_1$, $\forall s_2 \in S_2$. We now provide an example of a non-symmetric game involving two competing companies 1 and 2. In this game also, each company has to simultaneously decide which of the two products A, B, it will produce. Company 1 is better known for product A and if it happens that both companies produce A, company 1 prospers. If both companies produce B, then they share the profits equally. If one of them produces A and the other produces B, then company 2 prospers (perhaps due to its more aggressive marketing). The following payoff matrix captures the strategic situation facing the two companies.

1	2 A	B
A	4, 1	0, 4
B	1, 5	1, 1

4.9   A Duopoly Pricing Game

This is due to Bertrand (1883). There are two companies 1 and 2 which wish to maximize their profits. The demand as a function of a price p is given by a continuous and strictly decreasing function $x(p)$. The cost for producing each unit of product is c where $c > 0$. The companies simultaneously choose their prices p_1 and p_2. The amount of sales for each company is given by:

$$
\begin{aligned}
x_1(p_1, p_2) &= x(p_1) & \text{if} \quad p_1 < p_2 \\
&= \frac{x(p_1)}{2} & \text{if} \quad p_1 = p_2 \\
&= 0 & \text{if} \quad p_1 > p_2
\end{aligned}
$$

$$
\begin{aligned}
x_2(p_1, p_2) &= x(p_2) & \text{if} \quad p_2 < p_1 \\
&= \frac{x(p_2)}{2} & \text{if} \quad p_1 = p_2 \\
&= 0 & \text{if} \quad p_2 > p_1
\end{aligned}
$$

It is assumed that the firms incur production costs only for an output level equal to their actual sales. Given prices p_1 and p_2, the utilities of the two companies are:

$$
u_1(p_1, p_2) = (p_1 - c)\, x_1(p_1, p_2)
$$
$$
u_2(p_1, p_2) = (p_2 - c)\, x_2(p_1, p_2)
$$

Note that for this game, $N = \{1, 2\}$ and $S_1 = S_2 = [0, \infty)$. This is an infinite game since the strategy sets are infinite.

4.10   Tragedy of the Commons

The *Tragedy of the Commons* represents a type of social paradox or social tragedy. The problem involves a conflict over use of resources between individual interests and social interests. A village has n farmers represented by the set $N = \{1, 2, \ldots, n\}$. Each farmer has the option of keeping a sheep or not. If 1 corresponds to keeping a sheep and 0 corresponds to not keeping a sheep, the strategy sets are given by

$$S_1 = S_2 = \cdots = S_n = \{0, 1\}.$$

The utility from keeping a sheep (that arises because of milk, wool, etc.) is equal to 1 unit. The village has a limited stretch of grassland and when a sheep grazes on this, there is a damage to the environment, equal to 5 units. This damage to the environment is to be shared equally by the farmers.

Let s_i be the strategy of each farmer. Then $s_i \in \{0, 1\}$. The payoff to farmer i is given by:

$$u_i(s_1, \ldots, s_i, \ldots, s_n) = s_i - \left[\frac{5(s_1 + \cdots + s_n)}{n} \right]$$

For the case $n = 2$, the payoff matrix would be:

		2
1	0	1
0	0, 0	$-2.5, -1.5$
1	$-1.5, -2.5$	$-4, -4$

If $n > 5$, a farmer gains more utility by keeping a sheep rather than not having one. If $n < 5$, then the farmer gets less utility by keeping a sheep than not having one. If $n = 5$, the farmer can be indifferent between keeping a sheep and not keeping a sheep.

If the Government now imposes a pollution tax of 5 units to every farmer keeping a sheep, the payoff becomes:

$$u_i(s_1, \ldots, s_i, \ldots, s_n) = s_i - 5s_i - \frac{5(s_1 + \cdots + s_n)}{n}$$

Now every farmer will prefer not to keep a sheep. We will be analyzing this game in Chapters 5 and 6 to gain insights into this social situation.

4.11 Bandwidth Sharing Game

This problem is based on an example presented by Tardos and Vazirani [2]. There is a shared communication channel of maximum capacity 1. There are n users of this channel, and user i wishes to send x_i units of flow, where $x_i \in [0, 1]$. We have

$$N = \{1, 2, \ldots, n\}$$
$$S_1 = S_2 = \ldots = S_n = [0, 1].$$

If $\sum_{i \in N} x_i \geq 1$, then the transmission cannot happen since the capacity is exceeded, and the payoff to each player is zero. If $\sum_{i \in N} x_i < 1$, then assume that the following is the payoff to user i:

$$u_i(x_1, \ldots, x_n) = x_i \Big(1 - \sum_{j \in N} x_j \Big) \ \forall i \in N.$$

The above expression models the fact that the payoff to a player is proportional to the flow sent by the player but is negatively impacted by the total flow. The second term captures the fact that the quality of transmission deteriorates with the total bandwidth used. Note that the above is an infinite game (since the strategy sets are real intervals). We will show in Chapter 6 that an equilibrium outcome here is not socially optimal.

4.12 A Sealed Bid Auction

There is a seller who wishes to allocate an indivisible item to one of n prospective buyers in exchange for a payment. Here, $N = \{1, 2, \ldots, n\}$ represents the set of buying agents. Let $v_1, v_2, \ldots, v_n$ be the valuations of the players for the object. The n buying agents submit sealed bids and these bids need not be equal to the valuations. Assume that the sealed bid from player i ($i = 1, \ldots, n$) could be any real number greater than 0. Then the strategy sets of the players are: $S_i = (0, \infty)$ for $i = 1, \ldots, n$. Assume that the object is awarded to the agent with the lowest index among those who bid the highest. Let $b_1, \ldots, b_n$ be the bids from the n players. Then the allocation function will be:

$$y_i(b_1, \ldots, b_n) = \begin{cases} 1 & \text{if } b_i > b_j \text{ for } j = 1, \ldots, i-1; \quad b_i \geq b_j \text{ for } j = i+1, \ldots, n \\ 0 & \text{otherwise.} \end{cases}$$

In the first price sealed bid auction, the winner pays an amount equal to his bid, and the losers do not pay anything. In the second price sealed bid auction, the winner pays an amount equal to the highest bid among the players who do not win, and as usual the losers do not pay anything. The payoffs or utilities to the bidders in these two auctions are of the form:

$$u_i(b_1, \ldots, b_n) = y_i(b_1, \ldots, b_n)(v_i - t_i(b_1, \ldots, b_n))$$

where $t_i(b_1, \ldots, b_n)$ is the amount to be paid by bidder i in the auction when player i bids b_i $(i = 1, \ldots, n)$. Assume that $n = 4$, and suppose the valuations are $v_1 = 20$; $v_2 = 20$; $v_3 = 16$; $v_4 = 16$, and the bids are $b_1 = 10$; $b_2 = 12$; $b_3 = 8$; $b_4 = 14$. Then for both first price and second price auctions, we have the allocation $y_1(b) = 0$; $y_2(b) = 0$; $y_3(b) = 0$; $y_4(b) = 1$, where $b = (b_1, b_2, b_3, b_4)$. The payments for the first price auction are $t_1(b) = 0$; $t_2(b) = 0$; $t_3(b) = 0$; $t_4(b) = 14$ whereas the payments for the second price auction would be: $t_1(b) = 0$; $t_2(b) = 0$; $t_3(b) = 0$; $t_4(b) = 12$. The utilities can be easily computed from the valuations and the payments.

4.13   Pigou's Network Game

This example captures the effect of selfish routing when strategic players act independently of one another. A directed graph consists of two nodes S and T and there are two disjoint edges A and B connecting S to T (see Figure 4.1). A certain amount of traffic has to move from S to T. Each edge is associated with a cost function $c(\cdot)$ which describes the cost (for example travel time) from S to T, incurred by the users of that edge, as a function of the fraction of total traffic that is routed on that edge. Suppose $x \in [0, 1]$ denotes the fraction of traffic routed. On the edge A, the cost function is $c(x) = x \ \forall x \in [0, 1]$. On the edge B, the cost function is constant and equal to unity, that is, $c(x) = 1 \ \forall x \in [0, 1]$. A routing network of the above type is called a Pigou network [3].

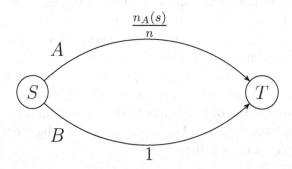

Fig. 4.1: A Pigou network

We shall consider a simple, stylized, discrete version of the above network with just two users, that is, $N = \{1, 2\}$. Each user has two strategies A and B corresponding to the two routes she may select. Thus we have $S_1 = S_2 = \{A, B\}$. Each user selects a route to be followed simultaneously and independent of the other user. A natural way of defining the payoff of a user for a strategy profile here would be negative of the cost of travel of the user. For example, suppose the strategy profile is (A, B) (player 1 selecting route A and player 2 selecting route B). The cost of travel for player 1 would be $\frac{1}{2}$ since the fraction of traffic routed through edge A is $\frac{1}{2}$. The payoff for player 1 becomes $-\frac{1}{2}$. The cost of travel for player 2 is 1 because the edge B is selected and the payoff becomes -1. The payoff matrix for this simple routing game is therefore given by

1	2	
	A	B
A	$-1, -1$	$-\frac{1}{2}, -1$
B	$-1, -\frac{1}{2}$	$-1, -1$

If we have n users, we have $N = \{1, \ldots, n\}$ and $S_1 = \ldots = S_n = \{A, B\}$. Let $s = (s_1, \ldots, s_n)$ be a strategy profile chosen by all the users. To define the payoff function, we shall first define $n_A(s)$ as the number of players who have chosen the route A in the strategy profile s. Similarly, $n_B(s)$ denotes the number of users who have chosen route B in the strategy profile s. Clearly, $n_A(s) + n_B(s) = n$ for all strategy profiles s. The payoff function is given by

$$u_i(s) = -\frac{n_A(s)}{n} \quad \text{if } s_i = A$$
$$= -1 \quad \text{if } s_i = B$$

We will analyze the above game in Chapter 6.

4.14 Braess Paradox Game

This game is developed on the lines of the game presented in the book by Easley and Kleinberg [4]. This game illustrates the Braess paradox which is named after the German mathematician Dietrich Braess. This paradox is usually associated with transportation networks and brings out the counter-intuitive fact that a transportation network with extra capacity added may actually perform worse (in terms of time delays) than when the extra capacity did not exist. Figure 4.2 shows a network that consists of a source S and a destination T, and two intermediate hubs A and B. It is required to travel from S to T. One route is via the hub A and the other route proceeds via the hub B.

Regardless of the number of vehicles on the route, it takes 25 minutes to travel from S to B or from A to T. On the other hand, the travel time from S to A takes time $\frac{m}{50}$ minutes where m is the number of vehicles on that link. Similarly, the travel time from B to T takes time $\frac{m}{50}$ minutes where m is the number of vehicles on that link. Assume that there are $n = 1000$ vehicles that wish to move from S to T. This means $N = \{1, 2, \ldots, 1000\}$. The strategy sets are $S_1 = \ldots = S_n = \{A, B\}$. Given a strategy profile $(s_1, \ldots, s_n)$, let $n_A(s_1, \ldots, s_n)$ $(n_B(s_1, \ldots, s_n))$ denote the number of vehicles taking the route via A (B). It is easy to note that

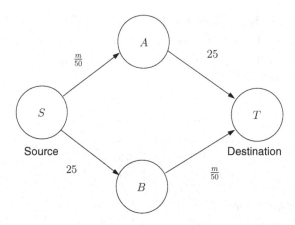

Fig. 4.2: A transportation network with four nodes

$n_A(s_1, \ldots, s_n) + n_B(s_1, \ldots, s_n) = n$. Since we wish to minimize travel time from S to T, it is convenient to define the utility of a player (in this case vehicle) as the negative of the travel time for that player from S to T. It is easy to see that

$$u_i(s_1, \ldots, s_n) = -25 - \frac{n_A(s_1, \ldots, s_n)}{50} \quad \text{if } s_i = A$$

$$= -25 - \frac{n_B(s_1, \ldots, s_n)}{50} \quad \text{if } s_i = B$$

This defines a strategic form game. Note that

$$u_i(A, A, \ldots, A) = u_i(B, B, \ldots, B) = -45$$

$$u_i(s_1, s_2, \ldots, s_n) = -35 \quad \text{whenever } n_A(s_1, \ldots, s_n) = n_B(s_1, \ldots, s_n) = 500$$

Let us say we now introduce a fast link from A to B to ease the congestion in the network (as a degenerate case, we will assume the travel time from A to B to be zero). Figure 4.3 depicts this new network with extra capacity added from A to B. Now the strategies available to each vehicle are to go from S to A to T (call this strategy A); S to B to T (call this strategy B); and S to A to B to T (call this strategy AB). So we have $S_1 = \ldots = S_n = \{A, B, AB\}$. Defining $n_A(s_1, \ldots, s_n), n_B(s_1, \ldots, s_n), n_{AB}(s_1, \ldots, s_n)$ on the same lines as before, we get

$$u_i(s_1, \ldots, s_n) = -25 - \frac{n_A(s_1, \ldots, s_n) + n_{AB}(s_1, \ldots, s_n)}{50} \quad \text{if } s_i = A$$

$$= -25 - \frac{n_B(s_1, \ldots, s_n) + n_{AB}(s_1, \ldots, s_n)}{50} \quad \text{if } s_i = B$$

$$= -\frac{n_A(s_1, \ldots, s_n) + n_{AB}(s_1, \ldots, s_n)}{50}$$

$$- \frac{n_B(s_1, \ldots, s_n) + n_{AB}(s_1, \ldots, s_n)}{50} \quad \text{if } s_i = AB$$

We will analyze the above two games in Chapters 5 and 6 and illustrate the Braess paradox.

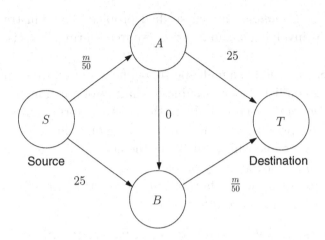

Fig. 4.3: Transportation network with an extra link from A to B

4.15 Summary and References

In this chapter, we presented many examples of strategic form games (also called normal form games) to gain an appreciation of how real world strategic situations could be abstracted as games. The examples we presented include:

- *Matching Pennies*, a two person zero-sum game and *Rock-Paper-Scissors* game, another two person zero-sum game. The games are called zero-sum because the sum of the utilities of the two players is zero in every outcome of the game. These are also called *strictly competitive games*.
- *BOS (Bach or Stravinsky) game*, also called the battle of the sexes game, captures a two player situation where the two players wish to coordinate with each other but they have different preferences for outcomes.
- *Coordination game* or the student's coordination game where two players derive a positive payoff only when they are together, however the payoff they derive when they are together depends on which actions they select.
- *Prisoner's Dilemma*, a classic two player game which illustrates many nuances of strategic conflict and cooperation. This is a game where rational and intelligent behavior does not lead to a socially optimal outcome.
- *Company's Dilemma* which shows how the prisoner's dilemma can be used to model a strategic situation facing two competing companies trying to outwit each other.
- *Non-Symmetric Company's Dilemma* which captures the strategic situation facing two companies which do not have a symmetric payoff structure.
- *Duopoly Pricing Game* which models the strategic situation facing two competing companies in deciding the price at which to sell a particular product.

- *Tragedy of the Commons*, a well studied problem that illustrates a common social paradox involving a conflict over resource sharing. This is a multi-person game.
- *Bandwidth Sharing* game, a multi-person game with infinite strategy sets which illustrates the conflict that arises due to sharing of a common resource.
- *Sealed Bid Auction*, which introduces the strategic form games underlying the well known first price auction and second price auction.
- *Pigou's Network* game which illustrates the notion of selfish routing by strategic agents acting independently of one another
- *Braess Paradox* game which faithfully captures the strategic conflict leading to the famous paradox in routing games.

The above examples are fairly representative of typical situations discussed in this book. We state cautiously that there are numerous other interesting and popular examples that we have left out in our discussion – in fact, we have covered only a minuscule subset of popular examples here. The following books also contain many illustrative examples of strategic form games: Osborne [1], Straffin [5], and Binmore [6], and Maschler, Solan, and Zamir [7].

The material discussed in this chapter draws upon mainly from three sources, namely the books by Myerson [8], Mascolell, Whinston, and Green [9], and Osborne and Rubinstein [1]. The paper by Tardos and Vazirani [2] is a fine introduction to concepts in game theory; we have taken many examples from their paper.

References

[1]   Martin J. Osborne and Ariel Rubinstein. *A Course in Game Theory*. Oxford University Press, 1994.

[2]   E. Tardos and V. Vazirani. "Introduction to game theory: Basic solution concepts and computational issues". In: *Algorithmic Game Theory*. Ed. by Noam Nisan, Tim Roughgarden, Eva Tardos, and Vijay Vazirani. Cambridge University Press, 2007, pp. 3–28.

[3]   T. Roughgarden and E. Tardos. "How bad is selfish routing?" In: *Journal of ACM* **49**(2) (2002), pp. 236–259.

[4]   David Easley and Jon Kleinberg. *Networks, Crowds, and Markets: Reasoning About a Highly Connected World*. Cambridge University Press, 2010.

[5]   Philip D. Straffin Jr. *Game Theory and Strategy*. The Mathematical Association of America, 1993.

[6]   Ken Binmore. *Fun and Games : A Text On Game Theory*. D. C. Heath & Company, 1992.

[7]   Michael Maschler, Eilon Solan, and Shmuel Zamir. *Game Theory*. Cambridge University Press, 2013.

[8]   Roger B. Myerson. *Game Theory: Analysis of Conflict*. Harvard University Press, Cambridge, Massachusetts, USA, 1997.

[9]   Andreu Mas-Colell, Michael D. Whinston, and Jerry R. Green. *Microeconomic Theory*. Oxford University Press, 1995.

[10]   Noam Nisan, Tim Roughgarden, Eva Tardos, and Vijay Vazirani (Editors). *Algorithmic Game Theory*. Cambridge University Press, 2007.

[11]   Martin J. Osborne. *An Introduction to Game Theory*. The MIT Press, 2003.

4.16 Exercises

(1) There are many interesting games that we have not discussed in this chapter. Explore other examples such as hawk and dove (also called chicken), cold war, pollution control, Cournot pricing game, ISP routing game, available from the literature, for example, the following books [10, 11, 5, 6, 7].

(2) There are n players. Each player announces a number in the set $\{1, ..., K\}$, where K is a fixed positive integer. A prize of \$1 is split equally between all the people whose number is closest to $\frac{2}{3}$ of the average number. Formulate this as a strategic form game.

(3) Develop the strategic form game for the Pigou network game for $n = 3$ and $n = 4$.

(4) Consider the following strategic form game (network formation game). The nodes of the network are the players: $N = \{1, 2, \ldots, n\}$. The strategy set S_i of player i is the set of all subsets of $N \setminus \{i\}$. A strategy of a node is to decide on with which other nodes it would like to have links. A strategy profile corresponds to a particular network or graph. Assume that δ where $0 < \delta < 1$ is the benefit that accrues to each node of a link while $c > 0$ is the cost to each node of maintaining the link. Further, assume that δ^k is the benefit that accrues from a k-hop relationship, where, k is the length of a shortest path between the two involved nodes. A link is formed under mutual consent while it can be broken unilaterally. Given a graph g formed out of a strategy profile, let the utility $u_i(g)$ of node i be given by

$$u_i(g) = \sum_{j \neq i} \delta^{l_{ij}(g)} - c.d_i(g)$$

where $l_{ij}(g)$ is the number of links in a shortest path between i and j and $d_i(g)$ is the degree of node i. Write down the strategy profiles corresponding to following structures of graphs assuming n nodes and compute the utilities of all individual nodes.

- Complete graph
- Straight line graph
- Star graph

Chapter 5

Dominant Strategy Equilibria

In the previous chapter, we presented several examples of strategic form games but we stopped short of analyzing the games. Commencing from this chapter, we start analyzing strategic form games. We define the notions of dominated strategies, dominating strategies, dominant strategies, and dominant strategy equilibria. We explore three categories of dominance: strong, weak, and very weak. We illustrate these notions through the examples of prisoner's dilemma, Braess paradox, and second price sealed bid auction.

We start the chapter with the notion of strong dominance. Subsequently, we introduce the notions of weak dominance and very weak dominance.

5.1 Strong Dominance

Definition 5.1 (Strongly Dominated Strategy). *Given a strategic form game* $\Gamma = \langle N, (S_i), (u_i) \rangle$, *a strategy* $s_i \in S_i$ *of player* i *is said to be strongly dominated by another strategy* $s_i' \in S_i$ *if*

$$u_i(s_i', s_{-i}) > u_i(s_i, s_{-i}) \ \ \forall s_{-i} \in S_{-i}$$

We also say strategy s_i' *strongly dominates strategy* s_i.

It is easy to note that player i will always prefer to play strategy s_i' over strategy s_i.

Definition 5.2 (Strongly Dominant Strategy). *A strategy* $s_i^* \in S_i$ *is said to be a strongly dominant strategy for player* i *if it strongly dominates every other strategy* $s_i \in S_i$. *That is,* $\forall s_i \neq s_i^*$,

$$u_i(s_i^*, s_{-i}) > u_i(s_i, s_{-i}) \ \ \forall s_{-i} \in S_{-i}$$

Definition 5.3 (Strongly Dominant Strategy Equilibrium). *A strategy profile* $(s_1^*, \ldots, s_n^*)$ *is called a strongly dominant strategy equilibrium of the game* $\Gamma = \langle N, (S_i), (u_i) \rangle$ *if,* $\forall i = 1, 2, \ldots, n$, *the strategy* s_i^* *is a strongly dominant strategy for player* i.

Example 5.1. Recall the prisoner's dilemma problem where $N = \{1, 2\}$ and $S_1 = S_2 = \{C, NC\}$ and the payoff matrix is given by:

1	2	
	NC	C
NC	$-2, -2$	$-10, -1$
C	$-1, -10$	$-5, -5$

Note that the strategy NC is strongly dominated by strategy C for player 1 since

$$u_1(C, NC) > u_1(NC, NC)$$
$$u_1(C, C) > u_1(NC, C)$$

Similarly, the strategy NC is strongly dominated by strategy C for player 2 since

$$u_2(NC, C) > u_2(NC, NC)$$
$$u_2(C, C) > u_2(C, NC)$$

Thus C is a strongly dominant strategy for player 1 and also for player 2. Therefore (C, C) is a strongly dominant strategy equilibrium for this game. □

   Note that if a (rational) player has a strongly dominant strategy, then we should expect the player to choose that strategy. On the other hand, if a player has a strongly dominated strategy, then we should expect the player not to play it.

5.2   Weak Dominance

Definition 5.4 (Weakly Dominated Strategy). *A strategy $s_i \in S_i$ is said to be weakly dominated by a strategy $s'_i \in S_i$ for player i if*

$$u_i(s'_i, s_{-i}) \geq u_i(s_i, s_{-i}) \ \forall s_{-i} \in S_{-i} \text{ and } u_i(s'_i, s_{-i}) > u_i(s_i, s_{-i}) \text{ for some } s_{-i} \in S_{-i}$$

The strategy s'_i is said to weakly dominate strategy s_i.

Note that strict inequality is to be satisfied for at least one s_{-i}.

Definition 5.5 (Weakly Dominant Strategy). *A strategy s^*_i is said to be a weakly dominant strategy for player i if it weakly dominates every other strategy $s_i \in S_i$.*

Definition 5.6 (Weakly Dominant Strategy Equilibrium). *Given a game $\Gamma = \langle N, (S_i), (u_i) \rangle$, a strategy profile $(s^*_1, \ldots, s^*_n)$ is called a weakly dominant strategy equilibrium if, $\forall i = 1, \ldots, n$, the strategy s^*_i is a weakly dominant strategy for player i.*

Example 5.2. Consider the following payoff matrix of a modified version of the prisoner's dilemma problem.

1	2	
	NC	C
NC	$-2,-2$	$-10,-2$
C	$-2,-10$	$-5,-5$

It is easy to note that C is a weakly dominant strategy for player 1 and also for player 2. Therefore the strategy profile (C, C) is a weakly dominant strategy equilibrium. $\quad\square$

5.3 Very Weak Dominance

Definition 5.7 (Very Weakly Dominated Strategy). *A strategy $s_i \in S_i$ is said to be very weakly dominated by a strategy $s_i' \in S_i$ for player i if*

$$u_i(s_i', s_{-i}) \geq u_i(s_i, s_{-i}) \ \forall s_{-i} \in S_{-i}$$

The strategy s_i' is said to very weakly dominate strategy s_i.

Note that strict inequality need not be satisfied for any s_{-i} unlike in the case of weak dominance where strict inequality must be satisfied for at least one s_{-i}.

Definition 5.8 (Very Weakly Dominant Strategy). *A strategy s_i^* is said to be a very weakly dominant strategy for player i if it very weakly dominates every other strategy $s_i \in S_i$.*

Definition 5.9 (Very Weakly Dominant Strategy Equilibrium). *A strategy profile $(s_1^*, \ldots, s_n^*)$ is called a very weakly dominant strategy equilibrium if, $\forall i = 1, \ldots, n$, the strategy s_i^* is a very weakly dominant strategy for player i.*

Note that every weakly dominant strategy equilibrium is trivially a very weakly dominant strategy equilibrium. We often use the notion of very weak dominance in mechanism design settings. In particular, this notion is typically used in defining *dominant strategy incentive compatibility* (Part 2 of the book).

Example 5.3. Consider the following payoff matrix of another modified version of the prisoner's dilemma problem.

1	2	
	NC	C
NC	$-2,-2$	$-5,-2$
C	$-2,-10$	$-5,-10$

It is easy to note that strategy C and strategy NC are very weakly dominant strategies for player 1 as well as player 2. Each of the four strategy profiles therefore constitutes a very weakly dominant strategy equilibrium. $\quad\square$

5.4   Illustrations of Dominant Strategy Equilibria

Example 5.4 (Tragedy of the Commons). We consider the tragedy of the commons example discussed in Chapter 4. Recall that

$$N = \{1, 2, \ldots, n\} \text{ is a set of farmers}$$
$$S_1 = S_2 = \cdots = S_n = \{0, 1\}.$$

Strategy 1 corresponds to keeping a sheep and strategy 0 corresponds to not keeping a sheep. Keeping a sheep gives a benefit of 1. However, when a sheep is kept, damage to the environment is 5. This damage is equally shared by all the farmers. For $i = 1, 2, \ldots, n$, we have

$$u_i(s_1, \ldots, s_n) = s_i - \frac{5}{n} \sum_{j=1}^{n} s_j = \left(\frac{n-5}{n}\right) s_i - \frac{5}{n} \sum_{j \neq i} s_j.$$

Case 1: $n < 5$. Given any $s_{-i} \in S_{-i}$,

$$u_i(0, s_{-i}) = -\frac{5}{n} \sum_{j \neq i} s_j$$
$$u_i(1, s_{-i}) = \left(\frac{n-5}{n}\right) - \frac{5}{n} \sum_{j \neq i} s_j.$$

Since $n < 5$, $\left(\frac{n-5}{n}\right) < 0$, and therefore, $u_i(0, s_{-i}) > u_i(1, s_{-i})$ $\forall s_{-i} \in S_{-i}$. It can be clearly seen that $(0, 0, \ldots, 0)$ is a strongly dominant strategy equilibrium. That is, there is no incentive for any farmer to keep a sheep.

Case 2: $n = 5$. Here we see that

$$u_i(0, s_{-i}) = u_i(1, s_{-i}) = -\frac{5}{n} \sum_{j \neq i} s_j.$$

Therefore,
$$u_i(0, s_{-i}) = u_i(1, s_{-i}) \, \forall s_{-i} \in S_{-i}.$$

It is easy to see that neither of the strategies here is a weakly dominant strategy or a strongly dominant strategy. On the other hand, each of the strategies is clearly a very weakly dominant strategy for every player. Thus every strategy profile is a very weakly dominant strategy equilibrium here.

Case 3: $n > 5$. Here

$$u_1(0, s_{-i}) = -\frac{5}{n} \sum_{j \neq i} s_j$$
$$u_i(1, s_{-i}) = \frac{n-5}{n} - \frac{5}{n} \sum_{j \neq i} s_j$$

Since $n > 5$, $\left(\frac{n-5}{n}\right) > 0$, and therefore, $u_i(0, s_{-i}) < u_i(1, s_{-i})$ $\forall s_{-i} \in S_{-i}$. Hence $(1, 1, \ldots, 1)$ is a strongly dominant strategy equilibrium. Thus if $n > 5$, it is best for all the farmers to keep a sheep. Now if the government decides to impose a pollution tax of 5 units for each sheep kept, we have

$$u_i(s_1, \ldots, s_n) = s_i - 5s_i - \frac{5}{n}\sum_{j=1}^{n} s_j = -4s_i - \frac{5}{n}s_i - \frac{5}{n}\sum_{j\neq i} s_j$$

Notice here that:

$$u_i(0, s_{-i}) = -\frac{5}{n}\sum_{j\neq i} s_j$$

$$u_i(1, s_{-i}) = -4 - \frac{5}{n} - \frac{5}{n}\sum_{j\neq i} s_j$$

This means whatever the value of n, the profile $(0, 0, \ldots, 0)$ is a strongly dominant strategy equilibrium. This is indeed a tragic situation for the farmers. $\square$

Example 5.5 (Braess Paradox Game). Recall the Braess paradox game (from Chapter 4) with an additional link introduced from A to B (Figure 4.3). In this game, it can be shown, for every player i, that

$$u_i(AB, s_{-i}) > u_i(A, s_{-i}) \ \forall \, s_{-i} \in S_{-i}$$

$$u_i(AB, s_{-i}) > u_i(B, s_{-i}) \ \forall \, s_{-i} \in S_{-i}$$

This shows that $(AB, AB, \ldots, AB)$ is a strongly dominant strategy equilibrium. Note that the above equilibrium profile leads to a total delay of 40 minutes. On the other hand, if 500 vehicles use the strategy A and the other 500 vehicles use the strategy B, the total delay for each vehicle is only 35 minutes. The paradox here is that the introduction of an additional link forces the strategy of AB on every vehicle (AB being a strongly dominant strategy for each vehicle) thereby leading to a delay that is higher than what it would be for a non-equilibrium profile. $\square$

Example 5.6 (Second Price Sealed Bid Auction). Consider the second price sealed bid auction for selling a single indivisible item discussed in Chapter 4. Let $b_1, b_2, \ldots, b_n$ be the bids (strategies) and we shall denote a bid profile (strategy profile) by $b = (b_1, b_2, \ldots, b_n)$. Assume that $v_i, b_i \in (0, \infty)$ for $i = 1, 2, \ldots, n$. Recall that the item is awarded to the bidder who has the lowest index among all the highest bidders, with the allocation function defined by:

$$\begin{aligned} y_i(b_1, \ldots, b_n) \ &= 1 \ \text{if} \quad b_i > b_j \ \text{for} \ j = 1, 2, \ldots, i-1 \ \text{and} \\ &\qquad\qquad\quad b_i \geq b_j \ \text{for} \ j = i+1, \ldots, n \\ &= 0 \ \text{else.} \end{aligned}$$

The payoff for each bidder is given by:

$$u_i(b_1, \ldots, b_n) = y_i(b_1, \ldots, b_n)(v_i - t_i(b_1, \ldots, b_n))$$

where $t_i(b_1, \ldots, b_n)$ is the amount paid by player i if she is the winning bidder. Being second price auction, the winner pays only the next highest bid. We now show that the strategy profile $(b_1, \ldots, b_n) = (v_1, \ldots, v_n)$ is a weakly dominant strategy equilibrium for this game.

To show this, consider bidder 1. His value is v_1 and bid is b_1. The other bidders have bids $b_2, \ldots, b_n$ and valuations $v_2, \ldots, v_n$. We consider the following cases.

> **Case 1:** $v_1 \geq \max(b_2, \ldots, b_n)$. There are two sub-cases here: $b_1 \geq \max(b_2, \ldots, b_n)$ and $b_1 < \max(b_2, \ldots, b_n)$.
>
> **Case 2:** $v_1 < \max(b_2, \ldots, b_n)$. There are two sub-cases here: $b_1 \geq \max(b_2, \ldots, b_n)$ and $b_1 < \max(b_2, \ldots, b_n)$.

We analyze these cases separately below.

Case 1: $v_1 \geq \max(b_2, \ldots, b_n)$.

We look at the following scenarios.

- Let $b_1 \geq \max(b_2, \ldots, b_n)$. This implies that bidder 1 is the winner, which implies that $u_1 = v_1 - \max(b_2, \ldots, b_n) \geq 0$.
- Let $b_1 < \max(b_2, \ldots, b_n)$. This means that bidder 1 is not the winner, which in turn means $u_1 = 0$.
- Let $b_1 = v_1$, then since $v_1 \geq \max(b_2, \ldots, b_n)$, we have $u_1 = v_1 - \max(b_2, \ldots, b_n)$.

Therefore, if $b_1 = v_1$, the utility u_1 is equal to the maximum utility obtainable. Thus, whatever the numerical values of $b_2, \ldots, b_n$, it is a best response for player 1 to bid v_1. Thus $b_1 = v_1$ is a very weakly dominant strategy for bidder 1.

Case 2: $v_1 < \max(b_2, \ldots, b_n)$.

As before, we look at the following scenarios.

- Let $b_1 \geq \max(b_2, \ldots, b_n)$. This implies that bidder 1 is the winner and the payoff is given by: $u_1 = v_1 - \max(b_2, \ldots, b_n) \ < 0$.
- Let $b_1 < \max(b_2, \ldots, b_n)$. This means bidder 1 is not the winner. Therefore $u_1 = 0$.
- If $b_1 = v_1$, then bidder 1 is not the winner and therefore $u_1 = 0$.

From the above analysis, it is clear that $b_1 = v_1$ is a best response strategy for player 1 in Case 2 also. Combining our analysis of Case 1 and Case 2, we have that

$$u_1(v_1, b_2, \ldots, b_n) \geq u_1(\hat{b}_1, b_2, \ldots, b_n) \ \forall \, \hat{b}_1 \in S_1 \ \ \forall \, (b_2, \ldots, b_n) \in S_2 \times \ldots \times S_n.$$

Also, we can show (and this is left as an exercise) that, for any $b_1' \neq v_1$, we can always find $b_2 \in S_2, b_3 \in S_3, \ldots, b_n \in S_n$, such that

$$u_1(v_1, b_2, \ldots b_n) > u_1(b_1', b_2, \ldots, b_n).$$

Thus $b_1 = v_1$ is a weakly dominant strategy for bidder 1. Using similar arguments, we can show that $b_i = v_i$ is a weakly dominant strategy for bidder i where $i = 2, 3, \ldots, n$. Therefore $(v_1, \ldots, v_n)$ is a weakly dominant strategy equilibrium.   □

5.5 Summary and References

In this chapter, we introduced the notions of a dominant strategy and dominant strategy equilibrium. Three different variations of this notion were introduced: strong dominance, weak dominance, and very weak dominance. The following points are to be noted.

- A strongly dominant strategy for a player means that the strategy when chosen by the player is strictly better than any other strategy, regardless of the strategies chosen by the other players.
- A very weakly dominant strategy for a player means that the strategy when chosen by the player is at least as good as any other strategy, regardless of the strategies chosen by the other players.
- A weakly dominant strategy for a player means that the strategy when chosen by the player is at least as good as any other strategy, regardless of the strategies chosen by the other players. In addition, it is strictly better than each of the other strategies of the player for at least one strategy profile chosen by the rest of the players.
- Dominant strategies may or may not exist. A strictly dominant strategy if it exists will be unique.
- A player would be happy to play a dominant strategy, if one exists (especially a strictly dominant strategy).
- We will be learning in Chapter 6 that any dominant strategy equilibrium is a pure strategy Nash equilibrium.

The material discussed in this chapter is mainly taken from the books by Myerson [1]; Mas-Colell, Whinston, and Green [2]; Shoham and Leyton-Brown [3].

References

[1] Roger B. Myerson. *Game Theory: Analysis of Conflict.* Harvard University Press, Cambridge, Massachusetts, USA, 1997.

[2] Andreu Mas-Colell, Michael D. Whinston, and Jerry R. Green. *Microeconomic Theory.* Oxford University Press, 1995.

[3] Yoam Shoham and Kevin Leyton-Brown. *Multiagent Systems: Algorithmic, Game-Theoretic, and Logical Foundations.* Cambridge University Press, New York, USA, 2009, 2009.

5.6 Exercises

(1) Show in a strategic form game that, for a player, a strongly dominant strategy, if one exists, is unique. What can you say about a weakly dominant strategy. How about a very weakly dominant strategy?

(2) Consider the following instance of the prisoners' dilemma problem.

1	2	
	NC	C
NC	$-4, -4$	$-2, -x$
C	$-x, -2$	$-x, -x$

Find the values of x for which:

   (a) the profile (C, C) is a strongly dominant strategy equilibrium.
   (b) the profile (C, C) is a weakly dominant strategy equilibrium but not a strongly dominant strategy equilibrium.
   (c) the profile (C, C) is a not even a weakly dominant strategy equilibrium.

In each case, say whether it is possible to find such an x. Justify your answer in each case.

(3) *First Price Auction.* Assume two bidders with valuations v_1 and v_2 for an object. Their bids are in multiples of some unit (that is, discrete). The bidder with higher bid wins the auction and pays the amount that he has bid. If both players bid the same amount, one of them gets the object with equal probability $\frac{1}{2}$. In this game,

   (a) Are any strategies strongly dominated?
   (b) Are any strategies weakly dominated?
   (c) Are any strategies very weakly dominated?

(4) *Second Price Auction.* We have shown that reporting true values in a second price auction leads to a very weakly dominant strategy equilibrium. Complete the proof that reporting true values is in fact a weakly dominant strategy equilibrium.

(5) Compute strongly or weakly dominant strategy equilibria of the Braess paradox game when the number 25 is replaced by the number 20 (Example 5.5).

(6) There are n departments in an organization. Each department can try to convince the central authority (of the organization) to get a certain budget allocated. If h_i is the number of hours of work put in by a department to make the proposal, let $c_i = w_i h_i^2$ be the cost of this effort to the department, where w_i is a constant. When the effort levels of the departments are $(h_1, h_2, \ldots, h_n)$, the total budget that gets allocated to all the departments is:

$$\alpha \sum_{i=1}^{n} h_i + \beta \prod_{i=1}^{n} h_i$$

where α and β are constants. Consider a game where the departments simultaneously and independently decide how many hours to spend on this effort. Show that a strongly dominant strategy equilibrium exists if and only if $\beta = 0$. Compute this equilibrium.

Chapter 6

Pure Strategy Nash Equilibria

Dominant strategy equilibria (strongly dominant, weakly dominant, very weakly dominant), if they exist, are very desirable, however, rarely do they exist because the conditions to be satisfied are quite demanding. A dominant strategy equilibrium requires that each player's strategy be a best response strategy against all possible strategy choices of the other players. We get the notion of *Nash equilibrium*, a central notion in game theory, if we only insist that each player's strategy offers a best response against the Nash equilibrium strategies of the other players. This solution concept is named after John Nash, one of the most celebrated game theorists of our times. In this chapter, we introduce the notion of pure strategy Nash equilibrium. We provide several examples to illustrate this notion. We show that pure strategy Nash equilibrium may not always exist. Often there could exist multiple Nash equilibria. We also show that the sum of utilities that players obtain in a Nash equilibrium may not be maximal. We present several interpretations that are possible for a Nash equilibrium. We also introduce the notions of *maxmin value*, *minmax value*, *maxmin strategy*, and *minmax strategy* in strategic form games and bring out the connection with pure strategy Nash equilibrium. Further, we introduce the notion of *subgame perfect equilibrium* in extensive form games.

6.1 The Notion of Nash Equilibrium

Definition 6.1 (Pure Strategy Nash Equilibrium). *Given a strategic form game* $\Gamma = \langle N, (S_i), (u_i) \rangle$, *the strategy profile* $s^* = (s_1^*, s_2^*, \ldots, s_n^*)$ *is called a pure strategy Nash equilibrium of* Γ *if*

$$u_i(s_i^*, s_{-i}^*) \geq u_i(s_i, s_{-i}^*) \ \forall s_i \in S_i, \ \forall i = 1, 2, \ldots, n.$$

Another way of stating the above is

$$u_i(s_i^*, s_{-i}^*) = \max_{s_i \in S_i} u_i(s_i, s_{-i}^*) \ \forall i = 1, 2, \ldots, n.$$

That is, each player's Nash equilibrium strategy is a best response to the Nash equilibrium strategies of the other players.

Note. In the above definition, we have implicitly assumed that the utilities represent benefits or profits to the players and therefore the players always seek to maximize their utilities. Occasionally, it happens that utilities can be expressed in a natural way in terms of costs or penalties rather than benefits or profits. In such a case, players will seek to minimize the utilities. In such a case, the inequality in the above definition would become $\leq$ instead of $\geq$. In this book, we consistently associate profits or benefits with utilities unless otherwise stated. Whenever costs are more natural to use, we will use a negative sign to the costs to define the utilities.

We now present an alternate way of describing a pure strategy Nash equilibrium (PSNE).

Definition 6.2 (Best Response Correspondence). *Given a strategic form game* $\Gamma = \langle N, (S_i), (u_i) \rangle$, *the best response correspondence for player i is the mapping* $b_i : S_{-i} \to 2^{S_i}$ *defined by*

$$b_i(s_{-i}) = \{s_i \in S_i : u_i(s_i, s_{-i}) \geq u_i(s_i', s_{-i}) \; \forall s_i' \in S_i\}.$$

That is, given a profile s_{-i} of strategies of the other players, $b_i(s_{-i})$ gives the set of all best response strategies of player i.

It can be seen that the strategy profile $(s_1^*, \ldots, s_n^*)$ is a pure strategy Nash equilibrium iff,

$$s_i^* \in b_i(s_{-i}^*), \quad \forall i = 1, \ldots, n.$$

Example 6.1 (The BOS Game). Recall the two player BOS game with the following payoff matrix:

	2	
1	A	B
A	$2,1$	$0,0$
B	$0,0$	$1,2$

There are two Nash equilibria here, namely (A, A) and (B, B). The profile (A, A) is a Nash equilibrium because

$$u_1(A, A) > u_1(B, A)$$
$$u_2(A, A) > u_2(A, B)$$

The profile (B, B) is a Nash equilibrium because

$$u_1(B, B) > u_1(A, B)$$
$$u_2(B, B) > u_2(B, A)$$

The best response sets are given by:

$$b_1(A) = \{A\}; \; b_1(B) = \{B\}; \; b_2(A) = \{A\}; \; b_2(B) = \{B\}$$

Since $A \in b_1(A)$ and $A \in b_2(A)$, (A, A) is a Nash equilibrium. Similarly since $B \in b_1(B)$ and $B \in b_2(B)$, (B, B) is a Nash equilibrium. The profile (A, B) is not a Nash equilibrium since $A \notin b_1(B)$; $B \notin b_2(A)$. $\qquad\square$

Example 6.2 (Prisoner's Dilemma). We consider the prisoner's dilemma problem which has the following payoff matrix:

1	2	
	NC	C
NC	$-2, -2$	$-10, -1$
C	$-1, -10$	$-5, -5$

Note that (C, C) is the unique Nash equilibrium here. To see why, we have to just look at the best response sets:

$$b_1(C) = \{C\}; \quad b_1(NC) = \{C\}; \quad b_2(C) = \{C\}; \quad b_2(NC) = \{C\}$$

Since (s_1^*, s_2^*) is a pure strategy Nash equilibrium iff $s_1^* \in b_1(s_2^*)$ and $s_2^* \in b_2(s_1^*)$, the only possible pure strategy Nash equilibrium here is (C, C). In fact as already seen, this is a strongly dominant strategy equilibrium.

A similar analysis holds for the version of Company's Dilemma game having the following payoff matrix.

1	2	
	A	B
A	$6, 6$	$0, 8$
B	$8, 0$	$3, 3$

In the note below, we generalize the observations we have just made. □

Note. Given a strategic form game $\Gamma = \langle N, (S_i), (u_i) \rangle$, a strongly (weakly) (very weakly) dominant strategy equilibrium $(s_1^*, \ldots s_n^*)$ is also a Nash equilibrium. This can be shown in a straightforward way (see Problem 1 in the exercises). The intuitive explanation for this is as follows. In a dominant strategy equilibrium, the equilibrium strategy of each player offers a best response irrespective of the strategies of the rest of the players. In a pure strategy Nash equilibrium, the equilibrium strategy of each player offers a best response against the Nash equilibrium strategies of the rest of the players. Thus, Nash equilibrium is a much weaker notion of equilibrium than a dominant strategy equilibrium.

Note. It is also clear that a Nash equilibrium need not be a dominant strategy equilibrium. As an immediate example, consider Example 6.1. The profiles (A, A) and (B, B) are both pure strategy Nash equilibria, however neither profile is a dominant strategy equilibrium. The reader can verify this immediately.

John F. Nash, Jr. is considered one of the most original mathematicians of the 20th Century. He was born in 1928 in Bluefield, West Virginia, USA. He completed his BS and MS in the same year (1948) at Carnegie Mellon University, majoring in Mathematics. He became a student of Professor Albert Tucker at Princeton University and completed his Ph.D. in Mathematics in 1950. His doctoral thesis (which had only 28 pages) proposed the brilliant notion of Nash Equilibrium, which helped expand the scope of game theory beyond two player zero-sum games.

The central result in his doctoral work settled the question of existence of a mixed strategy equilibrium in finite strategic form games. During his doctoral study, Nash also wrote a remarkable paper on the two player bargaining problem. He showed using an imaginative axiomatic approach that there exists a unique solution to the two person bargaining problem.

He worked as a professor of Mathematics at MIT in the Department of Mathematics where he did path-breaking work on algebraic geometry. He is also known for the Nash embedding theorem, which proves that any abstract Riemannian manifold can be isometrically realized as a sub-manifold of the Euclidean space. He is also known for his fundamental contributions to nonlinear parabolic partial differential equations.

The life and achievements of John Nash are fascinatingly captured in his biography *A Beautiful Mind* authored by Sylvia Nasar. This was later made into a popular movie with the same title. Professor Nash is currently at the Princeton University.

In 1994, John Nash was awarded the Nobel Prize in Economic Sciences, jointly with John C. Harsanyi and Reinhard Selten for their pioneering work in analyzing equilibria in the theory of non-cooperative games.

6.2 Illustrative Examples of Pure Strategy Nash Equilibrium

In this section, we present several examples of games with pure strategy Nash equilibria. We also present a couple of examples of games where a pure strategy Nash equilibrium does not exist.

Example 6.3 (Duopoly Pricing Game). Recall the duopoly pricing game discussed in Chapter 4. There are two companies 1 and 2 that wish to maximize their profits by choosing their prices p_1 and p_2. The utilities of the two companies are:

$$u_1(p_1, p_2) = (p_1 - c)\, x_1(p_1, p_2)$$
$$u_2(p_1, p_2) = (p_2 - c)\, x_2(p_1, p_2)$$

where $x_1(p_1, p_2)$ and $x_2(p_1, p_2)$ represent the amount of sales for the two companies when they choose the prices p_1 and p_2 (see Section 4.9). Note that $u_1(c, c) = 0$ and $u_2(c, c) = 0$. Also, it can be easily noted that

$$u_1(c, c) \geq u_1(p_1, c) \ \ \forall p_1 \in S_1$$

$$u_2(c, c) \geq u_2(c, p_2) \quad \forall p_2 \in S_2.$$

Therefore the strategy profile (c, c) is a pure strategy Nash equilibrium. The implication is that in the equilibrium, the companies set their prices equal to the marginal cost. The intuition behind this can be seen by imagining what would happen if both the companies set equal prices above marginal cost. Then the two companies would get half the market at a higher than marginal cost price. However, by lowering prices just slightly, a firm could capture the whole market, so both firms are driven to lower prices as much as they can. It does not make sense to price below marginal cost, because the firms would make a loss. Therefore, both firms will lower prices until they reach the marginal cost limit. $\qquad \square$

Example 6.4 (Tragedy of the Commons). Recall that $N = \{1, 2, \ldots, n\}$ is a set of farmers and the strategy sets are $S_1 = S_2 = \cdots = S_n = \{0, 1\}$. In the above, 1 corresponds to keeping a sheep and 0 corresponds to not keeping a sheep. Keeping a sheep gives a benefit of 1. However, when a sheep is kept, damage to the environment is 5. This damage is equally shared by all the farmers. Note that

$$u_i(s_1, \ldots, s_n) = s_i - \frac{5}{n} \sum_{j=1}^{n} s_j = \left(\frac{n-5}{n} \right) s_i - \frac{5}{n} \sum_{j \neq i} s_j \quad (i = 1, 2, \ldots, n).$$

When $n < 5$, we have shown in the previous chapter that $(0, 0, \ldots, 0)$ is a strongly dominant strategy equilibrium. That is, there is no incentive for any farmer to keep a sheep. When $n > 5$, we have shown that $(1, 1, \ldots, 1)$ is a strongly dominant strategy equilibrium. That is, keeping a sheep is a strongly dominant strategy for each farmer. Let us look at the case $n = 5$. Here,

$$u_i(0, s_{-i}) = -\frac{5}{n} \sum_{j \neq i} s_j$$

$$u_i(1, s_{-i}) = -\frac{5}{n} \sum_{j \neq i} s_j$$

Thus

$$u_i(0, s_{-i}) = u_i(1, s_{-i}), \quad \forall s_{-i} \in S_{-i} \; \forall i \in N.$$

This implies

$$b_i(s_{-i}) = \{0, 1\} \quad \forall s_{-i} \in S_{-i} \; \forall i \in N.$$

It can be seen that all the strategy profiles are Nash equilibria here. Also note that they are neither weakly dominant nor strongly dominant strategy equilibria.

If the government decides to impose a pollution tax of 5 units for each sheep kept, we have

$$u_i(s_1, \ldots, s_n) = s_i - 5s_i - \frac{5}{n} \sum_{j=1}^{n} s_j = -4s_i - \frac{5}{n} s_i - \frac{5}{n} \sum_{j \neq i} s_j$$

Here, note that

$$u_i(0, s_{-i}) = -\frac{5}{n} \sum_{j \neq i} s_j$$

$$u_i(1, s_{-i}) = -4 - \frac{5}{n} - \frac{5}{n} \sum_{j \neq i} s_j$$

This implies

$$b_i(s_{-i}) = \{0\} \quad \forall i \in N.$$

This means whatever the value of n, the profile $(0, 0, \ldots, 0)$ is a strongly dominant strategy equilibrium. $\qquad\square$

Example 6.5 (Bandwidth Sharing Game). Consider the bandwidth sharing game discussed in [1] and also presented in Chapter 4. We compute a Nash equilibrium for this game in the following way. Let x_i be the amount of flow that player i $(i = 1, \ldots, n)$ wishes to transmit on the channel and assume that

$$\sum_{i \in N} x_i < 1.$$

Recall that

$$u_i(x_1, \ldots, x_n) = x_i(1 - \sum_{j \in N} x_j) \, \forall i \in N.$$

Consider player i and define:

$$t_i = \sum_{j \neq i} x_j.$$

The payoff for player i is equal to

$$x_i(1 - t_i - x_i).$$

In order to maximize the above payoff, we have to choose

$$x_i^* = \underset{x_i \in [0,1]}{\arg\max} \; x_i(1 - t_i - x_i) = \frac{1 - t_i}{2} = \frac{1 - \sum_{j \neq i} x_j^*}{2}.$$

If this has to be satisfied for all $i \in N$, then we end up with n simultaneous equations

$$x_i^* = \frac{1 - \sum_{j \neq i} x_j^*}{2} \quad i = 1, \ldots, n.$$

We know that the profile $(x_1^*, \ldots, x_n^*)$ is a Nash equilibrium if and only if

$$u_i(x_i^*, x_{-i}^*) = \max_{x_i \in S_i} u_i(x_i, x_{-i}^*) \; \forall i = 1, \ldots, n.$$

It can be shown that the above set of simultaneous equations has the unique solution:

$$x_i^* = \frac{1}{1 + n} \quad i = 1, \ldots, n.$$

The profile $(\frac{1}{1+n},\ldots,\frac{1}{1+n})$ is thus a Nash equilibrium. The payoff for player i in the above Nash equilibrium is equal to

$$\left(\frac{1}{n+1}\right)\left(\frac{1}{n+1}\right).$$

Therefore the total payoff to all players combined is equal to

$$\frac{n}{(n+1)^2}.$$

As shown below, the above is not a happy situation. Consider the following profile

$$\left(\frac{1}{2n},\frac{1}{2n},\ldots,\frac{1}{2n}\right).$$

It is easy to show that the above is a non-equilibrium profile and that the profile gives each player a payoff

$$\frac{1}{2n}\left(1-\frac{n}{2n}\right)=\frac{1}{4n}.$$

Therefore the total payoff to all the players

$$=\frac{1}{4}>\frac{n}{(n+1)^2}.$$

Thus a non-equilibrium profile $(\frac{1}{2n},\frac{1}{2n},\ldots,\frac{1}{2n})$ provides higher payoff than a Nash equilibrium payoff. In general, like in the prisoner's dilemma problem, the equilibrium payoffs may not be the best possible outcome for the players individually or collectively or both. This is a limitation that Nash equilibrium payoffs often suffer from. □

Example 6.6 (Pigou's Network Game). Let us recall from Chapter 4, Pigou's network routing game (Figure 4.1). First, we consider the two player version where the payoff matrix is given by

1	2	
	A	B
A	$-1,-1$	$-\frac{1}{2},-1$
B	$-1,-\frac{1}{2}$	$-1,-1$

It is easy to see that the profiles (A,A), (A,B), and (B,A) are all pure strategy Nash equilibria. The remaining profile (B,B) is not a pure strategy Nash equilibrium because each player stands to gain by deviating unilaterally by playing strategy A instead of strategy B. The Nash equilibrium (A,A) leads to a total utility of -2 for the two agents while the other two equilibria lead to a total utility of $-\frac{3}{2}$.

Now let us consider the case when we have $n>2$ players. In this case, the profile $(A,A,\ldots,A)$ is a pure strategy Nash equilibrium and it yields a total utility of $-n$. If n is even, then the profile that produces the highest total utility is any profile in which half of the players play strategy A and the rest of the players play strategy B. The value of this total utility is $-((\frac{n}{2})(\frac{1}{2})-\frac{n}{2})$, which is equal to $-\frac{3n}{4}$. Notice that a non-equilibrium profile where half of the players play strategy A and the rest of the players play strategy B

produces a total utility that is greater than the total utility produced by a Nash equilibrium profile. Such a degradation in performance due to rationality of agents is discussed using the notion of *price of anarchy* in algorithmic game theory. The book by Nisan, Roughgarden, Tardos, and Vazirani [2] is an excellent source to probe further on this topic.   □

Example 6.7 (Braess Paradox Game). Here we consider the Braess paradox game which we discussed in Chapters 4 and 5. First consider that there is no link from A to B (Figure 4.2). Suppose $(s_1, \ldots, s_n)$ is any strategy profile such that

$$n_A(s_1, \ldots, s_n) = n_B(s_1, \ldots, s_n) = 500$$

That is, of the 1000 vehicles, exactly 500 take the route via A while the rest of the 500 vehicles take the route via B. Clearly, for such a strategy profile, $u_i(s_1, s_2, \ldots, s_n)$ is equal to -35 for all vehicles $i \in N$. Suppose vehicle i deviates from s_i with the rest of the vehicles retaining their strategies. The utility of vehicle i now becomes $(-25 - \frac{501}{50})$ which is less than -35. In fact, because of the unilateral deviation by vehicle i, the utility of all the 499 vehicles which were following the same route as vehicle i will now be better off whereas vehicle i and the rest of the 500 vehicles will be worse off. Thus all strategy profiles satisfying the above condition will be pure strategy Nash equilibria.

Now consider that an additional link is introduced from A to B (Figure 4.3). We have shown in Chapter 5 that the profile $(AB, AB, \ldots, AB)$ is a strongly dominant strategy equilibrium. Hence it is also a pure strategy Nash equilibrium. Note that the above equilibrium profile results in a total delay of 40 minutes.

On the other hand, consider a profile such that 500 vehicles use strategy A while the other 500 vehicles use strategy B. This profile is not a dominant strategy equilibrium or a Nash equilibrium but causes a total delay of only 35 minutes for each vehicle. As seen in Chapter 5, the paradox here is that the additional link introduced forces strategy AB on every vehicle (AB being a strongly dominant strategy for each vehicle) thereby causing a delay that is higher than what it would be for a non-equilibrium profile.   □

6.3   Games without a Pure Strategy Nash Equilibrium

Given a strategic form game, there is no guarantee that a pure strategy Nash equilibrium will exist. We provide several examples below.

Example 6.8 (Matching Pennies Game). Recall the matching pennies game discussed in Chapter 3 and the payoff matrix for this game:

	2	
1	A	B
A	$1, -1$	$-1, 1$
B	$-1, 1$	$1, -1$

It is easy to see that this game does not have a pure strategy Nash equilibrium. This shows that there is no guarantee that a pure strategy Nash equilibrium will exist. In Chapter 10, we will state sufficient conditions under which a given strategic form game is guaranteed to have a pure strategy Nash equilibrium. In the next chapter (Chapter 7), we define the notion of a mixed strategy Nash equilibrium and show that this game has a mixed strategy Nash equilibrium. □

Example 6.9. The rock-paper-scissors game, whose payoff matrix is shown below, does not have a pure strategy Nash equilibrium.

1	Rock	2 Paper	Scissors
Rock	0,0	−1,1	1,−1
Paper	1,−1	0,0	−1,1
Scissors	−1,1	1,−1	0,0

The non-symmetric company's dilemma game with the following payoff matrix also does not have a pure strategy Nash equilibrium.

1	2 A	B
A	4,1	0,4
B	1,5	1,1

We now provide an example of an infinite game that does not have a pure strategy Nash equilibrium. □

Example 6.10 (Procurement Exchange Game). This game is adapted from an example presented by Tardos and Vazirani [1]. Imagine a procurement exchange where buyers and sellers meet to match supply and demand for a particular product. Suppose that there are two sellers, 1 and 2, and three buyers A, B, and C. Because of certain constraints such as logistics, assume that

- A can only buy from seller 1.
- C can only buy from seller 2.
- B can buy from either seller 1 or seller 2.
- Each buyer has a maximum willingness to pay of 1 and wishes to buy one item.
- The sellers have enough items to sell.
- Each seller announces a price in the range $[0, 1]$.

Let s_1 and s_2 be the prices announced. It is easy to see that buyer A will buy an item from seller 1 at price s_1 and buyer C will buy an item from seller 2 at price s_2. If $s_1 < s_2$, then buyer B will buy an item from seller 1; if $s_1 > s_2$, buyer B will buy from seller 2. Assume that buyer B will buy from seller 1 if $s_1 = s_2$. The game can now be defined as follows:

$$N = \{1, 2\}$$
$$S_1 = S_2 = [0, 1]$$
$$u_1(s_1, s_2) = 2s_1 \text{ if } s_1 \le s_2$$
$$= s_1 \text{ if } s_1 > s_2$$
$$u_2(s_1, s_2) = 2s_2 \text{ if } s_1 > s_2$$
$$= s_2 \text{ if } s_1 \le s_2.$$

It is easy to observe that $u_2(1, s_2)$ has a value $2s_2$ for $0 \le s_2 < 1$. Therefore $u_2(1, s_2)$ increases when s_2 increases from 0, until s_2 reaches 1 when it suddenly drops to 1. Thus it is clear that a profile of the form $(1, s_2)$ cannot be a Nash equilibrium for any $s_2 \in [0, 1]$. Similarly, no profile of the form $(s_1, 1)$ can be a Nash equilibrium for any $s_1 \in [0, 1]$.

We now explore if there exists any Nash equilibrium (s_1^*, s_2^*), with $s_1^*, s_2^* \in [0, 1)$. There are two cases here.

Case 1: If $s_1^* \le \frac{1}{2}$, then the best response for player 2 would be to bid $s_2 = 1$ since that would fetch him the maximum payoff. However bidding $s_2 = 1$ is not an option here since the range of values for s_2 is $[0, 1)$.

Case 2: If $s_1^* > \frac{1}{2}$, then there are two cases: (1) $s_1^* \le s_2^*$ (2) $s_1^* > s_2^*$. Suppose $s_1^* \le s_2^*$. Then

$$u_1(s_1^*, s_2^*) = 2s_1^*$$
$$u_2(s_1^*, s_2^*) = s_2^*.$$

Choose s_2 such that $\frac{1}{2} < s_2 < s_1^*$. Then

$$
\begin{aligned}
u_2(s_1^*, s_2) &= 2s_2 \\
&> s_2^* \text{ since } 2s_2 > 1 \text{ and } s_2^* < 1 \\
&= u_2(s_1^*, s_2^*).
\end{aligned}
$$

Thus the players can improve upon (s_1^*, s_2^*) and hence (s_1^*, s_2^*) is not a Nash equilibrium.

Now, suppose, $s_1^* > s_2^*$. Then

$$u_1(s_1^*, s_2^*) = s_1^*$$
$$u_2(s_1^*, s_2^*) = 2s_2^*.$$

Now let us choose s_1 such that $1 > s_1 > s_1^*$. Then

$$u_1(s_1, s_2^*) = s_1 > s_1^* = u_1(s_1^*, s_2^*).$$

Thus the players can always improve upon (s_1^*, s_2^*). Therefore this game does not have a pure strategy Nash equilibrium. □

6.4   Interpretations of Nash Equilibrium

Nash equilibrium is an extensively discussed and debated topic in game theory. Many possible interpretations have been provided. Note that a Nash equilibrium is a profile of strategies of the n players, such that each player's choice is the player's best response given that the rest of the players play their Nash equilibrium strategies. By deviating from a Nash equilibrium strategy, a player will not be better off given that the other players do not deviate from their Nash equilibrium strategies. Following are several interpretations put forward by game theorists.

A common interpretation views a Nash equilibrium as a *prescription*. An adviser or a consultant to the n players would logically prescribe a Nash equilibrium strategy profile to the players. If the adviser recommends strategies that do not constitute a Nash equilibrium, then at least one player would find she is better off doing differently than advised. If the adviser prescribes strategies that do constitute a Nash equilibrium, then the players are happy because playing the prescribed strategy is best under the assumption that the other players will play their prescribed strategies. Thus a logical, rational, adviser would recommend a Nash equilibrium profile to the players. We have to be cautious however: A Nash equilibrium is an insurance against only unilateral deviations (that is, only one player at a time deviating from the equilibrium strategy). Two or more players deviating might result in players improving their payoffs compared to their equilibrium payoffs. For example, in the prisoner's dilemma problem, (C, C) is a Nash equilibrium. If both the players decide to deviate, then the resulting profile is (NC, NC), which is better for both the players. Note that (NC, NC) is not a Nash equilibrium.

Another common interpretation of Nash equilibrium is that of *prediction*. If the players are rational and intelligent, then a Nash equilibrium provides one possible, scientific prediction for the game. For example, a systematic elimination of strongly dominated strategies will lead to a reduced form that will include a Nash equilibrium (this will be illustrated in Chapter 7). Often, iterated elimination of strongly dominated strategies leads to a unique prediction which would be a Nash equilibrium.

An appealing interpretation of Nash equilibrium is that of a *self-enforcing agreement*. A Nash equilibrium can be viewed as an implicit or explicit agreement between the players. Once this agreement is reached, it does not need any external means of enforcement because it is in the self-interest of each player to follow this agreement if the others do. In a non-cooperative game, agreements cannot be enforced, hence, Nash equilibrium agreements are desirable in the sense of being sustainable under the assumption that only unilateral deviations are possible.

A natural, easily understood interpretation for Nash equilibrium has to do with *evolution and steady-state*. A Nash equilibrium is a potential convergence point of a dynamic adjustment process in which players adjust their behavior to that of other players in the game, constantly searching for strategy choices that will yield them the best results. This interpretation has been used to explain biological evolution. In this interpretation, Nash equilibrium is the outcome that results over time when a game is played repeatedly. A Nash equilibrium is like a long standing social convention that people are happy to maintain forever.

The above interpretations provide the most accepted points of view about Nash equilibrium in game theory. Holt and Roth [3] have published an insightful perspective on the notion of Nash equilibrium.

Note. Common knowledge of the game is a standard assumption in identifying a Nash equilibrium. It has been shown that the common knowledge assumption is quite strong and may not be required in its full strength. Suppose that each player is rational, knows his own payoff function, and knows the strategy choices of the others. This condition is weaker than common knowledge and is called mutual knowledge. Assuming mutual knowledge is adequate to identify a Nash equilibrium profile. For a detailed discussion of these concepts, the reader is referred to the paper by Aumann [4]. The book by Maschler, Solan, and Zamir [5] discusses these notions extensively with several illustrative examples.

Thomas Schelling received, jointly with Robert Aumann, the 2005 Nobel Prize in Economic Sciences for pioneering contributions that led to a clear understanding of conflict and cooperation through game theory analysis. Schelling's stellar contributions are best captured, among others, by several books that he has authored. The book *The Strategy of Conflict* that he wrote in 1960 is a classic work that initiated the study of bargaining and strategic behavior. It has been voted as one of the 100 most influential books since 1945. The notion of *focal point*, which is now called the *Schelling point* is introduced in this work to explain strategic behavior in the presence of multiple equilibria.

Another book entitled *Arms and Influence* is also a popularly cited work. A highlight of Schelling's work has been to use simple game theoretic models in an imaginative way to obtain deep insights into global problems such as the cold war, nuclear arms race, war and peace, etc.

Schelling was born on April 14, 1921. He received his Doctorate in Economics from Harvard University in 1951. During 1950-53, Schelling was in the team of foreign policy advisers to the US President, and ever since, he has held many policy making positions in public service. He has played an influential role in the global warming debate also. He was at Harvard University from 1958 to 1990. Since 1990, he has been a Distinguished University Professor at the University of Maryland, in the Department of Economics and the School of Public policy.

6.5 Existence of Multiple Nash Equilibria

We have seen several examples of strategic form games where multiple Nash equilibria exist. If a game has multiple Nash equilibria, then a fundamental question to ask is, which of these would get implemented? This question has been addressed by numerous game theorists, in particular, Thomas Schelling, who proposed the *focal point effect*. According to Schelling, anything that tends to focus the players' attention on one equilibrium may make them all expect it and hence fulfill it, like a self-fulfilling prophecy. Such a Nash equilibrium, which has some property that distinguishes it from all other equilibria is called a *focal equilibrium* or a *Schelling Point*.

Example 6.11. Consider the BOS game with the payoff matrix:

	2	
1	A	B
A	2,1	0,0
B	0,0	1,2

Here (A, A) and (B, B) are both Nash equilibria. If there is a special interest created about product A, then (A, A) may become the focal equilibrium. On the other hand, if there is a marketing blitz on product B, then (B, B) may become the focal equilibrium. □

6.6 Maxmin Values and Minmax Values

Given a Nash equilibrium, we have seen that the equilibrium strategy of a player provides a best response strategy assuming optimistically that the other players do not deviate from their equilibrium strategies. If a player wants to play so as to protect her payoff against any possible irrationality of the other players, then she has to plan for a worst case situation. Such situations lead to maxmin strategies.

Maxmin Value and Maxmin Strategy

The notion of a maxmin strategy of a player looks at the best possible payoff the player can guarantee herself even in the worst case when the other players are free to choose any strategies. We illustrate this notion using an example.

Example 6.12 (Maxmin Value). Consider the non-symmetric company's dilemma game (Section 4.8).

	2	
1	A	B
A	4,1	0,4
B	1,5	1,1

The above game does not have a pure strategy Nash equilibrium. If player 1 chooses strategy A, the minimum payoff he could get is 0 (when player 2 chooses strategy B). On the other hand, if player 1 chooses B, then the minimum he could get is 1 (when player 2 chooses A or B). Thus player 1 could decide to play strategy B and he is guaranteed to get a minimum payoff of 1, regardless of the strategy played by player 2. This payoff is called the *maxmin value* or *security value* of player 1 and the strategy B which assures him this payoff is called a *maxmin strategy* or a *security strategy*.

Similarly, if player 2 chooses strategy A, the minimum payoff she could get is 1 (when player 1 chooses strategy A). On the other hand, if player 2 chooses B, then the minimum she could get is again 1 (when player 1 chooses B). Thus whether player 2 plays strategy A or strategy B, she is guaranteed to get a minimum payoff of 1, regardless of player 1's strategy. Here, the payoff 1 is called the *maxmin value* or *security value* of player 2 and either of the strategies A, B, is called a *maxmin strategy* or *security strategy* of player 2. □

Suppose $\Gamma = \langle N, (S_i), (u_i) \rangle$ is any strategic form game. If player i chooses a strategy s_i, then the minimum payoff for this player would be

$$\min_{s_{-i} \in S_{-i}} u_i(s_i, s_{-i}).$$

Player i can choose a strategy in S_i that would maximize the above to obtain a payoff that he is guaranteed to obtain, irrespective of the strategies adopted by the rest of the players. This motivates the following definition.

Definition 6.3 (Maxmin Value and Maxmin Strategy). *Given a strategic form game,* $\Gamma = \langle N, (S_i), (u_i) \rangle$, *the maxmin value or security value of a player i ($i = 1, \ldots, n$) is given by:*

$$\underline{v_i} = \max_{s_i \in S_i} \min_{s_{-i} \in S_{-i}} u_i(s_i, s_{-i}).$$

Any strategy $s_i^* \in S_i$ that guarantees this payoff to player i is called a maxmin strategy or security strategy of player i.

Example 6.13. For the non-symmetric company's dilemma game, the maxmin value of player 1 is 1 and that of player 2 is also 1. Strategy B is a maxmin strategy of player 1 while strategy A is not a maxmin strategy for him. Strategies A and B are both maxmin strategies for player 2. This shows that a player may have multiple maxmin strategies. □

Note. If a player i plays a maxmin strategy and the other players play arbitrarily, then player i is always guaranteed to receive a payoff that is no less than $\underline{v_i}$. For this reason, a maxmin strategy is also called a *no-regret* strategy. In contrast, a Nash equilibrium strategy is not necessarily a no-regret strategy for a given player; other players deviating from their equilibrium strategies can cause the payoff of the player to become less than his payoff in the equilibrium.

The following proposition shows that the payoff of a player in a Nash equilibrium profile (if one exists) is at least the maxmin value of the player.

Proposition 6.1. *Suppose a strategic form game $\Gamma = \langle N, (S_i), (u_i) \rangle$ has a pure strategy Nash equilibrium $(s_1^*, \ldots, s_n^*)$. Then*

$$u_i(s_1^*, \ldots, s_n^*) \geq \underline{v_i} \ \forall i \in N.$$

Proof: First, we note that, $\forall i \in N$,

$$u_i(s_1^*, \ldots, s_n^*) = \max_{s_i \in S_i} u_i(s_i, s_{-i}^*).$$

Next we note that $\forall i \in N$,

$$u_i(s_i, s_{-i}^*) \geq \min_{s_{-i} \in S_{-i}} u_i(s_i, s_{-i}).$$

Combining the above two inequalities, it is clear that $\forall i \in N$, $u_i(s_1^*, \ldots, s_n^*) \geq \underline{v_i}$. ∎

Note. Given a strategic form game, a profile of maxmin strategies of the players can be regarded as another solution concept for the game. There could exist several such profiles. Clearly, these profiles are in general different from Nash equilibrium profiles. We will see, in Chapter 9, in the specific context of two player zero-sum games, that, every pure strategy Nash equilibrium profile (when one exists) will in fact also be a profile of maxmin strategies of the players.

Minmax Value

Informally, the minmax value of a player i is the lowest payoff that can be forced on the player i when the other players choose strategies that hurt player i the most. It is defined as follows.

Definition 6.4 (Minmax Value and Minmax Strategy). *Given a strategic form game, $\Gamma = \langle N, (S_i), (u_i) \rangle$, the minmax value of a player i ($i = 1, \ldots, n$) is given by:*

$$\overline{v_i} = \min_{s_{-i} \in S_{-i}} \max_{s_i \in S_i} u_i(s_i, s_{-i}).$$

Any strategy profile $s^*_{-i} \in S_{-i}$ of the other players that forces the payoff $\overline{v_i}$ on player i is called a minmax strategy profile (of the rest of the players) against player i.

Example 6.14. In the non-symmetric company's dilemma game, suppose we want to compute the minmax value of player 1. If player 2 plays strategy A, the maximum that player 1 could get is 4 (by playing strategy A). If player 2 plays strategy B, the maximum that player 1 could get is 1 (by playing strategy A or strategy B). Thus if player 2 plays strategy B, player 1 is forced to get a maximum payoff of 1, so the minmax value of player 1 is 1. The minmax strategy of player 2 against player 1 is clearly the strategy B. Similarly, the minmax value of player 2 is 4 and the minmax strategy of player 1 against player 2 is strategy A. □

Note that the minmax value of a player i is such that other players can guarantee that player i cannot receive more than the minmax value. Alternatively, it is indicative of the maximum resistance that player i can offer when the other players choose their strategies to hurt him most. On the other hand, the maxmin value of player i is the minimum payoff the player can guarantee himself of receiving. Intuitively, it is clear that the minmax value of a player must be greater than or equal to the maxmin value of that player. The following proposition formalizes this fact.

Proposition 6.2. *Consider a strategic form game $\Gamma = \langle N, (S_i), (u_i) \rangle$. Then*

$$\overline{v_i} \geq \underline{v_i} \ \forall i \in N.$$

Proof: Suppose s^*_{-i} is a minmax strategy against player i. This means

$$\overline{v_i} = \max_{s_i \in S_i} u_i(s_i, s^*_{-i}) \ \forall i \in N.$$

Note $\forall i \in N$ that

$$u_i(s_i, s_{-i}^*) \geq \min_{s_{-i} \in S_{-i}} u_i(s_i, s_{-i}) \ \forall s_i \in S_i.$$

Using the above two inequalities, we get

$$\overline{v_i} = \max_{s_i \in S_i} u_i(s_i, s_{-i}^*) \geq \max_{s_i \in S_i} \min_{s_{-i} \in S_{-i}} u_i(s_i, s_{-i}) = \underline{v_i} \ \forall i \in N.$$

Thus the minmax value of a player is no less than his maxmin value. ∎

The following proposition shows that the payoff of a player in a Nash equilibrium profile (if one exists) is at least the minmax value of the player.

Proposition 6.3. *Suppose a strategic form game* $\Gamma = \langle N, (S_i), (u_i) \rangle$ *has a pure strategy Nash equilibrium* $(s_1^*, \ldots, s_n^*)$. *Then*

$$u_i(s_1^*, \ldots, s_n^*) \geq \overline{v_i} \ \forall i \in N.$$

Proof: First, we note that $\forall i \in N$,

$$u_i(s_1^*, \ldots, s_n^*) = \max_{s_i \in S_i} u_i(s_i, s_{-i}^*).$$

Note that

$$\max_{s_i \in S_i} u_i(s_i, s_{-i}^*) \geq \min_{s_{-i} \in S_{-i}} \max_{s_i \in S_i} u_i(s_i, s_{-i}) \ \forall i \in N.$$

From the above, it is clear that

$$u_i(s_1^*, \ldots, s_n^*) \geq \overline{v_i} \ \forall i \in N.$$

∎

Note. The above discussion shows that the payoff of a player in a pure strategy Nash equilibrium (if one exists) is greater than or equal to the minmax value of the player which in turn is greater than or equal to the maxmin value of the player.

6.7   Equilibria in Extensive Form Games

We have studied extensive form games briefly in Chapter 3. We now revisit this important class of games and introduce a key solution concept called subgame perfect equilibrium. We discuss only extensive form games with perfect information.

Definition 6.5 (Subgame). *Given an extensive form game* Γ *and a non-terminal history* h, *the subgame following* h *is the part of the game that remains after the history* h *has occurred.*

Example 6.15. Consider the entry game shown in Figure 6.1(a). Figure 6.1(b) shows the only proper subgame of the entry game. Figure 6.2(a) shows another extensive form game. Figures 6.2(b) and 6.2(c) show the two proper subgames of this game. □

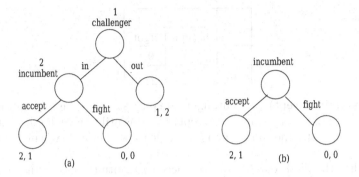

Fig. 6.1: Entry game and its subgame corresponding to history (in)

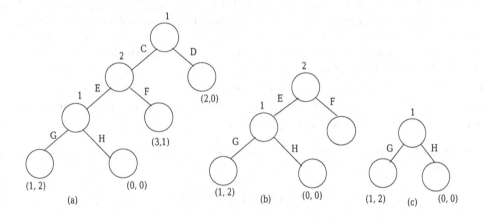

Fig. 6.2: Another game and its two subgames with history (C) and history (C, E)

Pure Strategy Nash Equilibria in Extensive Form Games

The notion of Nash equilibrium for extensive form games follows immediately through strategic form game representation of extensive form games. We can formally define a pure strategy Nash equilibrium as follows.

Definition 6.6. Given an extensive form game $\Gamma = \langle N, (A_i), \mathbb{H}, P, (\mathbb{I}_i), (u_i) \rangle$, a strategy profile $s^* = (s_1^*, \ldots, s_n^*)$ is called a pure strategy Nash equilibrium if $\forall i \in N$,

$$u_i(O(s_i^*, s_{-i}^*)) \geq u_i(O(s_i, s_{-i}^*)) \ \forall s_i \in S_i$$

where S_i is the set of all strategies of player i $(i = 1, 2, \ldots, n)$ and $O(.)$ denotes the outcome corresponding to a strategy profile.

Example 6.16. As an immediate example, consider the entry game (Figure 6.1(a)). The payoff matrix of strategic form game that is equivalent to the above game is given by

1	2	
	accept	fight
in	2, 1	0, 0
out	1, 2	1, 2

It is clear that both (in, accept) and (out, fight) are pure strategy Nash equilibria. Note that player 1 would prefer the equilibrium (in, accept) since his utility is higher in this equilibrium while player 2 would prefer the equilibrium (out, fight) since her utility is higher in this latter equilibrium.

Also, note that the Nash equilibrium (in, accept) is intuitive since the strategy *accept* is a valid and best response choice for player 2 in his decision node. The equilibrium (out, fight) is somewhat counter-intuitive because the strategy *out* played by player 1 will take player 1 to a leaf state, so player 2 is not called upon to play any strategy. However, the equilibrium (out, fight) can be explained through the following threat by player 2 to player 1: "I will fight you if you enter." Such a threat may not be a *credible threat* but it does capture the worst case scenario that could result when a player in the game deviates from rational behavior. The notion of subgame perfect equilibrium (which is discussed next) handles this issue in a logical way.

The notion of pure strategy Nash equilibrium in extensive form games ignores the sequential structure of the extensive form games. Nash equilibrium simply treats strategies as choices made once and for all before play begins. □

Example 6.17. In the extensive form game of Figure 6.2(a), recall the strategy sets of players 1 and 2:

$$S_1 = \{CG, CH, DG, DH\}$$
$$S_2 = \{E, F\}$$

The payoff matrix of the equivalent strategic form game is given by

1	2	
	E	F
CG	1, 2	3, 1
CH	0, 0	3, 1
DG	2, 0	2, 0
DH	2, 0	2, 0

There are three pure strategy Nash equilibria here, namely (DH, E), (DG, E), and (CH, F). □

Subgame Perfect Equilibrium

The notion of subgame perfect equilibrium (SGPE) takes into account every possible history in the game and ensures that each player's strategy is optimal given the strategies of the other players, not only at the start of the game but after every possible history. The following is a formal definition.

Definition 6.7 (Subgame Perfect Equilibrium). *Given an extensive form game* $\Gamma = \langle N, (A_i), \mathbb{H}, P, (\mathbb{I}_i), (u_i) \rangle$, *a strategy profile* $s^* = (s_1^*, \ldots, s_n^*)$ *is an SGPE if* $\forall i \in N$,

$$u_i(O_h(s_i^*, s_{-i}^*)) \geq u_i(O_h(s_i, s_{-i}^*)) \ \forall h \in \{x \in s_{\mathbb{H}} : P(x) = i\}; \ \forall s_i \in S_i$$

where $O_h(s_i^*, s_{-i}^*)$ *denotes the outcome corresponding to the history* h *in the strategy profile* (s_i^*, s_{-i}^*).

Example 6.18. In the entry game (Figure 6.1(a)), we have seen that both (in, accept) and (out, fight) are Nash equilibria. However the profile (out, fight) is not an SGPE because the action "fight" is not optimal for player 2 in the subgame corresponding to history (in). The rationale is that in case the challenger deviates from (out, fight) and plays "in", then player 2 is at a disadvantage since "fight" is not his best response.

In the case of extensive game shown in Figure 6.2(a), we have seen that the profiles (DH, E), (DG, E), and (CH, F) are all Nash equilibria. However, only the profile (DG, E) is a subgame perfect equilibrium. □

Nash Equilibrium and Subgame Perfect Equilibrium

From the definition of SGPE, it is clear that SGPE is a strategy profile that induces a Nash equilibrium in every subgame of the game. Thus an SGPE is always a Nash equilibrium whereas the converse is clearly not true as we have already seen in the examples.

In a Nash equilibrium of an extensive form game, each player's strategy is optimal given the strategies of the other players in the whole game. It may not be optimal in every subgame. However it will be optimal in any subgame that is reached when the players follow the Nash equilibrium strategies. On the other hand, an SGPE is such that each player's strategy is optimal in every possible history that may or may not occur if the players follow their strategies.

In a Nash equilibrium, each player has long experience of playing with other players and has correct beliefs about the actions of the other players. She believes they will not deviate from these actions and given these beliefs of wisdom, the Nash equilibrium strategy is optimal.

A subgame perfect equilibrium does not make such assumptions about the actions of the other players. The concept of SGPE takes into account the possibility of each player, even if on rare occasions, deviating from SGPE actions. Each player forms correct beliefs about other players' strategies and knows how the SGPE provides superior insurance against deviation by other players than a Nash equilibrium.

6.8 Summary and References

In this chapter, we introduced the central notion of pure strategy Nash equilibrium (PSNE). A PSNE is a strategy profile of the players, one strategy for each player, such that there is no benefit for any player to unilaterally deviate from his equilibrium strategy (that is with the other players not deviating from their equilibrium strategies). PSNE can also be defined as a profile of strategies such that every strategy in the profile is a best response strategy against the equilibrium strategies of the rest of the players. The following points merit special attention.

- A PSNE provides an insurance for each player against his own unilateral deviations only.
- A PSNE may not provide insurance for a player against unilateral deviations by any other player. For example, in prisoner's dilemma, (C, C) is a PSNE. If player 1 sticks to C and player 2 deviates to NC, player 1 improves his utility from -5 to -1.
- A PSNE does not provide insurance for a player against multilateral deviations by the players. An immediate example is again the prisoner's dilemma where both players deviating from (C, C) will take them to (NC, NC) which is strictly better for both of them.
- A PSNE may not correspond to a socially optimal outcome. This is once again exemplified by the prisoner's dilemma where the equilibrium profile (C, C) leads to a total utility of -10 while a non-equilibrium profile, (NC, NC) has a total utility of -4.
- A strategic form game need not have a PSNE (as shown by matching pennies and by the procurement exchange problem).
- A strategic form game may have multiple PSNEs and the payoffs for a player could be different in different PSNEs.
- Every dominant strategy equilibrium is also a PSNE.

A pure strategy Nash equilibrium could be interpreted in a wide variety of ways: (a) as a prescription by a mediator that the players would be happy to follow; (b) as a natural prediction for a repeated game; (c) as a self-enforcing agreement among the players; and (d) as a steady-state outcome of an evolutionary process. These interpretations have to be applied, with care and thought, to different modeling situations.

We have introduced the notion of a maxmin value or a security value of a player which represents the minimum guaranteed payoff to the player in the worst case scenario when the other players are free to play any strategies. We have also introduced the notion of a minmax value which is the lowest payoff that the other players can force on this player. If a pure strategy Nash equilibrium exists, we have shown that the payoff of any player under the equilibrium is greater than or equal to his minmax value which in turn is greater than or equal to his maxmin value.

We have also looked at the notion of Nash equilibrium and subgame perfect equilibrium of extensive form games. In this book, our focus is mostly on strategic form representation. We therefore do not elaborate further on extensive form games and subgame perfect equilibrium.

The material discussed in this chapter draws upon mainly from the books by Myerson [6] and Osborne and Rubinstein [7]. The paper by Tardos and Vazirani [1] is a fine introduction to concepts in game theory. In fact, we have taken many examples from their paper.

The books by Osborne [8], Straffin [9], Maschler, Solan, and Zamir [5], and Binmore [10] contain very interesting discussion on Nash equilibrium.

As is well known, the notion of Nash equilibrium was proposed by John Nash as part of his doctoral work which was published in [11, 12]. Holt and Roth [3] have published an insightful perspective on the notion of Nash equilibrium.

Most of the material in the section on subgame perfect equilibrium owes to the excellent discussion in the book by Osborne [8]. The reader is referred to that book for more details. Myerson's book [6] and the book by Maschler, Solan, and Zamir [5] have a detailed discussion of extensive form games.

References

[1]   E. Tardos and V. Vazirani. "Introduction to game theory: Basic solution concepts and computational issues". In: *Algorithmic Game Theory*. Ed. by Noam Nisan, Tim Roughgarden, Eva Tardos, and Vijay Vazirani. Cambridge University Press, 2007, pp. 3–28.

[2]   Noam Nisan, Tim Roughgarden, Eva Tardos, and Vijay Vazirani (Editors). *Algorithmic Game Theory*. Cambridge University Press, 2007.

[3]   Charles A. Holt and Alvin E. Roth. "The Nash equilibrium: A perspective". In: *Proceedings of the National Academy of Sciences* **101** (2004), pp. 3999–4002.

[4]   Robert J. Aumann. "Agreeing to disagree". In: *The Annals of Statistics* **4**(6) (1976), pp. 1236–1239.

[5]   Michael Maschler, Eilon Solan, and Shmuel Zamir. *Game Theory*. Cambridge University Press, 2013.

[6]   Roger B. Myerson. *Game Theory: Analysis of Conflict*. Harvard University Press, Cambridge, Massachusetts, USA, 1997.

[7]   Martin J. Osborne and Ariel Rubinstein. *A Course in Game Theory*. Oxford University Press, 1994.

[8]   Martin J. Osborne. *An Introduction to Game Theory*. The MIT Press, 2003.

[9]   Philip D. Straffin Jr. *Game Theory and Strategy*. The Mathematical Association of America, 1993.

[10]   Ken Binmore. *Fun and Games : A Text On Game Theory*. D. C. Heath & Company, 1992.

[11]   John F. Nash Jr. "Equilibrium points in n-person games". In: *Proceedings of the National Academy of Sciences* **36** (1950), pp. 48–49.

[12]   John F. Nash Jr. "Non-cooperative games". In: *Annals of Mathematics* **54** (1951), pp. 286–295.

6.9   Exercises

(1) Show in a strategic form game that any strongly (weakly) (very weakly) dominant strategy equilibrium is also a pure strategy Nash equilibrium.

(2) We have seen that a two player symmetric strategic form game is one in which $S_1 = S_2$ and $u_1(s_1, s_2) = u_2(s_2, s_1)$ $\forall s_1 \in S_1$ $\forall s_2 \in S_2$. Show in such a game

that the strategy profile (s_1^*, s_2^*) is a pure strategy Nash equilibrium if and only if the profile (s_2^*, s_1^*) is also a pure strategy Nash equilibrium.

(3) Find the pure strategy Nash equilibria, maxmin values, minmax values, maxmin strategies, and minmax strategies of the following game.

	2	
1	A	B
A	0, 1	1, 1
B	1, 1	1, 0

(4) Find the pure strategy Nash equilibria, maxmin values, minmax values, maxmin strategies, and minmax strategies of all the games discussed in Chapter 4 but not discussed in this chapter.

(5) Find the pure strategy Nash equilibria, maxmin values, minmax values, maxmin strategies, and minmax strategies of the following game.

	X	Y	Z
A	6, 6	8, 20	0, 8
B	10, 0	5, 5	2, 8
C	8, 0	20, 0	4, 4

(6) Find the pure strategy Nash equilibria, maxmin values, minmax values, maxmin strategies, and minmax strategies for the following two player game.

	A	B	C	D
A	5, 2	2, 6	1, 4	0, 4
B	0, 0	3, 2	2, 1	1, 1
C	7,0	2, 2	1, 5	5, 1
D	9, 5	1, 3	0, 2	4, 8

(7) Show in a strategic form game that a strongly dominant strategy of a player is also a maxmin strategy for the player. What about a weakly dominant strategy and a very weakly dominant strategy?

(8) In the Braess paradox game without the link from A to B, we have derived certain Nash equilibria (namely strategy profiles where 500 vehicles follow route A and the other 500 vehicles follow route B). Are these the only Nash equilibria? Also, in the extended game with a link from A to B, are there equilibria other than the profile corresponding to all vehicles following the route AB?

(9) Give examples of two player pure strategy games for the following situations

   (a) The game has a unique Nash equilibrium which is not a weakly dominant strategy equilibrium

   (b) The game has a unique Nash equilibrium which is a weakly dominant strategy equilibrium but not a strongly dominant strategy equilibrium

(c) The game has one strongly dominant or one weakly dominant strategy equilibrium and a second one which is only a Nash equilibrium

(10) *First Price Auction.* Assume two bidders with valuations v_1 and v_2 for an object. Their bids are in multiples of some unit (that is, discrete). The bidder with higher bid wins the auction and pays the amount that he has bid. If both bid the same amount, one of them gets the object with equal probability $\frac{1}{2}$. In this game, compute a pure strategy Nash equilibrium of the game.

(11) Compute a Nash equilibrium for the two person game with

$$S_1 = \{0,1\} \qquad S_2 = \{3,4\}$$

$$u_1(x,y) = -u_2(x,y) = |x - y| \quad \forall (x,y) \in \{0,1\} \times \{3,4\}$$

(12) Consider a strategic form game with $N = \{1,2\}$; $S_1 = S_2 = [a,b] \times [a,b]$ where a and b are positive real numbers such that $a < b$. That is, each player picks simultaneously a point in the square $[a,b] \times [a,b]$. Define the payoff functions:

$$u_1(s_1, s_2) = -u_2(s_1, s_2) = d(s_1, s_2)$$

where $d(s_1, s_2)$ is the Euclidean distance between the points s_1 and s_2. For this above game, compute all pure strategy Nash equilibria.

(13) Consider the game $\langle N, (S_i), (u_i) \rangle$ where $N = \{1, \ldots, n\}$ and $S_i = N \quad \forall i \in N$.

$$u_i(s_1, \ldots, s_n) = a_{ik} > 0 \qquad \text{if } s_1 = \cdots = s_n = k$$
$$= 0 \qquad \qquad \text{otherwise}$$

Compute all pure strategy Nash equilibria of this game.

(14) In the Pigou's network routing game, derive all pure strategy Nash equilibria for the cases $n = 3$ and $n = 4$. Generalize these findings to determine all pure strategy Nash equilibria for a general value of n.

(15) In the Pigou's network routing game, when n is even, show that the maximum social welfare is achieved by any profile in which the number of players choosing strategy A is the same as the number of players choosing strategy B. Investigate the case when n is odd.

(16) In the Pigou's network routing game, assume that the cost function on edge A is given by $c(x) = x^p \ \forall x \in [0,1]$ where p is a positive real constant. Determine the Nash equilibrium in this case.

(17) Consider the following strategic form game (network formation game). The nodes of the network are the players: $N = \{1, 2, \ldots, n\}$. The strategy set S_i of player i is the set of all subsets of $N \setminus \{i\}$. A strategy of a node is to decide on with which other nodes it would like to have links. A strategy profile corresponds to a particular network or graph. Assume that δ where $0 < \delta < 1$ is the benefit that accrues to each node of a link while $c > 0$ is the cost to each node of maintaining the link. Further, assume that δ^k is the benefit that accrues from a k-hop relationship, where, k is the length of a shortest path between the two

involved nodes. A link is formed under mutual consent while it can be broken unilaterally. Given a graph g formed out of a strategy profile, let the utility $u_i(g)$ of node i be given by

$$u_i(g) = \sum_{j \neq i} \delta^{l_{ij}(g)} - c.d_i(g)$$

where $l_{ij}(g)$ is the number of links in a shortest path between i and j and $d_i(g)$ is the degree of node i. Call a network efficient if it maximizes the sum of utilities of all nodes among all possible networks. Call a network pairwise stable if there is no incentive for any pair of unlinked nodes to form a link between them and there is no incentive for any node to delete any of its links. For this setting, prove the following two results.

- If $c < \delta - \delta^2$, the unique efficient network is the complete network
- If $c < \delta - \delta^2$, the unique pairwise stable network is the complete network

(18) Consider the so called ultimatum game where there are two players 1 and 2. Player 1 offers to player 2 an amount $0 \leq x \leq c$ where c is a constant. Player 2 either accepts this offer or rejects the offer. If player 2 accepts, then 2 receives x and 1 receives $c - x$. If player 2 rejects the offer, then both players end up with zero payoff. Write down the game tree, compute all Nash equilibria, and compute all SGPE.

(19) For the matching pennies game with observation, compute all Nash equilibria and all SGPE.

(20) For the sequential prisoner's dilemma problem where player 1 moves first and then player 2, compute all Nash equilibria and all SGPE.

(21) Find the Nash equilibria and SGPE of the following game.

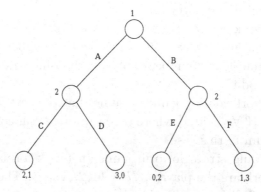

(22) **Programming Assignment.** Given a finite n-player strategic form game, develop a program that outputs

- all strongly dominant strategies;
- all weakly dominant strategies;

- all very weakly dominant strategies;
- a strongly dominant strategy equilibrium, if one exists;
- all weakly dominant strategy equilibria, if they exist;
- all very weakly dominant strategy equilibria, if they exist; and
- all pure strategy Nash equilibria, if they exist.
- maxmin values of all players and all their maxmin strategies
- minmax values of all players and all minmax strategy profiles against each player.

Chapter 7

Mixed Strategies and Mixed Strategy Nash Equilibrium

A natural generalization of pure strategies leads to mixed strategies. A mixed strategy of a player associates a probability distribution over the pure strategies of the player. Mixed strategies provide an elegant abstraction of real world strategic behavior of a player and enrich the space of possibilities when the game is played. In this chapter, we introduce the notions of a *mixed strategy* and a *mixed strategy Nash equilibrium*. We state and prove a crucial and useful theorem that provides necessary and sufficient conditions for a mixed strategy profile to be a mixed strategy Nash equilibrium. We present several examples that help gain an intuitive understanding of this important notion. We next discuss the notions of maxmin value and minmax value in mixed strategies. We also discuss the notion of *domination in mixed strategies* and illustrate iterated elimination of strongly dominated strategies.

7.1 Mixed Strategies

Consider a strategic form game: $\Gamma = \langle N, (S_i), (u_i) \rangle$. Recall that the elements of S_i are called *actions* or *pure strategies* of player i ($i = 1, \ldots, n$). If player i chooses a strategy in S_i according to a probability distribution, we have a mixed strategy or a randomized strategy. In the discussion that follows, we assume that S_i is a finite set for each $i = 1, 2, \ldots, n$.

Definition 7.1 (Mixed Strategy). *Given a player i with S_i as the set of pure strategies, a mixed strategy (also called randomized strategy) σ_i of player i is a probability distribution over S_i. That is, $\sigma_i : S_i \to [0,1]$ is a mapping that assigns to each pure strategy $s_i \in S_i$, a probability $\sigma_i(s_i)$ such that*

$$\sum_{s_i \in S_i} \sigma_i(s_i) = 1.$$

A pure strategy of a player, say $s_i \in S_i$, can be considered as a mixed strategy that assigns probability 1 to s_i and probability 0 to all other strategies of player i. Such a mixed strategy is called a *degenerate mixed strategy* and is denoted by $e(s_i)$ or simply by s_i.

If $S_i = \{s_{i1}, s_{i2}, \ldots, s_{im}\}$, then clearly, the set of all mixed strategies of player i is the set of all probability distributions on the set S_i. In other words, it is the set:

$$\Delta(S_i) = \left\{ (\sigma_{i1}, \ldots, \sigma_{im}) \in \mathbb{R}^m : \sigma_{ij} \geq 0 \text{ for } j = 1, \ldots, m \text{ and } \sum_{j=1}^{m} \sigma_{ij} = 1 \right\}.$$

The above set is called the *mixed extension* of S_i. Using the mixed extensions of strategy sets, we can define a mixed extension of the pure strategy game $\Gamma = \langle N, (S_i), (u_i) \rangle$. Let us denote the mixed extension of Γ by

$$\Gamma_{ME} = \langle N, (\Delta(S_i)), (U_i) \rangle.$$

Note that, for $i = 1, 2, \ldots, n$, U_i is a mapping that maps mixed strategy profiles to real numbers:

$$U_i : \Delta(S_1) \times \ldots \times \Delta(S_n) \to \mathbb{R}.$$

Given $\sigma_i \in \Delta(S_i)$ for $i = 1, \ldots, n$, a natural way of defining and computing $U_i(\sigma_1, \ldots, \sigma_n)$ is as follows. First, we make the standard assumption that the randomizations of individual players are mutually independent. This implies that given a mixed strategy profile $(\sigma_1, \ldots, \sigma_n)$, the random variables $\sigma_1, \ldots, \sigma_n$ are mutually independent. Therefore the joint probability of a pure strategy profile $(s_1, \ldots, s_n)$ is given by

$$\sigma(s_1, \ldots, s_n) = \prod_{i \in N} \sigma_i(s_i).$$

The payoff functions U_i are defined as

$$U_i(\sigma_1, \ldots, \sigma_n) = \sum_{(s_1, \ldots, s_n) \in S} \sigma(s_1, \ldots, s_n) \, u_i(s_1, \ldots, s_n).$$

Note that $U_i(\sigma_1, \ldots, \sigma_n)$ for $i = 1, \ldots, n$ is the expected payoff when the profiles $(s_1, \ldots, s_n)$ are chosen according to the joint distribution σ. In the sequel, when there is no confusion, we will write u_i instead of U_i. That is, instead of writing $U_i(\sigma_1, \ldots, \sigma_n)$, we will simply write $u_i(\sigma_1, \ldots, \sigma_n)$.

Example 7.1 (Mixed Strategies in the BOS Problem). Recall the BOS game discussed in Chapters 4 and 6, having the following payoff matrix:

1	2	
	A	B
A	2,1	0,0
B	0,0	1,2

Suppose (σ_1, σ_2) is a mixed strategy profile. This means that σ_1 is a probability distribution on $S_1 = \{A, B\}$, and σ_2 is a probability distribution on $S_2 = \{A, B\}$. Let us represent

$$\sigma_1 = (\sigma_1(A), \sigma_1(B)); \quad \sigma_2 = (\sigma_2(A), \sigma_2(B)).$$

We have $S = S_1 \times S_2 = \{(A, A), (A, B), (B, A), (B, B)\}$. We shall now compute the payoff functions u_1 and u_2. Note that, for $i = 1, 2$,

$$u_i(\sigma_1, \sigma_2) = \sum_{(s_1, s_2) \in S} \sigma(s_1, s_2) \, u_i(s_1, s_2).$$

The function u_1 can be computed as

$$\begin{aligned} u_1(\sigma_1, \sigma_2) &= \sigma_1(A)\sigma_2(A)u_1(A, A) + \sigma_1(A)\sigma_2(B)u_1(A, B) \\ &\quad + \sigma_1(B)\sigma_2(A)u_1(B, A) + \sigma_1(B)\sigma_2(B)u_1(B, B) \\ &= 2\sigma_1(A)\sigma_2(A) + \sigma_1(B)\sigma_2(B) \\ &= 2\sigma_1(A)\sigma_2(A) + (1 - \sigma_1(A))(1 - \sigma_2(A)) \end{aligned}$$

The above leads to

$$u_1(\sigma_1, \sigma_2) = 1 + 3\sigma_1(A)\sigma_2(A) - \sigma_1(A) - \sigma_2(A). \tag{7.1}$$

Similarly, we can show that

$$u_2(\sigma_1, \sigma_2) = 2 + 3\sigma_1(A)\sigma_2(A) - 2\sigma_1(A) - 2\sigma_2(A). \tag{7.2}$$

Suppose $\sigma_1 = \left(\frac{2}{3}, \frac{1}{3}\right)$ and $\sigma_2 = \left(\frac{1}{3}, \frac{2}{3}\right)$. Then it is easy to see that

$$u_1(\sigma_1, \sigma_2) = \frac{2}{3}; \quad u_2(\sigma_1, \sigma_2) = \frac{2}{3}.$$

The above two values are the same because of the structure of the payoff matrix here. $\square$

7.2 Mixed Strategy Nash Equilibrium

We now define the notion of a mixed strategy Nash equilibrium, which is a natural extension of the notion of pure strategy Nash equilibrium.

Definition 7.2 (Mixed Strategy Nash Equilibrium). *Given a strategic form game $\Gamma = \langle N, (S_i), (u_i) \rangle$, a mixed strategy profile $(\sigma_1^*, \ldots, \sigma_n^*)$ is called a Nash equilibrium if $\forall i \in N$,*

$$u_i(\sigma_i^*, \sigma_{-i}^*) \geq u_i(\sigma_i, \sigma_{-i}^*) \quad \forall \sigma_i \in \Delta(S_i).$$

Define the best response functions $b_i(.)$ as follows.

$$b_i(\sigma_{-i}) = \{\sigma_i \in \Delta(S_i) : u_i(\sigma_i, \sigma_{-i}) \geq u_i(\sigma_i', \sigma_{-i}) \ \forall \sigma_i' \in \Delta(S_i)\}.$$

Given σ_{-i}, $b_i(\sigma_{-i})$ is the set of all mixed strategies of player i, each of which is a best response mixed strategy of player i when the rest of the players are playing the strategy profile σ_{-i}. Then, clearly, a mixed strategy profile $(\sigma_1^*, \ldots, \sigma_n^*)$ is a Nash equilibrium iff

$$\sigma_i^* \in b_i(\sigma_{-i}^*) \ \forall i \in N.$$

Example 7.2 (Mixed Strategy Nash Equilibria for the BOS Game). Let (σ_1^*, σ_2^*) be a mixed strategy equilibrium of the BOS game. Then

$$u_1(\sigma_1^*, \sigma_2^*) \geq u_1(\sigma_1, \sigma_2^*) \quad \forall \sigma_1 \in \Delta(S_1)$$

$$u_2(\sigma_1^*, \sigma_2^*) \geq u_2(\sigma_1^*, \sigma_2) \quad \forall \sigma_2 \in \Delta(S_2).$$

Any solution that satisfies the above two sets of equations is a mixed strategy Nash equilibrium. The above two equations, making use of the expressions in equations (7.1) and (7.2), are equivalent to:

$$3\sigma_1^*(A)\sigma_2^*(A) - \sigma_1^*(A) \geq 3\sigma_1(A)\sigma_2^*(A) - \sigma_1(A) \ \forall \sigma_1 \in \Delta(S_1)$$

$$3\sigma_1^*(A)\sigma_2^*(A) - 2\sigma_2^*(A) \geq 3\sigma_1^*(A)\sigma_2(A) - 2\sigma_2(A) \ \forall \sigma_2 \in \Delta(S_2).$$

The above two equations are equivalent, respectively, to:

$$\sigma_1^*(A)\{3\sigma_2^*(A) - 1\} \geq \sigma_1(A)\{3\sigma_2^*(A) - 1\} \quad \forall \sigma_1 \in \Delta(S_1)$$

$$\sigma_2^*(A)\{3\sigma_1^*(A) - 2\} \geq \sigma_2(A)\{3\sigma_1^*(A) - 2\} \quad \forall \sigma_2 \in \Delta(S_2).$$

There are three possible cases.

- Case 1: $3\sigma_2^*(A) > 1$. This leads to the pure strategy Nash equilibrium (A, A).
- Case 2: $3\sigma_2^*(A) < 1$. This leads to the pure strategy Nash equilibrium (B, B).
- Case 3: $3\sigma_2^*(A) = 1$. This leads to the mixed strategy Nash equilibrium (σ_1^*, σ_2^*):

$$\sigma_1^*(A) = \frac{2}{3}; \ \ \sigma_1^*(B) = \frac{1}{3}; \ \ \sigma_2^*(A) = \frac{1}{3}; \ \ \sigma_2^*(B) = \frac{2}{3}.$$

It is easy to verify that $\sigma_1^* \in b_1(\sigma_2^*)$ and $\sigma_2^* \in b_2(\sigma_1^*)$.   □

7.3   Properties of Mixed Strategies

We shall now prove some interesting properties and results about mixed strategies. First we recall the definition of the familiar notion of a convex combination.

Definition 7.3 (Convex Combination). *Given real numbers $y_1, y_2, \ldots, y_n$, a convex combination of these numbers is a weighted sum of the form $\lambda_1 y_1 + \lambda_2 y_2 + \cdots + \lambda_n y_n$, where*

$$0 \leq \lambda_i \leq 1 \quad \text{for } i = 1, 2, \ldots, n; \quad \sum_{i=1}^{n} \lambda_i = 1$$

Proposition 7.1. *Let $\Gamma = \langle N, (S_i), (u_i) \rangle$ be a strategic form game. Then $u_i(\sigma_i, \sigma_{-i})$ can be expressed as the convex combination:*

$$u_i(\sigma_i, \sigma_{-i}) = \sum_{s_i \in S_i} \sigma_i(s_i) u_i(s_i, \sigma_{-i})$$

where

$$u_i(s_i, \sigma_{-i}) = \sum_{s_{-i} \in S_{-i}} \left(\prod_{j \neq i} \sigma_j(s_j) \right) u_i(s_i, s_{-i}).$$

Proof: First note that

$$u_i(\sigma_i, \sigma_{-i}) = \sum_{(s_1, \ldots, s_n) \in S} \left(\prod_{j \in N} \sigma_j(s_j) \right) u_i(s_i, s_{-i})$$

$$= \sum_{s_1 \in S_1} \sum_{s_2 \in S_2} \cdots \sum_{s_n \in S_n} \left(\prod_{j \in N} \sigma_j(s_j) \right) u_i(s_i, s_{-i})$$

$$= \sum_{s_i \in S_i} \sum_{s_{-i} \in S_{-i}} \left(\prod_{j \neq i} \sigma_j(s_j) \right) \sigma_i(s_i) \ u_i(s_i, s_{-i})$$

$$= \sum_{s_i \in S_i} \sigma_i(s_i) \left\{ \sum_{s_{-i} \in S_{-i}} \left(\prod_{j \neq i} \sigma_j(s_j) \right) u_i(s_i, s_{-i}) \right\}.$$

From the above, we immediately get:

$$u_i(\sigma_i, \sigma_{-i}) = \sum_{s_i \in S_i} \sigma_i(s_i) u_i(s_i, \sigma_{-i}). \qquad \blacksquare$$

The implication of this result is that the payoff for any player under a mixed strategy can be computed as a convex combination of the payoffs obtained when the player plays pure strategies with the rest of the players playing σ_{-i}.

We now bring out a few important observations about convex combinations in the context of mixed strategies with a simple example.

Example 7.3. Suppose $N = \{1, 2\}$, $S_1 = \{x_1, x_2, x_3, x_4, x_5\}$, and

$$u_1(\sigma_1, \sigma_2) = \sum_{s_1 \in S_1} \sigma_1(s_1) u_1(s_1, \sigma_2)$$

$$= \sigma_1(x_1) u_1(x_1, \sigma_2)$$

$$+ \sigma_1(x_2) u_1(x_2, \sigma_2) + \sigma_1(x_3) u_1(x_3, \sigma_2)$$

$$+ \sigma_1(x_4) u_1(x_4, \sigma_2) + \sigma_1(x_5) u_1(x_5, \sigma_2)$$

Suppose S_2 is some finite set. Let $u_1(x_1, \sigma_2) = 5$; $u_1(x_2, \sigma_2) = u_1(x_3, \sigma_2) = 10$; and $u_1(x_4, \sigma_2) = u_1(x_5, \sigma_2) = 20$. First note that the maximum value of the convex combination is 20 and this maximum value is attained when $\sigma_1(x_4) = 1$ or $\sigma_1(x_5) = 1$ or in general when $\sigma_1(x_4) + \sigma_1(x_5) = 1$. That is, when $\sigma_1(x_1) + \sigma_1(x_2) + \sigma_1(x_3) = 0$, or equivalently, when $\sigma_1(x_1) = \sigma_1(x_2) = \sigma_1(x_3) = 0$. Also, note that

$$\max_{\sigma_1 \in \Delta(S_1)} u_1(\sigma_1, \sigma_2) = 20; \quad \max_{\sigma_1 \in \Delta(S_1)} u_1(\sigma_1, \sigma_2) = \max_{s_1 \in S_1} u_1(s_1, \sigma_2)$$

Let $\rho \in \{\sigma_1 \in \Delta(S_1) : u_1(\sigma_1, \sigma_2) \geq u_1(\sigma_1', \sigma_2) \ \forall \sigma_1' \in \Delta(S_1)\}$.

$$\Longleftrightarrow \rho(x_4) + \rho(x_5) = 1$$
$$\Longleftrightarrow \rho(x_1) + \rho(x_2) + \rho(x_3) = 0$$
$$\Longleftrightarrow \rho(x_1) = \rho(x_2) = \rho(x_3) = 0$$
$$\Longleftrightarrow \rho(y) = 0 \ \forall \, y \notin \underset{s_1 \in S_1}{\arg\max} \ u_1(s_1, \sigma_2).$$

This example motivates the following important result.   □

Proposition 7.2. *Given a strategic form game* $\langle N, (S_i), (u_i) \rangle$*, then, for any* $\sigma \in \times_{i \in N} \Delta(S_i)$ *and for any player* $i \in N$*,*

$$\max_{\sigma_i \in \Delta(S_i)} u_i(\sigma_i, \sigma_{-i}) = \max_{s_i \in S_i} u_i(s_i, \sigma_{-i})$$

Furthermore

$$\rho_i \in \underset{\sigma_i \in \Delta(S_i)}{\arg\max} \ u_i(\sigma_i, \sigma_{-i})$$

iff

$$\rho_i(x) = 0 \ \ \forall x \notin \underset{s_i \in S_i}{\arg\max} \ u_i(s_i, \sigma_{-i})$$

Proof: The first step is to express $u_i(\sigma_i, \sigma_{-i})$ as a convex combination:

$$u_i(\sigma_i, \sigma_{-i}) = \sum_{s_i \in S_i} \sigma_i(s_i) u_i(s_i, \sigma_{-i})$$

The maximum value of a convex combination of values is simply the maximum of the values. Hence

$$\max_{\sigma_i \in \Delta(S_i)} u_i(\sigma_i, \sigma_{-i}) = \max_{s_i \in S_i} u_i(s_i, \sigma_{-i})$$

A mixed strategy $\rho_i \in \Delta(S_i)$ will attain this maximum value iff

$$\sum_{x \in X} \rho_i(x) = 1 \ \text{ where } \ X = \underset{s_i \in S_i}{\arg\max} \ u_i(s_i, \sigma_{-i})$$

The above is equivalent to: $\rho_i(x) = 0 \ \forall \, x \notin \underset{s_i \in S_i}{\arg\max} \ u_i(s_i, \sigma_{-i})$.   ∎

7.4 Necessary and Sufficient Conditions for a Profile to be a Mixed Strategy Nash Equilibrium

We now prove an extremely useful characterization for a mixed strategy Nash equilibrium profile. First we define the notion of support of a mixed strategy.

Definition 7.4 (Support of a Mixed Strategy). *Let* σ_i *be any mixed strategy of a player* i*. The support of* σ_i*, denoted by* $\delta(\sigma_i)$*, is the set of all pure strategies which have non-zero probabilities under* σ_i*, that is:*

$$\delta(\sigma_i) = \{s_i \in S_i : \sigma_i(s_i) > 0\}$$

Definition 7.5 (Support of a Mixed Strategy Profile). *Let $\sigma = (\sigma_1, \ldots, \sigma_n)$ be a mixed strategy profile with $\delta(\sigma_i)$ as the support of σ_i for $i = 1, \ldots, n$. Then the support $\delta(\sigma)$ of the profile σ is the Cartesian product of the individual supports, that is $\delta(\sigma_1) \times \ldots \times \delta(\sigma_n)$.*

Theorem 7.1. *The mixed strategy profile $(\sigma_1^*, \ldots, \sigma_n^*)$ is a mixed strategy Nash equilibrium iff $\forall i \in N$,*

(1) $u_i(s_i, \sigma_{-i}^*)$ is the same $\forall s_i \in \delta(\sigma_i^*)$ and
(2) $u_i(s_i, \sigma_{-i}^*) \geq u_i(s_i', \sigma_{-i}^*)$ $\forall s_i \in \delta(\sigma_i^*)$; $\forall s_i' \notin \delta(\sigma_i^*)$.

We refer to (1) and (2) above as condition (1) and condition (2), respectively, in the rest of this chapter. The theorem implies that the payoff for player i corresponding to any pure strategy having positive probability is the same and moreover is no less than the payoff corresponding to any pure strategy having zero probability (whenever all other players are playing their Nash equilibrium mixed strategies). The theorem is extremely useful in many contexts, including computation of Nash equilibria. We now prove this theorem.

Proof of Necessity: We are given that $(\sigma_1^*, \ldots, \sigma_n^*)$ is a Nash equilibrium. We have to show that the profile will satisfy conditions (1) and (2). It is clear from the definition of Nash equilibrium that $\forall i \in N$,

$$u_i(\sigma_i^*, \sigma_{-i}^*) \geq u_i(\sigma_i, \sigma_{-i}^*) \ \forall \sigma_i \in \Delta(S_i)$$

This implies that

$$u_i(\sigma_i^*, \sigma_{-i}^*) = \max_{\sigma_i \in \Delta(S_i)} u_i(\sigma_i, \sigma_{-i}^*)$$

Using Proposition (7.2) above, we can now write

$$u_i(\sigma_i^*, \sigma_{-i}^*) = \max_{s_i \in S_i} u_i(s_i, \sigma_{-i}^*)$$

This immediately implies by Proposition (7.1) that

$$\sum_{s_i \in S_i} \sigma_i^*(s_i) u_i(s_i, \sigma_{-i}^*) = \max_{s_i \in S_i} u_i(s_i, \sigma_{-i}^*) \ \forall i \in N$$

Since $\sigma_i^*(s_i) = 0 \ \forall s_i \notin \delta(\sigma_i)$, the above becomes

$$\sum_{s_i \in \delta(\sigma_i^*)} \sigma_i^*(s_i) u_i(s_i, \sigma_{-i}^*) = \max_{s_i \in S_i} u_i(s_i, \sigma_{-i}^*) \ \forall i \in N.$$

Suppose we have a convex combination $\pi_1 x_1 + \ldots + \pi_k x_k$ of numbers $x_1, \ldots, x_k$ with $\pi_i \neq 0 \ \forall i = 1, \ldots, k$, such that $\pi_1 + \ldots + \pi_k = 1$ and $\pi_1 x_1 + \ldots + \pi_k x_k = \max(x_1, \ldots, x_k)$, then, it is easy to see that

$$x_1 = x_2 = \ldots = x_k = \max(x_1, \ldots, x_k).$$

Using the above property, we obtain

$$u_i(s_i, \sigma_{-i}^*) = \max_{s_i \in S_i} u_i(s_i, \sigma_{-i}^*) \ \forall s_i \in \delta(\sigma_i^*); \ \forall i \in N.$$

This immediately implies that

$$u_i(s_i, \sigma_{-i}^*) = u_i(\sigma_i^*, \sigma_{-i}^*) \ \forall s_i \in \delta(\sigma_i^*); \ \forall i \in N.$$

It is clear from the above that

$$u_i(s_i, \sigma_{-i}^*) \geq u_i(s_i', \sigma_{-i}^*) \ \forall s_i \in \delta(\sigma_i^*); \ \forall s_i' \notin \delta(\sigma_i^*); \ \forall i \in N.$$

This proves the necessity.

Proof of Sufficiency: We are given that

(1) $u_i(s_i, \sigma_{-i}^*)$ has the same value, say, w_i, for all $s_i \in \delta(\sigma_i^*); \ \ \forall i \in N$

(2) $u_i(s_i, \sigma_{-i}^*) \geq u_i(s_i', \sigma_{-i}^*), \forall s_i \in \delta(\sigma_i^*); \ \ \forall s_i' \notin \delta(\sigma_i^*); \ \ \forall i \in N.$

To prove sufficiency, we have to show that $u(\sigma_1^*, \ldots, \sigma_n^*)$ is a mixed strategy Nash equilibrium. Consider for any $i \in N$,

$$
\begin{aligned}
u_i(\sigma_i^*, \sigma_{-i}^*) &= \sum_{s_i \in S_i} \sigma_i^*(s_i) u_i(s_i, \sigma_{-i}^*) \ \text{(Proposition 7.1)} \\
&= \sum_{s_i \in \delta(\sigma_i^*)} \sigma_i^*(s_i) u_i(s_i, \sigma_{-i}^*) \quad (\text{since } \sigma_i^*(s_i) = 0 \ \forall s_i \notin \delta(\sigma_i^*)) \\
&= \sum_{s_i \in \delta(\sigma_i^*)} \sigma_i^*(s_i).w_i \ \text{(Condition 1)} \\
&= w_i \\
&= \sum_{s_i \in S_i} \sigma_i(s_i) w_i \ \forall \sigma_i \in \Delta(S_i) \\
&\geq \sum_{s_i \in S_i} \sigma_i(s_i) u_i(s_i, \sigma_{-i}^*) \ \text{(Condition 2)} \\
&= u_i(\sigma_i, \sigma_{-i}^*).
\end{aligned}
$$

Thus the above inequality can be written as:

$$u_i(\sigma_i^*, \sigma_{-i}^*) \geq u_i(\sigma_i, \sigma_{-i}^*) \ \forall \sigma_i \in \Delta(S_i); \ \forall i \in N.$$

Therefore, $(\sigma_1^*, \ldots, \sigma_n^*)$ is a mixed strategy Nash equilibrium.   ∎

Implications of the Necessary and Sufficient Conditions

The necessary and sufficient conditions above have the following implications.

- Given a mixed strategy Nash equilibrium, each player gets the same payoff (as in the equilibrium) by playing *any pure strategy* having positive probability in her equilibrium mixed strategy.
- The above implies that the player can be indifferent about which of the pure strategies (having positive probability in her equilibrium mixed strategy) she will play. Of course, when this player plays only one of these pure strategies, then it may not be a best response for the other players to play their Nash equilibrium strategies.

- To verify whether or not a mixed strategy profile is a Nash equilibrium, it is enough to consider the effects of only pure strategy deviations (with the rest of the players playing their equilibrium strategies).

Another important implication is described in the following result.

Proposition 7.3. *Given $s_i \in S_i$, let $e(s_i)$ denote the degenerate mixed strategy that assigns probability 1 to s_i and probability 0 to all other strategies in S_i. The strategy profile $(s_i^*, \ldots, s_n^*)$ is a pure strategy Nash equilibrium of the game $\langle N, (S_i), (u_i) \rangle$ iff the mixed strategy profile $(e(s_1^*), \ldots, e(s_n^*))$ is a mixed strategy Nash equilibrium of the game $\langle N, (S_i), (u_i) \rangle$.*

Proof: First we prove the sufficiency. Let $(e(s_1^*), \ldots, e(s_n^*))$ be a mixed strategy Nash equilibrium. This

$$\implies u_i(e(s_i^*), e(s_{-i}^*)) \geq u_i(\sigma_i, e(s_{-i}^*)) \ \forall \sigma_i \in \Delta(S_i); \ \forall i \in N$$
$$\implies u_i(s_i^*, s_{-i}^*) \geq u_i(\sigma_i, s_{-i}^*) \ \forall \sigma_i \in \Delta(S_i); \ \forall i \in N$$
$$\implies u_i(s_i^*, s_{-i}^*) \geq u_i(e(s_i), s_{-i}^*) \ \forall s_i \in S_i; \ \forall i \in N$$
$$\implies u_i(s_i^*, s_{-i}^*) \geq u_i(s_i, s_{-i}^*) \ \forall s_i \in S_i; \ \forall i \in N$$
$$\implies (s_1^*, \ldots, s_n^*) \text{ is a pure strategy Nash equilibrium}$$

The above proves sufficiency. To prove the necessity, we proceed as follows. Given that $(s_1^*, \ldots, s_n^*)$ is a pure strategy Nash equilibrium

$$\implies u_i(s_i^*, s_{-i}^*) \geq u_i(s_i, s_{-i}^*) \ \forall s_i \in S_i \ \forall i \in N$$
$$\implies u_i(e(s_i^*), e(s_{-i}^*)) \geq u_i(s_i, e(s_{-i}^*)) \ \forall s_i \in S_i \ \forall i \in N$$
$$\implies u_i(e(s_i^*), e(s_{-i}^*)) = \max_{s_i \in S_i} u_i(s_i, e(s_{-i}^*)) \ \forall i \in N$$
$$\implies u_i(e(s_i^*), e(s_{-i}^*)) = \max_{\sigma_i \in \Delta(S_i)} u_i(\sigma_i, e(s_{-i}^*)) \ \forall i \in N \ \text{(By Prop. 7.2)}$$
$$\implies u_i(e(s_i^*), e(s_{-i}^*)) \geq u_i(\sigma_i, e(s_{-i}^*)) \ \forall \sigma_i \in \Delta(S_i); \ \forall i \in N$$
$$\implies (e(s_1^*), \ldots, e(s_n^*)) \text{ is a mixed strategy Nash equilibrium.}$$

The implication of the above is that to identify pure strategy equilibria of the game $\langle N, (\Delta(S_i)), (u_i) \rangle$, it is enough to look at the pure strategy game $\langle N, (S_i), (u_i) \rangle$. ∎

Mixed Strategy Nash Equilibria of the BOS Game

We consider again the BOS game with the payoff matrix:

1	2	
	A	B
A	2,1	0,0
B	0,0	1,2

First we verify that (A, A) is a Nash equilibrium. For this profile, we denote

$$\sigma_1^*(A) = 1; \quad \sigma_1^*(B) = 0; \quad \sigma_2^*(A) = 1; \quad \sigma_2^*(B) = 0$$

$$u_1(A, \sigma_2^*) = 2; \quad u_1(B, \sigma_2^*) = 0$$

Condition (1) of Theorem (7.1) is trivially true and condition (2) of that theorem is true because

$$u_1(A, \sigma_2^*) > u_1(B, \sigma_2^*)$$

These conditions are similarly satisfied for player 2 also. Hence (A, A) is a Nash equilibrium. Similarly, (B, B) is also a NE. Now, let us look at the candidate Nash equilibrium: $((\frac{2}{3}, \frac{1}{3}), (\frac{1}{3}, \frac{2}{3}))$. We denote:

$$\sigma_1^*(A) = \frac{2}{3} \quad \sigma_1^*(B) = \frac{1}{3}$$
$$\sigma_2^*(A) = \frac{1}{3} \quad \sigma_2^*(B) = \frac{2}{3}$$

First we examine the situation with player 1. Let us check condition (1).

$$u_1(A, \sigma_2^*) = \frac{1}{3}(2) + \frac{2}{3}(0) = \frac{2}{3}$$
$$u_1(B, \sigma_2^*) = \frac{1}{3}(0) + \frac{2}{3}(1) = \frac{2}{3}$$

Thus condition (1) is satisfied. Now, condition (2) is trivially satisfied since $\delta(\sigma_1^*) = \{A, B\}$, the entire set.

Let us examine the case of player 2. First we check condition (1).

$$u_2(\sigma_1^*, A) = \frac{2}{3}; \quad u_2(\sigma_1^*, B) = \frac{2}{3}.$$

Thus condition (1) is satisfied. As before, condition (2) is trivially satisfied.

Let us investigate if there are any other Nash equilibria. The equilibrium (A, A) corresponds to the support $\{A\} \times \{A\}$. The equilibrium (B, B) corresponds to the support $\{B\} \times \{B\}$. The equilibrium $((\frac{2}{3}, \frac{1}{3}), (\frac{1}{3}, \frac{2}{3}))$ corresponds to the support $\{A, B\} \times \{A, B\}$. We notice the following facts.

- There is no Nash equilibrium with support $\{A\} \times \{A, B\}$. If player 1 plays A, then player 2 has to play only A, which leads to the pure strategy Nash equilibrium (A, A). There is no way player will play B with non-zero probability.
- Similarly, there is no Nash equilibrium with any of the following supports:

$$\{B\} \times \{A, B\}$$
$$\{A, B\} \times \{A\}$$
$$\{A, B\} \times \{B\}$$
$$\{B\} \times \{A\}$$
$$\{A\} \times \{B\}$$

- Let us see if there is any other Nash equilibrium with support $\{A, B\} \times \{A, B\}$. To see this, let (σ_1^*, σ_2^*) defined by

$$\sigma_1^*(A) = x \quad \sigma_1^*(B) = 1 - x$$
$$\sigma_2^*(A) = y \quad \sigma_2^*(B) = 1 - y$$

be a Nash equilibrium such that neither $x \neq 0, x \neq 1, y \neq 0$ and $y \neq 1$ ($0 < x < 1; 0 < y < 1$). Then by condition (1) of the theorem, we have:

$$u_1(A, \sigma_2^*) = u_1(B, \sigma_2^*)$$
$$u_2(\sigma_1^*, A) = u_2(\sigma_1^*, B)$$

This implies $2y = 1 - y$ and $x = 2(1 - x)$. This in turn implies $y = \frac{1}{3}; \quad x = \frac{2}{3}$. This leads to the NE

$$\sigma_1^* = \left(\frac{2}{3}, \frac{1}{3}\right); \quad \sigma_2^* = \left(\frac{1}{3}, \frac{2}{3}\right)$$

The above equilibrium is the same as what we have discussed earlier. Thus the game does not have any other equilibria.

Mixed Strategy Nash Equilibria of the Coordination Game

Let us consider the coordination game with the payoff matrix:

	2	
1	A	B
A	10, 10	0, 0
B	0, 0	1, 1

In one interpretation of this game, the two players are students studying in a college and option A corresponds to staying in college and option B corresponds to going to a movie. We have already seen that (A, A) and (B, B) are pure strategy Nash equilibria. These correspond to the supports $\{A\} \times \{A\}$ and $\{B\} \times \{B\}$, respectively. It can be shown that the supports $\{A\} \times \{B\}; \{B\} \times \{A\}; \{A\} \times \{A, B\}; \{B\} \times \{A, B\}; \{A, B\} \times \{A\}; \{A, B\} \times \{B\}$ do not lead to any Nash equilibrium. We now investigate if there exists a Nash equilibrium with the support $\{A, B\} \times \{A, B\}$. Let $\sigma_1^* = (x, 1 - x); \quad \sigma_2^* = (y, 1 - y)$ with $x \neq 0, x \neq 1, y \neq 0, y \neq 1$ be a Nash equilibrium. Then condition (2) is trivially satisfied (since the support in each case is the entire strategy set). Let us check condition (1) which leads to:

$$u_1(A, \sigma_2^*) = u_1(B, \sigma_2^*)$$
$$u_2(\sigma_1^*, A) = u_2(\sigma_1^*, B)$$

The above equations are equivalent to

$$10y = 1 - y$$
$$10x = 1 - x$$

This leads to: $y = \frac{1}{11}$; $x = \frac{1}{11}$. This means $(\sigma_1^* = (\frac{1}{11}, \frac{10}{11})), \sigma_2^* = (\frac{1}{11}, \frac{10}{11}))$ is also a Nash equilibrium. This equilibrium looks somewhat counter-intuitive, however, a careful examination of conditions (1) and (2) of Theorem 7.1 explains why this must be a Nash equilibrium. Note that the players have no real preference over the probabilities with which they play their strategies. What actually determines these probabilities is the Nash equilibrium requirement to make the other player indifferent over her pure strategies in the support. Well, is it not common that students go off to a movie with a high probability rather than studying in the college? It is interesting that though staying in college gives higher payoff, the friends are more likely to meet in a movie if that is the (focal) equilibrium selected.

7.5 Maxmin Values and Minmax Values in Mixed Strategies

We have discussed in Section 6.6, the notions of maxmin values and minmax values in pure strategies. We now discuss these notions in the context of mixed strategies. For the sake of convenience, we use the same symbols $\underline{v_i}$ and $\overline{v_i}$ (that we have used in the context of pure strategies) to denote maxmin value and minmax value in mixed strategies. We hasten to add that the maxmin value of a player in mixed strategies is not necessarily equal to the maxmin value in pure strategies. Similar is the case with minmax values.

Maxmin Value in Mixed Strategies

Given a strategic form game, the maxmin value of a player is the highest payoff the player can guarantee himself even in the worst case when the other players are free to play any mixed strategies. This notion is formalized in the following definition.

Definition 7.6 (Maxmin Value in Mixed Strategies). *Given a strategic form game,* $\Gamma = \langle N, (S_i), (u_i) \rangle$, *the maxmin value or security value, in mixed strategies, of a player i (i = 1, \ldots, n) is given by:*

$$\underline{v_i} = \max_{\sigma_i \in \Delta(S_i)} \quad \min_{\sigma_{-i} \in \times_{j \neq i} \Delta(S_j)} u_i(\sigma_i, \sigma_{-i}).$$

Any mixed strategy $\sigma_i \in \Delta(S_i)$ *that guarantees this payoff to player i is called a maxmin mixed strategy or security strategy of player i.*

Note. A player may have multiple maxmin mixed strategies.

The following proposition shows that the payoff of a player in a mixed strategy Nash equilibrium is at least the maxmin value in mixed strategies of the player. The proof is similar to that of Proposition 6.1 which appears in Section 6.6.

Proposition 7.4. *Suppose a strategic form game* $\Gamma = \langle N, (S_i), (u_i) \rangle$ *has a mixed strategy Nash equilibrium* $(\sigma_1^*, \ldots, \sigma_n^*)$. *Then*

$$u_i(\sigma_1^*, \ldots, \sigma_n^*) \geq \underline{v_i} \ \forall i \in N$$

where $\underline{v_i}$ *is the maxmin value in mixed strategies of player i.*

Minmax Value in Mixed Strategies

Intuitively, the minmax value in mixed strategies of a player i is the lowest payoff that the other players will be able to force on the player i when they choose mixed strategies that hurt player i the most. It is defined as follows.

Definition 7.7 (Minmax Value in Mixed Strategies). *Given a strategic form game,* $\Gamma = \langle N, (S_i), (u_i) \rangle$, *the minmax value, in mixed strategies, of a player i* $(i = 1, \ldots, n)$ *is given by:*

$$\overline{v_i} = \min_{\sigma_{-i} \in \times_{j \neq i} \Delta(S_j)} \max_{\sigma_i \in \Delta(S_i)} u_i(\sigma_i, \sigma_{-i}).$$

Any mixed strategy profile σ_{-i} *that forces this payoff on player i is called a minmax mixed strategy profile (of the rest of the players) against player i.*

Intuitively, much like in the case of pure strategies, it is clear that the maxmin value in mixed strategies of a player must be less than or equal to the minmax value in mixed strategies of that player. The following proposition formalizes this fact. The proof proceeds on lines similar to that of Proposition 6.2 in Section 6.6.

Proposition 7.5. *Consider a strategic form game* $\Gamma = \langle N, (S_i), (u_i) \rangle$. *Then*

$$\overline{v_i} \geq \underline{v_i} \ \forall i \in N$$

where $\underline{v_i}$ *is the maxmin value in mixed strategies of player i and* $\overline{v_i}$ *is the minmax value in mixed strategies of player i.*

Note. It turns out that in two player strategic form games, the maxmin value in mixed strategies is in fact equal to the minmax value in mixed strategies. We emphasize that this need not be true in pure strategies.

The following proposition states that the payoff of a player in a mixed strategy Nash equilibrium profile (if one exists) is at least the minmax value of the player. The proof again proceeds on lines similar to the analogous proposition in Section 6.5 (Proposition 6.3).

Proposition 7.6. *Suppose a strategic form game* $\Gamma = \langle N, (S_i), (u_i) \rangle$ *has a mixed strategy Nash equilibrium* $(\sigma_1^*, \ldots, \sigma_n^*)$. *Then*

$$u_i(\sigma_1^*, \ldots, \sigma_n^*) \geq \overline{v_i} \ \forall i \in N$$

where $\overline{v_i}$ *is the minmax value in mixed strategies of player i.*

Note. The above discussion shows that the payoff of a player in a mixed strategy Nash equilibrium (if one exists) is greater than or equal to the minmax value in mixed strategies of the player which in turn is greater than or equal to the maxmin value in mixed strategies of the player.

7.6   Domination in Mixed Strategies

In this section, we define the notion of dominance in the context of mixed strategies and describe how elimination of dominated strategies simplifies equilibrium analysis.

Dominating Strategies and Dominated Strategies

Suppose $\langle N, (S_i), (u_i) \rangle$ is a strategic form game. In Chapter 5, we have discussed the notion of domination in the context of pure strategies. We now extend this notion to mixed strategies.

Definition 7.8 (Domination in Mixed Strategies). *Given two mixed strategies $\sigma_i, \sigma_i' \in \Delta(S_i)$ of player i, we say σ_i strictly dominates σ_i' if*

$$u_i(\sigma_i, \sigma_{-i}) > u_i(\sigma_i', \sigma_{-i}) \ \forall \sigma_{-i} \in \times_{j \neq i} \Delta(S_j).$$

We say σ_i weakly dominates σ_i' if

$$u_i(\sigma_i, \sigma_{-i}) \geq u_i(\sigma_i', \sigma_{-i}) \ \forall \sigma_{-i} \in \times_{j \neq i} \Delta(S_j) \ \text{ and }$$
$$u_i(\sigma_i, \sigma_{-i}) > u_i(\sigma_i', \sigma_{-i}) \ \text{ for some } \ \sigma_{-i} \in \times_{j \neq i} \Delta(S_j)$$

We say σ_i very weakly dominates σ_i' if

$$u_i(\sigma_i, \sigma_{-i}) \geq u_i(\sigma_i', \sigma_{-i}) \ \forall \sigma_{-i} \in \times_{j \neq i} \Delta(S_j)$$

In the cases above, we say the strategy σ_i' is strongly (weakly) (very weakly) dominated by σ_i.

Definition 7.9 (Dominant Mixed Strategy Equilibrium). *If the mixed strategy σ_i^* strongly (weakly) (very weakly) dominates all other strategies $\sigma_i' \in \Delta(S_i)$, we say σ_i^* is a strongly (weakly) (very weakly) dominant strategy of player i. A strategy profile $(\sigma_1^*, \cdots, \sigma_n^*)$ such that σ_i^* is a strictly (weakly) (very weakly) dominant strategy for player i, $\forall i \in N$, is called a strictly (weakly) (very weakly) dominant mixed strategy equilibrium.*

Note. Clearly, any dominant mixed strategy equilibrium is also a mixed strategy Nash equilibrium.

Note. A strictly dominant mixed strategy for any player, if one exists, is unique. Therefore a strictly dominant mixed strategy equilibrium, if one exists, is unique.

(a)

1	2	
	NC	C
NC	$-2, -2$	$-10, -1$
C	$-1, -10$	$-5, -5$

(b)

1	2
	C
NC	$-10, -1$
C	$-5, -5$

(c)

1	2
	C
C	$-5, -5$

Fig. 7.1: Prisoner's dilemma problem and elimination of strictly dominated strategies

Example 7.4. Consider the Prisoner's Dilemma game whose payoff matrix is reproduced in Figure 7.1(a) for ready reference.

Since the strategy NC is strictly dominated by strategy C for player 2, the player will never play NC. So, strategy NC of player 2 can be eliminated leading to the reduced payoff matrix as in Figure 7.1(b). Now the strategy NC of player 1 which is dominated by strategy C can also be eliminated, leading to the degenerate payoff matrix with a single entry corresponding to the profile (C, C), which in this case happens to be a strongly dominant strategy equilibrium. ☐

Example 7.5. Consider a two player game shown in Figure 7.2 (this game is a modified version of an example that appears in Shoham and Leyton-Brown [1]).

1	2		
	X	Y	Z
A	3,1	0,1	0,0
B	0,1	4,1	0,0
C	1,1	1,1	5,0

Fig. 7.2: A two player game to illustrate elimination of strictly dominated strategies

Note that the strategy Z of player 2 is strictly dominated by the strategy X and also the strategy Y. Therefore player 2 will never play strategy Z (whatever the strategy chosen by player 1). Thus strategy Z can be eliminated, leading to the reduced game as shown in Figure 7.3.

1	2	
	X	Y
A	3,1	0,1
B	0,1	4,1
C	1,1	1,1

Fig. 7.3: Game obtained after eliminating strategy Z of player 2

Now notice that none of the pure strategies of player 1 is dominated by any of the other pure strategies of player 1. However the strategy C is strictly dominated by the mixed strategy of player 1 that assigns equal probability to A and B. It has to be noted that the strategy C was not dominated by any mixed strategy in the original game. A strategy that was not dominated may thus become dominated when a strictly dominated strategy is eliminated. Also note that a pure strategy may not be dominated by any of the other pure strategies but could be dominated by a mixture of those pure strategies.

		2
1	X	Y
A	3,1	0,1
B	0,1	4,1

Fig. 7.4: Game obtained after eliminating strategy C

Figure 7.4 shows the game obtained after eliminating the strategy C of player 1. No more strategies can be eliminated from this game.   □

Iterated Elimination of Dominated Strategies

We have observed that elimination of strictly dominated strategies simplifies analysis of games. We shall formalize this as follows. Consider a finite strategic form game $\langle N, (S_i), (u_i)\rangle$. Let $k = 1, 2, \ldots, K$ denote the successive rounds in which strictly dominated strategies are eliminated. For each player $i \in N$, define the sets of strategies S_i^k as follows.

- $S_i^1 = S_i$
- $S_i^{k+1} \subseteq S_i^k$ for $k = 1, 2, \ldots, K - 1$.
- For $k = 1, 2, \ldots, K - 1$, all strategies $s_i \in S_i^k \setminus S_i^{k+1}$ are strictly dominated strategies which are eliminated in the kth round from the game in which the set of strategies of $j \in N$ is S_j^k.
- No strategy in S_i^K is strictly dominated in the game in which the set of strategies of each player $j \in N$ is S_j^K.

The above steps define the process of iterated elimination of strongly dominated strategies. The set of strategy profiles

$$\{(s_1, s_2, \ldots, s_n) : s_i \in S_i^K \quad \text{for} \quad i = 1, \ldots, n\}$$

is said to survive the iterated elimination of strictly dominated strategies.

Example 7.6. Consider the two player game of Figure 7.2 where $S_1 = \{A, B, C\}$; $S_2 = \{X, Y, Z\}$. For this game,

- $S_1^1 = S_1 = \{A, B, C\}$; $S_2^1 = S_2 = \{X, Y, Z\}$

- $S_1^2 = \{A, B, C\}$; $S_2^2 = \{X, Y\}$
- $S_1^3 = \{A, B\}$; $S_2^3 = \{X, Y\}$.

Therefore the strategy profiles $\{(A, X), (A, Y), (B, X), (B, Y)\}$ survive the iterated removal of strongly dominated strategies. $\qquad\square$

Note. Consider the set of all strategy profiles $(\sigma_1, \sigma_2, \ldots, \sigma_n)$ such that $\forall i \in N$, $\sigma_i(s_i) = 0$ for all strategies $s_i \in S_i$ that are eliminated during iterated removal of strongly dominated strategies. It can be proved that this set of strategy profiles will contain all mixed strategy Nash equilibria. If we are lucky (as it happened in the case of Prisoner's dilemma), the above set may be exactly the set of all Nash equilibria. In the other extreme case, it may as well be the entire set of all strategy profiles! Thus iterated removal of strongly dominated strategies may sometimes simplify Nash equilibrium computation. Of course, at many other times, this removal process may not lead to any simplifications as well.

Note. If the game is finite, iterated elimination of dominated strategies must end in a finite number of rounds. It can be shown that the order of removal of strongly dominated strategies does not affect the final outcome of the iterated elimination process. However, the order in which weakly or very weakly dominated strategies are eliminated does influence the final outcome of the process. It is to be noted that elimination of weakly or very weakly dominated strategies yields smaller reduced games compared to elimination of strongly dominated strategies.

7.7 Summary and References

A mixed strategy of a player is a probability distribution over the set of pure strategies of the player and represents a natural way for the player to randomize over her pure strategies. The following are some important observations in this chapter that need attention.

- The expected utility of a player under a mixed strategy profile can be obtained using the natural assumption that the players randomize their strategies independently of one another.
- A mixed strategy Nash equilibrium (MSNE) is a profile of mixed strategies of the players, one for each player, such that there is no benefit for any player to unilaterally deviate from his equilibrium mixed strategy (that is with the other players not deviating from their equilibrium mixed strategies). An MSNE can also be defined as a profile of mixed strategies such that every mixed strategy in the profile is a best response mixed strategy against the equilibrium mixed strategies of the rest of the players.
- Given a finite strategic form game, an MSNE can be characterized by the following two conditions: (a) The expected utility of each player, when all others are playing their equilibrium mixed strategies, is the same when the player chooses

to play any pure strategy that has non-zero probability in her equilibrium mixed strategy. (b) The above expected utility is greater than or equal to the expected utility of the player when she plays any pure strategy that has zero probability in her equilibrium mixed strategy (with all others are playing their equilibrium mixed strategies). The above characterization is extremely useful in computing MSNE of a finite game.

After discussing the notion of MSNE, we discussed the notions of maxmin value and minmax value of a player in the context of mixed strategies. The key result is that the payoff of a player in an MSNE will be no less than the minmax value of the player in mixed strategies which in turn is no less than the maxmin value of the player in mixed strategies. Also, in two player games, the maxmin value in mixed strategies is equal to the minmax value in mixed strategies.

We also discussed the notions of domination in mixed strategies and iterated elimination of dominated strategies.

The material discussed in this chapter draws upon mainly from the books by Myerson [2], Osborne and Rubinstein [3], and Maschler, Solan, and Zamir [4].

In this chapter, we have made an implicit assumption that the strategy sets are all finite and we have defined mixed strategies for only such games. However, mixed strategies can be naturally extended to infinite strategy sets by defining probability distributions over those sets.

The celebrated result by John Nash which states that every finite strategic form game is guaranteed to have at least one mixed strategy Nash equilibrium will be taken up for a detailed treatment in Chapter 10. Infinite games need not have a mixed strategy Nash equilibrium. Computation of Nash equilibria is an issue of intense interest. We will be covering that in Chapter 11. In Chapter 12, we discuss computational complexity issues related to Nash equilibrium computation.

The material on domination in mixed strategies is mostly called out from the books by Osborne [5], Shoham and Leyton-Brown [1], and Myerson [2]. The proofs for some of the problems mentioned above can also be found in these references.

References

[1] Yoam Shoham and Kevin Leyton-Brown. *Multiagent Systems: Algorithmic, Game-Theoretic, and Logical Foundations*. Cambridge University Press, New York, USA, 2009, 2009.

[2] Roger B. Myerson. *Game Theory: Analysis of Conflict*. Harvard University Press, Cambridge, Massachusetts, USA, 1997.

[3] Martin J. Osborne and Ariel Rubinstein. *A Course in Game Theory*. Oxford University Press, 1994.

[4] Michael Maschler, Eilon Solan, and Shmuel Zamir. *Game Theory*. Cambridge University Press, 2013.

[5] Martin J. Osborne. *An Introduction to Game Theory*. The MIT Press, 2003.

7.8 Exercises

(1) Let S be any finite set with n elements. Show that the set $\Delta(S)$, the set of all probability distributions over S, is a convex set.

(2) Given a strategic form game $\langle N, (S_i), (u_i) \rangle$, show for any two mixed strategies, σ_i^*, σ_i that

$$u_i(\sigma_i^*, \sigma_{-i}) > u_i(\sigma_i, \sigma_{-i}) \; \forall \sigma_{-i} \in \Delta(S_{-i})$$

if and only if

$$u_i(\sigma_i^*, s_{-i}) > u_i(\sigma_i, s_{-i}) \; \forall s_{-i} \in S_{-i}$$

(3) Show that any strictly dominant strategy in the game $\langle N, (S_i), (u_i) \rangle$ must be a pure strategy.

(4) Find the mixed strategy Nash equilibria for the matching pennies game:

	H	T
H	$1, -1$	$-1, 1$
T	$-1, 1$	$1, -1$

Also compute the maxmin value and minmax value in mixed strategies. Determine the maxmin mixed strategies of each player and the minmax mixed strategies against each player.

(5) Find the mixed strategy Nash equilibria for the rock-paper-scissors game:

1	2		
	Rock	Paper	Scissors
Rock	$0, 0$	$-1, 1$	$1, -1$
Paper	$1, -1$	$0, 0$	$-1, 1$
Scissors	$-1, 1$	$1, -1$	$0, 0$

Also compute the maxmin value and minmax value in mixed strategies. Determine the maxmin mixed strategies of each player and the minmax mixed strategies against each player.

(6) Consider the following two player zero-sum game where a, b, c, d are real numbers with $a > b$, $d > c$, $d > b$, and $a > c$. Compute all mixed strategy Nash equilibria for this game. Also compute the maxmin value and minmax value in mixed strategies. Determine the maxmin mixed strategies of each player and the minmax mixed strategies against each player.

1	2	
	A	B
A	$a, -a$	$b, -b$
B	$c, -c$	$d, -d$

(7) Find the mixed strategy Nash equilibria of the following game:

	A	B
A	2,2	1, 2
B	2,1	1, 1

Also compute the maxmin value and minmax value in mixed strategies. Determine the maxmin mixed strategies of each player and the minmax mixed strategies against each player.

(8) Find the mixed strategy Nash equilibria for the following game.

	A	B
A	6, 2	0, 0
B	0, 0	2, 6

If all these numbers are multiplied by 2, will the equilibria change?

(9) Consider any arbitrary two player game of the following type (with a,b,c,d any arbitrary real numbers):

	A	B
A	a, a	b, c
B	c, b	d, d

It is known that the game has a strongly dominant strategy equilibrium. Now prove or disprove: The above strongly dominant strategy equilibrium is the only possible mixed strategy equilibrium of the game.

(10) This game is called the *guess the average* game. There are n players. Each player announces a number in the set $\{1, \ldots, K\}$. A monetary reward of $1 is split equally between all the players whose number is closest to $\frac{2}{3}$ of the average number. Formulate this as a strategic form game. Show that the game has a unique mixed strategy Nash equilibrium, in which each player plays a pure strategy.

(11) Compute mixed strategy Nash equilibria, if any, for the two person game with

$$S_1 = [0, 1] \qquad S_2 = [3, 4]$$

$$u_1(x, y) = -u_2(x, y) = |x - y| \quad \forall (x, y) \in [0, 1] \times [3, 4]$$

(12) Consider a strategic form game with $N = \{1, 2\}$; $S_1 = S_2 = [a, b] \times [a, b]$ where a and b are positive real numbers such that $a < b$. That is, each player picks simultaneously a point in the square $[a, b] \times [a, b]$. Define the payoff functions:

$$u_1(s_1, s_2) = -u_2(s_1, s_2) = d(s_1, s_2)$$

where $d(s_1, s_2)$ is the Euclidean distance between the points s_1 and s_2. For this above game, compute all mixed strategy Nash equilibria.

(13) Compute all mixed strategy Nash equilibria for the Pigou network routing game (Chapters 4 and 6) for the cases $n = 2$ and $n = 3$. Can you generalize this result?

(14) There are two sellers 1 and 2 and there are three buyers A, B, and C.

- A can only buy from seller 1.
- C can only buy from seller 2.
- B can buy from either seller 1 or seller 2.
- Each buyer has a budget (maximum willingness to pay) of 1 and wishes to buy one item.
- The sellers have enough items to sell.
- Each seller announces a price as a real number in the range $[0, 1]$. Let s_1 and s_2 be the prices announced by sellers 1 and 2, respectively.
- Naturally, buyer A will buy an item from seller 1 at price s_1 and buyer C will buy an item from seller 2 at price s_2.
- In the case of buyer B, if $s_1 \leq s_2$, then he will buy an item from seller 1, otherwise he will buy from seller 2.

We have shown in Chapter 6 that the above game does not have pure strategy Nash equilibrium. Does this game have a mixed strategy Nash equilibrium?

(15) Consider a single player game with $N = \{1\}$ and $S_1 = [0, 1]$. Note that the set $[0, 1]$ is compact. Define the utility function as a discontinuous map:

$$u_1(s_1) = s_1 \quad \text{if } 0 \leq s_1 < 1$$
$$= 0 \quad \text{if } s_1 = 1$$

Show that the above game does not have a mixed strategy equilibrium.

(16) Consider a single player game with $N = \{1\}$ but with $S_1 = [0, 1)$ (not compact). Define the utility function as a continuous map:

$$u_1(s_1) = s_1 \quad \forall s_1 \in [0, 1]$$

Show that this game also does not have a mixed strategy equilibrium.

(17) Using the necessary and sufficient conditions for a mixed strategy Nash equilibrium, compute all mixed strategy Nash equilibria of the following problem:

	A	B
A	20, 0	0, 10
B	0, 90	20, 0

(18) Prove the following propositions.

- Suppose a strategic form game $\Gamma = \langle N, (S_i), (u_i) \rangle$ has a mixed strategy Nash equilibrium $(\sigma_1^*, \ldots, \sigma_n^*)$. Then

$$u_i(\sigma_1^*, \ldots, \sigma_n^*) \geq \underline{v_i} \quad \forall i \in N$$

where $\underline{v_i}$ is the maxmin value in mixed strategies of player i.
- Consider a strategic form game $\Gamma = \langle N, (S_i), (u_i) \rangle$. Then

$$\overline{v_i} \geq \underline{v_i} \quad \forall i \in N$$

where $\underline{v_i}$ is the maxmin value in mixed strategies of player i and $\overline{v_i}$ is the minmax value in mixed strategies of player i.

- Suppose a strategic form game $\Gamma = \langle N, (S_i), (u_i) \rangle$ has a mixed strategy Nash equilibrium $(\sigma_1^*, \ldots, \sigma_n^*)$. Then

$$u_i(\sigma_1^*, \ldots, \sigma_n^*) \geq \overline{v}_i \quad \forall i \in N$$

where $\overline{v}_i$ is the minmax value in mixed strategies of player i.

- Given a two player strategic form game, the maxmin value in mixed strategies is equal to the minmax value in mixed strategies.

(19) Apply iterative elimination of strongly dominated strategies to the following problem (Source: Myerson [2]).

		2	
1	X	Y	Z
A	2,3	3,0	0,1
B	0,0	1,6	4,2

(20) For the game shown below, apply the following elimination steps and observe the outcomes. What can you infer from these. (Source: Myerson [2]).

		2
1	X	Y
A	3,2	2,2
B	1,1	0,0
C	0,0	1,1

- Eliminate C followed by Y
- Eliminate B followed by X
- Eliminate B and C at the same time

(21) Show using the game below that the final outcomes of iterated elimination of weakly dominated strategies depends on the order of elimination (Source: Osborne [5]).

		2	
1	X	Y	Z
A	1,1	1,1	0,0
B	0,0	1,2	1,2

(22) Given a strategic form game $\langle N, (S_i), (u_i) \rangle$, consider the set of all strategy profiles $(\sigma_1, \ldots, \sigma_n)$ such that $\forall i \in N$, $\sigma(s_i) = 0$ for all strategies $s_i \in S_i$ that are eliminated during the iterated removal of strongly dominated strategies. Show that the above set includes all mixed strategy Nash equilibria.

Chapter 8

Utility Theory

Utilities play a central role in game theory. They capture the preferences that the players have for different outcomes in terms of real numbers thus enabling real-valued functions to be used in game theoretic analysis. So far we have implicitly assumed that utility functions can correctly and faithfully capture the preferences the players have for different outcomes. The utility theory developed by von Neumann and Morgenstern provides a scientific justification for this assumption. This chapter introduces and presents their axiomatic *utility theory*. The chapter also shows that any affine transformation preserves the properties of a utility function. The chapter presents a systematic procedure to compute von Neumann Morgenstern utilities. Finally the chapter presents an important categorization of players, based on their risk attitudes, as risk neutral, risk averse, or risk loving players.

8.1 Need for Utility Theory

The outcomes in a strategic form game are typically n-dimensional vectors of strategies, where n is the number of players. For example, consider the BOS game having the following payoff matrix:

1	2	
	A	B
A	$2,1$	$0,0$
B	$0,0$	$1,2$

For the above game, the set of outcomes is

$$X = \{(A, A),\ (A, B),\ (B, A),\ (B, B)\}$$

Each player has preferences on the different outcomes which can be expressed formally in terms of a binary relation usually called a *preference relation* defined on the set of outcomes X. The utility function of the player maps the outcomes to real numbers, so as to reflect the preference the player has for these outcomes. The utility function of player 1 is

$$u_1(A, A) = 2;\ u_1(A, B) = 0;\ u_1(B, A) = 0;\ u_1(B, B) = 1$$

The real numbers 2, 0, 0, 1 above capture the preference level that player 1 has for the four outcomes of the game. The utility function of player 2 is

$$u_2(A, A) = 1;\ u_2(A, B) = 0;\ u_2(B, A) = 0;\ u_2(B, B) = 2$$

Note that the utility function maps multi-dimensional information into real numbers to capture preferences by real numbers. The question arises whether it is possible at all to capture all the preferences without losing any information. Utility theory deals with this problem in a systematic and scientific way. There are many different utility theories which have been developed over the last century. The theory developed by von Neumann and Morgenstern [1] is one of the most influential among these and certainly the most relevant for game theory. In this chapter, we undertake a study of various issues involved in coming up with a satisfactory way of defining utilities in a game setting. The discussion is based on the development of these ideas in the books by Straffin [2], Maschler, Solan, and Zamir [3], Shoham and Leyton-Brown [4], and Myerson [5].

Ordinal Utilities

We motivate ordinal utilities with a simple example.

Example 8.1 (Ordinal Utilities). Consider a game with two players 1 and 2 and four outcomes, $X = \{x, y, z, w\}$. Suppose player 1 prefers x the most, followed by y, z, and w in that order. Let us denote this by, $x \succ y \succ z \succ w$. Assume that player 2's preferences are exactly the reverse, that is $w \succ z \succ y \succ x$. If it is required to assign real numbers to these outcomes to reflect the precedence ordering, then there are innumerable ways. One possible immediate assignment would be:

$$\text{Player 1}: x : 4;\ y : 3;\ z : 2;\ w : 1$$
$$\text{Player 2}: x : 2;\ y : 4;\ z : 6;\ w : 9.$$

Now consider another ordinal ranking to represent the preferences of player 1:

$$\text{Player 1}: x : 100;\ y : 50;\ z : 10;\ w : 0.$$

In the above ranking, the degrees of preferences of player 1 and also the ratios of differences of numbers are different from those in the earlier ranking.   □

Clearly, there exist uncountably infinite number of utility functions $u_1 : X \to \mathbb{R}$ and $u_2 : X \to \mathbb{R}$ that capture the preferences of players 1 and 2, respectively. In particular, if $\succeq_i$ $(i = 1, 2)$ represents the preference relation of player i, we are interested in a utility function u_i $(i = 1, 2)$ such that

$$x_1 \succeq_i x_2 \iff u_i(x_1) \geq u_i(x_2)$$

A scale on which larger numbers represent more preferred outcomes in a way that only the order of the numbers matters and not their absolute or relative magnitude is called an *ordinal scale*. Utility numbers determined from preferences in this way are called *ordinal utilities*. Note that the numerical values here only capture the order of preference of a player and may not capture the intensity or degree of the player's preferences.

Preferences over Lotteries

To describe the interaction of preferences when there is uncertainty about which outcome will be selected, the notion of a lottery (or probability distribution) is a natural tool that can be used. Suppose $X = \{x_1, x_2, \ldots, x_m\}$. Then a lottery on X is a probability distribution

$$\sigma = [p_1 : x_1; \; p_2 : x_2; \; \ldots; \; p_m : x_m]$$

Note that

$$p_j \geq 0 \text{ for } j = 1, 2, \ldots, m \text{ and } \sum_{j=1}^{m} p_j = 1.$$

We need to deal with preferences over lotteries and the utility function needs to be defined over the set of all lotteries $\Delta(X)$. We explain this with a simple example.

Example 8.2. Let the set of outcomes be $X = \{x, y, z, w\}$ as earlier. Consider the following two possibilities. In the first case, the outcomes x, y, z, w occur with probabilities $0.5, 0.2, 0.2, 0.1$ respectively and in the second case, the outcomes occur with probabilities $0.4, 0.3, 0.15, 0.15$, respectively. We shall represent these two possibilities by the lotteries σ_1, σ_2 defined over X:

$$\sigma_1 = [0.5 : x; \; 0.2 : y; \; 0.2 : z; \; 0.1 : w]; \quad \sigma_2 = [0.4 : x; \; 0.3 : y; \; 0.15 : z; \; 0.15 : w]$$

Now the question we would like to ask is which among these two lotteries is preferred by the player in a given setting. We have to define a utility function over the set of all lotteries on X to find a satisfactory answer to such a question. $\qquad \square$

The utility function over the lotteries should be such that one lottery is preferred to another lottery if and only if the number assigned to the first lottery is greater than or equal to the number assigned to the second lottery. von Neumann and Morgenstern came up with a beautiful theory for determining such utility functions. In fact, they showed that utility functions that are *linear in the probabilities of the lottery* will serve this purpose under an elegant axiomatic framework that they developed.

8.2 Axioms of von Neumann - Morgenstern Utility Theory

Let X as usual denote the set of outcomes. Consider a player i and suppose we focus on the preferences that the player has over the outcomes in X. These preferences can be expressed in the form of a binary relation $\succeq$ on X. Given $x_1, x_2 \in X$, let us define the following for the given player i:

- $x_1 \succeq x_2$: outcome x_1 is weakly preferred to outcome x_2
- $x_1 \succ x_2$: outcome x_1 is strictly preferred to outcome x_2
- $x_1 \sim x_2$: outcomes x_1 and x_2 are equally preferred (that is, player i is indifferent between x_1 and x_2)

Note immediately that

- $x_1 \succ x_2 \Longleftrightarrow x_1 \succeq x_2$ and $\neg(x_2 \succeq x_1)$
- $x_1 \sim x_2 \Longleftrightarrow x_1 \succeq x_2$ and $x_2 \succeq x_1$

It is clear that the relation $\succeq$ is reflexive.

We would like to extend binary relations $\succ$, $\succeq$, and $\sim$ to the set of lotteries to capture the preferences the players have on lotteries. We do this by presenting six axioms which represent natural and desirable properties that we would like preferences to satisfy. These axioms are: completeness, transitivity, substitutability, decomposability, monotonicity, and continuity. These were enunciated by von Neumann and Morgenstern. The first two axioms (completeness and transitivity) are properties of the preference relation over individual outcomes. The other four axioms provide the framework for extending the preference relation so as to apply for lotteries.

Axiom 1 (Completeness)

The completeness property means that every pair of outcomes is related by the preference relation. Moreover, the preference relation $\succeq$ induces an ordering on X which allows for ties among outcomes. This can be formally expressed as

$$x_1 \succ x_2; \text{ or } x_2 \succ x_1; \text{ or } x_1 \sim x_2 \ \forall x_1, x_2 \in X.$$

Axiom 2 (Transitivity)

This states that

$$x_1 \succeq x_2 \text{ and } x_2 \succeq x_3 \Longrightarrow x_1 \succeq x_3 \ \forall x_1, x_2, x_3 \in X.$$

To see why transitivity is natural requirement, we have to just visualize what would happen if transitivity is not satisfied. Suppose $x_1 \succeq x_2$ and $x_2 \succeq x_3$ but $x_3 \succ x_1$. Assume that the player in question is willing to pay a certain amount of money if she is allowed to exchange a current outcome with a more preferred outcome. Then the above three relationships will lead to the conclusion that the player is willing to pay a non-zero sum of money to exchange outcome x_3 with the same outcome! Such a situation is popularly known as a *money pump* situation and clearly leads to a problematic situation.

Axiom 3 (Substitutability)

This axiom is often called *independence*. If $x_1 \sim x_2$, then for all sequences of one or more outcomes $x_3, \ldots, x_m$, and sets of probabilities $p, p_3, \ldots, p_m$ such that

$$p + \sum_{j=3}^{m} p_j = 1,$$

the player is indifferent to the lotteries $\sigma_1 = [p : x_1; \; p_3 : x_3 ; \; \ldots \; ; \; p_m : x_m]$ and $\sigma_2 = [p : x_2; \; p_3 : x_3 ; \; \ldots \; ; \; p_m : x_m]$. We write this as $\sigma_1 \sim \sigma_2$ or

$$[p : x_1; \; p_3 : x_3 ; \; \ldots \; ; \; p_m : x_m] \sim [p : x_2; \; p_3 : x_3 ; \; \ldots \; ; \; p_m : x_m]$$

Substitutability implies that the outcome x_1 can always be substituted with outcome x_2 under the setting described above.

Example 8.3. Suppose a player who has just won a competition is given two options.

- Option 1: A tablet with probability 0.3 or a motorcycle with probability 0.7
- Option 2: A laptop with probability 0.3 or a motorcycle with probability 0.7

If the player is indifferent between a tablet and a laptop, then substitutability implies that he is indifferent between option 1, which is the lottery [0.3 : tablet; 0.7 : motorcycle], and option 2, which is the lottery [0.3 : laptop; 0.7 : motorcycle]. $\qquad \square$

Axiom 4 (Decomposability)

This axiom is often called *simplification of lotteries*. Suppose σ is a lottery over X and let $P_\sigma(x_i)$ denote the probability that x_i is selected by σ. The decomposability axiom states that

$$P_{\sigma_1}(x_i) = P_{\sigma_2}(x_i) \; \forall x_i \in X \implies \sigma_1 \sim \sigma_2 \; \forall \sigma_1, \sigma_2 \in \Delta(X)$$

Example 8.4. An example of σ for $X = \{x_1, x_2, x_3\}$ would be

$$\sigma = [0.6 : x_1; \; 0.4 : [0.4 : x_1; \; 0.6 : x_2]]$$

The above lottery is called a *compound lottery* since it has embedded within it another lottery. As a consequence of this axiom, the following lotteries will all be indifferent to a player:

$$\sigma_1 = [0.76 : x_1; \; 0.24 : x_2]$$

$$\sigma_2 = [0.6 : x_1; \; 0.4 : [0.4 : x_1; \; 0.6 : x_2]]$$

$$\sigma_3 = [0.4 : x_1; \; 0.6 : [0.6 : x_1; \; 0.4 : x_2]]$$

$$\sigma_4 = [0.5 : [0.8 : x_1; \; 0.2 : x_2]; \; 0.5 : [0.72 : x_1; \; 0.28 : x_2]]$$

Note that decomposability leads to simplifying a compound lottery into a simple lottery. $\quad \square$

Axiom 5 (Monotonicity)

Consider a player who strictly prefers outcome x_1 to outcome x_2. Suppose σ_1 and σ_2 are two lotteries over $\{x_1, x_2\}$. Monotonicity implies that the player would prefer the lottery that assigns higher probability to x_1. More formally, $\forall x_1, x_2 \in X$,

$$x_1 \succ x_2 \text{ and } 1 \geq p > q \geq 0 \Longrightarrow [p : x_1; \ 1 - p : x_2] \succ [q : x_1; \ 1 - q : x_2]$$

Intuitively, monotonicity means that players prefer more of a good thing.

Example 8.5. Suppose a player who has won a competition is given two options.
- Option 1: A laptop with probability 0.2 or a motorcycle with probability 0.8
- Option 2: A laptop with probability 0.3 or a motorcycle with probability 0.7

If the player prefers motorcycle to a laptop, then monotonicity implies that he would prefer option 1 which corresponds to the lottery [0.2 : laptop; 0.8 : motorcycle] over option 2 which corresponds to the lottery [0.3 : laptop; 0.7 : motorcycle]. □

Axiom 6 (Continuity)

This axiom states that $\forall x_1, x_2, x_3 \in X$,

$$x_1 \succ x_2 \text{ and } x_2 \succ x_3 \Longrightarrow \exists \, p \in [0, 1] \text{ such that } x_2 \sim [p : x_1; \ 1 - p : x_3]$$

The implication of the above axiom is that any outcome x_2 such that outcome x_1 is strictly preferred to x_2 but outcome x_2 is strictly preferred to another outcome x_3 will be indifferent to a player with $[p : x_1; \ 1 - p : x_3]$ for some probability p.

Example 8.6. Suppose a player who has won a competition can get a motorcycle (x_1) or a laptop (x_2) or a cellphone (x_3). Assume that the player strictly prefers a motorcycle over a laptop and strictly prefers a laptop over a cellphone. Then the continuity axiom asserts that there exists a probability $p \in [0, 1]$ such that the player is indifferent between the second preferred outcome laptop and the lottery which gives her a motorcycle with probability p or a cellphone with probability $(1 - p)$. □

We now state (without proof) a lemma and then state and prove an important theorem.

Lemma 8.1. *Suppose a relation $\succeq$ satisfies completeness, transitivity, decomposability, and monotonicity. Then if $x_1 \succ x_2$ and $x_2 \succ x_3$, there would exist a probability p such that*

$$x_2 \succ [q : x_1; 1 - q : x_3] \ \forall \, 0 \leq q < p$$

$$[r : x_1; 1 - r : x_3] \succ x_2 \ \forall \, 1 \geq r > p$$

The proof is left as an exercise (see exercises at the end of the chapter). Using axioms (1) to (6) and the above lemma, we are now in a position to state and prove the key result due to von Neumann and Morgenstern [1].

8.3 The von Neumann - Morgenstern Theorem

Theorem 8.1. *Given a set of outcomes $X = \{x_1, \ldots, x_m\}$ and a preference relation $\succeq$ on X that satisfies completeness, transitivity, substitutability, decomposability, monotonicity and continuity, there exists a utility function $u : X \to [0, 1]$ with the following two properties:*

(1) $u(x_1) \geq u(x_2)$ iff $x_1 \succeq x_2$, $\forall x_1, x_2 \in X$

(2) $u([p_1 : x_1; \ p_2 : x_2 \ ; \ \ldots \ ; \ p_m : x_m]) = \sum_{j=1}^{m} p_j u(x_j)$

Note. Condition (2) in the above theorem clearly specifies how to define the utility function over lotteries. Note that the right hand side is *linear* in the probabilities $p_1, \ldots, p_m$. This is a noteworthy feature of the von Neumann - Morgenstern utility function. A utility function that satisfies conditions (1) and (2) above is aptly called a *von Neumann – Morgenstern utility function*.

Proof : First we look at the degenerate case when $x_i \sim x_j \ \forall \ x_i, x_j \in X$. That is, the player is indifferent among all $x_i \in X$. Consider the function $u(x_i) = 0 \ \forall x_i \in X$. Part 1 of the theorem follows immediately. Part 2 follows from decomposability and substitutability and is left as an exercise.

If this degenerate case is not satisfied, then by completeness, there must exist at least one most preferred outcome and at least one least preferred outcome with the former different from the latter. Suppose $\bar{x} \in X$ is a most preferred outcome and $\underline{x} \in X$ is a least preferred outcome. Clearly, $\bar{x} \succ \underline{x}$. Now, given any $x_i \in X$, by continuity, there exists a probability p_i uniquely such that

$$x_i \sim [p_i : \bar{x}; \ 1 - p_i : \underline{x}].$$

Define $u : X \to [0, 1]$ as $u(x_i) = p_i \ \forall x_i \in X$. For this choice of u, we will now prove Part 1 and Part 2.

Proof of Part 1: Suppose $x_1, x_2 \in X$. Let us define two lotteries σ_1 and σ_2 in the following way, corresponding to x_1 and x_2, respectively:

$$x_1 \sim \sigma_1 = [\, u(x_1) : \bar{x}; \ 1 - u(x_1) : \underline{x} \,].$$

$$x_2 \sim \sigma_2 = [\, u(x_2) : \bar{x}; \ 1 - u(x_2) : \underline{x} \,].$$

We will show that $u(x_1) \geq u(x_2) \iff x_1 \succeq x_2$. First we prove that $u(x_1) \geq u(x_2) \implies x_1 \succeq x_2$. Suppose $u(x_1) > u(x_2)$. Since $\bar{x} \succ \underline{x}$, then by monotonicity we can conclude that

$$x_1 \sim \sigma_1 \succ \sigma_2 \sim x_2.$$

Using transitivity, substitutability, and decomposability, we get $x_1 \succ x_2$.

Suppose $u(x_1) = u(x_2)$. Then σ_1 and σ_2 are identical lotteries which means

$$x_1 \sim \sigma_1 \equiv \sigma_2 \sim x_2.$$

Transitivity now yields $x_1 \sim x_2$. We have thus shown that
$$u(x_1) \geq u(x_2) \implies x_1 \succeq x_2.$$
It remains to show that
$$x_1 \succeq x_2 \implies u(x_1) \geq u(x_2).$$
We show the above by proving the contrapositive:
$$u(x_1) < u(x_2) \implies x_2 \succ x_1.$$
Note that the contrapositive above can be written down by virtue of completeness. In fact, the above statement has already been proved when we showed above that
$$u(x_1) > u(x_2) \implies x_1 \succ x_2.$$
All that we have to do is to swap x_1 and x_2 to get the implication for the current case.

Proof of Part 2: First we define
$$u^* = u([p_1 : x_1; \quad p_2 : x_2; \quad \ldots; \quad p_m : x_m]).$$
By the definition of u, for each $x_j \in X$, we have
$$x_j \sim [u(x_j) : \bar{x}; \quad 1 - u(x_j) : \underline{x}].$$
Using substitutability, we can replace each x_j (in the definition of u^*) by the corresponding lottery. This yields
$$u^* = u([p_1 : [u(x_1) : \bar{x}; 1 - u(x_1) : \underline{x}] \ ; \ldots; \ p_m : [u(x_m) : \bar{x}; 1 - u(x_m) : \underline{x}]]).$$
Note that the above *nested* or *compound* lottery only selects between the two outcomes $\bar{x}$ and $\underline{x}$. Using decomposability, we get
$$u^* = u\left(\left[\left(\sum_{j=1}^{m} p_j u(x_j)\right) : \bar{x}; \quad \left(1 - \sum_{j=1}^{m} p_j u(x_j)\right) : \underline{x}\right]\right).$$
We can now use the definition of u to immediately obtain
$$u^* = \sum_{j=1}^{m} p_j u(x_j).$$
This proves Part 2 of the theorem. ∎

Example 8.7. Suppose a player who has won a competition is given two options.
- Option 1: A tablet with probability 0.3 or a motorcycle with probability 0.7
- Option 2: A cellphone with probability 0.3 or a laptop with probability 0.2 or a motorcycle with probability 0.5

Suppose the utility function of the player $u(\cdot)$ assigns real numbers 100, 200, 300, 400 to the outcomes cellphone, tablet, laptop, and motorcycle, respectively. Then the von Neumann – Morgernstern utility function assigns the number $(0.3)(200) + (0.7)(400)$ to option 1 and the number $(0.3)(100) + (0.2)(300) + (0.5)(400)$ to option 2. The expected utility of option 1 is therefore 340 and the expected utility of option 2 is 290. A rational player would clearly prefer option 1. □

8.4 Affine Transformations

In the above theorem, the range of the utility function is $[0, 1]$. It would be useful to have a utility function which is not confined to the range $[0, 1]$. The following result extends utility functions to a wider range of possibilities.

Proposition 8.1. *Every positive affine transformation $U(x)$ of a utility function $u(x)$ that satisfies $U(x) = au(x) + b$, where a and b are constants and $a > 0$, yields another utility function (in this case U) that satisfies properties (1) and (2) of Theorem 8.1.*

The proof of the result is left as an exercise. An interesting consequence of the above result is that some two player games which do not appear to be zero-sum are in fact zero-sum games, as seen by the following examples.

Example 8.8 (A Constant Sum Game). Consider the constant sum game shown in Figure 8.1. The constant sum here is equal to 1. By subtracting this constant sum from the utilities of one of the players (say player 2), we end up with the zero-sum game in Figure 8.2. □

	2	
1	*A*	*B*
A	$2, -1$	$5, -4$
B	$-6, 7$	$-1, 2$

Fig. 8.1: A constant sum game

	2	
1	*A*	*B*
A	$2, -2$	$5, -5$
B	$-6, 6$	$-1, 1$

Fig. 8.2: An equivalent zero-sum game

Example 8.9 (A Non-Zero Sum Game). Consider the two player non-zero, non-constant sum game shown in Figure 8.3. Using affine transformation $g(x) = \frac{1}{2}(x - 17)$ on the utilities of player 1, we get a zero-sum game shown in Figure 8.4. □

	2	
1	A	B
A	$27,-5$	$17,0$
B	$19,-1$	$23,-3$

Fig. 8.3: A non-zero sum game

	2	
1	A	B
A	$5,-5$	$0,0$
B	$1,-1$	$3,-3$

Fig. 8.4: An equivalent zero-sum game

8.5   Computing von Neumann - Morgenstern Utilities

Given a set of outcomes X, the theory of von Neumann - Morgenstern utilities provides a way of constructing utilities on those outcomes. The key observation is that the utilities can be constructed by asking the player concerned appropriate questions about lotteries. We explain this with an example (a simplified version of the one appearing in chapter 9 of [2]).

Suppose $X = \{x_1, x_2, x_3\}$ and assume without loss of generality that the player in question has the following preference ordering: $x_1 \succ x_2 \succ x_3$. We start by assigning numbers to the most preferred outcome x_1 and least preferred outcome x_3 in an arbitrary way, respecting only the fact that x_1 is assigned a larger number than x_3. Suppose we choose the numbers 200 and 100 respectively ($u(x_1) = 200; u(x_3) = 100$). We now try to fix a number for x_2. For this, we ask questions such as the following: would you prefer x_2 with probability 1 or a lottery that gives you x_1 with probability $\frac{1}{2}$ and x_3 with probability $\frac{1}{2}$. If the player prefers the certain event x_2 to the lottery, the implication is that x_2 ranks higher than the midpoint between x_1 and x_3, which means x_2 must be assigned a number greater than 150. This situation is pictorially depicted in Figure 8.5.

A possible next question to the player would be: Do you prefer x_2 for certain or the outcome x_1 with probability 0.75 and the outcome x_3 with probability 0.25 ? If the player prefers the lottery, then the situation will be depicted in Figure 8.6.

After a logical sequence of such questions, we would eventually find a lottery such that player 1 is indifferent between x_2 and a lottery, say, $[0.7 : x_1; \ 0.3 : x_3]$. This means we assign the number 170 to x_2 as shown in Figure 8.7.

The existence of a unique such solution is guaranteed by von Neumann - Morgenstern utility theory as long as our exploration is within the axiomatic framework.

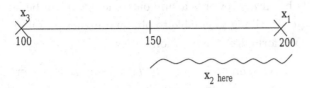

Fig. 8.5: Scenario 1

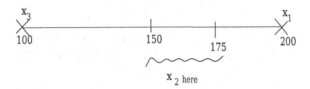

Fig. 8.6: Scenario 2

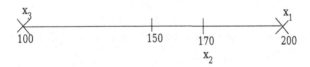

Fig. 8.7: Final assignment

8.6 Risk Attitudes of Players

In classic economics literature, three types of risk attitudes are considered: risk averse, risk neutral, and risk loving (or risk seeking). These three attitudes can be elegantly characterized using utility theory. We first provide a motivating example.

Example 8.10 (Risk Attitudes). Suppose a player who has won a competition is eligible to get a motorcycle (x_1) or a laptop (x_2) or a cellphone (x_3). Suppose his utilities for the individual outcomes are

$$u(x_1) = 1000; \quad u(x_2) = 200; \quad u(x_3) = 0$$

We know by utility theory that there exists a probability $p \in [0, 1]$ such that the player is indifferent between a sure outcome x_2 and the lottery $[p : x_1; (1 - p) : x_3]$. What this probability is will depend on the degree of risk the player is willing to take. If the player is risk neutral, this probability will be 0.2 (note that $200 = (0.2)1000 + (0.8)(0)$. A risk averse player will play it safe by tilting towards a sure outcome, so, p will be less than or equal to 0.2. A risk loving player is willing to gamble to obtain a higher payoff and p will be greater than or equal to 0.2. We formalize these notions below.   □

Suppose the set of outcomes $X = [-R, R]$ where R is a certain positive real number and assume that $x \in X$ represents the monetary reward a designated player receives in the game. Let $u_i(\cdot)$ be the von Neumann-Morgenstern utility function defined over lotteries on finite subsets of X for that player. As we have seen, $u_i(\cdot)$ can be determined from the utilities of the player for individual outcomes, say, $U_i : X \to \mathbb{R}$. Note that

$$U_i(x) = u_i([1 : x]) \ \forall x \in X$$

Suppose $\sigma = [p_1 : x_1; \ldots, p_m : x_m]$ is a lottery over the set of outcomes $\{x_1, \ldots, x_m\}$ where $x_j \in X \ \forall j = 1, \ldots, m$. Since $u_i(\cdot)$ is a von Neumann – Morgenstern utility function, we have

$$u_i(\sigma) = \sum_{j=1}^{m} p_j U_i(x_j)$$

Denote the expected monetary reward corresponding to σ by:

$$\mu_\sigma = \sum_{j=1}^{m} p_j x_j$$

Then we say player i is risk neutral if for all lotteries σ defined over finite subsets of X,

$$u_i(\sigma) = u_i([1 : \mu_\sigma]).$$

We say player i is risk averse if

$$u_i(\sigma) \leq u_i([1 : \mu_\sigma]).$$

We say player i is risk loving if

$$u_i(\sigma) \geq u_i([1 : \mu_\sigma]).$$

In order to determine if a given utility function is risk neutral or risk averse or risk loving, the above setup entails that we exhaustively check the condition for each and every σ which is not feasible at all. The following theorem provides a much more efficient way of determining the risk attitude of a player. We state this useful theorem without proof.

Theorem 8.2. *Suppose $x_1, x_2 \in \mathbb{R}$ represent any pair of monetary receipts by a player i. Then player i is risk neutral if $\forall p \in [0, 1]$,*

$$u_i([p : x_1; (1-p) : x_2]) = u_i([1 : px_1 + (1-p)x_2]) \ \forall x_1, x_2 \in \mathbb{R}$$

The player is risk averse if $\forall p \in [0, 1]$,

$$u_i([p : x_1; (1-p) : x_2]) \leq u_i([1 : px_1 + (1-p)x_2]) \ \forall x_1, x_2 \in \mathbb{R}$$

The player is risk loving if $\forall p \in [0, 1]$,

$$u_i([p : x_1; (1-p) : x_2]) \geq u_i([1 : px_1 + (1-p)x_2]) \ \forall x_1, x_2 \in \mathbb{R}$$

Note. The above theorem implies that the utility function of a risk averse player is concave while the utility function of a risk loving player is convex. Clearly, the utility function of a risk neutral player will be linear. Figures 8.8 and 8.9 depict utility functions that are risk averse and risk loving respectively.

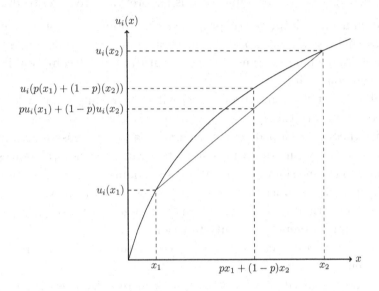

Fig. 8.8: Utility function of a risk averse player

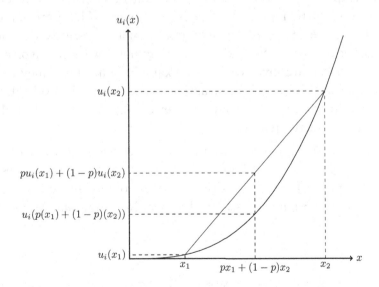

Fig. 8.9: Utility function of a risk loving player

8.7   Summary and References

A utility function defined in games maps multi-dimensional profiles into real numbers and the question arises whether such a mapping can capture all the preferences completely. This question was answered by von Neumann and Morgenstern through their utility theory. The key learnings of this chapter are provided below.

- von Neumann and Morgenstern proposed six axioms to express the desirable properties that we would expect a set of outcomes and preferences to satisfy. These are: completeness, transitivity, substitutability, decomposability, monotonicity, and continuity.
- To describe the interaction of preferences with uncertainty about which outcome is selected, the utility theory uses the notion of lotteries on the set of outcomes.
- The utility theory developed by von Neumann and Morgenstern guarantees the existence of a utility function that completely captures the preferences over lotteries on the outcome set when the above six axioms are satisfied. Interestingly, this utility function is linear in the probabilities in the lottery.
- Any affine transformation of a von Neumann Morgenstern utility function is also a von Neumann Morgenstern utility function.
- A systematic procedure can be used to compute von Neumann Morgenstern utilities given a set of outcomes.
- Based on the risk attitudes, players can be categorized as risk neutral, risk averse, or risk loving. The utility functions of these players will be linear, concave, and convex respectively.
- It is often tempting to interpret utilities in monetary terms. However, it is not always appropriate to represent utilities by money. There are many reasons for this. First, the utility of an individual is not necessarily dependent only on the amount of money. Second, money may not always be involved in every transaction that we are involved in. An example would be kidney exchange or barter transaction. Even in those situations where money is involved, the utility may not depend linearly on money. The exact dependence will be decided by the risk attitudes of the players.

The material of this chapter has been put together based on the treatment that appears in [4], [3], [2], and [5]. The reader must consult these references for more insights. The treatment [5] and [3] is rigorous and comprehensive. An exhaustive account appears in the original classic work of von Neumann and Morgenstern [1].

References

[1]   John von Neumann and Oskar Morgenstern. *Theory of Games and Economic Behavior*. Princeton University Press, 1944.
[2]   Philip D. Straffin Jr. *Game Theory and Strategy*. The Mathematical Association of America, 1993.

[3] Michael Maschler, Eilon Solan, and Shmuel Zamir. *Game Theory*. Cambridge University Press, 2013.

[4] Yoam Shoham and Kevin Leyton-Brown. *Multiagent Systems: Algorithmic, Game-Theoretic, and Logical Foundations*. Cambridge University Press, New York, USA, 2009, 2009.

[5] Roger B. Myerson. *Game Theory: Analysis of Conflict*. Harvard University Press, Cambridge, Massachusetts, USA, 1997.

8.8   Exercises

(1) Complete the proof of Lemma 8.1. (Proof is available in [4])

(2) Complete the proof of the result that affine transformations of a utility function do not affect properties (1) and (2) of the von Neumann – Morgenstern utilities (see Theorem 8.1).

(3) Straffin [2] describes a simple graphical way of investigating whether or not a given two player non-zero sum game is equivalent to a zero-sum game. This involves plotting of the utilities of player 1 and player 2 on the X-Y plane. This would be an instructive reading exercise.

(4) Prove Theorem 8.2 which provides a convenient characterization for risk neutral, risk averse, and risk loving players.

Chapter 9

Matrix Games

Two player zero-sum games describe strictly competitive situations involving two players. *Matrix games* are two player zero-sum games with finite strategy sets. Matrix games are interesting in many ways and their analysis is tractable due to their simplicity and special structure. It was shown by von Neumann and Morgenstern that linear programming can be used to solve these games. In this chapter, we first provide several examples of matrix games. Next we analyze matrix games in the context of pure strategies through key notions such as security level, security strategies, and saddle points. We show that pure strategy Nash equilibria, if they exist, are precisely the saddle points. Following this, we analyze matrix games in the context of mixed strategies. We show that the optimal strategies for the two players can be described by linear programs which are duals of each other. This leads to the main result in this chapter, the *minimax theorem*, which shows that every matrix game is guaranteed to have a mixed strategy Nash equilibrium.

A two person zero-sum game is a strategic form game $\langle \{1,2\}, (S_1, S_2), (u_1, u_2) \rangle$ such that $u_1(s_1, s_2) + u_2(s_1, s_2) = 0 \ \forall s_1 \in S_1; \ \forall s_2 \in S_2$. We also use the notation $\langle \{1,2\}, S_1, S_2, u_1, -u_1 \rangle$. A critical point to note is that a player maximizing her payoff is equivalent to minimizing the payoff of the other player. For this reason, these games are also called *strictly competitive games*. By convention, player 1 is called the *row player* and player 2 is called the *column player*.

In this chapter, we only discuss two player zero-sum games with finite strategy sets. Suppose $S_1 = \{s_{11}, s_{12}, \ldots, s_{1m}\}$ and $S_2 = \{s_{21}, s_{22}, \ldots, s_{2n}\}$. Without any confusion, we will assume from now on, that, $S_1 = \{1, 2, \ldots, m\}$ and $S_2 = \{1, 2, \ldots, n\}$ (the symbol n here is not to be confused with its usual meaning elsewhere in the book, namely the number of players in the game). Since the payoffs of one player are just the negative of the payoffs of the other player, these games can be represented by a matrix A with m rows and n columns with $a_{ij} = u_1(i, j) \ \forall i \in S_1$ and $\forall j \in S_2$. The number a_{ij} is the payoff to player 1 (row player) and $-a_{ij}$ is the payoff to player 2 (column player) when player 1 chooses strategy i and player 2 chooses strategy j. For this reason, these games are also aptly called matrix games. For brevity, we will just say A is a matrix game.

9.1 Examples of Matrix Games

Example 9.1 (Matching Pennies). Consider the standard matching pennies game, whose payoff matrix is given by the following table, assuming that strategy 1 corresponds to *heads* and strategy 2 corresponds to *tails*:

		2
1	1	2
1	$1, -1$	$-1, 1$
2	$-1, 1$	$1, -1$

The above matrix can be specified by a matrix A that includes only the payoffs of player 1:

$$A = \begin{bmatrix} 1 & -1 \\ -1 & 1 \end{bmatrix}$$

□

Example 9.2 (Rock-Paper-Scissors). We have already seen in Section 4.3 the rock-paper-scissors game where there are two players and each player has three possible strategies: 1 (rock); 2 (paper); and 3 (scissors). This is a matrix game with the following matrix:

$$A = \begin{bmatrix} 0 & -1 & 1 \\ 1 & 0 & -1 \\ -1 & 1 & 0 \end{bmatrix}$$

□

Example 9.3 (Product Prediction Game). Assume that there are two competing companies 1 and 2 that can produce one of three products X, Y, and Z, at a time. A company can only produce one product at a time and the payoff to the company depends on the products being produced by both companies. Suppose that when one company gets profit, the other company makes an equal amount of loss. Assuming X, Y, and Z as strategies 1, 2, and 3, respectively, we have $S_1 = S_2 = \{1, 2, 3\}$. An example payoff matrix is given by

$$A = \begin{bmatrix} 100 & 200 & 100 \\ 0 & -100 & 200 \\ -100 & 0 & -200 \end{bmatrix}$$

Each company has to decide simultaneously upon a product to produce. It would be of interest to predict which products the two companies will produce in equilibrium. □

Example 9.4 (A Constant Sum Game). An immediate generalization of a zero-sum game is a constant sum game: $\langle \{1, 2\}, S_1, S_2, u_1, u_2 \rangle$ such that $u_1(s_1, s_2) + u_2(s_1, s_2) = C$, $\forall s_1 \in S_1; s_2 \in S_2$ where C is a known constant. Any constant sum game can be transformed into a zero-sum game using a simple transformation (for example, by subtracting the constant from each payoff of one player) and can be analyzed as a zero-sum game. □

9.2 Pure Strategies in Matrix Games

In this section, we analyze matrix games when only pure strategies are allowed. First note that maximizing the payoff of any player is the same as minimizing the payoff of the other player. When the row player plays strategy i, the column player plays a strategy that will minimize the row player's payoff:

$$\min_{j \in S_2} a_{ij}$$

The above payoff is the minimum guaranteed payoff to the row player when she plays i. The row player will therefore look for a pure strategy i that maximizes the above. That is, a strategy i such that

$$\max_{i \in S_1} \min_{j \in S_2} a_{ij}$$

In other words, an optimal strategy for the row player is *maxminimization*. Note that the row player chooses a pure strategy that is best for her on the assumption that whatever she does, the column player will choose a strategy that will hurt her (row player) as much as possible. Such a strategy of the row player is called the *maxmin strategy* or *security strategy* of the row player.

Similarly, when the column player plays pure strategy j, he assures himself of a payoff equal to

$$\min_{i \in S_1} (-a_{ij}) = -\max_{i \in S_1} a_{ij}.$$

That is, he assures himself of losing no more than

$$\max_{i \in S_1} a_{ij}$$

The column player's optimal strategy will be to minimize this loss:

$$\min_{j \in S_2} \max_{i \in S_1} a_{ij}$$

This is called *minmaximization*. Such a strategy of the column player is called a *security strategy* of the column player.

Thus, the maxmin value and minmax value play a natural role in describing the optimal strategies of players in a matrix game. We have already defined the notions of maxmin value and minmax value in Chapter 6 and we recall these below.

Definition 9.1 (Maxmin Value). *Given a matrix game A, the maxmin value is defined as:*

$$\underline{v} = \max_{i \in S_1} \min_{j \in S_2} a_{ij}$$

Note. The maxmin value $\underline{v}$ is the minimum guaranteed payoff to the row player when the column player is free to play any strategy. A strategy of the row player that yields her the payoff $\underline{v}$ is called a maxmin strategy of the player.

Note. The maxmin value $\underline{v}$ is also called the *security level* of the row player or *lower value*. A maxmin strategy is also called a *security strategy* or *optimal strategy* of the row player.

Definition 9.2 (Minmax Value). *Given a matrix game A, the minmax value is defined as:*

$$\overline{v} = \min_{j \in S_2} \max_{i \in S_1} a_{ij}$$

Note. The value $\overline{v}$ is the maximum loss that the column player may suffer when the row player is free to play any strategy. The minmax value $\overline{v}$ is also called the upper value. A strategy of the column player that results in his getting the payoff $-\overline{v}$ is called a *security strategy* or *optimal strategy* of the column player.

Note. We have already shown in Section 6.5 that $\underline{v} \leq \overline{v}$. If $\underline{v} = \overline{v}$, then we have the following definition.

Definition 9.3 (Value in Pure Strategies). *Given a matrix game A, if $\underline{v} = \overline{v}$, the number $v = \underline{v} = \overline{v}$ is called the value of the matrix game in pure strategies.*

Example 9.5 (Maxmin Value and Minmax Value). Consider the matching pennies game. If the row player plays strategy 1, then the possible payoffs are 1 (if the column player plays strategy 1) or -1 (if the column player plays strategy 2) and hence the minimum payoff is -1. Similarly, if the row player plays strategy 2, the minimum payoff possible is -1. Thus the maxmin value is given by

$$\underline{v} = \max_i \min_j a_{ij} = \max\{-1, -1\} = -1$$

Both strategy 1 and strategy 2 are security strategies for the row player. The minmax value is given by

$$\overline{v} = \min_j \max_i a_{ij} = \min\{1, 1\} = 1$$

Here again, both strategy 1 and strategy 2 are security strategies for the column player. The game does not have a value since $\underline{v} \neq \overline{v}$.

Next we consider the rock-paper-scissors game. We have:

$$\underline{v} = \max_i \min_j a_{ij} = \max\{-1, -1, -1\} = -1$$
$$\overline{v} = \min_j \max_i a_{ij} = \min\{1, 1, 1\} = 1$$

This game, like the previous one, does not have a value since $\underline{v} \neq \overline{v}$.

Finally we consider the product prediction game. We have

$$\underline{v} = \max_i \min_j a_{ij} = \max\{100, -100, -200\} = 100$$
$$\overline{v} = \min_j \max_i a_{ij} = \min\{100, 200, 200\} = 100$$

Note that $\underline{v} = \bar{v}$ and the payoff $v = 100$, corresponding to the strategy profile $(1,1)$ is the value. Strategy 1 is row player's security strategy and strategy 1 is column player's security strategy.   □

9.3   Saddle Points and Pure Strategy Nash Equilibria

As observed in the examples above, given a matrix game A, the maxmin value $\underline{v}$ and the minmax value $\bar{v}$ always exist but they may not be equal. If they are equal, then the matrix is guaranteed to have one or more saddle points. We now define the notion of *saddle point* of a matrix.

Definition 9.4 (Saddle Point of a Matrix). *Given a matrix $A = [a_{ij}]$, the element a_{ij} is called a saddle point of A (or matrix game A) if*

$$a_{ij} \geq a_{kj} \quad \forall k = 1, \ldots, m; \text{ and}$$
$$a_{ij} \leq a_{il} \quad \forall l = 1, \ldots, n.$$

That is, the element a_{ij} is simultaneously a maximum in its column and a minimum in its row. Given a matrix game A, the strategies i and j are called the saddle point strategies of row player and column player, respectively.

We now make several key observations on saddle points. First we present two examples.

Example 9.6 (Saddle Points). Consider the product prediction game. We have seen that the value is $v = 100$ and this corresponds to the strategy profile $(1,1)$. Note that a_{11} is simultaneously a column maximum and a row minimum and therefore is a saddle point. We also make the following important additional observations.

- Saddle point strategy 1 is a best response strategy of the row player when the column player chooses saddle point strategy 1, and vice-versa. Hence the profile $(1,1)$ is a pure strategy Nash equilibrium. The strategy profile $(1,1)$ obviously satisfies the Nash equilibrium property namely the row player (the column player) will not be better off playing any other strategy when the column player (row player) sticks to the equilibrium strategy.
- The saddle point strategy profile $(1,1)$ remarkably satisfies the following property as well: The row player (column player) is not worse off by sticking to her saddle point strategy when the column player (row player) deviates from his saddle point strategy.
- By playing the saddle point strategy 1, the row player can assure herself a payoff of at least 100. By playing the saddle point strategy 1, the column player can assure himself that the row player will get a payoff of at most 100.
- If the row player gets a payoff of less than 100, then the row player can always do better by playing the saddle point strategy 1. If the row player gets a payoff of greater than 100, then the column player can always do better by playing saddle point strategy 1 and limiting the row player to a payoff of 100.

The above observations capture many properties satisfied by saddle point strategies.   □

Example 9.7. Let us look at a matrix game with the following matrix:

$$A = \begin{bmatrix} 5 & 3 & 5 & 3 \\ 2 & 1 & -1 & -2 \\ 4 & 3 & 5 & 3 \end{bmatrix}$$

$$\underline{v} = \max_i \ \min_j \ a_{ij} = \max\{3, -2, 3\} = 3$$
$$\overline{v} = \min_j \ \max_i \ a_{ij} = \min\{5, 3, 5, 3\} = 3$$

For the above game, note that $\underline{v} = \overline{v} = 3$. This game has four saddle points, namely a_{12}, a_{14}, a_{32}, and a_{34}, and they all yield the same payoff 3. Furthermore, all the four strategy profiles $(1,2), (1,4), (3,2), (3,4)$ also turn out to be pure strategy Nash equilibria. In fact, these are the only pure strategy Nash equilibria. □

The above two examples motivate and lead to the following results. First, the following theorem gives a necessary and sufficient condition for existence of a saddle point.

Theorem 9.1. *A matrix A has a saddle point if and only if $\underline{v} = \overline{v}$.*

The proof of the above is left as an exercise. The following proposition asserts that pure strategy Nash equilibria in matrix games are in fact the same as saddle points.

Proposition 9.1. *For a matrix game with payoff matrix A, a_{ij} is a saddle point if and only if the strategy profile (i, j) is a pure strategy Nash equilibrium.*

Proof: Suppose a_{ij} is a saddle point of A. We show that the outcome (i, j) is a PSNE. Since a_{ij} is a saddle point, a_{ij} is a maximum in column j and a_{ij} is a minimum in row i (which means $-a_{ij}$ is a maximum in row i). Together, these imply that the column player is playing a best response strategy against strategy i of the row player and the row player is playing a best response strategy with respect to strategy j of the column player. This in turn implies that (i, j) is a pure strategy Nash equilibrium. Thus if a_{ij} is a saddle point, then the profile (i, j) is a pure strategy Nash equilibrium.

If we assume that the profile (i, j) is a pure strategy Nash equilibrium, we can exactly reverse the above arguments and show that a_{ij} is a saddle point of A. ■

Note. The implication of the above proposition is that pure strategy Nash equilibria are endowed with substantial additional power in matrix games. Specifically, a pure strategy equilibrium strategy of a player also happens to be a security strategy or maxmin strategy of the player. This, of course, does not necessarily happen in games other than two player zero-sum games.

The following proposition brings out the interchangeability of saddle points in matrix games.

Proposition 9.2. *If in a matrix game with payoff matrix A, the elements a_{ij} and a_{hk} are both saddle points, then a_{ik} and a_{hj} are also saddle points. Also, all saddle points in the game yield the same respective payoffs to the players.*

Another way of stating this proposition would be to state that if (i, j) and (h, k) are pure strategy Nash equilibria, then (i, k) and (h, j) are also pure strategy Nash equilibria. The proof of this is left as an exercise. The proposition implies that if multiple saddle points exist, they are *interchangeable* in the sense that a player using any of her saddle point strategies against any of the other player's saddle point strategies will also result in a saddle point. Moreover the saddle points are *equivalent* in the sense that they all yield the same respective payoff value to the players.

9.4 Mixed Strategies in Matrix Games

We have seen that saddle points or pure strategy Nash equilibria may not exist in matrix games. However, when mixed strategies are allowed, equilibria are guaranteed to exist. Let $x = (x_1, \ldots, x_m)$ and $y = (y_1, \ldots, y_n)$ be the mixed strategies of the row player and the column player respectively. Note that a_{ij} is the payoff of the row player when the row player chooses row i and column player chooses column j with probability 1. The corresponding payoff for the column player is $-a_{ij}$. The expected payoff to the row player with the above mixed strategies x and y can be computed as:

$$= u_1(x, y)$$
$$= \sum_{i=1}^{m} \sum_{j=1}^{n} x_i y_j a_{ij}$$
$$= xAy \quad \text{where} \quad x = (x_1, \ldots, x_m); \ y = (y_1, \ldots, y_n); A = [a_{ij}]$$

We have slightly abused the notation in the above by using the vector y instead of its transpose (we do this throughout this chapter for the sake of convenience since the context is always clear). The expected payoff to column player $= -xAy$. When the row player plays x, she assures herself of an expected payoff

$$\min_{y \in \Delta(S_2)} xAy$$

The row player should therefore look for a mixed strategy x that maximizes the above. That is, an x such that

$$\max_{x \in \Delta(S_1)} \min_{y \in \Delta(S_2)} xAy$$

In other words, an optimal strategy for the row player is to do *maxminimization*. Note that the row player chooses a mixed strategy that is best for her on the assumption that whatever she does, the column player will choose a strategy that will hurt her (row player) as much as possible. Such a strategy of the row player is also aptly called a *security strategy* of the row player.

Similarly, when the column player plays y, she assures herself of a payoff

$$= \min_{x \in \Delta(S_1)} \ -xAy$$

$$= - \max_{x \in \Delta(S_1)} \ xAy$$

That is, she assures herself of losing no more than

$$\max_{x \in \Delta(S_1)} \ xAy$$

The column player's optimal strategy should be to minimize this loss:

$$\min_{y \in \Delta(S_2)} \max_{x \in \Delta(S_1)} \ xAy$$

This is called *minmaximization*. Such a strategy of the column player is also aptly called a *security strategy* of the column player.

We now state and prove an important lemma which asserts that when the row player plays x, among the best response strategies y of the column player, there is always at least one pure strategy.

Lemma 9.1. *Given a matrix game A and mixed strategies $x = (x_1, x_2, \ldots, x_m)$ and $y = (y_1, \ldots, y_n)$,*

$$\min_{y \in \Delta(S_2)} xAy = \min_{j} \sum_{i=1}^{m} a_{ij} x_i$$

Proof: For a given j, the summation

$$\sum_{i=1}^{m} a_{ij} x_i$$

gives the payoff to the row player when she adopts $x = (x_1, \ldots, x_m)$ and the column player adopts the pure strategy j. Therefore

$$\min_{j} \sum_{i=1}^{m} a_{ij} x_i$$

gives the minimum payoff that the row player gets when she plays x and when the column player is free to play any pure strategy. Since a pure strategy is a special case of mixed strategies, we have

$$\min_{j} \sum_{i=1}^{m} a_{ij} x_i \geq \min_{y \in \Delta(S_2)} xAy \tag{9.1}$$

On the other hand,

$$xAy = \sum_{j=1}^{n} y_j \left(\sum_{i=1}^{m} a_{ij} x_i \right)$$

$$\geq \sum_{j=1}^{n} y_j \left(\min_j \sum_{i=1}^{m} a_{ij} x_i \right)$$

$$= \min_j \sum_{i=1}^{m} a_{ij} x_i \quad \text{since} \quad \sum_{j=1}^{n} y_j = 1$$

Therefore, we have:

$$xAy \geq \min_j \sum_{i=1}^{m} a_{ij} x_i \ \forall \ x \in \Delta(S_1); \ \ \forall \ y \in \Delta(S_2)$$

This implies that

$$\min_{y \in \Delta(S_2)} xAy \geq \min_j \sum_{i=1}^{m} a_{ij} x_i \tag{9.2}$$

From equations (9.1) and (9.2), we have,

$$\min_{y \in \Delta(S_2)} xAy = \min_j \sum_{i=1}^{m} a_{ij} x_i$$

This completes the proof of the lemma. ∎

As an immediate corollary of the above lemma, it can be shown that

$$\max_{x \in \Delta(S_1)} xAy = \max_i \sum_{j=1}^{n} a_{ij} y_j$$

Using the above results, we can describe the optimization problems of the row player and the column player as follows.

Row Player's Optimization Problem (Maxminimization)

The optimization problem facing the row player can be expressed as

$$\text{maximize} \ \min_j \sum_{i=1}^{m} a_{ij} x_i$$

$$\text{subject to}$$

$$\sum_{i=1}^{m} x_i = 1$$

$$x_i \geq 0 \quad i = 1, \dots, m$$

Call the above problem P_1. Note that this problem can be succinctly expressed as

$$\max_{x \in \Delta(S_1)} \ \min_{y \in \Delta(S_2)} \ xAy$$

Column Player's Optimization Problem (Minmaximization)

The optimization problem facing the column player can be expressed as

$$\text{minimize } \max_i \sum_{j=1}^{n} a_{ij} y_j$$

subject to

$$\sum_{j=1}^{n} y_j = 1$$
$$y_j \geq 0 \quad j = 1, \ldots, n$$

Call the above problem P_2. Note that this problem can be succinctly expressed as

$$\min_{y \in \Delta(S_2)} \max_{x \in \Delta(S_1)} xAy$$

The following proposition shows that the problems P_1 and P_2 are equivalent to appropriate linear programs.

Proposition 9.3. *The problem P_1 is equivalent to the following linear program (we shall call this linear program LP_1):*

$$\text{Maximize} \qquad z$$
$$\text{subject to}$$
$$z - \sum_{i=1}^{m} a_{ij} x_i \quad \leq \quad 0 \quad j = 1, \ldots, n$$
$$\sum_{i=1}^{m} x_i = 1$$
$$x_i \geq 0 \quad i = 1, \ldots, m$$

Proof: Note that P_1 is a maximization problem and therefore by looking at the constraints

$$z - \sum_{i=1}^{m} a_{ij} x_i \leq 0 \quad j = 1, 2, \ldots, n,$$

any optimal solution (z^*, x^*) will satisfy one of the n inequalities in the above constraint. That is,

$$z^* = \sum_{i=1}^{m} a_{ij} x_i^* \quad \text{for some} \quad j \in \{1, \ldots, n\}$$

Let j^* be one such value of j. Then

$$z^* = \sum_{i=1}^{m} a_{ij^*} x_i^*$$

Because z^* is a feasible solution of LP_1, we have

$$\sum_{i=1}^{m} a_{ij^*} x_i^* \leq \sum_{i=1}^{m} a_{ij} x_i^* \quad \forall j = 1, \ldots, n$$

This means

$$\sum_{i=1}^{m} a_{ij^*} x_i^* = \min_j \sum_{i=1}^{m} a_{ij} x_i^*$$

If not, we have

$$z^* < \sum_{i=1}^{m} a_{ij} x_i \ \forall j = 1, 2, \ldots, n. \qquad \blacksquare$$

Thus the following two linear programs describe the optimization problems facing the row player and the column player.

Row Player's Linear Program (LP$_1$)

$$\begin{aligned}
&\text{maximize} \quad z \\
&\text{subject to} \\
&z - \sum_{i=1}^{m} a_{ij} x_i \leq 0 \quad j = 1, \ldots, n \\
&\sum_{i=1}^{m} x_i = 1 \\
&x_i \geq 0 \quad \forall i = 1, \ldots, m
\end{aligned}$$

Column Player's Linear Program (LP$_2$)

$$\begin{aligned}
&\text{minimize} \quad w \\
&\text{subject to} \\
&w - \sum_{j=1}^{n} a_{ij} y_j \geq 0 \quad i = 1, \ldots, m \\
&\sum_{j=1}^{n} y_j = 1 \\
&y_j \geq 0 \quad \forall j = 1, \ldots, n
\end{aligned}$$

Example 9.8 (Rock-Paper-Scissors Game). For the rock-paper-scissors game, recall the matrix of payoffs of row player:

$$A = \begin{bmatrix} 0 & -1 & 1 \\ 1 & 0 & -1 \\ -1 & 1 & 0 \end{bmatrix}$$

The problem P_1 would be:

$$\text{maximize } \min\{x_2 - x_3, \ -x_1 + x_3, \ x_1 - x_2\} \quad \text{subject to}$$

$$x_1 + x_2 + x_3 = 1$$

$$x_1 \geq 0; \ x_2 \geq 0; \ x_3 \geq 0$$

The above problem is equivalent to the linear program (LP_1):

$$\text{maximize } z \quad \text{subject to}$$

$$z \leq x_2 - x_3; \ z \leq -x_1 + x_3; \ z \leq x_1 - x_2.$$

$$x_1 + x_2 + x_3 = 1 \quad x_1 \geq 0; \ x_2 \geq 0; \ x_3 \geq 0.$$

In respect of the column player, the problem P_2 would be:

$$\text{minimize } \max\{-y_2 + y_3, \ y_1 - y_3, \ -y_1 + y_2\} \quad \text{subject to}$$

$$y_1 + y_2 + y_3 = 1$$

$$y_1 \geq 0; \ y_2 \geq 0; \ y_3 \geq 0$$

The above problem is equivalent to the linear program (LP_2):

$$\text{minimize } w \quad \text{subject to}$$

$$w \geq -y_2 + y_3; \ w \geq y_1 - y_3; \ w \geq -y_1 + y_2.$$

$$y_1 + y_2 + y_3 = 1; \ y_1 \geq 0; \ y_2 \geq 0; \ y_3 \geq 0.$$

The above linear programs enable us to compute the mixed strategy equilibria. $\square$

9.5 Minimax Theorem

This result is one of the important landmarks in the initial decades of game theory. This result was proved by von Neumann in 1928 using the Brouwer's fixed point theorem. Later, he and Morgenstern provided an elegant proof of this theorem using linear programming duality. The key implication of the minimax theorem is the existence of a mixed strategy Nash equilibrium in any matrix game.

Theorem 9.2 (Minimax Theorem). *For every matrix game with a $(m \times n)$ matrix A, there is a mixed strategy of the row player $x^* = (x_1^*, \ldots, x_m^*)$ and a mixed strategy of the column player $y^* = (y_1^*, \ldots, y_n^*)$ such that*

$$\max_{x \in \Delta(S_1)} x A y^* = \min_{y \in \Delta(S_2)} x^* A y$$

Moreover, the profile (x^*, y^*) is a mixed strategy Nash equilibrium.

Proof: Given a matrix A, we have defined linear programs LP_1 and LP_2 in the preceding section. The linear program LP_1 describes the optimal strategy of the row player while the linear program LP_2 describes the optimal strategy of the column player. First we make the observation that the linear program LP_2 is the dual of the linear program LP_1. We now invoke the strong duality theorem which states: *If an LP has an optimal solution, then its dual also has an optimal solution; moreover the optimal value of the dual is the same as the optimal value of the original (primal) LP*. See the mathematical appendix (Chapter 33) for a quick primer on LP duality.

To apply the strong duality theorem in the current scenario, we first observe that the problem P_1 has an optimal solution by the very nature of the problem. Since LP_1 is equivalent to the problem P_1, the immediate implication is that LP_1 has an optimal solution. Thus we have two linear programs LP_1 and LP_2 which are duals of each other and LP_1 has an optimal solution. Then by the strong duality theorem, LP_2 also has an optimal solution and the optimal value of LP_2 is the same as the optimal value of LP_1.

Let $z^*, x_1^*, \ldots, x_m^*$ be an optimal solution of LP_1. Then, we have

$$z^* = \sum_{i=1}^{m} a_{ij^*} x_i^* \quad \text{for some} \quad j^* \in \{1, \ldots, n\}$$

By the feasibility of an optimal solution in LP_1, we have

$$\sum_{i=1}^{m} a_{ij^*} x_i^* \le \sum_{i=1}^{m} a_{ij} x_i^* \quad \text{for} \quad j = 1, \ldots, n$$

This implies that

$$\sum_{i=1}^{m} a_{ij^*} x_i^* = \min_j \sum_{i=1}^{m} a_{ij} x_i^*$$
$$= \min_{y \in \Delta(S_2)} x^* A y \quad \text{(by Lemma 9.1)}$$

Thus

$$z^* = \min_{y \in \Delta(S_2)} x^* A y$$

Similarly, let $w^*, y_1^*, \ldots, y_n^*$ be an optimal solution of LP_2. Then

$$w^* = \sum_{j=1}^{n} a_{i^*j} y_j^* \quad \text{for some} \quad i^* \in \{1, \ldots, m\}$$

By the feasibility of an optimal solution in LP_2, we have

$$\sum_{j=1}^{m} a_{i^*j} y_j^* \ge \sum_{j=1}^{n} a_{ij} y_j^* \quad \text{for} \quad i = 1, 2, \ldots, m$$

This implies that

$$\sum_{j=1}^{n} a_{i^*j} y_j^* = \max_i \sum_{j=1}^{n} a_{ij} y_j^*$$

$$= \max_{x \in \Delta(S_1)} xAy^* \quad \text{(by Lemma 9.1)}$$

Therefore

$$w^* = \max_{x \in \Delta(S_1)} xAy^*.$$

By the strong duality theorem, the optimal values of the primal and the dual are the same and therefore $z^* = w^*$. This means that

$$\min_{y \in \Delta(S_2)} x^*Ay = \max_{x \in \Delta(S_1)} xAy^* \tag{9.3}$$

This proves the main part of the minimax theorem.

We now show that the mixed strategy profile (x^*, y^*) is a mixed strategy Nash equilibrium of the matrix game with matrix A. For this, consider

$$x^*Ay^* \geq \min_{y \in \Delta(S_2)} x^*Ay$$
$$= \max_{x \in \Delta(S_1)} xAy^*$$
$$\geq xAy^* \quad \forall x \in \Delta(S_1) \quad \text{(by equation (9.3))}$$

That is, $x^*Ay^* \geq xAy^* \ \forall x \in \Delta(S_1)$. This implies

$$u_1(x^*, y^*) \geq u_1(x, y^*) \ \forall x \in \Delta(S_1) \tag{9.4}$$

Further

$$x^*Ay^* \leq \max_{x \in \Delta(S_1)} xAy^*$$
$$= \min_{y \in \Delta(S_2)} x^*Ay$$
$$\leq x^*Ay \quad \forall y \in \Delta(S_2) \quad \text{(by (equation (9.3))}$$

That is, $x^*Ay^* \leq x^*Ay \ \forall y \in \Delta(S_2)$. This implies

$$u_2(x^*, y^*) \geq u_2(x^*, y) \ \forall y \in \Delta(S_2) \tag{9.5}$$

Equations (9.4) and (9.5) immediately imply that (x^*, y^*) is a mixed strategy Nash equilibrium. This means the minimax theorem guarantees the existence of a mixed strategy Nash equilibrium for any matrix game. ∎

Example 9.9. For the rock-paper-scissors game, it is easy to see that the linear programs LP_1 and LP_2 are duals of each other. Moreover, the optimal solution of LP_1 can be seen to be

$$x_1^* = \frac{1}{3}; \ x_2^* = \frac{1}{3}; \ x_3^* = \frac{1}{3}; \ z^* = 0$$

The optimal solution of LP_2 can be seen to be

$$y_1^* = \frac{1}{3}; \ y_2^* = \frac{1}{3}; \ y_3^* = \frac{1}{3}; \ w^* = 0$$

Thus $((\frac{1}{3}, \frac{1}{3}, \frac{1}{3}), (\frac{1}{3}, \frac{1}{3}, \frac{1}{3}))$ is a mixed strategy Nash equilibrium of the game. □

A Necessary and Sufficient Condition for Existence of Equilibrium

We now state a key theorem that provides necessary and sufficient conditions for a mixed strategy profile to be a Nash equilibrium in matrix games. We leave the proof of this as an exercise. The minimax theorem is used in a crucial way in proving this theorem.

Theorem 9.3. *Given a matrix game* $\langle \{1,2\}, S_1, S_2, u_1, -u_1 \rangle$, *a mixed strategy profile* (x^*, y^*) *is a Nash equilibrium if and only if*

$$x^* \in \arg\max_{x \in \Delta(S_1)} \ \min_{y \in \Delta(S_2)} \ xAy$$

and

$$y^* \in \arg\min_{y \in \Delta(S_2)} \ \max_{x \in \Delta(S_1)} \ xAy$$

Furthermore

$$
\begin{aligned}
u_1(x^*, y^*) &= -u_2(x^*, y^*) \\
&= x^* A y^* \\
&= \max_{x \in \Delta(S_1)} \ \min_{y \in \Delta(S_2)} \ xAy \\
&= \min_{y \in \Delta(S_2)} \ \max_{x \in \Delta(S_1)} \ xAy
\end{aligned}
$$

Note. A key point that must be noted in the context of matrix games, is that the two notions Nash equilibrium and maxmin strategy profile, which are in general different, turn out to be the same. Also, Nash equilibrium provides an insurance to each player not only against his own unilateral deviations but also against deviations by the other player.

9.6 Summary and References

Two player zero-sum games represent a well studied, well understood special class of strategic form games. If the strategy sets are finite, such a game can be conveniently represented by a matrix A where the element a_{ij} is the utility of the row player and $-a_{ij}$ is the utility of the column player when the row player plays pure strategy i and the column player plays pure strategy j. The following are the key results that we have covered in this chapter.

- When only pure strategies are allowed, an optimal strategy for the row player is to choose a strategy that maximizes the minimum payoff that she can get in each of her pure strategies. An optimal strategy for the column player is to choose a strategy that minimizes the maximum payoff that the row player gets in each of her (column player's) pure strategies (this is equivalent to minimizing the maximum loss that the column player may suffer in each of her pure strategies). These optimal strategies are also called security strategies of the players.

- The maxmin value or lower value is denoted by $\underline{v}$ and the minmax value or upper value is denoted by $\overline{v}$. It turns out that $\underline{v} \leq \overline{v}$. If $\underline{v} = \overline{v} = v$, then v is called the value. A value may or may not exist if only pure strategies are allowed.

- A saddle point of a matrix A is any element a_{ij} such that it is a row minimum and a column maximum at the same time. Given a matrix A, a saddle point exists if and only if $\underline{v} = \overline{v}$. A matrix may have zero or more saddle points. Furthermore, saddle points, if they exist, are precisely the pure strategy Nash equilibria of the game.

- If multiple saddle points exist, they all correspond to the same value (which is the value of the game). Also, saddle point strategies are interchangeable; that is, given a matrix game A, if a_{ij} and a_{hk} are both saddle points, then a_{ik} and a_{hj} are also saddle points.

- The saddle point strategies (also called optimal strategies) in matrix games are such that a saddle point strategy of a player not only offers a best response against unilateral deviations in his strategy but also against unilateral deviations in the other player's strategy.

- In a matrix game, we have seen that pure strategy Nash equilibria (or equivalently saddle points) may or may not exist. However, mixed strategy Nash equilibria always exist and this is a consequence of the minimax theorem of von Neumann and Morgenstern.

- The minimax theorem can be proved using LP duality. An optimal strategy of the row player can be computed using a linear program and the dual of this LP gives an optimal strategy for the column player. Using the strong duality theorem, the minimax theorem can be established.

- Mixed strategy Nash equilibria of matrix games can be computed by solving a linear program and therefore the worst case computational complexity of this problem is polynomial time (which is a rarity in Nash equilibrium computation).

The classic book by von Neumann and Morgenstern [1] contains a detailed exposition of matrix games, including the LP duality based approach to the minimax theorem. Another excellent reference is the book by Luce and Raiffa [2].

The book by Myerson [3] and the book on linear programming by Chvatal [4] have inspired the exposition in this chapter. Other books which can be consulted are the ones by Maschler, Solan, and Zamir [5], Osborne [6], by Rapoport [7], and by Straffin [8].

References

[1]   John von Neumann and Oskar Morgenstern. *Theory of Games and Economic Behavior.* Princeton University Press, 1944.
[2]   R.D. Luce and H. Raiffa. *Games and Decisions.* Wiley, New York, 1957.
[3]   Roger B. Myerson. *Game Theory: Analysis of Conflict.* Harvard University Press, Cambridge, Massachusetts, USA, 1997.

[4]   Vasek Chvatal. *Linear Programming*. W.H. Freeman & Company, 1983.

[5]   Michael Maschler, Eilon Solan, and Shmuel Zamir. *Game Theory*. Cambridge University Press, 2013.

[6]   Martin J. Osborne. *An Introduction to Game Theory*. The MIT Press, 2003.

[7]   Anatol Rapoport. *Two Person Game Theory*. Dover Publications, Inc., New York, USA, 1966.

[8]   Philip D. Straffin Jr. *Game Theory and Strategy*. The Mathematical Association of America, 1993.

9.7   Exercises

(1) Given a matrix $A = [a_{ij}]$, recall the definitions:

$$\underline{v} = \max_i \, \min_j \, a_{ij}$$

$$\overline{v} = \min_j \, \max_i \, a_{ij}$$

(a) Show that $\underline{v} \leq \overline{v}$. (b) Show that A has a saddle point if and only if $\underline{v} = \overline{v}$.

(2) In a matrix $A = [a_{ij}]$, if two elements a_{ij} and a_{hk} are saddle points, then show that a_{ik} and a_{hj} are also saddle points. An equivalent way of stating this proposition would be: if (i, j) and (h, k) are pure strategy Nash equilibria, then (i, k) and (h, j) are also pure strategy Nash equilibria.

(3) An $m \times m$ matrix is called a latin square if each row and each column is a permutation of $(1, \dots, m)$. Compute pure strategy Nash equilibria, if they exist, of a matrix game for which a latin square is the payoff matrix.

(4) Consider a matrix game with $|S_1| = |S_2|$ such that the matrix A is antisymmetric. Show that the value in mixed strategies is equal to zero.

(5) Consider the following game.

$$A = \begin{bmatrix} a & b \\ c & d \end{bmatrix}$$

Derive the conditions on the values of a, b, c, d for which the game is guaranteed to have a saddle point. Also, compute all mixed strategy Nash equilibria for the game.

(6) Suppose you are given a matrix game with 3 pure strategies for each player. Which numbers among $\{0, 1, \dots, 9\}$ cannot be the total number of *pure* strategy Nash equilibria for the game? Justify your answer.

(7) Give an example of a matrix game for each of the following cases:

- There exist only pure strategy Nash equilibria
- There exists exactly one Nash equilibrium
- There exist exactly two Nash equilibria
- There exist infinite number of Nash equilibria
- There exists a strongly dominant strategy equilibrium

(8) For the following matrix game, write down the primal and dual LPs and compute all Nash equilibria.

$$A = \begin{bmatrix} 2 & 3 \\ 4 & 1 \end{bmatrix}$$

(9) For the following matrix game,

- Compute maxmin and minmax values over pure strategies
- Compute all pure strategy Nash equilibria
- Compute maxmin and minmax values over mixed strategies
- Compute all mixed strategy Nash equilibria

$$A = \begin{bmatrix} 2 & 3 & 1 \\ 4 & 1 & 2 \\ 4 & 1 & 3 \end{bmatrix}$$

(10) For the above game, write down the primal and dual LPs and compute all Nash equilibria.

(11) For the following matrix game, formulate an appropriate LP and compute all mixed strategy equilibria.

$$A = \begin{bmatrix} 0 & 1 \\ \frac{1}{2} & 0 \\ -\frac{1}{2} & 1 \\ 0 & 0 \end{bmatrix}$$

(12) Complete the proof of Theorem 9.3 that provides a necessary and sufficient condition for a mixed strategy profile (x^*, y^*) to be a Nash equilibrium in a matrix game.

(13) **Programming Assignment**. Given a matrix game, write a program to formulate a linear program to compute mixed strategy Nash equilibria. An LP solver could be used to determine the equilibria.

Chapter 10

Existence of Nash Equilibrium

Existence of Nash equilibrium is a key question investigated extensively in game theory. For two person zero-sum games with finite strategy sets, we have seen in the previous chapter, the *minimax theorem*, which establishes the existence of at least one mixed strategy equilibrium. John Nash, in his brilliant work [1, 2], generalized the notion of an equilibrium to games with three or more players and also established the existence of at least one mixed strategy Nash equilibrium for every finite strategic form game. Nash equilibria in games turn out to be fixed points of appropriately defined mappings. In fact, the existence of equilibria in games is closely coupled with fixed point theorems such as *Brouwer's fixed point theorem* [3] and *Kakutani's fixed point theorem* [4]. We study these important results in this chapter. We also present *Sperner's lemma*, a celebrated result in combinatorics, which can also be used to prove fixed point theorems and the Nash theorem. Mathematical preliminaries required for a clear understanding of this chapter are included in the mathematical appendix (Chapter 33).

This chapter is structured as follows. We start the chapter by defining correspondences and fixed points, and by stating two fixed point theorems, namely, Brouwer's theorem and Kakutani's theorem. Following this, we show that pure strategy Nash equilibria and mixed strategy Nash equilibria are fixed points of appropriately defined correspondences.

Next, we state and prove a theorem that provides sufficient conditions for the existence of a pure strategy Nash equilibrium in strategic form games. The proof of this theorem crucially uses Kakutani's fixed point theorem. Subsequently, we state and prove the Nash theorem which again uses Kakutani's theorem.

Following this, we provide an alternative way of proving the Nash theorem through Sperner's lemma. First we state and prove Sperner's lemma. Next we show how Brouwer's fixed point theorem can be proved using Sperner's lemma. Following this, we show how the Nash theorem can be proved using Brouwer's fixed point theorem.

Finally, we provide a brief overview of results on existence of Nash equilibrium in infinite games.

10.1   Correspondences and Fixed Point Theorems

Suppose n and k are positive integers. Given a set $X \subset \mathbb{R}^n$ and another set $Y \subset \mathbb{R}^k$, a correspondence or a set function f from X to Y assigns to each $x \in X$, a subset of Y (including Y), that is $f(x) \subseteq Y$ for each $x \in X$. We denote it as $f : X \rightrightarrows Y$. Such a function is also often called a set-valued function.

Note that when $f(x)$ contains exactly one element for each x, f simply becomes an ordinary function.

Graph of a Correspondence

Let $X \subset \mathbb{R}^n$ and let $Y \subset \mathbb{R}^k$ be a closed set. The graph of the correspondence $f : X \rightrightarrows Y$ is the set $\{(x, y) : x \in X, y \in f(x)\}$.

Closed Graph Correspondence

Given $X \subset \mathbb{R}^n$ and a closed set $Y \subset \mathbb{R}^k$, the correspondence $f : X \rightrightarrows Y$ is said to have a closed graph if for any two sequences $x^m \to x \in X$ and $y^m \to y \in Y$, with $x^m \in X$ and $y^m \in f(x^m)$ for every m, we have $y \in f(x)$.

Upper Hemicontinuity

Given $X \subset \mathbb{R}^n$ and a closed set $Y \subset \mathbb{R}^k$, the correspondence $f : X \rightrightarrows Y$ is said to be upper hemicontinuous (uhc) if it has a closed graph and the images of compact sets are bounded.

The above definition also implies that the images of compact sets are in fact compact. Upper hemicontinuity of correspondences is a natural generalization of the notion of continuity of functions.

Fixed Point Theorems

Fixed point theorems provide very useful results for establishing the existence of solutions of an equilibrium system of equations. The idea is to formulate the problem as the search for a fixed point of a suitably constructed function or correspondence.

Fixed Point of a Function

Let $X \subset \mathbb{R}^n$ and $f : X \to X$ be a mapping. A point $x \in X$ is called a *fixed point* of f if $f(x) = x$.

As an immediate example, suppose $X : [0, 1] \to [0, 1]$ and $f(x) = x^2$. f has two fixed points 0 and 1 since $f(0) = 0$ and $f(1) = 1$.

Brouwer's Fixed Point Theorem

This famous theorem which dates back to 1912 [3] can be used to show that every two player zero-sum game has at least one mixed strategy Nash equilibrium. The statement of the theorem is as follows.

Theorem 10.1 (Brouwer's Fixed Point Theorem). *Let $X \subset \mathbb{R}^n$ be non-empty, compact and convex. If $f : X \to X$ is continuous, then f has a fixed point.*

Fixed Point of a Correspondence

Let $X \subset \mathbb{R}^n$ and $f : X \rightrightarrows X$ be a correspondence. A point $x \in X$ is called a fixed point of f if $x \in f(x)$.

Kakutani's Fixed Point Theorem

This famous theorem due to Kakutani [4] is used extensively in game theory. In fact, John Nash used it in his doctoral work to prove the existence of a mixed Nash equilibrium in finite strategic form games. The theorem is also used in arriving at sufficient conditions for existence of a pure strategy Nash equilibrium in finite games.

Theorem 10.2 (Kakutani's Fixed Point Theorem). *Suppose that $X \subset \mathbb{R}^n$ is a non-empty, compact, and convex subset of $\mathbb{R}^n$. Let $f : X \rightrightarrows X$ be a correspondence such that*

(a) f is upper hemicontinuous
(b) $f(x) \subset X \ \forall x \in X$ is non-empty and convex.

Then f has a fixed point in X.

10.2 Nash Equilibrium as a Fixed Point

In this section, we show that pure strategy Nash equilibria and mixed strategy Nash equilibria of strategic form games are fixed points of appropriately defined correspondences.

Pure Strategy Nash Equilibrium as a Fixed Point

Consider a strategic form game $\Gamma = \langle N, (S_i), (u_i) \rangle$. We have seen that a strategy profile $(s_1^*, \dots, s_n^*)$ is a pure strategy Nash equilibrium iff

$$s_i^* \in b_i(s_{-i}^*) \quad \forall\, i \in N$$

where b_i is the best response correspondence (which, for each $s_{-i} \in S_{-i}$ gives the set of all best response strategies of player i against s_{-i}):

$$b_i(s_{-i}) = \{s_i \in S_i : u_i(s_i, s_{-i}) \geq u_i(s'_i, s_{-i}) \ \forall s'_i \in S_i\}.$$

Let us define the composite correspondence $b : S \rightrightarrows S$ as follows:

$$b(s_1, \ldots, s_n) = b_1(s_{-1}) \times \ldots \times b_n(s_{-n})$$

We know that $s^* = (s_1^*, \ldots, s_n^*)$ is a Nash equilibrium iff $s_i^* \in b_i(s_{-i}^*) \ \forall i \in N$. This is equivalent to:

$$(s_1^*, \ldots, s_n^*) \in b_1(s_{-1}^*) \times \cdots \times b_n(s_{-n}^*)$$

which in turn means

$$(s_1^*, \ldots, s_n^*) \in b(s_1^*, \ldots, s_n^*)$$

This is the same as saying that s^* is a fixed point of the correspondence $b(.)$.

Example 10.1. We provide below the payoff matrix of the prisoner's dilemma problem for ready reference.

1	2	
	NC	C
NC	$-2, -2$	$-10, -1$
C	$-1, -10$	$-5, -5$

Note that $S_1 = S_2 = \{C, NC\}$ and $b_1(C) = b_1(NC) = b_2(C) = b_2(NC) = \{C\}$. The best response correspondence for different profiles is given by

$$
\begin{aligned}
b(NC, NC) &= b_1(C) \times b_2(C) = \{(C, C)\} \\
b(NC, C) &= b_1(C) \times b_2(NC) = \{(C, C)\} \\
b(C, NC) &= b_1(NC) \times b_2(C) = \{(C, C)\} \\
b(C, C) &= b_1(NC) \times b_2(NC) = \{(C, C)\}.
\end{aligned}
$$

The last equality above clearly implies that (C, C) is a Nash equilibrium.   □

Mixed Strategy Nash Equilibrium as a Fixed Point

Now consider mixed strategies. Recall that a mixed strategy profile $(\sigma_1^*, \ldots, \sigma_n^*)$ is a Nash equilibrium iff

$$\sigma_i^* \in b_i(\sigma_{-i}^*) \ \forall \ i \in N$$

where b_i the best response correspondence defined by

$$b_i(\sigma_{-i}) = \{\sigma_i \in \Delta(S_i) : u_i(\sigma_i, \sigma_{-i}) \geq u_i(\sigma'_i, \sigma_{-i}) \ \forall \ \sigma'_i \in \Delta(S_i)\}.$$

Let us define the composite correspondence

$$b : \Delta(S_1) \times \ldots \times \Delta(S_n) \rightrightarrows \Delta(S_1) \times \ldots \times \Delta(S_n)$$

on the same lines as we defined earlier in the case of pure strategies:

$$b(\sigma_1, \ldots, \sigma_n) = b_1(\sigma_{-1}) \times \ldots \times b_n(\sigma_{-n})$$

Clearly, a mixed strategy profile $\sigma^* = (\sigma_1^*, \ldots, \sigma_n^*)$ is a Nash equilibrium iff $\sigma^* \in b(\sigma^*)$, that is, iff σ^* is a fixed point of the best response correspondence b.

10.3 Sufficient Conditions for Existence of Pure Strategy Nash Equilibria

In this section, we state and prove an important result due to Debreu (1952)[5]. This result provides sufficient conditions for existence of pure strategy Nash equilibria. We first state and prove an important lemma.

Lemma 10.1. *Suppose the sets $S_1, S_2, \ldots, S_n$ are non-empty, compact, and convex subsets of some Euclidean space. Further assume $u_i : S_1 \times \cdots \times S_n \to \mathbb{R}$ is continuous in $(s_1, \ldots, s_n)$, and $u_i(s_i, s_{-i})$ quasi-concave in s_i. Then the best response correspondence of player i defined by*

$$b_i(s_{-i}) = \{s_i \in S_i : u_i(s_i, s_{-i}) \geq u_i(s_i', s_{-i}) \, \forall s_i' \in S_i\}$$

is (a) non-empty for each $s_{-i} \in S_{-i}$, (b) convex valued for each $s_{-i} \in S_{-i}$, and (c) upper hemicontinuous.

Proof: First we show that $b_i(s_{-i})$ is non-empty. Note that $b_i(s_{-i})$ is the set of maximizers of a continuous function u_i over a compact set S (S is compact since $S_1, \ldots, S_n$ are compact). Therefore by Weierstrass's theorem, the function u_i attains a maximum and hence $b_i(s_{-i})$ is non-empty.

Next we show that $b_i(s_{-i})$ is convex-valued. It is given that u_i is quasi-concave in s_i. This means $u_i(\cdot, s_{-i})$ is quasi-concave on S_i. Fix s_{-i} and call $u_i(x, s_{-i}) = u_i(x)$. By definition of quasi-concavity, each of the sets $U_f(a) = \{x \in S_i : u_i(x) \geq a\}$ is convex $\forall a \in \mathbb{R}$. Let

$$a = \max_{x \in S_i} u_i(x)$$

This is guaranteed to exist, thanks to Weierstrass's theorem. Then the definition implies that the set of all maximizers of a quasi-concave function is a convex set. Therefore $b_i(s_{-i})$ is a convex set.

Now we prove that b_i is upper hemicontinuous. For this, we have to show:

(1) b_i has a closed graph. That is, for any sequence $(s_i^n, s_{-i}^n) \to (s_i, s_{-i})$ such that $s_i^n \in b_i(s_{-i}^n) \, \forall n$, we have that $s_i \in b_i(s_{-i})$.

(2) b_i maps compact sets into bounded sets. It is easy to see that the set $U_c = b_i(s_{-i})$ is bounded.

To show (1), we are given that $(s_i^n, s_{-i}^n) \to (s_i, s_{-i})$ with $s_i^n \in b_i(s_{-i}^n) \, \forall n$. This implies that $u_i(s_i^n, s_{-i}^n) \geq u_i(s_i', s_{-i}^n) \, \forall s_i' \in S_i \, \forall n$. Since u_i is continuous, we have

$$u_i(s_i^n, s_{-i}^n) \to u_i(s_i, s_{-i})$$
$$u_i(s_i', s_{-i}^n) \to u_i(s_i', s_{-i})$$

This implies that

$$u_i(s_i, s_{-i}) \geq u_i(s_i', s_{-i}) \, \forall s_i' \in S_i$$

which in turn implies that $s_i \in b_i(s_{-i})$. This shows that b_i has a closed graph. ∎

Theorem 10.3. *Given a strategic form game $\Gamma = \langle N, (S_i), (u_i) \rangle$, a pure strategy Nash equilibrium exists if $\forall i \in N$,*

(1) S_i *is a non-empty, convex, and compact subset (of some Euclidean space)*

(2) $u_i(s_1, \ldots, s_n)$ *is continuous in* $(s_1, \ldots, s_n)$

(3) $u_i(s_i, s_{-i})$ *is quasi-concave in* s_i.

Proof: Recall that a pure strategy Nash equilibrium is a fixed point of the best response correspondence $b : S \rightrightarrows S$:

$$b(s_1, \ldots, s_n) = b_1(s_{-1}) \times \cdots \times b_n(s_{-n})$$

Note that $S = S_1 \times \cdots S_n$ is non-empty, compact, and convex since each S_i is non-empty, compact, and convex. Also note by the Lemma 10.1 that $b(\cdot)$ is a non-empty, convex-valued, and upper hemicontinuous correspondence. The correspondence b satisfies all the conditions of Kakutani's fixed point theorem and therefore we can now apply the theorem to conclude that the correspondence b has a fixed point which is precisely a pure strategy Nash equilibrium. This proves the result. ∎

We now make the following observations.

- The above result does not apply to games which have finite strategy sets with two or more elements because such sets are not convex.
- The result provides only a sufficient condition. We have seen many finite games having pure strategy Nash equilibria. These examples show that the conditions are not necessary.
- The result does not say when a Nash equilibrium is unique.
- In the above theorem, quasi-concavity cannot be relaxed as shown by the example that follows.

Example 10.2. Consider the game with $N = \{1, 2\}$ where each player picks a point on the unit square simultaneously. The payoffs are defined as

$$u_1(s_1, s_2) = d(s_1, s_2) \quad \forall \, s_1, s_2 \in [1, 2] \times [1, 2]$$

$$u_2(s_1, s_2) = -d(s_1, s_2) \quad \forall \, s_1, s_2 \in [1, 2] \times [1, 2]$$

where $d(s_1, s_2)$ is the Euclidean distance between the points s_1 and s_2. In this game, if the two players pick the same location, there is an incentive for player 1 to deviate. On the other hand, if they pick different locations, there is an incentive for player 2 to deviate. Hence there does not exist any pure strategy Nash equilibrium for this game. □

10.4 The Nash Theorem

We are now finally ready to prove the Nash theorem.

Theorem 10.4. *Every finite strategic form game* $\Gamma = \langle N, (S_i), (u_i) \rangle$ *has at least one mixed strategy Nash equilibrium.*

Proof: To prove this result, we proceed as follows. Let $S_i = \{s_{i1}, \ldots, s_{im_i}\}$. Note that

$$\Delta(S_i) = \left\{ (x_1, \ldots, x_{m_i}) \in \mathbb{R}^{m_i} : 0 \leq x_j \leq 1 \; \forall j = 1, \ldots, m_i; \; \sum_{j=1}^{m_i} x_j = 1 \right\}$$

Thus $\Delta(S_i) \subset \mathbb{R}^{m_i}$. In fact $\Delta(S_i) \subset [0, 1]^{m_i}$, which means

$$\Delta(S_1) \times \ldots \times \Delta(S_n) \subset [0, 1]^{m_1} \times \ldots \times [0, 1]^{m_n}$$

(1) Clearly, $\Delta(S_i)$, which is the collection of all probability distributions over S_i, is non-empty $\forall i = 1, \ldots, n$.

(2) Now we show that $\Delta(S_i)$ is convex. Let $\lambda \in (0, 1)$ be any number. Consider any two elements of $\Delta(S_i)$, $x = (x_1, \ldots, x_{m_i})$ and $y = (y_1, \ldots, y_{m_i})$ and consider any convex combination:

$$\lambda x + (1 - \lambda)y = \lambda(x_1, \ldots, x_{m_i}) + (1 - \lambda)(y_1, \ldots, y_{m_i})$$
$$= (\lambda x_1 + (1 - \lambda)y_1, \ldots, \lambda x_{m_i} + (1 - \lambda)y_{m_i})$$

Clearly, $0 \leq \lambda x_j + (1 - \lambda)y_j \leq 1 \; \forall j = 1, \ldots, m_i; \; \forall \lambda \in (0, 1)$. Consider

$$\sum_{j=1}^{m_i} \lambda x_j + (1 - \lambda)y_j = \sum_{j=1}^{m_i} \lambda x_j + \sum_{j=1}^{m_i} (1 - \lambda)y_j$$
$$= \lambda + (1 - \lambda) = 1$$

Therefore, $\lambda x + (1 - \lambda)y \in \Delta(S_i)$ and hence $\Delta(S_i)$ is convex.

(3) Next we have to show that $\Delta(S_i)$ is compact for $i = 1, \ldots, n$. Since $\Delta(S_i) \subset \mathbb{R}^{m_i}$, compactness is equivalent to closedness and boundedness. Since $\Delta(S_i) \subset [0, 1]^{m_i}$, boundedness is immediate. The proof of closedness is left as an exercise.

(4) Next we show that $u_i(\sigma_1, \ldots, \sigma_n)$ is continuous in $(\sigma_1, \ldots, \sigma_n)$. Recall that

$$u_i(\sigma_1, \ldots, \sigma_n) = \sum_{(s_1, \ldots, s_n) \in S} \left(\prod_{j=1}^{n} \sigma_j(s_j) \right) u_i(s_1, \ldots, s_n)$$

Using the above expression, it can be shown that $u_i(\sigma_1, \ldots, \sigma_n)$ is continuous. This is left as an exercise.

(5) Finally we need to show that $u_i(\sigma_1, \ldots, \sigma_n)$ is quasi-concave in σ_i. This is left as an exercise.

(1), (2), (3), (4), and (5) will enable the conditions of Kakutani's fixed point theorem to be satisfied and as a consequence, the correspondence b has a fixed point, thus proving the Nash theorem. ∎

Needless to say, the above theorem only provides sufficient conditions for the existence of equilibria. The conditions are not necessary, which means that even if these conditions are not satisfied, Nash equilibria may still exist. As an immediate example, we have shown (in Chapter 5) the existence of Nash equilibrium (in fact, a weakly dominant strategy equilibrium) for the strategic form game underlying the Vickrey auction (this example has infinite strategy sets).

10.5 Sperner's Lemma

Sperner's Lemma is a fascinating result in combinatorics due to Emanuel Sperner, a celebrated 20th century mathematician from Germany. The lemma is immensely valuable in proving important theorems in fixed point theory and game theory. In particular, the lemma can be used to prove Brouwer's fixed point theorem, Kakutani's fixed point theorem, and the Nash theorem. To state Sperner's lemma, we need the following setup. The material in this section is based on the discussion in the book by Vohra [6].

Setup for Sperner's Lemma

Consider a triangle with vertices A, B, and C and triangulate it (that is, divide the triangle into smaller triangles) in the following way. Identify midpoints of AC, BC, and AB say X, Y, and Z, respectively and make a triangle out of X, Y, and Z. This results in four smaller triangles. If we repeat the procedure on each of these four triangles, we obtain 16 triangles, as depicted in Figure 10.1 (let us call all the smaller triangles baby triangles). The triangulation can be continued further to result in 64, 256, ..., baby triangles.

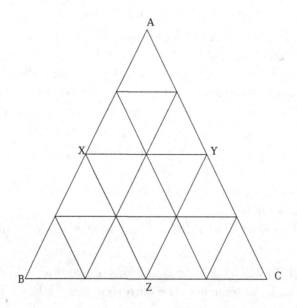

Fig. 10.1: Triangulation into 16 triangles

Suppose we follow the rules below for *labeling* or *coloring* the vertices of all the baby triangles.

(1) Vertices along the edge AB can only be labeled with A or B but not C.

(2) Vertices along the edge AC can only be labeled with A or C but not B.

(3) Vertices along the edge BC can only be labeled with B or C but not A.

(4) Vertices lying completely inside the original big triangle can be labeled with A or B or C.

Identify all the baby triangles such that the three vertices have three distinct colors A, B, C. Let us shade all such baby triangles. Among these shaded baby triangles, there will be two types: (a) those in which the vertices A, B, C appear in clockwise fashion (b) those in which the vertices A, B, C appear in counter-clockwise fashion. We will distinguish these two kinds of shaded baby triangles through different kinds of shades.

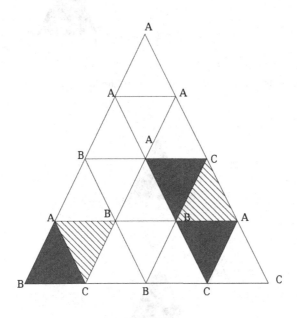

Fig. 10.2: Triangulation with $N_C = 2$; $N_{AC} = 3$

For example, Figure 10.2 shows a triangulation with 16 baby triangles where the vertices are labeled following the rules above. Baby triangles where vertices labeled A, B, C appear in clockwise fashion have one kind of shading while baby triangles where vertices labeled A, B, C appear in counter-clockwise fashion have a darker type of shading. Note that there are two shaded baby triangles of the clockwise type and three shaded triangles of the counter-clockwise type. Let N_C (N_{AC}) be the number of shaded triangles of clockwise (counter-clockwise) type.

Figures 10.3 and 10.4 show two other instances of triangulations with one shaded triangle and three shaded triangles respectively.

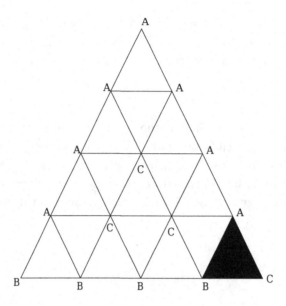

Fig. 10.3: A triangulation with 16 triangles and $N_C = 0$; $N_{AC} = 1$

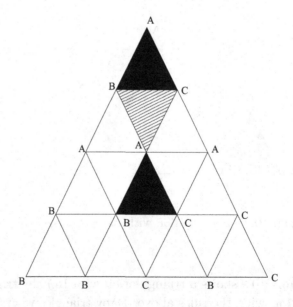

Fig. 10.4: A triangulation with 16 triangles, $N_C = 1$; $N_{AC} = 2$

Sperner's Lemma and Proof

Sperner's lemma states that the number of baby triangles ($N_C + N_{AC}$) having A, B, C as vertex labels following the above labeling rules is always odd. In fact, the lemma asserts that $N_{AC} = 1 + N_C$. This remarkable result can be proved as follows. The proof relies on labeling the edges and triangles in the following way.

- If the vertices of an edge have the same label, the edge is labeled with 0.
- If the vertices of an edge have different labels, and the labels appear in counter-clockwise sense (same sense as in the original big triangle), the edge is labeled with 1.
- If the vertices of an edge have different labels, and the labels appear in clockwise sense, the edge is labeled with -1.
- For each baby triangle, add the above numbers on the edges and write the sum in a little circle in the middle of the triangle. Call this sum as *Sperner number* of the baby triangle.

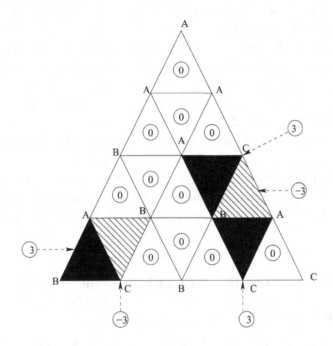

Fig. 10.5: Triangulation of Figure 10.2 with Sperner numbers included for each triangle

Figure 10.5 shows the triangulation of Figure 10.2 with the Sperner numbers included for each of the 16 baby triangles. In general, with the above numbering scheme, there exist four possibilities.

(1) The three vertices are different and are labeled counter-clockwise (Sperner number = 3).

(2) The three vertices are different and are labeled clockwise (Sperner number = -3).

(3) The three vertices have the same label (Sperner number = 0).

(4) Two vertices have the same label and the third vertex has a different label (Sperner number $= 0$).

Let us analyze a typical edge of the big triangle. Suppose we focus on edge AB. On this edge, there are smaller edges (belonging to the baby triangles). Note that

- number 1 on a small edge indicates a change from A to B.
- number -1 indicates a change from B to A.
- number 0 indicates no change.

The above cases are illustrated in Figure 10.5.

On the edge AB of the big triangle, the overall change is from A to B. Therefore the sum of the numbers on all small edges along AB must be equal to 1. Similarly, the sum of all numbers on all small edges along BC is 1 and this sum is again equal to 1 on AC. Thus the sum of all numbers on all small edges lying along the outer edges of the big triangle is equal to 3.

Now let us analyze the numbers along all small edges inside the big triangle. Each small edge inside is a part of two baby triangles and is labeled either 0 on both the triangles or 1 on one triangle and -1 on the other triangle. Thus the numbers on all small inside edges add up to zero. Thus the sum of all numbers on all edges of all baby triangles is equal to 3.

Notice that the sum of all Sperner numbers inside all baby triangles must be the same as the sum of all numbers on all the edges and hence is equal to 3. Clearly, the Sperner number of a shaded baby triangle is either 3 (for the counter-clockwise case) or -3 (for the clockwise case) and the Sperner number for each of the other baby triangles is 0. This means $N_{AC} = 1 + N_C$ and therefore $N_C + N_{AC}$ must be an odd number.

10.6   Sperner's Lemma to Brouwer's Fixed Point Theorem

Brouwer's Fixed Point Theorem

Let us recall Brouwer's fixed point theorem for ready reference [3]. The theorem states that if $X \subset \mathbb{R}^n$ is a compact and convex subset of $\mathbb{R}^n$ and $f : X \to X$ is a continuous function, then f has a fixed point, that is, there exists an $x \in X$ such that $f(x) = x$. To prove the Brouwer's theorem, we first state and prove a supporting lemma. We prove this supporting lemma using Sperner's lemma. The proof given here closely follows the one that appears in [6]. First we define the n-simplex.

Definition 10.1 (n-Simplex). *The n-simplex is defined as the set*

$$\Delta^n = \{x \in \mathbb{R}^n : x_i \geq 0 \text{ for } i = 1, 2, \ldots, n; \sum_{i=1}^{n} x_i = 1\}$$

Note immediately that Δ^n is simply the collection of all probability distributions $(x_1, x_2, \ldots, x_n)$. This set can be shown to be convex and compact (left as an exercise).

Lemma 10.2. *If $f : \Delta^n \to \Delta^n$ is a continuous function, then f has a fixed point. That is, there exists an $x \in \Delta^n$ such that $f(x) = x$.*

Proof: This lemma can be proved easily for $n = 1$ and $n = 2$. For a proof for $n = 2$, see [6]. We present the proof for $n = 3$ using Sperner's lemma. The proof can be generalized in a natural way for $n > 3$. So let us show that if a function $f : \Delta^3 \to \Delta^3$ is continuous, then it has a fixed point. Suppose that f does not have a fixed point. Let $f(x) = (f_1(x), f_2(x), f_3(x))$. The set Δ^3 is a two dimensional triangle which can be triangulated in the standard way yielding smaller baby triangles. The first subdivision leads to 4 triangles, the second subdivision leads to 16 triangles, and so on. Let us focus on the mth subdivision. Suppose we color the vertices (1,2, or 3) following the rule below:

$$c(x) = \min\{i : f_i(x) < x_i\}$$

This is a well defined rule if f does not have a fixed point. To show this, suppose it is not a well defined rule. That would mean

$$f_i(x) \geq x_i \text{ for } i = 1, 2, 3, \text{ for some } (x_1, x_2, x_3) \in \Delta^3$$

Since $x, f(x) \in \Delta^3$, we have $x_1 + x_2 + x_3 = 1$ and $f_1(x) + f_2(x) + f_3(x) = 1$ which implies that

$$f_i(x) = x_i \text{ for } i = 1, 2, 3$$

This contradicts our assumption that f has no fixed point.

The above coloring scheme satisfies the setup for the Sperner's lemma. This is seen as follows.

- Note that $c(1, 0, 0) = 1; c(0, 1, 0) = 2; c(0, 0, 1) = 3$. That is, the three corners of the big triangle have three different colors.
- Suppose x is a point on an edge of the triangle Δ^3. For example, suppose x is a point on the edge between (1,0,0) and (0,1,0). Note that

$$x = \lambda(1, 0, 0) + (1 - \lambda)(0, 1, 0) = (\lambda, (1 - \lambda), 0)$$

  for a suitable value of λ, $0 \leq \lambda \leq 1$. Our coloring rule can be applied to show that

$$c\,(\lambda,\ 1 - \lambda,\ 0) = 1 \text{ or } 2$$

This means that points on the boundaries of Δ^3 have colors in accordance with the requirements of Sperner's lemma.

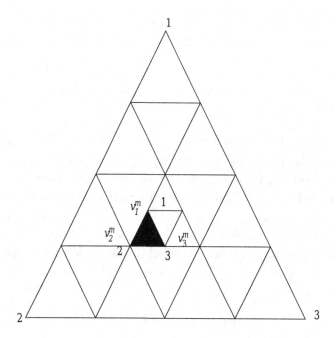

Fig. 10.6: A triangulation showing a baby triangle with three distinct colors on the mth subdivision

Applying Sperner's Lemma to the current situation, we conclude that in the mth subdivision of Δ^3, there must exist a baby triangle with corners (v_1^m, v_2^m, v_3^m) that are differently colored. See Figure 10.6. Without loss of generality, we have

$$c\left(v_1^m\right) = 1; \; c\left(v_2^m\right) = 2; \; c\left(v_3^m\right) = 3$$

Let $m \to \infty$ and consider the infinite sequence

$$\{v_1^m\}_{m \geq 1}$$

This sequence may itself not have a limit but since Δ^3 is a compact set, the above sequence has a convergent subsequence. For an appropriate subsequence $\{v_1^l\}_{l \geq 1}$, we therefore get that

$$v_1^l \to x \in \Delta^3 \text{ for some } x$$

Similarly, we can show that $v_2^l \to x$ and $v_3^l \to x$. Since the function $f : \Delta^3 \to \Delta^3$ is continuous, we have

$$f(v_1^l) \to f(x)$$
$$f(v_2^l) \to f(x)$$
$$f(v_3^l) \to f(x)$$

Since $c(v_1^l) = 1$, $f_1(v_1^l)$ is strictly less than the first component of v_1^l. Since $c(v_2^l) = 2$, $f_2(v_2^l)$ is strictly less than the second component of v_2^l. Since $c(v_3^l) = 3$, $f_3(v_3^l)$ is strictly less than the third component of v_3^l. This would imply that

$$f_1(x) \leq x_1; \; f_2(x) \leq x_2; \; f_3(x) \leq x_3$$

The above implies that

$$\sum_{i=1}^{3} f_i(x) \leq \sum_{i=1}^{3} x_i$$

However, since $f : \Delta^3 \to \Delta^3$, we have

$$\sum_{i=1}^{3} f_i(x) = \sum_{i=1}^{3} x_i = 1$$

The above is possible if and only if

$$f_i(x) = x_i \text{ for } i = 1, 2, 3$$

which contradicts our original assumption that f does not have a fixed point. This then proves the lemma. ∎

Based on this lemma, we now prove Brouwer's fixed point theorem.

Proof of Brouwer's Fixed Point Theorem

The proof crucially uses a result on the topological equivalence of compact and convex sets. The result says that if X is compact and convex, with a dimension of $(n-1)$, then X and Δ^n are topologically equivalent in the following sense: there exist mappings $g : X \to \Delta^n$ and $g^{-1} : \Delta^n \to X$ such that both g and g^{-1} are continuous. Now define $h : \Delta^n \to \Delta^n$ as follows.

$$h(x) = g(f(g^{-1}(x)))$$

Since f and g are continuous, so is h and by invoking Lemma 10.2, h will have a fixed point, say x^*. That is

$$h(x^*) = g(f(g^{-1}(x^*))) = x^*$$

This immediately implies that

$$f(g^{-1}(x^*)) = g^{-1}(x^*)$$

which implies that $g^{-1}(x^*)$ is a fixed point of $f : X \to X$. This proves Brouwer's fixed point theorem. ∎

10.7 Proving Nash Theorem using Brouwer's Theorem

Consider a finite strategic form game $\Gamma = \langle N, (S_i), (u_i) \rangle$ with $N = \{1, 2, \ldots, n\}$. Let us use the notation:

$$S_i = \{s_{ij} : j = 1, 2, \ldots, m_i\} \text{ where } m_i = |S_i|; \ i = 1, \ldots, n$$

We now prove, using Brouwer's fixed point theorem, that a finite strategic form game such as above will always have at least one mixed strategic equilibrium (which is the

Nash Theorem). As usual, let $\Delta(S_i)$ denote the set of all probability distributions on S_i and define

$$M = \Delta(S_1) \times \ldots \times \Delta(S_n)$$

Each $\sigma \in M$ is a vector with $\sum_{i \in N} |S_i|$ components. Suppose s_{ik} is a particular pure strategy of player i and let σ_{ik} be the component in σ corresponding to s_{ik}. Define a mapping $f : M \to M$ that maps vectors from M into itself. Given $\sigma \in M, f(\sigma)$ has as many components as σ and let $f_{ik}(\sigma)$ be the component in $f(\sigma)$ corresponding to pure strategy s_{ik}. Recall that we can represent $\sigma = (\sigma_i, \sigma_{-i})$. Consider

$$f_{ik}(\sigma) = \frac{\sigma_{ik} + \max(0, u_i(s_{ik}, \sigma_{-i}) - u_i(\sigma_i, \sigma_{-i}))}{\sum_{s_{ij} \in S_i} [\sigma_{ij} + \max(0, u_i(s_{ij}, \sigma_{-i}) - u_i(\sigma_i, \sigma_{-i}))]}$$

Note that the denominator above is certainly greater than or equal to 1 since

$$\sum_{s_{ij} \in S_i} \sigma_{ij} = 1$$

Also, we have

$$\sum_{j=1}^{|S_i|} f_{ij}(\sigma) = 1 \quad \text{for } i = 1, 2, \ldots, n$$

Clearly, $f : M \to M$ is a well defined mapping. It can be verified that f is continuous and therefore by Brouwer's theorem, f has a fixed point. That is, there exists a $\sigma^* \in M$ such that $f(\sigma^*) = \sigma^*$. This means that $\forall i \in N$, $\forall s_{ik} \in S_i$, we have

$$\sigma_{ik}^* = f(\sigma_{ik}^*) = \frac{\sigma_{ik}^* + \max(0, u_i(s_{ik}, \sigma_{-i}^*) - u_i(\sigma_i^*, \sigma_{-i}^*))}{\sum_{s_{ij} \in S_i} [\sigma_{ij}^* + \max(0, u_i(s_{ij}, \sigma_{-i}^*) - u_i(\sigma_i^*, \sigma_{-i}^*))]}$$

We now consider two cases. In case 1,

$$\sum_{s_{ij} \in S_i} [\max(0, u_i(s_{ik}, \sigma_{-i}^*) - u_i(\sigma_i^*, \sigma_{-i}^*))] = 0 \; \forall \, i \in N$$

and in case 2, the above sum is > 0 for at least some $i \in N$. In case 1, we will get

$$u_i(s_{ij}, \sigma_{-i}^*) - u_i(\sigma_i^*, \sigma_{-i}^*) \leq 0 \; \forall \; s_{ij} \in S_i \; \forall \, i \in N$$

which immediately implies that $(\sigma_i^*, \sigma_{-i}^*)$ is a Nash equilibrium.

In case 2, there will exist at least one agent i and strategy $s_{ik} \in S_i$ such that

$$\max(0, u_i(s_{ik}, \sigma_{-i}^*) - u_i(\sigma_i^*, \sigma_{-i}^*)) > 0$$

This implies that

$$\sigma_{ik}^* = \frac{\max(0, u_i(s_{ik}, \sigma_{-i}^*) - u_i(\sigma_i^*, \sigma_{-i}^*))}{\sum_{s_{ij} \in S_i} [\max(0, u_i(s_{ij}, \sigma_{-i}^*) - u_i(\sigma_i^*, \sigma_{-i}^*))]}$$

This in turn implies $\sigma_{ik}^* \neq 0$ which implies $\sigma_{ik}^* > 0$. Based on the above, we can show that

$$u_i(s_{ik}, \sigma_{-i}^*) > u_i(\sigma_i^*, \sigma_{-i}^*) \text{ iff } \sigma_{ik}^* > 0 \; \forall s_{ik} \in S_i.$$

This leads to a contradiction since $u_i(\sigma_i^*, \sigma_{-i}^*)$ is a convex combination of $u_i(s_{ik}, \sigma_{-i}^*)$ such that $s_{ik} \in S_i$ and $\sigma_{ik}^* > 0$. Notice that:

$$u_i(\sigma_i^*, \sigma_{-i}^*) = \sum_{s_{ik} \in \delta(\sigma_i^*)} u_i(s_{ik}, \sigma_{-i}^*) > \sum_{s_{ik} \in \delta(\sigma_i^*)} u_i(\sigma_i^*, \sigma_{-i}^*) = u_i(\sigma_i^*, \sigma_{-i}^*)$$

Hence only case 1 can happen and thus $(\sigma_i^*, \sigma_{-i}^*)$ is a Nash equilibrium. ∎

10.8   Existence of Nash Equilibrium in Infinite Games

Consider a strategic form game but with infinite strategy sets. Now the definition of mixed strategies and equilibrium analysis requires a more technical treatment. In particular the strategy sets are required to be compact metric spaces to make the games amenable for mathematical analysis. Myerson [7] provides an excellent description of the technical issues involved here. A prominent result on existence of mixed strategy Nash equilibrium in this setting is due to Glicksberg [8]. Before stating this result, we define a few relevant notions.

Continuous Games

A strategic form game with finite number of players, $\langle N, (S_i), (u_i) \rangle$ is called a continuous game if $\forall \, i \in N$, the strategy set S_i is a non-empty, compact metric space and u_i is a continuous function.

ε-Nash Equilibrium

Given a real number $\varepsilon > 0$, a strategy profile $(\sigma_1^*, \dots, \sigma_n^*)$ of a strategic form game $\langle N, (S_i), (u_i) \rangle$ is said to be an ε-Nash equilibrium if $\forall \, i \in N$,

$$u_i(\sigma_i^*, \sigma_{-i}^*) \geq u_i(\sigma_i, \sigma_{-i}^*) - \varepsilon \;\; \forall \sigma_i \in \Delta(S_i)$$

Note immediately that an ε-Nash equilibrium becomes a Nash equilibrium when $\varepsilon = 0$.

Glicksberg's Results

We now state two results, due to Glicksberg [8].

(1) Every continuous game has a Nash equilibrium.
(2) Every continuous game has an ε-Nash equilibrium for all $\varepsilon > 0$. This is a consequence of the above.

We now provide two examples to show that continuity and compactness are necessary for the above result.

Example 10.3 (Necessity of Continuity). Consider a game with $N = \{1\}$ and $S_1 = [0, 1]$ (compact). Define the utility function as a discontinuous map:

$$\begin{aligned} u_1(s_1) &= s_1 \quad \text{if } 0 \leq s_1 < 1 \\ &= 0 \quad \text{if } s_1 = 1 \end{aligned}$$

It can be shown that the above game does not have a mixed strategy equilibrium.   □

Example 10.4 (Necessity of Compactness). Consider again a game with $N = \{1\}$ but with $S_1 = [0, 1)$ (not compact). Define the utility function as a continuous map:

$$u_1(s_1) = s_1 \;\; \forall s_1 \in [0, 1)$$

It can be shown that this game also does not have a mixed strategy equilibrium. ☐

Some Key Results

Dasgupta and Maskin [9, 10] have come up with sufficient conditions for existence of Nash equilibrium in discontinuous games. Simon [11], Renny [12], and Carmona [13] provide updates on existence results in discontinuous games. Myerson [7] brings out the technical issues involved in a detailed way. Moon [14] provides an up-to-date survey.

10.9 Summary and References

In this chapter, we have addressed the crucial issue of existence of PSNE and MSNE. The following is the sequence of results presented.

- PSNE and MSNE of strategic form games are fixed points of appropriately defined best response correspondences.
- A finite strategic form game need not have a pure strategy Nash equilibrium. We have shown certain sufficient conditions under which a PSNE is guaranteed to exist.
- *Nash Existence Theorem*: Every finite strategic form game has at least one mixed strategy Nash equilibrium. The proof crucially uses the Kakutani fixed point theorem.
- We have stated and proved Sperner's lemma, a well known result in combinatorics. We have shown how this lemma can be used to prove the Brouwer's fixed point theorem and the Nash existence theorem.
- We have discussed certain results on the existence of Nash equilibrium in games with a finite number of players but with infinite strategy sets.

The existence of Nash equilibrium is the classic result that was first published in [1, 2]. The presentation in this chapter is based on the books by Myerson [7], Mas-Colell, Whinston, and Green [15], and Vohra [6]. The books by Shoham and Leyton-Brown [16] and by Maschler, Solan, and Zamir [17] also contain elegant proofs for the Nash theorem.

References

[1]   John F. Nash Jr. "Equilibrium points in *n*-person games". In: *Proceedings of the National Academy of Sciences* **36** (1950), pp. 48–49.

[2]   John F. Nash Jr. "Non-cooperative games". In: *Annals of Mathematics* **54** (1951), pp. 286–295.

[3]   L. E. J. Brouwer. "Uber abbildung von mannig-faltigkeiten". In: *Mathematishche Annalen* **71** (1912), pp. 97–115.

[4]   Shizuo Kakutani. "A generalization of Brouwers fixed point theorem". In: *Duke Mathematical Journal* **8**(3) (1941), pp. 457–459.

[5] Gerard Debreu. "A social equilibrium existence theorem". In: *Proceedings of the National Academy of Sciences* **38**(10) (1952), pp. 886–893.

[6] Rakesh Vohra. *Advanced Mathematical Economics*. Cambridge University Press, 2009.

[7] Roger B. Myerson. *Game Theory: Analysis of Conflict*. Harvard University Press, Cambridge, Massachusetts, USA, 1997.

[8] I. Glicksberg. "A further generalization of the Kakutani fixed point theorem with applications to Nash equilibrium points". In: *Proceedings of the National Academy of Sciences* **3** (1952), pp. 170–174.

[9] P. Dasgupta and E. Maskin. "The existence of equilibrium in discontinuous economic games, I: Theory". In: *The Review of Economic Studies* **53**(1) (1986), pp. 1–26.

[10] P. Dasgupta and E. Maskin. "The existence of equilibrium in discontinuous economic games, II: Applications". In: *The Review of Economic Studies* **53**(1) (1986), pp. 27–42.

[11] L. K. Simon. "Games with discontinuous payoffs". In: *The Review of Economic Studies* **54**(4) (1987), pp. 569–597.

[12] P. J. Reny. "On the existence of pure and mixed strategy Nash equilibria in discontinuous games". In: *Econometrica* **67**(5) (1999), pp. 1029–1056.

[13] Guilherme Carmona. "An existence result for discontinuous games". In: *Journal of Economic Theory* **144**(3) (2009), pp. 1333–1340.

[14] Moon Chetry. *A survey on computational methods for Nash equilibrium*. Tech. rep. 2010.

[15] Andreu Mas-Colell, Michael D. Whinston, and Jerry R. Green. *Microeconomic Theory*. Oxford University Press, 1995.

[16] Yoam Shoham and Kevin Leyton-Brown. *Multiagent Systems: Algorithmic, Game-Theoretic, and Logical Foundations*. Cambridge University Press, New York, USA, 2009, 2009.

[17] Michael Maschler, Eilon Solan, and Shmuel Zamir. *Game Theory*. Cambridge University Press, 2013.

10.10 Exercises

(1) Recall the definition of n-simplex:

$$\Delta^n = \{x \in \mathbb{R}^n : x_i \geq 0 \text{ for } i = 1, 2, \ldots, n; \sum_{i=1}^{n} x_i = 1\}$$

Note that Δ^n is the collection of all probability distributions $(x_1, x_2, \ldots, x_n)$. Show that this set is convex and compact.

(2) Complete the proof of the following sub-result in Section 10.5 on Nash theorem: $\Delta(S_i)$ is closed for each $i \in N$.

(3) Following the definition of Δ^n above, if $f : \Delta \rightarrow \Delta$ is a continuous function, then show that f has a fixed point. Similarly, if $f : \Delta^2 \rightarrow \Delta^2$ is a continuous function, then show that f has a fixed point.

(4) Consider a strategic form game with $N = \{1, 2\}$:

$$u_1(s_1, s_2) = d(s_1, s_2) \quad \forall \, s_1, s_2 \in [1, 2] \times [1, 2]$$

$$u_2(s_1, s_2) = -d(s_1, s_2) \quad \forall \, s_1, s_2 \in [1, 2] \times [1, 2]$$

where $d(s_1, s_2)$ is the Euclidean distance between the points s_1 and s_2. We have shown that this game does not have pure strategy Nash equilibria. Does this game have mixed strategy Nash equilibria?

(5) Consider a game with $N = \{1\}$ and $S_1 = [0, 1]$. Define the utility function as a discontinuous map:

$$u_1(s_1) = s_1 \quad \text{if } 0 \le s_1 < 1$$
$$= 0 \quad \text{if } s_1 = 1$$

Show that the above game does not have a mixed strategy equilibrium.

(6) Consider again a game with $N = \{1\}$ but with $S_1 = [0, 1]$. Define the utility function as a continuous map:

$$u_1(s_1) = s_1 \ \forall s_1 \in [0, 1]$$

Show that the above game does not have a mixed strategy equilibrium.

Chapter 11

Computation of Nash Equilibria

Computing Nash equilibria is one of the fundamental computational problems in game theory. In fact, this is one of the actively investigated problems in theoretical computer science in recent times. In this chapter, we provide some insights into this problem using illustrative examples. In particular, we show how the necessary and sufficient conditions for a profile to be a mixed strategy equilibrium (presented in Chapter 7) can be used to set up an algorithmic procedure to compute mixed strategy Nash equilibria. In the next chapter, we look into the computational complexity of this problem.

11.1 Supports and Nash Equilibria

Support of a Mixed Strategy Profile

Consider the strategic form game $\Gamma = \langle N, (S_i), (u_i) \rangle$. Given a mixed strategy σ_i of player i, recall that the support of σ_i, denoted by $\delta(\sigma_i)$ is defined as the set of all pure strategies of player i which have a non-zero probability in σ_i:

$$\delta(\sigma_i) = \{ s_i \in S_i \ : \ \sigma_i(s_i) > 0 \}$$

Given a mixed strategy profile $\sigma = (\sigma_1, \ldots, \sigma_n)$, the support of σ is defined in a natural way as the Cartesian product of all the individual supports:

$$\delta(\sigma_1, \ldots, \sigma_n) = \delta(\sigma_1) \times \ldots \times \delta(\sigma_n)$$

This is the set of all pure strategy profiles that would have positive probability if the players chose their strategies according to σ. We make the immediate observation that every mixed strategy Nash equilibrium has to be associated with a support. For a finite game, we have a finite number of supports and each support can be investigated for giving rise to Nash equilibria.

Before proceeding further, we recall the necessary and sufficient condition that we presented in Chapter 7: Given a strategic form game $\langle N, (S_i), (u_i) \rangle$, the mixed strategy profile $(\sigma_1, \ldots, \sigma_n)$ is a Nash equilibrium iff $\forall i \in N$,

(1) $u_i(s_i, \sigma_{-i})$ is the same for all $s_i \in \delta(\sigma_i)$

(2) $u_i(s_i, \sigma_{-i}) \geq u_i(s_i', \sigma_{-i}) \ \forall s_i \in \delta(\sigma_i), \ \forall s_i' \in S_i \setminus \delta(\sigma_i)$.

We will refer to the above two conditions as condition (1) and condition (2) respectively in the rest of this chapter.

Example 11.1. Consider the following version of the BOS game:

1	2 A	B
A	3, 1	0, 0
B	0, 0	1, 3

For the above game, the set of all possible supports is given by: $\{A\} \times \{A\}$, $\{A\} \times \{B\}$, $\{B\} \times \{A\}$, $\{B\} \times \{B\}$, $\{A\} \times \{A, B\}$, $\{B\} \times \{A, B\}$, $\{A, B\} \times \{A\}$, $\{A, B\} \times \{B\}$, $\{A, B\} \times \{A, B\}$. For this game, we have already seen that (A, A) and (B, B) are pure strategy Nash equilibria. These correspond to the supports $\{A\} \times \{A\}$ and $\{B\} \times \{B\}$, respectively. We now compute a third equilibrium which in this case has the support $\{A, B\} \times \{A, B\}$. To do this, we use conditions (1) and (2) above. If (σ_1^*, σ_2^*) is a Nash equilibrium with support $\{A, B\} \times \{A, B\}$, then condition (1) would mean that

$$u_1(A, \sigma_2^*) = u_1(B, \sigma_2^*)$$
$$u_2(\sigma_1^*, A) = u_2(\sigma_1^*, B)$$

Note that

$$u_1(A, \sigma_2^*) = 3\sigma_2^*(A)$$
$$u_1(B, \sigma_2^*) = \sigma_2^*(B)$$
$$u_2(\sigma_1^*, A) = \sigma_1^*(A)$$
$$u_2(\sigma_1^*, B) = 3\sigma_1^*(B)$$

We therefore have

$$3\sigma_2^*(A) = \sigma_2^*(B)$$
$$\sigma_1^*(A) = 3\sigma_1^*(B)$$

Since $\sigma_1^*(A) + \sigma_1^*(B) = \sigma_2^*(A) + \sigma_2^*(B) = 1$, we get

$$\sigma_1^* = \left(\frac{3}{4}, \frac{1}{4}\right) \quad \text{and} \quad \sigma_2^* = \left(\frac{1}{4}, \frac{3}{4}\right)$$

Note that the above strategy profile trivially satisfies condition (2) above and therefore the profile is a Nash equilibrium. We now generalize the above process of finding a Nash equilibrium. □

11.2   A General Algorithm for Finding Nash Equilibria of Finite Strategic Form Games

The first observation we make is that although there are infinitely many (in fact uncountably so) mixed strategy profiles, there are only finitely many subsets of $S_1 \times S_2 \times \ldots \times S_n$ that can be supports of Nash equilibria. Note that the number of supports of a mixed strategy of a player i is precisely the number of non-empty subsets of S_i, which is equal to $2^{|S_i|} - 1$. Therefore the total number of supports of mixed strategy profiles would be

$$(2^{|S_1|} - 1) \times (2^{|S_2|} - 1) \times \ldots \times (2^{|S_n|} - 1).$$

One can sequentially consider one support at a time and search for Nash equilibria with that support. In doing this, the conditions (1) and (2) would be extremely useful.

Equations to be Solved

Let $X_i \subseteq S_i$ be a non-empty subset of S_i which will represent our current guess as to which strategies of player i have positive probability in a Nash equilibrium. That is, our current guess of a support for Nash equilibrium is $X_1 \times X_2 \times \ldots \times X_n$. If there exists a Nash equilibrium with this support, then, by the above result, there must exist numbers $w_1, \ldots, w_n$ and mixed strategies $\sigma_1, \ldots, \sigma_n$ such that

$$w_i = u_i(s_i, \sigma_{-i}) \ \forall s_i \in X_i \ \forall i \in N$$

This expands to:

$$w_i = \sum_{s_{-i} \in S_{-i}} \left(\prod_{j \neq i} \sigma_j(s_j) \right) u_i(s_i, s_{-i}) \tag{11.1}$$

The above condition asserts that each player i must get the same payoff, denoted by w_i, by playing any of the pure strategies having positive probability in the mixed strategy σ_i. Next we need to satisfy

$$w_i \geq u_i(s_i, \sigma_{-i}) \ \forall s_i \in S_i \setminus X_i \ \forall i \in N$$

The above expands to:

$$w_i \geq \sum_{s_{-i} \in S_{-i}} \left(\prod_{j \neq i} \sigma_j(s_j) \right) u_i(s_i, s_{-i}) \quad \forall s_i \in S_i \setminus X_i \ \forall i \in N \tag{11.2}$$

The above condition ensures that the pure strategies in X_i produce payoffs that are no worse than the payoffs produced by pure strategies in $S_i \setminus X_i$. Next, we have

$$\sigma_i(x_i) > 0 \quad \forall x_i \in X_i \ \forall i \in N \tag{11.3}$$

The condition above states that the probability of each pure strategy of a player in the support of the mixed strategy must be greater than zero. The next set of constraints is:

$$\sigma_i(s_i) = 0 \quad \forall s_i \in S_i \setminus X_i \ \forall i \in N \tag{11.4}$$

The above condition asserts that the probability of each pure strategy of a player not in the support of the mixed strategy must be zero. Finally, we need

$$\sum_{x_i \in S_i} \sigma_i(x_i) = 1 \quad \forall i \in N \tag{11.5}$$

The above ensures that each σ_i is a probability distribution over S_i.

We need to find $w_1, w_2, \ldots, w_n$ and $\sigma_1(s_1)$ $\forall s_1 \in S_1$, $\sigma_2(s_2)$ $\forall s_2 \in S_2$, $\ldots$, and $\sigma_n(s_n)$ $\forall s_n \in S_n$, such that the above equations (11.1) – (11.5) are satisfied. Then $(\sigma_1, \ldots, \sigma_n)$ is a Nash equilibrium and w_i is the expected payoff to player i in that Nash equilibrium. On the other hand, if there is no solution that satisfies (11.1)–(11.5), then there is no Nash equilibrium having support $X_1 \times \ldots \times X_n$. The number of unknowns in the above is $n + |S_1| + \cdots + |S_n|$, where the first term n corresponds to the variables $w_1, w_2, \ldots, w_n$ while $|S_i|$ corresponds to the variables $\sigma_i(s_i)$, $s_i \in S_i$.

- Eq. (11.1) leads to $|X_1| + |X_2| + \cdots + |X_n|$ equations.
- Eq. (11.2) leads to $|S_1 \setminus X_1| + \cdots + |S_n \setminus X_n|$ equations.
- Eq. (11.3) leads to $|X_1| + \cdots + |X_n|$ equations
- Eq. (11.4) leads to $|S_1 \setminus X_1| + \cdots + |S_n \setminus X_n|$ equations.
- Eq. (11.5) leads to n equations.

Thus we have a total of $n + \sum_{i \in N} |S_i|$ variables and $n + 2 \sum_{i \in N} |S_i|$ equations. For example, if we have 2 players with 3 strategies each, we will have 8 variables and 14 equations. We make the following observations.

Note. From (11.1) and (11.2), we see that the resulting equations are in general non-linear because of the term

$$\prod_{j \neq i} \sigma_j(s_j).$$

Note. If there are only two players, then we will have only linear equations. The number of these equations will be $2 + 2|S_1| + 2|S_2|$ while the number of variables will be $2 + |S_1| + |S_2|$. These numbers correspond to each individual support. The maximum number of supports to be examined is:

$$\prod_{i \in N} \left(2^{|S_i|} - 1 \right)$$

So even for a two player game, the number of equations to be solved can become unmanageable.

Note. If the number of players exceeds 2, then not only do we have a huge number of equations, we also have to deal with non-linearity. For two player games, the resulting equations constitute a problem which is known as the *linear complementarity problem* (LCP). With three or more players, the equations constitute the so called *nonlinear complementarity problem* (NLCP). We do not provide any more details about LCPs and NLCPs here; the interested reader is referred to the comprehensive book by Murty [1].

11.3 An Example for Computing Nash Equilibrium

This illustrative example is taken from Myerson's book [2]. This is a two player game with payoff matrix as shown.

	2		
1	L	M	R
T	7, 2	2, 7	3, 6
B	2, 7	7, 2	4, 5

Clearly, $S_1 = \{T, B\}$; $S_2 = \{L, M, R\}$. A support for this game is of the form $X_1 \times X_2$ where $X_1 \subseteq S_1$, $X_2 \subseteq S_2$, $X_1 \neq \emptyset$, $X_2 \neq \emptyset$. The number of such supports is equal to $(2^2 - 1)(2^3 - 1)$, which is 21. These supports are: $\{T\} \times \{L\}$, $\{T\} \times \{M\}$, $\{T\} \times \{R\}$, $\{T\} \times \{L, M\}$, $\{T\} \times \{L, R\}$, $\{T\} \times \{M, R\}$, $\{T\} \times \{L, M, R\}$; $\{B\} \times \{L\}$, $\{B\} \times \{M\}$, $\{B\} \times \{R\}$, $\{B\} \times \{L, M\}$, $\{B\} \times \{L, R\}$, $\{B\} \times \{M, R\}$, $\{B\} \times \{L, M, R\}$; $\{T, B\} \times \{L\}$, $\{T, B\} \times \{M\}$, $\{T, B\} \times \{R\}$, $\{T, B\} \times \{L, M\}$, $\{T, B\} \times \{L, R\}$, $\{T, B\} \times \{M, R\}$, $\{T, B\} \times \{L, M, R\}$. Our analysis proceeds as follows.

- Let us look for a Nash equilibrium in which player 1 plays pure strategy T. Player 2's best response for this is the pure strategy M. If player 2 plays M, player 1's best response is B. Thus there is no Nash equilibrium in which player 1 plays pure strategy T and this rules out the first 7 supports.
- Now let us look for a Nash equilibrium in which player 1 plays pure strategy B. If player 1 chooses B, player 2 would choose L. Player 1's best response to L is T. This immediately implies that there is no Nash equilibrium in which player 1 plays pure strategy B. Thus the second set of 7 supports can be ruled out.
- As a consequence of the above two facts, in any Nash equilibrium, player 1 must randomize between T and B with positive probabilities for both T and B.
- Let us see what happens if player 2 chooses a pure strategy. If player 2 chooses L, player 1 chooses T; If player 2 chooses M, 1 chooses B; If player 2 chooses R, player 1 chooses B. Thus when player 2 plays a pure strategy, the best response of player 1 is also a pure strategy. However we have seen that in any Nash equilibrium, player 1 has to give positive probability to both the strategies T and B. Therefore, there is no Nash equilibrium in which player 2 plays a pure strategy and supports $\{T, B\} \times \{L\}$, $\{T, B\} \times \{M\}$, $\{T, B\} \times \{R\}$ can be dropped from the potential list of Nash equilibria.

The above discussion shows that the game does not have any pure strategy Nash equilibria. Also, the game does not have any Nash equilibria in which a player plays only a pure strategy. This leaves only the following supports for further exploration:

- *Candidate Support 1*: $\{T, B\} \times \{L, M, R\}$
- *Candidate Support 2*: $\{T, B\} \times \{M, R\}$
- *Candidate Support 3*: $\{T, B\} \times \{L, M\}$
- *Candidate Support 4*: $\{T, B\} \times \{L, R\}$

Candidate Support 1: $\{T, B\} \times \{L, M, R\}$

Player 1 must get the same payoff from T and B. This leads to

$$w_1 = 7\sigma_2(L) + 2\sigma_2(M) + 3\sigma_2(R) \tag{11.6}$$
$$w_1 = 2\sigma_2(L) + 7\sigma_2(M) + 4\sigma_2(R) \tag{11.7}$$

Similarly, player 2 must get the same payoff from each of L, M, R:

$$w_2 = 2\sigma_1(T) + 7\sigma_1(B) \tag{11.8}$$
$$w_2 = 7\sigma_1(T) + 2\sigma_1(B) \tag{11.9}$$
$$w_2 = 6\sigma_1(T) + 5\sigma_1(B) \tag{11.10}$$

In addition, we have

$$\sigma_1(T) + \sigma_1(B) = 1 \tag{11.11}$$
$$\sigma_2(L) + \sigma_2(M) + \sigma_2(R) = 1 \tag{11.12}$$

we have 7 equations in 7 unknowns. However,

$$(11.8), (11.9), (11.10) \implies \sigma_1(T) = \sigma_1(B) = \frac{1}{2}$$

whereas

$$(11.9), (11.10), (11.11) \implies \sigma_1(T) = \frac{3}{4}; \quad \sigma_1(B) = \frac{1}{4}$$

Thus this system of equations does not even have a solution and surely will not lead to a Nash equilibrium profile.

Candidate Support 2: $\{T, B\} \times \{M, R\}$

Here we get the equations

$$w_1 = 2\sigma_2(M) + 3\sigma_2(R)$$
$$w_1 = 7\sigma_2(M) + 4\sigma_2(R)$$
$$w_2 = 7\sigma_1(T) + 2\sigma_1(B)$$
$$w_2 = 6\sigma_1(T) + 5\sigma_1(B)$$
$$\sigma_1(T) + \sigma_1(B) = 1$$
$$\sigma_2(L) + \sigma_2(M) + \sigma_2(R) = 1$$
$$\sigma_2(L) = 0$$

The solution is

$$\sigma_1(T) = \frac{3}{4}; \quad \sigma_1(B) = \frac{1}{4}$$
$$\sigma_2(M) = -\frac{1}{4}; \quad \sigma_2(R) = \frac{5}{4}$$

but the solution leads to negative numbers and thus is not valid.

Candidate Support 3: $\{T, B\} \times \{L, M\}$

We get the equations

$$w_1 = 7\sigma_2(L) + 2\sigma_2(M)$$
$$w_1 = 2\sigma_2(L) + 7\sigma_2(M)$$
$$w_2 = 2\sigma_1(T) + 7\sigma_1(B)$$
$$w_2 = 7\sigma_1(T) + 2\sigma_1(B)$$
$$\sigma_1(T) + \sigma_1(B) = 1$$
$$\sigma_2(L) + \sigma_2(M) = 1$$
$$\sigma_2(R) = 0$$

These equations have a unique solution:

$$\sigma_1(T) = \sigma_1(B) = \frac{1}{2}; \quad \sigma_2(L) = \sigma_2(M) = \frac{1}{2}; \quad \sigma_2(R) = 0; \quad w_1 = w_2 = 4.5.$$

Before we can declare this as a Nash equilibrium, we need to do one more check. Note that $\sigma_2(R) = 0$. So we have to check whether player 2 actually prefers L and M over R. We have to check what payoff player 2 would get when he plays R against player 1 playing σ_1.

$$u_2(\sigma_1, R) = \sigma_1(T)u_2(T, R) + \sigma_1(B)u_2(B, R)$$
$$= \frac{1}{2} \times 6 + \frac{1}{2} \times 5 = 5.5 > 4.5.$$

This means player 2 would not be willing to choose σ_2 when player 1 plays σ_1; player 2 would prefer to play pure strategy R instead. Thus this solution is also not a Nash equilibrium.

Candidate Support 4: $\{T, B\} \times \{L, R\}$

The equations here are:

$$w_1 = 7\sigma_2(L) + 3\sigma_2(R)$$
$$w_1 = 2\sigma_2(L) + 4\sigma_2(R)$$
$$w_2 = 2\sigma_1(T) + 7\sigma_1(B)$$
$$w_2 = 6\sigma_1(T) + 5\sigma_1(B)$$
$$\sigma_1(T) + \sigma_1(B) = 1$$
$$\sigma_2(L) + \sigma_2(R) + \sigma_2(M) = 1$$
$$\sigma_2(M) = 0$$
$$\sigma_1(T), \sigma_1(B), \sigma_2(L), \sigma_2(R) \geq 0$$
$$w_2 \geq \sigma_1(T)u_2(T, M) + \sigma_2(B)u_2(B, M)$$

The unique solution of the above system of equations is

$$\sigma_1(T) = \frac{1}{3} \quad \sigma_1(B) = \frac{2}{3}$$

$$\sigma_2(L) = \frac{1}{6} \quad \sigma_2(M) = 0 \quad \sigma_2(R) = \frac{5}{6}$$

$$w_1 = \frac{8}{3} \quad w_2 = \frac{16}{3}$$

Moreover,

$$u_2(\sigma_1, M) = 7\left(\frac{1}{3}\right) + 2\left(\frac{2}{3}\right) = \frac{11}{3} \leq \frac{16}{3}$$

This is certainly a Nash equilibrium. Thus the mixed profile

$$\left(\left(\frac{1}{3}, \frac{2}{3}\right), \left(\frac{1}{6}, 0, \frac{5}{6}\right)\right)$$

is the unique mixed strategy Nash equilibrium of the given game. Note that

$$u_2(\sigma_1, M) = \sigma_1(T)u_2(T, M) + \sigma_1(B)u_2(B, M) = \frac{11}{3}$$

$$u_2(\sigma_1, L) = u_2(\sigma_1, R) = \frac{16}{3}$$

11.4   Summary and References

In this chapter, we have outlined an algorithmic procedure for computing mixed strategy Nash equilibria in finite games based on the necessary and sufficient conditions for a strategy profile to be a MSNE. For two person games, the above leads to a linear complementarity problem while for games with more than two players, the above leads to a non-linear complementarity problem.

For the past five decades, game theorists and more recently theoretical computer scientists have sought to develop efficient algorithms for computing Nash equilibria of finite games. One of the early breakthroughs was the *complementary pivot algorithm* developed by Lemke and Howson [3] in 1964 for bimatrix games (that is, two player non-zero sum games). This was immediately followed by Mangasarian's algorithm [4] for bimatrix games. Scarf [5], in 1967, developed an algorithm for the case of three or more players. Rosenmuller [6] generalized the Lemke-Howson algorithm in 1971 to the case of games with three or more players. In the same year, Wilson [7] proposed a new algorithm for computing equilibria of games with three or more players. All of these algorithms have a worst case running time that is exponential in the size of the strategy sets and number of players.

McKelvey and McLennan wrote in 1996 an excellent survey paper on equilibrium computation algorithms [8]. Murty treats the complementarity problems in a comprehensive way in his book [1]. During the past decade, there has been intense renewed activity on developing more efficient algorithms. Notable efforts include the works of Govindan and Wilson [9] who used a global Newton method; Porter, Nudelman, and Shoham [10]; and Sandholm, Gilpin, and Conitzer [11]. The well known journal *Economic Theory* published a special issue on computation of Nash equilibria in finite games edited by von Stengel in 2010 [12]. This special issue summarizes the current state-of-the-art on this problem by leading researchers. The edited volume by Nisan, Roughgarden, Tardos, and Vazirani [13] also has survey articles on this problem.

Software Tools

Surprisingly, there are not many software tools available for computational game theory. The most notable is the tool GAMBIT [14] which is powerful, user-friendly, and freely downloadable. This tool is useful for finite non-cooperative games (both extensive form and strategic form). The tool GAMUT [15] is also quite useful and freely downloadable. At the Indian Institute of Science, the tool NECTAR (Nash Equilibrium Computation Algorithms and Resources) [16] has been developed over the years.

References

[1] K.G. Murty. *Linear Complementarity, Linear and Nonlinear Programming.* Helderman-Verlag, 1988.

[2] Roger B. Myerson. *Game Theory: Analysis of Conflict.* Harvard University Press, Cambridge, Massachusetts, USA, 1997.

[3] C. E. Lemke and J. T. Howson Jr. "Equilibrium points of bi-matrix games". In: *Journal of the Society for Industrial and Applied Mathematics* **12** (1964), pp. 413–423.

[4] O. L. Mangasarian. "Equilibrium points of bimatrix games". In: *Journal of the Society for Industrial and Applied Mathematics* **12** (1964), pp. 778–780.

[5] Herbert E. Scarf. "The core of an *n*-person game". In: *Econometrica* **35** (1967), pp. 50–69.

[6] J. Rosenmuller. "On a generalization of the Lemke-Howson algorithm to noncooperative *n*-person games". In: *SIAM Journal on Applied Mathematics* **21** (1971), pp. 73–79.

[7] R. Wilson. "Computing equilibria of *n*-person games". In: *SIAM Journal on Applied Mathematics* **21** (1971), pp. 80–87.

[8] R. D. McKelvey and A. McLennan. "Computation of equilibria in finite games". In: *Handbook of Computational Economics.* Ed. by J. Rust, H. Amman, and D. Kendrick. Elsevier, 1996, pp. 87–142.

[9] S. Govindan and R. Wilson. "A global Newton method to compute Nash equilibria". In: *Journal of Economic Theory* **110**(1) (2003), pp. 65–86.

[10] R. Porter, E. Nudelman, and Y. Shoham. "Simple Search Methods for Finding a Nash Equilibrium". In: *Games and Economic Behavior* **63**(2) (2008), pp. 642–662.

[11] T. Sandholm, A. Gilpin, and V. Conitzer. "Mixed-integer programming methods for finding Nash equilibria". In: *Proceedings of the American Association of Artificial Intelligence, AAAI-2005.* 2005, pp. 495–501.

[12] Bernard Von Stengel. "Special Issue on Computation of Nash Equilibria in Finite Games". In: *Economic Theory* **42**(1) (2010).

[13] Noam Nisan, Tim Roughgarden, Eva Tardos, and Vijay Vazirani (Editors). *Algorithmic Game Theory.* Cambridge University Press, 2007.

[14] The GAMBIT Project. *GAMBIT: Software.* www.gambit-project.org, 2005.

[15]   E. Nudelman, J. Wortman, Y. Shoham, and K. Leyton-Brown. "Run the GAMUT: A comprehensive approach to evaluating game-Theoretic algorithms". In: *Proceedings of the Third International Joint Conference on Autonomous Agents and Multiagent Systems, AAMAS-2004*. 2004, pp. 880–887.

[16]   Game Theory Laboratory. *NECTAR: Software*. Department of Computer Science and Automation, Indian Institute of Science, Bangalore, India. http://lcm.csa.iisc.ernet.in/nectar, 2010.

11.5   Exercises

(1) Find the mixed strategy Nash equilibria for the following game.

	H	T
H	1, 1	0, 1
T	1, 0	0, 0

(2) Find the mixed strategy Nash equilibria for the following game.

	A	B
A	6, 2	0, 0
B	0, 0	2, 6

(3) Find all mixed strategy equilibria for the following game

	A	B	C
A	-3, -3	-1, 0	4, 0
B	0, 0	2, 2	3, 1
C	0,0	2, 4	3, 3

(4) Show that the pure strategy profile (a_2, b_2) is the unique mixed strategy Nash equilibrium of the following game.

			2	
1	b_1	b_2	b_3	b_4
a_1	0,7	2,5	7,0	0,1
a_2	5,2	3,3	5,2	0,1
a_3	7,0	2,5	0,7	0,1
a_4	0,0	0,−2	0,0	10,−1

(5) Consider the following game

		2		
1	LL	L	M	R
U	100, 2	−100, 1	0,0	−100, −100
D	−100, −100	100, 49	1,0	100,2

What are the Nash equilibria of this game.

(6) Compute all Nash equilibria for the following game for each $a \in (1, \infty)$

	2	
A	$a, 0$	$1, 2 - a$
B	$1, 1$	$0,0$

(7) Consider the following game where the numbers a, b, c, d, k_1, k_2 are strictly positive real numbers.

	H_1	H_2
P_1	$a, -k_1 a$	$b, -k_1 b$
P_2	$c, -k_2 c$	$d, -k_2 d$

For the above two player non-zero sum game, write down the necessary and sufficient conditions for mixed strategy Nash equilibrium and compute all mixed strategy Nash equilibria.

(8) Consider a 3 person game with $S_1 = S_2 = S_3 = \{1, 2, 3, 4\}$. If $u_i(x, y, z) = x + y + z + 4i$ for each $i = 1, 2, 3$, show that the game has a unique Nash equilibrium.

(9) Suppose

$$u_1(x, y, z) = 10 \qquad \text{if } x = y = z$$
$$= 0 \qquad \text{otherwise}$$

Describe all pure strategy Nash equilibria and show that mixed strategy Nash equilibria lead to smaller payoffs than pure Nash equilibria.

Chapter 12

Complexity of Computing a Nash Equilibrium

One of the central questions that theoretical computer scientists have investigated in recent times with much interest and intensity is the issue of complexity of computing a (mixed strategy) Nash equilibrium of a finite strategic form game. Thanks to the Nash theorem, at least one Nash equilibrium is guaranteed to exist for finite strategic form games and the problem of finding a Nash equilibrium therefore belongs to the class of total search problems (that is, search problems where a solution is guaranteed to exist). A large body of literature exists on this problem and this chapter attempts to bring out some salient aspects of the main results available on this problem. This chapter is based on the papers listed in the bibliography of this chapter, in particular, the survey article written by Daskalakis, Goldberg, and Papadimitriou [1].

12.1   Problems: NASH, BROUWER

First we introduce the two important problems NASH and BROUWER which are both total search problems.

- NASH: Given a finite strategic form game, find a mixed strategy Nash equilibrium of the game. There could be potentially a number of mixed strategy Nash equilibria but we are interested in any one sample equilibrium.
- BROUWER: Given a continuous function f on the set $[0,1]^m$ (which is a compact and convex set), find a fixed point of the function f, that is, find an $x \in [0,1]^m$ such that $f(x) = x$. Note that m is a finite positive integer here and potentially f may have multiple fixed points. We are interested in only finding any one of those.

Instead of an exact Nash equilibrium or an exact fixed point, it is often convenient to work with an approximate Nash equilibrium or an approximate fixed point. Given a real number $\varepsilon > 0$ (howsoever small), an ε-Nash equilibrium is a profile of mixed strategies where any player can only improve her expected payoff by at most ε by switching to any other strategy. Similarly, an ε-fixed point of a function $f : [0,1]^m \to [0,1]^m$ is a point $x \in [0,1]^m$ such that

$$d(f(x), x) \leq \varepsilon$$

where d is a metric (or distance function) defined on $[0, 1]^m$. We now state two problems ε-NASH and ε-BROUWER as follows.

- ε-NASH: Given a finite strategic form game and a real number $\varepsilon > 0$, compute an ε-Nash equilibrium of the game.
- ε-BROUWER: Given an efficient algorithm to evaluate a continuous function $f : [0, 1]^m \to [0, 1]^m$, a desired accuracy $\varepsilon > 0$, and a distance metric d on $[0, 1]^m$, compute a point $x \in [0, 1]^m$ such that $d(f(x), x) \leq \varepsilon$.

In the above definitions, a few technical subtleties have been left out for ease of presentation and the interested reader is referred to [1] for more details. Clearly, the problem ε-NASH (ε-BROUWER) is no more complex than NASH (BROUWER) which involves computing an exact value. Therefore any hardness result for ε-NASH (ε-BROUWER) will automatically carry over to NASH (BROUWER). From now on, for ease of presentation, we will refer to ε-NASH (ε-BROUWER) as NASH (BROUWER).

The main result presented in this chapter is that the problem NASH is $\mathbb{PPAD}$-complete where $\mathbb{PPAD}$ is a complexity class of total search problems (short for *Polynomial Parity Argument for Directed graphs*). We now describe this class $\mathbb{PPAD}$ and a problem called EOL (End of Line Problem) which is a $\mathbb{PPAD}$-complete problem.

12.2 The Class $\mathbb{PPAD}$

The Classes $\mathbb{P}$, $\mathbb{NP}$, $\mathbb{NPC}$

First we recall the classes $\mathbb{P}$ and $\mathbb{NP}$. $\mathbb{P}$ is the class of all decision problems or search problems which are solvable in polynomial time by a deterministic Turing machine. $\mathbb{NP}$ is the class of all problems solvable in polynomial time by a non-deterministic Turing machine. We say a problem X is $\mathbb{NP}$-hard if every problem belonging to $\mathbb{NP}$ can be reduced to the problem X. Reduction of a problem Y to a problem X means that there is an efficient algorithm (that is, a polynomial time algorithm on a deterministic Turing machine) that takes as input an instance of Y and outputs an instance of X so that any solution to the instance of X can be transformed into a solution of the original instance of Y using an efficient algorithm. Finally, an $\mathbb{NP}$-complete problem X is a problem which is not only $\mathbb{NP}$-hard but also belongs to $\mathbb{NP}$. In order to show that a problem Y is $\mathbb{NP}$-complete, it is enough to show that an $\mathbb{NP}$-complete problem X can be reduced to the problem Y. Also, it is useful to observe that the class $\mathbb{NP}$ consists of all problems which can be reduced to any $\mathbb{NP}$-complete problem.

The Classes TFNP and PPAD

Papadimitriou (see for example [2]) proposed the complexity class TFNP (Total Function Non-deterministic Polynomial time) to describe all search problems for which every instance has a solution. An example would be FACTOR which takes as input an integer and determines all its prime factors. An immediate relevant example is NASH which finds an exact or ε-Nash equilibrium of a finite strategic form game. Papadimitriou also proposed a classification of total search problems based on certain "arguments" which are non-constructive steps that are used in proving that every instance of the total search problem has a solution. This leads to the following classes of total search problems.

- PPA (Polynomial Parity Argument): If a graph has a node of odd degree, then it must have at least one other node of odd degree. This is called the parity argument (PA) and the class of total search problems which use this argument are grouped under the class PPA. Formally, a problem is in PPA if there is a polynomial time reduction to the problem of finding an odd degree vertex given another odd degree vertex in a graph that is represented by a polynomial sized circuit.
- PPAD (Polynomial Parity Argument for Directed Graphs): Given a directed graph, the in-degree (out-degree) of a node is the number of incoming (outgoing) arcs. A node is said to be unbalanced if its in-degree and out-degree are different. The PPAD argument says that if a directed graph has an unbalanced node, then there must exist at least one other unbalanced node.

The relationship between the various classes of total search problems is depicted in Figure 12.1. (The figure nonchalantly assumes that $\mathbb{P} \subsetneq \mathbb{NP}$. If $\mathbb{P} = \mathbb{NP}$, then all the classes will collapse into one).

It is interesting to think about how hard the problems in PPAD are. If $\mathbb{P} = \mathbb{NP}$, then this issue is settled since PPAD which is a subset of NP will itself be equal to $\mathbb{P}$. If $\mathbb{P} \neq \mathbb{NP}$ (as is widely believed), then there is strong evidence to believe that PPAD contains hard problems. For several decades now, theoretical computer scientists have tried in vain to design efficient algorithms for some problems which are in PPAD (for example, BROUWER, NASH, and the End-of-Line problem which will be introduced in the next section). Thus unless $\mathbb{P} = \mathbb{NP}$, we can safely believe that PPAD does contain computationally hard problems.

The EOL Problem

The EOL (End-of-Line) problem is the best known PPAD-complete problem. It is a special case of the following total search problem: Given a directed graph G and a designated unbalanced vertex of G, find some other unbalanced vertex in G. The EOL problem assumes that every vertex G has at most one incoming edge and at most one outgoing edge. With this restriction, the given graph must be a set of paths

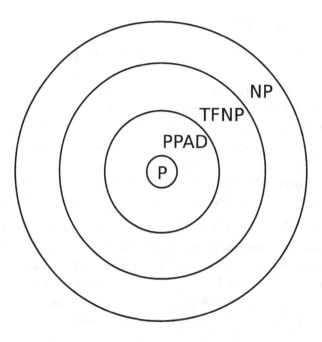

Fig. 12.1: Relationships among different relevant complexity classes

and cycles. Figure 12.2 provides a few representative examples of such graphs.

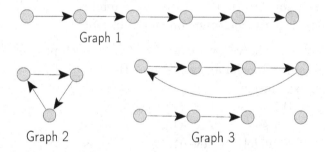

Fig. 12.2: Some examples of the EOL problem

The EOL problem further assumes that each vertex in a graph with, say 2^n vertices, is labeled with a unique binary string of length n. The edges in the graph are described using a predecessor function p and a successor function s defined on the set of vertices. If (v, v') is an edge in the graph, then $s(v) = v'$ and $p(v') = v$ have the obvious meaning. Note that the entire graph is represented using binary strings as vertices and by defining the p and s functions. With this representation, the EOL problem starts with a designated unbalanced vertex and seeks to find some other unbalanced vertex.

It has been shown that the EOL problem is $\mathbb{PPAD}$-complete. Two immediate consequences of this fact are the following:

- A problem X is $\mathbb{PPAD}$-complete if EOL can be reduced to the problem X.
- A problem $Y \in \mathbb{PPAD}$ if Y can be reduced to EOL.

One of the major results proved in recent times is that the problem NASH is $\mathbb{PPAD}$-complete. The proof of this result has taken several years of effort (see the bibliography) and the final steps in the proof was contributed by Daskalakis in his doctoral dissertation which won the ACM Doctoral Dissertation Award in 2008.

12.3 NASH is $\mathbb{PPAD}$-complete

We only provide an outline of the proof of this result. The proof proceeds in two stages.

- First it is shown that NASH $\in \mathbb{PPAD}$. This is shown by reducing NASH to EOL.
- Second, it is shown that NASH is $\mathbb{PPAD}$-complete. This is shown by reducing EOL to NASH.

The proof in both directions above uses the problem BROUWER.

NASH *is in* $\mathbb{PPAD}$

It has been shown that BROUWER can be reduced to EOL using the Sperner's lemma. We refer the reader to [1] for details. Therefore, BROUWER $\in \mathbb{PPAD}$. It has also been shown that NASH can be reduced to BROUWER (see [1]). Since NASH can be reduced to BROUWER, we have that NASH can be reduced to EOL which means that NASH $\in \mathbb{PPAD}$.

NASH *is* $\mathbb{PPAD}$-*complete*

First it is shown that BROUWER is $\mathbb{PPAD}$-complete. This is done by showing that EOL can be reduced to BROUWER by encoding a directed graph in terms of a continuous, easy-to-compute function. BROUWER can be reduced to NASH using interesting arguments [1]. Since BROUWER is $\mathbb{PPAD}$-complete and BROUWER can be reduced to NASH, we have that NASH is $\mathbb{PPAD}$-complete.

For detailed proofs of all the above results, the reader is referred to [1] and other relevant papers in the bibliography.

12.4 Some Observations

The fact that NASH is $\mathbb{PPAD}$-complete and therefore computationally a hard problem (unless $\mathbb{P} = \mathbb{NP}$) raises some questions about whether it is practical to use it as a solution concept. Efficient computation of Nash equilibrium is crucial for many reasons [3].

- In many practical situations such as game playing, multiagent reasoning, auctions, etc., quick computation of equilibrium is extremely useful.
- If players in a game can only invest polynomial computation in a game, then it is important that Nash equilibrium or any chosen solution concept is computable in polynomial time.

The result that NASH is $\mathbb{PPAD}$-complete almost rules out the possibility of a polynomial time algorithm for computing Nash equilibrium. Notwithstanding this, Nash equilibrium is bound to retain its pre-eminent position as a premier solution concept due to its intuitive, natural, and technically rigorous development. We now summarize a few important results relevant to computation of Nash equilibrium.

- Though NASH is $\mathbb{PPAD}$-complete, it is unlikely to be $\mathbb{NP}$-complete, as argued by Nimrod Megiddo [1]: Suppose we have a reduction from the $\mathbb{NP}$-complete problem SAT to NASH. Since NASH is a total search problem and SAT is not a total search problem, the above reduction would mean that the solution of any instance of NASH tells us whether or not the SAT instance has a solution. This enables us to design a non-deterministic algorithm to verify that an instance of SAT has no solution. Complexity theorists believe that such an algorithm for SAT is as unlikely as $\mathbb{P} = \mathbb{NP}$.
- Chen, Deng, and Teng [4] have ruled out the existence of a fully polynomial time approximation scheme (FPTAS) for computing an ε-Nash equilibrium for finite strategic form games. This means there is no algorithm that can compute an ε-Nash equilibrium with a running time that is polynomial in the size of the game (number of players and number of strategies) and polynomial in $1/\varepsilon$.
- On the other hand, it is open whether there exists a polynomial time approximation scheme (PTAS) for computing an ε-Nash equilibrium (that is an algorithm that computes an ε-Nash equilibrium with running time that is polynomial in the size of the game but depends arbitrarily on $1/\varepsilon$).
- Lipton, Markakis, and Mehta [5] have shown the existence of a sub-exponential algorithm for computing an ε-Nash equilibrium.
- It is worth recalling here that the complexity of computing Nash equilibria in matrix games (two player zero-sum game) is polynomial, thanks to the linear programming formulation of von Neumann and Morgenstern. The complexity of this problem for two player non-zero-sum games and beyond is unlikely to be polynomial time unless we are looking at very special cases. Numerous algorithms have been proposed over the last 50 years, however these algorithms either have worst case exponential time complexity or their complexity is not even known. For a survey of these algorithms, the reader is referred to McKelvey and McLennan [6].

For more details and insights, the reader is referred to the excellent survey paper by Daskalakis, Goldberg, and Papadimitriou [1].

12.5   Summary and References

In this chapter, we have outlined that the problem of computing a mixed strategy Nash equilibrium in a finite strategic form game is $\mathbb{PPAD}$-complete where the class $\mathbb{PPAD}$ consists of all search problems for which every instance has a solution and the proof of existence of solution is based on the PPAD argument. PPAD stands for *polynomial parity argument for directed graphs* and the PPAD argument says that if a directed graph has an unbalanced node (that is in-degree not equal to out-degree), then there must exist at least one other unbalanced node.

As already stated, much of the content in this chapter owes to the survey paper by Daskalakis, Goldberg, and Papadimitriou [1]. The detailed proofs of results are available in [7, 1, 4]. There are many other survey articles on both complexity and algorithmic issues in the volume on Algorithmic Game Theory edited by Nisan, Roughgarden, Tardos, and Vazirani [8], The papers by Conitzer and Sandholm [9] and Roughgarden [3] are also expository. There is a good discussion in the book by Shoham and Leyton-Brown [10]. Other useful references include [5, 11].

References

[1]   C. Daskalakis, P. W. Goldberg, and C. H. Papadimitriou. "The complexity of computing a Nash equilibrium". In: *Communications of the ACM* **52**(2) (2009), pp. 89–97.

[2]   C.H. Papadimitriou. "The complexity of finding Nash equilibria". In: *Algorithmic Game Theory*. Ed. by Noam Nisan, Tim Roughgarden, Eva Tardos, and Vijay Vazirani. Cambridge University Press, 2007, pp. 29–52.

[3]   T. Roughgarden. "Algorithmic game theory". In: *Communications of the ACM* **53**(7) (2010), pp. 78–86.

[4]   Xi Chen, Xiaotie Deng, and Shang-Hua Teng. "Settling the complexity of two-player Nash equilibrium". In: *Journal of ACM* **56**(3) (2009).

[5]   R. J. Lipton, E. Markakis, and A. Mehta. "Playing large games using simple strategies". In: *Proceedings of the 4th ACM Conference on Electronic Commerce, EC-2003*. ACM. 2003, pp. 36–41.

[6]   R. D. McKelvey and A. McLennan. "Computation of equilibria in finite games". In: *Handbook of Computational Economics*. Ed. by J. Rust, H. Amman, and D. Kendrick. Elsevier, 1996, pp. 87–142.

[7]   C. Daskalakis. "The complexity of computing a Nash equilibrium". In: *Proceedings of the 38th Annual ACM Symposium on Theory of Computing, STOC-2006*. ACM. 2006, pp. 71–78.

[8]   Noam Nisan, Tim Roughgarden, Eva Tardos, and Vijay Vazirani (Editors). *Algorithmic Game Theory*. Cambridge University Press, 2007.

[9]   Vincent Conitzer and Tuomas Sandholm. "Complexity Results about Nash Equilibria". In: *Proceedings of the Eighteenth International Joint Conference on Artificial Intelligence, IJCAI-2003, Acapulco, Mexico*. 2003, pp. 765–771.

[10]   Yoam Shoham and Kevin Leyton-Brown. *Multiagent Systems: Algorithmic, Game-Theoretic, and Logical Foundations*. Cambridge University Press, New York, USA, 2009, 2009.

[11]   K. Etessami and M. Yannakakis. "On the complexity of Nash equilibria and other fixed points". In: *48th Annual IEEE Symposium on Foundations of Computer Science, FOCS-2007*. IEEE. 2007, pp. 113–123.

Chapter 13

Bayesian Games

We have so far studied strategic form games with complete information, where the the entire game is common knowledge to the players. We will now study games with incomplete information, where at least one player has *private information* about the game which the other players may not know. While complete information games provide a convenient and useful abstraction for strategic situations, incomplete information games are more realistic. Incomplete information games are central to the theory of mechanism design. In this chapter, we study a particular form of these games called *Bayesian games* and introduce the important notion of *Bayesian Nash equilibrium*.

13.1 Games with Incomplete Information

A game with *incomplete information* is one in which, when the players are ready to make a move, at least one player has *private information* about the game which the other players may not know. The initial private information that a player has, just before making a move in the game, is called the *type* of the player. For example, in an auction involving a single indivisible item, each player has a valuation for the item, and typically this player would know this valuation deterministically while the other players may only have probabilistic information about how much this player values the item.

Definition 13.1 (Strategic Form Game with Incomplete Information).
A strategic form game with incomplete information is defined as a tuple $\Gamma = \langle N, (\Theta_i), (S_i), (p_i), (u_i) \rangle$ *where*

- $N = \{1, 2, \ldots, n\}$ *is the set of players.*
- Θ_i *is the set of types of player i where $i = 1, 2, \ldots, n$.*
- S_i *is the set of actions or pure strategies of player i where $i = 1, 2, \ldots, n$.*
- *The belief function p_i is a mapping from Θ_i into $\Delta(\Theta_{-i})$, the set of probability distributions over Θ_{-i}. That is, for any possible type $\theta_i \in \Theta_i$, p_i specifies a probability distribution $p_i(.|\theta_i)$ over the set Θ_{-i} representing player i's beliefs about the types of the other players if his own type were θ_i;*

- *The payoff function $u_i : \Theta_1 \times \ldots \times \Theta_n \times S_1 \times \ldots \times S_n \to \mathbb{R}$ assigns to each profile of types and each profile of actions, a payoff that player i would get.*

When we study such a game, we assume that

(1) Each player i knows the entire structure of the game as defined above.
(2) Each player i knows his own type $\theta_i \in \Theta_i$. The player learns his type through some signals and each element in his type set is a summary of the information gleaned from the signals.
(3) The above facts are common knowledge among all the players in N.
(4) The exact type of a player is not known deterministically to the other players who however have a probabilistic guess of what this type is. The belief functions p_i describe these conditional probabilities. Note that the belief functions p_i are also common knowledge among the players.

Bayesian Games

John Harsanyi (joint winner of the Nobel Prize in Economic Sciences in 1994 with John Nash and Reinhard Selten) proposed in 1968, *Bayesian* games to represent games with incomplete information. We first define the notion of consistency which is a natural and reasonable assumption to make in games with incomplete information.

Definition 13.2 (Consistency of Beliefs). *We say beliefs $(p_i)_{i \in N}$ are consistent if there is some common prior distribution over the set of type profiles Θ such that each player's beliefs given his type are just the conditional probability distributions that can be computed from the prior distribution.*

If the game is finite, beliefs are consistent if there exists some probability distribution $\mathbb{P} \in \Delta(\Theta)$ such that

$$p_i(\theta_{-i}|\theta_i) = \frac{\mathbb{P}(\theta_i, \theta_{-i})}{\displaystyle\sum_{t_{-i} \in \Theta_{-i}} \mathbb{P}(\theta_i, t_{-i})} \quad \forall \theta_i \in \Theta_i; \ \forall \theta_{-i} \in \Theta_{-i}; \ \forall i \in N.$$

In a consistent model, differences in beliefs among players can be logically explained by differences in information. If the model is not consistent, differences in beliefs among players can only be explained by differences of opinion that cannot be derived from any differences in information and must be simply assumed a priori [1]. When consistency of beliefs is satisfied, we refer to the games as *Bayesian games*.

 In 1994, **John Charles Harsanyi** was awarded the Nobel Prize in Economic Sciences, jointly with Professor John Nash and Professor Reinhard Selten, for their pioneering analysis of equilibria in non-cooperative games. Harsanyi is best known for his work on games with incomplete information and in particular Bayesian games, which he published as a series of three celebrated papers titled *Games with incomplete information played by Bayesian players* in the Management Science journal in 1967 and 1968.

His work on analysis of Bayesian games is of foundational value to mechanism design since mechanisms crucially use the framework of games with incomplete information. Harsanyi is also acclaimed for his intriguing work on *utilitarian ethics*, where he applied game theory and economic reasoning in political and moral philosophy. Harsanyi's collaboration with Reinhard Selten on the topic of equilibrium analysis resulted in a celebrated book entitled *A General Theory of Equilibrium Selection in Games* (MIT Press, 1988).

John Harsanyi was born in Budapest, Hungary, on May 29, 1920. He got two doctoral degrees – the first one in philosophy from the University of Budapest in 1947 and the second one in economics from Stanford University in 1959. His adviser at Stanford University was Professor Kenneth Arrow, who got the Economics Nobel Prize in 1972. Harsanyi worked at the University of California, Berkeley, from 1964 to 1990 when he retired. He died on August 9, 2000, in Berkeley, California.

 **Reinhard Selten**, a joint winner of the Nobel prize in economic sciences along with John Nash and John Harsanyi, is a key contributor to the theory of incomplete information games besides John Harsanyi. In fact Harsanyi refers to the type agent representation of Bayesian games as the *Selten game*. Selten is best known for his fundamental work on extensive form games and their transformation to strategic form through a representation called the agent normal form. Selten is also widely known for his deep work on bounded rationality.

Selten is also widely regarded as a pioneer of experimental economics. Harsanyi and Selten, in their remarkable book *A General Theory of Equilibrium Selection in Games* (MIT Press, 1988), develop a general framework to identify a unique equilibrium as the solution of a given finite strategic form game. Their solution can be thought of as the limit of an evolutionary process.

Selten was born in Breslau (currently in Poland but formerly in Germany) on October 5, 1930. He earned a doctorate in Mathematics from Frankfurt University, working with Professor Ewald Burger and Professor Wolfgang Franz. He is currently a Professor Emeritus at the University of Bonn, Germany.

The phrases *actions* and *strategies* are used differently in the Bayesian game context. A strategy for a player i in Bayesian games is defined as a mapping from

Θ_i to S_i. A strategy s_i of a player i, therefore, specifies a pure action for each type of player i; $s_i(\theta_i)$ for a given $\theta_i \in \Theta_i$ would specify the pure action that player i would play if his type were θ_i. The notation $s_i(.)$ is used to refer to the pure action of player i corresponding to an arbitrary type from his type set. When it is convenient, we use $a_i \in S_i$ to represent a typical action of player i.

13.2   Examples of Bayesian Games

Example 13.1 (A Two Player Bargaining Game). This example is taken from the book by Myerson [1]. There are two players, player 1 (seller) and player 2 (buyer). Player 1 wishes to sell an indivisible item and player 2 is interested in buying this item. Each player knows what the object is worth to himself but thinks that its value to the other player may be any integer from 1 to 100 with probability $\frac{1}{100}$. The type of the seller has the natural interpretation of being the willingness to sell (minimum price at which the seller is prepared to sell the item), and the type of the buyer has the natural interpretation of being the willingness to pay (maximum price the buyer is prepared to pay for the item). Assume that each player will simultaneously announce a bid between 0 and 100 for trading the object. If the buyer's bid is greater than or equal to the seller's bid they will trade the object at a price equal to the average of their bids; otherwise no trade occurs. For this game:

$$N = \{1, 2\}$$
$$\Theta_1 = \Theta_2 = \{1, 2, \ldots, 100\}$$
$$S_1 = S_2 = \{0, 1, 2, \ldots, 100\}$$
$$p_1(\theta_2|\theta_1) = \frac{1}{100} \; \forall \theta_1 \in \Theta_1; \; \forall \theta_2 \in \Theta_2$$
$$p_2(\theta_1|\theta_2) = \frac{1}{100} \; \forall \theta_1 \in \Theta_1; \; \forall \theta_2 \in \Theta_2$$
$$u_1(\theta_1, \theta_2, s_1, s_2) = \frac{s_1 + s_2}{2} - \theta_1 \quad \text{if } s_2 \geq s_1$$
$$= 0 \qquad\qquad \text{if } s_2 < s_1$$
$$u_2(\theta_1, \theta_2, s_1, s_2) = \theta_2 - \frac{s_1 + s_2}{2} \quad \text{if } s_2 \geq s_1$$
$$= 0 \qquad\qquad \text{if } s_2 < s_1.$$

Note that the beliefs p_1 and p_2 are consistent with the prior:

$$\mathbb{P}(\theta_1, \theta_2) = \frac{1}{10000} \; \forall \theta_1 \in \Theta_1 \; \forall \theta_2 \in \Theta_2$$

where

$$\Theta_1 \times \Theta_2 = \{1, \ldots, 100\} \times \{1, \ldots, 100\}.$$

□

Example 13.2 (A Sealed Bid Auction). Consider a seller who wishes to sell an indivisible item through an auction. Let there be two prospective buyers who bid for this item. The buyers have their individual valuations for this item. These valuations could be considered as the types of the buyers. Here the game consists of the two bidders, namely the buyers, so $N = \{1, 2\}$. The two bidders submit bids, say b_1 and b_2 for the item. Let us say that the one who bids higher is awarded the item with a tie resolved in favor of bidder 1. The winner determination function therefore is:

$$
\begin{aligned}
f_1(b_1, b_2) &= \quad 1 \text{ if } b_1 \geq b_2 \\
&= \quad 0 \text{ if } b_1 < b_2
\end{aligned}
$$

$$
\begin{aligned}
f_2(b_1, b_2) &= \quad 1 \text{ if } b_1 < b_2 \\
&= \quad 0 \text{ if } b_1 \geq b_2.
\end{aligned}
$$

Assume that the valuation set for each buyer is the real interval $[0, 1]$ and also that the strategy set for each buyer is again $[0, 1]$. This means $\Theta_1 = \Theta_2 = [0, 1]$ and $S_1 = S_2 = [0, 1]$. If we assume that each player believes that the other player's valuation is chosen according to an independent uniform distribution, then note that

$$
p_1([x, y] | \theta_1) = y - x \ \forall \ 0 \leq x \leq y \leq 1; \ \forall \theta_1 \in \Theta_1.
$$

$$
p_2([x, y] | \theta_2) = y - x \ \forall \ 0 \leq x \leq y \leq 1; \ \forall \theta_2 \in \Theta_2.
$$

In a first price auction, the winner will pay what is bid by her, and therefore the utility function of the players is given by

$$
u_i(\theta_1, \theta_2, b_1, b_2) = f_i(b_1, b_2)(\theta_i - b_i); \ i = 1, 2.
$$

This completes the definition of the Bayesian game underlying a first price auction involving two bidders. One can similarly develop the Bayesian game for the second price sealed bid auction. Note that only u_1 and u_2 would be different in the case of second price auction. $\square$

13.3 Type Agent Representation and the Selten Game

This is a representation of Bayesian games that enables a Bayesian game to be transformed to a strategic form game (with complete information). Given a Bayesian game

$$
\Gamma = \langle N, (\Theta_i), (S_i), (p_i), (u_i) \rangle
$$

the Selten game is an equivalent strategic form game

$$
\Gamma^s = \langle N^s, (S_{\theta_i})_{\substack{\theta_i \in \Theta_i \\ i \in N}}, (U_{\theta_i})_{\substack{\theta_i \in \Theta_i \\ i \in N}} \rangle.
$$

The idea used in formulating a Selten game is to have *type agents*. Each player in the original Bayesian game is now replaced with a number of type agents; in fact, a player is replaced by exactly as many type agents as the number of types in the type set of that player. We can safely assume that the type sets of the players are mutually disjoint. The set of players in the Selten game is given by:

$$N^s = \bigcup_{i \in N} \Theta_i.$$

Note that each type agent of a particular player can play precisely the same actions as the player himself. This means that for every $\theta_i \in \Theta_i$,

$$S_{\theta_i} = S_i.$$

The payoff function U_{θ_i} for each $\theta_i \in \Theta_i$ is the conditional expected utility to player i in the Bayesian game given that θ_i is his actual type. It is a mapping with the following domain and co-domain:

$$U_{\theta_i} : \left(\underset{i \in N}{\times} \underset{\theta_i \in \Theta_i}{\times} S_i \right) \to \mathbb{R}.$$

We will explain the way U_{θ_i} is derived using an example. This example is developed, based on the illustration in the book by Myerson [1].

Example 13.3 (Selten Game for a Bayesian Pricing Game). Consider two firms, company 1 and company 2. Company 1 produces a product x_1 whereas company 2 produces either product x_2 or product y_2. The product x_2 is somewhat similar to product x_1 while the product y_2 is a different line of product. The product to be produced by company 2 is a closely guarded secret, so it can be taken as private information of company 2. We thus have $N = \{1, 2\}$, $\Theta_1 = \{x_1\}$, and $\Theta_2 = \{x_2, y_2\}$. Each firm has to choose a price for the product it produces, and this is the strategic decision to be taken by the company. Company 1 has the choice of choosing a low price a_1 or a high price b_1 whereas company 2 has the choice of choosing a low price a_2 or a high price b_2. We therefore have $S_1 = \{a_1, b_1\}$ and $S_2 = \{a_2, b_2\}$. The type of company 1 is common knowledge since Θ_1 is a singleton. Therefore, the belief probabilities of company 2 about company 1 are given by $p_2(x_1|x_2) = 1$ and $p_2(x_1|y_2) = 1$. Let us assume the belief probabilities of company 1 about company 2 to be $p_1(x_2|x_1) = 0.6$ and $p_1(y_2|x_1) = 0.4$. Let the utility functions for the two possible type profiles $(\theta_1 = x_1, \theta_2 = x_2)$ and $(\theta_1 = x_1, \theta_2 = y_2)$ be given as in Tables 13.1 and 13.2.

1	2	
	a_2	b_2
a_1	1, 2	0, 1
b_1	0, 4	1, 3

Table 13.1: u_1 and u_2 for $\theta_1 = x_1; \theta_2 = x_2$

This completes the description of the Bayesian game. We now derive the equivalent Selten game. We have

$$N^s = \Theta_1 \cup \Theta_2 = \{x_1, x_2, y_2\}$$
$$S_{x_1} = S_1 = \{a_1, b_1\}$$
$$S_{x_2} = S_{y_2} = S_2 = \{a_2, b_2\}.$$

	2	
1	a_2	b_2
a_1	$1, 3$	$0, 4$
b_1	$0, 1$	$1, 2$

Table 13.2: u_1 and u_2 for $\theta_1 = x_1; \theta_2 = y_2$

Note that

$$U_{\theta_i} : S_1 \times S_2 \times S_2 \to \mathbb{R} \ \ \forall \theta_i \in \Theta_i, \forall i \in N$$

$$S_1 \times S_2 \times S_2 = \{(a_1, a_2, a_2), (a_1, a_2, b_2), (a_1, b_2, a_2), (a_1, b_2, b_2),$$
$$(b_1, a_2, a_2), (b_1, a_2, b_2), (b_1, b_2, a_2), (b_1, b_2, b_2)\}.$$

The above gives the set of all strategy profiles of all the type agents. A typical strategy profile can be represented as $(s_{x_1}, s_{x_2}, s_{y_2})$. This could also be represented as $(s_1(.), s_2(.))$ where the strategy s_1 is a mapping from Θ_1 to S_1, and the strategy s_2 is a mapping from Θ_2 to S_2. In general, for an n player Bayesian game, a pure strategy profile is of the form

$$((s_{\theta_1})_{\theta_1 \in \Theta_1}, (s_{\theta_2})_{\theta_2 \in \Theta_2}, \ldots, (s_{\theta_n})_{\theta_n \in \Theta_n}).$$

An equivalent way to write this would be $(s_1(.), s_2(.), \ldots, s_n(.))$, where s_i is a mapping from Θ_i to S_i for $i = 1, 2, \ldots, n$. The payoffs for type agents (in the Selten game) are obtained as conditional expectations over the type profiles of the rest of the agents. For example, let us compute the payoff $U_{x_1}(a_1, a_2, b_2)$, which is the expected payoff obtained by type agent x_1 (belonging to player 1) when this type agent plays action a_1 and the type agents x_2 and y_2 of player 2 play the actions a_2 and b_2 respectively. In this case, the type of player 1 is known, but the type of player could be x_2 or y_2 with probabilities given by the belief function $p_1(.|x_1)$. The following conditional expectation gives the required payoff.

$$U_{x_1}(a_1, a_2, b_2) = p_1(x_2|x_1) \ u_1(x_1, x_2, a_1, a_2)$$
$$+ p_1(y_2|x_1) \ u_1(x_1, y_2, a_1, b_2)$$
$$= (0.6)(1) + (0.4)(0)$$
$$= 0.6.$$

It can be similarly shown that

$$U_{x_1}(b_1, a_2, b_2) = 0.4$$
$$U_{x_2}(a_1, a_2, b_2) = 2$$
$$U_{x_2}(a_1, b_2, b_2) = 1$$
$$U_{y_2}(a_1, a_2, b_2) = 4$$
$$U_{y_2}(a_1, a_2, a_2) = 3.$$

From the above, we see that

$$U_{x_1}(a_1, a_2, b_2) > U_{x_1}(b_1, a_2, b_2)$$
$$U_{x_2}(a_1, a_2, b_2) > U_{x_2}(a_1, b_2, b_2)$$
$$U_{y_2}(a_1, a_2, b_2) > U_{y_2}(a_1, a_2, a_2).$$

We can immediately conclude that the action profile (a_1, a_2, b_2) is a Nash equilibrium of the Selten game. Another way of representing this profile would be (s_1^*, s_2^*) where $s_1^*(x_1) = a_1$ and $s_2^*(x_2) = a_2$; $s_2^*(y_2) = b_2$. □

Payoff Computation in Selten Game

From now on, when there is no confusion, we will use u instead of U. In general, given a Bayesian game $\Gamma = \langle N, (\Theta_i), (S_i), (p_i), (u_i) \rangle$, suppose $(s_1, \ldots, s_n)$ is a strategy profile where for $i = 1, \ldots, n$, s_i is a mapping from Θ_i to S_i. Assume the current type of player i to be θ_i. Then the expected utility to player i is given by

$$u_i((s_i, s_{-i})|\theta_i) = \mathbb{E}_{\theta_{-i}}\left[(u_i(\theta_i, \theta_{-i}, s_i(\theta_i), s_{-i}(\theta_{-i}))\right]$$

For a finite Bayesian game, the above immediately translates to

$$u_i((s_i, s_{-i})|\theta_i) = \sum_{t_{-i} \in \Theta_{-i}} p_i(t_{-i}|\theta_i)(u_i(\theta_i, t_{-i}, s_i(\theta_i), s_{-i}(t_{-i}))$$

With this setup, we now define the notion of Bayesian Nash equilibrium.

13.4   Bayesian Nash Equilibrium

Definition 13.3 (Pure Strategy Bayesian Nash Equilibrium). *A pure strategy Bayesian Nash equilibrium in a Bayesian game*

$$\Gamma = \langle N, (\Theta_i), (S_i), (p_i), (u_i) \rangle$$

can be defined in a natural way as a pure strategy Nash equilibrium of the equivalent Selten game. That is, a profile of strategies $(s_1^*, \ldots, s_n^*)$ is a pure strategy Bayesian Nash equilibrium if $\forall i \in N$; $\forall s_i : \Theta_i \to S_i$; $\forall \theta_i \in \Theta_i$,

$$u_i((s_i^*, s_{-i}^*) \mid \theta_i) \geq u_i((s_i, s_{-i}^*) \mid \theta_i)$$

That is, $\forall i \in N$; $\forall a_i \in S_i$; $\forall \theta_i \in \Theta_i$,

$$\mathbb{E}_{\theta_{-i}}\left[u_i(\theta_i, \theta_{-i}, s_i^*(\theta_i), s_{-i}^*(\theta_{-i}))\right] \geq \mathbb{E}_{\theta_{-i}}\left[u_i(\theta_i, \theta_{-i}, a_i, s_{-i}^*(\theta_{-i}))\right]$$

Example 13.4 (Bayesian Pricing Game). Consider the Bayesian pricing game being discussed. We make the following observations.

- When $\theta_2 = x_2$, the strategy b_2 is strongly dominated by a_2. Thus player 2 chooses a_2 when $\theta_2 = x_2$.

- When $\theta_2 = y_2$, the strategy a_2 is strongly dominated by b_2 and therefore player 2 chooses b_2 when $\theta_2 = y_2$.
- When the action profiles are (a_1, a_2) or (b_1, b_2), player 1 has payoff 1 regardless of the type of player 2. In all other profiles, payoff of player 1 is zero.
- Since $p_1(x_2|x_1) = 0.6$ and $p_1(y_2|x_1) = 0.4$, player 1 thinks that the type x_2 of player 2 is more likely than type y_2.

The above arguments imply that a pure strategy Bayesian Nash equilibrium in the above example is given by:

$$(s_{x_1}^* = a_1, s_{x_2}^* = a_2, s_{y_2}^* = b_2)$$

thus validating what we have already shown. In the above equilibrium, the strategy of company 1 is to price the product low whereas the strategy of company 2 is to price the product low if it produces x_2 and to price the product high if it produces y_2. It can be seen that the above is the unique pure strategy Bayesian Nash equilibrium for this game.

The above example clearly illustrates the ramification of analyzing each matrix separately. If it is common knowledge that player 2's type is x_2, then the unique Nash equilibrium is (a_1, a_2). If it is common knowledge that player 2 has type y_2, then we get (b_1, b_2) as the unique Nash equilibrium. However, in a Bayesian game, the type of player 2 is not common knowledge, and hence the above prediction based on analyzing the matrices separately would be wrong. $\qquad\square$

Example 13.5 (First Price Sealed Bid Auction). Consider again the example of first price sealed bid auction with two prospective buyers. Here the two buyers are the players. Each buyer submits a sealed bid, $b_i \geq 0$ $(i = 1, 2)$. The sealed bids are looked at, and the buyer with the higher bid is declared the winner. If there is a tie, buyer 1 is declared the winner. The winning buyer pays to the seller an amount equal to his bid. The losing bidder does not pay anything.

Let us make the following assumptions:

(1) θ_1, θ_2 are independently drawn from the uniform distribution on $[0, 1]$.
(2) The sealed bid of buyer i takes the form $b_i(\theta_i) = \alpha_i \theta_i$, where $\alpha_i \in (0, 1]$. This assumption implies that player i bids a fraction α_i of his value; this is a reasonable assumption that implies a linear relationship between the bid and the value. Each buyer knows that the bids are of the above form. Buyer 1 (buyer 2) seeks to compute an appropriate value for α_1 (α_2).

Buyer 1's problem is now to bid in order to maximize his expected payoff:

$$\max_{b_1 \geq 0}(\theta_1 - b_1)P\{b_2(\theta_2) \leq b_1\}.$$

Since the bid of player 2 is $b_2(\theta_2) = \alpha_2 \theta_2$ and $\theta_2 \in [0, 1]$, the maximum bid of buyer 2 is α_2. Buyer 1 knows this and therefore $b_1 \in [0, \alpha_2]$. Also,

$$P\{b_2(\theta_2) \leq b_1\} = P\{\alpha_2 \theta_2 \leq b_1\}$$
$$= P\{\theta_2 \leq \frac{b_1}{\alpha_2}\}$$
$$= \frac{b_1}{\alpha_2} \text{ (since } \theta_2 \text{ is uniform over } [0, 1]).$$

Thus buyer 1's problem is:

$$\max_{b_1 \in [0, \alpha_2]} (\theta_1 - b_1) \frac{b_1}{\alpha_2}.$$

The solution to this problem is

$$b_1(\theta_1) = \begin{cases} \frac{\theta_1}{2} & \text{if } \frac{\theta_1}{2} \leq \alpha_2 \\ \alpha_2 & \text{if } \frac{\theta_1}{2} > \alpha_2. \end{cases}$$

We can show on similar lines that

$$b_2(\theta_2) = \begin{cases} \frac{\theta_2}{2} & \text{if } \frac{\theta_2}{2} \leq \alpha_1 \\ \alpha_1 & \text{if } \frac{\theta_2}{2} > \alpha_1. \end{cases}$$

Let $\alpha_1 = \alpha_2 = \frac{1}{2}$. Then we get

$$b_1(\theta_1) = \frac{\theta_1}{2} \; \forall \, \theta_1 \in \Theta_1 = [0, 1]$$

$$b_2(\theta_2) = \frac{\theta_2}{2} \; \forall \, \theta_2 \in \Theta_2 = [0, 1].$$

If $b_2(\theta_2) = \frac{\theta_2}{2}$, the best response of buyer 1 is $b_1(\theta_1) = \frac{\theta_1}{2}$ since $\alpha_1 = \frac{1}{2}$. Similarly, if $b_1(\theta_1) = \frac{\theta_1}{2}$, the best response of buyer 2 is $b_2(\theta_2) = \frac{\theta_2}{2}$ since $\alpha_2 = \frac{1}{2}$. This implies that the profile $\left(\frac{\theta_1}{2}, \frac{\theta_2}{2} \right) \; \forall \theta_1 \in \Theta_1, \forall \theta_2 \in \Theta_2$ is a Bayesian Nash equilibrium of the Bayesian game underlying the first price auction (under the setting that we have considered). $\qquad \square$

13.5 Dominant Strategy Equilibria

Dominant strategy equilibria of Bayesian games can again be defined using the Selten game representation. We only define the notion of *very weakly dominant strategy equilibrium* and leave the definitions of *weakly dominant strategy equilibrium* and *strongly dominant strategy equilibrium* to the reader.

Definition 13.4 (Very Weakly Dominant Strategy Equilibrium). *Given a Bayesian game*

$$\Gamma = \langle N, (\Theta_i), (S_i), (p_i), (u_i) \rangle$$

a profile of strategies $(s_1^*, \ldots, s_n^*)$ *is called a very weakly dominant strategy equilibrium if* $\forall i \in N; \; \forall s_i : \Theta_i \to S_i; \; \forall s_{-i} : \Theta_{-i} \to S_{-i}; \; \forall \theta_i \in \Theta_i$

$$u_i((s_i^*, s_{-i}) \mid \theta_i) \geq u_i((s_i, s_{-i}) \mid \theta_i)$$

That is, $\forall i \in N; \; \forall a_i \in S_i; \; \forall \theta_i \in \Theta_i; \; \forall s_{-i} : \Theta_{-i} \to S_{-i};$,

$$\mathbb{E}_{\theta_{-i}} \left[u_i(\theta_i, \theta_{-i}, s_i^*(\theta_i), s_{-i}(\theta_{-i})) \right] \geq \mathbb{E}_{\theta_{-i}} \left[u_i(\theta_i, \theta_{-i}, a_i, s_{-i}(\theta_{-i})) \right]$$

A close examination of the above definition (note the presence of s_{-i} on the left hand side as well as the right hand side) shows that the notion of dominant strategy equilibrium is independent of the belief functions, and this is what makes it a very powerful notion and a very strong property. The notion of dominant strategy equilibrium is used extensively in mechanism design theory to define *dominant strategy implementation*. Often very weakly dominant strategy equilibrium is used in these settings.

Example 13.6 (Second Price Auction). We have shown above that the first price sealed bid auction has a Bayesian Nash equilibrium. Now we consider the second price sealed bid auction with two bidders and show that it has a weakly dominant strategy equilibrium. Let us say buyer 2 announces his bid as b_2. There are two cases.

(1) $\theta_1 \geq b_2$
(2) $\theta_1 < b_2$

Case 1: $\theta_1 \geq b_2$

Let b_1 be the bid of buyer 1. Here there are two cases.

- If $b_1 \geq b_2$, then the payoff for buyer 1 is $\theta_1 - b_2 \geq 0$.
- If $b_1 < b_2$, then the payoff for buyer 1 is 0.
- Thus in this case, the maximum payoff possible is $\theta_1 - b_2 \geq 0$.

If $b_1 = \theta_1$ (that is, buyer 1 announces his true valuation), then payoff for buyer 1 is $\theta_1 - b_2$, which happens to be the maximum possible payoff as shown above. Thus announcing θ_1 is a best response to buyer 1 whatever the announcement of buyer 2.

Case 2: $\theta_1 < b_2$

Here again there are two cases: $b_1 \geq b_2$ and $b_1 < b_2$.

- If $b_1 \geq b_2$, then the payoff for buyer 1 is $\theta_1 - b_2$, which is negative.
- If $b_1 < b_2$, then buyer 1 does not win and payoff for him is zero.
- Thus in this case, the maximum payoff possible is 0.

If $b_1 = \theta_1$, payoff for buyer 1 is 0. By announcing $b_1 = \theta_1$, his true valuation, buyer 1 gets zero payoff, which in this case is a best response.

We can now make the following observations about this example.

- Bidding his true valuation is optimal for buyer 1 regardless of the bid of buyer 2.
- Similarly bidding his true valuation is optimal for buyer 2 whatever the bid of buyer 1.
- This means truth revelation is a very weakly dominant strategy for each player, and $(s_1^*(\theta_1) = \theta_1, s_2^*(\theta_2) = \theta_2)$ is a very weakly dominant strategy equilibrium.

We leave it to the reader to show that the equilibrium is in fact a weakly dominant strategy equilibrium as well. $\qquad \square$

13.6 Summary and References

In this chapter, we have introduced strategic form games with incomplete information. We summarize the main points of this chapter below.

- In a game with incomplete information, every player, in addition to strategies (actions), also has private information which is called the type of the player. Each player has a type set. Also, each player has a probabilistic guess about the types of the rest of the players. The utilities depend not only on the actions chosen by the players but also the types of the players. Bayesian games provide a common way of representing strategic form games with incomplete information.
- Harsanyi and Selten have developed a theory of Bayesian games. The central idea of their theory is to transform a Bayesian game into a strategic form game with complete information using the so called type agent representation. The resulting strategic form games with complete information are called Selten games.
- A strategy of a player in a Bayesian game is a mapping from the player's type set to his action set. Using these mappings, different notions of equilibrium can be defined. Bayesian Nash equilibrium is a natural extension of pure strategy Nash equilibrium to the case of Bayesian games.
- We have illustrated the computation of Bayesian Nash equilibrium and dominant strategy equilibria using the familiar examples of first price auction and second price auction, respectively.

The material discussed in this chapter is mainly drawn from the the book by Myerson [1]. John Harsanyi wrote a series of three classic papers introducing, formalizing, and elaborating upon Bayesian games. These papers [2, 3, 4] appeared in 1967 and 1968.

References

[1] Roger B. Myerson. *Game Theory: Analysis of Conflict*. Harvard University Press, Cambridge, Massachusetts, USA, 1997.
[2] John C. Harsanyi. "Games with incomplete information played by Bayesian players. Part I: The basic model". In: *Management Science* **14** (1967), pp. 159–182.
[3] John C. Harsanyi. "Games with incomplete information played by Bayesian players. Part II: Bayesian equilibrium points". In: *Management Science* **14** (1968), pp. 320–334.
[4] John C. Harsanyi. "Games with incomplete information played by Bayesian players. Part III: The basic probability distribution of the game". In: *Management Science* **14** (1968), pp. 486–502.

13.7 Exercises

(1) Write down the definitions of weakly dominant strategy equilibrium and strongly dominant strategy equilibrium for Bayesian games.
(2) Consider the example of first price sealed bid auction with two buyers which we discussed in this chapter. What is the common prior with respect to which the beliefs of the two players are consistent?
(3) We have shown for the second price auction that bidding true valuations is a

very weakly dominant strategy equilibrium. Show that this equilibrium is weakly dominant as well. Also, show that this equilibrium is not strongly dominant.

(4) Consider two agents 1 and 2 where agent 1 is the seller of an indivisible item and agent 2 is a prospective buyer of the item. The type θ_1 of agent 1 (seller) can be interpreted as the willingness to sell of the agent (minimum price at which agent 1 is willing to sell). The type θ_2 of agent 2 (buyer) has the natural interpretation of willingness to pay (maximum price the buyer is willing to pay). Assume that $\Theta_1 = \Theta_2 = [0,1]$ and that each agent thinks that the type of the other agent is uniformly distributed over the real interval $[0,1]$. Define the following protocol. The seller and the buyer are asked to submit their bids b_1 and b_2 respectively. Trade happens if $b_1 \leq b_2$ and trade does not happen otherwise. If trade happens, the buyer gets the item and pays the seller an amount $\frac{(b_1+b_2)}{2}$. Compute a Bayesian Nash equilibrium of the Bayesian game here.

(5) **Programming Assignment**. Given a finite Bayesian game, write a program to transform it into a Selten game and compute all Bayesian Nash equilibria (if they exist) and all dominant strategy equilibria (if they exist).

PART 2

MECHANISM DESIGN

Mechanism design is the art of designing games so that they exhibit desirable equilibrium behavior. In this part (Chapters 14-24), we study fundamental principles and key issues in mechanism design.

- In Chapter 14, we introduce mechanisms with simple, illustrative examples and discuss the key notions of *social choice functions*, *direct mechanisms*, and *indirect mechanisms*. In Chapter 15, we bring out the principles underlying implementation of social choice functions by mechanisms. In Chapter 16, we define the important notion of incentive compatibility and bring out the difference between dominant strategy incentive compatibility (DSIC) and Bayesian incentive compatibility (BIC). We prove the *revelation theorem*, an important fundamental result. Chapter 17 is devoted to two key impossibility results: the Gibbard-Satterwaite theorem and the Arrow theorem.
- Chapters 18-22 are devoted to different classes of quasilinear mechanisms which are either DSIC or BIC. In Chapter 18, we study VCG (Vickrey-Clarke-Groves) mechanisms, by far the most extensively investigated class of mechanisms. Chapter 19 contains an exploration of mechanism design space in quasilinear environment, including Bayesian mechanisms. In Chapter 20, we discuss auctions which are a popular example of mechanisms. In Chapter 21, we study optimal mechanisms, in particular the Myerson auction. In Chapter 22, we study the sponsored search auction problem in detail to illustrate a compelling application of mechanism design.
- In Chapter 23, we discuss *implementation in Nash equilibrium* which assumes a complete information setting. Finally, Chapter 24 provides a brief description of important advanced topics in mechanism design.

Chapter 14

Introduction to Mechanism Design

Mechanism design can be viewed as the *reverse engineering* of games or equivalently as the *art of designing the rules of a game to achieve a specific desired outcome*. The main focus of mechanism design is to create institutions or protocols that satisfy certain desired objectives, assuming that the individual agents, interacting through the institution, will act strategically and may hold private information that is relevant to the decision at hand. We commence our discussion of mechanism design with this chapter. We introduce mechanisms through simple examples and trace the evolution of mechanism design theory from the 1960s. Mechanisms induce a game among strategic agents in order to realize a system-wide objective or social choice function, in an equilibrium of the game. Mechanisms could be direct or indirect. In this chapter, we define the key notions of *social choice function*, *direct mechanism*, and *indirect mechanism*. We provide several illustrative examples of social choice functions.

14.1 Mechanism Design: Common Examples and History

Mechanism design is concerned with settings where a policy maker (or social planner) faces the problem of aggregating the *announced preferences* of multiple agents into a collective (or social), system-wide decision when the *actual preferences* of the agents are not publicly known. Thus mechanism design requires the designer to solve a *decision or optimization problem with incomplete information or incomplete specification*. The essential technique that mechanism design uses is to induce a game among the agents in such a way that in an equilibrium of the induced game, the desired system-wide solution is implemented. Informally, a mechanism makes the players do what the social planner would like them to do.

Mechanisms: Two Common Examples

Mechanisms have been used and practiced from times immemorial. For example, auctions, which provide a popular instance of mechanisms, have been in vogue for several centuries.

Cake Cutting Problem

The following popular stories capture the idea behind mechanisms quite strikingly (see Figure 14.1). The first story is that of a mother with two kids, who has to design a mechanism to make her kids share a cake equally. The mother is the social planner in this case. If the mother slices the cake into two equal pieces and distributes one piece to each of the kids, the solution is not necessarily acceptable to the kids because each kid will be left with the perception that he/she got the smaller of the two pieces. On the other hand, consider the following mechanism: (1) One of the kids would slice the cake into two pieces and (2) the other kid gets the chance to pick up any of the pieces, leaving the remaining piece to the kid who sliced the cake into two pieces. Child 1, who cuts the cake will slice it exactly into two equal halves (in *his* eyes), as any other division will leave him with the smaller piece (since child 2 will pick the larger of the two slices). Child 2 is happy because she gets to choose and also chooses what in *her* eyes is the larger of the two slices. This mechanism implements the desirable outcome of the kids sharing the cake equally and further each kid has every reason to be happy about this mechanism.

Fig. 14.1: Mechanism design for cake cutting

Baby's Mother Problem

The second story is from ancient wisdom. This is attributed to several wise people, notably King Solomon. In India, it is attributed independently to (a) Birbal who was an adviser to King Akbar in the late 1500s and to (b) Tenali Rama, who was a popular poet and adviser in the court of King Sri Krishna Devaraya of the Vijayanagara dynasty in the early 1500s. In this fable, two women come to the king with a baby, each claiming to be the baby's mother, seeking justice (see Figure 14.2). The clueless king turns to his adviser to solve the problem. The adviser suggests the following mechanism: slice the baby into two equal pieces and give one piece each to the two mothers. Upon which, one of the women (the real mother) immediately pleads with the king not to slice the baby. The adviser and the king, after watching the reactions and body languages of the two mothers immediately ordered that the baby be handed over to the real mother. This is an example of a truth elicitation mechanism.

Fig. 14.2: Mechanism design for truth elicitation

Mechanisms such as above are ubiquitous in everyday life. We implicitly or explicitly use mechanisms in many activities in day-to-day life, be it family related, profession related, or society related. The emergence of game theory during the 1940s and 1950s helped develop a formal theory of mechanism design starting from the 1960s.

Mechanism Design: A Brief History

Leonid Hurwicz (Nobel laureate in Economic Sciences in 2007) first introduced the notion of mechanisms with his work in 1960 [1]. He defined a mechanism as a communication system in which participants send messages to each other and perhaps to a *message center* and a pre-specified rule assigns an outcome (such as allocation of goods and payments to be made) for every collection of received messages. William Vickrey (Nobel laureate in Economic Sciences in 1996) wrote a classic paper in 1961 [2] which introduced the celebrated Vickrey auction (second price auction). To this day, the Vickrey auction continues to enjoy a special place in the annals of mechanism design and can be described as one of the earliest landmarks in mechanism design. John Harsanyi (Nobel laureate in Economic Sciences in 1994 jointly with John Nash and Reinhard Selten) developed the theory of games with incomplete information, in particular Bayesian games, through a series of three seminal papers in 1967-68 [3, 4, 5]. Harsanyi's work later proved to be of foundational value to mechanism design. Hurwicz [6] introduced the key notion of incentive compatibility in 1972. This notion allowed mechanism design to incorporate the incentives of rational players and opened up mechanism design. Edward Clarke [7] and Theodore Groves [8] came up with a generalization of Vickrey mechanisms and helped define a broad class of so called dominant strategy incentive compatible mechanisms in the quasi-linear environment.

Leonid Hurwicz, Eric Maskin, and Roger Myerson were jointly awarded the Nobel prize in Economic Sciences in 2007 for having laid the foundations of mechanism design theory. Hurwicz, born in 1917, is the oldest winner of the Nobel prize. It was Hurwicz who first introduced the notion of mechanisms with his work in 1960 [1]. He defined a mechanism as a communication system in which participants send messages to each other and perhaps to a *message center* and a pre-specified rule assigns an outcome (such as allocation of goods and payments to be made) for every collection of received messages.

Hurwicz introduced the key notion of incentive compatibility in 1972 [6]. This notion allowed mechanism design to incorporate the incentives of rational players and opened up the area of mechanism design. The notion of incentive compatibility plays a central role in the revelation theorem, which is a fundamental result in mechanism design theory. Hurwicz is also credited with many important possibility and impossibility results in mechanism design. For example, he showed that, in a standard exchange economy, no incentive compatible mechanism that satisfies individual rationality can produce Pareto optimal outcomes. Hurwicz's work in game theory and mechanism design demonstrated, beyond doubt, the value of using analytical methods in modeling economic institutions.

Hurwicz was, until his demise on June 24, 2008, Regents Professor Emeritus in the Department of Economics at the University of Minnesota. He taught there in the areas of welfare economics, public economics, mechanisms and institutions, and mathematical economics.

 **Eric Maskin** is credited with many pioneering contributions to mechanism design. One of his most creative contributions was his work on implementation theory, which addresses the following problem: Given a social goal, can we characterize when we can design a mechanism whose equilibrium outcomes coincide with the outcomes that are desirable according to that goal? Maskin [9] gave a general solution to this problem. He brilliantly showed that if social goals are to be implementable, then they must satisfy a certain kind of *monotonicity* (Maskin Monotonicity). He also showed that monotonicity guarantees implementation under certain mild conditions (at least three players and no veto power). He has also made major contributions to dynamic games. One of his early contributions was to formalize the Revelation Theorem to the setting of Bayesian incentive compatible mechanisms.

Maskin was born on December 12, 1950, in New York City. He earned an A.B. in Mathematics and a Ph.D. in Applied Mathematics from Harvard University in 1976. He taught at the Massachusetts Institute of Technology during 1977–1984 and at Harvard University during 1985–2000. During 2000-2011, he was the Albert O. Hirschman Professor of Social Science at the Institute for Advanced Study in Princeton, NJ, USA. Since 2011, he is Adams University Professor in the Department of Economics at the Harvard University, Cambridge, Massachusetts, USA.

 **Roger Bruce Myerson** has contributed to several areas in game theory and mechanism design, and his contributions have left a deep impact in the area. He was instrumental in conceptualizing and proving the revelation theorem in mechanism design for Bayesian implementations in its greatest generality. His work on optimal auctions in 1981 is a landmark result and has led to an extensive body of further work in the area of optimal auctions. He has also made major contributions in bargaining with incomplete information and cooperative games with incomplete information. His textbook *Game Theory: Analysis of Conflict* is a scholarly and comprehensive reference text that embodies all important results in game theory in a rigorous, yet insightful way. Myerson has also worked on economic analysis of political institutions and written several influential papers in this area including recently on democratization and the Iraq war.

Myerson was born on March 29, 1951. He received his A.B., S.M., and Ph.D., all in Applied Mathematics from Harvard University. He completed his Ph.D. in 1976, working with the legendary Kenneth Arrow. He was a Professor of Economics at the Kellogg School of Management in Northwestern University during 1976-2001. Since 2001, he has been the Glen A. Lloyd Distinguished Service Professor of Economics at the University of Chicago.

There were two major advances in mechanism design in the 1970s. The first was the *revelation principle* which essentially showed that direct mechanisms are the same as indirect mechanisms. This meant that mechanism theorists needed to worry only about direct mechanisms, leaving the development of real-world mechanisms (which are mostly indirect mechanisms) to mechanism designers and practitioners. Alan Gibbard [10] formulated the revelation principle for dominant strategy incentive compatible mechanisms. This was later extended to Bayesian incentive compatible mechanisms through several independent efforts [11] – Eric Maskin and Roger Myerson (both Nobel laureates in Economic Sciences in 2007) had a leading role to play in this. In fact, Myerson developed the revelation principle in its greatest generality [11]. The second major advance in mechanism design in the 1970s was on *implementation theory* which addresses the following problem: can a mechanism be designed so that all its equilibria are optimal? Maskin [9] gave the first general solution to this problem.

Mechanism design has made phenomenal advances during 1980s, 1990s, 2000s, and during the past few years. It has found widespread applicability in a variety of disciplines. These include: design of auctions, markets, and trading institutions [11, 12, 13, 14], regulation and auditing [11], social choice theory [11], computer science [15], resource allocation to strategic agents, electronic commerce and web-based applications [16], etc. This list is by no means exhaustive.

14.2   Mechanism Design Environment

The following provides a general setting for formulating, analyzing, and solving mechanism design problems.

- There are n agents, $1, 2, \ldots, n$, with $N = \{1, 2, \ldots, n\}$. The agents are rational and intelligent, and interact strategically among themselves towards making a collective decision.
- X is a set of *alternatives* or *outcomes*. The agents are required to make a collective choice from the set X.
- Prior to making the collective choice, each agent privately observes his preferences over the alternatives in X. This is modeled by supposing that agent i privately observes a parameter or signal θ_i that determines his preferences. The value of θ_i is known to agent i and may not be known to the other agents. θ_i is called a *private value* or *type* of agent i.
- We denote by Θ_i the set of private values of agent i, $i = 1, 2, \ldots, n$. The set of all type profiles is given by $\Theta = \Theta_1 \times \ldots \times \Theta_n$. A typical type profile is represented as $\theta = (\theta_1, \ldots, \theta_n)$.
- We assume that there is a common prior $\mathbb{P} \in \Delta(\Theta)$. To ensure consistency of beliefs, individual belief functions $p_i : \Theta_i \to \Delta(\Theta_{-i})$ (where Θ_{-i} is the set of type profiles of agents other than i) can all be derived from the common prior.

- Individual agents have preferences over outcomes that are represented by a utility function $u_i : X \times \Theta_i \to \mathbb{R}$. Given $x \in X$ and $\theta_i \in \Theta_i$, the value $u_i(x, \theta_i)$ denotes the payoff that agent i, having type $\theta_i \in \Theta_i$, receives from an outcome $x \in X$. In the more general case, u_i depends not only on the outcome and the type of player i, but could depend on the types of the other players as well, and so $u_i : X \times \Theta \to \mathbb{R}$. We restrict our attention to the former case in this book since most situations discussed in this book fall into the former category.

- The set of outcomes X, the set of players N, the type sets Θ_i $(i = 1, \ldots, n)$, the common prior distribution $\mathbb{P} \in \Delta(\Theta)$, and the payoff functions u_i $(i = 1, \ldots, n)$ are assumed to be *common knowledge* among all the players. The specific type θ_i observed by agent i is private information of agent i.

Social Choice Functions

Since the preferences of the agents depend on the realization of their types $\theta = (\theta_1, \ldots, \theta_n)$, it is logical and natural to make the collective decision depend on θ. This leads to the definition of a social choice function.

Definition 14.1 (Social Choice Function). *Suppose $N = \{1, 2, \ldots, n\}$ is a set of agents with the type sets $\Theta_1, \Theta_2, \ldots, \Theta_n$ respectively. Given a set of outcomes X, a social choice function is a mapping $f : \Theta_1 \times \ldots \times \Theta_n \to X$ that assigns to each possible type profile $(\theta_1, \theta_2, \ldots, \theta_n)$, an outcome from the set X. The outcome corresponding to a type profile is called a social choice or collective choice for that type profile.*

We will be presenting several examples of social choice functions subsequently in this chapter. We provide an immediate example here in an informal way.

Example 14.1 (Shortest Path Problem with Incomplete Information).
Consider a connected directed graph with a source vertex and a destination vertex identified. Let the graph have n edges, each owned by a rational and intelligent agent. Let the set of agents be denoted by $N = \{1, 2, \ldots, n\}$. Assume that the cost of the edge is private information of the agent owning the edge and let θ_i be this private information for agent i $(i = 1, 2, \ldots, n)$. Let us say that a social planner is interested in finding a shortest path from the source vertex to the destination vertex. The social choice function here maps each type profile $(\theta_1, \ldots, \theta_n)$ (which is in fact a profile of edge costs) to a shortest path corresponding to those edge costs. The social planner knows everything about the graph except the costs of the edges. So, the social planner first needs to extract this information from each agent and then find a shortest path from the source vertex to the destination vertex. Thus there are two problems facing the social planner, which are described below. $\qquad\square$

Preference Elicitation Problem

Consider a social choice function $f : \Theta_1 \times \ldots \times \Theta_n \to X$. The types $\theta_1, \ldots, \theta_n$ of the individual agents are private information of the agents. Hence for the social choice $f(\theta_1, \ldots, \theta_n)$ to be chosen when the individual types are $\theta_1, \ldots, \theta_n$, each agent must disclose its true type to the social planner. However, given a social choice function f, a given agent may not find it in its best interest to reveal this information truthfully. This is called the *preference elicitation* problem or the *information revelation* problem.

Preference Aggregation Problem

Once all the agents report their types, the profile of reported types has to be transformed to an outcome, based on the social choice function. Let θ_i be the true type and $\hat{\theta}_i$ the reported type of agent i $(i = 1, \ldots, n)$. The process of computing $f(\hat{\theta}_1, \ldots, \hat{\theta}_n)$ is called the *preference aggregation* problem.

Example 14.2. In the current example of shortest path problem with incomplete information, the preference elicitation problem is to elicit the true values of the costs of the edges from the respective edge owners. The preference aggregation problem is to compute a shortest path from the source vertex to the destination vertex, given the structure of the graph and the (reported) costs of the edges. The preference aggregation problem is often an optimization problem like for instance in the current example. □

Figure 14.3 provides a pictorial representation of all the elements in a mechanism design environment.

14.3   Direct and Indirect Mechanisms

One can view mechanism design as the process of solving an incompletely specified optimization problem where the specification is first elicited and then the underlying optimization problem or decision problem is solved. Specification elicitation is basically the preference elicitation or type elicitation problem. To elicit the type information from the agents in a truthful way, there are broadly two kinds of approaches, which are aptly called *direct mechanisms* and *indirect mechanisms*. We define these below. In these definitions, we assume that the set of agents N, the set of outcomes X, the sets of types $\Theta_1, \ldots, \Theta_n$, the common prior $\mathbb{P} \in \Delta(\Theta)$, and the utility functions $u_i : X \times \Theta_i \to \mathbb{R}$ are given and are common knowledge.

Definition 14.2 (Direct Mechanism). *Suppose $f : \Theta_1 \times \ldots \times \Theta_n \to X$ is a social choice function. A direct mechanism (also called a direct revelation mechanism) corresponding to f consists of the tuple $(\Theta_1, \Theta_2, \ldots, \Theta_n, f(.))$.*

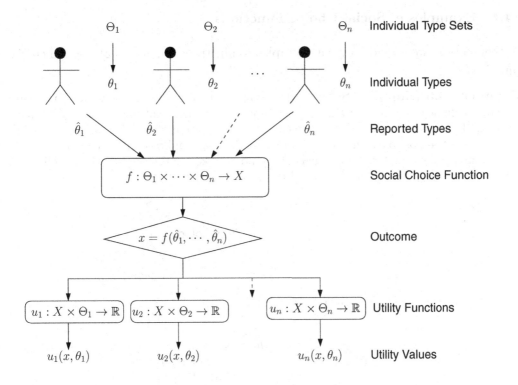

Fig. 14.3: Mechanism design environment

The idea of a direct mechanism is to *directly* seek the type information from the agents by asking them to reveal their true types.

Definition 14.3 (Indirect Mechanism). *An indirect mechanism (also called an indirect revelation mechanism) consists of a tuple* $(S_1, S_2, \ldots, S_n, g(.))$ *where* S_i *is a set of possible actions for agent* i *(i = 1, 2, \ldots, n) and* $g : S_1 \times S_2 \times \ldots \times S_n \to X$ *is a function that maps each action profile to an outcome.*

The idea of an indirect mechanism is to provide a choice of actions to each agent and specify an outcome for each action profile. This induces a game among the players and the strategies played by the agents in an equilibrium of this game will indirectly reflect their original types. The idea behind and the difference between direct mechanisms and indirect mechanisms will become clear in the next chapter when we discuss implementation of social choice functions by mechanisms.

Note that a direct mechanism corresponding to $f : \Theta_1 \times \ldots \times \Theta_n \to X$ is a special case of an indirect mechanism $(S_1, S_2, \ldots, S_n, g(.))$ with $S_i = \Theta_i \; \forall i \in N$ and $g = f$.

14.4 Examples of Social Choice Functions

In this section, we provide several examples to illustrate the notion of a social choice function.

Example 14.3 (Supplier Selection). Suppose there is a buyer who wishes to procure a certain volume of an item that is produced by two suppliers, call them 1 and 2. We have $N = \{1, 2\}$. Supplier 1 is known to use technology a_1 to produce these items, while supplier 2 uses one of two possible technologies, (1) a superior, high end technology a_2 and (2) a low end technology b_2. The technology elements could be taken as the types of the suppliers, so we have $\Theta_1 = \{a_1\}$; $\Theta_2 = \{a_2, b_2\}$. See Figure 14.4.

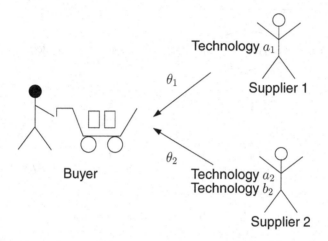

Fig. 14.4: A procurement scenario with two suppliers

Let us define three outcomes (alternatives) x, y, z for this situation. The alternative x means that the entire volume required is sourced from supplier 1 while the alternative z means that the entire volume required is sourced from supplier 2. The alternative y indicates that 50% of the requirement is sourced from supplier 1 and the rest is sourced from supplier 2.

Assume that the buyer already has a long-standing relationship with supplier 1, this supplier is the preferred one. However, because of the superiority of technology a_2 over a_1 and b_2, the buyer may like to source at least a certain fraction of requirement from supplier 2 if supplier 2 uses technology a_2. The payoff functions below reflect the above facts:

$$u_1(x, a_1) = 100; \ u_1(y, a_1) = 50; \ u_1(z, a_1) = 0$$

$$u_2(x, a_2) = 0; \ u_2(y, a_2) = 50; \ u_2(z, a_2) = 100$$

$$u_2(x, b_2) = 0; \ u_2(y, b_2) = 50; \ u_2(z, b_2) = 25.$$

Note that $\Theta = \{(a_1, a_2), (a_1, b_2)\}$. Consider the social choice function $f(a_1, a_2) = y$ and $f(a_1, b_2) = x$. This means that when supplier 2 uses technology a_2, the buyer would like to procure from both the suppliers, whereas if supplier 2 uses technology b_2, the buyer would rather source the entire requirement from supplier 1. Note that the technology used by supplier 2 is private information and is not known to the buyer.

Likewise, there are eight other social choice functions that one can define here. These are included below.

$$f(a_1, a_2) = x; \quad f(a_1, b_2) = x$$
$$f(a_1, a_2) = x; \quad f(a_1, b_2) = y$$
$$f(a_1, a_2) = x; \quad f(a_1, b_2) = z$$
$$f(a_1, a_2) = y; \quad f(a_1, b_2) = y$$
$$f(a_1, a_2) = y; \quad f(a_1, b_2) = z$$
$$f(a_1, a_2) = z; \quad f(a_1, b_2) = x$$
$$f(a_1, a_2) = z; \quad f(a_1, b_2) = y$$
$$f(a_1, a_2) = z; \quad f(a_1, b_2) = z.$$

It would be interesting to look into the practical meaning and implications of these social choice functions. □

Example 14.4 (Selling an Indivisible Object). A typical selling situation involves a seller, a pool of buyers, and objects to be sold. We consider a simple abstraction of the problem by considering a selling agent (call the agent 0) and two buying agents (call them 1 and 2), so we have $N = \{0, 1, 2\}$. See Figure 14.5.

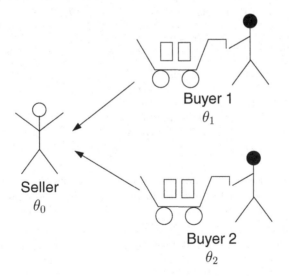

Fig. 14.5: A selling scenario with two buying agents

The seller wishes to sell an indivisible object to one of the buyers in return for a monetary payment. An outcome here can be represented by $x = (y_0, y_1, y_2, t_0, t_1, t_2)$ where y_0, y_1, y_2 indicate the allocations and t_0, t_1, t_2 indicate the payments. For $i = 0, 1, 2$, y_i takes value 1 if the object is allocated to player i and takes the value 0 otherwise; t_i is the payment received by agent i. The set X of all feasible outcomes is given by

$$X = \{(y_0, y_1, y_2, t_0, t_1, t_2) : y_i \in \{0, 1\}, \sum_{i=0}^{2} y_i = 1, t_i \in \mathbb{R}, \ i \in N\}.$$

For $x = (y_0, y_1, y_2, t_0, t_1, t_2)$, we can define the utilities for buyers $1, 2$ in a natural way as follows:

$$u_i(x, \theta_i) = u_i((y_0, y_1, y_2, t_0, t_1, t_2), \theta_i) = y_i \theta_i + t_i \ ; \quad i = 1, 2$$

where $\theta_i \in \mathbb{R}_+$ can be viewed as agent i's valuation of the object. Such utility functions are said to be of *quasi-linear* form (because it is linear in some of the variables and possibly non-linear in the other variables). We will be studying such utility forms quite extensively from Chapter 18 onwards. We make the following assumptions regarding valuations.

- The seller has a *known* value θ_0 for the object. That is, $\Theta_0 = \{\theta_0\}$.
- Let $\Theta_i \subseteq \mathbb{R}_+$ be the set of all possible valuations of buyer i ($i = 1, 2$) for the object. The type sets are common knowledge. The exact type of a buyer before playing the game is private information of the buyer. The type of a buyer is to be viewed as the *willingness to pay* (maximum price above which the buyer is not interested in buying the item).

Consider the following social choice function.

- The selling agent allocates the object to the buyer with the highest willingness to buy. If both the buyers have the same type, the seller will allocate the object to buyer 1.
- The allocated buyer, say buyer i, pays an amount equal to θ_i to the selling agent.

The above social choice function $f(\theta) = (y_0(\theta), y_1(\theta), y_2(\theta), t_0(\theta), t_1(\theta), t_2(\theta))$, which we will call SCF1 from now on, can be precisely written, $\forall \theta = (\theta_0, \theta_1, \theta_2) \in \Theta_0 \times \Theta_1 \times \Theta_2$, as

$$\begin{aligned}
y_0(\theta) &= 0 \\
y_1(\theta) &= 1 \quad \text{if } \theta_1 \geq \theta_2 \\
&= 0 \quad \text{if } \theta_1 < \theta_2 \\
y_2(\theta) &= 1 \quad \text{if } \theta_1 < \theta_2 \\
&= 0 \quad \text{if } \theta_1 \geq \theta_2 \\
t_1(\theta) &= -y_1(\theta)\, \theta_1 \\
t_2(\theta) &= -y_2(\theta)\, \theta_2 \\
t_0(\theta) &= -(t_1(\theta) + t_2(\theta)).
\end{aligned}$$

Suppose we consider another social choice function, which has the same allocation rule as the one we have just studied but has a different payment rule. The winning buyer now pays the seller an amount equal to the second highest willingness to buy (as usual, the losing buyer does not pay anything to the seller). The new social choice function, which we will call SCF2, will be the following: For any $\theta = (\theta_0, \theta_1, \theta_2) \in \Theta_0 \times \Theta_1 \times \Theta_2$,

$$\begin{aligned}
y_0(\theta) &= 0 \\
y_1(\theta) &= 1 \quad \text{if } \theta_1 \geq \theta_2 \\
&= 0 \quad \text{if } \theta_1 < \theta_2 \\
y_2(\theta) &= 1 \quad \text{if } \theta_1 < \theta_2 \\
&= 0 \quad \text{if } \theta_1 \geq \theta_2 \\
t_1(\theta) &= -y_1(\theta)\, \theta_2 \\
t_2(\theta) &= -\, y_2(\theta)\, \theta_1 \\
t_0(\theta) &= -(t_1(\theta) + t_2(\theta)).
\end{aligned}$$

It is instructive to write down the above SCFs in the case of more than two buyers. □

We now define a complementary social choice function that describes the reverse of selling, namely buying. Our abstraction here consists of one buying agent and two selling agents.

Example 14.5 (Procurement of an Indivisible Object). We consider a buying agent (call the agent 0) and two selling agents (call them 1 and 2), so we have $N = \{0, 1, 2\}$. See Figure 14.6. An indivisible object is to be procured from one of the sellers in return for a monetary payment. An outcome here can be represented by $x = (y_0, y_1, y_2, t_0, t_1, t_2)$. The numbers y_0, y_1, y_2 indicate the allocations and t_0, t_1, t_2 indicate the payments. For $i = 1, 2$, y_i takes value 1 if the object is procured from seller i and takes the value 0 otherwise; y_0 takes the value 0 when the buyer receives the object and takes the value 1 if the buyer does not receive the object. t_i $(i = 0, 1, 2)$ is the payment received by agent i (or monetary transfer to agent i).

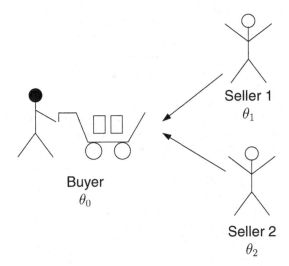

Fig. 14.6: A procurement scenario with two sellers

The set X of all feasible outcomes is given by

$$X = \{(y_0, y_1, y_2, t_0, t_1, t_2) : y_i \in \{0, 1\}, \sum_{i=0}^{2} y_i = 1, t_i \in \mathbb{R}, \ i = 0, 1, 2\}.$$

For $x = (y_0, y_1, y_2, t_0, t_1, t_2)$, the utilities of the selling agents $1, 2$ can be defined in a natural way to be of the form:

$$u_i(x, \theta_i) = u_i((y_0, y_1, y_2, t_0, t_1, t_2), \theta_i) = -y_i\theta_i + t_i \ ; \ \ i = 1, 2$$

where $\theta_i \in \mathbb{R}_+$ can be viewed as seller i's valuation or cost (also called willingness to sell) of the object. We make the following assumptions regarding valuations.

- The buyer has a *known* value θ_0 for the object. That is, $\Theta_0 = \{\theta_0\}$. This valuation does not depend on the choice of the seller from whom the item is purchased.

- Let $\Theta_i \subseteq \mathbb{R}_+$ be the set of all types of agent i $(i = 1,2)$. These sets are common knowledge. However, the exact value of θ_i before playing the game is private information of player i $(i = 1,2$. The type of a seller is to be viewed as the *willingness to sell* (minimum price below which the seller is not interested in selling the item).

Consider the following social choice function.

- The buyer buys the object from the seller with the lowest willingness to sell. If both the sellers have the same type, the buyer will buy the object from seller 1.
- The buyer pays to the allocated seller, say seller i, an amount equal to θ_i.

The above social choice function $f(\theta) = (y_0(\theta), y_1(\theta), y_2(\theta), t_0(\theta), t_1(\theta), t_2(\theta))$ can be precisely written $\forall \theta = (\theta_0, \theta_1, \theta_2) \in \Theta_0 \times \Theta_1 \times \Theta_2$ as

$$
\begin{aligned}
y_0(\theta) &= 0 \\
y_1(\theta) &= 1 \quad \text{if } \theta_1 \leq \theta_2 \\
&= 0 \quad \text{if } \theta_1 > \theta_2 \\
y_2(\theta) &= 1 \quad \text{if } \theta_1 > \theta_2 \\
&= 0 \quad \text{if } \theta_1 \leq \theta_2 \\
t_1(\theta) &= y_1(\theta)\,\theta_1 \\
t_2(\theta) &= y_2(\theta)\,\theta_2 \\
t_0(\theta) &= -(t_1(\theta) + t_2(\theta)).
\end{aligned}
$$

Suppose we consider another social choice function, which has the same allocation rule as the one we have just studied but has a different payment rule. The buyer now pays the winning seller a payment equal to the second lowest willingness to sell (as usual, the losing seller does not receive any payment). The new social choice function will be the following.

$$
\begin{aligned}
y_0(\theta) &= 0 \\
y_1(\theta) &= 1 \quad \text{if } \theta_1 \leq \theta_2 \\
&= 0 \quad \text{if } \theta_1 > \theta_2 \\
y_2(\theta) &= 1 \quad \text{if } \theta_1 > \theta_2 \\
&= 0 \quad \text{if } \theta_1 \leq \theta_2 \\
t_1(\theta) &= y_1(\theta)\,\theta_2 \\
t_2(\theta) &= y_2(\theta)\,\theta_1 \\
t_0(\theta) &= -(t_1(\theta) + t_2(\theta)).
\end{aligned}
$$

It is instructive to write down the above SCFs in the case of more than two sellers. $\qquad \square$

Example 14.6 (Bilateral Trade).

Consider two agents 1 and 2 where agent 1 is the seller of an indivisible object and agent 2 is a prospective buyer of the good. See Figure 14.7. An outcome here is of the form $x = (y_1, y_2, t_1, t_2)$ where $y_i = 1$ if agent i gets the object and t_i denotes the payment received by agent i $(i = 1,2)$. A natural set of outcomes here is

$$
X = \{(y_1, y_2, t_1, t_2) : \ y_1 + y_2 = 1; \ y_1, y_2 \in \{0, 1\}\}.
$$

The utility of the agent i $(i = 1,2)$ would be of the form

$$
u_i((y_1, y_2, t_1, t_2), \theta_i) = y_i \theta_i + t_i.
$$

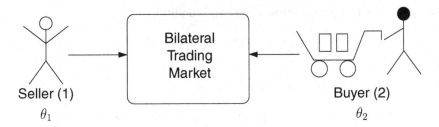

Fig. 14.7: A bilateral trade environment

The type θ_1 of agent 1 (seller) can be interpreted as the willingness to sell of the agent (minimum price at which agent 1 is willing to sell). The type θ_2 of agent 2 (buyer) has the natural interpretation of willingness to pay (maximum price the buyer is willing to pay). A social choice function here would be $f(\theta) = (y_1(\theta), y_2(\theta), t_1(\theta), t_2(\theta))$ defined as

$$
\begin{aligned}
y_1(\theta_1, \theta_2) &= 1 \quad \theta_1 > \theta_2 \\
&= 0 \quad \theta_1 \leq \theta_2 \\
y_2(\theta_1, \theta_2) &= 1 \quad \theta_1 \leq \theta_2 \\
&= 0 \quad \theta_1 > \theta_2 \\
t_1(\theta_1, \theta_2) &= \quad y_2(\theta_1, \theta_2) \left(\frac{\theta_1 + \theta_2}{2} \right) \\
t_2(\theta_1, \theta_2) &= -y_2(\theta_1, \theta_2) \left(\frac{\theta_1 + \theta_2}{2} \right).
\end{aligned}
$$

Note that the money the buyer pays (which is equal to the money the seller receives) in case trade happens is equal to half of $\theta_1 + \theta_2$. $\qquad \square$

Example 14.7 (Funding a Public Project). Consider a set of individuals $N = \{1, 2, \ldots, n\}$ who have a stake in a common infrastructure, for example, a bridge, community building, Internet infrastructure, etc. For example, the agents could be firms forming a business cluster and interested in creating a shared infrastructure. The cost of the project is to be shared by the agents themselves since there is no source of external funding. Let $k = 1$ indicate that the project is taken up, with $k = 0$ indicating that the project is dropped. Let $t_i \in \mathbb{R}$ denote the payment received by agent i (which means $-t_i$ is the payment made by agent i) for each $i \in N$. Let the cost of the project be C. Since the agents have to fund the project themselves,

$$
C \leq -\sum_{i \in N} t_i \quad \text{if } k = 1
$$

$$
0 \leq -\sum_{i \in N} t_i \quad \text{if } k = 0
$$

Combining the above two possibilities, we get the condition

$$\sum_{i \in N} t_i \le -kC \; ; \;\; k \in \{0, 1\}.$$

Thus, a natural set of outcomes for this problem is:

$$X = \{(k, t_1, \ldots, t_n) : k \in \{0, 1\}, \; t_i \in \mathbb{R} \; \forall i \in N, \; \sum_{i \in N} t_i \le -kC\}.$$

We assume the utility of agent i, when its type is θ_i corresponding to an outcome $(k, t_1, t_2, \ldots, t_n)$ to be given by

$$u_i((k, t_1, \ldots, t_n), \theta_i) = k\theta_i + t_i.$$

The type θ_i of agent i has the natural interpretation of being the willingness to pay of agent i (maximum amount that agent i is prepared to pay) towards the project. A social choice function in this context is $f(\theta) = (k(\theta), t_1(\theta), \ldots, t_n(\theta))$ given by

$$k(\theta) = \begin{cases} 1 \text{ if } \sum_{i \in N} \theta_i \ge C \\ 0 \text{ otherwise} \end{cases}$$

$$t_i(\theta) = -\left(\frac{k(\theta)C}{n}\right).$$

The way $k(\theta)$ is defined ensures that the project is taken up only if the combined willingness to pay of all the agents is at least the cost of the project. The definition of $t_i(\theta)$ above follows the egalitarian principle, namely that the agents share the cost of the project equally among themselves. □

All the examples above illustrate how a meaningful social choice choice function may be defined in a given setting.

14.5   Summary and References

In this chapter, we introduced concepts and building blocks of mechanism design with examples and definitions. In particular:

- We started with two common examples (cake cutting and baby's mother problems) and traced the history of developments in mechanism design.
- We introduced the building blocks of a mechanism design environment such as social choice functions, preference elicitation, preference aggregation, direct mechanisms, and indirect mechanisms.
- We next gave several examples to illustrate the notion of social choice functions: selecting suppliers; selling an indivisible object; buying an indivisible object; bilateral trade; and funding a public project.

The next chapter is devoted to explaining how social choice functions may be implemented by direct mechanisms and indirect mechanisms.

The examples discussed in this chapter are mainly based on the examples presented by Mas-Colell, Whinston, and Green [12] and the monograph by Narahari, Garg, Ramasuri, and Hastagiri [16]. The scientific background document available on the Nobel Prize website [11] provides an excellent introduction and overview.

References

[1] L. Hurwicz. "Optimality and informational efficiency in resource allocation processes". In: *Mathematical Methods in the Social Sciences*. Ed. by K.J. Arrow and S. Karlin. Stanford University Press, Palo Alto, California, USA, 1960.

[2] William Vickrey. "Counterspeculation, auctions, and competitive sealed tenders". In: *Journal of Finance* **16**(1) (1961), pp. 8–37.

[3] John C. Harsanyi. "Games with incomplete information played by Bayesian players. Part I: The basic model". In: *Management Science* **14** (1967), pp. 159–182.

[4] John C. Harsanyi. "Games with incomplete information played by Bayesian players. Part II: Bayesian equilibrium points". In: *Management Science* **14** (1968), pp. 320–334.

[5] John C. Harsanyi. "Games with incomplete information played by Bayesian players. Part III: The basic probability distribution of the game". In: *Management Science* **14** (1968), pp. 486–502.

[6] L. Hurwicz. "On informationally decentralized systems". In: *Decision and Organization*. Ed. by C.B. McGuire and R. Radner. North-Holland, Amsterdam, 1972.

[7] E. Clarke. "Multi-part pricing of public goods". In: *Public Choice* **11** (1971), pp. 17–23.

[8] T. Groves. "Incentives in teams". In: *Econometrica* **41** (1973), pp. 617–631.

[9] Eric Maskin. "Nash equilibrium and welfare optimality". In: *Review of Economic Studies* **66** (1999), pp. 23–38.

[10] A. Gibbard. "Manipulation of voting schemes". In: *Econometrica* **41** (1973), pp. 587–601.

[11] The Nobel Foundation. *The Sveriges Riksbank Prize in Economic Sciences in Memory of Alfred Nobel 2007: Scientific Background*. Tech. rep. The Nobel Foundation - Stockholm, Sweden, 2007.

[12] Andreu Mas-Colell, Michael D. Whinston, and Jerry R. Green. *Microeconomic Theory*. Oxford University Press, 1995.

[13] Paul Milgrom. *Putting Auction Theory to Work*. Cambridge University Press, Cambridge, UK, 2004.

[14] The Economic Sciences Prize Committee. *Stable matching: Theory, Evidence, and Practical Design - The Sveriges Riksbank Prize in Economic Sciences in Memory of Alfred Nobel 2012: Scientific Background*. Tech. rep. The Nobel Foundation, Stockholm, Sweden, 2012.

[15] Noam Nisan, Tim Roughgarden, Eva Tardos, and Vijay Vazirani (Editors). *Algorithmic Game Theory*. Cambridge University Press, 2007.

[16] Y. Narahari, Dinesh Garg, Ramasuri Narayanam, and Hastagiri Prakash. *Game Theoretic Problems in Network Economics and Mechanism Design Solutions*. Springer, London, 2009.

14.6 Exercises

(1) In the cake cutting problem, if there were three children rather than two, what would be some appropriate mechanisms for fair sharing of the cake?

(2) Write down the type sets, outcomes, and social choice function in the cake cutting problem.

(3) Write down the type sets, outcomes, and social choice function in the baby's mother problem.

(4) Write down the social choice functions SCF1 and SCF2 assuming one selling agent and n buying agents.

(5) Write down social choice functions analogous to SCF1 and SCF2 when we have a procurement situation with one buying agent and n selling agents.

Chapter 15

Implementation of Social Choice Functions by Mechanisms

In the last chapter, we introduced several key notions: social choice functions, direct mechanisms, and indirect mechanisms. In the current chapter, we explain the process by which a social choice function can be realized through a direct mechanism or an indirect mechanism through illustrative examples. The main example considered is that of a selling agent who wishes to allocate an object to one of two buying agents against a monetary payment. We first define three natural social choice functions SCF1, SCF2, and SCF3, and explore their implementability by direct mechanisms. Next we turn to indirect mechanisms for implementing these social choice functions (first price auction and second price auction) and bring out the idea behind indirect mechanisms. Our discussion of direct and indirect mechanisms leads to the key notions of *dominant strategy implementation* and *Bayesian Nash implementation* followed by the notions of *dominant strategy incentive compatibility* and *Bayesian incentive compatibility*.

15.1 Implementation by Direct Mechanisms

We start with the example on supplier selection from the previous chapter to motivate implementation by direct mechanisms.

Supplier Selection Problem

Example 15.1 (Supplier Selection). Recall Example 14.3 where $N = \{1, 2\}$; $X = \{x, y, z\}$; $\Theta_1 = \{a_1\}$; , $\Theta_2 = \{a_2, b_2\}$ and $\Theta = \{(a_1, a_2), (a_1, b_2)\}$. The payoff functions are reproduced here for ready reference:

$$u_1(x, a_1) = 100; \quad u_1(y, a_1) = 50; \quad u_1(z, a_1) = 0$$
$$u_2(x, a_2) = 0; \quad u_2(y, a_2) = 50; \quad u_2(z, a_2) = 100$$
$$u_2(x, b_2) = 0; \quad u_2(y, b_2) = 50; \quad u_2(z, b_2) = 25.$$

Suppose the social planner (in this case, the buyer) wishes to implement the social choice function f with $f(a_1, a_2) = y$ and $f(a_1, b_2) = x$. Announcing this as the social choice function, let us say the social planner asks the agents to reveal their types. Agent 1 has nothing to reveal since its type is common knowledge (as his type set is a singleton). We will now check whether agent 2 would be willing to truthfully reveal its type.

- If $\theta_2 = a_2$, then, because $f(a_1, a_2) = y$ and $f(a_1, b_2) = x$ and $u_2(y, a_2) > u_2(x, a_2)$, agent 2 is happy to reveal a_2 as its type.
- However if $\theta_2 = b_2$, then because $u_2(y, b_2) > u_2(x, b_2)$ and $f(a_1, b_2) = x$, agent 2 would wish to lie and claim that its type is a_2 and not b_2.

Thus though the social planner would like to implement an SCF $f(\cdot)$, the social planner would be unable to implement the above SCF since one of the agents (in this case agent 2) does not find it a best response to reveal the true type.

On the other hand, let us say the social planner wishes to implement the social choice function f given by $f(a_1, a_2) = z$ and $f(a_1, b_2) = y$. One can show in this case that the SCF can be implemented. Table 15.1 lists all the nine SCFs and their implementability. □

SCF		Implementable
$f(a_1, a_2)$	$f(a_1, b_2)$	
x	x	✓
x	y	✗
x	z	✗
y	x	✗
y	y	✓
y	z	✗
z	x	✗
z	y	✓
z	z	✓

Table 15.1: Social choice functions and their implementability

Selling an Indivisible Object

We now consider three social choice functions in the context of the problem of a selling agent (agent 0) seeking to allocate a single indivisible object to one of two buying agents (agents 1 and 2) against a monetary payment (See Figure 15.1). We have already defined two such social choice functions SCF1 and SCF2 in the previous chapter. We recall those functions and also define a third social choice function SCF3. We first consider SCF1. Note that $\Theta = \Theta_0 \times \Theta_1 \times \Theta_2$. The function $f(\theta) = (y_0(\theta), y_1(\theta), y_2(\theta), t_0(\theta), t_1(\theta), t_2(\theta))\ \forall \theta = (\theta_0, \theta_1, \theta_2) \in \Theta$ is defined as

$$y_0(\theta) = 0$$
$$y_1(\theta) = 1 \quad \text{if } \theta_1 \geq \theta_2$$
$$ = 0 \quad \text{if } \theta_1 < \theta_2$$
$$y_2(\theta) = 1 \quad \text{if } \theta_1 < \theta_2$$
$$ = 0 \quad \text{if } \theta_1 \geq \theta_2$$

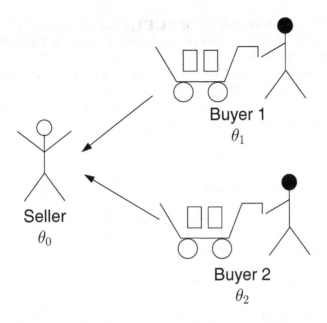

Fig. 15.1: A selling scenario with two buying agents

$$t_1(\theta) = -y_1(\theta)\, \theta_1$$
$$t_2(\theta) = -y_2(\theta)\, \theta_2$$
$$t_0(\theta) = -(t_1(\theta) + t_2(\theta)).$$

Note that the object is allocated to whichever buyer has higher valuation (with a tie resolved in favor of agent 1) and the winning buyer has to pay her valuation to the seller. We note that the social choice function is attractive to the seller since the seller will capture all of the benefits that are generated by the object. The social choice function SCF2 is different from SCF1 in that the payment to be made by the winning buyer is equal to the second highest valuation. So, only the following terms will be different in SCF2:

$$t_1(\theta) = -y_1(\theta)\, \theta_2$$
$$t_2(\theta) = -y_2(\theta)\, \theta_1$$

We define a third social choice function, SCF3, which has the same allocation rule as SCF1 and SCF2 but the payment by the winning buyer is equal to half her valuation. This is represented as:

$$t_1(\theta) = -y_1(\theta)\, \frac{\theta_1}{2}$$
$$t_2(\theta) = -y_2(\theta)\, \frac{\theta_2}{2}$$

We now investigate the implementability, through direct mechanisms, of SCF1, SCF2, and SCF3.

Example 15.2 (Implementability of SCF1). Let us assume that θ_1 and θ_2 are drawn independently from a uniform distribution over $[0,1]$. The following analysis show that SCF1 is not implementable.

Suppose buyer 2 announces his true value θ_2. Let us say the valuation of buyer 1 is θ_1 and he announces $\hat{\theta}_1$. If $\theta_2 \leq \hat{\theta}_1$, then buyer 1 is the winner and his utility will be $\theta_1 - \hat{\theta}_1$. If $\theta_2 > \hat{\theta}_1$, then buyer 2 is the winner and buyer 1's utility is zero. Since buyer 1 wishes to maximize his expected utility, he solves the problem

$$\max_{\hat{\theta}_1}(\theta_1 - \hat{\theta}_1)\, P\{\theta_2 \leq \hat{\theta}_1\}$$

Since θ_2 is uniformly distributed on $[0,1]$,

$$P\{\theta_2 \leq \hat{\theta}_1\} = \hat{\theta}_1$$

Thus buyer 1 tries to solve the problem:

$$\max_{\hat{\theta}_1}(\theta_1 - \hat{\theta}_1)\hat{\theta}_1$$

This problem has the solution

$$\hat{\theta}_1 = \frac{\theta_1}{2}$$

Thus if buyer 2 is truthful, the best response for buyer 1 is to announce $\frac{\theta_1}{2}$.

Similarly if buyer 1 always announces his true valuation θ_1, then the best response of buyer 2 is to announce $\frac{\theta_2}{2}$ when his true type is θ_2. Thus there is no incentive for the buyers to announce their true valuations. A social planner who wishes to realize the above social choice function finds that rational players will not reveal their true private values. Thus SCF1 cannot be implemented. □

Example 15.3 (Implementability of SCF2). We now show that the function SCF2 can be implemented. Suppose θ_i is the true valuation of buyer i $(i = 1, 2)$. Let us say buyer 2 announces his valuation as $\hat{\theta}_2$. There are two cases: (1) $\theta_1 \geq \hat{\theta}_2$ and (2) $\theta_1 < \hat{\theta}_2$.

Case 1: $\theta_1 \geq \hat{\theta}_2$

Let $\hat{\theta}_1$ be the announcement of buyer 1. Here there are two cases.

- If $\hat{\theta}_1 \geq \hat{\theta}_2$, then buyer 1 wins and his payoff is $\theta_1 - \hat{\theta}_2 \geq 0$.
- If $\hat{\theta}_1 < \hat{\theta}_2$, then buyer 1 does not win and his payoff is 0.
- Thus in this case, the maximum payoff possible is $\theta_1 - \hat{\theta}_2 \geq 0$.

If $\hat{\theta}_1 = \theta_1$ (that is, buyer 1 announces his true valuation), then payoff for buyer 1 equals $\theta_1 - \hat{\theta}_2$, which happens to be the maximum possible payoff as shown above. Thus announcing θ_1 is a best response for buyer 1 whenever $\theta_1 \geq \hat{\theta}_2$.

Case 2: $\theta_1 < \hat{\theta}_2$

Here again there are two cases: $\hat{\theta}_1 \geq \hat{\theta}_2$ and $\hat{\theta}_1 < \hat{\theta}_2$.

- If $\hat{\theta}_1 \geq \hat{\theta}_2$, then buyer 1 wins and his payoff is $\theta_1 - \hat{\theta}_2$ which is negative.

- If $\hat{\theta}_1 < \hat{\theta}_2$, then buyer 1 does not win and payoff for him is zero.
- Thus in this case, the maximum payoff possible is 0.

If $\hat{\theta}_1 = \theta_1$, payoff for buyer 1 is 0. By announcing $\hat{\theta}_1 = \theta_1$, his true valuation, buyer 1 gets zero payoff, which in this case is a best response.

We can now make the following observations about this example. Reporting his true valuation is optimal for buyer 1 regardless of what buyer 2 reports. Similarly announcing his true valuation is optimal for buyer 2 whatever the announcement of buyer 1 may be. More formally, reporting true type is a weakly dominant strategy for each player. Thus this social choice function can be implemented even though the valuations (types) are private information. □

Example 15.4 (Implementability of SCF3). Again, suppose θ_1 and θ_2 are the true valuations of buyers 1 and 2, respectively. Assume that buyer 2 reports his true type θ_2. Suppose buyer 1 has type θ_1, then his optimal report $\hat{\theta}_1$ is obtained by solving

$$\max_{\hat{\theta}_1} \left(\theta_1 - \frac{\hat{\theta}_1}{2} \right) P\{\theta_2 \le \hat{\theta}_1\}$$

This is the same as

$$\max_{\hat{\theta}_1} \left(\theta_1 - \frac{\hat{\theta}_1}{2} \right) \hat{\theta}_1$$

This yields $\hat{\theta}_1 = \theta_1$. Thus it is optimal in expectation for buyer 1 to reveal his true private value if buyer 2 reveals his true value. The same situation applies to buyer 2. Thus, a best response for each agent, given that the other agent truthfully reports his true type, is to report his true type. This implies that SCF3 can be implemented. □

Note. It is important to see the difference in the implementability of SCF2 and SCF3. In the case of SCF2, reporting truth is a best response whatever the other agent reports. In the case of SCF3, reporting truth is a best response in expectation over the type reports of the other agent if the other agent also reports truthfully. We say SCF2 is implementable in dominant strategy equilibrium and SCF3 is implementable in Bayesian Nash equilibrium. We wish to emphasize again that SCF1 is not implementable.

15.2 Implementation by Indirect Mechanisms

The examples above have shown us a possible way in which one can try to implement a social choice function. The protocol we followed for implementing the social choice functions was:

- Announce the social choice function $f : \Theta_1 \times \ldots \times \Theta_n \to X$.
- Ask each agent $i = 1, \ldots, n$ to announce his type θ_i.

- Given announcements $(\hat{\theta}_1, \ldots, \hat{\theta}_n)$ by the agents, choose the outcome $x = f(\hat{\theta}_1, \ldots, \hat{\theta}_n) \in X$.

It is natural to call such a method of trying to implement an SCF as a *direct revelation mechanism* or simply a *direct mechanism*. Another approach to implementing a social choice function is through an *indirect way*. Here the mechanism makes the agents interact through an institutional framework in which there are rules governing the actions the agents would be allowed to play and in which there is a way of transforming these actions into an outcome. The design of the mechanism is such that the actions the agents choose will invariably depend on their private values and become the strategies of the players. Auctions provide a common example of indirect mechanisms and we illustrate below two commonly used auctions, first price auction (FPA) and second price auction (SPA).

Example 15.5 (First Price Sealed Bid Auction for Selling). Consider the seller (agent 0) and two potential buyers (agents 1, 2) as before. The seller plays the role of an auctioneer and the buyers play the role of bidders in the auction. Each buyer is asked to submit a sealed bid, $b_i \geq 0$ $(i = 1, 2)$. The sealed bids are examined and the buyer with the higher bid is declared the winner. If there is a tie, assume that buyer 1 is declared the winner. The winning buyer pays to the seller an amount equal to his bid. The losing bidder does not pay anything.

We emphasize the subtle difference between the situations in Example 15.2 and the current example. In Example 15.2 (direct mechanism), each buyer is asked to announce (directly) his type (valuation for the object), whereas in the current example 15.5 (indirect mechanism), each buyer is asked to submit a bid for the object. The intent is that the bid submitted will depend on the type. Based on the type, the buyer has a strategy for bidding. So it becomes a game and in an equilibrium of the game, the strategies, hopefully, will indirectly reveal the types of the players.

Let us make the following assumptions:

(1) θ_1, θ_2 are independently drawn from the uniform distribution on $[0, 1]$.
(2) The sealed bid of buyer i takes the form $b_i(\theta_i) = \alpha_i \theta_i$, where $\alpha_i \in (0, 1]$. That the bid will be of the above form is known to both the bidders. The values of α_1, α_2 are not known however and the bidders have to compute these in order to determine their best response bids.

Buyer 1's problem is now to bid in a way so as to maximize his payoff:

$$\max_{b_1 \geq 0} \ (\theta_1 - b_1) \, P\{b_2(\theta_2) \leq b_1\}$$

Since the bid of player 2 is $b_2(\theta_2) = \alpha_2 \theta_2$ and $\theta_2 \in [0, 1]$, the maximum bid of buyer 2 is α_2. Buyer 1 knows this and therefore $b_1 \in [0, \alpha_2]$. Also,

$$P\{b_2(\theta_2) \leq b_1\} = P\{\alpha_2 \theta_2 \leq b_1\}$$

$$= P\left\{\theta_2 \leq \frac{b_1}{\alpha_2}\right\}$$

$$= \frac{b_1}{\alpha_2} \text{ since } \theta_2 \text{ is uniform over } [0, 1]$$

Thus buyer 1's problem is:

$$\max_{b_1 \in [0, \alpha_2]} (\theta_1 - b_1) \frac{b_1}{\alpha_2}$$

The solution to this problem is

$$b_1(\theta_1) = \begin{cases} \frac{\theta_1}{2} & \text{if } \frac{\theta_1}{2} \leq \alpha_2 \\ \alpha_2 & \text{if } \frac{\theta_1}{2} > \alpha_2 \end{cases}$$

We can show on similar lines that

$$b_2(\theta_2) = \begin{cases} \frac{\theta_2}{2} & \text{if } \frac{\theta_2}{2} \leq \alpha_1 \\ \alpha_1 & \text{if } \frac{\theta_2}{2} > \alpha_1 \end{cases}$$

Let $\alpha_1 = \alpha_2 = \frac{1}{2}$. Then we get

$$b_1(\theta_1) = \frac{\theta_1}{2} \quad \forall \theta_1 \in \Theta_1 = [0, 1]$$

$$b_2(\theta_2) = \frac{\theta_2}{2} \quad \forall \theta_2 \in \Theta_2 = [0, 1]$$

Note that if $b_2(\theta_2) = \frac{\theta_2}{2}$, we have $\alpha_2 = \frac{1}{2}$ and $\frac{\theta_1}{2} \leq \alpha_2$ and therefore the best response of buyer 1 is $b_1(\theta_1) = \frac{\theta_1}{2}$. Similarly if $b_1(\theta_1) = \frac{\theta_1}{2}$, we have $\alpha_1 = \frac{1}{2}$ and $\frac{\theta_2}{2} \leq \alpha_1$ and therefore the best response of buyer 2 is $b_2(\theta_2) = \frac{\theta_2}{2}$. Hence the profile $\left(\frac{\theta_1}{2}, \frac{\theta_2}{2}\right)$ is a Bayesian Nash equilibrium of an underlying Bayesian game. This equilibrium can be computed by the rational and intelligent bidders.

This means there is a Bayesian Nash equilibrium of an underlying Bayesian game (induced by the indirect mechanism namely the first price sealed bid auction) that yields the outcome $f(\theta) = (y_0(\theta), y_1(\theta), y_2(\theta), t_0(\theta), t_1(\theta), t_2(\theta))$ such that $\forall \theta = (\theta_0, \theta_1, \theta_2) \in \Theta$,

$$y_0(\theta) = 0$$
$$y_1(\theta) = 1 \quad \text{if } \theta_1 \geq \theta_2$$
$$\quad = 0 \quad \theta_1 < \theta_2$$
$$y_2(\theta) = 1 \quad \text{if } \theta_1 < \theta_2$$
$$\quad = 0 \quad \theta_1 \geq \theta_2$$
$$t_1(\theta) = -y_1(\theta) \frac{\theta_1}{2}$$
$$t_2(\theta) = -y_2(\theta) \frac{\theta_2}{2}$$
$$t_0(\theta) = -(t_1(\theta) + t_2(\theta))$$

Note that the social choice function that is realized above is SCF3. We emphasize that it is neither SCF1 nor SCF2. $\qquad \square$

Example 15.6 (Second Price Sealed Bid Auction).

Example 15.6 (Second Price Sealed Bid Auction). In this indirect mechanism, each buyer is asked to submit a sealed bid $b_i \geq 0$. The bids are examined and the buyer with higher bid is declared the winner. In case there is a tie, buyer 1 is declared the winner.

The winning buyer will pay to the seller an amount equal to the second highest bid. The losing bidder does not pay anything.

In this case, we can show that $b_i(\theta_i) = \theta_i$ for $i = 1, 2$ constitutes a weakly dominant strategy for each player. The arguments are identical to those in Example 15.3.

Thus the game induced by the indirect mechanism second price sealed bid auction has a weakly dominant strategy in which the social choice function SCF2 is implemented.   □

Summary of Examples

We can summarize the main points of the current chapter so far as follows.

- The social choice function SCF1 cannot be implemented by a direct mechanism. We still have not investigated if SCF1 can perhaps be implemented by an indirect mechanism.
- The function SCF2 can be implemented in dominant strategies by a direct mechanism. Also, the indirect mechanism, namely second price auction implements SCF2 in dominant strategies.
- The function SCF3 is implemented in Bayesian Nash equilibrium by a direct mechanism. Also the indirect mechanism, namely first price auction, implements it in Bayesian Nash equilibrium.

15.3   Bayesian Game Induced by a Mechanism

Recall that a mechanism is an institution or a framework with a set of rules that prescribe the actions available to players and specify how these action profiles are transformed into outcomes. A mechanism specifies an action set for each player. The outcome function gives the rule for obtaining outcomes from action profiles. Given:

(1) a set of agents $N = \{1, 2, \ldots, n\}$,
(2) type sets $\Theta_1, \ldots, \Theta_n$,
(3) a common prior $\mathbb{P} \in \Delta(\Theta)$ and belief functions $p_i : \Theta_i \to \Delta(\Theta_{-i})$ $(i = 1, \ldots, n)$ that can be derived from $\mathbb{P}$,
(4) a set of outcomes X,
(5) utility functions $u_1, \ldots, u_n$, with $u_i : X \times \Theta_i \to \mathbb{R}$,

a mechanism $\mathscr{M} = (S_1, \ldots, S_n, g(\cdot))$ induces among the players, a Bayesian game $\langle N, (\Theta_i), (S_i), (p_i), (U_i) \rangle$ where

$$U_i(\theta_1, \ldots, \theta_n, s_1, \ldots, s_n) = u_i(g(s_1, \ldots, s_n), \theta_i).$$

We will use the symbol u_i instead of U_i whenever there is no confusion.

Strategies in the Induced Bayesian Game

For $i = 1, 2, \ldots, n$, a strategy s_i for agent i in the induced Bayesian game is a mapping $s_i : \Theta_i \to S_i$. Thus, given a type $\theta_i \in \Theta_i$, $s_i(\theta_i)$ will give the action of player i corresponding to θ_i. The strategy $s_i(.)$ will specify actions corresponding to types. In the auction scenario, the bid b_i of player i is a function of the valuation θ_i. For example, $b_i(\theta_i) = \alpha_i \theta_i$ is a particular strategy for player i.

Example 15.7 (Bayesian Game Induced by First Price Auction).

First, note that $N = \{0, 1, 2\}$. The type sets are $\Theta_0, \Theta_1, \Theta_2$, and the common prior is some known distribution $\mathbb{P} \in \Delta(\Theta)$. The set of outcomes is

$$X = \{(y_0, y_1, y_2, t_0, t_1, t_2) : y_i \in \{0, 1\}, y_0 + y_1 + y_2 = 1, t_i \in \mathbb{R} \; \forall i \in N\}$$

The utility functions for the buyers 1 and 2 are given by

$$u_i((y_0, y_1, y_2, t_0, t_1, t_2), \theta_i) = y_i \theta_i + t_i; \quad i = 1, 2$$

The strategy sets are given by

$$S_0 = \{\theta_0\}; \; S_1 = \mathbb{R}_+ \; ; \; S_2 = \mathbb{R}_+$$

Note that θ_0 is some known valuation the seller has for the object. Since S_0 is a singleton, the bid of the seller is common knowledge. We include it in the following only for the sake of completeness. The outcome rule $g(\cdot)$ for bid profiles $b = (b_0, b_1, b_2) \in S_0 \times S_1 \times S_2$ is given by

$$g(b) = (y_0(b), y_1(b), y_2(b), t_0(b), t_1(b), t_2(b))$$

such that $\forall (b_0, b_1, b_2) \in S_0 \times S_1 \times S_2$,

$$
\begin{aligned}
y_0(b_0, b_1, b_2) &= 0 \\
y_1(b_0, b_1, b_2) &= 1 && \text{if } b_1 \geq b_2 \\
&= 0 && \text{if } b_1 < b_2 \\
y_2(b_0, b_1, b_2) &= 1 && \text{if } b_1 < b_2 \\
&= 0 && \text{if } b_1 \geq b_2 \\
t_1(b_0, b_1, b_2) &= -y_1(b_0, b_1, b_2) \, b_1 \\
t_2(b_0, b_1, b_2) &= -y_2(b_0, b_1, b_2) \, b_2 \\
t_0(b_0, b_1, b_2) &= -(t_1(b_0, b_1, b_2) + t_2(b_0, b_1, b_2)).
\end{aligned}
$$

If we specify the common prior $\mathbb{P}$ and the belief functions, it would complete the specification of the Bayesian game induced by the first price auction. □

15.4 Implementation of a Social Choice Function by a Mechanism

We now formalize the notion of implementation of a social choice function by a mechanism.

Definition 15.1 (Implementation of an SCF). *We say a mechanism $\mathcal{M} = ((S_i)_{i \in N}, g(\cdot))$, where $g : S_1 \times \ldots \times S_n \to X$, implements the social choice function $f(\cdot)$ if there is a pure strategy equilibrium $s^*(\cdot) = (s_1^*(\cdot), \ldots, s_n^*(\cdot))$ of the Bayesian game Γ induced by $\mathcal{M}$ such that $g(s_1^*(\theta_1), \ldots, s_n^*(\theta_n)) = f(\theta_1, \ldots, \theta_n), \, \forall (\theta_1, \ldots, \theta_n) \in \Theta$.*

Figure 15.2 depicts all the building blocks involved in the implementation of a social choice function by an indirect mechanism.

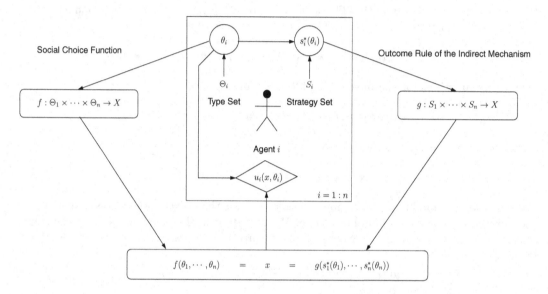

Fig. 15.2: The idea behind implementation by an indirect mechanism

Note that a direct mechanism corresponding to a social choice function $f(\cdot)$ is a special case of an indirect mechanism with the strategy sets same as the type sets and the outcome rule $g(\cdot)$ same as the social choice function $f(\cdot)$. It goes without saying that a Bayesian game is induced by a direct mechanism as well.

Depending on the nature of the underlying equilibrium, two ways of implementing an SCF $f(\cdot)$ are standard in the literature.

Definition 15.2 (Implementation in Dominant Strategies). *We say a mechanism $\mathcal{M} = ((S_i)_{i \in N}, g(\cdot))$ implements the social choice function $f(\cdot)$ in dominant strategy equilibrium if there is a weakly dominant strategy equilibrium $s^*(\cdot) = (s_1^*(\cdot), \ldots, s_n^*(\cdot))$ of the Bayesian game Γ induced by $\mathcal{M}$ such that*

$$g(s_1^*(\theta_1), \ldots, s_n^*(\theta_n)) = f(\theta_1, \ldots, \theta_n) \, \forall (\theta_1, \ldots, \theta_n) \in \Theta.$$

Since a strongly dominant strategy equilibrium is automatically a weakly dominant strategy equilibrium, the above definition applies to the strongly dominant case also. In the latter case, we could say the implementation is in strongly dominant strategy equilibrium. The definition also applies to very weakly dominant strategy equilibria and often times this is the implementation that is considered.

Note that the second price auction implements SCF2 in weakly dominant strategy equilibrium. We have also shown that SCF2 can be implemented through a direct mechanism in (weakly) dominant strategies. The latter statement is technically stated by saying that SCF2 is dominant strategy incentive compatible (more about this in the next chapter).

Definition 15.3 (Implementation in Bayesian Nash Equilibrium). *We say that a mechanism $\mathcal{M} = ((S_i)_{i \in N}, g(\cdot))$ implements the social choice function $f(\cdot)$ in Bayesian Nash equilibrium if there is a pure strategy Bayesian Nash equilibrium $s^*(\cdot) = (s_1^*(\cdot), \ldots, s_n^*(\cdot))$ of the game Γ induced by $\mathcal{M}$ such that*

$$g\left(s_1^*(\theta_1), \ldots, s_n^*(\theta_n)\right) = f\left(\theta_1, \ldots, \theta_n\right) \ \forall \left(\theta_1, \ldots, \theta_n\right) \in \Theta.$$

Note that the first price auction implements SCF3 in Bayesian Nash equilibrium. We have also shown that SCF3 can be implemented through a direct mechanism in Bayesian Nash equilibrium. The latter statement is technically stated by saying that SCF3 is Bayesian incentive compatible (more about this in the next chapter).

Finally, note that SCF1 cannot be implemented using a direct mechanism. In fact, as shown in the next chapter, there is no indirect mechanism that can implement SCF1.

Key Facts about Implementation

Note the requirement on existence of a pure strategy Bayesian Nash equilibrium for the game Γ induced by $\mathcal{M}$. Naturally we must be wary of the possibility that such an equilibrium may not exist.

On the other hand, the game Γ may have more than one equilibrium, but the above definition requires only that *one of them* induces outcomes in accordance with the SCF $f(\cdot)$. Implicitly, then, the above definition assumes that, if multiple equilibria exist, the agents will play the equilibrium that the mechanism designer (social planner) wants.

Another implicit assumption of the above definition is that the game induced by the mechanism is a simultaneous move game, that is all the agents, after learning their types, choose their actions simultaneously.

We have talked about two broad categories of implementations: dominant strategy implementation (DSI) and Bayesian Nash implementation (BNI). It is easy to see that DSI implies BNI but BNI need not imply DSI. Apart from these two broad categories, we can consider other solution concepts for games and define implementability in those equilibria. Examples include: Nash equilibrium (complete information), subgame perfect equilibrium, etc. Chapter 24 treats implementation in Nash equilibrium in detail. At this point, we only state that implementation in

Nash equilibrium is stronger than BNI but weaker than DSI.

The *revelation theorem* which is a fundamental result in mechanism design shows that direct mechanisms and indirect mechanisms are equivalent. Indirect mechanisms (for example, auctions) are appealing and useful because they provide us with practical ways of implementing social choice functions. Direct mechanisms provide an abstraction which is valuable in developing the theory of mechanism design. The revelation theorem is covered in detail in the next chapter.

15.5   Summary and References

In this chapter, we have investigated the process of implementing a social choice function through a direct mechanism or an indirect mechanism. The following are the salient points to be noted.

- A direct mechanism for a social choice function works by trying to extract the private information (types) from the agents truthfully. An indirect mechanism (such as an auction where agents bid) tries to extract truthful information by inducing the agents to play certain strategies that indirectly capture the private information.
- Not all social choice functions can be implemented by direct mechanisms, as shown by the social choice function SCF1.
- Social choice functions such as SCF2 can be implemented by a direct mechanism in dominant strategies.
- Social choice functions such as SCF3 cannot be implemented by a direct mechanism in dominant strategies but may be implemented by a direct mechanism in Bayesian Nash equilibrium.
- A direct mechanism (corresponding to an SCF) induces a Bayesian game among the agents and the induced Bayesian game may have a dominant strategy equilibrium or a Bayesian Nash equilibrium or none. If reporting true types is an equilibrium, then we say the direct mechanism implements the SCF and we say the SCF is incentive compatible.
- Given an SCF, an indirect mechanism is said to implement the SCF if the mechanism induces a Bayesian game having an equilibrium that produces precisely the outcomes of the SCF through the mechanism's outcome rule.

In the next chapter, we show that direct mechanisms and indirect mechanisms are in fact equivalent. This is the central idea of the revelation theorem. The next chapter also defines the key notion of incentive compatibility.

Chapter 24 introduces the notion of implementation in Nash equilibrium in the complete information setting. The chapter also talks about the notion of *strong implementation* which means that the outcomes of the social choice function are reproduced in every equilibrium of the induced Bayesian game.

The contents of this chapter, especially SCF1, SCF2, and SCF3, are based on the examples discussed in the book by Mas-Colell, Whinston, and Green [1]. The procurement versions (buying scenarios) of SCF1, SCF2, and SCF3 are discussed in detail in the monograph by Narahari, Garg, Narayanam, and Prakash [2].

References

[1] Andreu Mas-Colell, Michael D. Whinston, and Jerry R. Green. *Microeconomic Theory*. Oxford University Press, 1995.
[2] Y. Narahari, Dinesh Garg, Ramasuri Narayanam, and Hastagiri Prakash. *Game Theoretic Problems in Network Economics and Mechanism Design Solutions*. Springer, London, 2009.

15.6 Exercises

(1) Investigate the implementability of the eight social choice functions (supplier selection problem) presented in Table 15.1.

(2) Think about what would be an indirect mechanism for implementing social choice functions of the type presented for the supplier selection problem.

(3) Consider a buying scenario with one buying agent (agent 0) and two selling agents (agents 1, 2). Modify the social choice functions SCF1, SCF2, SCF3 to represent the buying scenario and call the new social choice functions BUY1, BUY2, and BUY3 respectively. Write down these three new social choice functions in the usual notation.

(4) Show that the social choice function BUY1 cannot be implemented by a direct mechanism.

(5) Show that BUY2 and BUY3 can be implemented by appropriate direct mechanisms.

(6) Show that the mechanism *lowest price procurement auction* implements BUY3 in Bayesian Nash equilibrium (Hint: see [2]).

(7) Show that BUY2 is implementable in dominant strategy equilibrium by the mechanism *second lowest price procurement auction*.

(8) In some of the examples discussed in this chapter, it is assumed that a tie between agent 1 and agent 2 will be resolved in favor of agent1. Investigate what would happen in these examples if the tie is resolved in favor of agent 1 or agent 2 using a Bernoulli random variable.

(9) Consider two agents 1 and 2 where agent 1 is the seller of an indivisible item and agent 2 is a prospective buyer of the item. An outcome here is of the form $x = (y_1, y_2, t_1, t_2)$ where $y_i = 1$ if agent i gets the item and t_i denotes the payment received by agent i $(i = 1, 2)$. A natural set of outcomes here is

$$X = \{(y_1, y_2, t_1, t_2) : y_1 + y_2 = 1; \ y_1, y_2 \in \{0, 1\}\}.$$

Define the utilities of the agents i $(i = 1, 2)$ appropriately. The type θ_1 of agent

1 (seller) can be interpreted as the willingness to sell of the agent (minimum price at which agent 1 is willing to sell). The type θ_2 of agent 2 (buyer) has the natural interpretation of willingness to pay (maximum price the buyer is willing to pay). Assume that $\Theta_1 = \Theta_2 = [0, 1]$ and that each agent thinks that the type of the other agent is uniformly distributed over the real interval $[0, 1]$. Define the social choice function $f(\theta) = (y_1(\theta), y_2(\theta), t_1(\theta), t_2(\theta))$ by

$$y_1(\theta_1, \theta_2) = 1 \quad \theta_1 > \theta_2$$
$$= 0 \quad \theta_1 \leq \theta_2$$
$$y_2(\theta_1, \theta_2) = 1 \quad \theta_1 \leq \theta_2$$
$$= 0 \quad \theta_1 > \theta_2$$
$$t_1(\theta_1, \theta_2) = y_2(\theta_1, \theta_2) \left(\frac{\theta_1 + \theta_2}{2} \right)$$
$$t_2(\theta_1, \theta_2) = -y_2(\theta_1, \theta_2) \left(\frac{\theta_1 + \theta_2}{2} \right).$$

Now define the following indirect mechanism. The seller and the buyer are asked to submit their bids b_1 and b_2 respectively. Trade happens if $b_1 \leq b_2$ and trade does not happen otherwise. If trade happens, the buyer gets the item and pays the seller an amount $\frac{(b_1 + b_2)}{2}$. Will this indirect mechanism implement the above social choice function?

Chapter 16

Incentive Compatibility and Revelation Theorem

In mechanism design, the notion of incentive compatibility is of fundamental importance and the revelation theorem is a key result. This chapter first presents the notions of *dominant strategy incentive compatibility* (DSIC) and *Bayesian incentive compatibility* (BIC) in a formal way. Next, it develops the revelation theorem for dominant strategy equilibrium followed by the revelation theorem for Bayesian Nash equilibrium. Finally the chapter describes two important properties of social choice functions in which a social planner would be interested: *ex-post efficiency* and *non-dictatorship*.

16.1 Incentive Compatibility

We have already seen that mechanism design involves the preference elicitation problem and the preference aggregation problem. The preference elicitation problem seeks to collect truthful information from the agents about their types. In order to elicit truthful information, the idea is to make truth revelation a best response for the agents, consistent with rationality and intelligence assumptions. Offering incentives is a way of achieving this; incentive compatibility essentially refers to offering the right incentives that make agents reveal their types truthfully. There are broadly two types of incentive compatibility: (1) Truth revelation is a best response for each agent irrespective of what is reported by the other agents; (2) truth revelation is a best response for each agent in expectation of the types of the rest of the agents. The first one is called dominant strategy incentive compatibility (DSIC), and the second one is called Bayesian Nash incentive compatibility (BIC). Since truth revelation is always with respect to types, only direct revelation mechanisms are relevant when formalizing the notion of incentive compatibility. The notion of incentive compatibility was first introduced by Leonid Hurwicz [1].

Definition 16.1 (Incentive Compatibility (IC)). *A social choice function $f :$ $\Theta_1 \times \ldots \times \Theta_n \to X$ is said to be incentive compatible (or truthfully implementable) if the Bayesian game induced by the direct revelation mechanism $\mathscr{D} = ((\Theta_i)_{i \in N}, f(\cdot))$ has a pure strategy equilibrium $s^*(\cdot) = (s_1^*(\cdot), \ldots, s_n^*(\cdot))$ in which $s_i^*(\theta_i) = \theta_i, \forall \theta_i \in \Theta_i, \forall i \in N$.*

That is, truth revelation by each agent constitutes an equilibrium of the game induced by $\mathscr{D}$. It is easy to infer that if an SCF $f(\cdot)$ is incentive compatible then the direct revelation mechanism $\mathscr{D} = ((\Theta_i)_{i \in N}, f(\cdot))$ can implement it. This means the social choice function $f(\cdot)$ can be realized by *directly* asking the agents to report their types and using this type information in $f(\cdot)$ to determine the social outcome.

We emphasize again the point that the induced Bayesian game may have no equilibrium, exactly one equilibrium, or two or more equilibria. The above definition requires at least one of them to induce outcomes that are identical to those of the social choice function. Thus the above definition assumes that, if multiple equilibria exist, the agents will play the truth revealing equilibrium that the mechanism designer (social planner) wants.

Based on the type of equilibrium concept used, two types of incentive compatibility are defined: dominant strategy incentive compatibility and Bayesian incentive compatibility.

Dominant Strategy Incentive Compatibility

Definition 16.2 (Dominant Strategy Incentive Compatibility (DSIC)).
A social choice function $f : \Theta_1 \times \ldots \times \Theta_n \to X$ *is said to be dominant strategy incentive compatible (or truthfully implementable in dominant strategies) if the direct revelation mechanism* $\mathscr{D} = ((\Theta_i)_{i \in N}, f(\cdot))$ *has a weakly dominant strategy equilibrium* $s^*(\cdot) = (s_1^*(\cdot), \ldots, s_n^*(\cdot))$ *in which* $s_i^*(\theta_i) = \theta_i, \forall \theta_i \in \Theta_i, \forall i \in N$.

That is, truth revelation by each agent constitutes a weakly dominant strategy equilibrium of the game induced by $\mathscr{D}$. Other phrases which are often used for DSIC are *strategy-proof*, *cheat-proof*, *straightforward*, and *truthful*. In a few cases, the weakly dominant strategy equilibrium could turn out to be a strongly dominant strategy equilibrium as well. Also, often times, we find it convenient to relax the weakly dominant strategy equilibrium to be a very weakly dominant strategy equilibrium.

Example 16.1 (Dominant Strategy Incentive Compatibility of SCF2).
We have seen in the previous chapter that the social choice function SCF2 can be realized by a direct revelation mechanism in dominant strategies. As a consequence, for each $\theta = (\theta_1, \ldots, \theta_n) \in \Theta$, the profile $(\theta_1, \ldots, \theta_n)$ can be shown to be a (weakly) dominant strategy equilibrium of the induced Bayesian game. This means SCF2 is DSIC. Also, SCF2 is implemented by the second price auction (which is an indirect mechanism) in dominant strategy equilibrium.   □

Necessary and Sufficient Condition for DSIC

Using the definition of a weakly dominant strategy equilibrium in Bayesian games (Chapter 13), the following necessary and sufficient condition for an SCF $f(\cdot)$ to be dominant strategy incentive compatible can be derived:

$$u_i \left(f \left(\theta_i, \theta_{-i} \right), \theta_i \right) \geq u_i (f(\theta_i', \theta_{-i}), \theta_i)$$

$$\forall \theta_i' \in \Theta_i, \ \forall \theta_i \in \Theta_i, \ \forall \theta_{-i} \in \Theta_{-i}, \ \forall i \in N. \tag{16.1}$$

The above condition says that the SCF $f(.)$ is DSIC if and only if for each agent i $(i = 1, 2, \ldots, n)$, it is always a best response for agent i to report his true type θ_i, irrespective of what is reported by the rest of the agents.

Bayesian Incentive Compatibility

Definition 16.3 (Bayesian Incentive Compatibility (BIC)). *A social choice function* $f : \Theta_1 \times \ldots \times \Theta_n \to X$ *is said to be Bayesian incentive compatible (or truthfully implementable in Bayesian Nash equilibrium) if the direct revelation mechanism* $\mathscr{D} = ((\Theta_i)_{i \in N}, f(\cdot))$ *has a Bayesian Nash equilibrium* $s^*(\cdot) = (s_1^*(\cdot), \ldots, s_n^*(\cdot))$ *in which* $s_i^*(\theta_i) = \theta_i, \forall \theta_i \in \Theta_i, \forall i \in N$.

That is, truth revelation by each agent constitutes a Bayesian Nash equilibrium of the game induced by $\mathscr{D}$.

Example 16.2 (Bayesian Incentive Compatibility of SCF3). We have seen in the previous chapter that the social choice function SCF3 can be realized by a direct revelation mechanism in Bayesian Nash sense. As a consequence, for each $\theta = (\theta_1, \ldots, \theta_n) \in \Theta$, the profile $(\theta_1, \ldots, \theta_n)$ can be shown to be a Bayesian Nash equilibrium of the induced Bayesian game. This means that SCF3 is BIC. Also, SCF3 is implemented by the first price auction (which is an indirect mechanism) in Bayesian Nash equilibrium. $\qquad \square$

Necessary and Sufficient Condition for BIC

Using the definition of a Bayesian Nash equilibrium in Bayesian games (Chapter 14), the following necessary and sufficient condition for an SCF $f(\cdot)$ to be Bayesian incentive compatible can be derived:

$$E_{\theta_{-i}} \left[u_i \left(f \left(\theta_i, \theta_{-i} \right), \theta_i \right) | \theta_i \right] \geq E_{\theta_{-i}} [u_i (f(\theta_i', \theta_{-i}), \theta_i) | \theta_i]$$

$$\forall \theta_i' \in \Theta_i, \ \forall \theta_i \in \Theta_i, \ \forall i \in N. \tag{16.2}$$

where the expectation is taken over the distribution of type profiles of agents other than agent i. Recall from Chapter 14 that we have used $p_i : \Theta_i \to \Delta(\Theta_{-i})$ to denote the belief probability distributions of player i about the type profiles of the rest of the agents, for different types of player i. That is, $p_i(\theta_i)$ represents the belief distribution of player i when his type is θ_i about the type profiles of the rest of the agents. Also, recall that $p_i(\cdot)$ is derived from a common prior $\mathbb{P} \in \Delta(\Theta)$.

The above condition says that the SCF $f(.)$ is BIC if and only if for each agent i $(i = 1, 2, \ldots, n)$, whenever the other agents report their types truthfully, it is a best response in expectation for agent i to report his true type θ_i.

Note. If a social choice function $f(\cdot)$ is dominant strategy incentive compatible then it is also Bayesian incentive compatible. The proof of this follows trivially from the fact that a weakly dominant strategy equilibrium is clearly also a Bayesian Nash equilibrium.

16.2   The Revelation Principle for Dominant Strategy Equilibrium

The revelation principle basically illustrates the relationship between an indirect revelation mechanism $\mathcal{M}$ and a direct revelation mechanism $\mathcal{D}$ with respect to a given SCF $f(\cdot)$. This result enables us to restrict our inquiry about truthful implementation of an SCF to the class of direct revelation mechanisms only.

Theorem 16.1. *Suppose that there exists a mechanism $\mathcal{M} = (S_1, \ldots, S_n, g(\cdot))$ that implements the social choice function $f(\cdot)$ in dominant strategy equilibrium. Then $f(\cdot)$ is dominant strategy incentive compatible.*

Proof: It is given that $\mathcal{M} = (S_1, \ldots, S_n, g(\cdot))$ implements $f(\cdot)$ in dominant strategies. This implies there exists a weakly dominant strategy equilibrium $s^*(\cdot) = (s_1^*(\cdot), \ldots, s_n^*(\cdot))$ of the underlying Bayesian game such that

$$g\left(s_1^*(\theta_1), \ldots, s_n^*(\theta_n)\right) = f\left(\theta_1, \ldots, \theta_n\right) \ \forall \left(\theta_1, \ldots, \theta_n\right) \in \Theta \qquad (16.3)$$

The above equilibrium condition implies that

$$u_i(g(s_i^*(\theta_i), s_{-i}(\theta_{-i})), \theta_i) \geq u_i(g(a_i, s_{-i}(\theta_{-i})), \theta_i); \ \ \forall a_i \in S_i; \ \forall \theta_i \in \Theta_i;$$
$$\forall \theta_{-i} \in \Theta_{-i}; \ \forall s_{-i}(\cdot) \in S_{-i}; \ \forall i \in N. \qquad (16.4)$$

Condition (16.4) implies, in particular, that

$$u_i(g(s_i^*(\theta_i), s_{-i}^*(\theta_{-i})), \theta_i) \geq u_i(g(s_i^*(\theta_i'), s_{-i}^*(\theta_{-i})), \theta_i)$$
$$\forall \theta_i' \in \Theta_i, \ \forall \theta_i \in \Theta_i, \ \forall \theta_{-i} \in \Theta_{-i} \ \forall i \in N. \quad (16.5)$$

Conditions (16.3) and (16.5) together imply that

$$u_i\left(f\left(\theta_i, \theta_{-i}\right), \theta_i\right) \geq u_i(f(\theta_i', \theta_{-i}), \theta_i), \forall \theta_i' \in \Theta_i, \ \forall \theta_i \in \Theta_i, \ \forall \theta_{-i} \in \Theta_{-i}, \ \forall i \in N.$$

But this is precisely condition (16.1), the necessary and sufficient condition for $f(\cdot)$ to be truthfully implementable in dominant strategies. ∎

The idea behind the revelation principle can be understood with the help of Figure 16.1. In this picture, **DSI** represents the set of all social choice functions that are implementable in dominant strategies and **DSIC** is the set of all social choice functions that are dominant strategy incentive compatible. The picture depicts the obvious fact that **DSIC** is a subset of **DSI** and illustrates the revelation theorem by showing that the set difference between these two sets is the empty set, thus implying that **DSIC** is precisely the same as **DSI**.

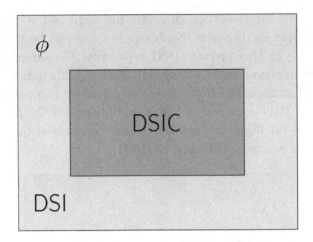

DSI: Dominant Strategy Implementable
DSIC: Dominant Strategy Incentive Compatible
DSI \ DSIC = ϕ

Fig. 16.1: Revelation principle for dominant strategy equilibrium

16.3 The Revelation Principle for Bayesian Nash Equilibrium

Theorem 16.2. *Suppose that there exists a mechanism $\mathcal{M} = (S_1, \ldots, S_n, g(\cdot))$ that implements the social choice function $f(\cdot)$ in Bayesian Nash equilibrium. Then $f(\cdot)$ is Bayesian incentive compatible.*

Proof: It is known that $\mathcal{M} = (S_1, \ldots, S_n, g(\cdot))$ implements $f(\cdot)$ in Bayesian Nash equilibrium. This means there exists a Bayesian Nash equilibrium $s^*(\cdot) = (s_1^*(\cdot), \ldots, s_n^*(\cdot))$ of the underlying Bayesian game such that

$$g\left(s_1^*(\theta_1), \ldots, s_n^*(\theta_n)\right) = f\left(\theta_1, \ldots, \theta_n\right) \ \forall (\theta_1, \ldots, \theta_n) \in \Theta \qquad (16.6)$$

Bayesian Nash equilibrium condition implies that

$$E_{\theta_{-i}}\left[u_i(g(s_i^*(\theta_i), s_{-i}^*(\theta_{-i})), \theta_i)|\theta_i\right] \geq E_{\theta_{-i}}\left[u_i(g(a_i, s_{-i}^*(\theta_{-i})), \theta_i)|\theta_i\right]$$
$$\forall a_i \in S_i, \ \forall \theta_i \in \Theta_i, \ \forall i \in N. \qquad (16.7)$$

Condition (16.7) implies, in particular, that

$$E_{\theta_{-i}}\left[u_i(g(s_i^*(\theta_i), s_{-i}^*(\theta_{-i})), \theta_i)|\theta_i\right] \geq E_{\theta_{-i}}\left[u_i(g(s_i^*(\theta_i'), s_{-i}^*(\theta_{-i})), \theta_i)|\theta_i\right]$$
$$\forall \theta_i' \in \Theta_i, \ \forall \theta_i \in \Theta_i, \ \forall i \in N. \qquad (16.8)$$

Conditions (16.6) and (16.8) together imply that

$$E_{\theta_{-i}}\left[u_i\left(f\left(\theta_i, \theta_{-i}\right), \theta_i\right)|\theta_i\right] \geq E_{\theta_{-i}}\left[u_i(f(\theta_i', \theta_{-i}), \theta_i)|\theta_i\right], \forall \theta_i' \in \Theta_i, \ \forall \theta_i \in \Theta_i, \ \forall i \in N.$$

But this is precisely condition (16.2), the necessary and sufficient condition for $f(\cdot)$ to be Bayesian incentive compatible. ∎

In a way similar to the revelation principle for dominant strategy equilibrium, the revelation principle for Bayesian Nash equilibrium can be explained with the help of Figure 16.2. In this picture, **BNI** represents the set of all social choice functions which are implementable in Bayesian Nash equilibrium and **BIC** is the set of all social choice functions which are Bayesian incentive compatible. The picture depicts the fact that **BIC** is a subset of **BNI** and illustrates the revelation theorem by showing that the set difference between these two sets is the empty set, thus implying that **BIC** is precisely the same as **BNI**.

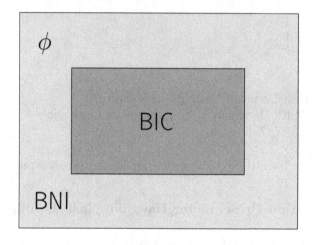

BNI: Bayesian Nash Implementable
BIC: Bayesian Incentive Compatible
BNI \ BIC $= \phi$

Fig. 16.2: Revelation principle for Bayesian Nash equilibrium

Figure 16.3 provides a high level view of both the revelation theorems that we have seen in this chapter. The revelation theorems essentially imply that indirect mechanisms are the same as direct mechanisms in terms of the collection of social choice functions that can be implemented. The theorems have enabled mechanism design theorists to focus only on direct mechanisms for developing theoretical results. Indirect mechanisms are required by practitioners to design practical, imaginative ways of realizing the outcomes of the social choice functions.

16.4 Properties of Social Choice Functions

We have seen that a mechanism facilitates a solution to both the preference elicitation problem and preference aggregation problem, if the mechanism can implement the desired social choice function $f(\cdot)$. It is obvious that some SCFs are implementable and the others are not. Before we look into the question of characterizing

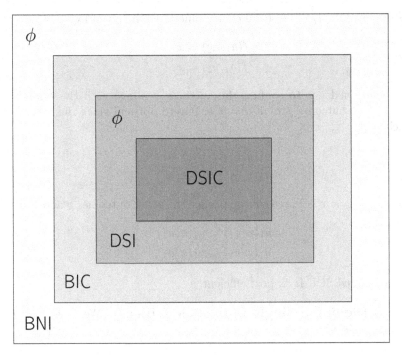

BNI: Bayesian Nash Implementable   DSI: Dominant Strategy Implementable
BIC: Bayesian Incentive Compatible   DSIC: Dominant Strategy Incentive Compatible
BNI \ BIC = ϕ DSI \ DSIC = ϕ

Fig. 16.3: Combined view of revelation theorems for dominant strategy equilibrium and Bayesian Nash equilibrium

the space of implementable social choice functions, it is important to know which properties a social planner would like the social choice function to possess. In this section, we highlight two desirable properties of an SCF: ex-post efficiency and non-dictatorship. Other key properties will be introduced appropriately in future chapters.

Ex-Post Efficiency

Definition 16.4 (Ex-Post Efficiency). *A social choice function $f : \Theta \to X$ is said to be ex-post efficient (or Paretian) if for every profile of agents' types, $\theta \in \Theta$, the outcome $f(\theta)$ is a Pareto optimal outcome. The outcome $f(\theta)$ is Pareto optimal if there does not exist any $x \in X$ such that:*

$$u_i(x, \theta_i) \geq u_i(f(\theta), \theta_i) \, \forall \, i \in N \text{ and } u_i(x, \theta_i) > u_i(f(\theta), \theta_i) \text{ for some } i \in N.$$

Example 16.3 (Supplier Selection Problem). Consider the supplier selection problem (Example 14.3). Let the social choice function f be given by

$$f(a_1, a_2) = x$$
$$f(a_1, b_2) = x.$$

The reader is cautioned not to confuse the outcome x above with the symbol x used in Definition 16.4. The outcome $f(a_1, a_2) = x$ is Pareto optimal since the other outcomes y and z are such that

$$u_1(y, a_1) < u_1(x, a_1)$$
$$u_1(z, a_1) < u_1(x, a_1).$$

The outcome $f(a_1, b_2) = x$ is Pareto optimal since the other outcomes y and z are such that

$$u_1(y, a_1) < u_1(x, a_1)$$
$$u_1(z, a_1) < u_1(x, a_1).$$

Thus the above defined SCF is ex-post efficient. $\square$

Example 16.4 (Selling a Single Indivisible Object). We have looked at three social choice functions, SCF1, SCF2, SCF3, in the previous chapter. The reader can verify that all these SCFs are ex-post efficient. $\square$

We state below a useful proposition which can be proved easily by contradiction. The proof is left as an exercise.

Proposition 16.1. *Suppose* $f : \Theta \rightarrow X$ *is a social choice function such that* $\forall \theta \in \Theta$,

$$\sum_{i=1}^{n} u_i(f(\theta), \theta_i) \geq \sum_{i=1}^{n} u_i(x, \theta_i) \ \forall x \in X$$

That is, the outcome chosen in every type profile maximizes the sum of utilities of the agents. Then the SCF $f(\cdot)$ *is ex-post efficient.*

Non-Dictatorship

We define this through a dictatorial social choice function.

Definition 16.5 (Dictatorship). *A social choice function* $f : \Theta \rightarrow X$ *is said to be dictatorial if there exists an agent* $d \in N$ *such that* $\forall \theta \in \Theta$,

$$u_d(f(\theta), \theta_d) \geq u_d(x, \theta_d) \ \forall x \in X.$$

Such an agent is called a dictator. A social choice function that does not contain a dictator is said to be non-dictatorial.

Intuitively, a dictator is an agent for whom all outcomes of the social choice function turn out to be most favored outcomes. Note that multiple dictators could exist for a given social choice function.

Example 16.5 (Supplier Selection Problem). Let the social choice function f in Example 14.3 be given by

$$f(a_1, a_2) = x; \quad f(a_1, b_2) = x.$$

It is easy to see that agent 1 is a dictator and hence this is a dictatorial SCF. On the other hand, consider the following SCF:

$$f(a_1, a_2) = x; \quad f(a_1, b_2) = y.$$

One can verify that this is not a dictatorial SCF. □

16.5 Summary and References

This chapter was devoted to the revelation theorem which is a central result in mechanism design theory. Intuitively, the revelation theorem says that direct mechanisms and indirect mechanisms are equivalent. The following are the salient points of this chapter.

- A social choice function is said to be incentive compatible if reporting true types constitutes an equilibrium of the Bayesian game induced by the direct mechanism corresponding to the SCF. If the equilibrium is a dominant strategy equilibrium, we say the SCF is DSIC. If the equilibrium is only a Bayesian Nash equilibrium, we say the SCF is BIC.

- Intuitively, DSIC means that reporting true types is a best response strategy for each agent irrespective of what is reported by the other agents. BIC means that reporting true types is a best response strategy in expectation for each agent whenever all other agents also report their types truthfully. Clearly, DSIC implies BIC but not vice-versa.

- The revelation theorem for dominant strategy equilibrium states that if there exists an indirect mechanism that implements an SCF in dominant strategies, there will also exist a direct mechanism that implements the SCF in dominant strategies (that is the SCF is DSIC). The revelation theorem for Bayesian Nash equilibrium states that if there exists an indirect mechanism that implements an SCF in Bayesian Nash equilibrium, there will also exist a direct mechanism that implements the SCF in Bayesian Nash equilibrium (that is the SCF is BIC).

- We defined two important properties of a SCF namely ex-post efficiency and non-dictatorship. Ex-post efficiency implies that all outcomes of the SCF are Pareto optimal, which is desirable. A dictator in a SCF is an agent such that every outcome of the SCF is a most favored outcome for the dictator. An SCF that does not contain a dictator is said to be non-dictatorial. These two properties will be crucially used in the next chapter.

The proofs for the revelation theorems presented in this chapter are based on the ones presented in the book by Mas-Colell, Whinston, and Green [2]. The monograph by Narahari, Garg, Narayanam, and Prakash [3] is another useful reference.

References

[1]   L. Hurwicz. "On informationally decentralized systems". In: *Decision and Organization*. Ed.
       by C.B. McGuire and R. Radner. North-Holland, Amsterdam, 1972.
[2]   Andreu Mas-Colell, Michael D. Whinston, and Jerry R. Green. *Microeconomic Theory*. Oxford University Press, 1995.
[3]   Y. Narahari, Dinesh Garg, Ramasuri Narayanam, and Hastagiri Prakash. *Game Theoretic Problems in Network Economics and Mechanism Design Solutions*. Springer, London, 2009.

16.6   Exercises

(1) Recall the cake-cutting problem in Chapter 14. A mother wants to distribute a cake equally between two of her children. She designs the following mechanism: one of the children will cut the cake and the other child will get the first chance to pick up the cake. The mechanism ensures that the social choice function (namely the cake is distributed equally between the two children) is implemented in dominant strategies. Now consider the case where there are 3 children instead of 2. For this problem, suggest (i) a mechanism which will implement the SCF in dominant strategies and (ii) a mechanism which will implement the SCF in Bayesian Nash equilibrium but not in dominant strategies. Prove your results with simple, brief, logical arguments.

(2) Show that the social choice functions SCF1 and SCF2 we defined in Chapter 15 are ex-post efficient. How about SCF3?

(3) Consider a seller who is faced with a single buyer. The type set of the buyer is $\Theta = \{0, 1, 2\}$. The set of outcomes is $X = \{a, b, c\}$. The valuation function of the buyer is $v(a, \theta) = 0 \ \forall \ \theta \in \Theta$; $v(b, \theta) = \frac{\theta}{2} \ \forall \ \theta \in \Theta$; $v(c, \theta) = \theta \ \forall \ \theta \in \Theta$. Write down all incentive compatible social choice functions for this setting. Note that there is only one agent here.

(4) Let $N = \{1, 2\}$; $\Theta_1 = \{a_1, b_1\}$; $\Theta_2 = \{a_2, b_2\}$; $X = \{x, y, z\}$; and

$$u_1(x, a_1) = 100; \ \ u_1(y, a_1) = 50; \ \ u_1(z, a_1) = 0$$
$$u_1(x, b_1) = 50; \ \ u_1(y, b_1) = 100; \ \ u_1(z, b_1) = 40$$
$$u_2(x, a_2) = 0; \ \ u_2(y, a_2) = 50; \ \ u_2(z, a_2) = 100$$
$$u_2(x, b_2) = 50; \ \ u_2(y, b_2) = 30; \ \ u_2(z, b_2) = 100$$

For the above environment, suggest a social choice function in each case listed below (EPE - ex-post efficient; BIC - Bayesian Incentive Compatible; DSIC - dominant strategy incentive compatible; D- Dictatorial; ND - Non-dictatorial).

- An SCF which is EPE, DSIC, D
- An SCF which is EPE, DSIC, ND
- An SCF which is not EPE but is DSIC, ND
- An SCF which is EPE, BIC (under a suitable prior), but not DSIC
- An SCF which is EPE, not BIC (under some prior), not DSIC

(5) Show that the social choice function representing the following situation is ex-post efficient. There are n agents and an indivisible good is to be allocated to one of them. The good is allocated to an agent having highest valuation and the total amount received by all the agents together is zero.

(6) Derive the following necessary and sufficient condition for a social choice function $f(\cdot)$ to be DSIC:

$$u_i\left(f\left(\theta_i, \theta_{-i}\right), \theta_i\right) \geq u_i(f(\theta_i', \theta_{-i}), \theta_i), \quad \forall \theta_i' \in \Theta_i, \ \forall \theta_i \in \Theta_i, \ \forall \theta_{-i} \in \Theta_{-i}, \ \forall i \in N.$$

(7) Derive the following necessary and sufficient condition for a social choice function $f(\cdot)$ to be BIC:

$$E_{\theta_{-i}}\left[u_i\left(f\left(\theta_i, \theta_{-i}\right), \theta_i\right) | \theta_i\right] \geq E_{\theta_{-i}}[u_i(f(\theta_i', \theta_{-i}), \theta_i) | \theta_i], \quad \forall \theta_i' \in \Theta_i, \ \forall \theta_i \in \Theta_i, \ \forall i \in N.$$

(8) Can a given social choice function have more than one dictator? Prove your result.

(9) Suppose $f : \Theta \to X$ is a social choice function such that $\forall \theta \in \Theta$,

$$\sum_{i=1}^{n} u_i(f(\theta), \theta_i) \geq \sum_{i=1}^{n} u_i(x, \theta_i) \ \forall x \in X$$

That is, the outcome chosen in every type profile maximizes the sum of utilities of the agents. Then show that the SCF $f(\cdot)$ is ex-post efficient.

(10) Consider two agents 1 and 2 where agent 1 is the seller of an indivisible item and agent 2 is a prospective buyer of the item. An outcome here is of the form $x = (y_1, y_2, t_1, t_2)$ where $y_i = 1$ if agent i gets the item and t_i denotes the payment received by agent i $(i = 1, 2)$. A natural set of outcomes here is

$$X = \{(y_1, y_2, t_1, t_2) : \ y_1 + y_2 = 1; \ y_1, y_2 \in \{0, 1\}.$$

Define the utilities of the agents i $(i = 1, 2)$ appropriately. The type θ_1 of agent 1 (seller) can be interpreted as the willingness to sell of the agent (minimum price at which agent 1 is willing to sell). The type θ_2 of agent 2 (buyer) has the natural interpretation of willingness to pay (maximum price the buyer is willing to pay). Assume that $\Theta_1 = \Theta_2 = [0, 1]$ and that each agent thinks that the type of the other agent is uniformly distributed over the real interval $[0, 1]$. Define the social choice function $f(\theta) = (y_1(\theta), y_2(\theta), t_1(\theta), t_2(\theta))$ by

$$y_1(\theta_1, \theta_2) = 1 \quad \theta_1 > \theta_2$$
$$= 0 \quad \theta_1 \leq \theta_2$$
$$y_2(\theta_1, \theta_2) = 1 \quad \theta_1 \leq \theta_2$$
$$= 0 \quad \theta_1 > \theta_2$$
$$t_1(\theta_1, \theta_2) = y_2(\theta_1, \theta_2)\frac{\theta_1 + \theta_2}{2}$$
$$t_2(\theta_1, \theta_2) = -y_2(\theta_1, \theta_2)\frac{\theta_1 + \theta_2}{2}.$$

Is this social choice function DSIC? Is it BIC?

(11) **Programming Assignment**. Given a set of players, their finite type sets, a finite set of outcomes, utility values, and a social choice function, design and implement a software tool to determine if a given SCF is ex-post efficient, DSIC, and dictatorial. Also, given belief probability distributions, investigate if a given SCF is BIC.

Chapter 17

The Gibbard-Satterthwaite Impossibility Theorem

In this chapter, we discuss two impossibility theorems which have shaped the research and advances in mechanism design theory. The first one is the *Gibbard-Satterthwaite theorem* which essentially shows under some technical conditions that dominant strategy incentive compatibility can only be achieved by dictatorial social choice functions. Remarkably, the theorem also opens up attractive opportunities for implementing interesting, useful mechanisms under practical settings such as the quasilinear environment. We provide a proof of this theorem. The chapter also introduces the celebrated *Arrow's impossibility theorem* which is a related, important, and much earlier result in social choice theory. In this chapter, we also present all the preliminary paraphernalia required for understanding the two theorems.

17.1   Preliminaries

We have seen in the last section that dominant strategy incentive compatibility is an extremely desirable property of social choice functions. However the DSIC property, being a strong one, precludes certain other desirable properties to be satisfied. In this section, we discuss the Gibbard-Satterthwaite impossibility theorem (GS theorem, for short), which shows that the DSIC property will force a social choice function to be dictatorial in an unrestricted utility environment. In fact, in the process, even ex-post efficiency will have to be sacrificed. One can say that the GS theorem has shaped the course of research in mechanism design during the 1970s and beyond, and is therefore a landmark result in mechanism design theory. The GS theorem is credited independently to Gibbard [1] and Satterthwaite [2]. The GS theorem is partly based on the famous Arrow's impossibility theorem which also we discuss in this chapter. We commence our discussion of the GS theorem with a motivating example.

Example 17.1 (Supplier Selection Problem). We recall Example 14.3. We have $N = \{1, 2\}$, $X = \{x, y, z\}$, $\Theta_1 = \{a_1\}$, and $\Theta_2 = \{a_2, b_2\}$. Consider the following utility functions (note that the utility functions $u_1(\cdot, a_1)$ and $u_2(\cdot, a_2)$ are the same as in Example 14.3 while the utility function $u_2(\cdot, b_2)$ is different).

Allan Gibbard is currently Richard B. Brandt Distinguished University Professor of Philosophy at the University of Michigan. His classic paper *Manipulation of Voting Schemes: A General Result* published in Econometrica (Volume 41, Number 4) in 1973 presents the famous impossibility theorem which is the subject of this chapter. The result was also independently developed by Mark Satterthwaite. Professor Gibbard's current research interests are in ethical theory. He is the author of two widely popular books: *Thinking How to Live* (2003 - Harvard University Press) and *Wise Choices, Apt Feelings* (1990 - Harvard University Press and Oxford University Press).

Mark Satterthwaite is currently A.C. Buehler Professor in Hospital and Health Services Management and Professor of Strategic Management and Managerial Economics at the Kellogg School of Management, Northwestern University. He is a microeconomic theorist with keen interest in how healthcare markets work. His paper *Strategy-proofness and Arrow's Conditions: Existence and Correspondence Theorems for Voting Procedures and Social Welfare Functions* published in the Journal of Economic Theory (Volume 10, April 1975) presented a brilliant reinterpretation of Arrow's impossibility theorem, which is now known as the Gibbard-Satterthwaite Theorem. He has authored a large number of scholarly papers in the areas of dynamic matching in markets, organizational dynamics, and mechanism design.

$$u_1(x, a_1) = 100; \quad u_1(y, a_1) = 50; \quad u_1(z, a_1) = 0$$
$$u_2(x, a_2) = 0; \quad u_2(y, a_2) = 50; \quad u_2(z, a_2) = 100$$
$$u_2(x, b_2) = 30; \quad u_2(y, b_2) = 60; \quad u_2(z, b_2) = 20.$$

We observe for this example that the DSIC and BIC notions are identical since the type of player 1 is common knowledge and hence player 1 always reports the true type (since the type set is a singleton). Consider the social choice function f given by $f(a_1, a_2) = x$; $f(a_1, b_2) = x$. It can be seen that this SCF is ex-post efficient.

To investigate DSIC, suppose the type of player 2 is a_2. If player 2 reports his true type, then the outcome is x. If he misreports his type as b_2, then also the outcome is x. Hence there is no incentive for player 2 to misreport. A similar situation presents itself when the type of player 2 is b_2. Thus f is DSIC.

In both the type profiles, the outcome happens to be the most favorable one for player 1, that is, x. Therefore, player 1 is a dictator and f is dictatorial. Thus the above function is ex-post efficient and DSIC, but dictatorial.

Now, let us consider a different SCF h defined by $h(a_1, a_2) = y$; $h(a_1, b_2) = x$. Following similar arguments as above, h can be shown to be ex-post efficient and nondictatorial but not DSIC. Table 17.1 lists all the nine possible social choice functions in this scenario and the combination of properties each function satisfies.

i	$f_i(a_1, a_2)$	$f_i(a_1, b_2)$	EPE	DSIC	NON-DICT
1	x	x	✓	✓	×
2	x	y	✓	×	✓
3	x	z	×	×	✓
4	y	x	✓	×	✓
5	y	y	✓	✓	✓
6	y	z	×	×	✓
7	z	x	✓	✓	✓
8	z	y	✓	✓	×
9	z	z	×	✓	✓

Table 17.1: Social choice functions and properties satisfied by them

Note that the situation is quite desirable with the following SCFs.

$$f_5(a_1, a_2) = y; \quad f_5(a_1, b_2) = y$$
$$f_7(a_1, a_2) = z; \quad f_7(a_1, b_2) = x.$$

The reason is that the above functions are ex-post efficient, DSIC, and also nondictatorial. Unfortunately however, such desirable situations do not occur in general. In the present case, the desirable situation does occur due to certain reasons that will be clear soon. $\square$

In a general setting, ex-post efficiency, DSIC, and nondictatorial properties can never be satisfied simultaneously. In fact, even DSIC and nondictatorial properties cannot coexist. This is the implication of the powerful Gibbard-Satterthwaite theorem.

17.2 The Gibbard-Satterthwaite Theorem

We will build up some notation before presenting the theorem.

Rational Preference Relations

We have already seen that the preference of an agent i, over the outcome set X, when its type is θ_i, can be described by means of a *utility function* $u_i(\cdot, \theta_i) : X \to \mathbb{R}$, which assigns a real number to each element in X. A utility function $u_i(\cdot, \theta_i)$ always induces a *unique* preference relation $\succsim$ on X which can be described in the following manner:

$$x \succsim y \Leftrightarrow u_i(x, \theta_i) \geq u_i(y, \theta_i).$$

The above preference relation is often called a *rational preference relation* and it is formally defined as follows.

Definition 17.1 (Rational Preference Relation). *We say that a relation $\succsim$ on the set X is a rational preference relation if it possesses the following three properties:*

(1) Reflexivity: $\forall\, x \in X$, we have $x \succsim x$.
(2) Completeness: $\forall\, x, y \in X$, we have that $x \succsim y$ or $y \succsim x$ (or both).
(3) Transitivity: $\forall\, x, y, z \in X$, if $x \succsim y$ and $y \succsim z$, then $x \succsim z$.

The following proposition establishes the relationship between rational preference relations and utility functions.

Proposition 17.1.

(1) If a preference relation $\succsim$ on X is induced by some utility function $u_i(\cdot, \theta_i)$, then it will be a rational preference relation.
(2) For any given rational preference relation $\succsim$ on X, there may not exist a utility function that induces it. However, when the set X is finite, given any rational preference relation, there will certainly exist a utility function that induces it.
(3) For a given rational preference relation $\succsim$ on X, there might be several utility functions that induce it. Indeed, if the utility function $u_i(\cdot, \theta_i)$ induces $\succsim$, then $u_i'(x, \theta_i) = f(u_i(x, \theta_i))$ is another utility function that will also induce $\succsim$, where $f : \mathbb{R} \to \mathbb{R}$ is a strictly increasing function.

Strict-Total Preference Relations

We now define a special class of rational preference relations that satisfy the anti-symmetry property also.

Definition 17.2 (Strict-Total Preference Relation). *We say that a rational preference relation $\succsim$ is strict-total if it possesses the antisymmetry property, in addition to reflexivity, completeness, and transitivity. Antisymmetry means that, for any $x, y \in X$ such that $x \succsim y$ as well as $y \succsim x$, the outcomes x and y are the same.*

　　The strict-total preference relation is also known as a *linear order relation* because it satisfies the properties of the usual *greater than or equal to* relationship on the real line. Let us denote the set of all rational preference relations and strict-total preference relations on the set X by $\mathscr{R}$ and $\mathscr{P}$, respectively. It is easy to see that $\mathscr{P} \subset \mathscr{R}$.

Ordinal Preference Relations

In a mechanism design problem, for agent i, the preferences over the set X are described in the form of a utility function $u_i : X \times \Theta_i \to \mathbb{R}$. That is, for every possible type $\theta_i \in \Theta_i$ of agent i, we can define a utility function $u_i(\cdot, \theta_i)$ over the set X. Let this utility function induce a rational preference relation $\succsim_i (\theta_i)$ over X. The set $\mathscr{R}_i = \{ \succsim_i (\theta_i) : \theta_i \in \Theta_i \}$ is known as the set of ordinal preference relations for agent i. It is easy to see that $\mathscr{R}_i \subset \mathscr{R} \;\; \forall \, i \in N$.

With all the above notions in place, we are now in a position to state the GS theorem.

Theorem 17.1 (Gibbard-Satterthwaite Impossibility Theorem). *Consider a social choice function $f : \Theta \to X$. Suppose that*

(1) The outcome set X is finite and $|X| \geq 3$,
(2) $\mathscr{R}_i = \mathscr{P} \;\; \forall \, i \in N$,
(3) f is an onto mapping, that is, the image of SCF $f(\cdot)$ is the set X.

Then the social choice function f is dominant strategy incentive compatible iff it is dictatorial.

The implication of condition (2) above is that each agent will exhibit all possible strict-total preferences over outcomes through its different types. Thus the preference structure is as *rich* as it could possibly be. The implication of condition (3) is that every outcome in X is possible under the social choice mapping $f(.)$. Figure 17.1 shows a pictorial representation of the GS theorem. The figure depicts two classes F_1 and F_2 of social choice functions. The class F_1 is the set of all SCFs that satisfy conditions (1) and (2) of the theorem while the class F_2 is the set of all SCFs that satisfy condition (3) of the theorem. The class GS is the set of all SCFs in the intersection of F_1 and F_2 which are DSIC. The functions in the class GS have to be necessarily dictatorial.

Implications of the GS Theorem

One way to get around the impossible situation described by the GS Theorem is to hope that at least one of the conditions (1), (2), and (3) of the theorem does not hold. We discuss each of the possibilities below.

- Condition (1) asserts that $|X| \geq 3$. This condition is violated only if $|X| = 1$ or $|X| = 2$. The case $|X| = 1$ corresponds to a trivial situation and is not of interest. The case $|X| = 2$ is more interesting but is of only limited interest. A public project problem where only a go or no-go decision is involved and there are no payments involved corresponds to this situation.
- Condition (2) asserts that $\mathscr{R}_i = \mathscr{P} \; \forall i \in N$. This means that the preferences of each agent cover the entire space of strict total preference relations on X. That is, each agent has an extremely rich set of preferences. If we are able to

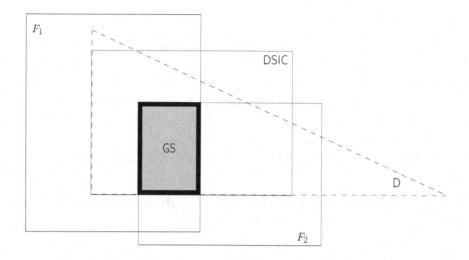

F_1 : Set of all SCFs for which $|X| \geq 3$ and $\mathscr{R}_i = \mathscr{P} \; \forall \; i \in N$
F_2 : Set of all onto SCFs
DSIC: Set of all dominant strategy incentive compatible SCFs
D   : Set of all dictatorial SCFs
GS   : $F_1 \cap F_2 \cap \text{DSIC}$

Fig. 17.1: An illustration of the Gibbard-Satterthwaite theorem

somehow restrict the preferences, we can hope to violate this condition. One can immediately note that this condition was violated in the motivating example (Example 17.1, the supplier selection problem). The celebrated class of VCG mechanisms has been derived by restricting the preferences to the quasilinear domain. This will be discussed in detail in Chapter 18.

- Condition (3) asserts that f is an onto function. Note that this condition also was violated in Example 17.1. This provides one more route for getting around the GS Theorem.

Another way of escaping from the undesirable implications of the GS Theorem is to settle for a weaker form of incentive compatibility than DSIC. We have already discussed Bayesian incentive compatibility (BIC) which only guarantees that reporting true types is a best response in expectation for each agent whenever all other agents also report their true types. Following this route leads us to Bayesian incentive compatible mechanisms. These are discussed in detail in Chapter 19.

The GS Theorem is a significant result that influenced the course of mechanism design research in the 1970s and 1980s.

17.3 Proof of Gibbard Satterthwaite Theorem

We start with a few definitions and concepts: lower contour sets, weak preference reversal property, and monotonicity.

Definition 17.3 (Lower Contour Set). *Given an outcome* $x \in X$, *and agent* $i \in N$ *and a type of agent* i, $\theta_i \in \Theta_i$, *the lower contour set* $L_i(x, \theta_i)$ *is defined as*

$$L_i(x, \theta_i) = \{y \in X \; : \; u_i(x, \theta_i) \geq u_i(y, \theta_i)\}$$

The lower contour set of agent i corresponding to a type θ_i and an outcome x consists of all outcomes which produce equal or less utility than $u_i(x, \theta_i)$.

Weak Preference Reversal Property

Recall the necessary and sufficient condition for DSIC of a social choice function $f(.)$:

$$u_i(f(\theta_i, \theta_{-i}), \; \theta_i) \; \geq \; u_i(f(\hat{\theta}_i, \theta_{-i}), \; \theta_i) \; \forall \; \theta_i \in \Theta_i; \; \forall \; \hat{\theta}_i \in \Theta_i; \; \forall \; \theta_{-i} \in \Theta_{-i}; \; \forall i \in N$$

Consider an agent $i \in N$ and let θ_i', $\theta_i'' \in \Theta_i$ be any two possible types. If the function $f(.)$ is DSIC, then the above necessary and sufficient condition yields the following two inequalities:

$$u_i(f(\theta_i', \theta_{-i}), \; \theta_i') \; \geq \; u_i(f(\theta_i'', \theta_{-i}), \; \theta_i') \; \forall \theta_{-i} \in \Theta_{-i}$$
$$u_i(f(\theta_i'', \theta_{-i}), \; \theta_i'') \; \geq \; u_i(f(\theta_i', \theta_{-i}), \; \theta_i'') \; \forall \theta_{-i} \in \Theta_{-i}$$

Clearly, the preference ranking of the outcomes $f(\theta_i', \theta_{-i})$ and $f(\theta_i'', \theta_{-i})$ *weakly reverses* when the type changes from θ_i' to θ_i''. This motivates the following definition.

Definition 17.4 (Weak Preference Reversal Property). *Consider an agent* $i \in N$ *and let* θ_i', $\theta_i'' \in \Theta_i$ *be any two possible types. Given* $\theta_{-i} \in \Theta_{-i}$, *we say the SCF* $f(.)$ *satisfies the weak preference reversal property for agent* i *and for types* θ_i', θ_i'' *if the following inequalities are satisfied.*

$$u_i(f(\theta_i', \theta_{-i}), \; \theta_i') \; \geq \; u_i(f(\theta_i'', \theta_{-i}), \; \theta_i')$$
$$u_i(f(\theta_i'', \theta_{-i}), \; \theta_i'') \; \geq \; u_i(f(\theta_i', \theta_{-i}), \; \theta_i'')$$

It can be shown that, if a social choice function $f(.)$ is such that the above weak preference reversal property holds for all possible pairs $\theta_i', \theta_i'' \in \Theta_i$ and for all $\theta_{-i} \in \Theta_{-i}$ ($\forall i \in N$), then $f(.)$ is DSIC [3]. Thus DSIC can also be characterized as being equivalent to the weak preference reversal property being satisfied for all agents $i \in N$ and for all $\theta_i', \theta_i'' \in \Theta_i$ and for all $\theta_{-i} \in \Theta_{-i}$. In terms of lower contour sets, the above observations can be summarized as the following proposition.

Proposition 17.2. *A social choice function* $f : \theta \to X$ *is DSIC iff* $\forall i \in N$, $\forall \theta_{-i} \in \Theta_{-i}$ *and all pairs* $\theta_i', \theta_i'' \in \Theta_i$, *the following inequalities are satisfied.*

$$f(\theta_i'', \theta_{-i}) \; \in \; L_i(f(\theta_i', \theta_{-i}), \; \theta_i') \; \text{ and } \; f(\theta_i', \theta_{-i}) \; \in \; L_i(f(\theta_i'', \theta_{-i}), \; \theta_i'')$$

Monotonicity

Monotonicity is an important property of a social choice function and plays a crucial role in mechanism design theory. Suppose $\theta \in \Theta$ and $f(\theta) = x \in X$. Let the type profile θ change to $\theta' \in \Theta$ and assume that in the new type profile θ', no agent finds that some alternative which was weakly worse than x under type θ, becomes strictly preferred to x. That is, there does not exist an agent i such that an outcome $y \in X$ that was (weakly) worse than x under θ will become strictly better than x under θ'. Then monotonicity of $f(.)$ means that x must continue to be the social choice in θ', that is $f(\theta') = x$. This is formalized in the following definition.

Definition 17.5 (Monotonicity). *A social choice function $f : \Theta \to X$ is monotonic if $\forall \theta \in \Theta,\ \forall \theta' \in \Theta\ (\theta' \neq \theta)$,*

$$L_i(f(\theta), \theta_i) \subset L_i(f(\theta), \theta_i') \ \forall\ i \in N \Longrightarrow f(\theta') = f(\theta)$$

The above means that, for each agent i, outcomes which were weakly worse than $f(\theta)$ under θ_i, will continue to be weakly worse than $f(\theta)$ under θ_i'.

Proof of Gibbard-Satterthwaite Theorem

The proof is simple in one direction: Suppose all the conditions $(1) - (3)$ are satisfied and $f(.)$ is dictatorial, it can be shown easily that $f(.)$ is DSIC. This is left as an exercise.

In the other direction, we are given that conditions $(1) - (3)$ are satisfied and $f(.)$ is DSIC. We have to show that $f(.)$ is dictatorial. The proof of this proceeds in three steps. We have followed here closely the proof approach given by Mas-Colell, Whinston, and Green [3].

Step 1 : Showing that $f(.)$ is Monotonic

We are given that $f(.)$ is DSIC. Consider two profiles $\theta = (\theta_1, \theta_2, \ldots, \theta_n)$ and $\theta' = (\theta_1', \theta_2', \ldots, \theta_n')$ such that

$$L_i(f(\theta), \theta_i) \subset L_i(f(\theta), \theta_i') \ \forall i \in N$$

Consider the outcome $f(\theta_1', \theta_2, \ldots, \theta_n)$. Then by the weak preference reversal property, we have

$$f(\theta_1', \theta_2, \ldots, \theta_n) \in L_1(f(\theta_1, \theta_2, \ldots, \theta_n), \theta_1)$$

The above two equations imply that

$$f(\theta_1', \theta_2, \ldots, \theta_n) \in L_1(f(\theta_1, \theta_2, \ldots, \theta_n), \theta_1')$$

From the above inclusion, it follows that

$$f(\theta_1, \theta_2, \ldots, \theta_n) \succsim_1 (\theta_1') f(\theta_1', \theta_2, \ldots, \theta_n)$$

By the weak preference reversal property, we again have

$$f(\theta_1, \theta_2, \ldots, \theta_n) \in L_1(f(\theta_1', \theta_2, \ldots, \theta_n), \theta_1')$$

which implies

$$f(\theta_1', \theta_2, \ldots, \theta_n) \succsim_1 (\theta_1') f(\theta_1, \theta_2, \ldots, \theta_n)$$

Since $\mathscr{R}_i = \mathscr{P}$ $\forall i \in N$, no two alternatives can be indifferent in the preference relation $\succsim_1 (\theta_1')$. Therefore it must be that

$$f(\theta_1', \theta_2, \ldots, \theta_n) = f(\theta_1, \theta_2, \ldots, \theta_n)$$

On similar lines, it can be shown that

$$f(\theta_1', \theta_2', \theta_3, \ldots, \theta_n) = f(\theta_1, \theta_2, \ldots, \theta_n)$$

Extending the above argument iteratively we get what we need for monotonicity of $f(.)$:

$$f(\theta_1', \theta_2', \ldots, \theta_n') = f(\theta_1, \theta_2, \ldots, \theta_n)$$

Step 2 : Showing that $f(.)$ is Ex-Post Efficient

Here we show that $f(.)$ is ex-post efficient if $|X| \geq 3$; $\mathscr{R}_i = \mathscr{P}$ $\forall i \in N$; $f(\Theta) = X$, and $f(.)$ is monotonic. We prove this by contradiction. Suppose $f(.)$ is not ex-post efficient. Then, there exists a type profile $\theta \in \Theta$ and an outcome $y \in X$, $y \neq f(\theta)$, such that

$$u_i(y, \theta_i) > u_i(f(\theta), \theta_i) \ \forall \ i \in N$$

The above involves only strict inequality because no two alternatives can be indifferent for any agent as $\mathscr{R}_i = \mathscr{P}$ $\forall i \in N$. Since f is onto, there exists a type profile $\theta' \in \Theta$ such that $f(\theta') = y$. Therefore, we have

$$u_i(f(\theta'), \theta_i) > u_i(f(\theta), \theta_i) \ \forall i \in N$$

Choose $\theta'' \in \Theta$ such that $\forall \ i \in N$,

$$u_i(f(\theta'), \theta_i'') > u_i(f(\theta), \theta_i'') > u_i(z, \theta_i'') \ \forall \ z \neq f(\theta), f(\theta')$$

The above choice is certainly possible since all preferences in $\mathscr{P}$ are allowed and $|X| \geq 3$. We now invoke monotonicity by first showing that

$$L_i(f(\theta'), \theta_i') \subset L_i(f(\theta'), \theta_i'') \ \forall \ i \in N$$

To show the above, we show that

$$x \in L_i(f(\theta'), \theta_i') \implies x \in L_i(f(\theta'), \theta_i'') \ \forall x \in X$$

First note that if $x = f(\theta)$ or $x = f(\theta')$, then clearly, $x \in L_i(f(\theta'), \theta_i'')$, so there is nothing to show. If $x \neq f(\theta), f(\theta')$, then

$$x \in L_i(f(\theta'), \theta_i') \implies u_i(x, \theta_i') \leq u_i(f(\theta'), \theta_i')$$

We know that $u_i(x, \theta_i'') \leq u_i(f(\theta'), \theta_i'')$ which immediately implies that $x \in L_i(f(\theta'), \theta_i'')$.

Now invoking monotonicity, we get

$$f(\theta'') = f(\theta')$$

We can also show that $L_i(f(\theta), \theta_i) \subset L_i(f(\theta), \theta_i'') \; \forall i \in N$. Monotonicity again implies that

$$f(\theta'') = f(\theta)$$

The above is a contradiction, since $f(\theta') \neq f(\theta)$. This in turn implies that f must be ex-post efficient.

Step 3 : Showing that $f(.)$ is Dictatorial

We are given that $f(\cdot)$ is DSIC and EPE and we have to show that $f(\cdot)$ is dictatorial. This result can be obtained as a corollary of the Arrow's impossibility result (see the next section).   ∎

Some Notes and Observations

We make the following important observations about the GS theorem.

Note. It may be noted that the finiteness of X is not required for GS Theorem. However, if X is not finite, the assumption about agents being expected utility maximizers may not be compatible with the condition $\mathcal{R}_i = \mathcal{P} \; \forall i \in N$ [3]. If X is not finite, the GS Theorem will still hold if $\mathcal{R}_i$ for each $i \in N$ is the set of all continuous preferences on X [3].

Note. If $|X| = 2$, the GS theorem is not true. We have already seen this earlier in this section while discussing Example 17.1.

Note. When $\mathcal{R}_i = \mathcal{P} \; \forall i \in N$, it may be noted that any ex-post efficient social choice function must have $f(\Theta) = X$.

Note. The GS theorem holds even if the assumption (2) is relaxed to $\mathcal{P} \subset \mathcal{R}_i \; \forall i \in N$.

Note. We have already seen (Definition 16.5) that $f : \Theta \to X$ is dictatorial on $Y \subset X$ if there exists an agent $d \in N$ such that $\forall \, \theta \in \Theta$,

$$u_d(f(\theta), \theta_d) \geq u_d(y, \theta_d) \, \forall y \in Y$$

The GS theorem holds good under the following special setting also: suppose X is finite, $|f(\Theta)| \geq 3$, and $\mathcal{P} \subset \mathcal{R}_i \; \forall i \in N$. Then $f(.)$ is DSIC iff $f(.)$ is dictatorial on $f(\Theta)$.

Kenneth Joseph Arrow received the Nobel Prize in Economic Sciences in 1972, jointly with John R. Hicks, for their pioneering contributions to general economic equilibrium theory and welfare theory. Arrow is regarded as one of the most influential economists of all time. With his path-breaking contributions in social choice theory, general equilibrium analysis, endogenous growth theory, and economics of information, Kenneth Arrow is truly a legend of economics. Three of his doctoral students, John Harsanyi, Michael Spencer, and Roger Myerson are also Economics Nobel laureates.

The famous Arrow impossibility theorem was one of the outstanding results included in his classic book in 1951 *Social Choice and Individual Values*, which itself was inspired by his doctoral work. The theorem was first published in the *Journal of Political Economy* in 1950. This theorem is perhaps the most important result in welfare economics and also has far-reaching ramifications for mechanism design theory.

Kenneth Arrow was born in the New York City on August 23, 1921. He earned his doctorate from Columbia University in 1951, working with Professor Harold Hotelling. He is a recipient of the von Neumann Theory Prize in 1986, and he was awarded in 2004 the National Medal of Science, the highest scientific honor in the United States. His joint work with Gerard Debreu on general equilibrium theory is also a major landmark that was prominently noted in the Nobel Prize awarded to Gerard Debreu in 1983. Arrow is currently the Joan Kenney Professor of Economics and Professor of Operations Research, Emeritus, at Stanford University.

17.4 Arrow's Impossibility Theorem

The need to aggregate preference orderings of individual players into a single social preference ordering arises in many contexts. The Arrow's theorem is a landmark result that shows that when there are at least three outcomes, there is no method that can aggregate the individual preference orderings into a social preference ordering while meeting certain desirable criteria. Following are these criteria:

- *Unanimity*: If every player prefers alternative x to alternative y, then the social ordering also prefers x to y.
- *Pairwise Independence*: If every player's preference between x and y remains unchanged, then in the social ordering also, the preference between x and y remains unchanged (even if the preferences of the players between other pairs such as x and z; y and z; and z and w change).
- *No Dictator Property*: No single player possesses the power to completely dictate the social ordering.

Arrow's impossibility theorem has shaped the discipline of social choice theory in many significant ways. It has been used extensively in proving many important results in microeconomics including the Gibbard-Satterthwaite theorem.

Before discussing this result, we first set up some relevant notation. Consider a set of agents $N = \{1, 2, \ldots, n\}$ and a set of outcomes X. Let $\succsim_i$ be a rational preference relation of agent i ($i \in N$). For example, $\succsim_i$ could be induced by $u_i(., \theta_i)$ where θ_i is a certain type of agent i. Each agent is thus naturally associated with a set $\mathscr{R}_i$ of rational preference relations derived from the utility functions $u_i(., \theta_i)$ where $\theta_i \in \Theta_i$.

Given a rational preference relation $\succsim_i$, denote by $\succ_i$ the relation defined by

$$(x, y) \in \succ_i \text{ iff } (x, y) \in \succsim_i \text{ and } (y, x) \notin \succsim_i .$$

The relation $\succ_i$ is said to be the *strict total preference relation* derived from $\succsim_i$. Note that $\succ_i = \succsim_i$ if $\succsim_i$ itself is a strict total preference relation. Given an outcome set X, a strict total preference relation can be simply represented as an ordered tuple of elements of X.

As usual $\mathscr{R}$ and $\mathscr{P}$ denote, respectively, the set of all rational preference relations and strict total preference relations on the set X. Let $\mathscr{A}$ be any nonempty subset of $\mathscr{R}^n$. We define a *social welfare functional* as a mapping from $\mathscr{A}$ to $\mathscr{R}$.

Definition 17.6 (Social Welfare Functional). *Given* $N = \{1, 2, \ldots, n\}$, *an outcome set* X, *and a set of profiles* $\mathscr{A}$ *of rational preference relations of the agents,* $\mathscr{A} \subset \mathscr{R}^n$, *a social welfare functional is a mapping* $W : \mathscr{A} \longrightarrow \mathscr{R}$.

Note that a social welfare functional W aggregates a given profile of rational preference relations $(\succsim_1, \ldots, \succsim_n) \in \mathscr{A}$, into a single rational preference relation $\succsim$.

Example 17.2 (Social Welfare Functional). Consider the example of the supplier selection problem discussed earlier, where $N = \{1, 2\}$, $X = \{x, y, z\}$, $\Theta_1 = \{a_1\}$, and $\Theta_2 = \{a_2, b_2\}$. Recall the utility functions:

$$u_1(x, a_1) = 100; \quad u_1(y, a_1) = 50; \quad u_1(z, a_1) = 0$$
$$u_2(x, a_2) = 0; \quad u_2(y, a_2) = 50; \quad u_2(z, a_2) = 100$$
$$u_2(x, b_2) = 30; \quad u_2(y, b_2) = 60; \quad u_2(z, b_2) = 20.$$

The utility function u_1 leads to the following strict preference relation:

$$\succsim_{a_1} = (x, y, z).$$

The utility function u_2 leads to the strict total preference relations:

$$\succsim_{a_2} = (z, y, x); \quad \succsim_{b_2} = (y, x, z).$$

Let the set $\mathscr{A}$ be defined as

$$\mathscr{A} = \{(\succsim_{a_1}, \succsim_{a_2}), (\succsim_{a_1}, \succsim_{b_2})\}.$$

An example of a social welfare functional here would be the mapping W_1 given by

$$W_1(\succsim_{a_1}, \succsim_{a_2}) = (x, y, z); \quad W_1(\succsim_{a_1}, \succsim_{b_2}) = (y, x, z).$$

Another example would be the mapping W_2 given by

$$W_2(\succsim_{a_1}, \succsim_{a_2}) = (x, y, z); \quad W_2(\succsim_{a_1}, \succsim_{b_2}) = (z, y, x).$$

Several such social welfare functionals can be defined here. □

Note the difference between a social choice function and a social welfare functional. In the case of a social choice function, the preferences are summarized in terms of types and each type profile is mapped to a social outcome. On the other hand, a social welfare functional maps a profile of individual preferences to a social preference relation. Recall that the type of an agent determines a preference relation on the set X through the utility function.

We now define three properties of a social welfare functional: *unanimity* (also called *Paretian property*); *pairwise independence* (also called *independence of irrelevant alternatives* (IIA)), and *dictatorship*.

Definition 17.7 (Unanimity). *A social welfare functional $W : \mathscr{A} \longrightarrow \mathscr{R}$ is said to be unanimous if $\forall (\succsim_1, \ldots, \succsim_n) \in \mathscr{A}$ and $\forall x, y \in X$,*

$$(x, y) \in \succsim_i \ \forall i \in N \implies (x, y) \in W_p(\succsim_1, \ldots, \succsim_n)$$

where $W_p(\succsim_1, \ldots, \succsim_n)$ is the strict preference relation derived from $W(\succsim_1, \ldots, \succsim_n)$.

The above definition means that, for all pairs $x, y \in X$, whenever x is preferred to y for every agent, then x is also socially preferred to y (in a strict way).

Example 17.3 (Unanimity). For the setting in Example 17.2, recall

$$W_1(\succsim_{a_1}, \succsim_{a_2}) = W_1((x, y, z), (z, y, x)) = (x, y, z)$$

$$W_1(\succsim_{a_1}, \succsim_{b_2}) = W_1((x, y, z), (y, x, z)) = (y, x, z).$$

In order to check unanimity, we need to check only the following pairs for which both the two players have the same preference order:

- $(y, z) \in \succsim_{a_1}, (y, z) \in \succsim_{b_2}$, and $(y, z) \in W_1(\succsim_{a_1}, \succsim_{b_2})$; and
- $(x, z) \in \succsim_{a_1}, (x, z) \in \succsim_{b_2}$, and $(x, z) \in W_1(\succsim_{a_1}, \succsim_{b_2})$.

Thus W_1 is unanimous. On the other hand, consider

$$W_2((x, y, z), (z, y, x)) = (x, y, z); \quad W_2((x, y, z), (y, x, z)) = (z, y, x)$$

Here $(y, z) \in \succsim_{a_1}$ and $(y, z) \in \succsim_{b_2}$ but $(y, z) \notin W_2(\succsim_{a_1}, \succsim_{b_2})$. So W_2 is not unanimous. □

We now introduce pairwise independence or independence of irrelevant alternatives (IIA). This property implies that the social preference between x and y will depend only on the individual preferences between x and y. More specifically, given two profiles ($\succsim_1, \ldots, \succsim_n$) and ($\succsim'_1, \ldots, \succsim'_n$) such that for all players $i \in N$, the outcomes x and y have the same order in $\succsim_1$ and $\succsim'_1$, then the outcomes x and y will have the same order in $W(\succsim_1, \ldots, \succsim_n)$ and $W(\succsim'_1, \ldots, \succsim'_n)$. Note that preferences between other pairs such as x and z; y and z; and z and w do not matter here (this explains why this property is called independence of irrelevant alternatives). The formal definition of this key notion is given below.

Definition 17.8 (Pairwise Independence). *The social welfare functional* $W : \mathscr{A} \longrightarrow \mathscr{R}$ *is said to satisfy pairwise independence if:*

$$\forall x, y \in X, \ \forall (\succsim_1, \ldots, \succsim_n), (\succsim_1', \ldots, \succsim_n') \in \mathscr{A} \text{ satisfying}$$

$$(x, y) \in \succsim_i \ \Leftrightarrow \ (x, y) \in \succsim_i' \text{ and } (y, x) \in \succsim_i \Leftrightarrow (y, x) \in \succsim_i' \ \forall i \in N,$$

we have that

$$(x, y) \in W(\succsim_1, \ldots, \succsim_n) \Leftrightarrow (x, y) \in W(\succsim_1', \ldots, \succsim_n'); \text{ and}$$

$$(y, x) \in W(\succsim_1, \ldots, \succsim_n) \Leftrightarrow (y, x) \in W(\succsim_1', \ldots, \succsim_n').$$

Example 17.4 (Pairwise Independence). Consider the example as before and let

$$W_3(\succsim_{a_1}, \succsim_{a_2}) = W_3((x, y, z), (z, y, x)) = (x, y, z)$$

$$W_3(\succsim_{a_1}, \succsim_{b_2}) = W_3((x, y, z), (y, x, z)) = (y, z, x).$$

Here agent 1 prefers x to y in both the profiles while agent 2 prefers y to x in both the profiles. However in the first case, x is socially preferred to y while in the second case y is socially preferred to x. Thus the social preference between x and y is not dependent solely on the individual preferences between x and y. This shows that W_3 is not pairwise independent. On the other hand, consider W_4 given by

$$W_4((x, y, z), (z, y, x)) = (x, y, z)$$

$$W_4((x, y, z), (y, x, z)) = (z, x, y).$$

Now this social welfare functional satisfies pairwise independence. □

The pairwise independence property is a very appealing property since it ensures that the social ranking between any pair of alternatives x and y does not in any way depend on alternatives other than x and y or the relative positions of these other alternatives in the individual preferences. Secondly, the pairwise independence property has a connection to the weak preference reversal property, which we have studied earlier in this chapter. Recall that weak preference reversal property is quite crucial in ensuring dominant strategy incentive compatibility of social choice functions. Finally, the pairwise independence property leads to a natural decomposition of the problem of social ranking. For instance, if we wish to determine a social ranking on the outcomes of a subset Y of X, we do not need to worry about individual preferences on the set $X \backslash Y$.

We next introduce the dictatorship property which means that there exists a player (called a dictator) who calls all the shots: the social preference ordering is always the same as the preference ordering of the dictator. In other words, there exists a player whose preferences always prevail. Ideally we would like the social welfare functional to be non-dictatorial.

Definition 17.9 (Dictatorship). *A social welfare functional* $W : \mathscr{A} \longrightarrow \mathscr{R}$ *is called a dictatorship if there exists an agent,* $d \in N$*, called the dictator such that* $\forall x, y \in X$ *and* $\forall (\succsim_1, \ldots, \succsim_n) \in \mathscr{A}$*, we have*

$$(x, y) \in \succsim_d \Longrightarrow (x, y) \in W_p(\succsim_1, \ldots, \succsim_n).$$

This means that whenever the dictator prefers x to y, then x is also socially preferred to y, irrespective of the preferences of the other agents. A social welfare functional that does not have a dictator is said to be nondictatorial.

Example 17.5 (Dictatorship). Consider the social welfare functional

$$W_5((x, y, z), (z, y, x)) = (x, y, z)$$

$$W_5((x, y, z), (y, x, z)) = (x, y, z).$$

It is clear that agent 1 is a dictator here. On the other hand, the social welfare functional

$$W_3((x, y, z), (z, y, x)) = (x, y, z)$$

$$W_3((x, y, z), (y, x, z)) = (y, z, x)$$

is not dictatorial. □

The dream of a social planner would be to implement a social welfare functional that is unanimous, satisfies the pairwise independence property, and is nondictatorial. Unfortunately, this belongs to the realm of impossible situations when the preference profiles of the agents are *rich*. This is the essence of the Arrow's Impossibility Theorem, which is stated next.

Theorem 17.2 (Arrow's Impossibility Theorem). *Suppose*

(1) $|X| \geq 3$*,*
(2) $\mathscr{A} = \mathscr{R}^n$ *or* $\mathscr{A} = \mathscr{P}^n$*.*

Then every social welfare functional $W : \mathscr{A} \longrightarrow \mathscr{R}$ *that is unanimous and satisfies pairwise independence is dictatorial.*

The theorem was first enunciated in [4] and elaborated later in [5]. For a proof of this theorem, we refer the reader to Proposition 21.C.1 of Mas-Colell, Whinston, and Green [3]. Arrow's Impossibility Theorem is pictorially depicted in Figure 17.2. The set P denotes the set of all Paretian or unanimous social welfare functionals. The set IIA denotes the set of all social welfare functionals that satisfy independence of irrelevant alternatives (or pairwise independence). The diagram shows that the intersection of P and IIA is necessarily a subset of D, the class of all dictatorial social welfare functionals.

The Gibbard-Satterthwaite theorem has close connections to Arrow's Impossibility Theorem. The property of unanimity of social welfare functionals is related

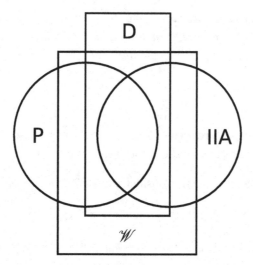

$\mathscr{W}$: Set of all social welfare functionals with $\mathscr{A} = \mathscr{R}^n$ or $\mathscr{P}^n$

P   : Set of all paretian or unanimous functionals

IIA : Set of all functionals satisfying independence of irrelevant alternatives
      or pairwise independence

D   : Dictatorial social welfare functionals

Fig. 17.2: An illustration of Arrow's impossibility theorem

to ex-post efficiency of social choice functions. The notions of dictatorship of so-cial welfare functionals and social choice functions are closely related. The pairwise independence property of social welfare functionals has intimate connections with the DSIC property of social choice functions through the weak preference reversal property and monotonicity. We do not delve deep into this here; interested readers are referred to the book of Mas-Colell, Whinston, and Green [3] (Chapters 21 and 23).

To conclude this section, we state a corollary of the Arrow's impossibility theorem which is critically used in the proof of the Gibbard-Satterthwaite theorem. This is Proposition 21.E.1 in the book by Mas-Colell, Whinston, and Green [3].

Proposition 17.3. *Suppose* $|X| \geq 3$ *and the domain of admissible preferences is either* $\mathscr{A} = \mathscr{R}^n$ *or* $\mathscr{A} = \mathscr{P}^n$. *Then every weakly Paretian and monotonic social choice function* $f : \mathscr{A} \longrightarrow X$ *is dictatorial.*

17.5 Summary and References

The GS theorem essentially states that DSIC can only be achieved by dictatorial social choice functions when (a) the outcome set is finite and there are at least three elements (b) all possible strict preferences over outcomes are possible for every agent (c) the SCF produces every possible outcome. On the face of it, the GS theorem clearly gives disappointing news to mechanism designers. However, by carefully looking at the conditions under which the theorem holds, mechanism design researchers have unearthed many interesting possibilities as follows.

- Restriction of the preferences to the quasilinear setting has led to the popular VCG (Vickrey-Clarke-Groves) mechanisms which achieve dominant strategy incentive compatibility and allocative efficiency in general practical situations
- Relaxation of DSIC to BIC has led to a variety of Bayesian mechanisms such as the dAGVA mechanism which satisfy BIC, AE, and also strict budget balance.

The famous Arrow's impossibility result predates the GS theorem by almost two decades and provides technical support to prove the GS theorem. Arrow's theorem is in the broader area of social choice theory and states under similar technical conditions that unanimity and independence of irrelevant alternatives cannot coexist with non-dictatorship.

There are many alternate proofs for the Gibbard-Satterthwaite theorem and the Arrow's impossibility theorem. The proof provided here for the GS theorem is based on the treatment available in the book by Mas-Colell, Whinston, and Green [3]. Sen has provided an elegant direct proof of the Gibbard-Satterthwaite theorem in [6].

References

[1]   A. Gibbard. "Manipulation of voting schemes". In: *Econometrica* **41** (1973), pp. 587–601.

[2]   M.A. Satterthwaite. "Strategy-proofness and Arrow's conditions: Existence and correspondence theorem for voting procedure and social welfare functions". In: *Journal of Economic Theory* **10** (1975), pp. 187–217.

[3]   Andreu Mas-Colell, Michael D. Whinston, and Jerry R. Green. *Microeconomic Theory*. Oxford University Press, 1995.

[4]   Kenneth J. Arrow. "A difficulty in the concept of social welfare". In: *Journal of Political Economy* **58**(4) (1950), pp. 328–346.

[5]   Kenneth J. Arrow. *Social Choice and Individual Values*. Yale University Press, 1951.

[6]   Arunava Sen. "Another direct proof of the Gibbarad-Satterthwaite theorem". In: *Economics Letters* **70** (2001), pp. 381–385.

Chapter 18

Vickrey-Clarke-Groves (VCG) Mechanisms

VCG mechanisms constitute an extensively studied special class of *mechanisms with money*. They are derived using the idea of violating one of the necessary conditions of the Gibbard-Satterthwaite theorem. VCG mechanisms assume a restricted environment called the *quasilinear environment* in which no social choice function can be dictatorial and moreover the mechanism can be elegantly decomposed into an allocation rule and a payment rule. Further the ex-post efficiency property can be separated into two properties, *allocative efficiency* (a property of the allocation rule) and *strict budget balance* (a property of the payment rule). VCG mechanisms are appealing because they satisfy allocative efficiency as well as dominant strategy incentive compatibility. We discuss the quasilinear environment first followed by *Groves mechanisms* (which are the most general among VCG mechanisms). Then we discuss the *Clarke mechanism* (also called pivotal mechanism) of which the Vickrey mechanism is a special case. We provide several examples to illustrate VCG mechanisms.

18.1   The Quasilinear Environment

In the quasilinear environment, an outcome $x \in X$ is a vector of the form $x = (k, t_1, \ldots, t_n)$, where k is an element of a set K, which is called the set of *project choices* or *allocations*. The set K is usually assumed to be finite. The term $t_i \in \mathbb{R}$ represents the monetary transfer to agent i. If $t_i > 0$, then, by convention, agent i receives an amount of money equal to t_i and if $t_i < 0$, agent i pays an amount of money equal to t_i. It is important to note that an outcome is decomposed into an allocation part and a payment part. The set of alternatives X is therefore

$$X = \{(k, t_1, \ldots, t_n) : k \in K; \ t_i \in \mathbb{R}; \ \forall i \in N\}.$$

Often, we deal with a system in which the n agents have no external source of funding and we make the implicit assumption:

$$\sum_{i \in N} t_i \leq 0.$$

This condition is known as the *weak budget balance* condition. When this condition is assumed, the set of alternatives will become:

$$X = \left\{ (k, t_1, \ldots, t_n) : k \in K; \ t_i \in \mathbb{R} \ \forall \ i \in N; \ \sum_{i \in N} t_i \leq 0 \right\}.$$

An outcome of a social choice function $f : \Theta \to X$ in quasilinear environment takes the form $f(\theta) = (k(\theta), t_1(\theta), \ldots, t_n(\theta))$ where, for every $\theta \in \Theta$, we have $k(\theta) \in K$. If weak budget balance is satisfied, we have in addition, $\sum_i t_i(\theta) \leq 0 \ \forall \theta \in \Theta$.

Note. We clarify the use of symbols k and $k(\theta)$ and the symbols t_i and $t_i(\theta)$. If the type profile θ is implicit and clear, we simply use k and t_i. Whenever θ is required to be explicitly mentioned, we use $k(\theta)$ and $t_i(\theta)$. Note that $k(\cdot)$ is a mapping from Θ to K while $t_i(\cdot)$ for $i = 1, \ldots, n$ is a mapping from Θ to $\mathbb{R}$.

For a direct revelation mechanism $\mathscr{D} = ((\Theta_i)_{i \in N}, f(\cdot))$ in this environment, the agent i's utility function takes the quasilinear form

$$u_i(x, \theta_i) = u_i((k, t_1, \ldots, t_n), \theta_i) = v_i(k, \theta_i) + m_i + t_i$$

where m_i is agent i's initial endowment of the money and the function $v_i(\cdot, \cdot)$ is known as agent i's valuation function.

Recall from our discussion of mechanism design environment (Chapter 16) that the utility functions $u_i(\cdot)$ are assumed to be common knowledge. In the context of a quasilinear environment, this implies that for any given type θ_i of any agent i, the social planner and every other agent j have a way of knowing the function $v_i(., \theta_i)$, $t_i(\theta)$, and m_i.

Immediate examples of quasilinear environment include many of the previously discussed examples, such as the first price and second price auctions (Example 14.4), bilateral trade (Example 14.6), the public project problem (Example 14.7), etc. In the quasilinear environment, we can define two important properties of a social choice function, namely, allocative efficiency and budget balance.

Allocative Efficiency

Allocative efficiency is a property of the allocation function $k(\cdot)$ in quasilinear environment.

Definition 18.1 (Allocative Efficiency (AE)). *We say that a social choice function* $f(\cdot) = (k(\cdot), t_1(\cdot), \ldots, t_n(\cdot))$ *is allocatively efficient if for each* $\theta \in \Theta$, $k(\theta)$ *satisfies the following condition*

$$k(\theta) \in \arg\max_{k \in K} \sum_{i=1}^{n} v_i(k, \theta_i).$$

Equivalently,

$$\sum_{i=1}^{n} v_i(k(\theta), \theta_i) = \max_{k \in K} \sum_{i=1}^{n} v_i(k, \theta_i).$$

The above definition implies that for every $\theta \in \Theta$, the allocation $k(\theta)$ will maximize the sum of the values of the players. In other words, every allocation is a value maximizing allocation, or the objects are allocated to the players who value the objects most. This is an extremely desirable property to have for any social choice function. Often, we will be using the symbol $k^*(\cdot)$ for a function $k(\cdot)$ that satisfies Equation (18.1), to indicate that it maximizes the total value in all allocations.

Note. The above definition implicitly assumes that for any given θ, the function $\sum_{i=1}^{n} v_i(., \theta_i) : K \to \mathbb{R}$ attains a maximum over the set K.

Example 18.1 (Public Project Problem). Consider the public project problem with two agents $N = \{1, 2\}$. Let the cost of the public project be 50 units of money. Let the type sets of the two players be given by $\Theta_1 = \Theta_2 = \{20, 60\}$. Each agent either has a low willingness to pay, 20, or a high willingness to pay, 60. Let the set of project choices be $K = \{0, 1\}$, with 1 indicating that the project is taken up and 0 indicating that the project is dropped.

Assume that if $k = 1$, then the two agents will equally share the cost of the project by paying 25 each. If $k = 0$, the project is not taken up and agents do not pay anything. Consider the valuation function:

$$v_i(k, \theta_i) = k(\theta_i - 25).$$

This means, if $k = 0$, the agents derive zero value while if $k = 1$, the value derived is the willingness to pay minus 25. Define the following allocation function:

$$k(\theta_1, \theta_2) = 0 \text{ if } \theta_1 = \theta_2 = 20$$
$$= 1 \text{ otherwise.}$$

This means, the project is taken up only when at least one of the agents has a high willingness to pay. We can see that this function is allocatively efficient.

(θ_1, θ_2)	k	$v_1(k, \theta_1)$ when $k = 0$	$v_2(k, \theta_2)$ when $k = 0$	$v_1(k, \theta_1)$ when $k = 1$	$v_2(k, \theta_2)$ when $k = 1$
$(20, 20)$	0	0	0	-5	-5
$(20, 60)$	1	0	0	-5	35
$(60, 20)$	1	0	0	35	-5
$(60, 60)$	1	0	0	35	35

Table 18.1: Values for different type profiles when $v_i(k, \theta_i) = k(\theta_i - 25)$

This may be easily inferred from Table 18.1, which shows the values derived by the agents for different type profiles. The second column gives the actual value of k. □

Example 18.2 (A Non-Allocatively Efficient SCF). Let the v function be defined as under:
$$v_i(k, \theta_i) = k\theta_i \qquad i = 1, 2.$$

With respect to the above function, the allocation function k defined in Example 18.1 is not allocatively efficient. The values for different type profiles are shown in Table 18.2. If

(θ_1, θ_2)	k	$v_1(k, \theta_1)$ when $k = 0$	$v_2(k, \theta_2)$ when $k = 0$	$v_1(k, \theta_1)$ when $k = 1$	$v_2(k, \theta_2)$ when $k = 1$
$(20, 20)$	0	0	0	20	20
$(20, 60)$	1	0	0	20	60
$(60, 20)$	1	0	0	60	20
$(60, 60)$	1	0	0	60	60

Table 18.2: Values for different type profiles when $v_i(k, \theta_i) = k\theta_i$

the type profile is $(20, 20)$, the allocation is $k = 0$ and the total value of allocation is 0. However, the total value is 40 when the allocation is $k = 1$. This immediately shows that k is not allocatively efficient. $\qquad\square$

Budget Balance

Budget balance is a property of the payment functions $t_1(\cdot), \ldots, t_n(\cdot)$ in quasilinear environment.

Definition 18.2 (Budget Balance (BB)). *We say that a social choice function* $f(\cdot) = (k(\cdot), t_1(\cdot), \ldots, t_n(\cdot))$ *is budget balanced if for each* $\theta \in \Theta$, $t_1(\theta), \ldots, t_n(\theta)$ *satisfy the following condition:*

$$\sum_{i \in N} t_i(\theta) = 0. \qquad (18.1)$$

Conventionally, this property is called *strong budget balance* (SBB), and the property of having

$$\sum_{i \in N} t_i(\theta) \leq 0$$

is called *weak budget balance* (WBB). In this book, we will use the term budget balance (BB) to refer to strong budget balance.

Budget balance ensures that the total receipts are equal to total payments. This means that the system is a closed one, with no surplus and no deficit. The weak budget balance property means that the total payments are greater than or equal to total receipts. Suppose we have a bilateral trading system where there is a set of sellers and a set of buyers who are exchanging objects with monetary transfers.

Suppose $t_i(\theta)$ is the payment received by agent i $(i = 1, 2, \ldots, n)$ when the type profile is θ. There are three possibilities here.

Strictly Budget Balanced

This corresponds to the case when the sum of all monetary transfers of all agents in all type profiles is equal to zero. This means the sum total of payments made by the agents is equal to the sum total of payments received by the agents. This is a happy situation because monetary transfers happen in such a way that there is no surplus or deficit. Such a trading institution can run by itself (in fact in a completely decentralized way).

Weakly Budget Balanced

This corresponds to the case when the sum of all monetary transfers of all agents in all type profiles is less than or equal to zero. This means that the sum total of payments made by the agents is at least as high as the sum total of payments received and there is a surplus. This surplus could be consumed by the market maker or the broker who runs the trading institution.

Not Budget Balanced

Here it will happen that in at least one type profile, the sum total of payments made by the agents is strictly less than the sum total of payments received by the agents, so there is a deficit of money. In this situation, in order to maintain budget balance, there must be an outside agency supplying the deficit. This is a situation that we would like to avoid. In general, the budget balance property has to be carefully interpreted in the context of the specific institutional framework being studied.

Note. In this chapter, we assume that the set of feasible outcomes is given by

$$X = \left\{ (k, t_1, \ldots, t_n) : k \in K; \ t_i \in \mathbb{R}; \ \forall i \in N; \ \sum_{i \in N} t_i \leq 0 \right\}.$$

As a consequence of this, all social choice functions discussed in this chapter are WBB by design. In the next chapter, we will be discussing a broader class of social choice functions that may or may not be WBB.

Important Consequences of Quasilinearity

We now prove the following two consequences of quasilinearity:

- No social choice function in quasilinear environment is dictatorial.
- In quasilinear environment, ex-post efficiency is equivalent to allocative efficiency together with budget balance.

The first lemma summarizes an important fact about social choice functions in quasilinear environment. This fact enables us to get around the impossible situation created by condition (2) of the Gibbard-Satterthwaite theorem (Theorem 17.1).

Lemma 18.1. *No social choice function with at least two agents in quasilinear environment is dictatorial.*

Proof: Suppose that a social choice function, $f(\cdot)$, is dictatorial in the quasilinear environment. This means that there exists a dictator, say $d \in N$, such that for each $\theta \in \Theta$, we have

$$u_d(f(\theta), \theta_d) \geq u_d(x, \theta_d) \ \forall x \in X.$$

Since the environment is quasilinear, we have

$$u_d(f(\theta), \theta_d) = v_d(k(\theta), \theta_d) + t_d(\theta).$$

Since we are currently assuming that a social choice function is WBB (see note above), there are only two possibilities given a $\theta \in \Theta$: Either the sum of payments is equal to zero or less than to zero. Consider the following alternative $x \in X$:

$$x = \begin{cases} (k(\theta), (t_i = t_i(\theta))_{i \neq d}, t_d = t_d(\theta) - \sum_{i=1}^n t_i(\theta)) & : & \sum_{i=1}^n t_i(\theta) < 0 \\ (k(\theta), (t_i = t_i(\theta))_{i \neq d,j}, t_d = t_d(\theta) + \epsilon, t_j = t_j(\theta) - \epsilon) & : & \sum_{i=1}^n t_i(\theta) = 0 \end{cases}$$

where $\epsilon > 0$ is any arbitrary real number, and j is any agent other than d. It is easy to verify, for the above outcome x, that we have $u_d(x, \theta_d) > u_d(f(\theta), \theta_d)$, which contradicts the assumption that d is a dictator. ∎

We emphasize that allocative efficiency is a property of the allocation function while budget balance is a property of the payment function. If the environment is quasilinear, these two properties together are equivalent to ex-post efficiency. The following lemma states this result.

Lemma 18.2. *A social choice function $f(\cdot) = (k(\cdot), t_1(\cdot), \ldots, t_n(\cdot))$ is ex-post efficient in quasilinear environment if and only if it is allocatively efficient and budget balanced.*

Proof: Let us assume that $f(\cdot) = (k(\cdot), t_1(\cdot), \ldots, t_n(\cdot))$ is allocatively efficient and budget balanced. This implies that for any $\theta \in \Theta$, we have

$$\sum_{i=1}^n u_i(f(\theta), \theta_i) = \sum_{i=1}^n v_i(k(\theta), \theta_i) + \sum_{i=1}^n t_i(\theta)$$

$$= \sum_{i=1}^n v_i(k(\theta), \theta_i) + 0$$

$$\geq \sum_{i=1}^n v_i(k, \theta_i) + \sum_{i=1}^n t_i; \ \forall \, x = (k, t_1, \ldots, t_n) \in X$$

$$= \sum_{i=1}^n u_i(x, \theta_i); \ \forall \, x = (k, t_1, \ldots, t_n) \in X.$$

That is, if the SCF is allocatively efficient and budget balanced, then for any type profile θ of the agent, the outcome chosen by the social choice function will be such that it maximizes the total utility derived by all the agents under any allocation. This will automatically imply that the SCF is ex-post efficient (see Proposition 16.1).

To prove the other direction of the lemma, we proceed in two parts. In the first part, we show that if $f(\cdot)$ is not allocatively efficient, then, it cannot be ex-post efficient and in the second part, we will show that if $f(\cdot)$ is not budget balanced then it cannot be ex-post efficient. These two facts together will imply that if $f(\cdot)$ is ex-post efficient, then it will have to be allocatively efficient and budget balanced, thus completing the proof of the lemma.

To prove the first part, let us assume that $f(\cdot)$ is not allocatively efficient. This means that there exists a $\theta \in \Theta$ and a $k' \in K$ such that

$$\sum_{i=1}^{n} v_i(k', \theta_i) > \sum_{i=1}^{n} v_i(k(\theta), \theta_i).$$

This implies that there exists at least one agent j such that $v_j(k', \theta_i) > v_j(k(\theta), \theta_i)$. Now consider the following alternative x given by

$$\left(k', (t_i = t_i(\theta) + v_i(k(\theta), \theta_i) - v_i(k', \theta_i))_{i \neq j}, t_j = t_j(\theta) + v_j(k(\theta), \theta_j) - v_j(k', \theta_j) + \varepsilon\right)$$

where $\varepsilon > 0$. It is easy to verify that $u_i(x, \theta_i) = u_i(f(\theta), \theta_i) \, \forall \, i \neq j$ and $u_j(x, \theta_j) > u_j(f(\theta), \theta_j)$, implying that $f(\cdot)$ is not ex-post efficient.

To prove the second part, we assume that $f(\cdot)$ is not budget balanced. This means that there exists at least one agent j such that $t_j(\theta) < 0$. Let us consider the following alternative x:

$$x = \left(k', (t_i = t_i(\theta))_{i \neq j}, t_j = t_j(\theta) + \varepsilon\right).$$

It is easy to verify that for the above alternative x, we have

$$u_i(x, \theta_i) = u_i(f(\theta), \theta_i) \, \forall \, i \neq j \text{ and } u_j(x, \theta_j) > u_j(f(\theta), \theta_j),$$

implying that $f(\cdot)$ is not ex-post efficient. ∎

In view of Lemma 18.1, the social planner need not worry about the existence of a dictator in any social choice function in a quasilinear environment and the planner can explore whether there exists any SCF that is both EPE and DSIC. Furthermore, in the light of Lemma 18.2, we can say that the social planner can look for an SCF that is AE, SBB, and DSIC. Once again the question arises whether there could exist social choice functions which satisfy all these three properties – AE, SBB, and DSIC. We explore this and other questions in the forthcoming sections.

18.2 Groves Mechanisms

The main result in this section is that in the quasilinear environment, there exist social choice functions that are both allocatively efficient and dominant strategy incentive compatible. These are in general called the VCG (Vickrey–Clarke–Groves) mechanisms.

The VCG mechanisms are named after their famous inventors William Vickrey, Edward Clarke, and Theodore Groves. It was Vickrey who introduced the famous Vickrey auction (second price sealed bid auction) in 1961 [1]. To this day, the Vickrey auction continues to enjoy a special place in the annals of mechanism design. Clarke [2] and Groves [3] came up with a generalization of the Vickrey mechanisms and helped define a broad class of dominant strategy incentive compatible mechanisms in the quasilinear environment. VCG mechanisms are by far the most extensively used among quasilinear mechanisms. They derive their popularity from their mathematical elegance and the strong properties they satisfy for many practical settings.

The Groves Theorem

The following celebrated result provides a sufficient condition for an allocatively efficient social choice function in quasilinear environment to be dominant strategy incentive compatible. We will refer to this theorem in the sequel as Groves theorem, rather than Groves' theorem. The Groves theorem is one of the landmark results in mechanism design theory.

William Vickrey is the inventor of the famous *Vickrey Auction*, which is considered a major breakthrough in the design of auctions. He showed that the second price sealed bid auction enjoys the strong property of dominant strategy incentive compatibility, in his classic paper *Counterspeculation, Auctions, and Competitive Sealed Tenders* which appeared in the Journal of Finance in 1961. This work demonstrated for the first time the value of game theory in designing auctions. Apart from this famous auction, Vickrey is known for an early version of revenue equivalence theorem, a key result in auction theory.

Vickrey is also known for pioneering work in congestion pricing, where he introduced the idea of pricing roads and services as a natural means of regulating heavy demand. His ideas were subsequently put into practice in London city transportation. The Nobel prize in economic sciences in 1996 was jointly won by James A. Mirrlees and William Vickrey for their fundamental contributions to the economic theory of incentives under asymmetric information. However, just three days before the prize announcement, Vickrey passed away on October 11, 1996.

Vickrey was born on June 21, 1914 in Victoria, British Columbia. He earned a Ph.D. from Columbia University in 1948. His doctoral dissertation titled *Agenda for Progressive Taxation* is considered a pioneering piece of work. He taught at Columbia from 1946 until his retirement in 1982.

Edward Clarke distinguished himself as a senior economist with the Office of Management and Budget (Office of Information and Regulatory Affairs) involved in transportation regulatory affairs. He is a graduate of Princeton University and the University of Chicago, where he received an MBA and a Ph.D. (1978). He has worked in public policy at the city/regional (Chicago), state, federal, and international levels.

In public economics, he developed the demand revealing mechanism for public project selection, which was noted in the Nobel Committee's award of the 1996 Nobel Prize in Economics to William Vickrey. Clarke's paper *Multi-part Pricing of Public Goods* in the journal Public Choice in 1971 is a classic in mechanism design. Among VCG mechanisms, Clarke's mechanism is a natural and popular approach used in mechanism design problems.

Theodore Groves is credited with the most general among the celebrated class of VCG mechanisms. In a classic paper entitled *Incentives in Teams* published in Econometrica in 1973, Groves proposed a general class of allocatively efficient, dominant strategy incentive compatible mechanisms.

The Groves mechanism generalizes the Clarke mechanism (proposed in 1971), which in turn generalizes the Vickrey auction proposed in 1961. Groves earned a doctorate in economics at the University of California, Berkeley, and he is currently a Professor of Economics at the University of California, San Diego.

Theorem 18.1 (Groves Theorem). *Let the SCF $f(\cdot) = (k^*(\cdot), t_1(\cdot), \ldots, t_n(\cdot))$ be allocatively efficient. Then $f(\cdot)$ is dominant strategy incentive compatible if it satisfies the following payment structure (the Groves payment (incentive) scheme):*

$$t_i(\theta_i, \theta_{-i}) = \left[\sum_{j \neq i} v_j(k^*(\theta), \theta_j) \right] + h_i(\theta_{-i}) \ \forall \, i = 1, \ldots, n \qquad (18.2)$$

where $h_i : \Theta_{-i} \to \mathbb{R}$ is any arbitrary function.

Proof: The proof is by contradiction. Suppose $f(\cdot)$ satisfies both allocative efficiency and the Groves payment structure but is not DSIC. This implies that $f(\cdot)$ does not satisfy the following necessary and sufficient condition for DSIC:

$$u_i(f(\theta_i, \theta_{-i}), \theta_i) \geq u_i(f(\theta_i', \theta_{-i}), \theta_i) \ \forall \theta_i' \in \Theta_i \ \forall \theta \in \Theta \ \forall \theta_{-i} \in \Theta_{-i} \ \forall i \in N.$$

This implies that there exists at least one agent i for which the above is false. Let i be one such agent. That is, for agent i,

$$u_i(f(\theta_i', \theta_{-i}), \theta_i) > u_i(f(\theta_i, \theta_{-i}), \theta_i)$$

for some $\theta_i \in \Theta_i$, for some $\theta_{-i} \in \Theta_{-i}$, and for some $\theta'_i \in \Theta_i$. Expanding the expression for u_i above, we obtain that, for agent i, there would exist $\theta_i \in \Theta_i, \theta'_i \in \Theta_i, \theta_{-i} \in \Theta_{-i}$ such that

$$v_i(k^*(\theta'_i, \theta_{-i}), \theta_i) + t_i(\theta'_i, \theta_{-i}) + m_i > v_i(k^*(\theta_i, \theta_{-i}), \theta_i) + t_i(\theta_i, \theta_{-i}) + m_i.$$

Recall the Groves payment structure:

$$t_i(\theta_i, \theta_{-i}) = \left[\sum_{j \neq i} v_j(k^*(\theta_i, \theta_{-i}), \theta_j) \right] + h_i(\theta_{-i})$$

$$t_i(\theta'_i, \theta_{-i}) = \left[\sum_{j \neq i} v_j(k^*(\theta'_i, \theta_{-i}), \theta_j) \right] + h_i(\theta_{-i})$$

Substituting these, we get

$$v_i(k^*(\theta'_i, \theta_{-i}), \theta_i) + \sum_{j \neq i} v_j(k^*(\theta'_i, \theta_{-i}), \theta_j) > v_i(k^*(\theta_i, \theta_{-i}), \theta_i) + \sum_{j \neq i} v_j(k^*(\theta_i, \theta_{-i}), \theta_j),$$

which implies

$$\sum_{i=1}^{n} v_i(k^*(\theta'_i, \theta_{-i}), \theta_i) > \sum_{i=1}^{n} v_i(k^*(\theta_i, \theta_{-i}), \theta_i).$$

The above contradicts the fact that $f(\cdot)$ is allocatively efficient. This completes the proof.   ∎

The following are a few immediate and interesting implications of the above theorem.

Note. Given the announcements θ_{-i} of agents $j \neq i$, the monetary transfer to agent i depends on his announced type only through the project choice $k^*(\theta_i, \theta_{-i})$.

Note. The change in the monetary transfer of agent i when his type changes from θ_i to θ'_i is equal to the effect that the corresponding change in project choice has on total value of the rest of the agents. That is,

$$t_i(\theta_i, \theta_{-i}) - t_i(\theta'_i, \theta_{-i}) = \sum_{j \neq i} \left[v_j(k^*(\theta_i, \theta_{-i}), \theta_j) - v_j(k^*(\theta'_i, \theta_{-i}), \theta_j) \right].$$

Another way of describing this is to say that the change in monetary transfer to agent i reflects exactly the *externality* he is imposing on the other agents.

After the famous result of Groves, a direct revelation mechanism in which the implemented SCF is allocatively efficient and satisfies the Groves payment scheme is called a *Groves Mechanism*.

Definition 18.3 (Groves Mechanisms). *A direct revelation mechanism, $\mathcal{D} = ((\Theta_i)_{i \in N}, f(\cdot))$ in which $f(\cdot) = (k(\cdot), t_1(\cdot), \ldots, t_n(\cdot))$ satisfies allocative efficiency (18.1) and Groves payment rule (18.2) is known as a Groves mechanism.*

In mechanism design parlance, Groves mechanisms are often referred to as Vickrey–Clarke–Groves (VCG) mechanisms because the Clarke mechanism is a special case of the Groves mechanism, and the Vickrey mechanism is a special case of the Clarke mechanism. We will discuss this relationship later in this chapter.

The Groves theorem provides a sufficiency condition under which an allocatively efficient SCF will be DSIC. The following theorem due to Green and Laffont [4] provides a set of conditions under which the condition of Groves Theorem also becomes a necessary condition for an allocatively efficient SCF to be DSIC. In this theorem, we let $\mathscr{F}$ denote the set of all possible functions $f : K \to \mathbb{R}$.

Theorem 18.2 (First Characterization Theorem of Green–Laffont).
Suppose for each agent $i \in N$ that $\{v_i(.,\theta_i) : \theta_i \in \Theta_i\} = \mathscr{F}$, that is, every possible valuation function from K to $\mathbb{R}$ arises for some $\theta_i \in \Theta_i$. Then any allocatively efficient social choice function $f(\cdot)$ will be dominant strategy incentive compatible if and only if it satisfies the Groves payment scheme given by Equation (18.2).

Note that in the above theorem, every possible valuation function from K to $\mathbb{R}$ arises for each $\theta_i \in \Theta_i$. In the following characterization theorem, again due to Green and Laffont [4], $\mathscr{F}$ is replaced with $\mathscr{F}_c$ where $\mathscr{F}_c$ denotes the set of all possible continuous functions $f : K \to \mathbb{R}$.

Theorem 18.3 (Second Characterization Theorem of Green–Laffont).
Suppose for each agent $i \in N$ that $\{v_i(.,\theta_i) : \theta_i \in \Theta_i\} = \mathscr{F}_c$, that is, every possible continuous valuation function from K to $\mathbb{R}$ arises for some $\theta_i \in \Theta_i$. Then any allocatively efficient social choice function $f(\cdot)$ will be dominant strategy incentive compatible if and only if it satisfies the Groves payment scheme given by Equation (18.2).

18.3 Clarke (Pivotal) Mechanisms

Groves mechanisms were reported in 1973 [3]. A special class of Groves mechanisms was developed earlier by Clarke in 1971 [2] and these are known as the *Clarke* mechanisms, or the *pivotal* mechanisms. The Clarke mechanism is a special case of the Groves mechanism in the sense of using a natural special form for the function $h_i(\cdot)$. In the Clarke mechanism, the function $h_i(\cdot)$ is given by the following relation:

$$h_i(\theta_{-i}) = -\sum_{j \neq i} v_j(k^*_{-i}(\theta_{-i}), \theta_j) \ \forall \, \theta_{-i} \in \Theta_{-i}, \forall \, i = 1, \ldots, n \qquad (18.3)$$

where $k^*_{-i}(\theta_{-i}) \in K_{-i}$ is a project choice that is allocatively efficient if the system consisted of all agents other than agent i. The set K_{-i} above is the set of project choices available when agent i is absent. Formally, $k^*_{-i}(\theta_{-i})$ must satisfy the following condition.

$$\sum_{j\neq i} v_j(k^*_{-i}(\theta_{-i}), \theta_j) \geq \sum_{j\neq i} v_j(k, \theta_j) \ \forall k \in K_{-i} \tag{18.4}$$

Substituting the value of $h_i(\cdot)$ from Equation (18.3) in Equation (18.2), we get the following expression for agent i's monetary transfer in the Clarke mechanism:

$$t_i(\theta) = \left[\sum_{j\neq i} v_j(k^*(\theta), \theta_j)\right] - \left[\sum_{j\neq i} v_j(k^*_{-i}(\theta_{-i}), \theta_j)\right] \ \forall i = 1, \ldots, n. \tag{18.5}$$

The above payment rule has an appealing interpretation: Given a type profile $\theta = (\theta_1, \ldots, \theta_n)$, the monetary transfer to agent i is given by the total value of all agents other than i under an efficient allocation when agent i is present in the system minus the total value of all agents other than i under an efficient allocation when agent i is absent in the system. Another appealing interpretation of Clarke's payment rule can be derived as follows. We can write

$$t_i(\theta_i, \theta_{-i}) = \sum_{j\in N} v_j(k^*(\theta), \theta_j) - v_i(k^*(\theta), \theta_i) - \sum_{j\neq i} v_j(k^*_{-i}(\theta_{-i}), \theta_j)$$

$$= \sum_{j\in N} v_j(k^*(\theta), \theta_j) - \sum_{j\neq i} v_j(k^*_{-i}(\theta_{-i}), \theta_j) - v_i(k^*(\theta), \theta_i).$$

The difference in the first two terms represents the marginal contribution of agent i to the system. Thus the Clarke mechanism gives an additional incentive to every allocated agent, namely that agent's marginal contribution to the mechanism. This additional incentive is key to inducing truth from the agents (in a dominant strategy sense).

The Clarke mechanism is also known as the pivotal mechanism since each *allocated* agent plays a *pivotal* role in deciding the value received by the other agents due to his presence in the society of players.

18.4　Examples of VCG Mechanisms

VCG mechanisms derive their popularity on account of the elegant mathematical and economic properties that they have and the rich first level insights they provide during the process of designing mechanisms for a mechanism design problem. For this reason, invariably, the first choice of mechanisms for mechanism design researchers are always VCG mechanisms. However, VCG mechanisms do have many limitations. The virtues and limitations of VCG mechanisms are captured by Ausubel and Milgrom [5], whereas a recent paper by Rothkopf [6] summarizes the practical limitations of applying VCG mechanisms. In this section, we provide a number of examples to illustrate some interesting nuances of VCG mechanisms.

Example 18.3 (Vickrey Auction for a Single Indivisible Item). Consider 5 bidders $\{1, 2, 3, 4, 5\}$, with valuations $v_1 = 20; v_2 = 15; v_3 = 12; v_4 = 10; v_5 = 6$, participating in a sealed bid auction for a single indivisible item. If Vickrey auction is the mechanism used, then a dominant strategy for the agents is to bid their valuations. Agent 1 with valuation 20 will be the winner, and the monetary transfer to agent 1

$$= \sum_{j \neq 1} v_j(k^*(\theta), \theta_j) - \sum_{j \neq 1} v_j(k^*_{-1}(\theta_{-1}), \theta_j)$$
$$= 0 - 15 = -15.$$

This means agent 1 would pay an amount equal to 15, which happens to be the second highest bid (in this case the second highest valuation). Note that 15 is the change in the total value of agents other than agent 1 when agent 1 drops out of the system. This is the externality that agent 1 imposes on the rest of the agents. This externality becomes the payment of agent 1 when he wins the auction.

Another way of determining the payment by agent 1 is to compute his marginal contribution to the system (refer to the discussion in the previous section). The total value in the presence of agent 1 is 20, while the total value in the absence of agent 1 is 15. Thus the marginal contribution of agent 1 is 5. The above marginal contribution is given as a discount to agent 1 by the Vickrey payment mechanism, and agent 1 pays $20 - 5 = 15$. Such a discount is known as the *Vickrey discount*. □

Example 18.4 (Vickrey Auction for Multiple Identical Items). Consider the same set of bidders as above but with the difference that there are 3 identical items available for auction. Each bidder wants only one item. If we apply the Clarke mechanism for this situation, bidders 1, 2, and 3 become the winners. The payment by bidder 1

$$= \sum_{j \neq 1} v_j(k^*(\theta), \theta_j) - \sum_{j \neq 1} v_j(k^*_{-1}(\theta_{-1}), \theta_j)$$
$$= (15 + 12) - (15 + 12 + 10)$$
$$= -10.$$

Thus bidder 1 pays an amount equal to the highest non-winning bid. Similarly, one can verify that the payment to be made by the other two winners (namely agent 2 and agent 3) is also equal to 10. This payment is consistent with their respective marginal contributions.

Marginal contribution of agent 1 $= (20 + 15 + 12) - (15 + 12 + 10) = 10$

Marginal contribution of agent 2 $= (20 + 15 + 12) - (20 + 12 + 10) = 5$

Marginal contribution of agent 3 $= (20 + 15 + 12) - (20 + 15 + 10) = 2$.

In the above example, let the demand by agent 1 be 2 units with the rest of agents continuing to have unit demand. Now the allocation will allocate 2 units to agent 1 and 1 unit to agent 2.

Payment by agent 1 $= 15 - (15 + 12 + 10) = -22$

Payment by agent 2 $= 40 - (40 + 12) = -12$.

This is because the marginal contribution of agent 1 and agent 2 are given by: agent 1: $55 - 37 = 18$; agent 2: $55 - 52 = 3$. $\qquad\square$

Example 18.5 (A VCG Mechanism for the Public Project Problem).

Consider the public project problem discussed in Example 18.1. We shall compute the Clarke payments by each agent for each type of profile. We will also compute the utilities. First consider the type profile $(20, 20)$. Since $k(20, 20) = 0$, the values derived by either agent is zero. Hence the Clarke payment by each agent is zero, and the utilities are also zero.

Next consider the type profile $(60, 20)$. Note that $k(60, 20) = 1$. Agent 1 derives a value 35 and agent 2 derives a value -5. If agent 1 is not present, then agent 2 is left alone and the allocation will be 0 since its willingness to pay is 20. Thus the value to agent 2 when agent 1 is not present is 0. This means

$$t_1(60, 20) = -5 - 0 = -5.$$

This implies agent 1 would pay an amount 5 in addition to 25, which is its contribution to the cost of the project. The above payment is consistent with the marginal contribution of agent 1, which is equal to $(60 - 25) + (20 - 25) - 0 = 35 - 5 = 30$.

We can now determine the utility of agent 1, which will be

$$u_1(60, 20) = v_1(60, 20) + t_1(60, 20) = 35 - 5 = 30.$$

To compute $t_2(60, 20)$, we first note that the value to the agent 1 when agent 2 is not present is $(60 - 50)$. Therefore

$$t_2(60, 20) = 35 - 10 = 25.$$

This means agent 2 receives 25; of course, this is besides the amount of 25 it pays towards the cost of the project. Now

$$u_2(60, 20) = v_2(60, 20) + t_2(60, 20) = -5 + 25 = 20.$$

(θ_1, θ_2)	$t_1(\theta_1, \theta_2)$	$t_2(\theta_1, \theta_2)$	$u_1(\theta_1, \theta_2)$	$u_2(\theta_1, \theta_2)$
(20, 20)	0	0	0	0
(60, 20)	-5	25	30	20
(20, 60)	25	-5	20	30
(60, 60)	25	25	60	60

Table 18.3: Payments and utilities for different type profiles

Likewise, we can compute the payments and utilities of the agents for all the type profiles. Table 18.3 provides these values. $\qquad\square$

Example 18.6 (Strategy Proof Network Formation). Consider the problem of forming a supply chain as depicted in Figure 18.1. The node S represents a starting state

and T represents a target state; A and B are two intermediate states. SP_1, SP_2, SP_3, SP_4 are four different service providers. In the figure, the service providers are represented as

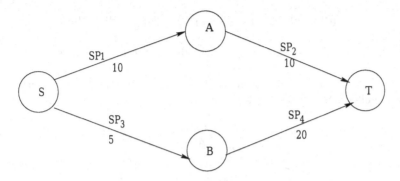

Fig. 18.1: A network formation problem - case 1

owners of the respective edges. The cost of providing service (willingness to sell) is indicated on each edge. The problem is to procure a path from S to T having minimum cost. Let (y_1, y_2, y_3, y_4) represent the allocation vector. The feasible allocation vectors are

$$K = \{(1, 1, 0, 0), (0, 0, 1, 1)\}.$$

Among these, the allocation $(1, 1, 0, 0)$ is allocatively efficient since it minimizes the cost of allocation. We shall define the value as follows:

$$v_i((y_1, y_2, y_3, y_4); \theta_i) = -y_i\theta_i.$$

The above manner of defining the values reflects the fact that cost minimization is the same as value maximization. Applying Clarke's payment rule, we obtain

$$t_1(\theta) = -10 - (-25) = 15$$
$$t_2(\theta) = -10 - (-25) = 15.$$

If we compute the marginal contributions, we find that each of the agents makes a marginal contribution of 5 which is added to the value in deciding the payment. The utilities for these two agents are

$$u_1(\theta) = -10 + 15 = 5$$
$$u_2(\theta) = -10 + 15 = 5.$$

The payments and utilities for SP_3 and SP_4 are zero. Let us study the effect of changing the willingness to sell of SP_4. Let us make it as 15. Then, we find that both the allocations $(1, 1, 0, 0)$ and $(0, 0, 1, 1)$ are allocatively efficient. If we choose the allocation $(1, 1, 0, 0)$, we get the payments as

$$t_1(\theta) = 10; \quad t_2(\theta) = 10; \quad u_1(\theta) = 0; \quad u_2(\theta) = 0.$$

This means that the payments to the service providers are equal to the costs. There is no surplus payment to the winning agents. In this case, the mechanism is friendly to the buyer and unfriendly to the sellers.

If we make the willingness to sell of SP_4 as 95, the allocation $(1,1,0,0)$ is efficient and we get the payments as

$$t_1(\theta) = 90; \quad t_2(\theta) = 90; \quad u_1(\theta) = 80; \quad u_2(\theta) = 80.$$

In this case, the mechanism is extremely unfriendly to the buyer but is very attractive to the sellers.

Let us introduce one more edge from B to A corresponding to a new service provider SP_5 and see the effect. See Figure 18.2.

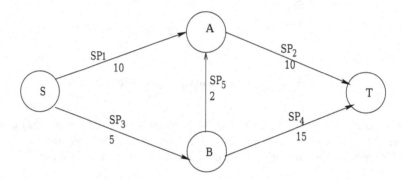

Fig. 18.2: A network formation problem - case 2

The efficient allocation here is $(0, 1, 1, 0, 1)$. The payments are

$$t_2(\theta) = 13; \quad t_3(\theta) = 8; \quad t_5(\theta) = 5; \quad u_2(\theta) = 3; \quad u_3(\theta) = 3; \quad u_5(\theta) = 3.$$

This shows that the total payments to be made by the buyer is 26 whereas the total payment if the service provider SP_5 were absent is 20. Thus in spite of an additional agent being available, the payment to the buyer is higher. This shows a kind of non-monotonicity exhibited by the Clarke payment rule. ☐

The above examples have illustrated many characteristic features of VCG mechanisms when applied to practical problems of interest.

18.5 Summary and References

Vickrey-Clarke-Groves mechanisms represent a prominent class of mechanisms in the quasilinear environment satisfying DSIC and AE. The salient points discussed in this chapter include the following.

- In the quasilinear setting, each outcome of a given social choice function can be decomposed into an allocation part and a payment part. The utilities depend linearly on the values and the payments where the values are (possibly non-linear) functions of the allocation and the private types.

- A remarkable property satisfied SCFs in quasilinear environment is that they are non-dictatorial. Another elegant property is that ex-post efficiency is the same as allocative efficiency plus strict budget balance. Allocative efficiency means that in every outcome, the sum of the values of the allocation (social welfare of the allocation) is maximized. Strict budget balance means that in every outcome, the sum total of payments by the agents is equal to the sum total of receipts by the agents.

- The Vickrey auction mechanism is a special case of the Clarke mechanism which in turn is a special case of the Groves mechanism. The Groves theorem states that an allocatively efficient SCF with Groves payment structure will satisfy the extremely desirable DSIC property. The Groves payment formula is based on the principle that the monetary transfer to an agent could depend on the types of the other agents in an arbitrary way but should depend on the type of the agent only through the effect of its type on the allocation.

- The Clarke mechanism can be derived as a special case of the Groves mechanism by requiring that the payment is decided by the values of the rest of the agents when the agent is dropped from the game. The Clarke mechanism proves that the agents report truthfully when their respective marginal contributions are offered to them as additional incentives.

- The Vickrey auction is essentially the Clarke mechanism applied to auctioning multiple units of a single type of item. When the Clarke mechanism is applied to a combinatorial auction (to be introduced in Chapter 20), we call the mechanism a generalized Vickrey auction (GVA).

The Vickrey auction is the pioneering contribution of William Vickrey [1] while the celebrated pivotal mechanism was developed by Clarke [2] and a generalization of Clarke's mechanisms were developed by Groves [3]. The original papers written by these celebrities are a must-read for mechanism design students.

References

[1] William Vickrey. "Counterspeculation, auctions, and competitive sealed tenders". In: *Journal of Finance* **16**(1) (1961), pp. 8–37.

[2] E. Clarke. "Multi-part pricing of public goods". In: *Public Choice* **11** (1971), pp. 17–23.

[3] T. Groves. "Incentives in teams". In: *Econometrica* **41** (1973), pp. 617–631.

[4] J.R. Green and J.J. Laffont. *Incentives in Public Decision Making*. North-Holland, Amsterdam, 1979.

[5] L.M. Ausubel and P. Milgrom. "The lovely but lonely Vickrey auction". In: *Combinatorial Auctions*. Ed. by P. Cramton, Y. Shoham, and R. Steinberg. The MIT Press, Cambridge, Massachusetts, 2006, pp. 17–40.

[6] M. Rothkopf. "Thirteen reasons why the Vickrey-Clarke-Groves process is not practical". In: *Operations Research* **55**(2) (2007), pp. 191–197.

18.6   Exercises

(1) Consider five selling agents $\{1, 2, 3, 4, 5\}$, with valuations $v_1 = 20; v_2 = 15; v_3 = 12; v_4 = 10; v_5 = 6$, participating in a sealed bid procurement auction for a single indivisible item. These valuations are to be viewed as the willingness to sell values of the bidders. If Vickrey auction is the mechanism used, then compute the allocation and payment. If the buyer wishes to procure three objects instead of one object, and each bidder can supply at most one object, then compute the allocation and payments. Finally, if the buyer wishes to buy 6 objects and each bidder is willing to supply up to two objects, compute the allocation and payments.

(2) Consider an exchange where a single unit of an item is traded. There are 4 sellers S1, S2, S3, S4 and 3 buyers B1, B2, and B3. Here are the bids from the buyers and the asks from the sellers for the single item. The objective is to maximize the surplus in the exchange.

S1: 10   S2: 12   S3: 14   S4: 16
B1: 8   B2: 12   B3: 18

(a) Define the surplus of the exchange as the total amount of money paid by the buyers minus the total amount of money received by the sellers. Call an allocation surplus maximizing if it maximizes the surplus of the exchange. Find a surplus maximizing allocation for this exchange. (b) Assuming that Vickrey pricing is used, what will be the payment? (c) Will the mechanism satisfy budget balance?

(3) Consider a forward auction for sale of m identical objects. Let there be n bidders where $n > m$. The valuations of the bidders for the object are $v_1, \ldots, v_n$, respectively. Each bidder is interested in at most one unit. For this auction scenario, write down an allocation rule that is allocatively efficient. What will be the Clarke payment in this case? Do you see any difficulty? How can you overcome the difficulty, if any?

(4) Consider an auction for selling a single indivisible item where the bidder with the highest bid is declared as the winner and the winner pays an amount equal to twice the bid of the bidder with the lowest valuation among the rest of the agents. As an example consider 5 bidders with valuations 20, 15, 12, 10, 8. The bidder with valuation 20 is declared the winner and will pay an amount $= 16$. On the other hand, if there are only three bidders with values 20, 15, 12, the first bidder wins but has to pay 24. Is this mechanism a Clarke mechanism? Is the mechanism a Groves mechanism? Is the mechanism incentive compatible?

(5) **Programming Assignment.** Implement the Clarke mechanism. Identify the inputs to this program carefully. The output must be an efficient allocation and a payment vector for any given type profile. The implementation can also be generalized to Groves mechanisms.

Chapter 19

Mechanism Design Space in Quasilinear Environment

We have seen that mechanism design is concerned with design of institutions or protocols which minimize the economic losses arising from private information and self-interest. The trade-offs involved in designing mechanisms with desirable properties such as incentive compatibility, allocative efficiency, and budget balance are quite complex and there is a sea of literature comprising possibility results and impossibility theorems. In this chapter, we study some of these tradeoffs. We introduce an important mechanism called the *dAGVA mechanism* which achieves allocative efficiency as well as strict budget balance, by relaxing DSIC to BIC. We also introduce another important property, namely, *individual rationality* (also known as *voluntary participation*) and study additional tradeoffs that arise due to this property. Our discussion assumes quasilinear preferences. Towards the end of this chapter, we discuss a special case of the quasilinear environment called the *linear environment*. For this special environment, we present a characterization developed by Myerson for BIC social choice functions.

19.1 Groves Mechanisms and Strict Budget Balance

In Chapter 18, we implicitly assumed that weak budget balance property is satisfied by all the mechanisms discussed in that chapter. In general, however, it is not true. Note that a Groves mechanism, which we discussed at length in the previous chapter, always satisfies the properties of AE and DSIC. Therefore, if a Groves mechanism is strictly budget balanced, then it will solve the problem of the social planner because it will then be ex-post efficient and dominant strategy incentive compatible. By looking at the definition of the Groves mechanism, one can conclude that it is the functions $h_i(\cdot)$ for $i = 1, \ldots, n$ that decide whether or not the Groves mechanism is budget balanced. The natural question that arises now is whether there exists a way of defining functions $h_i(\cdot)$ for $i = 1, \ldots, n$ such that the Groves mechanism is budget balanced. In what follows, we first present the Green-Laffont theorem which asserts that Groves mechanisms cannot be strictly budget balanced in a general setting. Next, we show that there is a practically relevant special setting in which Groves mechanisms can be made strictly budget balanced.

Possibility and Impossibility Results for Budget Balance

Green and Laffont [1] showed that in a quasilinear environment, if the set of possible types for each agent is sufficiently rich then ex-post efficiency and DSIC cannot be achieved together. The precise statement is given in the form of the following theorem. Recall the notation $\mathscr{F}$ which denotes the set of of all functions from the set K of project choices to $\mathbb{R}$.

Theorem 19.1 (Green–Laffont Impossibility Theorem). *Suppose for each agent $i \in N$ that $\mathscr{F} = \{v_i(., \theta_i) : \theta_i \in \Theta_i\}$, that is, every possible valuation function from K to $\mathbb{R}$ arises for some $\theta_i \in \Theta_i$. Then there is no social choice function that is ex-post efficient and DSIC.*

Thus, the above theorem says that if the set of possible types for each agent is sufficiently rich, then there is no hope of finding a way to define the functions $h_i(\cdot)$ in Groves payment scheme such that we have $\sum_{i=1}^{n} t_i(\theta) = 0$. However, one special case in which a positive result arises is summarized in the form of the following possibility result.

Theorem 19.2 (Budget Balance of Groves Mechanisms). *If there is at least one agent whose preferences are known (that is, the type set is a singleton) then it is possible to choose the functions $h_i(\cdot)$ so that $\sum_{i=1}^{n} t_i(\theta) = 0$.*

Proof: Let agent i be such that his preferences are known, that is $\Theta_i = \{\theta_i\}$. In view of this condition, it is easy to see that for an allocatively efficient social choice function $f(\cdot) = (k^*(\cdot), t_1(\cdot), \ldots, t_n(\cdot))$, the allocation $k^*(\cdot)$ depends only on the types of the agents other than i. That is, the allocation $k^*(\cdot)$ is a mapping from Θ_{-i} to K. Let us define the functions $h_j(\cdot)$ in the following manner:

$$
h_j(\theta_{-j}) = \begin{cases} h_j(\theta_{-j}) & : \quad j \neq i \\ -\sum_{r \neq i} h_r(\theta_{-r}) - (n-1)\sum_{r=1}^{n} v_r(k^*(\theta), \theta_r) & : \quad j = i. \end{cases}
$$

It is easy to see that under the above definition of the functions $h_i(\cdot)$, we will have $t_i(\theta) = -\sum_{j \neq i} t_j(\theta)$ and therefore strict budget balance is achieved. ∎

19.2 Clarke Mechanisms and Weak Budget Balance

Recall from the definition of Groves mechanisms that, for weak budget balance, we should choose the functions $h_i(\theta_{-i})$ for $i = 1, \ldots, n$ in a way that the weak budget balance condition $\sum_{i=1}^{n} t_i(\theta) \leq 0$ is satisfied. In this sense, the Clarke mechanism is a useful special case because it achieves weak budget balance under fairly general settings. In order to understand these general sufficiency conditions, we define the following quantities:

$$B^*(\theta) = \left\{ k \in K : k \in \arg\max_{k \in K} \sum_{j=1}^{n} v_j(k, \theta_j) \right\}$$

$$B^*(\theta_{-i}) = \left\{ k \in K_{-i} : k \in \arg\max_{k \in K_{-i}} \sum_{j \neq i} v_j(k, \theta_j) \right\}.$$

In the above, $B^*(\theta)$ is the set of project choices that are allocatively efficient when all the agents are present in the system. Similarly, $B^*(\theta_{-i})$ is the set of project choices that are allocatively efficient if all agents except agent i were present in the system.

Using the above quantities, we define the following property of a direct revelation mechanism in quasilinear environment.

Definition 19.1 (No Single Agent Effect). *We say that mechanism $\mathcal{M}$ has no single agent effect if for each agent i, for each $\theta \in \Theta$, and for each $k^*(\theta) \in B^*(\theta)$, we have a $k \in K_{-i}$ such that*

$$\sum_{j \neq i} v_j(k, \theta_j) \geq \sum_{j \neq i} v_j(k^*(\theta), \theta_j).$$

The above property means that there would not exist an agent i such that the sum of values of all agents other than i under an AE allocation in the presence of agent i is strictly greater than the sum of values of all agents other than i under an AE allocation in the absence of agent i. Such an agent, if one exists, essentially *weakens* the other agents by its absence.

We now state and prove the following proposition that gives a sufficiency condition for Clarke mechanism to be weakly budget balanced.

Proposition 19.1. *If the Clarke mechanism has no single agent effect, then the monetary transfer to each agent would be non-positive, that is, $t_i(\theta) \leq 0 \ \forall \theta \in \Theta; \ \forall i = 1, \ldots, n$. In such a situation, the Clarke mechanism would satisfy the weak budget balance property.*

Proof: Note that by virtue of no single agent effect, for each agent i, each $\theta \in \Theta$, and each $k^*(\theta) \in B^*(\theta)$, there exists a $k \in K_{-i}$ such that

$$\sum_{j \neq i} v_j(k, \theta_j) \geq \sum_{j \neq i} v_j(k^*(\theta), \theta_j).$$

However, by definition of $k_{-i}^*(\theta_{-i})$, given by Equation (18.4), we have

$$\sum_{j \neq i} v_j(k_{-i}^*(\theta_{-i}), \theta_j) \geq \sum_{j \neq i} v_j(k, \theta_j) \ \forall k \in K_{-i}.$$

Combining the above two facts, we get

$$\sum_{j \neq i} v_j(k^*(\theta), \theta_j) - \sum_{j \neq i} v_j(k_{-i}^*(\theta_{-i}), \theta_j) \leq 0 \ \forall i \in N$$

That is, $t_i(\theta) \le 0 \ \forall i \in N$. This immediately implies

$$\sum_{i=1}^{n} t_i(\theta) \le 0.$$

This shows that the the Clarke mechanism is weakly budget balanced when there is no single agent effect.   ∎

Redistribution Mechanisms

These are Groves mechanisms which are weakly budget balanced and in addition they try to minimize the budget imbalance while preserving the AE and DSIC properties. Here the idea is to start with a Clarke mechanism which clearly includes an allocation that is AE and payments are determined using the Clarke payment rule. The payments are then redistributed among the agents in such a way that the budget imbalance is reduced without sacrificing either AE or DSIC. This is an important class of mechanisms called redistribution mechanisms. Examples of these mechanisms may be found in [2, 3, 4, 5].

19.3   Individual Rationality

Individual rationality is also often referred to as voluntary participation property. Individual rationality of a social choice function essentially means that each agent gains a utility that is no less than he would get without participating in a mechanism that implements the social choice function. There are three stages at which individual rationality constraints (also called participation constraints) may be relevant in a mechanism design situation. Suppose $\overline{u_i}(\theta_i)$ denotes the utility that agent i receives by withdrawing from the mechanism when his type is θ_i.

Ex-Post Individual Rationality

These constraints become relevant when any agent i is given a choice to withdraw from the mechanism at the *ex-post stage*, that is, after all the agents have announced their types and an outcome in X has been chosen. Then, to ensure agent i's participation, we must satisfy the following *ex-post participation (or individual rationality) constraints*

$$u_i(f(\theta_i, \theta_{-i}), \theta_i) \ge \overline{u_i}(\theta_i) \ \forall \ (\theta_i, \theta_{-i}) \in \Theta.$$

Interim Individual Rationality

Let the agent i be allowed to withdraw from the mechanism at the *interim stage* that arises after the agents have learned their type but before they have chosen their actions in the mechanism. In such a situation, the agent i will participate in the mechanism only if his interim expected utility $E_{\theta_{-i}}[u_i(f(\theta_i, \theta_{-i}), \theta_i)|\theta_i]$ from social choice function $f(\cdot)$, when his type is θ_i, is at least $\overline{u_i}(\theta_i)$. Thus, *interim participation (or individual rationality) constraints* for agent i require that

$$E_{\theta_{-i}}[u_i(f(\theta_i, \theta_{-i}), \theta_i)|\theta_i] \geq \overline{u_i}(\theta_i) \ \forall \, \theta_i \in \Theta_i.$$

Ex-Ante Individual Rationality

Let agent i be allowed to withdraw from participation in a mechanism even at *ex-ante stage*, that is, before the agents learn their type. In such a situation, the agent i will participate voluntarily in the mechanism only if his ex-ante expected utility $E_\theta[u_i(f(\theta_i, \theta_{-i}), \theta_i)]$ from social choice function $f(\cdot)$ is at least $E_{\theta_i}[\overline{u_i}(\theta_i)]$. Note that E_θ indicates that the expectation is taken by an agent not only over the types of the other agents but also over his own types. Thus, *ex-ante participation (or individual rationality) constraints* for agent i require that

$$E_\theta[u_i(f(\theta_i, \theta_{-i}), \theta_i)] \geq E_{\theta_i}[\overline{u_i}(\theta_i)].$$

The following proposition establishes a relationship among the three different participation constraints discussed above. The proof is straightforward and is left as an exercise.

Proposition 19.2. *For any social choice function $f(\cdot)$, we have*

$$f(\cdot) \ \text{is ex-post IR} \Longrightarrow f(\cdot) \ \text{is interim IR} \Longrightarrow f(\cdot) \ \text{is ex-ante IR}.$$

19.4 VCG Mechanisms and Individual Rationality

We motivate the importance of the individual rationality property through an example.

Example 19.1 (Public Project Problem). Consider the public project problem with

$$N = \{1, 2\}; \ K = \{0, 1\}; \ \Theta_1 = \Theta_2 = \{20, 60\}.$$

Further assume that the cost of the project is 50, so that the set of feasible outcomes is:

$$X = \{(k, t_1, t_2) : k \in \{0, 1\}; \ t_1, t_2 \in \mathbb{R}; \ -(t_1 + t_2) \leq 50\}$$

Consider the following allocation function:

$$k^*(\theta_1, \theta_2) = 0 \ \text{if} \ \theta_1 = \theta_2 = 20$$
$$= 1 \ \text{otherwise}.$$

Define the valuation function as:

$$v_i(k^*(\theta_1, \theta_2), \theta_i) = k^*(\theta_1, \theta_2)(\theta_i - 25) \ \forall \theta_1 \in \Theta_1; \ \forall \theta_2 \in \Theta_2$$

We have already shown in Chapter 18 that the above allocation function is allocatively efficient. Therefore we can use the Groves payment rule and make the following social choice function DSIC:

$$f(\theta) = (k^*(\theta), t_1(\theta), t_2(\theta)),$$

where $t_1(\theta)$ and $t_2(\theta)$ satisfy the Groves payment rule. Suppose the above mechanism is ex-post individually rational with $\overline{u_i}(\theta_i) = 0 \ \forall \ \theta_i \in \Theta_i; \ i = 1, 2$. This means

$$u_i(f(\theta_1, \theta_2), \theta_i) \geq 0 \ \forall \theta_1 \in \Theta_1; \ \theta_2 \in \Theta_2$$

In particular, we have $u_1(f(20, 60), 20) \geq 0$ which is equivalent to:

$$v_1(k^*(20, 60), 20) + t_1(20, 60) \geq 0$$

Since $v_1(k^*(20, 60), 20) = -5$, we get $-t_1(20, 60) \leq -5$. Now consider $t_1(60, 60)$. Since the social choice function is DSIC, we have

$$u_1(f(60, 60), 60) \geq u_1(f(20, 60), 60)$$

which implies

$$v_1(k^*(60, 60), 60) + t_1(60, 60) \geq v_1(k^*(20, 60), 60) + t_1(20, 60)$$

Since $v_1(k^*(60, 60), 60) = 35$ and $v_1(k^*(20, 60), 60) = 35$, the above implies that $-t_1(60, 60) \leq -5$. Similarly by symmetry, we have $-t_2(60, 60) \leq -5$, which means

$$-t_1(60, 60) - t_2(60, 60) \leq -10$$

The above shows that the sum total of payments made by the agents is less than or equal to -10 and since the project cost is 50, the above leads to an infeasible outcome. We arrived at this based on our assumption that the social choice function is ex-post individually rational. Therefore the above mechanism does not satisfy individual rationality. This clearly means that the agents, of their own accord, will not participate voluntarily in the mechanism. $\square$

Clarke Mechanisms and Individual Rationality

The following proposition investigates the individual rationality of the Clarke mechanism. First, we provide two definitions.

Definition 19.2 (Choice Set Monotonicity). *We say that a mechanism $\mathscr{M}$ is choice set monotone if the set of feasible outcomes X (weakly) grows as additional agents are introduced into the system. An implication of this property is $K_{-i} \subseteq K \ \forall \ i = 1, \ldots, n$.*

Intuitively, choice set monotonicity means that as more agents become available, the feasible outcomes progressively become richer.

Definition 19.3 (No Negative Externality). *Consider a choice set monotone mechanism $\mathscr{M}$. We say that the mechanism $\mathscr{M}$ has no negative externality if for* *each agent i, each $\theta \in \Theta$, and each $k^*_{-i}(\theta_{-i}) \in B^*(\theta_{-i})$, we have*

$$v_i(k^*_{-i}(\theta_{-i}), \theta_i) \geq 0.$$

Intuitively, the above property means that every agent has a non-negative value for any project choice that is allocatively efficient in the absence of that agent. That is in the absence of this agent, the rest of the agents will not hurt this agent.

We now state and prove a proposition which provides a sufficient condition for the ex-post individual rationality of the Clarke mechanism. Recall from Section 19.3 the notation $\overline{u_i}(\theta_i)$, which represents the utility that agent i receives by withdrawing from the mechanism.

Proposition 19.3 (Ex-Post Individual Rationality of Clarke Mechanism).
Consider a Clarke mechanism in which

(1) $\overline{u_i}(\theta_i) = 0 \ \forall \theta_i \in \Theta_i; \ \forall \ i = 1, \ldots, n,$
(2) the mechanism satisfies choice set monotonicity property, and
(3) the mechanism satisfies no negative externality property.

Then the Clarke mechanism is ex-post individual rational.

Proof: Recall that utility $u_i(f(\theta), \theta_i)$ of an agent i in Clarke mechanism is given by

$$u_i(f(\theta), \theta_i) = v_i(k^*(\theta), \theta_i) + \left[\sum_{j \neq i} v_j(k^*(\theta), \theta_j)\right] - \left[\sum_{j \neq i} v_j(k^*_{-i}(\theta_{-i}), \theta_j)\right]$$

$$= \left[\sum_{j} v_j(k^*(\theta), \theta_j)\right] - \left[\sum_{j \neq i} v_j(k^*_{-i}(\theta_{-i}), \theta_j)\right].$$

By virtue of choice set monotonicity, we know that $k^*_{-i}(\theta_{-i}) \in K$. Therefore, we have

$$u_i(f(\theta), \theta_i) \geq \left[\sum_{j} v_j(k^*_{-i}(\theta_{-i}), \theta_j)\right] - \left[\sum_{j \neq i} v_j(k^*_{-i}(\theta_{-i}), \theta_j)\right]$$

$$= v_i(k^*_{-i}(\theta_{-i}), \theta_i)$$

$$\geq 0 = \overline{u_i}(\theta_i).$$

The last step follows since the mechanism has no negative externality. ∎

Example 19.2 (Individual Rationality in Sealed Bid Auctions). Let us consider the example of first-price sealed bid auction. If for each possible type θ_i, the utility $\overline{u_i}(\theta_i)$ derived by the agents i from not participating in the auction is 0, then it is easy to see that the SCF would be ex-post IR.

Let us next consider the example of a second-price sealed bid auction. If for each possible type θ_i, the utility $\overline{u_i}(\theta_i)$ derived by the agents i from not participating in the auction is 0, then it is easy to see that the SCF would be ex-post IR. Moreover, the ex-post IR of this auction also follows directly from Proposition 19.3 because this is a special case of the Clarke mechanism satisfying all the required conditions in the proposition. □

19.5   The dAGVA Mechanism

The quasilinear environment provided us with an escape route from the Gibbard-Satterthwaite theorem and we were able to construct mechanisms that are AE and DSIC. However, these mechanisms do not satisfy budget balance as we realized in Theorem 19.1. Our quest for mechanisms that satisfy both AE and BB (that is ex-post efficiency) leads us to relaxing DSIC to BIC. This is what is achieved by the dAGVA (d'Aspremont, Gérard-Varet, and Arrow) mechanism. This mechanism is also known as the AVG mechanism.

The following theorem, due to d'Aspremont and Gérard-Varet [6] and Arrow [7] establishes that in quasilinear environments, there exist social choice functions that are both ex-post efficient and Bayesian incentive compatible.

Theorem 19.3 (The dAGVA Theorem). *Let the social choice function* $f(\cdot) = (k^*(\cdot), t_1(\cdot), \ldots, t_n(\cdot))$ *be allocatively efficient and the types of the agents be statistically independent of each other (that is, the joint density of types is the product of marginal densities). This social choice function is Bayesian incentive compatible if the payments satisfy:*

$$t_i(\theta_i, \theta_{-i}) = \xi_i(\theta_i) + h_i(\theta_{-i}) \; \forall \theta_i \in \theta_i; \; \forall \theta_{-i} \in \Theta_{-i}; \; \forall i \in N$$

$$\text{where} \quad \xi_i(\theta_i) = E_{\tau_{-i}} \left[\sum_{j \neq i} v_j(k^*(\theta_i, \tau_{-i}), \tau_j) \right] \qquad (19.1)$$

As in the Groves payment scheme, $h_i : \Theta_{-i} \to \mathbb{R}$ *is any arbitrary function.*

Proof: We are given that the social choice function $f(\cdot) = (k^*(\cdot), t_1(\cdot), \ldots, t_n(\cdot))$ is allocatively efficient, that is, it satisfies the condition (18.1); the types are statistically independent of each other; and the payments are determined according to the dAGVA payment scheme (19.1). We will set out to prove the necessary and sufficient condition for an SCF $f(\cdot)$ to be BIC:

$$E_{\theta_{-i}} \left[u_i \left(f(\theta_i, \theta_{-i}), \theta_i \right) | \theta_i \right] \geq E_{\theta_{-i}} [u_i(f(\theta_i', \theta_{-i}), \theta_i) | \theta_i], \; \forall \theta_i' \in \Theta_i, \; \forall \theta_i \in \Theta_i, \; \forall i \in N.$$

We first note that

$$E_{\theta_{-i}} \left[u_i(f(\theta_i, \theta_{-i}), \theta_i) | \theta_i \right] = E_{\theta_{-i}} \left[v_i(k^*(\theta_i, \theta_{-i}), \theta_i) + t_i(\theta_i, \theta_{-i}) | \theta_i \right].$$

Since θ_i and θ_{-i} are statistically independent, the expectation can be taken without conditioning on θ_i. Using equation (19.1), the term $E_{\theta_{-i}} \left[u_i(f(\theta_i, \theta_{-i}), \theta_i) | \theta_i \right]$ can be written as

$$E_{\theta_{-i}} \left[v_i(k^*(\theta_i, \theta_{-i}), \theta_i) + h_i(\theta_{-i}) + E_{\tau_{-i}} \left[\sum_{j \neq i} v_j(k^*(\theta_i, \tau_{-i}), \tau_j) \right] \right]$$

This simplifies to

$$E_{\theta_{-i}} \left[\sum_{j=1}^{n} v_j(k^*(\theta_i, \theta_{-i}), \theta_j) \right] + E_{\theta_{-i}} [h_i(\theta_{-i})].$$

Since $k^*(\cdot)$ is efficient allocation, it satisfies (18.1) and we get,

$$\sum_{j=1}^{n} v_j(k^*(\theta_i, \theta_{-i}), \theta_j) \geq \sum_{j=1}^{n} v_j(k^*(\theta_i', \theta_{-i}), \theta_j) \; \forall \; \theta_i' \in \Theta_i.$$

Thus we get, $\forall \; \theta_i' \in \Theta_i$, $\forall \theta_i \in \Theta_i$, and $\forall i \in N$,

$$E_{\theta_{-i}} \left[\sum_{j=1}^{n} v_j(k^*(\theta_i, \theta_{-i}), \theta_j) \right] + E_{\theta_{-i}}[h_i(\theta_{-i})]$$

$$\geq E_{\theta_{-i}} \left[\sum_{j=1}^{n} v_j(k^*(\theta_i', \theta_{-i}), \theta_j) \right] + E_{\theta_{-i}}[h_i(\theta_{-i})].$$

Again by making use of statistical independence we can rewrite the above inequality in the following form

$$E_{\theta_{-i}} \left[u_i(f(\theta_i, \theta_{-i}), \theta_i) | \theta_i \right] \geq E_{\theta_{-i}} \left[u_i(f(\theta_i', \theta_{-i}), \theta_i) | \theta_i \right] ; \; \forall \; \theta_i' \in \Theta_i; \; \forall \theta_i \in \Theta_i; \; \forall i \in N.$$

This proves that $f(\cdot)$ is BIC. ∎

Note. Observe that when agents $j \neq i$ announce their types truthfully, agent i finds that truth revelation is a best response strategy, in expectation over the type profiles of the rest of the agents.

After the results of d'Aspremont and Gérard-Varet [6] and Arrow [7], a direct revelation mechanism in which the SCF is allocatively efficient and satisfies the dAGVA payment scheme (19.1) is called as *dAGVA mechanism/expected externality mechanism/expected Groves mechanism*.

Definition 19.4 (dAGVA Mechanism). *A direct revelation mechanism,* $\mathscr{D} = ((\Theta_i)_{i \in N}, f(\cdot))$ *in which* $f(\cdot) = (k^*(\cdot), t_1(\cdot), \dots, t_n(\cdot))$ *satisfies allocative efficiency and the dAGVA payment scheme is known as dAGVA or expected externality or expected Groves mechanism.*

The dAGVA Mechanism and Strict Budget Balance

We now show that the functions $h_i(\cdot)$ above can be chosen so that $\sum_{i=1}^{n} t_i(\theta) = 0$. Consider

$$\xi_j(\theta_j) = E_{\tau_{-j}} \left[\sum_{l \neq j} v_l(k^*(\theta_j, \tau_{-j}), \tau_l) \right] \; \forall \; i = 1, \dots, n$$

Let us choose

$$h_i(\theta_{-i}) = -\left(\frac{1}{n-1} \right) \sum_{j \neq i} \xi_j(\theta_j) \; \forall \; i = 1, \dots, n.$$

In view of the above definitions, we note that

$$t_i(\theta) = \xi_i(\theta_i) - \left(\frac{1}{n-1}\right)\sum_{j\neq i}\xi_j(\theta_j)$$

This implies

$$\sum_{i=1}^n t_i(\theta) = \sum_{i=1}^n \xi_i(\theta_i) - \left(\frac{1}{n-1}\right)\sum_{i=1}^n\sum_{j\neq i}\xi_j(\theta_j)$$

After simplification, we obtain

$$\sum_{i=1}^n t_i(\theta) = \sum_{i=1}^n \xi_i(\theta_i) - \left(\frac{1}{n-1}\right)\sum_{i=1}^n (n-1)\xi_i(\theta_i)$$

Expanding all the terms on the right hand side and simplifying, we obtain

$$\sum_{i=1}^n t_i(\theta) = 0.$$

This shows that the dAGVA mechanism can be made strictly budget balanced with a judicious choice of $h_i(.)$ functions.

Example 19.3. Consider the dAGVA mechanism for the three agents case, that is, $N = \{1,2,3\}$. The payments for the three agents would be:

$$t_1(\theta) = \xi_1(\theta_1) - \frac{1}{2}\left[\xi_2(\theta_2) + \xi_3(\theta_3)\right]$$

$$t_2(\theta) = \xi_2(\theta_2) - \frac{1}{2}\left[\xi_1(\theta_1) + \xi_3(\theta_3)\right]$$

$$t_3(\theta) = \xi_3(\theta_3) - \frac{1}{2}\left[\xi_1(\theta_1) + \xi_2(\theta_2)\right]$$

Clearly, $t_1(\theta) + t_2(\theta) + t_3(\theta) = 0$. This situation can be better understood with the help of Figure 19.1, which depicts the above payments in the form of a graph. □

As shown in Figure 19.1, the budget balanced payment structure of the agents in the above mechanism can be given an elegant graph theoretic interpretation. Imagine a directed graph $G = (V, A)$ where V is the set of $n+1$ vertices, numbered $0, 1, \ldots, n$, and A is the set of $[n + n(n-1)]$ directed arcs. The vertices starting from 1 through n correspond to the n agents involved in the system and the vertex numbered 0 corresponds to the social planner. The set A consists of two types of the directed arcs: (1) Arcs $0 \to i$ $\forall i = 1, \ldots, n$ and (2) Arcs $i \to j$ $\forall i, j \in \{1, 2, \ldots, n\}; i \neq j$.

Each of the arcs $0 \to i$ carries a flow of $t_i(\theta)$ and each of the arcs $i \to j$ carries a flow of $\frac{\xi_i(\theta_i)}{n-1}$. Thus the total outflow from a node $i \in \{1, 2, \ldots, n\}$ is $\xi_i(\theta_i)$ and total inflow to the node i from nodes $j \in \{1, 2, \ldots, n\}$ is $-h_i(\theta_{-i}) = \left(\frac{1}{n-1}\right)\sum_{j\neq i}\xi_j(\theta_j)$. Thus for node i, $t_i(\theta) - h_i(\theta_{-i})$ is the net inflow which it is receiving from node 0

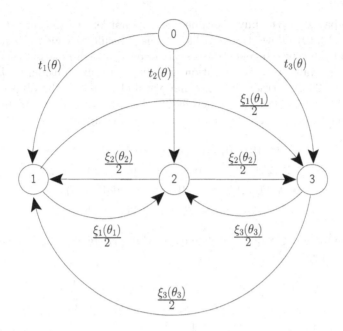

Fig. 19.1: Payment structure showing budget balance in the dAGVA mechanism

in order to respect the flow conservation constraint. Thus, if $t_i(\cdot)$ is positive then the agent i receives the money from the social planner and if it is negative, then the agent pays the money to the social planner. Looking at the flow conservation equation for node 0, it is clear the total payment received by the planner from the agents and total payment made by the planner to the agents will add up to zero. The flow from node i to node j can be justified as follows. Each agent i first evaluates the expected total valuation that would be generated together by all other agents in his absence, which turns out to be $\xi_i(\theta_i)$. Now, agent i divides it equally among the other agents and pays to every other agent an amount equivalent to this. Note that the allocation itself will explicitly take into account the presence of agent i.

Example 19.4 (Bilateral Trading Market). There are two players, player 1 (seller) and player 2 (buyer). Player 1 wishes to sell an indivisible item and player 2 is interested in buying this item. Player 1's type is the willingness to sell (minimum price at which the seller is prepared to sell the item), and has two possible values $\{10, 20\}$. Player 2's type is the willingness to buy (maximum price the buyer is prepared to pay for the item) and has two possible values $\{10, 20\}$. Each player can be in any of the two types with equal probability of 0.5. If the buyer's type is greater than or equal to the seller's announced type, they will trade the object; otherwise no trade occurs. Thus the allocation function $k(\theta_1, \theta_2)$ allocates the object to the buyer (player 2) if $\theta_1 \leq \theta_2$ and the object will remain with the seller (player 1) if $\theta_1 > \theta_2$. This allocation function can be shown to be allocatively efficient (see exercise). We shall now use k^* instead of k to emphasize that k is allocatively efficient.

The values of the players in different type profiles can be derived as follows. Note that whenever trade happens, the seller's value is the negative of his willingness to sell while the buyer's value is his willingness to buy. Whenever trade does not happen, the seller's value is his willingness to pay while the buyer's value is zero. First let us consider $v_1(k^*(10,10),10)$. The type profile $(10,10)$ allows trade to happen as a result of which the seller (agent 1) loses the item and the buyer (agent 2) gains the item. The willingness to sell of agent 1 is 10 and therefore the value in this allocation is -10. Similarly, consider $v_1(k^*(20,10),20)$. In the type profile $(20,10)$, trade does not happen and therefore the object remains with the seller. Since the willingness to sell here is 20, the value of agent 1 in this allocation is 20. Likewise, we can compute all the values and the following provides all the values.

$$v_1(k^*(10,10),10) = -10; \quad v_1(k^*(20,10),20) = 20$$
$$v_1(k^*(10,20),10) = -10; \quad v_1(k^*(20,20),20) = -20$$
$$v_2(k^*(10,10),10) = 10; \quad v_2(k^*(20,10),10) = 0$$
$$v_2(k^*(10,20),20) = 20; \quad v_2(k^*(20,20),20) = 20.$$

We now compute the ξ values as defined in the strictly budget balanced version of dAGVA payment scheme. We get:

$$\xi_1(10) = \frac{1}{2}v_2(k^*(10,10),10) + \frac{1}{2}v_2(k^*(10,20),20) = \frac{1}{2}(10+20) = 15$$

$$\xi_1(20) = \frac{1}{2}v_2(k^*(20,10),10) + \frac{1}{2}v_2(k^*(20,20),20) = \frac{1}{2}(0+20) = 10$$

$$\xi_2(10) = \frac{1}{2}v_1(k^*(10,10),10) + \frac{1}{2}v_1(k^*(20,10),20) = \frac{1}{2}(-10+20) = -5$$

$$\xi_2(20) = \frac{1}{2}v_1(k^*(10,20),10) + \frac{1}{2}v_1(k^*(20,20),20) = \frac{1}{2}(-10-20) = -15$$

The payments will be:

$$t_1(10,10) = \xi_1(10) - \xi_2(10) = 15 - (-5) = 20$$
$$t_1(10,20) = \xi_1(10) - \xi_2(20) = 15 - (-15) = 30$$
$$t_1(20,10) = \xi_1(20) - \xi_2(10) = 10 - (-5) = 15$$
$$t_1(20,20) = \xi_1(20) - \xi_2(20) = 10 - (-15) = 25$$

The payments of the buyer will be exactly the reverse. It is easy to see that this is not individually rational for the buyer. $\square$

The dAGVA Mechanism and Individual Rationality

We have seen that the dAGVA mechanism satisfies AE, SBB, and BIC. One would be curious to know whether it satisfies individual rationality also. Unfortunately, the following theorem rules out that possibility at least for a bilateral trade setting.

The Myerson–Satterthwaite Theorem

The Myerson–Satterthwaite Theorem is an impossibility result and it asserts that in a bilateral trade setting, there is no SCF that satisfies AE, SBB, BIC, and Interim IR all together. The precise statement of the theorem is as follows.

Theorem 19.4 (Myerson–Satterthwaite Impossibility Theorem).

Consider a bilateral trade setting in which the buyer and seller are risk neutral, the valuations θ_1 and θ_2 are drawn independently from the intervals $[\underline{\theta_1}, \overline{\theta_1}] \subset \mathbb{R}$ and $[\underline{\theta_2}, \overline{\theta_2}] \subset \mathbb{R}$ with strict positive densities, and $(\underline{\theta_1}, \overline{\theta_1}) \bigcap (\underline{\theta_2}, \overline{\theta_2}) \neq \emptyset$. Then there is no Bayesian incentive compatible social choice function that is ex-post efficient and gives every buyer and every seller nonnegative expected utilities from participation.

The term *risk neutral* has already been elaborated in Chapter 8 (see Section 8.6). For a proof of the above theorem, refer to Proposition 23.E.1 of the book by Mas-Colell, Whinston, and Green [8].

19.6 Mechanism Design Space in Quasilinear Environment

Figure 19.2 shows the space of mechanisms taking into account all the results we have studied so far. This figure summarizes all the results we have seen in the previous chapter and the current one. A careful look at the diagram suggests why designing a mechanism that satisfies a specified combination of properties is a quite intricate exercise.

A designer of mechanisms (with money) in a quasilinear setting has to weigh in the tradeoffs in a judicious way while selecting a particular mechanism for his current application. This is where the possibility and impossibility theorems become important. An intelligent social planner will first identify the key properties required for a given application and examines if all of these key properties are in the realm of the possible. If not, the social planner will have to filter out one or more properties from the list and come up finally with a mechanism that fits the application best. As new applications emerge in the Internet era and new properties become relevant, research in mechanism design these days is all about how to design the most appropriate mechanisms satisfying the most desirable subset of properties.

19.7 Linear Environment

The linear environment is a special, often-studied, subclass of the quasilinear environment. This environment is a restricted version of the quasilinear environment in the following sense.

(1) Each agent i's type lies in an interval $\Theta_i = [\underline{\theta_i}, \overline{\theta_i}] \subset \mathbb{R}$ with $\underline{\theta_i} < \overline{\theta_i}$.
(2) Agents' types are statistically independent, that is, the density $\phi(\cdot)$ has the form $\phi_1(\cdot) \times \ldots \times \phi_n(\cdot)$.
(3) $\phi_i(\theta_i) > 0 \ \forall \ \theta_i \in [\underline{\theta_i}, \overline{\theta_i}] \ \forall \ i = 1, \ldots, n$.
(4) Each agent i's utility function takes the following form

$$u_i(x, \theta_i) = \theta_i v_i(k) + m_i + t_i.$$

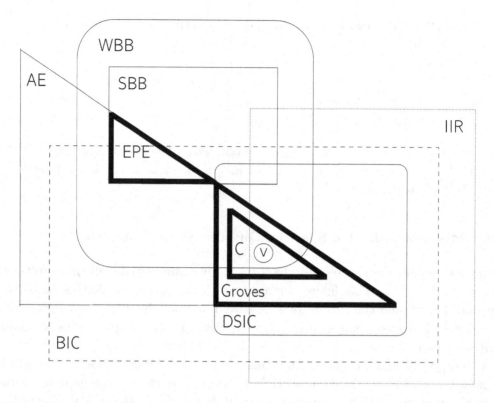

AE   : Allocative Efficient   EPE : Ex-Post Efficient
SBB   : Strict Budget Balanced   IIR : Interim Individually Rational
WBB   : Weak Budget Balanced   C   : Clarke Mechanism
BIC   : Bayesian Incentive Compatible   V   : Vickrey Auction
DSIC : Dominant Strategy Incentive Compatible

Fig. 19.2: Mechanism design space in quasilinear environment

The linear environment has very interesting properties in terms of being able to obtain a characterization of the class of BIC social choice functions. Before we present Myerson's Characterization Theorem for BIC social choice functions in a linear environment, we define the following quantities with respect to any social choice function $f(\cdot) = (k(\cdot), t_1(\cdot), \ldots, t_n(\cdot))$ in this environment.

- Let $\bar{t}_i(\hat{\theta}_i) = E_{\theta_{-i}}[t_i(\hat{\theta}_i, \theta_{-i})]$ be agent i's expected transfer given that he announces his type to be $\hat{\theta}_i$ and that all agents $j \neq i$ truthfully reveal their types.
- Let $\bar{v}_i(\hat{\theta}_i) = E_{\theta_{-i}}[v_i(\hat{\theta}_i, \theta_{-i})]$ be agent i's expected "benefits" given that he announces his type to be $\hat{\theta}_i$ and that all agents $j \neq i$ truthfully reveal their types.
- Let $U_i(\hat{\theta}_i | \theta_i) = E_{\theta_{-i}}[u_i(f(\hat{\theta}_i, \theta_{-i}), \theta_i) | \theta_i]$ be agent i's expected utility when his type is θ_i, he announces his type to be $\hat{\theta}_i$, and all agents $j \neq i$ truthfully reveal

their types. It is easy to verify from the previous two definitions that

$$U_i(\hat{\theta}_i | \theta_i) = \theta_i \overline{v_i}(\hat{\theta}_i) + \overline{t_i}(\hat{\theta}_i).$$

- Let $U_i(\theta_i) = U_i(\theta_i | \theta_i)$ be the agent i's expected utility conditional on his type being θ_i when he and all other agents report their true types. It is easy to verify that

$$U_i(\theta_i) = \theta_i \overline{v_i}(\theta_i) + \overline{t_i}(\theta_i).$$

Myerson's Characterization Theorem

With the above notation in place, we now present Myerson's [9] theorem for characterizing the BIC social choice functions in this environment.

Theorem 19.5 (Myerson's Characterization Theorem). *In linear environment, a social choice function $f(\cdot) = (k(\cdot), t_1(\cdot), \ldots, t_n(\cdot))$ is BIC if and only if, for all $i = 1, \ldots, n$,*

(1) $\overline{v_i}(\cdot)$ is nondecreasing,
(2) $U_i(\theta_i) = U_i(\underline{\theta_i}) + \int_{\underline{\theta_i}}^{\theta_i} \overline{v_i}(s) ds \ \forall \, \theta_i \in \Theta_i.$

For a proof of the above theorem, refer to Proposition 23.D.2 of the book by Mas-Colell, Whinston, and Green [8]. The above theorem shows that to identify all BIC social choice functions in a linear environment, we can proceed as follows: First identify which functions $k(\cdot)$ lead every agent i's expected benefit function $\overline{v_i}(\cdot)$ to be nondecreasing. Then, for each such function identify transfer functions $\overline{t_1}(\cdot), \ldots, \overline{t_n}(\cdot)$ that satisfy the second condition of the above proposition. Substituting for $U_i(\cdot)$ in the second condition above, we get that expected transfer functions are precisely those that satisfy, for $i = 1, \ldots, n$,

$$\overline{t_i}(\theta_i) = \overline{t_i}(\underline{\theta_i}) + \underline{\theta_i} \, \overline{v_i}(\underline{\theta_i}) - \theta_i \overline{v_i}(\theta_i) + \int_{\underline{\theta_i}}^{\theta_i} \overline{v_i}(s) ds$$

for some constant $\overline{t_i}(\underline{\theta_i})$. Finally, choose any set of transfer functions $t_1(\cdot), \ldots, t_n(\cdot)$ such that for all θ_i, $E_{\theta_{-i}}[t_i(\theta_i, \theta_{-i})] = \overline{t_i}(\theta_i)$. In general, there are many such functions, $t_i(\cdot, \cdot)$; one, for example, is simply $t_i(\theta_i, \theta_{-i}) = \overline{t_i}(\theta_i)$.

19.8 Summary and References

In this chapter, we have looked into a variety of possibilities and impossibilities for mechanisms under quasilinear preferences.

- First we looked at Groves mechanisms (which satisfy AE and DSIC) and budget balance. The Green-Laffont theorem rules out strict budget balance of Groves mechanisms. An escape route is the scenario in which the type set of one of the players is common knowledge.

- Next we looked at Clarke mechanisms and weak budget balance. We showed that under a sufficient condition (called no single agent effect), Clarke mechanisms are weakly budget balanced. Redistribution mechanisms are those which minimize the budget imbalance while preserving AE and DSIC.

- Following this, we defined an important property called individual rationality (IR) which ensures that every agent would participate in the mechanism voluntarily. This property could be defined at three stages of the game: ex-ante, interim, and ex-post. We showed that VCG mechanism are not necessarily IR and proved that Clarke mechanisms are IR if two conditions (choice set monotonicity and no negative externality) are satisfied.

- The next topic we discussed was the dAGVA mechanism which is also called the expected Groves mechanism. The dAGVA mechanism satisfies BIC, AE, and SBB but is not IR. The mechanism is tailor made for two sided market settings such as bilateral trade.

- We consolidated all the results that we have examined in mechanism design under quasilinear preferences and Figure 19.3 captures the intricate possibilities and impossibilities.

- To conclude the chapter, we discussed an important special case of quasilinear setting called the linear environment and presented a key result by Myerson which gives a characterization of BIC mechanisms in linear environment. This result ties up BIC with monotonicity and will be crucially used in subsequent chapters while proving the revenue equivalence theorem (for single item auctions) and in setting up the results for optimal auctions.

References

[1] J.R. Green and J.J. Laffont. *Incentives in Public Decision Making*. North-Holland, Amsterdam, 1979.

[2] R. Cavallo. "Optimal decision making with minimal waste: strategy-proof redistribution of VCG payments". In: *Proceedings of the Fifth International Joint Conference on Autonomous Agents and Multiagent Systems, AAMAS-2006*. 2006, pp. 882–889.

[3] H. Moulin. "Almost budget balanced VCG mechanisms to assign multiple objects". In: *Journal of Economic Theory* **144** (2009), pp. 96–119.

[4] M. Guo and V. Conitzer. "Worst-case optimal redistribution of VCG payments in multiunit auctions". In: *Games and Economic Behavior* **67** (2010), pp. 69–98.

[5] Sujit Gujar and Y. Narahari. "Redistribution mechanisms for assignment of heterogeneous objects". In: *Journal of Artificial Intelligence Research* **41** (2011), pp. 131–154.

[6] C. d'Aspremont and L.A. Gérard-Varet. "Incentives and incomplete information". In: *Journal of Public Economics* **11** (1979), pp. 25–45.

[7] K. Arrow. "The property rights doctrine and demand revelation under incomplete information". In: *Economics and Human Welfare*. Ed. by M. Boskin. Academic Press, New York, 1979.

[8] Andreu Mas-Colell, Michael D. Whinston, and Jerry R. Green. *Microeconomic Theory*. Oxford University Press, 1995.

[9] Roger B. Myerson. "Optimal auction design". In: *Mathematics of Operations Research* **6**(1) (1981), pp. 58–73.

19.9 Exercises

(1) Consider that there are two agents, each of them holding a single indivisible object. Suppose $\Theta_1 = \{1,2\}$; $\Theta_2 = \{2,3\}$. Consider the following direct mechanism where the two agents report their types. Agent 1 wins if her report is greater than or equal to the report of player 2; otherwise player 2 wins. Whoever wins becomes the seller and whoever loses becomes the buyer and the object held by the winner is bought by the loser. Design a (strictly) budget balanced dAGVA mechanism for the above problem.

(2) Consider two agents 1 and 2 with $\Theta_1 = \{1,2,3\}$ and $\Theta_2 = \{2,3\}$. Each of these agents has a single indivisible item to sell to the other. A dAGVA mechanism decides who will sell. Assume that agent 1 sells if his bid is less than or equal to that of agent 2, in which case agent 2 will buy the item from agent 1. If the bid of agent 1 is greater than that of agent 2, then agent 2 sells and agent 1 buys it from agent 2. Payments are decided by the dAGVA mechanism. Design a strictly budget balanced dAGVA mechanism for this problem.

(3) Consider a selling agent 0 and two buying agents 1, 2. The buying agents submit sealed bids to buy a single indivisible item. Let θ_1 and θ_2 be the willingness to pay of the buyers. Let us define the usual allocation function:

$$y_1(\theta_1, \theta_2) = 1 \text{ if } \theta_1 \geq \theta_2$$
$$= 0 \text{ else}$$
$$y_2(\theta_1, \theta_2) = 1 \text{ if } \theta_1 < \theta_2$$
$$= 0 \text{ else.}$$

Let $\Theta_1 = \Theta_2 = [0, 1]$ and assume that the bids from the bidders are i.i.d. uniform distributions on $[0, 1]$. Also assume that $\Theta_0 = \{0\}$. Assuming that the dAGVA mechanism is used, compute the payments.

(4) Consider a sealed bid auction with one buyer and two selling agents. There is a single indivisible item which the buyer wishes to buy. The bidders are symmetric with independent private values distributed uniformly over $[0, 1]$. Whoever bids lower will be selected to sell the item. Suppose the dAGVA payment rule is used. Compute the payment that the winner will receive. How about the loser?

(5) Consider a bilateral trade setting in which each $\theta_i(i = 1, 2)$ is independently drawn from a uniform distribution on $[0, 1]$. Compute the payments in the dAGVA mechanism. Verify that truth telling is a Bayesian Nash equilibrium.

(6) Consider again a bilateral trade setting in which each $\theta_i(i = 1, 2)$ is independently drawn from a uniform distribution on $[0,1]$. Suppose now that by refusing to participate in the mechanism a seller with valuation θ_1 receives expected utility θ_1 (he simply consumes the good), whereas a buyer with valuation θ_2 receives expected utility 0. Show that in the dAGVA mechanism there is a type of buyer or seller who will strictly prefer not to participate.

(7) Show by means of an example that when the buyer and seller in a bilateral trade

setting both have a discrete set of possible valuations, social choice functions may exist that are Bayesian incentive compatible, ex-post efficient, and individually rational. (*Hint:* It is enough to consider each agent to have two possible types.)

(8) **Programming Assignment.** Implement the dAGVA mechanism. Identify the inputs to this program carefully. The output must be an efficient allocation and a payment vector for any given type profile.

Chapter 20

Auctions

Auctions are ubiquitous these days in real-world e-commerce and e-business transactions and numerous other applications on the web. Auctions provide a natural example of *mechanisms with money*. Mechanism design theory provides a principled way of designing auctions to ensure that desirable properties are satisfied. In this chapter, we discuss different types of auctions and key mechanism design issues. In particular, we discuss four basic types of auctions for selling or procuring a single indivisible item: English auction, Dutch auction, first price auction, and second price auction (Vickrey auction). We discuss a key result concerning the above four auctions, namely the *revenue equivalence theorem*. We also introduce *combinatorial auctions*.

An auction is a mechanism to allocate a set of goods to a set of bidders on the basis of bids announced by the bidders. Auctions have been used for trading of objects for thousands of years. In the recent times, the use of auctions in web-based applications has grown dramatically. These applications include traditional ones such as sale of paintings and memorabilia to more current applications such as auctions for Internet advertising space, keyword auctions on search engine websites, industrial procurement auctions, auctions for spectrum allocation, auctions for airport slot allocation, etc. There is therefore a great deal of interest in the theory and practical applications of auctions.

There are excellent books [1, 2, 3] and survey articles [4, 5, 6] on auctions. More recently, several survey papers have focused on combinatorial auctions [7, 8, 9, 10].

20.1 Auction Types and Desirable Properties

Classification of Auctions

Kalagnanam and Parkes [9] have suggested a framework for classifying auctions based on six major criteria as outlined below.

(1) *Resources*: Resources are entities over which negotiations in an auction are conducted. Resources could be a single item or multiple items, with a single or multiple units of each item. Multiple item auctions are called combinatorial auctions.

(2) *Market Structure*: There are three types of market structures in auctions. In a *forward auction*, a single seller sells resources to multiple buyers. In a *reverse auction*, a single buyer attempts to source resources from multiple suppliers, as is common in procurement. Auctions with multiple buyers and sellers are called *double auctions* or *exchanges*.

(3) *Preference Structure*: The preferences define an agent's utility for different outcomes in the auction. For example, when multiple units of an item are involved, agents could indicate a decreasing marginal utility for additional units. If an object has multiple attributes such as cost, lead time, quality, reliability, etc., an agent's preference structure could capture the importance the agent attaches to the attributes.

(4) *Bid Structure*: The structure of the bids within the auction defines the flexibility with which agents can express their resource requirements. For a simple single unit, single item commodity, the bids required are simply the willingness to buy or willingness to sell. For a multiunit identical items setting, the bids need to specify price and quantity. This introduces the possibility for allowing volume discounts. With multiple items, bids may specify preferences on bundles.

(5) *Winner Determination*: Other phrases which are used synonymously with winner determination are *market clearing*, *bid evaluation*, *bid allocation*, or simply *allocation*. In the case of forward auctions, winner determination refers to choosing an optimal subset of buyers who would be awarded the items. In the case of reverse auctions, winner determination refers to choosing an optimal subset of sellers who would be awarded the contracts for supplying the required items. In the case of an exchange, winner determination refers to determining an optimal match between buyers and sellers. The computational complexity of the winner determination problem is an important issue to be considered in designing auctions.

(6) *Information Feedback*: An auction protocol may be with information feedback or without information feedback. In a single round auction, agents submit bids without receiving feedback (such as price signals) from the auction. In multi-round auctions, agents can adjust bids in response to information feedback from the auction. Feedback about the state of the auction is usually characterized by a *price signal* and a *tentative allocation*, and provides useful information about the bids of winning agents which helps an agent to revise its own bids.

Auctions: Desirable Properties

We now provide an intuitive idea about desirable properties that an auction designer looks for. Not all of these can be realized simultaneously as we have seen in the previous chapter. Depending on the context, the auction designer has to carefully choose a maximal subset of these properties that can be simultaneously achieved.

Solution Equilibrium

The solution of a mechanism is in equilibrium, if no agent wishes to change its bid, given the information it has about other agents. Many types of equilibria can be computed given the assumptions about the preferences of agents (buyers and sellers), rationality, and information availability. We are already familiar with different types of equilibria: *Bayesian Nash equilibrium*, *ex-post Nash equilibrium*, and *strongly/weakly/very-weakly dominant strategy equilibrium*.

Incentive Compatibility

An auction is said to be incentive compatible if the agents optimize their expected utilities by bidding their true valuations of the resources. Depending on the equilibrium achieved by truthful bidding, an incentive compatible auction is qualified as Bayesian incentive compatible or dominant strategy incentive compatible. If a mechanism is DSIC, each agent's decision depends only on its local information and there is no need whatsoever for the agent to model or compute the strategies of the other agents. In the case of BIC, computation of equilibrium strategies will require information about the prior. Ex-post incentive compatibility (EPIC) (which will be discussed in Chapter 23) is another kind of incentive compatibility – stronger than BIC but weaker than DSIC.

Allocative Efficiency

Allocative efficiency is achieved when the social utility (sum of utilities) of all the winners is maximized. Allocative efficiency ensures that the resources are allocated to the agents who value them most.

Individual Rationality

An auction is said to be individually rational (or is said to have voluntary participation property) if its allocations do not make any agent worse off than if the agent had not participated in the mechanism. That is, every agent gains a nonnegative utility by participating in the mechanism.

Budget Balance

An auction is said to be *weakly* budget balanced if, in all feasible outcomes, the payments by buyers exceed or equal to the receipts of sellers. An auction is said to be *strongly* budget balanced if the net monetary transfer is zero. In other words, budget balance ensures that the auctioneer or mechanism designer does not make losses.

Revenue Maximization or Cost Minimization

In an auction where a seller is auctioning a set of items, the seller would like to maximize total revenue earned. On the other hand, in a procurement auction, the buyer would like to procure at minimum cost. Often, rather than revenue maximization, the goal of the seller will be profit maximization, where profit is revenue minus cost. In an exchange setting where there are multiple buyers and multiple sellers, maximization of surplus where surplus is the total amount of receipts minus total amount of payments could be the objective.

Fairness

Winner determination algorithms, especially those based on heuristics, could lead to different sets of winners at different times. Since there could be multiple optimal solutions, different sets of winners could be produced by different algorithms. This creates a perception of unfairness and can influence bidders' willingness to participate in auctions. Bidders who lose even though they could have won with a different algorithm could end up feeling unfairly treated.

Cheatproofness

An auction should be robust to false name attacks and innumerable other types of manipulations by the bidders.

20.2 Canonical Mechanisms for a Single Indivisible Item Auction

There are four basic types of auctions when a single indivisible item is to be sold or bought. We discuss the case of selling or forward auction here. When a single indivisible item is to be bought or procured, the four types of auctions can be used in a *reverse* way. These are then called *reverse auctions* or *procurement auctions*.

English Auction

This is also called an open cry auction or an ascending bid auction. Here, the going price starts at a low level and is successively raised until only one bidder remains in the fray. This can be done in several ways: (a) an auctioneer announces prices, (b) bidders call the bids themselves, or (c) bids are submitted electronically. At any point of time, each bidder knows the level of the current best bid. The winning bidder pays the latest going price.

Dutch Auction

This is also called a descending bid auction. Here, the auctioneer announces an initial (high) price and then keeps lowering the price in successive rounds until one of the bidders accepts the current price. The winner pays the current price.

First Price Sealed Bid Auction

Here, potential buyers submit sealed bids and the highest bidder is awarded the item. If multiple highest bidders are available, a suitable tie-breaking rule is applied to select the winner. The winning bidder pays the price that he has bid.

Second Price Sealed Bid Auction

This is the classic Vickrey auction. Recall that potential buyers submit sealed bids and the allocation is as in the first price auction. The winning bidder pays a price equal to the second highest bid (which is also the highest losing bid).

Example 20.1 (Canonical Auctions). Consider the following scenario. There is a seller who wishes to auction a property. There are two prospective buyers for this property. The first buyer has a willingness to pay of Rs. 10 million for the property and the second bidder has a willingness to pay of Rs. 15 million. Each bidder does not know the willingness to pay of the other bidder.

English Auction

A typical English auction may progress like this. The first bidder bids Rs. 5 million and then the second bidder places a bid of Rs. 6 million. The first bidder may now increase his bid to Rs. 8 million. The second bidder may then increase her bid to Rs. 9 million. The first bidder may again revise his bid to Rs. 9.5 Million. The second bidder now revises her bid to Rs. 10 million. Now, the first bidder will not increase his bid anymore. So the second bidder will receive the property by paying Rs. 10 million.

Dutch Auction

A typical Dutch auction would proceed as follows. The seller declares a price Rs. 20 million. No agent is willing to purchase at that price. The seller drops the price to Rs. 18 million. Still no agent would be willing to buy. The seller continues to drop the price, say, to Rs. 16 million, Rs. 14 million, Rs. 12 million, Rs. 11 million. At Rs. 11 million, the second bidder may decide to buy it, since she might (though she does not know the valuation of the first bidder) apprehend that the first agent may express his intent to buy before her. Note that Rs. 11 million is lower than what the second bidder is willing to pay.

First Price Sealed Bid Auction

Suppose the first bidder bids Rs. 9 million and the second one bids Rs. 11 million. The second bidder will win and pay Rs. 11 million, which is his bid, to the seller.

Second Price Sealed Bid Auction (Vickrey Auction)

Each bidder knows that if he wins, he has to pay the other's bid. Truthful bidding is a weakly dominant strategy here. So the first bidder will bid Rs. 10 million and the second bidder will bid Rs. 15 million. The second bidder will receive the property by paying Rs. 10 million which is the second highest bid. □

20.3   Revenue Equivalence of First Price and Second Price Auctions

In this section, we prove under some conditions that the expected revenue to the seller is the same in the first price auction and second price auction. We in fact prove a more general result on the revenue equivalence of two auctions which are natural generalizations of first price auction and second price auction.

Consider a seller who wishes to sell an indivisible object in which n buying agents $\{1, \ldots, n\}$ are interested. Suppose θ_i is the type of buying agent i ($i = 1, \ldots, n$ where θ_i denotes the willingness to buy of agent i. Assume that $y_i(\theta)$ is the probability of agent i getting the object when the vector of announced types is $\theta = (\theta_1, \ldots, \theta_n)$. The expected payoff to the buyer i with a type profile $\theta = (\theta_1, \ldots, \theta_n)$ will be $y_i(\theta)\theta_i + t_i(\theta)$ where $t_i(\theta)$ is the monetary transfer to player i when the type profile is θ (linear environment – see Section 19.7). The set of allocations is given by

$$K = \left\{ (y_1, \ldots, y_n) : y_i \in [0, 1] \; \forall i = 1, \ldots, n; \sum_{i=1}^{n} y_i \leq 1 \right\}.$$

As earlier, let $\overline{y_i}(\hat{\theta}_i) = E_{\theta_{-i}}[y_i(\hat{\theta}_i, \theta_{-i})]$ be the expected probability that agent i gets the object conditional to announcing his type as $\hat{\theta}_i$, with the rest of the agents announcing their types truthfully. Similarly, $\overline{t_i}(\hat{\theta}_i) = E_{\theta_{-i}}[t_i(\hat{\theta}_i, \theta_{-i})]$ denotes the expected payment received by agent i conditional to announcing his type as $\hat{\theta}_i$, with the rest of the agents announcing their types truthfully. Then,

$$U_i(\theta_i) = \overline{y_i}(\theta_i)\theta_i + \overline{t_i}(\theta_i)$$

denotes the expected payoff to agent i when all the buying agents announce their types truthfully. We now state and prove an important proposition.

Theorem 20.1. *Consider an auction scenario with:*

(1) n risk-neutral bidders (buyers) $1, 2, \ldots, n$

(2) The valuation of bidder i ($i = 1, \ldots, n$) is a real interval $[\underline{\theta_i}, \overline{\theta_i}] \subset \mathbb{R}$ with $\underline{\theta_i} < \overline{\theta_i}$.

(3) The valuation of bidder i ($i = 1, \ldots, n$) is drawn from $[\underline{\theta_i}, \overline{\theta_i}]$ with a strictly positive density $\phi_i(.) > 0$. Let $\Phi_i(.)$ be the cumulative distribution function.

(4) The types of the bidders are statistically independent.

Suppose that a given pair of Bayesian Nash equilibria of two different auction procedures are such that:

- *For every bidder i, for each possible realization of $(\theta_1, \ldots, \theta_n)$, bidder i has an identical probability of getting the object in the two auctions.*
- *Every bidder i has the same expected payoff in the two auctions when his valuation for the object is at its lowest possible level.*

Then the two auctions generate the same expected revenue to the seller.

Before proving the theorem, to appreciate on the first assumption above, namely risk neutrality, we point the reader to Section 8.6 where we discussed three different types of risk attitudes of players: risk averse, risk neutral, and risk loving. In brief, a bidder is risk neutral if his utility is a linear function of the money held by him.

Proof: By the revelation principle, it is enough that we investigate two BIC social choice functions in this auction setting. It is sufficient to show that two separate BIC social choice functions having (a) the same allocation functions $(y_1(\theta), \ldots, y_n(\theta))$ $\forall \theta \in \Theta$, and (b) the same values of $U_1(\underline{\theta_1}), \ldots, U_n(\underline{\theta_n})$ will generate the same expected revenue to the seller.

We first derive an expression for the seller's expected revenue given any BIC mechanism.

$$\text{Expected revenue to the seller} = \sum_{i=1}^{n} E_\theta[-t_i(\theta)]. \tag{20.1}$$

Now, we have:

$$E_\theta[-t_i(\theta)] = E_{\theta_i}[-E_{\theta_{-i}}[t_i(\theta)]]$$

$$= \int_{\underline{\theta_i}}^{\overline{\theta_i}} [\overline{y_i}(\theta_i)\theta_i - U_i(\theta_i)]\phi_i(\theta_i)d\theta_i$$

$$= \int_{\underline{\theta_i}}^{\overline{\theta_i}} \left[[\overline{y_i}(\theta_i)\theta_i - U_i(\underline{\theta_i})] - \int_{\underline{\theta_i}}^{\theta_i} \overline{y_i}(s)ds \right] \phi_i(\theta_i)d\theta_i.$$

The last step is an implication of Myerson's characterization of Bayesian incentive compatible functions in linear environment (see Section 19.7). The above expression is now equal to

$$\left[\int_{\underline{\theta_i}}^{\overline{\theta_i}} \left(\overline{y_i}(\theta_i)\theta_i - \int_{\underline{\theta_i}}^{\theta_i} \overline{y_i}(s)ds \right) \phi_i(\theta_i)d\theta_i \right] - U_i(\underline{\theta_i}).$$

We first simplify

$$\int_{\underline{\theta_i}}^{\overline{\theta_i}} \left(\int_{\underline{\theta_i}}^{\theta_i} \overline{y_i}(s)ds \right) \phi_i(\theta_i)d\theta_i$$

by applying integration by parts with $\int_{\underline{\theta_i}}^{\theta_i} \overline{y_i}(s)ds$ as the first function. This yields

$$\int_{\underline{\theta_i}}^{\overline{\theta_i}} \overline{y_i}(\theta_i)d\theta_i - \int_{\underline{\theta_i}}^{\overline{\theta_i}} \overline{y_i}(\theta_i)\Phi_i(\theta_i)d\theta_i$$

which is equal to:

$$\int_{\underline{\theta_i}}^{\overline{\theta_i}} \overline{y_i}(\theta_i)[1 - \Phi_i(\theta_i)]d\theta_i.$$

Therefore we get

$$E_{\theta_i}[-\overline{t_i}(\theta_i)] = -U_i(\underline{\theta_i}) + \left[\int_{\underline{\theta_i}}^{\overline{\theta_i}} \overline{y_i}(\theta_i) \left\{ \theta_i - \frac{1 - \Phi_i(\theta_i)}{\phi_i(\theta_i)} \right\} \phi_i(\theta_i)d\theta_i \right]$$

$$= -U_i(\underline{\theta_i}) + \left[\int_{\underline{\theta_1}}^{\overline{\theta_1}} \cdots \int_{\underline{\theta_n}}^{\overline{\theta_n}} y_i(\theta_1, \ldots, \theta_n) \right.$$
$$\left. \times \left(\theta_i - \frac{1 - \Phi_i(\theta_i)}{\phi_i(\theta_i)} \right) \left(\prod_{j=1}^{n} \phi_j(\theta_j) \right) d\theta_n \ldots d\theta_1 \right]$$

since

$$\overline{y_i}(\theta_i) = \int_{\underline{\theta_1}}^{\overline{\theta_1}} \cdots \int_{\underline{\theta_n}}^{\overline{\theta_n}} y_i(\theta_1, \ldots, \theta_n) \left(\prod_{j=1}^{n} \phi_j(\theta_j) \right) \underbrace{d\theta_n \ldots d\theta_1}_{\text{without } d\theta_i}.$$

Therefore the expected revenue of the seller

$$= \left[\int_{\underline{\theta_1}}^{\overline{\theta_1}} \cdots \int_{\underline{\theta_n}}^{\overline{\theta_n}} \sum_{i=1}^{n} y_i(\theta_1, \ldots, \theta_n) \left(\theta_i - \frac{1 - \Phi_i(\theta_i)}{\phi_i(\theta_i)} \right) \right] \left(\prod_{j=1}^{n} \phi_j(\theta_j) \right) d\theta_n \ldots d\theta_1$$
$$- \sum_{i=1}^{n} U_i(\underline{\theta_i}).$$

By looking at the above expression, we see that any two Bayesian incentive compatible social choice functions that generate the same functions $(y_1(\theta), \ldots, y_n(\theta))$ and the same values of $(U_1(\underline{\theta_1}), \ldots, U_n(\underline{\theta_n}))$ generate the same expected revenue to the seller.   ■

Note. The first price auction and the second price auction satisfy the conditions of the above theorem:

- In both the auctions, the bidder with the highest valuation wins the auction.
- Bidders' valuations are drawn from some real interval $[\underline{\theta_i}, \overline{\theta_i}]$ and a bidder with valuation at the lower limit of the interval has a payoff of zero in both the auctions.

Thus the theorem can be applied to the equilibria of the two auctions: Note that in the case of the first price auction, it is a Bayesian Nash equilibrium while in the case of the second price auction, it is a weakly dominant strategy equilibrium. Thus these two auctions generate the same expected revenue to the seller.

We are now in a position to state and informally prove an important result, the *revenue equivalence theorem*, in the context of auctioning a single indivisible item. The article by McAfee and McMillan [4] and the book by Vijay Krishna [1] provide excellent references for this topic and much of the discussion in this section is based on the above references.

20.4   Revenue Equivalence Theorem

This important theorem states that the four canonical auctions for a single indivisible item produce the same expected revenue to the seller under a benchmark model.

The Benchmark Model

There are four assumptions that are key to the revenue equivalence theorem: (1) risk neutrality of bidders; (2) bidders have independent private values; (3) bidders are symmetric; (4) payments depend on bids alone. These are described below in more detail.

(1) Risk Neutrality of Bidders

It is assumed in the benchmark model that all the bidders are risk neutral. This immediately implies that the utility function of each bidder is linear in the money held by the bidder. See Section 8.6 for more details.

(2) Independent Private Values Model

In the independent private values model, each bidder knows precisely how much he values the item. However, each bidder may not know the valuation of the item for the other bidders. Each bidder perceives any other bidder's valuation as drawn from some known probability distribution. Also, each bidder knows that the other bidders and the seller regard his own valuation as being drawn from some known probability distribution. More formally, let $N = \{1, 2, \ldots, n\}$, as usual, be the set of bidders. The independent private values assumption presupposes a probability distribution Φ_i from which bidder i ($i \in N$) draws his valuation v_i. Only bidder i observes his own valuation v_i, but all other bidders and the seller only know the distribution Φ_i. The probability distributions of the bidders are mutually independent.

An appropriate example of this assumption is provided by the auction of a rare painting in which the bidders are consumers buying for their own use and not for resale.

A popular model that is different from the above model is the *common value model*. Here, if V is the *unobserved* true value of the item, then the bidders' perceived values $v_i, i = 1, \ldots, n$ are independent draws from some probability distribution $H(v_i|V)$. All bidders know the distribution H. An example is provided by the sale of a rare painting that is being bid for by bidders who intend to resell it. The rare painting has one single objective value, namely its market price. However, no one knows its true market price. The bidders, if they gain access to useful but different bits of information, will have different guesses about how much the painting is objectively worth.

Suppose a bidder comes to know the valuation of another bidder for the painting. If the situation is described by the common value model, then the above provides useful information about the likely true value of the item, and the bidder would perhaps change his own valuation in the light of this. If the situation is described by the independent private values model, the bidder has definite valuation for the painting, and learning about others' valuations will not make him change his own valuation. He might perhaps, for strategic reasons, change his bid.

Real world auction situations are likely to contain aspects of both the independent private values model and the common value model. It is assumed in the benchmark model that the independent private values assumption holds.

(3) Symmetry

This assumption implies that all the bidders have the same set of possible valuations, and further they draw their valuations using the same probability distribution function Φ. That is, $\Phi_1 = \Phi_2 = \ldots = \Phi_n = \Phi$.

(4) Dependence of Payments on Bids Alone

It is assumed that the payment to be made by the winner to the seller is a function of bids alone.

Theorem 20.2 (Revenue Equivalence Theorem). *Consider a seller or an auctioneer seeking to sell a single indivisible item in which n bidders are interested. For the benchmark model (bidders are risk neutral, bidders have independent private values, bidders are symmetric, and payments depend only on bids), all the four basic auction types (English auction, Dutch auction, first price auction, and second price auction) yield the same expected revenue to the seller.*

Note. The result may seem somewhat counter intuitive. For example, it might seem that receiving the highest bid in a first price sealed bid auction must be better for the seller than receiving the second highest bid, as in second price auction. However, it is to be noted that bidders act differently in different auction situations. In particular, they bid more aggressively in a second price auction than in a first price auction.

Proof: The proof proceeds in three parts. In Part 1, we show that the first price auction and the second price auction yield the same expected revenue in their respective equilibria. In Part 2, we show that the Dutch auction and the first price auction produce the same outcome. In Part 3, we show that the English auction and the second price auction yield the same outcome. We caution the readers that our proof is intuition based but informal and we refer the readers to [1] for a rigorous proof of this result.

Part 1: Revenue Equivalence of First Price and Second Price Auctions

We have already shown that first price auction and the second price auction satisfy the conditions of Theorem 20.1. It is clear that the two auctions generate the same expected revenue to the seller. In fact, it can be shown in any *symmetric* auction setting (where the bidders' valuations are independently drawn from identical distributions) that the conditions of Theorem 20.1 will be satisfied by any Bayesian Nash equilibrium of the first price auction and the weakly dominant strategy equilibrium of the second price sealed bid auction.

Part 2: Revenue Equivalence of Dutch Auction and First Price Auction

To see this, consider the situation facing a bidder in these two auctions. In each case, the bidder must choose how high to bid without knowing the other bidders' valuations. If he wins, the price he pays equals his own bid. This result is true irrespective of which of the assumptions in the benchmark model apply. We point out that the equilibrium in the underlying Bayesian game in the two cases here is a Bayesian Nash equilibrium.

Part 3: Revenue Equivalence of English Auction and Second Price Auction

The outcomes of the English auction and the second price auction satisfy a weakly dominant strategy equilibrium. That is, each bidder has a well defined best response bid regardless of how high he believes the other agents will bid. In the second price auction, the weakly dominant strategy is to bid true valuation. In the English auction, the weakly dominant strategy is to remain in the bidding process until the price reaches the bidder's own valuation.

First we analyze the English auction. Note that a bidder drops out as soon the going price exceeds his valuation. The second last bidder drops out as soon as the price exceeds his own valuation. This leaves only one bidder in the fray and he wins the auction. Note that the winning bidder's valuation is the highest among all the bidders and he earns some payoff in spite of the monopoly power of the seller. Only the winning bidder knows how much payoff he receives because only he knows his own valuation. Suppose the valuations of the n bidders are $v_{(1)}, v_{(2)}, \ldots, v_{(n)}$. Since the bidders are symmetric, these valuations are draws from the same distribution and without loss of generality, assume that these are in descending order. The winning bidder gets a payoff of $v_{(1)} - v_{(2)}$.

Next we analyze the second price auction. In the second price auction, the bidder's choice of bid determines only whether or not he wins; the amount he pays if he wins is beyond his control. We have already shown that each bidder's equilibrium strategy is to bid his valuation for the item. The payment here is equal to the true valuation of the bidder with the second highest valuation. Thus the expected payments and hence the expected revenue to the seller are the same in English auction and the second price auction. ∎

Some Observations

We now make a few important observations on the revenue equivalence theorem.

Equivalence in Expectation

The theorem does not imply that the outcomes of the four auction forms are always exactly the same. They are only equal in expectation. Note that in the English auction or the second price auction, the price exactly equals the valuation of the bidder with the second highest valuation. In Dutch auction or the first price auction, the price is the expectation of the second highest valuation conditional on the winning bidder's own valuation. The above two prices will be equal only by accident; however, they are equal in expectation.

Variance of Revenue

The revenue equivalence theorem does not prescribe under what circumstances a particular one among the four candidate auctions would serve the purpose best. When the assumptions of the benchmark model are relaxed, particular auction forms emerge as being superior.

It has been shown in the literature that variance of revenue is lower in English auction or second price auction than in Dutch auction or first price auction. Hence if the seller were risk averse, he would choose English or second price rather than Dutch or first price.

Bidding Complexity

The bidding strategy is very simple in the English auction and the second price auction. In the English auction, a bidder remains in bidding until the price reaches his valuation. In the second price auction, he submits a sealed bid equal to his own valuation. On the other hand, the bidding logic is quite complex in the Dutch auction and the first price auction. Here the bidder bids some amount less than his true valuation. Exactly how much less depends upon the probability distribution of the other bidders' valuations and the number of competing bidders. Finding the Nash equilibrium bid is a non-trivial computational problem.

20.5   Combinatorial Auctions

A combinatorial auction is one where the bids correspond to bundles or combinations of different items. In a *forward combinatorial auction*, a bundle of different types of objects is available with the seller; the buyers are interested in purchasing certain subsets of the items. In a *reverse combinatorial auction*, a bundle of different types of objects is required by the buyer; several sellers are interested in selling subsets of the objects to the buyer. There is a rich body of literature on combinatorial auctions, for example see the volume edited by Cramton, Shoham, and Steinberg [3].

To illustrate a simple combinatorial auction, we provide an example below.

	A	B	AB
Agent 1	*	*	10
Agent 2	5	*	*
Agent 3	*	5	*

Table 20.1: Valuations of agents for bundles in scenario 1

Generalized Vickrey Auction

Generalized Vickrey auction (GVA) refers to an auction that results when the Clarke mechanism is applied to a combinatorial auction. Let a seller be interested in auctioning two items A and B. Let there be three buying agents $\{1, 2, 3\}$. With a slight abuse of notation, let us denote the subsets $\{A\}$, $\{B\}$, $\{A, B\}$ by A, B, and AB, respectively. These are called combinations or bundles. Assume that the agents have *valuations* for the bundles as shown in Table 20.1. In the above table, each starred entry indicates that the agent is not interested in that bundle. Note from Table 20.1 that agent 1 values bundle AB at 10 and does not have any valuation for bundle A and bundle B. Agent 2 is only interested in bundle A and has a valuation of 5 for this bundle. Agent 3 is only interested in bundle B and has a valuation of 5 for this bundle.

If we apply the Clarke mechanism to this situation, the bids from the agents will be identical to the valuations because of the DSIC property of the Clarke mechanism. There are two allocatively efficient allocations, namely: (1) allocate bundle AB to agent 1; (2) allocate bundle A to agent 2 and bundle B to agent 3. Each of these allocations has a total value of 10. Suppose we choose allocation (2), which awards bundle A to agent 2 and bundle B to agent 3. To compute the payments to be made by agents 2 and 3, we have to use the Clarke payment rule. For this, we analyze what would happen in the absence of agent 2 and agent 3 separately. If agent 2 is absent, the allocation will award the bundle AB to agent 1 resulting in a total value of 10. Therefore, the Vickrey discount to agent 2 is $10 - 10 = 0$, which means payment to be made by agent 2 is $5 + 0 = 5$. Similarly the Vickrey discount to agent 3 is also 0 and the payment to be made by agent 3 is also equal to 5. The total revenue to the seller is $5 + 5 = 10$. Even if allocation (1) is chosen (that is, award bundle AB to agent 1), the total revenue to the seller remains as 10. This is a situation where the seller is able to capture the entire consumer surplus.

A contrasting situation will result if the valuations are as shown in Table 20.2. In this case, the winning allocation is: award bundle A to agent 2 and bundle B to agent 3, resulting in a total value of 20. If agent 2 is not present, the allocation will be to award bundle AB to agent 1, thus resulting in a total value of 10. Similarly, if agent 3 were not present, the allocation would be to award bundle AB to agent 1, thus resulting in a total value of 10. This would mean a Vickrey discount of 10 each

	A	B	AB
Agent 1	*	*	10
Agent 2	10	*	*
Agent 3	*	10	*

Table 20.2: Valuations of agents for bundles in scenario 2

	A	B	AB
Agent 1	*	*	10
Agent 2	2	*	*
Agent 3	*	2	*

Table 20.3: Valuations of agents for bundles in scenario 3

to agent 2 and agent 3, which in turn means that the payment to be made by agent 2 and agent 3 is 0 each! This represents a situation where the seller will end up with a zero revenue in the process of guaranteeing allocative efficiency and dominant strategy incentive compatibility. Worse still, if agent 2 and agent 3 are both the false names of a single agent, then the auction itself is seriously manipulated!

We now study a third scenario where the valuations are as described in Table 20.3. Here, the allocation is to award bundle AB to agent 1, resulting in a total value of 10. If agent 1 were absent, the allocation would be to award bundle A to agent 2 and bundle B to agent 3, which leads to a total value of 4. The Vickrey discount to agent 1 is therefore $10 - 4 = 6$, and the payment to be made by agent 1 is 4. The revenue to the seller is also 4. Contrast this scenario with scenario 2, where the valuations of bidders 2 and 3 were higher, but they were able to win the bundles by paying nothing. This shows that the GVA mechanism is not foolproof against bidder collusion (in this case, bidders 2 and 3 can collude and deny the bundle to agent 1 and also seriously reduce the revenue to the seller).

It has been shown that GVA has the desirable properties of DSIC, AE, WBB, and IR. However, in general, applying Clarke mechanism to combinatorial auctions involves solving up to $(n+1)$ winner determination problems, where n is the number of agents. These problems are often NP-hard

Combinatorial Auctions: To Probe Further

Combinatorial auctions have found widespread applications in numerous network economics situations. The edited volume by Cramton, Shoham, and Steinberg [3] is a comprehensive source of information on different aspects of combinatorial auctions.

There are also many survey articles on combinatorial auctions. These include: de Vries and Vohra [7], Pekec and Rothkopf [8], Narahari and Dayama [10], and Blumrosen and Nisan [11].

20.6 Summary and References

In this chapter, we have looked into various aspects of auctions and auction design. Specifically, we have covered the following topics.

- Desirable properties of auctions, based on the context, include incentive compatibility, allocative efficiency or welfare maximization, budget balance, individual rationality, revenue maximization (or cost minimization), etc.
- There are numerous types of auctions: single item - single unit; single item - multiunit; multi-item - single unit; multi-item - multiunit; multi-attribute, etc.
- For auctioning a single indivisible item, four canonical auctions are commonly considered: English auction, Dutch auction, first price sealed bid auction, second price sealed bid auction (Vickrey auction). The revenue equivalence theorem states that these four auctions produce the same expected revenue to the auctioneer under a standard benchmark model. For more details on the revenue equivalence theorem, the reader is referred to the papers by Myerson [12], McAfee and McMillan [4], Klemperer [13], and the books by Milgrom [2] and Krishna [1].
- Combinatorial auctions represent auctions for multiple item types. The generalized Vickrey auction (GVA) is essentially the Clarke mechanism applied to combinatorial auctions.

We must mention here that we have covered in this chapter only a few key results in auctions. In fact, we have only covered a limited variety of auctions in this chapter. For more details on auctions, there are excellent survey articles [4, 5, 6] and books [1, 2, 3] devoted to auctions. Recent survey papers have focused on combinatorial auctions [7, 8, 9, 10]. Procurement auctions are very popular in industrial settings. A survey as well as a case study appear in [14].

In the next chapter, we discuss optimal auctions which maximize revenue or minimize cost to the auctioneer subject to incentive compatibility and individual rationality. In the chapter following that, we present the case study of sponsored search auctions on the web and bring out the role of mechanism design in creating these auctions.

References

[1]   Vijay Krishna. *Auction Theory*. Academic Press, San Diego, California, USA, 2002.
[2]   Paul Milgrom. *Putting Auction Theory to Work*. Cambridge University Press, Cambridge, UK, 2004.

[3]   P. Cramton, Y. Shoham, and R. Steinberg (Editors). *Combinatorial Auctions*. The MIT Press, Cambridge, Massachusetts, 2005.

[4]   R. P. McAfee and J. McMillan. "Auctions and bidding". In: *Journal of Economic Literature* **25**(2) (1987), pp. 699–738.

[5]   P. Milgrom. "Auctions and bidding: A primer". In: *Journal of Economic Perspectives* **3**(3) (1989), pp. 3–22.

[6]   E. Wolfstetter. "Auctions: An introduction". In: *Economic Surveys* **10** (1996), pp. 367–421.

[7]   S. de Vries and R.V. Vohra. "Combinatorial auctions: A survey". In: *INFORMS Journal of Computing* **15**(1) (2003), pp. 284–309.

[8]   A. Pekec and M.H. Rothkopf. "Combinatorial auction design". In: *Management Science* **49** (2003), pp. 1485–1503.

[9]   J.R. Kalagnanam and D.C. Parkes. "Auctions, bidding, and exchange design". In: *Handbook of Quantitative Supply Chain Analysis: Modeling in the E-Business Era*. Ed. by D. Simchi-Levi, S.D. Wu, and Z.J. Shen. Kluwer Academic Publishers, New York, 2005.

[10] Y. Narahari and P. Dayama. "Combinatorial auctions for electronic business". In: *Sadhana - Indian Academy Proceedings in Engineering Sciences* **30**(3) (2003), pp. 179–212.

[11] L. Blumrosen and N. Nisan. "Combinatorial auctions". In: *Algorithmic Game Theory*. Ed. by Noam Nisan, Tim Roughgarden, Eva Tardos, and Vijay Vazirani. Cambridge University Press, 2007, pp. 267–300.

[12] Roger B. Myerson. "Optimal auction design". In: *Mathematics of Operations Research* **6**(1) (1981), pp. 58–73.

[13] P. Klemperer. "Why every economist should learn some auction theory". In: *Advances in Economics and Econometrics: Invited Lectures to 8th World Congress of the Econometric Society*. Ed. by M. Dewatripont, L. Hansen, and S. Turnovsky. Cambridge University Press, Cambridge, UK, 2003.

[14] Charles H. Rosa Devadatta Kulkarni Pankaj Dayama T.S. Chandrashekar Y. Narahari and Jeffrey D. Tew. "Auction based mechanisms for electronic procurement". In: *IEEE Transactions on Automation Science and Engineering* **4**(3) (2006), pp. 297–321.

20.7 Exercises

(1) (Second price auction with budget). Consider a second price auction for a single indivisible item. Suppose each bidder i has a value $v_i > 0$ and a budget $c_i > 0$. If a bidder wins the object and has to pay higher than the budget, the bidder will simply drop out from the auction but is charged with a small penalty $\epsilon > 0$. Compute a bid in the auction for each player i which will be a weakly dominant strategy for the player.

(2) Consider a single-item, multi-unit exchange with two selling agents and two buying agents. The selling agents specify marginally decreasing, piecewise constant *asks* and buying agents specify marginally decreasing, piecewise constant *bids*. It is required to maximize the total surplus (total receipts minus total payments by the exchange). The asks received from the sellers are:

```
Ask-1: ((1-50, 10), (51-150, 8), (151-200, 6))
           (the above means  unit price of Rs. 10 for the 50 items;
           unit price of Rs. 8 for the next 100 items;
           unit price of Rs. 6 for the next 50 items)
```

Ask-2: ((1-50, 12), (51-100, 10), (101-200, 6))

The bids received from the buying agents are:

Bid-1: ((1-50, 12), (51-100, 11), (101-150, 10))

Bid-2: ((1-75, 12), (76-150, 10))

Assume that Clarke mechanism is used. For this problem:

- Compute a surplus maximizing allocation for the given bids.
- What is the payment required to be made by the two buyers?
- What is the payment received by the two sellers?

(3) The GVA mechanism is used by a buyer for procuring a bundle $\{A, B, C, D, E\}$. The following are the bids received from 5 sellers.

- Seller 1: (A, 20), (B, 30), (AB, 45)
- Seller 2: (B, 25), (C, 35), (BC, 50)
- Seller 3: (C, 30), (D, 40), (CD, 60)
- Seller 4: (D, 35), (E, 45), (DE, 70)
- Seller 5: (E, 40), (A, 15), (EA, 50)

Assume XOR bids (that is, at most one bid will be selected from any seller). Compute the allocation and the payments that the winning bidders will receive. Is this mechanism individually rational? Why?

(4) Apply the GVA mechanism to the following combinatorial auction scenario. There are three bidders and two objects. The valuation matrix is as follows.

	{1}	{2}	{1,2}
Bidder 1	6	10	10
Bidder 2	8	5	8
Bidder 3	8	0	9

(5) **Programming Project**. It would be useful to set up a web-based auction house to implement a variety of auctions. Such a platform will enable experimenting with various auction mechanisms.

Chapter 21

Optimal Mechanisms and Myerson Auction

In this chapter, we introduce the notion of an *optimal mechanism* and discuss in detail a particular case of an optimal auction for selling a single indivisible object. The *Myerson auction* is a well known mechanism to solve this problem. This auction proposes an allocation policy and a payment protocol for maximizing the expected revenue of the seller ensuring at the same time that incentive compatibility and individual rationality properties are satisfied.

21.1   Optimal Mechanisms

A key problem that a social planner is faced with is to decide which direct revelation mechanism (or equivalently, social choice function) is *optimal* for a given problem. We now attempt to formalize the notion of optimality of social choice functions and optimal mechanisms.

Social Utility Function

We first define the concept of a *social utility function*.

Definition 21.1 (Social Utility Function). *A social utility function is a mapping $w : \mathbb{R}^n \to \mathbb{R}$ that aggregates each profile $(u_1, \ldots, u_n) \in \mathbb{R}^n$ of individual utility values of the agents into a social utility.*

Consider a mechanism design problem and a direct revelation mechanism $\mathscr{D} = ((\Theta_i)_{i \in N}, f(\cdot))$ proposed for the problem. Let $(\theta_1, \ldots, \theta_n)$ be the type profile of the agents and assume for a moment that they will all reveal their true types when requested by the planner. In such a case, the social utility that would be realized by the social planner for a type profile θ of the agents is given by:

$$w(u_1(f(\theta), \theta_1), \ldots, u_n(f(\theta), \theta_n)). \tag{21.1}$$

However, the agents, being strategic, may not reveal their true types unless it is a best response for them to do so. In general, rationality of the agents implies that the agents report their types according to a strategy suggested by an equilibrium $s^*(\cdot) = (s_1^*(\cdot), \ldots, s_n^*(\cdot))$ of the Bayesian game induced by the mechanism. In such a case, the social utility that would be realized by the social planner for a type profile θ of the agents is given by

$$w(u_1(f(s^*(\theta)), \theta_1), \ldots, u_n(f(s^*(\theta)), \theta_n)). \tag{21.2}$$

In some instances, the above equilibrium, if one exists, may turn out to be a dominant strategy equilibrium. In general, it is a Bayesian Nash equilibrium. It will be perfect if any of these equilibria corresponds to truthful reporting of types by all the players.

Optimal Mechanism Design Problem

In view of the above notion of a social utility function, it is clear that the objective of a social planner would be to look for a social choice function $f(\cdot)$ that would maximize the expected social utility for a given social utility function $w(\cdot)$, subject to certain natural and reasonable constraints. The desirable constraints may include any combination of all the previously studied properties of a social choice function, such as ex-post efficiency, incentive compatibility, and individual rationality. This set of social choice functions is known as a *set of feasible social choice functions* and is denoted by F. Thus, the problem of a social planner can now be cast as an optimization problem where the objective is to maximize the expected social utility, and the constraint is that the social choice function must be chosen from the feasible set F. This problem is known as the *optimal mechanism design* problem and the solution of the problem would be a social choice function $f^*(\cdot) \in F$, which is used to define the optimal mechanism $\mathscr{D}^* = ((\Theta_i)_{i \in N}, f^*(\cdot))$ for the problem being studied.

Depending on whether the agents are honest or rational entities, the optimal mechanism design problem will take one of two different forms.

$$\begin{array}{c} \text{maximize} \\ f(\cdot) \in F \end{array} E_\theta \left[w(u_1(f(\theta), \theta_1), \ldots, u_n(f(\theta), \theta_n)) \right] \tag{21.3}$$

$$\begin{array}{c} \text{maximize} \\ f(\cdot) \in F \end{array} E_\theta \left[w(u_1(f(s^*(\theta)), \theta_1), \ldots, u_n(f(s^*(\theta)), \theta_n)) \right] \tag{21.4}$$

The problem (21.3) is relevant when the agents are honest and always reveal their true types whereas the problem (21.4) is relevant when the agents are strategic. One might ask how to define the set of feasible social choice functions F. There is no unique definition of this set and it is mostly based on a subjective judgment of the social planner and on the problem being modeled. The choice of the set F depends on the desirable properties the social planner would wish to have in the optimal social choice function $f^*(\cdot)$. The various choices include:

$$F_{\text{DSIC}} = \{f : \Theta \to X | f(\cdot) \text{ is dominant strategy incentive compatible}\}$$
$$F_{\text{BIC}} = \{f : \Theta \to X | f(\cdot) \text{ is Bayesian incentive compatible}\}$$
$$F_{\text{EPIR}} = \{f : \Theta \to X | f(\cdot) \text{ is ex-post individual rational}\}$$
$$F_{\text{IIR}} = \{f : \Theta \to X | f(\cdot) \text{ is interim individual rational}\}$$

$$F_{\text{EAIR}} = \{f : \Theta \to X | f(\cdot) \text{ is ex-ante individual rational}\}$$
$$F_{\text{EPE}} = \{f : \Theta \to X | f(\cdot) \text{ is ex-post efficient}\}.$$

The set of feasible social choice functions F may be either any one of the above sets or intersection of any combination of the above sets.

21.2 Myerson's Optimal Auction

Myerson's optimal auction [1] is a landmark result in mechanism design theory. Myerson chooses $F = F_{BIC} \cap F_{IIR}$ as the set of feasible social choice functions. In the literature, this particular feasible set is known as *incentive feasible set* due to Myerson [1]. Note that if the agents are honest, then the sets F_{DSIC} and F_{BIC} will be equal to the whole set of all the social choice functions. If the agents are strategic, the set $F = F_{BIC} \cap F_{IIR}$ is an appropriate choice for a feasible set. BIC ensures incentive compatibility that is not too strong to be satisfied and so is reasonable. IIR assumes that players know their types but do not know the types of the other players (which is quite realistic) and guarantees that every player participates voluntarily.

In this section, we specifically consider the problem of a seller (also the auctioneer in this case) who would like to auction a single indivisible object and assume that there are n buying agents or bidders ($N = \{1, \ldots, n\}$) interested in the object. Suppose there is no reserve price (minimum price below which the auctioneer is not prepared to sell the object). The objective here is to maximize the expected revenue of the auctioneer. We discuss an optimal mechanism developed by Myerson [1] for this problem.

We assume that each bidder i's type (valuation for the object) lies in an interval $\Theta_i = [\underline{\theta_i}, \overline{\theta_i}]$. We impose the following additional conditions.

(1) The auctioneer and the bidders are risk neutral (see Section 8.6 for more details).
(2) The types of the bidders are statistically independent, that is, the joint density $\phi(\cdot)$ has the form $\phi_1(\cdot) \times \ldots \times \phi_n(\cdot)$
(3) $\phi_i(\cdot) > 0 \ \forall \ i = 1, \ldots, n$
(4) We consider a general form of the outcome set X by allowing a random assignment of the object. We consider $y_i(\theta)$ to be buyer i's probability of getting the object when the vector of announced types is $\theta = (\theta_1, \ldots, \theta_n)$. Thus, the new outcome set is given by

$$X = \Big\{ (y_0, \ldots, y_n, t_0, \ldots, t_n) | y_0 \in [0,1], t_0 \geq 0, y_i \in [0,1], t_i \leq 0 \ \forall \ i = 1, \ldots, n,$$

$$\sum_{i=1}^{n} y_i \leq 1; \ \sum_{i=0}^{n} t_i = 0 \Big\}$$

Note that the condition $\sum_{i=1}^{n} y_i < 1$ will imply that there is no trade. The utility functions of the agents $i = 1, \ldots, n$ are given by

$$u_i(f(\theta), \theta_i) = u_i((y_0(\theta), \ldots, y_n(\theta), t_0(\theta), \ldots, t_n(\theta)), \theta_i) = \theta_i y_i(\theta) + t_i(\theta)$$

Viewing $y_i(\theta) = v_i(k(\theta))$ (where $k(\theta)$ is the project choice corresponding to type profile θ) in conjunction with the second and third conditions above, we can claim that the underlying environment here is linear (see Section 19.7 for definition of linear environment).

In the above example, the seller or the auctioneer is the social planner looking for an optimal direct revelation mechanism to sell the object. Myerson's [1] idea was that the auctioneer must use a social choice function which is Bayesian incentive compatible and interim individual rational and would fetch the maximum expected revenue to the auctioneer. Thus, in this problem, the set of feasible social choice functions is given by $F = F_{BIC} \cap F_{IIR}$. The objective is to maximize the total expected revenue of the seller which is given by

$$E_\theta \left[w(u_1(f(\theta), \theta_1), \ldots, u_n(f(\theta), \theta_n)) \right] = -E_\theta \left[\sum_{i=1}^{n} t_i(\theta) \right]$$

Note that in the above objective function, we have used $f(\theta)$ and not $f(s^*(\theta))$. This is because in the set of feasible social choice functions, we are considering only BIC social choice functions and for these functions we have $s^*(\theta) = \theta \ \forall \ \theta \in \Theta$. Thus, Myerson's optimal auction design problem can be formulated as the following optimization problem.

$$\underset{f(\cdot) \in F}{\text{maximize}} \quad - E_\theta \left[\sum_{i=1}^{n} t_i(\theta) \right] \tag{21.5}$$

where

$$F = \{ f(\cdot) = (y_1(\cdot), \ldots, y_n(\cdot), t_1(\cdot), \ldots, t_n(\cdot)) | f(\cdot) \text{ is BIC and IIR} \}.$$

We now invoke Myerson's characterization theorem (Section 19.7) to the above situation. First we recall the following notation:

- $\overline{t_i}(\hat{\theta}_i) = E_{\theta_{-i}}[t_i(\hat{\theta}_i, \theta_{-i})]$ is bidder i's expected transfer when he announces his type to be $\hat{\theta}_i$ and that all the bidders $j \neq i$ truthfully reveal their types;
- $\overline{y_i}(\hat{\theta}_i) = E_{\theta_{-i}}[y_i(\hat{\theta}_i, \theta_{-i})]$ is the expected probability that bidder i would receive the object given that he announces his type to be $\hat{\theta}_i$ and all bidders $j \neq i$ truthfully reveal their types; and
- $U_i(\theta_i) = \theta_i \overline{y_i}(\theta_i) + \overline{t_i}(\theta_i)$ (we can take unconditional expectation because types are independent).

We can say that an SCF $f(\cdot)$ in the above context would be BIC iff it satisfies the following two conditions

(1) $\overline{y_i}(\cdot)$ is non-decreasing in θ_i for all $i = 1, \ldots, n$

(2) $U_i(\theta_i) = U_i(\underline{\theta_i}) + \int_{\underline{\theta_i}}^{\theta_i} \overline{y_i}(s)ds \ \forall\, \theta_i \in \Theta_i; \ \forall\, i = 1, \ldots, n$

Also, we can invoke the definition of interim individual rationality to assert that the SCF $f(\cdot)$ in the above context would be interim IR iff it satisfies the following conditions

$$U_i(\theta_i) \geq 0 \ \forall \theta_i \in \Theta_i; \ \forall\, i = 1, \ldots, n$$

where it is assumed that the expected utility of not participating in the mechanism is 0.

In view of the above setup, the optimal auction design problem (21.5) can be rewritten as follows.

$$\underset{(y_i(\cdot),\, U_i(\cdot))_{i \in N}}{\text{maximize}} \quad \sum_{i=1}^{n} \int_{\underline{\theta_i}}^{\overline{\theta_i}} (\theta_i \overline{y_i}(\theta_i) - U_i(\theta_i))\, \phi_i(\theta_i) d\theta_i \tag{21.6}$$

subject to

(i) $\overline{y_i}(\cdot)$ is non-decreasing in $\theta_i \ \forall\, i = 1, \ldots, n$

(ii) $y_i(\theta) \in [0, 1], \sum_{i=1}^{n} y_i(\theta) \leq 1 \ \forall i = 1, \ldots, n, \forall\, \theta \in \Theta$

(iii) $U_i(\theta_i) = U_i(\underline{\theta_i}) + \int_{\underline{\theta_i}}^{\theta_i} \overline{y_i}(s)ds \ \forall\, \theta_i \in \Theta_i; \ \forall\, i = 1, \ldots, n$

(iv) $U_i(\theta_i) \geq 0 \ \forall\, \theta_i \in \Theta_i; \ \forall\, i = 1, \ldots, n$

We first note that if constraint (iii) is satisfied then constraint (iv) will be satisfied iff $U_i(\underline{\theta_i}) \geq 0 \ \forall\, i = 1, \ldots, n$. As a result, we can replace the constraint (iv) with

(iv') $U_i(\underline{\theta_i}) \geq 0 \ \forall\, i = 1, \ldots, n$

Next, substituting for $U_i(\theta_i)$ in the objective function from constraint (iii), we get

$$\sum_{i=1}^{n} \int_{\underline{\theta_i}}^{\overline{\theta_i}} \left(\theta_i \overline{y_i}(\theta_i) - U_i(\underline{\theta_i}) - \int_{\underline{\theta_i}}^{\theta_i} \overline{y_i}(s)ds \right) \phi_i(\theta_i) d\theta_i$$

Integrating by parts the above expression, the auctioneer's problem can be written as one of choosing the $y_i(\cdot)$ functions and the values $U_1(\underline{\theta_1}), \ldots, U_n(\underline{\theta_n})$ to maximize

$$\int_{\underline{\theta_1}}^{\overline{\theta_1}} \cdots \int_{\underline{\theta_n}}^{\overline{\theta_n}} \left[\sum_{i=1}^{n} y_i(\theta_i) J_i(\theta_i) \right] \left[\prod_{i=1}^{n} \phi_i(\theta_i) \right] d\theta_n \ldots d\theta_1 - \sum_{i=1}^{n} U_i(\underline{\theta_i})$$

subject to constraints (i), (ii), and (iv'), where

$$J_i(\theta_i) = \left(\theta_i - \frac{1 - \Phi_i(\theta_i)}{\phi_i(\theta_i)} \right) = \left(\theta_i - \frac{\overline{\Phi_i}(\theta_i)}{\phi_i(\theta_i)} \right)$$

where, $\Phi_i(\cdot)$ is the cumulative distribution function corresponding to the density $\phi_i(\cdot)$ and we denote $\overline{\Phi_i}(\theta_i) = 1 - \Phi_i(\theta_i)$. The quantities $J_i(\theta_i)$'s are called *virtual valuations*. It is evident that solution must have $U_i(\underline{\theta_i}) = 0$ for all $i = 1, \ldots, n$. Hence, the auctioneer's problem reduces to choosing functions $y_i(\cdot)$ to maximize

$$\int\limits_{\underline{\theta_1}}^{\overline{\theta_1}} \cdots \int\limits_{\underline{\theta_n}}^{\overline{\theta_n}} \left[\sum_{i=1}^{n} y_i(\theta_i) J_i(\theta_i)\right] \left[\prod_{i=1}^{n} \phi_i(\theta_i)\right] d\theta_n \ldots d\theta_1$$

subject to constraints (i) and (ii).

Let us ignore constraint (i) for the moment. Then inspection of the above expression indicates that $y_i(\cdot)$ is a solution to this relaxed problem iff for all $i = 1, \ldots, n$, we have

$$y_i(\theta) = \begin{cases} 0 & : \text{ if } J_i(\theta_i) < \max\{0, \max_{h \neq i} J_h(\theta_h)\} \\ 1 & : \text{ if } J_i(\theta_i) > \max\{0, \max_{h \neq i} J_h(\theta_h)\} \end{cases} \tag{21.7}$$

Note that $J_i(\theta_i) = \max\{0, \max_{h \neq i} J_h(\theta_h)\}$ is a zero probability event.

In other words, if we ignore the constraint (i), then, $y_i(\cdot)$ is a solution to this relaxed problem iff the object is allocated to a bidder who has highest non-negative value for $J_i(\theta_i)$. Now, recall the definition of $\overline{y_i}(\cdot)$. It is easy to write down the following expression

$$\overline{y_i}(\theta_i) = E_{\theta_{-i}}\left[y_i(\theta_i, \theta_{-i})\right] \tag{21.8}$$

Now, if we assume that $J_i(\cdot)$ is non-decreasing in θ_i then it is easy to see that above solution $y_i(\cdot)$, given by (21.7), will be non-decreasing in θ_i, which in turn implies, by looking at expression (21.8), that $\overline{y_i}(\cdot)$ is non-decreasing in θ_i. Thus, the solution to this relaxed problem actually satisfies constraint (i) under the assumption that $J_i(\cdot)$ is non-decreasing. Assuming that $J_i(\cdot)$ is non-decreasing, the solution given by (21.7) seems to be the solution of the optimal mechanism design problem. The condition that $J_i(\cdot)$ is non-decreasing in θ_i is met by many of the common distribution functions, for example, uniform and exponential.

So far we have computed the allocation rule for the optimal mechanism and now we turn our attention to the payment rule. The payment rule $t_i(\cdot)$ must satisfy $\forall i \in N$,

$$\overline{t_i}(\theta_i) = E_{\theta_{-i}}[t_i(\theta_i, \theta_{-i})] = U_i(\theta_i) - \theta_i \overline{y_i}(\theta_i) = \int\limits_{\underline{\theta_i}}^{\theta_i} \overline{y_i}(s)ds - \theta_i \overline{y_i}(\theta_i) \tag{21.9}$$

Looking at the above formula, we can say that if the payment rule $t_i(\cdot)$ satisfies the following formula (21.10), then it would also satisfy the formula (21.9).

$$t_i(\theta_i, \theta_{-i}) = \int\limits_{\underline{\theta_i}}^{\theta_i} y_i(s, \theta_{-i})ds - \theta_i y_i(\theta_i, \theta_{-i}) \quad \forall \theta \in \Theta \tag{21.10}$$

The above formula can be rewritten more intuitively, as follows. For any vector θ_{-i}, let us define

$$z_i(\theta_{-i}) = \inf \{\theta_i | J_i(\theta_i) > 0 \text{ and } J_i(\theta_i) \geq J_j(\theta_j) \; \forall \; j \neq i\}$$

Then $z_i(\theta_{-i})$ is the infimum of all winning bids for bidder i against θ_{-i}, so

$$y_i(\theta_i, \theta_{-i}) = \begin{cases} 1 & : \quad \text{if } \theta_i > z_i(\theta_{-i}) \\ 0 & : \quad \text{if } \theta_i < z_i(\theta_{-i}) \end{cases}$$

This gives us

$$\int_{\underline{\theta_i}}^{\theta_i} y_i(s, \theta_{-i}) ds = \begin{cases} \theta_i - z_i(\theta_{-i}) & : \quad \text{if } \theta_i \geq z_i(\theta_{-i}) \\ 0 & : \quad \text{if } \theta_i < z_i(\theta_{-i}) \end{cases}$$

Finally, the formula (21.10) becomes

$$t_i(\theta_i, \theta_{-i}) = \begin{cases} -z_i(\theta_{-i}) & : \quad \text{if } \theta_i \geq z_i(\theta_{-i}) \\ 0 & : \quad \text{if } \theta_i < z_i(\theta_{-i}) \end{cases}$$

That is bidder i must pay only when he is allocated the object and he pays an amount equal to his lowest possible winning bid. This completes the specification of the payment rule.

Some Observations on Myerson's Auction

Monotone Assumption on Virtual Valuations

The assumption that the virtual valuation function $J_i(\cdot)$ is monotone non-decreasing in θ_i $(i = 1, \ldots, n)$ is satisfied if each of the distributions $\phi_i(\cdot)$ is such that its hazard rate:

$$\frac{\phi_i}{(1 - \Phi_i)}$$

is monotone increasing. This condition is satisfied by many popular distributions such as uniform and exponential. In case this assumption is violated, there is a work-around using the so called *ironing* procedure described by Myerson [1]. The idea is to use a nearest monontonic transformation of the virtual valuations instead of the actual virtual valuations.

Myerson's Auction is DSIC

While formulating the optimal auction problem, the incentive compatibility requirement is only BIC. However, it turns out that the Myerson auction is in fact DSIC [1] which is a happy byproduct of the way the auction is designed.

Game Theory and Mechanism Design

Myerson's Auction is not Allocatively Efficient

When the various bidders have differing distribution function $\Phi_i(\cdot)$ then, the bidder who has the largest value of $J_i(\theta_i)$ is *not* necessarily the bidder who has bid the highest amount for the object. Thus Myerson's optimal auction need not be allocatively efficient and therefore, need not be ex-post efficient.

Symmetric Bidders

If the bidders are symmetric, that is, $\Theta_1 = \ldots = \Theta_n = \Theta$ and $\Phi_1(\cdot) = \ldots = \Phi_n(\cdot) = \Phi(\cdot)$, then the allocation rule would be precisely the same as that of first price and second price auctions. In such a case the object would be allocated to the highest bidder. In such a situation, the optimal auction would also become allocatively efficient. Also, note that in such a case the payment rule that we described above would coincide with the payment rules in second price auction. In other words, the second price auction (Vickrey auction) is the optimal auction when the bidders are symmetric. Therefore, many a time, the optimal auction is also known as *modified Vickrey auction.*

21.3   Efficient Optimal Auctions

Krishna and Perry [2] have argued in favor of an auction which will maximize the revenue subject to AE, DSIC, and IIR constraints. The Green Laffont theorem (Chapter 18) tells us that any DSIC and AE mechanism is necessarily a VCG mechanism. So, we have to look for a VCG mechanism which will maximize the revenue to the seller. Krishna and Perry [2] define *social utility* as the value of an efficient allocation:

$$SW(\theta) = \sum_{j=1}^{n} v_j(k^*(\theta), \theta_j)$$

$$SW_{-i}(\theta) = \sum_{j \neq i} v_j(k^*(\theta), \theta_j)$$

With these functions, we can write the payment rule in Clarke's pivotal mechanism as

$$t_i(\theta) = SW_{-i}(0, \theta_{-i}) - SW_{-i}(\theta)$$

That is, payment by the agent i is the externality he is imposing by reporting type to be θ_i rather than zero. The authors of [2] generalize it. Fix a vector, $s = (s_1, s_2, \ldots, s_n) \in \Theta$ called as *basis* because it defines the payment rule. The *VCG mechanism with basis s* is defined by

$$t_i(\theta|s_i) = SW(s_i, \theta_{-i}) - SW_{-i}(\theta)$$

It can be seen that this new mechanism is also DSIC. Now choosing an appropriate basis, one can always find an optimal auction in the class of VCG mechanisms. Krishna and Perry [2] have shown that the classical Vickrey auction is an optimal and efficient auction for a single indivisible item. They have also shown that the Vickrey auction is an optimal one among VCG mechanisms for multiunit auctions, when all the bidders have downward sloping demand curves.

21.4 Summary and References

In this chapter, we have described the Myerson auction which represents an important result in mechanism design theory. The Myerson auction maximizes the expected revenue of an auctioneer (or seller) who seeks to allocate a single indivisible item to one of a set of bidders, subject to Bayesian incentive compatibility and interim individual rationality. In fact, it turns out that the auction is also DSIC though it may not be allocatively efficient. When the bidders are symmetric, the Myerson auction turns out to be AE and in fact the same as the Vickrey auction. The Myerson auction can also be developed for buying a single indivisible item.

Before describing the Myerson auction, we set up the optimal mechanism design problem. An appropriate feasible set of mechanisms for determining an optimal mechanism is the so called incentive feasible set which is the set of all SCFs that are BIC as well as interim individual rational.

After describing the Myerson auction, we briefly described efficient optimal auctions which are auctions that maximize the revenue subject to AE, DSIC, and IIR. Vickrey auction again turns out to be an efficient optimal auction for a single indivisible item.

For a detailed treatment of the Myerson auction, the classic paper by Myerson [1] and the excellent textbook by Vijay Krishna [2] are highly recommended.

Riley and Samuelson [3] also independently studied the problem of design of an optimal auction for selling a single indivisible object. They assume the bidders to be symmetric.

The Myerson optimal mechanism for the reverse auction setting has been presented in the monograph by Narahari, Garg, Narayanam, and Prakash [4].

The Myerson auction has been extended and enhanced in many ways in the context of many applications. The next chapter (Chapter 22) discusses an application and extension of the Myerson auction to the problem of sponsored search auctions.

References

[1]   Roger B. Myerson. "Optimal auction design". In: *Mathematics of Operations Research* **6**(1) (1981), pp. 58–73.

[2]   Vijay Krishna. *Auction Theory*. Academic Press, San Diego, California, USA, 2002.

[3]   J.G. Riley and W.F. Samuelson. "Optimal auctions". In: *American Economic Review* **71**(3) (1981), pp. 383–392.

[4]   Y. Narahari, Dinesh Garg, Ramasuri Narayanam, and Hastagiri Prakash. *Game Theoretic Problems in Network Economics and Mechanism Design Solutions*. Springer, London, 2009.

21.5   Exercises

(1) Consider a sealed bid auction with one seller and two buying agents. There is a single indivisible item which the seller wishes to sell. The bidders are symmetric with independent private values distributed uniformly over $[0, 1]$. Whoever bids higher will be allocated the item. For this auction:

- What is the equilibrium bidding strategy of a bidder in the first price auction?
- What is the expected revenue in the first price auction?
- What is the expected revenue in the second price auction?
- What is the expected revenue in the Myerson auction?

(2) Myerson auction is clearly Bayesian incentive compatible (since it is one of the constraints). The Myerson auction has also be shown to be dominant strategy incentive compatible. Attempt a proof of this.

(3) Develop the Myerson auction for the case of a reverse auction where an auctioneer wishes to buy an indivisible object to minimize the expected cost subject to BIC and IIR constraints (Hint: see [4]).

(4) Examine the difficulties encountered in applying Myerson auction to the case when instead of one single indivisible object, we have multiple identical objects. In particular, look at the case when you have two objects.

Chapter 22

Mechanism Design for Sponsored Search Auctions

The sponsored search auction problem was introduced briefly as an example in Chapter 1. In this chapter, we study this problem in more detail to demonstrate a compelling application of mechanism design. We first present a mechanism design formulation of this problem. Using this formulation, we describe two well known mechanisms for sponsored search auctions – *generalized second price* (GSP) and *Vickrey-Clarke-Groves* (VCG). We then present an optimal auction mechanism (OPT) which is an extension of the Myerson's optimal auction mechanism discussed in the previous chapter. The *OPT mechanism* maximizes the search engine's expected revenue subject to Bayesian incentive compatibility and individual rationality of the bidders. We then make a comparative study of GSP, VCG, and OPT mechanisms. This chapter is based on the paper [1] and also on Chapter 3 in [2].

The advertisers-supported web site is one of the successful business models in the web landscape. In a relatively short time, advertising on the Internet has been embraced by advertisers and marketers across all industry sectors. Sponsored search is now a key determinant of revenue performance of any search engine company. Our interest in this chapter lies in studying sponsored search based advertising as a mechanism design problem.

22.1 Sponsored Search Auction

When an Internet user (which we will sometimes refer to as the user, searcher, or customer) enters a keyword (that is a search phrase) into a search engine, the user gets back a page with results, containing both the links most relevant to the query and the sponsored links, that is, paid advertisements . When a sponsored link is clicked, the user is sent to the respective advertiser's web page. The advertiser then pays the search engine a certain amount of money for directing the user to its web page. Figure 22.1 depicts the result of a search performed on Google using the keyword *camera*. There are two different stacks – the left stack contains links that are most relevant to the query term, and the right stack contains the sponsored links. Often, a few sponsored links are placed immediately above of the search results. These sponsored links are clearly distinguishable from the actual search results.

However, the visibility of a sponsored search link depends on its location (slot) on the result page. Typically, a number of merchants (advertisers) are interested

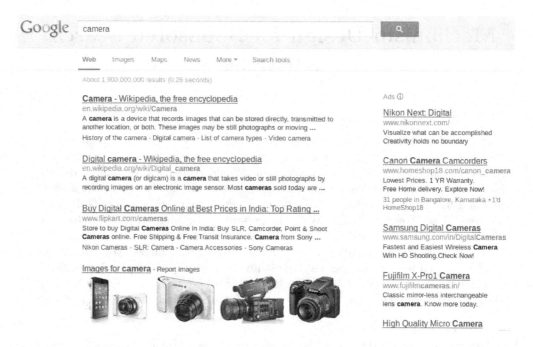

Fig. 22.1: Result of a search performed on Google

in advertising alongside the search results of a keyword. However, the number of slots available to display the sponsored links is limited. Therefore, against every search performed by the user, the search engine faces the problem of matching the advertisers to the slots. In addition, the search engine also needs to decide on a price to be charged to each advertiser. An advertiser naturally prefers a slot with higher visibility. Hence, search engines need a system for allocating the slots to advertisers and deciding on a price to be charged to each advertiser. Due to increasing demands for advertising space, most search engines are currently using auction mechanisms for this purpose. These auctions are called sponsored search auctions. In a typical sponsored search auction, advertisers are invited to submit bids on keywords, that is, the maximum amount they are willing to pay for a user clicking on the advertisement (**ad** for short). This is typically referred by the term Cost-Per-Click (CPC). Based on the bids submitted by the advertisers for a particular keyword, the search engine (which we will sometimes refer to as the auctioneer or the seller) picks a subset of advertisements along with the order in which to display them. The actual price charged also depends on the bids submitted by the advertisers.

22.2 Sponsored Search Auction as a Mechanism Design Problem

Consider a search engine that has received a query from a user, and it immediately faces the problem of invoking an auction for selling its advertising space among the available advertisers for this particular query word. Let us assume the following.

(1) There are n advertisers interested in this particular keyword, and $N = \{1, 2, \ldots, n\}$ represents the set of these advertisers. Also, there are m slots available with search engine to display the ads and $M = \{1, 2, \ldots, m\}$ represents the set of these advertising slots.

(2) α_{ij} is the probability that a user will click on the ith advertiser's **ad** if it is displayed in j^{th} position (slot), where the first position refers to the top most position. We assume that α_{ij} satisfy the following condition:

$$1 \geq \alpha_{i1} \geq \alpha_{i2} \geq \ldots \geq \alpha_{im} \geq 0 \; \forall i \in N. \tag{22.1}$$

Note, here we are assuming that click probability α_{ij} does not depend on which other advertiser has been allocated to what other position. We refer to this assumption as *absence of allocative externality* among the advertisers.

(3) Each advertiser precisely knows the value derived out of each click performed by any user on his ad. We assume this value is independent of the position of the **ad** and only depends on whether a user clicks on the **ad** or not. However, the advertiser does not know the values derived by the other advertisers out of a single user-click. Formally, this is modeled by supposing that advertiser i observes a parameter or signal θ_i that represents his value for each user click. The parameter θ_i is referred to as advertiser i's *type*. The set of possible types of advertiser i is denoted by Θ_i.

(4) Each advertiser perceives any other advertiser's valuation as a draw from some probability distribution. Similarly, each advertiser knows that the other advertisers regard his own valuation as a draw from some probability distribution. More precisely, for advertiser i, $i = 1, 2, \ldots, n$, there is some cumulative distribution function $\Phi_i(\cdot)$ from which he draws his valuation θ_i. Let $\phi_i(\cdot)$ be the corresponding probability density function. We assume that θ_i takes values from a closed real interval $\left[\underline{\theta_i}, \overline{\theta_i}\right]$. That is, $\Theta_i = \left[\underline{\theta_i}, \overline{\theta_i}\right]$. We also assume that any advertiser's valuation is statistically independent from any other advertiser's valuation. That is, $\Phi_i(\cdot), i = 1, 2, \ldots, n$ are mutually independent. We refer to this assumption as *independent private values assumption.*

(5) Each advertiser i is rational and intelligent in the sense of maximizing an expected value of a utility function $u_i : X \times \Theta_i \rightarrow \mathbb{R}$, where X is the set of outcomes, which will be defined shortly.

(6) The probability distribution functions $\Phi_i(\cdot)$, the type sets $\Theta_1, \ldots, \Theta_n$, and the utility functions $u_i(\cdot)$ are common knowledge among the advertisers. Note that utility function $u_i(\cdot)$ of advertiser i depends on both the outcome x and the type θ_i. Although the type θ_i is not common knowledge, by saying that $u_i(\cdot)$

is common knowledge we mean that for any given type θ_i, the auctioneer (that is, search engine in this case) and every other advertiser can evaluate the utility function of advertiser i.

In view of the above modeling assumptions, the sponsored search auction problem can now be precisely stated as follows. For any search phrase, each interested advertiser i, bids an amount $b_i \geq 0$, which depends on his actual type θ_i. Now each time the search engine receives this search phrase, the search engine determines, based on the bid vector $(b_1, \ldots, b_n)$, (a) the winning advertisers along with the order in which their ads will be displayed against the search results and (b) the amount that will be paid by each advertiser if the user clicks on his ad. These are called *allocation* and *payment rules*, respectively. A sponsored search auction can be viewed as an *indirect mechanism* $\mathscr{M} = ((B_i)_{i \in N}, g(\cdot))$, where $B_i \subset \mathbb{R}^+$ is the set of bids that an advertiser i can ever report to the search engine and $g(\cdot)$ is the allocation and payment rule. Note, if we assume that for each advertiser i, the set of bids B_i is the same as type set Θ_i, then indirect mechanism $\mathscr{M} = ((B_i)_{i \in N}, g(\cdot))$ becomes a direct revelation mechanism $\mathscr{D} = ((\Theta_i)_{i \in N}, f(\cdot))$, where $f(\cdot)$ becomes the allocation and payment rule. In the rest of this chapter, we will assume that $B_i = \Theta_i \ \forall \, i = 1, \ldots, n$. Thus, in view of this assumption, we can regard a sponsored search auction as a direct revelation mechanism.

The various components of a typical sponsored search mechanism design problem are listed below.

Outcome Set X

An outcome in the case of a sponsored search auction may be represented by a vector $x = (y_{ij}, p_i)_{i \in N, j \in M}$, where y_{ij} is the probability that advertiser i is allocated to the slot j, and p_i denotes the price-per-click charged from advertiser i. The set of feasible alternatives is then

$$X = \left\{ (y_{ij}, p_i)_{i \in N, j \in M} \,\middle|\, y_{ij} \in [0,1] \ \forall i \in N, \ \forall j \in M; \ \sum_{i=1}^{n} y_{ij} \leq 1 \ \forall j \in M, \sum_{j=1}^{m} y_{ij} \leq 1 \ \forall i \in N, \right.$$
$$\left. p_i \geq 0 \ \forall i \in N \right\}.$$

Note that randomized outcomes are also included in the above outcome set. This implies that randomized mechanisms are also part of the design space.

Utility Function of Advertisers $u_i(\cdot)$

The utility function of advertiser i can be given, for $x = (y_{ij}, p_i)_{i \in N, j \in M}$, by

$$u_i(x, \theta_i) = \left(\sum_{j=1}^{m} y_{ij} \alpha_{ij} \right) (\theta_i - p_i).$$

Social Choice Function $f(\cdot)$ (Allocation and Payment Rules)

The general structure of the allocation and payment rule for this case is

$$f(b) = (y_{ij}(b), p_i(b))_{i \in N, j \in M}$$

where $b = (b_1, \ldots, b_n)$ is a bid vector of the advertisers. The functions $y_{ij}(\cdot)$ form the allocation rule, and the functions $p_i(\cdot)$ form the payment rule.

Linear Environment

Through a slight modification in the definition of allocation rule, payment rule, and utility functions, we can show that a sponsored search auction is indeed a direct revelation mechanism in a linear environment (see Section 19.7). To transform the underlying environment to a linear one, we redefine the allocation and payment rule as below.

$$f(b) = (y(b), t_i(b))_{i \in N, j \in M}$$

where $y(b) = (y_{ij}(b))_{i \in N, j \in M}$ and $t_i(b) = \left(\sum_{j=1}^{m} y_{ij}(b) \alpha_{ij} \right) p_i(b)$. The quantity $t_i(b)$ can be viewed as the expected payment made by the advertiser i to the search engine against every search query received by the search engine, and when the bid vector of the advertisers is $b = (b_1, \ldots, b_n)$.

Now, we can rewrite the utility functions in following manner:

$$u_i(f(b), \theta_i) = \theta_i v_i(y(b)) - t_i(b)$$

where $v_i(y(b)) = \left(\sum_{j=1}^{m} y_{ij}(b) \alpha_{ij} \right)$. The quantity $v_i(y(b))$ can be interpreted as the probability that advertiser i will receive a user click whenever there is a search query received by the search engine and when the bid vector of the advertisers is $b = (b_1, \ldots, b_n)$. Now, it is easy to verify that the underlying environment here is *linear*.

In what follows, we illustrate three basic mechanisms for sponsored search auctions with respect to the above model.

- Generalized first price (GFP) mechanism
- Generalized second price (GSP) mechanism
- Vickrey-Clarke-Groves (VCG) mechanism

For each of these mechanisms, we describe the allocation rule $y_{ij}(\cdot)$ and payment rule $p_i(\cdot)$.

22.3 Generalized First Price (GFP) Mechanism

The allocation and payment rules under this mechanism are the following [3].

GFP: Allocation Rule

In this mechanism, the m advertising slots are allocated to advertisers in *descending order of their bids*. Let $b^{(k)}$ be the kth highest element in $(b_1, \ldots, b_n)$. Similarly, let $(b_{-i})^{(k)}$ be the kth highest element in $(b_1, \ldots, b_{i-1}, b_{i+1}, \ldots, b_n)$. In view of these definitions, we can say that if $b = (b_1, b_2, \ldots, b_n)$ is the profile of bids received from the n advertisers, then the first slot is allocated to the advertiser whose bid is equal to $b^{(1)}$. Similarly, the second slot is allocated to the advertiser whose bid is equal to $b^{(2)}$, and so on. That is, for all $i \in N$ and all $j \in M$,

$$y_{ij}(b) = \begin{cases} 1 & : \quad \text{if } b_i = b^{(j)} \\ 0 & : \quad \text{otherwise.} \end{cases} \tag{22.2}$$

If two advertisers have the same bid, then the tie can be broken by an appropriate rule.

GFP: Payment Rule

Every time a user clicks on a sponsored link, an advertiser pays an amount equal to the amount of the advertiser's bid. That is, if $b = (b_1, b_2, \ldots, b_n)$ is the profile of bids received from the n advertisers then, for all $i \in N$,

$$p_i(b) = \begin{cases} b_i & : \quad \text{if advertiser } i\text{'s \textbf{ad} is displayed} \\ 0 & : \quad \text{otherwise.} \end{cases} \tag{22.3}$$

22.4   Generalized Second Price (GSP) Mechanism

The primary motivation for this auction mechanism was instability of the GFP mechanism. In particular, it has been shown by Edelman, Ostrovsky, and Schwarz [3] that under the GFP mechanism, truth telling is not an equilibrium bidding strategy for the advertisers, and this fact leads to instability in the system, which in turn leads to inefficient investments on behalf of the advertisers. The GFP mechanism also creates volatile prices, which in turn cause allocative inefficiencies.

GSP: Allocation Rule

GSP: Allocation Rule 1

This rule is the same as the allocation rule of GFP mechanisms, that is, the slots are allocated to the advertisers in descending order of their bids.

GSP: Allocation Rule 2

In this rule, the first slot is allocated to the advertiser $i \in N$ for whom the quantity $\alpha_{i1} b_i$ is the maximum. If there is a tie then it is broken by an appropriate rule. Now this advertiser is removed from the set N, and an advertiser among the remaining ones is chosen for whom $\alpha_{j2}b_j$ (where $j \in N \setminus \{i\}$) is a maximum. The second slot is allocated to this advertiser. In similar fashion, all the other slots are allocated.

GSP: Allocation Rule 3

Here, for each advertiser, an estimated *Click-Through-Rate (CTR)* is computed. This is the ratio of the number of clicks received by the **ad** to the number of times the **ad** was displayed against the search results. Now the advertisers are ranked in decreasing order of the *ranking scores*, where ranking score of an advertiser is defined as the product of the advertiser's bid and estimated *CTR*. In the rest of the chapter, we assume that click probabilities depend only on the positions of the ads and are independent of the identities of the advertisers. That is, $\alpha_{1j} = \alpha_{2j} = \ldots = \alpha_{nj} = \alpha_j \; \forall j \in M$. We also assume that the allocation rule in a GSP mechanism is the same as the allocation rule 2, which would be the same as allocation rule 1 because of the previous assumption.

GSP: Payment Rule

In this auction mechanism, every time a user clicks on a sponsored link, an advertiser pays an amount equal to the bid of the advertiser who is just below him in the ranking of the displayed ads plus a minimum increment. The advertiser whose ad appears at the bottom-most position is charged the amount of the highest bid among the disqualified bids plus the minimum increment. If there is no such bid then he is charged nothing. If $b = (b_1, b_2, \ldots, b_n)$ is the profile of bids received from the n advertisers, then because of the assumptions we made earlier regarding the allocation rule in the GSP mechanism, the price per click that is charged to an advertiser i would be given by

$$p_i(b) = \begin{cases} \sum_{j=1}^{m} \left(b^{(j+1)} y_{ij}(b) \right) & : \text{ if either } m < n \text{ or } n \leq m \text{ but } b_i \neq b^{(n)} \\ 0 & : \text{ otherwise} \end{cases}$$

where $b^{(j+1)}$ is the $(j+1)^{th}$ highest bid which is the same as the bid of an advertiser whose **ad** is allocated to position $(j+1)$. We have ignored the small increment because all the future analysis and results are insensitive to this amount.

22.5 Vickrey–Clarke–Groves (VCG) Mechanism

On the face of it, the GSP mechanism appears to be a generalized version of the well known Vickrey auction, which is used for selling a single indivisible object. But as shown by Edelman, Ostrovsky, and Schwarz [3], and also shown in the later part of this chapter, the GSP mechanism is indeed not a generalization of the classical Vickrey auction to the setting where a set of ranked objects is being sold. In this section, our objective is to develop the Clarke mechanism for the sponsored search auction. We refer to this as the VCG mechanism, following standard practice.

VCG: Allocation Rule

By definition, the VCG mechanism is allocatively efficient. Therefore, in the case of a sponsored search auction, the allocation rule $y^*(\cdot)$ in the VCG mechanism is

$$y^*(\cdot) = \frac{\arg\max}{y(\cdot)} \sum_{i=1}^{n} b_i v_i(y(b)) = \frac{\arg\max}{y_{ij}(\cdot)} \sum_{i=1}^{n} \sum_{j=1}^{m} (b_i \alpha_{ij}) y_{ij}(b). \qquad (22.4)$$

In the previous section, we have already seen that the greedy allocation rule is a solution to (22.4). Moreover, under the assumption that click probabilities are independent of advertisers' identities, the allocation $y^*(\cdot)$ allocates the slots to the advertisers in the decreasing order of their bids. That is, if $b = (b_1, b_2, \ldots, b_n)$ is the profile of bids received from the n advertisers then $y^*(\cdot)$ must satisfy the following condition:

$$y_{ij}^*(b) = \begin{cases} 1 & : & b_i = b^{(j)} \\ 0 & : & \text{otherwise.} \end{cases} \qquad (22.5)$$

We state below an interesting observation regarding GFP and GSP mechanisms, which is based on the above observations.

Proposition 22.1. *If click probabilities depend only on the positions of the ads and are independent of the identities of the advertisers, then*

(1) The GFP mechanism is allocatively efficient.

(2) The GSP mechanism is allocatively efficient if it uses allocation rule 2, which is the same as allocation rule 3.

(3) The allocation rule for the VCG mechanism, which is an efficient allocation, is given by (22.5). Moreover, this allocation rule is precisely the same as the GFP allocation rule and allocation rule 3.

VCG: Payment Rule

As per the definition of the VCG mechanism, the expected payment $t_i(b)$ made by an advertiser i, when the profile of the bids submitted by the advertisers is $b = (b_1, \ldots, b_n)$, must be calculated using the following Clarke's payment rule:

$$t_i(b) = \left[\sum_{j \neq i} b_j v_j(y^*(b)) \right] - \left[\sum_{j \neq i} b_j v_j(y_{-i}^*(b)) \right] \qquad (22.6)$$

where $y_{-i}^*(\cdot)$ is an efficient allocation of the slots among the advertisers when advertiser i is removed from the scene. Substituting value of $y^*(\cdot)$ from Equation (22.5) and making use of the fact that $v_i(y^*(b)) = \sum_{j=i}^{m} y_{ij}^*(b) \alpha_j$, Equation (22.6) can be written as follows:

Case 1 ($m < n$):

$$t^{(j)}(b) = \alpha_j p^{(j)}(b)$$

$$= \begin{cases} \beta_j b^{(j+1)} + t^{(j+1)}(b) & : \quad \text{if } 1 \le j \le (m-1) \\ \alpha_m b^{(m+1)} & : \quad \text{if } j = m \\ 0 & : \quad \text{if } m < j \le n \end{cases} \tag{22.7}$$

where

- $t^{(j)}(b)$ is the expected payment made by the advertiser whose **ad** is displayed in j^{th} position, for every search query received by the search engine and when the bid profile of the advertisers is $b = (b_1, \ldots, b_n)$,
- $p^{(j)}(b)$ is the payment made by the advertiser, whose **ad** is displayed in j^{th} position, for every click made by the user and when the bid profile of the advertisers is $b = (b_1, \ldots, b_n)$,
- $\beta_j = (\alpha_j - \alpha_{j+1})$, and
- $b^{(j)}$ has its usual interpretation.

Case 2 ($n \le m$):

$$t^{(j)}(b) = \alpha_j p^{(j)}(b)$$

$$= \begin{cases} \beta_j b^{(j+1)} + t^{(j+1)}(b) & : \quad \text{if } 1 \le j \le (n-1) \\ 0 & : \quad \text{if } j = n. \end{cases} \tag{22.8}$$

Unfolding of Equations (22.7) and (22.8) results in the following expressions for payments:

Case 1 ($m < n$):

$$p^{(j)}(b) = \frac{1}{\alpha_j} t^{(j)}(b) = \begin{cases} \frac{1}{\alpha_j}\left[\sum_{k=j}^{m-1} \beta_k b^{(k+1)}\right] + \frac{\alpha_m}{\alpha_j} b^{(m+1)} & : \quad \text{if } 1 \le j \le (m-1) \\ b^{(m+1)} & : \quad \text{if } j = m \\ 0 & : \quad \text{if } m < j \le n. \end{cases} \tag{22.9}$$

Case 2 ($n \le m$):

$$p^{(j)}(b) = \frac{1}{\alpha_j} t^{(j)}(b) = \begin{cases} \frac{1}{\alpha_j}\sum_{k=j}^{n-1} \beta_k b^{(k+1)} & : \quad \text{if } 1 \le j \le (n-1) \\ 0 & : \quad \text{if } j = n. \end{cases} \tag{22.10}$$

Thus, we can say that Equation (22.5) describes the allocation rule for the VCG mechanism and Equations (22.9) and (22.10) describe the payment rule for the VCG mechanism.

22.6 Optimal (OPT) Mechanism

In this section, our goal is to compute the allocation and payment rule $f(\cdot)$ that results in an optimal mechanism for the sponsored search auction. This calls for extending Myerson's optimal auction to the case of the sponsored search auction. We follow a line of attack that is similar to that of Myerson [4]. Recall that we formulated the sponsored search auction as a direct revelation mechanism $\mathscr{D} = ((\Theta_i)_{i \in N}, f(\cdot))$ in a linear environment, where the utility function of an advertiser i is given by

$$u_i(f(b), \theta_i) = \left(\sum_{j=1}^{m} y_{ij}(b)\alpha_j \right)(\theta_i - p_i(b))$$

$$= v_i(y(b))(\theta_i - p_i(b))$$

$$= \theta_i v_i(y(b)) + t_i(b)$$

where

- $v_i(y(b)) = \left(\sum_{j=1}^{m} y_{ij}(b)\alpha_j \right)$ is the valuation function of the advertiser i and can be interpreted as the probability that advertiser i will receive a user click whenever there is a search query received by the search engine and when the bid vector of the advertisers is b.
- $t_i(b) = v_i(y(b))p_i(b)$ can be viewed as the expected payment made by advertiser i to the search engine against every search query received by the search engine and when the bid vector of the advertisers is b.

OPT: Allocation Rule

It is convenient to define

- $\bar{t}_i(b_i) = E_{\theta_{-i}}[t_i(b_i, \theta_{-i})]$ is the expected payment made by advertiser i when he bids an amount b_i and all the advertisers $j \neq i$ bid their true types.
- $\bar{v}_i(b_i) = E_{\theta_{-i}}[v_i(y(b_i, \theta_{-i}))]$ is the probability that advertiser i will receive a user click if he bids an amount b_i and all the advertisers $j \neq i$ bid their true types.
- $U_i(\theta_i) = \theta_i \bar{v}_i(\theta_i) - \bar{t}_i(\theta_i)$ gives advertiser i's expected utility from the mechanism conditional on his type being θ_i when he and all other advertisers bid their true types.

The problem of designing an optimal mechanism for the sponsored search auction can now be written as one of choosing functions $y_{ij}(\cdot)$ and $U_i(\cdot)$ to solve:

Maximize

$$\sum_{i=1}^{n} \int_{\underline{\theta_i}}^{\overline{\theta_i}} (\theta_i \bar{v}_i(\theta_i) - U_i(\theta_i)) \, \phi_i(\theta_i) d\theta_i \qquad (22.11)$$

subject to

(i) $\overline{v}_i(\cdot)$ is non-decreasing $\forall i \in N$

(ii) $y_{ij}(\theta) \in [0,1], \sum_{j=1}^{m} y_{ij}(\theta) \leq 1, \sum_{i=1}^{n} y_{ij}(\theta) \leq 1 \ \forall i \in N, \ \forall j \in M, \ \forall \theta \in \Theta$

(iii) $U_i(\theta_i) = U_i(\underline{\theta_i}) + \int_{\underline{\theta_i}}^{\theta_i} \overline{v}_i(s)ds \ \forall i \in N, \ \forall \theta_i \in \Theta_i$

(iv) $U_i(\theta_i) \geq 0 \ \forall i \in N, \ \forall \theta_i \in \Theta_i$.

In the above formulation, the objective function is the total expected payment received by the search engine from all the advertisers. Note that constraints (iv) are the advertisers' interim individual rationality constraints while constraint (ii) is the feasibility constraint. Constraints (i) and (iii) are the necessary and sufficient conditions for the allocation and payment rule $f(\cdot) = (y_{ij}(\cdot), t_i(\cdot))_{i \in N, j \in M}$ to be Bayesian incentive compatible (Myerson's characterization theorem – Section 19.7). These constraints are taken from [4] and have already been presented in Chapter 21.

We have a critical observation to make here. Note that in the above optimization problem, we have replaced the bid b_i by the actual type θ_i. This is because we are imposing the Bayesian incentive compatibility constraints on the allocation and payment rule, and, hence, every advertiser will bid his true type. Thus, while dealing with the OPT mechanism, we can safely interchange θ_i and b_i for any $i \in N$.

Note first that if constraint (iii) is satisfied, then constraint (iv) will be satisfied iff $U_i(\underline{\theta_i}) \geq 0 \ \forall i \in N$. As a result, we can replace the constraint (iv) with

(iv') $U_i(\underline{\theta_i}) \geq 0 \ \forall i \in N$.

Next, substituting for $U_i(\theta_i)$ in the objective function from constraint (iii), we get

$$\sum_{i=1}^{n} \int_{\underline{\theta_i}}^{\overline{\theta_i}} \left(\overline{v}_i(\theta_i)\theta_i - U_i(\underline{\theta_i}) - \int_{\underline{\theta_i}}^{\theta_i} \overline{v}_i(s)ds \right) \phi_i(\theta_i)d\theta_i.$$

Integrating by parts the above expression, the search engine's problem can be written as one of choosing the $y_{ij}(\cdot)$ functions and the values $U_1(\underline{\theta_1}), \ldots, U_n(\underline{\theta_n})$ to maximize

$$\int_{\underline{\theta_1}}^{\overline{\theta_1}} \cdots \int_{\underline{\theta_n}}^{\overline{\theta_n}} \left[\sum_{i=1}^{n} v_i(y(\theta_i, \theta_{-i}))J_i(\theta_i) \right] \left[\prod_{i=1}^{n} \phi_i(\theta_i) \right] d\theta_n \ldots d\theta_1 - \sum_{i=1}^{n} U_i(\underline{\theta_i})$$

subject to constraints (i), (ii), and (iv'), where

$$J_i(\theta_i) = \theta_i - \frac{1 - \Phi_i(\theta_i)}{\phi_i(\theta_i)}.$$

It is evident that the solution must have $U_i(\underline{\theta_i}) = 0$ for all $i = 1, 2, \ldots, n$. Hence, the search engine's problem reduces to choosing functions $y_{ij}(\cdot)$ to maximize

$$\int_{\underline{\theta_1}}^{\overline{\theta_1}} \cdots \int_{\underline{\theta_n}}^{\overline{\theta_n}} \left[\sum_{i=1}^{n} v_i(y(\theta_i, \theta_{-i}))J_i(\theta_i) \right] \left[\prod_{i=1}^{n} \phi_i(\theta_i) \right] d\theta_n \ldots d\theta_1$$

subject to constraints (i) and (ii).

Let us ignore the constraint (i) for the moment. Then an inspection of the above expression indicates that $y_{ij}(\cdot)$ is a solution to this relaxed problem iff for all $i = 1, 2, \ldots, n$ we have

$$
y_{ij}(\theta) = \begin{cases} 0 & \forall j = 1, 2, \ldots, m & : & \text{if } J_i(\theta_i) < 0 \\ 1 & \forall j = 1, 2, \ldots, m < n & : & \text{if } J_i(\theta_i) = J^{(j)} \\ 1 & \forall j = 1, 2, \ldots, n \le m & : & \text{if } J_i(\theta_i) = J^{(j)} \\ 0 & & : & \text{otherwise} \end{cases} \tag{22.12}
$$

where $J^{(j)}$ is the jth highest value among $J_i(\theta_i)$s.

In other words, if we ignore the constraint (i) then $y_{ij}(\cdot)$ is a solution to this relaxed problem if and only if no slot is allocated to any advertiser having negative value $J_i(\theta_i)$, and the rest of the advertisers' ads are displayed in the same order as the values of $J_i(\theta_i)$. That is, the first slot is allocated to the advertiser who has the highest nonnegative value for $J_i(\theta_i)$, the second slot is allocated to the advertiser who has the second highest nonnegative value for $J_i(\theta_i)$, and so on.

Now, recall the definition of $\bar{v}_i(\cdot)$. It is easy to write down the following expression:

$$
\bar{v}_i(\theta_i) = E_{\theta_{-i}} \left[v_i(y(\theta_i, \theta_{-i})) \right] \tag{22.13}
$$

$$
= E_{\theta_{-i}} \left[\sum_{j=1}^{m} y_{ij}(\theta_i, \theta_{-i}) \alpha_j \right]. \tag{22.14}
$$

Now if we assume that $J_i(\cdot)$ is nondecreasing in θ_i, it is easy to see that the above solution $y_{ij}(\cdot)$, given by (22.12), will be nondecreasing in θ_i, which in turn implies, by looking at expression (22.14), that $\bar{v}_i(\cdot)$ is nondecreasing in θ_i. Thus, the solution to this relaxed problem actually satisfies constraint (i) under the assumption that $J_i(\cdot)$ is nondecreasing. Assuming that $J_i(\cdot)$ is nondecreasing, the solution given by (22.12) appears to be the solution of the optimal mechanism design problem for sponsored search auction. Note that in Equation (22.12), we have written the allocation rule $J_i(\cdot)$ as a function of actual type profile θ of the advertisers rather than the bid vector b. This is because in an OPT mechanism, each advertiser bids his true type, and we have $b_i = \theta_i \; \forall \, i = 1, \ldots, n$.

The condition that $J_i(\cdot)$ is nondecreasing in θ_i is met by most distribution functions such as uniform and exponential. In the rest of this chapter, we will work with the assumption that for every advertiser i, $J_i(\cdot)$ is nondecreasing in θ_i.

It is interesting to note that in the above allocation rule, the condition $J_i(.) > 0$ for qualifying an advertiser to display his/her **ad** can be expressed more conveniently in the form of reserve price in the following sense. For each advertiser i, we first compute the value of θ_i at which we have $J_i(\theta_i) = 0$. We call this value aptly as the *reserve price* of advertiser i. Now the allocation rule says that we first discard all those advertisers whose bid is less than their corresponding reserve price. Among the remaining advertisers, we allocate the advertisers in decreasing order of their $J_i(\theta_i)$ values. Further, if the advertisers are symmetric then the reserve price will be the same for all the advertisers, and moreover if $J_i(.)$ is nondecreasing in θ_i then among the qualified advertisers, the allocation rule will be the same as the GFP allocation rule. This interpretation of the allocation rule is the same as the allocation rule in [5] under the parallel case. This observation leads to the following proposition.

Proposition 22.2. *If the advertisers have nonidentical distribution functions $\Phi_i(\cdot)$ then the advertiser who has the kth largest value of $J_i(b_i)$ is not necessarily the advertiser who has bid the kth highest amount. Thus the OPT mechanism need not be allocatively efficient and, therefore, need not be ex post efficient.*

Proposition 22.3. *If the advertisers are symmetric in following sense*

- $\Theta_1 = \ldots = \Theta_n = \Theta$
- $\Phi_1(\cdot) = \ldots = \Phi_n(\cdot) = \Phi(\cdot)$

and for every advertiser i, we have $J_i(\cdot) > 0$ and $J_i(\cdot)$ is nondecreasing, then

- $J_1(\cdot) = \ldots = J_n(\cdot) = J(\cdot)$.
- *The rank of an advertiser in the decreasing order sequence of $J_1(b_1), \ldots, J_n(b_n)$ is precisely the same as the rank of the same advertiser in the decreasing order sequence of $b_1, \ldots, b_n$.*
- *For a given bid vector b, the OPT mechanism results in the same allocation as suggested by the GFP, the GSP, and the VCG mechanisms.*
- *The OPT mechanism is allocatively efficient.*

OPT: Payment Rule

Now we compute the payment rule. Again, following Myerson's line of attack, the optimal expected payment rule $t_i(\cdot)$ must be chosen in such a way that it satisfies

$$\bar{t}_i(\theta_i) = E_{\theta_{-i}}[t_i(\theta_i, \theta_{-i})] = \theta_i \bar{v}_i(\theta_i) - U_i(\theta_i) = \theta_i \bar{v}_i(\theta_i) - \int_{\underline{\theta_i}}^{\theta_i} \bar{v}_i(s)ds. \quad (22.15)$$

Looking at the above formula, we can say that if the payment rule $t_i(\cdot)$ satisfies the following formula (22.16) then it would also satisfy formula (22.15).

$$t_i(\theta_i, \theta_{-i}) = \theta_i v_i(y(\theta_i, \theta_{-i})) - \int_{\underline{\theta_i}}^{\theta_i} v_i(y(s, \theta_{-i}))ds \ \forall \theta \in \Theta \quad (22.16)$$

The above formula can be rewritten in a more intuitive way, for which we need to define the following quantities for any vector θ_{-i}:

Case 1 $(m < n)$:

$$z_{i1}(\theta_{-i}) = \inf\left\{\theta_i | J_i(\theta_i) > 0 \text{ and } J_i(\theta_i) \geq J_{-i}^{(1)}\right\}$$

$$z_{i2}(\theta_{-i}) = \inf\left\{\theta_i | J_i(\theta_i) > 0 \text{ and } J_{-i}^{(1)} > J_i(\theta_i) \geq J_{-i}^{(2)}\right\}$$

$$\vdots = \vdots$$

$$z_{im}(\theta_{-i}) = \inf\left\{\theta_i | J_i(\theta_i) > 0 \text{ and } J_{-i}^{(m-1)} > J_i(\theta_i) \geq J_{-i}^{(m)}\right\}.$$

Case 2 $(n \leq m)$:

$$z_{i1}(\theta_{-i}) = \inf\left\{\theta_i | J_i(\theta_i) > 0 \text{ and } J_i(\theta_i) \geq J_{-i}^{(1)}\right\}$$

$$z_{i2}(\theta_{-i}) = \inf\left\{\theta_i | J_i(\theta_i) > 0 \text{ and } J_{-i}^{(1)} > J_i(\theta_i) \geq J_{-i}^{(2)}\right\}$$

$$\vdots = \vdots$$

$$z_{in}(\theta_{-i}) = \inf\left\{\theta_i | J_i(\theta_i) > 0 \text{ and } J_{-i}^{(n-1)} > J_i(\theta_i)\right\}.$$

In the above definitions, $J_{-i}^{(k)}$ is the kth highest value among the following $(n-1)$ values

$$J_1(\theta_1), \ldots, J_{i-1}(\theta_{i-1}), J_{i+1}(\theta_{i+1}), \ldots, J_n(\theta_n).$$

The quantity $z_{ik}(\theta_{-i})$ is the infimum of all the bids for advertiser i that can make him win the kth slot against the bid vector θ_{-i} from the other advertisers. In view of the above definitions, we can write

Case 1 $(m < n)$:

$$v_i(y(\theta_i, \theta_{-i})) = \begin{cases} \alpha_1 & : \text{ if } \theta_i \geq z_{i1}(\theta_{-i}) \\ \alpha_2 & : \text{ if } z_{i1}(\theta_{-i}) > \theta_i \geq z_{i2}(\theta_{-i}) \\ \vdots & : \vdots \\ \alpha_m & : \text{ if } z_{i(m-1)}(\theta_{-i}) > \theta_i \geq z_{im}(\theta_{-i}) \\ 0 & : \text{ if } z_{im}(\theta_{-i}) > \theta_i. \end{cases}$$

Case 2 $(n \leq m)$:

$$v_i(y(\theta_i, \theta_{-i})) = \begin{cases} \alpha_1 & : \text{ if } \theta_i \geq z_{i1}(\theta_{-i}) \\ \alpha_2 & : \text{ if } z_{i1}(\theta_{-i}) > \theta_i \geq z_{i2}(\theta_{-i}) \\ \vdots & : \vdots \\ \alpha_n & : \text{ if } z_{i(n-1)}(\theta_{-i}) > \theta_i. \end{cases}$$

This gives us the following expressions for $\int_{\underline{\theta_i}}^{\theta_i} v_i(y(s, \theta_{-i}))ds$. In these expressions, r is the position of advertiser i's ad.

Case 1 $(m < n)$:

$$\begin{cases} \alpha_r(\theta_i - z_{ir}(\theta_{-i})) + \sum_{j=(r+1)}^{m} \alpha_j \left(z_{i(j-1)}(\theta_{-i}) - z_{ij}(\theta_{-i})\right) & : \quad \text{if } 1 \le r \le (m-1) \\ \alpha_m(\theta_i - z_{im}(\theta_{-i})) & : \quad \text{if } r = m \\ 0 & : \quad \text{otherwise.} \end{cases}$$

Case 2 $(n \le m)$:

$$\begin{cases} \alpha_r(\theta_i - z_{ir}(\theta_{-i})) + \sum_{j=(r+1)}^{n} \alpha_j \left(z_{i(j-1)}(\theta_{-i}) - z_{ij}(\theta_{-i})\right) & : \quad \text{if } 1 \le r \le (n-1) \\ \alpha_n(\theta_i - z_{in}(\theta_{-i})) & : \quad \text{if } r = n. \end{cases}$$

Substituting the above value for $\int_{\underline{\theta_i}}^{\theta_i} v_i(y(s, \theta_{-i}))ds$ in formula (22.16), we get

Case 1 $(m < n)$:

$$p_i(\theta_i, \theta_{-i}) = \frac{1}{\alpha_r} t_i(\theta_i, \theta_{-i}) = \begin{cases} \frac{\alpha_m}{\alpha_r} z_{im}(\theta_{-i}) + \frac{1}{\alpha_r} \sum_{j=r}^{m-1} \beta_j z_{ij}(\theta_{-i}) : \text{ if } 1 \le r \le (m-1) \\ z_{im}(\theta_{-i}) & : \text{ if } r = m \\ 0 & : \text{ otherwise.} \end{cases} \quad (22.17)$$

Case 2 $(n \le m)$:

$$p_i(\theta_i, \theta_{-i}) = \frac{1}{\alpha_r} t_i(\theta_i, \theta_{-i}) = \begin{cases} \frac{\alpha_n}{\alpha_r} z_{in}(\theta_{-i}) + \frac{1}{\alpha_r} \sum_{j=r}^{n-1} \beta_j z_{ij}(\theta_{-i}) : \text{ if } 1 \le r \le (n-1) \\ z_{in}(\theta_{-i}) & : \text{ if } r = n \\ 0 & : \text{ otherwise.} \end{cases} \quad (22.18)$$

The above relations say that an advertiser i must pay only when his **ad** receives a click, and he pays the amount equal to $p_i(\theta)$. Note that in above relations, we have expressed the payment rule $p_i(\cdot)$ as a function of actual type profile θ of the advertisers rather than the bid vector b. This is because in an OPT mechanism, each advertiser bids his true type, and we have $b_i = \theta_i \ \forall \ i = 1, \ldots, n$.

Thus, we can say that Equation (22.12) describes the allocation rule for the OPT mechanism and Equations (22.17) and (22.18) describe the payment rule for the OPT mechanism.

In what follows, we discuss an important special case of the OPT mechanism when the advertisers are symmetric.

OPT Mechanism and Symmetric Advertisers

Let us assume that advertisers are symmetric in the following sense:

- $\Theta_1 = \ldots = \Theta_n = \Theta = [L, U] \subset \mathbb{R}$.

- $\Phi_1(\cdot) = \ldots = \Phi_n(\cdot) = \Phi(\cdot)$.

Also, we assume that

- $J(\cdot)$ is non-decreasing over the interval $[L, U]$.
- $J(x) > 0 \ \forall \, x \in [L, U]$.

Note that if $J(L) > 0$ then we must have $L > 0$.

Proposition 22.3 shows that if the advertisers are symmetric then the allocation rule under the OPT mechanism is the same as the GFP, the GSP, and the VCG mechanisms. Coming to the payment rule, it is easy to verify that if advertiser i is allocated the slot r for the bid vector (θ_i, θ_{-i}) then we should have

Case 1 ($m < n$):

$$
z_{ij}(\theta_{-i}) = \begin{cases} \theta^{(j)} & : \text{ if } 1 \leq j \leq (r-1) \\ \theta^{(j+1)} & : \text{ if } r \leq j \leq m. \end{cases}
\tag{22.19}
$$

Case 2 ($n \leq m$):

$$
z_{ij}(\theta_{-i}) = \begin{cases} \theta^{(j)} & : \text{ if } 1 \leq j \leq (r-1) \\ \theta^{(j+1)} & : \text{ if } r \leq j \leq (n-1) \\ L & : \text{ if } j = n. \end{cases}
\tag{22.20}
$$

If we substitute Equations (22.19) and (22.20) into Equations (22.17) and (22.18), then we get the following payment rule for the OPT mechanism when the advertisers are symmetric:

Case 1 ($m < n$):

$$
p_i(\theta_i, \theta_{-i}) = \frac{1}{\alpha_r} t_i(\theta_i, \theta_{-i}) = \begin{cases} \frac{\alpha_m}{\alpha_r} \theta^{(m+1)} + \frac{1}{\alpha_r} \sum_{j=r}^{m-1} \beta_j \theta^{(j+1)} & : \text{ if } 1 \leq r \leq (m-1) \\ \theta^{(m+1)} & : \text{ if } r = m \\ 0 & : \text{ otherwise.} \end{cases}
\tag{22.21}
$$

Case 2 ($n \leq m$):

$$
p_i(\theta_i, \theta_{-i}) = \frac{1}{\alpha_r} t_i(\theta_i, \theta_{-i}) = \begin{cases} \frac{\alpha_n}{\alpha_r} L + \frac{1}{\alpha_r} \sum_{j=r}^{n-1} \beta_j \theta^{(j+1)} & : \text{ if } 1 \leq r \leq (n-1) \\ L & : \text{ if } r = n \\ 0 & : \text{ otherwise.} \end{cases}
\tag{22.22}
$$

Compare the above equations with the payment rule of the VCG mechanism given by Equations (22.9) and (22.10). This comparison leads to the following proposition:

Proposition 22.4. *If the advertisers are symmetric in following sense*

- $\Theta_1 = \ldots = \Theta_n = \Theta = [L, U]$

- $\Phi_1(\cdot) = \ldots = \Phi_n(\cdot) = \Phi(\cdot)$

and for every advertiser i, we have $J_i(\cdot) > 0$ and $J_i(\cdot)$ is non-decreasing over the interval $[L, U]$, then

- *the payment rule for Case 1 coincides with the corresponding payment rule in the VCG mechanism,*
- *and the payment rule for the Case 2 differs from the corresponding payment rule of the VCG mechanism just by a constant amount L.*

Note that L cannot be zero because of the assumption that $J(L) > 0$.

22.7 Summary and References

This chapter was devoted to applying mechanism design to a popular current problem namely sponsored search auctions (SSA) on the web. The discussion brings out how mechanism design can be used in the context of a real-world application. The following provides the sequence in which the results were discussed.

- The SSA problem was formulated as a mechanism design problem in quasilinear environment. In fact, the quasilinear setting here turns out to be a linear setting.
- In the above mechanism design framework, the allocation rule and the payment rule of the earliest mechanism that was used, namely GFP (generalized first price) mechanism, were derived.
- Next the allocation rule and payment rule for the GSP (generalized second price) mechanism were derived. Search engines commonly use the GSP mechanism or its variants. The allocation rule and payment rule for the Clarke mechanism as applied to this setting were derived.
- A new mechanism was proposed, OPT, that generalizes Myerson auction to the SSA setting. The generalized mechanism involves exploiting the intrinsic structure of the SSA problem to extend the virtual functions defined by Myerson.

Mechanism design for sponsored search auctions has been a major topic of research in the recent years. The annual ACM conference on Electronic Commerce (now rechristened as the ACM Conference on Economics and Computation) is a rich source of the current state-of-the-art in this area.

References

[1] Dinesh Garg and Y. Narahari. "An optimal mechanism for sponsored search auctions and comparison with other mechanisms". In: *IEEE Transactions on Automation Science and Engineering* **6**(4) (2009), pp. 641–657.

[2] Y. Narahari, Dinesh Garg, Ramasuri Narayanam, and Hastagiri Prakash. *Game Theoretic Problems in Network Economics and Mechanism Design Solutions*. Springer, London, 2009.

[3]   B. Edelman, M. Ostrovsky, and M. Schwarz. "Internet advertising and the generalized second price auction: Selling billions of dollars worth of keywords". In: *American Economic Review* **97**(1) (2007), pp. 242–259.

[4]   Roger B. Myerson. "Optimal auction design". In: *Mathematics of Operations Research* **6**(1) (1981), pp. 58–73.

[5]   Juan Feng. "Optimal mechanism for selling a set of commonly ranked objects". In: *Marketing Science* **27**(3) (2008), pp. 501–512.

22.8   Exercises

(1) Consider 5 bidders $\{1, 2, 3, 4, 5\}$ with valuations $v_1 = 20; v_2 = 15; v_3 = 12; v_4 = 10; v_5 = 6$ participating in a sponsored search auction where there are 3 sponsored slots. What will be the result of applying the GSP, VCG, and optimal auctions here?

(2) In the above problem, instead of three sponsored slots, let there be three identical items on auction. Let the demand by agent 1 be 2 units with the rest of agents having unit demand. What will be the result of applying the GSP and VCG auctions here?

(3) Assume in a sponsored search auction with three slots that the valuations of a given bidder for any of the three slots is the same. Also assume that the click probability for the three slots is the same. Now consider 5 bidders $\{1, 2, 3, 4, 5\}$ with valuations $v_1 = 15; v_2 = 14; v_3 = 12; v_4 = 10; v_5 = 8$ participating in the sponsored search auction. What will be the result of applying the GSP, VCG, and optimal auctions here?

Chapter 23

Implementation in Ex-Post Nash Equilibrium

So far, we have studied implementation of social choice functions in dominant strategy equilibrium or in Bayesian Nash equilibrium. In this chapter, we discuss implementation in *ex-post Nash equilibrium* which applies to a *complete information setting*. We bring out the connection of ex-post Nash implementation to the important notion of monotonicity which was developed by Eric Maskin, Nobel laureate in Economic Sciences in 2007.

23.1 Implementation in Multiple Equilibria

While defining implementation of a social choice function $f : \Theta \to X$ by a mechanism $\mathscr{M} = (S_1, \ldots, S_n; \ g(.))$, we carefully stated that, in each $\theta \in \Theta$, there exists an equilibrium of the game induced by $\mathscr{M}$ in which the outcome $f(\theta)$ of the social choice function is reproduced. We did not address the issue of what is to be done if in a given $\theta \in \Theta$, the induced game has multiple equilibria. In the other equilibria, the outcome may not be $f(\theta)$. We have therefore implicitly assumed that the players will play the equilibrium that the social planner desires if there are two or more equilibria. We see this with the following example.

Example 23.1 (Multiple Equilibria Problem). This example is taken from the book by Mas-Colell, Whinston, and Green [1]. Consider the public project problem with $N = \{1, 2\}$ (see Section 14.4). A decision must be made on whether or not to take up the public project. The allocation $k = 0$ indicates that the project is not undertaken and the allocation $k = 1$ means that the project is undertaken. Suppose each of the two players has the following type set

$$\Theta_1 = \Theta_2 = \{\theta_L, \theta_H\}$$

where the types indicate the valuations the agents have for the project. Here θ_H indicates a higher valuation and θ_L indicates the lower valuation. Suppose that $\theta_H > 0 > \theta_L$ with $\theta_H + \theta_L > 0$. As per standard convention, the types of the agents are statistically independent with

$$\mathbb{P}(\theta_1 = \theta_L) = \mathbb{P}(\theta_2 = \theta_L) = \lambda \in (0, 1)$$

The following project choice function is allocatively efficient:

$$k^*(\theta_1, \theta_2) = 0 \text{ if } \theta_1 = \theta_2 = \theta_L$$
$$= 1 \text{ otherwise}$$

For this problem, we can invoke the dAGVA mechanism (Chapter 19) and for each $(\theta_1, \theta_2) \in \Theta_1 \times \Theta_2$, reporting true types by both the players constitutes a Bayesian Nash equilibrium of the game induced by the mechanism. Recall that the monetary transfer to agent i is given by

$$t_i(\theta_i, \theta_{-i}) = E_{\theta'_{-i}}[\theta'_{-i}k^*(\theta_i, \theta'_{-i})] + h_i(\theta_{-i})$$

However, for this problem, the above is not the only Bayesian Nash equilibrium. In particular, we show below that both agents reporting θ_H also constitutes a Bayesian Nash equilibrium.

Suppose agent 2 always announces θ_H. Then whatever agent 1 announces (θ_L or θ_H), the project choice will be $k = 1$ and the project is undertaken. The direct benefit for agent 1 will be θ_L if its type is θ_L and will be θ_H if its type is θ_H. Therefore, agent 1's best response strategy will be to announce a type that minimizes the expected payment. Payment for agent 1 if it announces θ_L is equal to $(1 - \lambda)\theta_H + h_i(\theta_H)$. Payment for agent 1 if it announces θ_H is equal to $\lambda\theta_L + (1 - \lambda)\theta_H + h_i(\theta_H)$. Thus agent 1 would prefer to announce θ_H regardless of its true type if agent 2 announces θ_H. A similar analysis holds when agent 1 announces θ_H and we evaluate agent 2's best response announcement. Thus (θ_H, θ_H) constitutes another Bayesian Nash equilibrium.   □

Strong Implementation

The foregoing example suggests that a social planner who wishes to implement a social choice function has to additionally ensure that the equilibrium that is reached by the induced game is the desired one. This is not at all a trivial problem. However, there is a stronger notion of implementation which ensures that the social choice function is implemented by all equilibria of the induced game. In such a case, the social planner will be fully confident that the mechanism will definitely implement the desired SCF. We define this notion next.

Definition 23.1 (Strong Implementation).
A mechanism $\mathcal{M} = (S_1, \ldots, S_n; g(.))$ is said to strongly implement a social choice function $f : \Theta_1 \times \ldots \times \Theta_n \to X$ if every equilibrium strategy profile $(s_1^*(.), \ldots, s_n^*(.))$ of the game induced by M is such that

$$g(s_1^*(\theta_1), \ldots, s_n^*(\theta_n)) = f(\theta_1, \ldots, \theta_n) \ \forall \ (\theta_1, \ldots, \theta_n) \in \Theta$$

Strong implementation is automatically achieved if the implementation is in strongly dominant strategy equilibrium. If the implementation is in weakly dominant strategy equilibrium, strong implementation is more difficult. Achieving strong implementation in Bayesian Nash equilibrium is clearly the most difficult of all.

23.2 Implementation in Nash Equilibrium

Suppose each agent, in addition to observing its own type, is also able to observe the types of the rest of the agents. Such a situation becomes a *complete information setting*. While the players are able to observe the entire type profile θ, the social planner may not be aware of the type profile. So, in order to implement a social choice function in this setting, the social planner has to come up with a mechanism that would induce a game among the agents, leading to a Nash equilibrium, $s^*(\theta)$, in which the outcome $f(\theta)$ corresponding to the type profile θ is reproduced. Maskin [2, 3] has pioneered fundamental work on this topic and we shall discuss this with an example [4].

Example 23.2 (Implementation in Nash Equilibrium). Suppose $N = \{1,2\}$ and $X = \{x, y, z, w\}$. The players could be in one of two states, θ_A and θ_B. The set of states here (analogous to set of type profiles) is given by

$$\Theta = \{\theta_A, \theta_B\}$$

Note that we do not separately mention the individual types of the agents since we are studying a complete information setting where each agent observes the entire type profile. In these two states, suppose the agents have the following preferences over the elements of the outcome set $X = \{x, y, z, w\}$. The preferences in the state $\theta = \theta_A$ are:

$$1 : x \succ y \succ z \succ w; \quad 2 : w \succ y \succ z \succ x$$

The preferences in the state $\theta = \theta_B$ are:

$$1 : w \succ x \succ z \succ y; \quad 2 : y \succ x \succ z \succ w$$

We have chosen to give the rankings over the outcomes rather than the actual utility values here. However one can work with utility values as well.

The above is a relabeled version of the illustrative example presented by Maskin in his Nobel prize lecture [4]. The two players correspond to two representative consumers of energy. The social planner is the energy authority. The outcomes x, y, z, w correspond respectively to four potential sources of energy namely gas, oil, coal, and nuclear power. Player 1 is a convenience-conscious consumer while player 2 is a safety-conscious consumer of energy. The state θ_A corresponds to a state where the consumers of energy are not too much concerned about future needs and future possibilities while the state θ_B refers to an opposite situation where the consumers weigh in the future options and possibilities carefully. In these two states, the two consumers have preferences over the four different sources of energy which have been described above. The aim of the energy authority is to aggregate their preferences and implement a social choice function that is desirable and acceptable to the consumers. Suppose the energy authority wishes to implement the social choice function

$$f(\theta_A) = y; \quad f(\theta_B) = x$$

An immediate observation we can make about the above SCF is it is ex-post efficient. Further its outcomes are either the first ranked preference or the second ranked preference of the two consumers. $\qquad\square$

Example 23.3 (Implementability by a Direct Mechanism). We will now investigate if the above SCF can be implemented by a direct mechanism. The social planner can ask the two players to report the state and

- choose y if both announce θ_A,
- choose x if both announce θ_B, and
- choose y with probability 0.5 and x with probability 0.5 if their announcements are different

Note that the best response of agent 1 is to announce θ_B whatever the announcement by agent 2 and whatever the state. This is because agent 2 prefers x to y in both the states. Clearly, agent 1 is able to increase the probability of realizing its preferred outcome

- from 0.5 to 1 if agent 2 announces θ_A
- from 0 to 0.5 if agent 2 announces θ_B

Similarly, the best response of agent 2, whatever the announcement by agent 1 and whatever the state, would be to report θ_A since agent 2 prefers y to x. Thus the rational behavior of agents 1 and 2 implies that, in each state, the outcome is an equal probability randomization between x and y. Thus there is only a 50 percent probability that the outcome is $f(\theta)$. $\square$

Example 23.4 (Implementability by an Indirect Mechanism). Now we investigate the possibility of implementing the social choice function through an indirect mechanism. Suppose $S_1 = \{U, D\}$ and $S_2 = \{L, R\}$ and the outcome rule $g(.)$ is defined by the following matrix:

	2	
1	L	R
U	y	z
D	w	x

First we analyze the situation when the state is $\theta = \theta_A$. Agent 2 has to choose between L and R and it turns out that L is a dominant strategy for agent 2. This is because when agent 2 plays L,

- if agent 1 plays U, then the outcome is y which agent 2 prefers to z
- if agent 1 plays D, then the outcome is w which agent 2 prefers to x

When agent 2 plays its dominant strategy L, it is a best response for agent 1 to play U since the outcome y is better than w for agent 1. Thus, when $\theta = \theta_A$, the strategy profile (U, L) is the best response strategy profile and in fact, is the unique Nash equilibrium. Most importantly, the outcome realized in this Nash equilibrium is y and since $f(\theta_A) = y$, we are able to implement the outcome of the social choice function in the state θ_A.

A similar analysis can be conducted when $\theta = \theta_B$ and it turns out that (D, R) will be the unique Nash equilibrium in this case, leading to the outcome x which is precisely $f(\theta_B)$. Thus in both the states, the social choice function is realized even though the social planner does not know what the state is. Moreover, the two agents are interested in their own preferences and not concerned about what the social choice function is. We say that the indirect mechanism implements the social choice function in Nash equilibrium. The point to remember that this is a complete information setting in which all the agents know the entire type profile or the complete state information. $\square$

Connection to Monotonicity

Maskin [2, 3] investigated under what conditions a social choice function can be implemented in Nash equilibrium and came up with the notion of *monotonicity* which is often called *Maskin monotonicity*. Maskin established that monotonicity is a necessary condition for implementability in Nash equilibrium and also proved that monotonicity together with another property called *no veto power* will be sufficient for implementability. We have formally defined monotonicity in Chapter 17 and we now apply this notion to the example we are currently discussing. We first summarize the monotonicity property in an intuitive manner as follows [4]. Suppose $f(\theta) = x$ where θ is some state (or type profile) and x is some outcome. Consider another state θ'. In the states θ and θ', the players will have their preferences over the outcomes. If, while going from θ to θ', the outcome x does not fall in any player's ranking relative to any other outcome, then monotonicity requires that the outcome produced by θ' be the same as before, that is $f(\theta') = x$. If, while going from θ to θ', the outcome x does fall in some player's ranking relative to some outcome, then monotonicity does not impose any restriction on the outcome $f(\theta')$.

Example 23.5 (Application of Monotonicity). Recall the preferences in the example that we are currently discussing. The preferences in the state $\theta = \theta_A$ are:

$$1 : x \succ y \succ z \succ w; \quad 2 : w \succ y \succ z \succ x$$

The preferences in the state $\theta = \theta_B$ are:

$$1 : w \succ x \succ z \succ y; \quad 2 : y \succ x \succ z \succ w$$

The social choice function is $f(\theta_A) = y$; $f(\theta_B) = x$. When we go from θ_A to θ_B, the outcome y falls in the ranking of agent 1, relative to both z and w. Thus the fact that $f(\theta_B)$ is not equal to y does not violate monotonicity. Similarly, when we go from θ_B to θ_A, we notice that x falls in the ranking of agent 2, relative to z as well as w. Therefore, the fact that $f(\theta_A)$ is not equal to x does not violate monotonicity.

Suppose the preferences in the state $\theta = \theta_B$ are changed as follows (with preferences in the state $\theta = \theta_A$ remaining as before):

$$1 : x \succ y \succ z \succ w; \quad 2 : y \succ x \succ z \succ w$$

Let us say the social choice function is $f(\theta_A) = y$; $f(\theta_B) = w$. When we go from θ_A to θ_B, notice that the outcome $f(\theta_A) = y$ does not fall in the rankings of the two agents. Thus for monotonicity to hold, $f(\theta_B)$ must be the same as $f(\theta_A)$ which is not true here since $f(\theta_B) = w$ and not equal to y. Thus by Maskin's result, this SCF cannot be implemented in Nash equilibrium. The reader is asked to verify this as an exercise. □

23.3 Implementability in Complete Information Setting

As observed in the foregoing examples, a complete information setting is one where each agent has full knowledge about the entire type profile (or state). The social planner, however, does not observe the state and in order to implement a social choice function, makes the agents play a game with the hope that equilibrium play will yield the outcomes of the social choice function. A complete information setting is a special case of the general mechanism design environment that we have studied in all earlier chapters. It is special in the sense that all agents receive signals about the types of other agents that are perfectly correlated. Our aim is to define implementation and incentive compatibility in such an environment using the notion of Nash equilibrium.

Definition 23.2. We say a mechanism $\mathcal{M} = (S_1, \ldots, S_n; g(.))$ implements a social choice function $f : \Theta_1 \times \ldots \times \Theta_n \to X$ in Nash equilibrium if $\forall \theta \in \Theta$, there exists a Nash equilibrium $s^*(\theta) = (s_1^*(\theta), \ldots, s_n^*(\theta))$ such that $g(s^*(\theta)) = f(\theta)$. We say $\mathcal{M}$ strongly implements $f(.)$ in Nash equilibrium if $\forall \theta \in \Theta$, every Nash equilibrium yields the outcome $f(\theta)$.

Often the phrase *implementation in ex-post Nash equilibrium* is also used. The first observation we make is that if a social choice function is dominant strategy implementable, it will be certainly implementable in Nash equilibrium because a dominant strategy equilibrium is also a Nash equilibrium. Moreover, the presence of complete information does not affect dominant strategy implementation in any way since an agent's belief about the types of other agents does not in any way affect the agent's dominant strategies. The second observation we make is that a social choice function that is implementable in Nash equilibrium is also implementable in Bayesian Nash equilibrium since a Nash equilibrium is a (degenerate) Bayesian Nash equilibrium.

Definition 23.3 (Ex-Post Nash Incentive Compatibility (EPIC)). *A social choice function $f : \Theta \to X$ is said to be EPIC if complete information game induced by the direct revelation mechanism $\mathcal{D} = (\Theta, f(\cdot))$ has a Nash equilibrium $s^*(\cdot) = (s_1^*(\cdot), \ldots, s_n^*(\cdot))$ such that $s_i^*(\theta) = \theta \; \forall \theta \in \Theta$, $\forall i \in N$. We say $f(\cdot)$ is strongly EPIC if $\forall \theta \in \Theta$, every Nash equilibrium yields the outcome $f(\theta)$.*

Note. Clearly, EPIC is stronger than Bayesian incentive compatibility but much weaker than dominant strategy incentive compatibility. A social choice function is EPIC if for all players $i \in N$ and for all type profiles $(\theta_i, \theta_{-i}) \in \Theta$, whenever all other players report their true types, it is optimal for player i also to report his true type. In the case of BIC, for each player $i \in N$ and $\forall \theta_i \in \Theta_i$, reporting true type is optimal in expectation, where the expectation is taken over the belief distribution $p_i(\theta_i) \in \Delta(\Theta_{-i})$.

It turns out that any social choice function $f(.)$ can be implemented in Nash equilibrium if $n \geq 3$ as shown by the following discussion. Consider the mechanism where each player i (for $i = 1, \ldots, n$) simultaneously announces a type profile (or state) $\theta^i \in \Theta$. If at least $(n-1)$ agents announce the same profile, say θ^*, then select the outcome $f(\theta^*)$, otherwise select a fixed, arbitrary outcome $x_0 \in X$. Suppose the current state is θ and consider the profile of announcements $(\theta, \theta, \ldots, \theta)$. This profile is a Nash equilibrium since any single agent unilaterally deviating from this profile would still guarantee that the outcome does not change from $f(\theta)$.

Monotonicity: Necessary Condition for Implementability

Though, every social choice function, technically speaking, can be implemented in the above way, the implementation is somewhat contrived. If the implementation is a *strong* implementation, then this situation is effectively avoided. This provides a compelling case for asking the following question: in the complete information setting, which social choice functions can be strongly implemented in Nash equilibrium. A partial answer to this question is provided by the following powerful proposition (due to Maskin [2]) which states that monotonicity is a necessary condition.

Proposition 23.1. *If a social choice function $f(.)$ can be strongly implemented in Nash equilibrium, then $f(.)$ must be monotonic.*

Proof: First we recall the definition of lower contour set and monotonicity. Given an outcome $x \in X$, and agent $i \in N$ and a type of agent i, $\theta_i \in \Theta_i$, the lower contour set $L_i(x, \theta_i)$ is defined as

$$L_i(x, \theta_i) = \{y \in X : u_i(x, \theta_i) \geq u_i(y, \theta_i)\}$$

A social choice function $f : \Theta \to X$ is monotonic if $\forall \theta \in \Theta$, $\forall \theta' \in \Theta(\theta' \neq \theta)$,

$$L_i(f(\theta), \theta_i) \subset L_i(f(\theta), \theta_i') \ \forall \, i \in N \implies f(\theta') = f(\theta)$$

Suppose the mechanism $\mathcal{M} = (S_1, \ldots, S_n; g(.))$ strongly implements the social choice function $f(.)$. This means when the profile is θ, every Nash equilibrium results in the outcome $f(\theta)$. That is, there must exist a strategy profile $s^*(.) = (s_1^*(.), \ldots, s_n^*(.))$ such that

$$g(s^*(\theta)) = f(\theta) \ \text{ and } \ g(s_i', s_{-i}^*) \in L_i(f(\theta), \theta_i) \ \forall \, s_i' \in S_i \ \forall i \in N$$

Suppose $f(.)$ is not monotonic. Then there would exist a $\theta' \in \Theta$ such that

$$L_i(f(\theta), \theta_i) \subset L_i(f(\theta), \theta_i') \ \forall \, i \in N \ \text{ but } \ f(\theta') \neq f(\theta)$$

However, $s^*(.)$ is also a Nash equilibrium under θ' because

$$g(s_i', s_{-i}^*) \in L_i(f(\theta), \theta_i') \ \forall \, s_i' \in S_i \ \forall i \in N$$

Thus $\mathcal{M}$ does not strongly implement $f(.)$ which is a contradiction to our supposition that $f(.)$ is not monotonic.

Sufficient Condition for Implementability

Maskin [2, 4] also showed that in combination with (what Maskin calls) an innocuous property called *no veto power*, monotonicity provides a sufficient condition for implementability in Nash equilibrium, as long as there are at least three agents in the system. This is summarized in the following definition and proposition.

Definition 23.4 (No Veto Power). *A social choice function $f(.)$ is said to satisfy* no veto power *property if $\forall \theta \in \Theta$, if it happens in θ that a particular outcome $x \in X$ is a highest ranked outcome for all players, except possibly one, then $f(\theta) = x$.*

Proposition 23.2. *If $n \geq 3$, $f(.)$ is monotonic, and $f(.)$ satisfies no veto power property, then $f(.)$ can be strongly implemented in Nash equilibrium.*

23.4 Summary and References

This chapter has provided a brief introduction to *implementation in complete information environment*, a topic that has been inspired by the pioneering work of Eric Maskin [4]. Our discussion centered around implementation in ex-post Nash equilibrium which automatically implies a complete information environment. This is in contrast to the earlier chapters where the setting was one of incomplete information.

The main result that was stated in this chapter is that monotonicity is a necessary condition for implementability in ex-post Nash equilibrium. Moreover, monotonicity together with another condition called no veto power provides a sufficient condition for implementability in ex-post Nash equilibrium.

Much of this material in this chapter is based on the relevant material from Chapter 23 of the book by Mas-Colell, Whinston, and Green [1] and the Nobel prize lecture by Maskin [4].

References

[1]   Andreu Mas-Colell, Michael D. Whinston, and Jerry R. Green. *Microeconomic Theory*. Oxford University Press, 1995.

[2]   Eric Maskin. "Nash equilibrium and welfare optimality". In: *Review of Economic Studies* **66** (1999), pp. 23–38.

[3]   Eric Maskin. "The theory of implementation in Nash equilibrium: A survey". In: *Social Goals and Social Organization: Essays in Honor of Elishs Pazner*. Ed. by L. Hurwicz, D. Schmeidler, and H. Sonnenschein. Cambridge University Press, Cambridge, UK, 1985.

[4]   Eric Maskin. *Mechanism design: How to implement social goals*. Tech. rep. Prize Lecture, The Nobel Foundation, Stockholm, Sweden, December 2007.

Chapter 24

Further Topics in Mechanism Design

Mechanism design is a vast area with a riches of results. In this book, we have thus far covered some essential aspects and key results in mechanism design. We now provide a brief glimpse of some additional key topics in mechanism design. We caution that no particular logical order has been followed while discussing the topics. We also alert the reader that the treatment is at best superficial. Pointers to the relevant literature are provided wherever appropriate. The topics listed in this chapter are by no means exhaustive.

24.1   Characterization of DSIC Mechanisms

We have seen that a direct revelation mechanism is specified as $\mathscr{D} = ((\Theta_i)_{i \in N}, f(.))$, where f is the underlying social choice function and Θ_i is the type set of agent i. A valuation function of each agent i, $v_i(\cdot, \cdot)$, associates a value of the allocation chosen by f to agent i. An elegant characterization of DSIC social choice functions has been obtained by Roberts [1]. The work of Roberts generalizes the Green–Laffont characterization theorems (Theorems 18.2 and 18.3) in the following way. Recall that the Green-Laffont theorems assert that an allocatively efficient and DSIC social choice function in the above unconstrained setting has to be necessarily a Groves mechanism. The result of Roberts asserts that all DSIC mechanisms are variations of the VCG mechanism. These variants are often referred to as the *weighted VCG mechanisms*. In a weighted VCG mechanism, weights are given to the agents and to the outcomes. The resulting social choice function is said to be an *affine maximizer*. First we define the notion of an affine maximizer and next state the Roberts' Theorem.

Definition 24.1. A social choice function f is called an affine maximizer if for some subrange $A' \subset X$, for some agent weights $w_1, w_2, \ldots, w_n \in \mathbb{R}^+$, and for some outcome weights $c_x \in \mathbb{R}$, and for every $x \in A'$, we have that

$$f(\theta_1, \theta_2, \ldots, \theta_n) \in \arg\max_{x \in A'} \left\{ c_x + \sum_i w_i v_i(x) \right\}.$$

Theorem 24.1 (Roberts' Theorem). *If $|X| \geq 3$ and for each agent $i \in N$, Θ_i is unconstrained, then any DSIC social choice function f has nonnegative weights $w_1, w_2, \ldots, w_n$ (not all of them zero) and constants $\{c_x\}_{x \in X}$, such that for all $\theta \in \Theta$,*

$$f(\theta) \in \arg\max_{x \in X} \left\{ \sum_{i=1}^{n} w_i v_i(x) + c_x \right\}.$$

For a proof of this important theorem, we refer the reader to the work by Roberts [1]. Lavi, Mu'alem, and Nisan have provided two more proofs for the theorem – interested readers might refer to their paper [2] as well.

The result of Roberts asserts that all DSIC mechanisms in an unconstrained setting are variations of the VCG mechanisms. Note that these mechanisms need not be AE in general. Thus, under an unconstrained setting, if we need both DSIC and AE, we have to employ only a VCG mechanism. Even if we are willing to sacrifice AE, we still have to use a weighted VCG mechanism to achieve DSIC.

24.2   Dominant Strategy Implementation of BIC Rules

Clearly, dominant strategy incentive compatibility is stronger and much more desirable than Bayesian incentive compatibility. A striking reason for this is any Bayesian implementation assumes that the private information structure is common knowledge. It also assumes that the social planner knows a common prior distribution. In many cases, this requirement might be quite demanding. Also, a slight mis-specification of the common prior may lead the equilibrium to shift quite dramatically. This may result in unpredictable effects; for example it might cause an auction to behave in a highly non-optimal manner.

A dominant strategy implementation overcomes these problems in a simple way since the equilibrium strategy does not depend upon the common prior distribution. We would therefore wish to have a DSIC implementation. Since the class of BIC social choice functions is much richer than DSIC social choice functions, one would like to ask the question: Can we implement a BIC SCF as a DSIC rule with the same expected interim utilities to all the players? Mookherjee and Stefan [3] have answered this question by characterizing BIC rules that can be equivalently implemented in dominant strategies. When certain sufficient conditions are satisfied, a BIC social choice function could be implemented without having to worry about a common prior. The article by Mookherjee and Stefan [3] may be consulted for further details.

24.3   Interdependent Values

We have so far assumed that the private values or signals observed by the agents are independent of one another. This is a reasonable assumption in some situations.

However, in the real world, there are environments where the valuation of agents might depend upon the information available or observed by the other agents. We will take a look at two examples.

Example 24.1. Consider an auction for a rare painting. There is no guarantee that the painting is an original one or a plagiarized version. If all the agents knew that the painting is not an original one, they would have a very low value for it independent of one another, whereas on the other hand, they would have a high value for it when it is genuine. Suppose the agents have no knowledge about its authenticity. In such a case, if a certain bidder happens to get information about its genuineness, the valuations of all the other agents will naturally depend upon this signal (indicating the authenticity of the painting) observed by this agent. □

Example 24.2. Consider an auction for oil drilling rights. At the time of the auction, prospective buyers usually carry out geological tests and their private valuations depend upon the results of these tests. If a prospective buyer knew the results of the tests of the others, that buyer's willingness to pay for the drilling rights would be modulated suitably based on the information available. □

The interdependent private value models have been studied in the mechanism design literature. For example, there exists a popular model called the *common value model* (which we have already seen in Section 20.4). As another example, consider a situation when a seller is trying to sell an indivisible object. The value of the received object for the bidders depends upon each others' private signals. Also, the private signals observed by the agents are interdependent. In such a scenario, Cremer and McLean [4] have designed an auction that extracts a revenue from the bidders, which is equal to what could have been extracted when the actual signals of the bidders are known. In this auction, it is an ex-post Nash equilibrium for the agents to report their true types. This auction is interim individually rational but may not be ex-post individually rational. McAfee and Reny [5] have derived general results in the context of mechanism design with correlated information. Mezzetti [6] has designed a two stage mechanism that guarantees allocative efficiency and ex-post incentive compatibility.

24.4 Other Forms of Implementability

We have discussed three different types of implementation: dominant strategy implementation, Bayesian Nash implementation, and ex-post Nash implementation. A number of other concepts have been explored for implementation of social choice functions. These include (we provide one principal reference in each case):

- subgame perfect equilibrium [7]
- Undominated Nash equilibrium [8]

- Dominance solvability [9]
- Trembling hand perfect equilibrium [10]
- Strong equilibrium [11]

24.5   Key Current Topics

Mechanism design is currently an actively and intensely researched area and there are many emerging topics. Prominent ones include mechanism design without money [12], dynamic mechanism design [13], mechanisms with learning [14], computational social choice (which includes computational voting theory) [15], and mechanisms for crowdsourcing [16]. We have only mentioned a few of the topics here and the reader must look into current literature to get an idea of several exciting new developments and trends in this area.

24.6   Computational Issues in Mechanism Design

We have seen several possibility and impossibility results in the context of mechanism design. While every possibility result is a good news, there could be still be challenges involved in actually implementing such a mechanism. For example, we have seen that the GVA mechanism (Chapter 20) is an allocatively efficient and dominant strategy incentive compatible mechanism for combinatorial auctions. A major difficulty with GVA is the computational complexity involved in determining the allocation and the payments. Both the allocation and payment determination problems are NP-hard, being instances of the weighted set packing problem (in the case of forward auction) or the weighted set covering problem (in the case of reverse auction). In fact, if there are n agents, then in the worst case, the payment determination may involve solving as many as n NP-hard problems, so overall, as many as $(n + 1)$ NP-hard problems will need to be solved for implementing the GVA mechanism. Moreover, approximately solving any one of these problems may compromise properties such as efficiency and/or incentive compatibility of the mechanism.

In mechanism design, computations are involved at two levels: first, at the agent level and secondly at the mechanism level [17, 18]. Complexity at the agent level involves strategic complexity (complexity of computing an optimal strategy) and valuation complexity (computation required to provide preference information within a mechanism). Complexity at the mechanism level includes communication complexity (how much communication is required between agents and the mechanism to compute an outcome) and winner determination complexity (computation required to determine an outcome given the strategies of the agents). Typically, insufficient computation leading to approximate solutions is not an option for mechanism design since properties such as incentive compatibility, allocative efficiency, individual rationality, etc., may be compromised.

For a detailed description of computational complexity issues in mechanism design, the reader is referred to the excellent survey articles [17, 18].

24.7 Summary and References

Mechanism design is a vast area embodying a rich collection of results. In the previous ten chapters, we have covered some basics and key results:

(1) Building blocks mechanism design
(2) Social choice functions and mechanisms
(3) Incentive compatibility and revelation theorem
(4) Gibbard-Satterthwaite theorem and its implications
(5) Quasilinear environment and VCG mechanisms
(6) Bayesian mechanisms and mechanism design space in quasilinear environment
(7) Auctions and revenue equivalence theorem
(8) Optimal mechanisms and Myerson auction
(9) Application of mechanism design to sponsored search auctions
(10) Implementation in ex-post Nash equilibrium

To say the least, the above topics only provide a first level peek into this deep subject. In this current chapter, we listed a few other important topics and provided pointers to the literature. Hopefully after reading through the above chapters, the reader is in a position to undertake a deeper dive into mechanism design.

For a microeconomics oriented treatment of mechanism design, the readers could refer to textbooks, such as the ones by Mas-Colell, Whinston, and Green [19] (Chapter 23); Green and Laffont [20]; and Laffont [21]. There is an excellent recent survey article by Nisan [22], which targets a computer science audience. There are many other informative survey papers on mechanism design - for example by Myerson [23], Serrano [24], and Jackson [25, 26]. The Nobel Prize website has a scholarly technical summary of mechanism design theory [27]. The recent edited volume on *Algorithmic Game Theory* by Nisan, Roughgarden, Tardos, and Vazirani [28] also has many interesting overview articles related to mechanism design.

References

[1]   K. Roberts. "The characterization of implementable choice rules". In: *Aggregation and Revelation of Preferences*. Ed. by J.J. Laffont. North-Holland, Amsterdam, 1979, pp. 321–349.

[2]   R. Lavi, A. Mu'alem, and N. Nisan. *Two simplified proofs for Roberts' theorem*. Tech. rep. School of Computer Science and Engineering, The Hebrew University of Jerusalem, Israel, 2004.

[3]   D. Mookherjee and S. Reichelstein. "Dominant strategy implementation of Bayesian incentive compatible allocation rules". In: *Journal of Economic Theory* 56(2) (1992), pp. 378–399.

[4]   J. Cremer and R.P McLean. "Optimal selling strategies under uncertainty for a discriminating monopolist when demands are interdependent". In: *Econometrica* 53(2) (1985), pp. 345–361.

[5] R. Preston McAfee and Philip J. Reny. "Correlated information and mechanism design". In: *Econometrica* **60**(2) (1992), pp. 395–421.

[6] Claudio Mezzetti. "Mechanism design with interdependent valuations: Efficiency". In: *Econometrica* **72**(5) (2004), pp. 1617–1626.

[7] J. Moore and R. Repullo. "Subgame perfect implementation". In: *Econometrica* **56** (1988), pp. 1191–1220.

[8] T. Palfrey and S. Srivastava. "Nash implementation using undominated strategies". In: *Econometrica* **59** (1991), pp. 479–501.

[9] Herve Moulin. "Dominance solvable voting schemes". In: *Econometrica* **47** (1979), pp. 1337–1351.

[10] Tomas Sjostrom. "Implementation in perfect equilibria". In: *Social Choice and Welfare* **10** (1993), pp. 97–106.

[11] Bhaskar Dutta and Arunava Sen. "Implementation under strong equilibrium: A complete characterization". In: *Journal of Mathematical Economics* **20** (1991), pp. 46–67.

[12] James Schummer and Rakesh Vohra. "Mechanim design without money". In: *Algorithmic Game Theory*. Ed. by Noam Nisan, Tim Roughgarden, Eva Tardos, and Vijay Vazirani. Cambridge University Press, 2007, pp. 243–266.

[13] Dirk Bergemann and Juuso Vlimki. "The dynamic pivot mechanism". In: *Econometrica* **78**(2) (2010), pp. 771–789.

[14] Akash Das Sharma, Sujit Gujar, and Y. Narahari. "Truthful multi-armed bandit mechanisms for multi-slot sponsored search auctions". In: *Current Science* **103**(9) (2012), pp. 1064–1077.

[15] Vincent Conitzer Felix Brandt and Ulle Endriss. "Computational social choice". In: *Multiagent Systems*. Ed. by G. Weiss. MIT Press, 2013.

[16] Swaprava Nath et al. "Mechanism design for time critical and cost critical task execution via crowdsourcing". In: *Proceedings of the 8th International Workshop on Internet and Network Economics (WINE - 2012)*. Springer Lecture Notes in Computer Science. 2012.

[17] J.R. Kalagnanam and D.C. Parkes. "Auctions, bidding, and exchange design". In: *Handbook of Quantitative Supply Chain Analysis: Modeling in the E-Business Era*. Ed. by D. Simchi-Levi, S.D. Wu, and Z.J. Shen. Kluwer Academic Publishers, New York, 2005.

[18] T. Sandholm. "Computing in mechanism design". In: *The New Palgrave Dictionary of Economics*. Second Edition, Palgrave Macmillan, 2008.

[19] Andreu Mas-Colell, Michael D. Whinston, and Jerry R. Green. *Microeconomic Theory*. Oxford University Press, 1995.

[20] J.R. Green and J.J. Laffont. *Incentives in Public Decision Making*. North-Holland, Amsterdam, 1979.

[21] J.J. Laffont. *Fundamentals of Public Economics*. The MIT Press, Cambridge, Massachusetts, 1988.

[22] Noam Nisan, Tim Roughgarden, Eva Tardos, and Vijay Vazirani (Editors). *Algorithmic Game Theory*. Cambridge University Press, 2007.

[23] Roger B. Myerson. "Mechanism design". In: *The New Palgrave Dictionary of Economics*. Ed. by J. Eatwell, M. Milgate, and P. Newman. Norton, New York, 1989, pp. 191–206.

[24] R. Serrano. "The theory of implementation of social choice rules". In: *SIAM Review* **46** (2004), pp. 377–414.

[25] M.O. Jackson. "A crash course in implementation theory". In: *Social Choice and Welfare* **18** (2001), pp. 655–708.

[26] M.O. Jackson. "Mechanism theory". In: *Encyclopedia of Life Support Systems*. Ed. by U. Derigs. EOLSS Publishers, 2003.

[27] The Nobel Foundation. *The Sveriges Riksbank Prize in Economic Sciences in Memory of Alfred Nobel 2007: Scientific Background*. Tech. rep. The Nobel Foundation - Stockholm, Sweden, 2007.

[28] N. Nisan. "Introduction to mechanism design (for computer scientists)". In: *Algorithmic Game Theory*. Ed. by Noam Nisan, Tim Roughgarden, Eva Tardos, and Vijay Vazirani. Cambridge University Press, 2007, pp. 209–242.

PART 3

COOPERATIVE GAME THEORY

In this part, we study cooperative games, starting with a discussion on *correlated strategies* and *correlated equilibrium* (Chapter 25). The *Nash bargaining problem* represents one of the earliest and most influential results in cooperative game theory. Chapter 26 describes the problem and proves the Nash bargaining result. We introduce in Chapter 27, *multiplayer coalitional games* or *characteristic form games*. In particular, we introduce *transferable utility games* (TU games) with several illustrative examples. Chapters 28-30 are devoted to solution concepts in cooperative game theory. In Chapter 28, we study the *core*, a central notion in cooperative game theory and in Chapter 29, we study the *Shapley value*, a popular solution concept. We also introduce the Shapley-Shubik power index and the Banzhaf power index. In Chapter 30, we briefly study five other important solution concepts in cooperative game theory: *Stable Sets*, *Bargaining Sets*, *Kernel*, *Nucleolus*, and *Gately Point*. Chapter 31 is devoted to the interesting topic of matching algorithms.

Chapter 25

Correlated Strategies and Correlated Equilibrium

We commence our study of cooperative game theory with a discussion of games and solution concepts that enable us to capture cooperation among players. In this chapter, we first study *games with contracts* followed by *games with communication*. We introduce the notion of *correlated strategies* and show how these strategies capture cooperative actions of players. We then define and illustrate the notion of *correlated equilibrium* and bring out its connection to Nash equilibrium.

The motivation to look at games with cooperation is the fact that in many games, Nash equilibria yield non-optimal payoffs compared to certain non-equilibrium outcomes. Let us consider the following modified version of the prisoner's dilemma problem [1] whose payoff matrix is shown in Figure 25.1.

1	2	
	x_2	y_2
x_1	2, 2	0, 6
y_1	6, 0	1, 1

Fig. 25.1: Payoff matrix of a modified version of prisoner's dilemma game

Note in the above that the unique equilibrium (which happens to be a strictly dominant strategy equilibrium) is (y_1, y_2) that yields a payoff profile $(1, 1)$. The non-equilibrium outcome (x_1, x_2) yields higher payoffs $(2, 2)$. In situations like these, the players may like to transform the game to extend the set of equilibria to include better outcomes. There could be several ways of achieving this transformation:

- The players may communicate among themselves to coordinate their moves
- The players may formulate agreements in the form of contracts
- The players may decide to play the game repeatedly

25.1 Games with Contracts

In a game with contracts, a player who signs a contract is required to play according to a designated strategy which is called a correlated strategy. Contracts transform games with less desirable equilibria to games with more desirable equilibria. We illustrate contracts and correlated strategies through the examples below.

Example 25.1 (Modified Prisoner's Dilemma with a Contract).
In the game shown in Figure 25.1, let us say the two players sign the following contract (call it contract 1).

(1) If both players sign this contract, then player 1 (player 2) chooses to play the strategy x_1 (x_2).
(2) If the contract is signed by only player 1, player 1 would choose y_1.
(3) If the contract is signed by only player 2, player 2 would choose y_2.

Call the action of signing the contract by player i ($i = 1, 2$) as a_i. We can now expand the strategy sets as $S_1 = \{x_1, y_1, a_1\}$ and $S_2 = \{x_2, y_2, a_2\}$. The transformed game has the payoff matrix shown in Figure 25.2.

1	2		
	x_2	y_2	a_2
x_1	2, 2	0, 6	0, 6
y_1	6, 0	1, 1	1, 1
a_1	6, 0	1, 1	2, 2

Fig. 25.2: Payoff matrix with contract 1

The transformed game now has a new equilibrium (a_1, a_2) which is a weakly dominant strategy equilibrium yielding payoffs $(2, 2)$. The profile (y_1, y_2) continues to be an equilibrium but is not a dominant strategy equilibrium. $\square$

Example 25.2 (Modified Prisoner's Dilemma with Additional Contract).
Even better payoffs could be achieved if a second contract (call it contract 2) is introduced in addition to contract 1 above. This additional contract commits the players to a correlated strategy. This contract is as follows.

- If both players sign this new contract, then a coin will be tossed. In the event of a *heads*, they will implement (x_1, y_2) and in the event of a *tails*, they will implement (y_1, x_2).
- If player 1 alone signs this new contract, then player 1 chooses y_1.
- If player 2 alone signs this new contract, then player 2 chooses y_2.

If b_1 and b_2 represent the actions of players 1 and 2 corresponding to signing of this new contract, the extended payoff matrix would be as shown in Figure 25.3. This new game has the following equilibria:

- (y_1, y_2) with payoffs $(1, 1)$
- (a_1, a_2) with payoffs $(2, 2)$
- (b_1, b_2) with payoffs $(3, 3)$
- $((0, 0, \frac{2}{3}, \frac{1}{3}), (0, 0, \frac{2}{3}, \frac{1}{3}))$ where the mixed strategy $(0, 0, \frac{2}{3}, \frac{1}{3})$ for player 1 means a_1 with probability $\frac{2}{3}$ and b_1 with probability $\frac{1}{3}$. This equilibrium leads to a payoff of $\frac{5}{3}$ for both player 1 and player 2.

It turns out that none of the above equilibria are dominant strategy equilibria. $\square$

1	2			
	x_2	y_2	a_2	b_2
x_1	$2,2$	$0,6$	$0,6$	$0,6$
y_1	$6,0$	$1,1$	$1,1$	$1,1$
a_1	$6,0$	$1,1$	$2,2$	$1,1$
b_1	$6,0$	$1,1$	$1,1$	$3,3$

Fig. 25.3: Modified prisoner's dilemma with contract 1 and contract 2

25.2 Correlated Strategies

The choice of pure strategies by players in a game may be correlated perhaps because the players are observing the same or related random events before making their choices. A correlated strategy captures the above feature. Moreover, a correlated strategy, as illustrated in the examples above, also captures cooperative play by the members of a coalition.

Definition 25.1 (Correlated Strategy). *Let* $\Gamma = \langle N, (S_i), (u_i) \rangle$ *be a strategic form game. A correlated strategy for a non-empty subset* C *(also called coalition) of the players is any probability distribution over the set of possible combinations of pure strategies that these players can choose.*

In other words, a correlated strategy, τ_C for a given coalition C belongs to $\Delta(S_C)$ where

$$S_C = \times_{i \in C} \ S_i$$

N is called the *grand coalition* and the symbol τ_N denotes a correlated strategy of the grand coalition.

Example 25.3 (Correlated Strategies). Let $N = \{1, 2, 3\}; S_1 = \{x_1, y_1\}; S_2 = \{x_2, y_2\}; S_3 = \{x_3, y_3, z_3\}$. If $C = \{2, 3\}$, then

$$S_C = S_2 \times S_3 = \{(x_2, x_3), (x_2, y_3), (x_2, z_3), (y_2, x_3), (y_2, y_3), (y_2, z_3)\}$$

A correlated strategy for the coalition C is a probability distribution on S_C. For example, $(\frac{1}{4}, \frac{1}{4}, \frac{1}{4}, \frac{1}{12}, \frac{1}{12}, \frac{1}{12})$ would correspond to (x_2, x_3) with probability $\frac{1}{4}$, (x_2, y_3) with probability $\frac{1}{4}$, and so on. □

Note. A correlated strategy $\tau_C \in \Delta(\times_{i \in C} S_i)$ can be implemented as follows. A reliable mediator or a referee picks randomly a profile of pure strategies in S_C according to distribution τ_C. The mediator asks each player to play the strategy chosen in this pure strategy profile.

Note. Let S, as usual, denote:

$$S = S_N = \times_{i \in N} \ S_i$$

Suppose $\alpha \in \Delta(S)$ is any correlated strategy for all players. Let $U_i(\alpha)$ denote the expected payoff to player i when α is implemented. It can be easily seen that

$$U_i(\alpha) = \sum_{s \in S} \alpha(s) u_i(s)$$

Let $U(\alpha) = (U_1(\alpha), \ldots, U_n(\alpha))$ denote the *expected payoff allocation* to players when they implement α.

Note. Given any allocation in the set $\{U(\alpha) : \alpha \in \Delta(S)\}$, there exists a contract such that if all the players signed this contract, then they would get this expected payoff allocation.

Note. The set of possible expected payoff allocations $\{U(\alpha) : \alpha \in \Delta(S)\}$ can be shown to be a *closed and convex* subset of $\mathbb{R}^n$. When there is no confusion, we will use $u(\alpha)$ instead of $U(\alpha)$.

Correlated Strategies and Mixed Strategies

It is important to understand the difference between a correlated strategy and a mixed strategy profile. A correlated strategy for the grand coalition N is a member of $\Delta(\times(S_i))$ whereas a mixed strategy profile is a member of $\times(\Delta(S_i))$. Given any mixed strategy profile σ of all players, we can always find a correlated strategy of all players α such that $u_i(\alpha) = u_i(\sigma) \ \forall i \in N$. However, given a correlated strategy α of all the players, it may not always be possible to find any mixed strategy profile σ such that $u_i(\sigma) = u_i(\alpha) \ \forall i \in N$.

Contract Signing Game

A vector of correlated strategies of all possible coalitions is called a *contract*. More formally, a contract is defined as follows.

Definition 25.2 (Contract). *Consider the vector* $\tau = (\tau_C)_{C \subseteq N}$. *Note that*

$$\tau \in \times_{C \subseteq N} \ (\Delta(\times_{i \in C} \ S_i)).$$

The vector τ of correlated strategies of all coalitions is a contract.

Note that τ_C for $C \subseteq N$ gives the correlated strategy that would be implemented by players in C if C were the set of players to sign the contract. Clearly, a contract defines (in fact induces) an extended game and this extended game is called the *contract signing game.*

Example 25.4 (Contract in terms of Correlated Strategies). We have discussed two contracts in the context of the modified prisoner's dilemma. Note that contract 1 is described by $(\tau_1, \tau_2, \tau_{\{1,2\}})$ where $\tau_1 = (x_1 : 0, y_1 : 1)$; $\tau_2 = (x_2 : 0, y_2 : 1)$; $\tau_{\{1,2\}} = ((x_1, x_2) : 1;\ (x_1, y_2) : 0;\ (y_1, x_2) : 0;\ (y_1, y_2) : 0)$. The payoff matrix in Figure 25.2 defines the contract signing game induced by contract 1. Contract 2 is given by $(\tau_1, \tau_2, \tau_{\{1,2\}})$ where $\tau_1 = (x_1 : 0, y_1 : 1)$; $\tau_2 = (x_2 : 0, y_2 : 1)$; $\tau_{\{1,2\}} = ((x_1, x_2) : 0;\ (x_1, y_2) : \frac{1}{2};\ (y_1, x_2) : \frac{1}{2};\ (y_1, y_2) : 0)$. The payoff matrix in Figure 25.3 defines the contract signing game induced by contract 1 and contract 2. $\qquad\square$

Concept of Individual Rationality

Clearly, players may not be willing to sign any contract that is proposed. For example, in the modified prisoner's dilemma game of Figure 25.1, player 1 will not agree to sign a contract that would commit the players to implement (x_1, y_2) since it gives him a payoff 0. Player 1 can always guarantee himself a payoff of 1 by not signing anything and simply choosing y_1. We now investigate which contracts a player would be really interested in signing. In Chapters 6 and 7, we have already seen the notion of a *security level* or *maxmin value* for a player, which is the minimum guaranteed payoff the player can assure himself when the rest of the players are free to play any strategies. The following provides a natural way of defining such a security level:

$$v_i = \max_{\tau_i \in \Delta(S_i)} \min_{s_{N-i} \in S_{N-i}} u_i(\tau_i, s_{N-i})$$

where

$$S_{N-i} = S_{N \setminus \{i\}};\ \ s_{N-i} \in S_{N-i}.$$

The expected utility $u_i(\tau_i, s_{N-i})$ is given by:

$$u_i(\tau_i, s_{N-i}) = \sum_{s_i \in S_i} \tau_i(s_i) u_i(s_i, s_{N-i}).$$

For example, in the modified prisoner's dilemma problem (Figure 25.1), $v_1 = v_2 = 1$.

Individually Rational Correlated Strategy

It is reasonable for player i to sign a contract to play a correlated strategy α only if $u_i(\alpha) \geq v_i$. This is called the *individual rationality* or *participation* constraint for player i. This leads to the following definition.

Definition 25.3 (Individually Rational Correlated Strategy). *A correlated strategy*

$$\alpha \in \Delta(S_1 \times \cdots \times S_n)$$

for all the players in N is said to be individually rational *if*

$$u_i(\alpha) \geq v_i\ \ \forall i \in N.$$

It can be shown, using a two player zero-sum game interpretation of the above situation, that the security level v_i also satisfies

$$v_i = \min_{\tau_{N-i} \in \Delta(S_{N-i})} \max_{s_i \in S_i} u_i(s_i, \tau_{N-i})$$

where

$$\tau_{N-i} = \tau_{N \setminus \{i\}} \in \Delta(S_{N-i}).$$

The expected utility $u_i(s_i, \tau_{N-i})$ is given by

$$u_i(s_i, \tau_{N-i}) = \sum_{s_{N-i} \in S_{N-i}} \tau_{N-i}(s_{N-i}) u_i(s_i, s_{N-i}).$$

v_i is the best expected payoff that player i is guaranteed to get against any correlated strategy that the other players could use against player i. A *minmax correlated strategy* against player i is any correlated strategy $\tau_{N-i} \in \Delta(S_{N-i})$ of the rest of the players which forces the payoff of player i to be equal to his minmax value v_i.

Equilibria of the Contract Signing Game

Suppose the players make their decisions about which contract to sign independently. Then, the following proposition holds.

Proposition 25.1. *Given any individually rational correlated strategy α, there exists a contract τ with $\tau_N = \alpha$ such that all players signing this contract is a Nash equilibrium of the contract signing game.*

Proof: Let $\alpha \in \Delta(S)$ be an individually rational correlated strategy. That is

$$u_i(\alpha) \geq v_i \ \forall i \in N$$

Consider the contract $\tau = (\tau_C)_{C \subseteq N}$ such that $\tau_N = \alpha$ and τ_{N-i} is a minmax strategy against player i. τ_C for all other coalitions (that is, coalitions other than $N, N-1, \ldots, N-n$) could be chosen arbitrarily. Let $(a_1, \ldots, a_n)$ be the profile of contract signing strategies for this contract. Note that this profile corresponds to the situation when all the players sign the contract. Now,

$$u_i(a_1, \ldots, a_n) = u_i(\alpha) \quad \text{(since } \tau_N = \alpha).$$

Therefore, we get for all $i \in N$,

$$u_i(a_1, \ldots, a_n) \geq v_i$$

For any $s_i \in S_i$ such that $s_i \neq a_i$, note that the profile (s_i, a_{-i}) corresponds to the situation when player i plays s_i and the rest of the players sign the contract. We have,

$$u_i(s_i, a_{-i}) = u_i(s_i, \tau_{N-i}) \leq v_i$$

since τ_{N-i} is a minmax strategy against player i. Therefore,

$$u_i(a_i, a_{-i}) \geq u_i(s_i, a_{-i}) \ \forall s_i \in S_i \ \forall i \in N$$

Thus $(a_1, a_2, \ldots, a_n)$ is a Nash equilibrium of the contract signing game. ∎

Thus any individually rational correlated strategy $\alpha \in \Delta(S)$ will lead to a contract such that all players signing the contract is a Nash equilibrium of the contract signing game. It also turns out that in any Nash equilibrium of a contract signing game, the expected payoffs for players would be at least their respective security levels. This is stated in the next proposition.

Proposition 25.2. *Consider any Nash equilibrium (s_i^*, s_{-i}^*) of a contract signing game induced by a correlated strategy α. Then, $u_i(s_i^*, s_{-i}^*) \geq v_i \; \forall i \in N$.*

Proof: Consider any Nash equilibrium (s_i^*, s_{-i}^*) of a contract signing game and suppose $u_i(s_i^*, s_{-i}^*) < v_i$ for some player i. Now player i can decide not to sign the contract and instead play the strategy that guarantees him the minmax value v_i. This immediately provides the contradiction. ∎

Following the two propositions above, it is clear that

$$\{u(\alpha) : \alpha \in \Delta(S) \text{ and } u_i(\alpha) \geq v_i \; \forall i \in N\}$$

is exactly the set of payoff allocations that can be achieved in Nash equilibria of the contract signing game when every player has the option to sign nothing and choose an action in S_i. This set is also the set of expected payoff allocations corresponding to individually rational correlated strategies. This set can be shown to be *closed and convex*.

Example 25.5 (Payoff Allocations in the Modified Prisoner's Dilemma).
Consider the modified prisoner's dilemma game with payoff matrix as in Figure 25.1. The expected payoff in a correlated strategy is a convex combination of the payoffs in different strategy profiles and hence the set of all payoff allocations for the above game is the convex set with extreme points $(0, 6)$, $(6, 0)$, and $(1, 1)$. See Figure 25.4. Note that this set is also closed and that the point $(2, 2)$ is in the interior of this convex set. The set of possible expected payoff allocations satisfying individual rationality is the triangle with corners at $(1, 1)$, $(5, 1)$, and $(1, 5)$ as shown. This is because $v_1 = 1$ and $v_2 = 1$ for this example. Note that this set is also closed and convex. □

25.3 Games with Communication

We have so far seen how contracts can transform a game with less desirable equilibria to a game with more desirable equilibria. However, in many situations, players may not be able to commit themselves to binding contracts. The reasons for this could be many [1]:

- Player's strategies may not be observable to the enforcers of contracts.
- There may not be adequate sanctions to guarantee compliance with contracts.

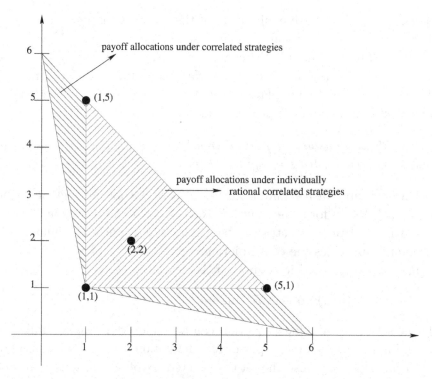

Fig. 25.4: Payoff allocation vectors under correlated strategies for the modified prisoner's dilemma problem

- Player's strategies might actually involve inalienable rights (that is, players may not be able to transfer their rights).

In these above situations also, it may still be possible for the players to communicate and coordinate among themselves, and achieve a self-enforcing equilibrium with desirable payoff structures. Such games correspond to *games with communication*. A game with communication is one, in which, in addition to the strategy options explicitly specified, the players have a range of implicit options to communicate with each other. A game with communication need not have any contracts. Such a game may still achieve interesting results in spite of contracts being absent.

Example 25.6 (A Game with Communication). Consider a two player game having the payoff matrix shown in Figure 25.5. Clearly, this game has three Nash equilibria.

- (x_1, x_2) with payoff allocation $(5, 1)$
- (y_1, y_2) with allocation $(1, 5)$
- Mixed strategy Nash equilibrium $((\frac{1}{2}, \frac{1}{2}), (\frac{1}{2}, \frac{1}{2}))$ which yields the outcome $(2.5, 2.5)$.

Note that (y_1, x_2) is not a Nash equilibrium though it is clearly a desirable outcome. It can be realized through a binding contract. However, if contracts cannot be used, we are not sure whether we can achieve the payoff profile $94, 4)$ or even anything better than

	2	
1	x_2	y_2
x_1	5, 1	0, 0
y_1	4, 4	1, 5

Fig. 25.5: A two player game to illustrate games with communication

(2.5, 2.5). It turns out that correlated strategies exist that achieve a better allocation than (2.5, 2.5) as shown by the following example. ☐

Example 25.7 (Correlated Strategy 1). Let us say players choose to toss a coin and select the outcome (x_1, x_2) with probability $\frac{1}{2}$ and the outcome (y_1, y_2) with probability $\frac{1}{2}$. This refers to the following correlated strategy

$$\alpha = \left((x_1, x_2); \frac{1}{2}; (x_1, y_2) : 0; (y_1, x_2) : 0; (y_1, y_2) : \frac{1}{2} \right)$$

Note that $u_1(\alpha) = u_2(\alpha) = 3$. To implement this correlated strategy, players can toss a coin and choose the outcome (x_1, x_2) in the event of a *heads* and choose the outcome (y_1, y_2) in the event of a *tails*. In order to implement this, communication and coordination are required. The outcome suggested by this correlated strategy will be *self-enforcing* since neither player will gain by unilaterally deviating from this.

The above correlated strategy can also be implemented with the help of a trusted mediator who helps the players to communicate and share information: the mediator recommends, randomly, with probability 0.5 each the profiles (x_1, x_2) and (y_1, y_2). Assume that each player comes to know only the strategy recommended to him by the mediator.

- Player 1, if recommended x_1 by the mediator thinks that player 2 is recommended x_2. Believing that player 2 obeys the recommendation x_2, player 1 finds it a best response to choose x_1 and thus accepts the mediator's recommendation.
- Player 1, if recommended y_1 by the mediator thinks that player 2 is recommended y_2. Believing that player 2 obeys the recommendation y_2, player 1 finds it a best response to choose y_1 and again accepts the mediator's recommendation.
- Player 2, if recommended x_2 by the mediator thinks that player 1 is recommended x_1. Believing that player 1 obeys the recommendation x_1, player 2 finds it a best response to choose x_2 and thus accepts the mediator's recommendation.
- Player 2, if recommended y_2 by the mediator thinks that player 1 is recommended y_1. Believing that player 1 obeys the recommendation y_1, player 2 finds it a best response to choose y_2 and again accepts the mediator's recommendation.

Thus mediation can also be used to implement the above correlated strategy. ☐

Example 25.8 (Correlated Strategy 2). We now explore a different correlated strategy that can be realized with the help of a mediator. Consider the correlated strategy

$$\alpha = \left((x_1, x_2) : \frac{1}{3}; (x_1, y_2) : 0; (y_1, x_2) : \frac{1}{3}; (y_1, y_2) : \frac{1}{3} \right)$$

Note that $u_1(\alpha) = u_2(\alpha) = \frac{10}{3}$. To implement this correlated strategy, the mediator recommends, randomly, with probability $\frac{1}{3}$, each of the profiles $(x_1, x_2), (y_1, y_2), (y_1, x_2)$. Again assume that each player comes to know only the strategy recommended to him by the mediator.

- Suppose the mediator recommends x_1 to player 1. Then player 1 knows that player 2 is recommended x_2. When player 2 plays x_2 (as recommended by the mediator), it is a best response for player 1 to play x_1, so he would be happy to play x_1 and thus accept the recommendation of the mediator.
- Suppose the mediator recommends y_1 to player 1. Then player 1 knows that the mediator would recommend the mixed strategy $x_2 : 0.5; y_2 : 0.5$ to player 2. When player 2 plays the above mixed strategy, then player 1 gets a payoff of 2.5 if he plays x_1 and gets a payoff of 2.5 even if he plays y_1. Thus player 1 can be indifferent between x_1 and y_1 and will not mind accepting the recommendation of the mediator to play y_1.

The above shows that player 1 would be happy to follow the recommendation of the mediator if player 1 expected player 2 also to follow the recommendation of the mediator.

Similarly, it can be shown that player 2 would be happy to do as recommended by the mediator under the belief that player 1 would do as recommended by the mediator.

The above shows that the two players can reach a self-enforcing understanding to obey the mediator if the mediator recommends the correlated strategy

$$\left((x_1, x_2) : \frac{1}{3}; \ (x_1, y_2) : 0; \ (y_1, x_2) : \frac{1}{3}; \ (y_1, y_2) : \frac{1}{3} \right)$$

In other words, even though the mediator's recommendation is not binding on the two players, the two players find it in their best interest to follow it. Thus there is a Nash equilibrium of the transformed game with mediated communication without contracts. This is the idea behind the notion of *correlated equilibrium* which is discussed next. □

25.4 Correlated Equilibrium

Consider the following setup of a game with communication. Let $\Gamma = \langle N, (S_i), (u_i) \rangle$ be any finite strategic form game. Assume that there is a mediator who chooses a pure strategy profile $(s_1, \ldots, s_n)$ according to a probability distribution $\alpha \in \Delta(S)$ which is common knowledge among the players. The observer recommends to player i $(i = 1, \ldots, n)$ the pure strategy s_i but does not reveal s_{-i} to player i. Based on the recommendation, the player either obeys it or chooses any other strategy from his strategy set S_i. Let $\delta_i : S_i \to S_i$ describe player i's choice of a strategy based on the mediator's recommendation. That is, $\delta_i(s_i)$ gives the strategy that the player i chooses to play when the mediator recommends s_i to him. $\delta_i(s_i) = s_i$ means that the player i obeys the mediator when the mediator recommends s_i.

Definition 25.4 (Correlated Equilibrium). *Given a finite strategic form game* $\Gamma = \langle N, (S_i), (u_i) \rangle$, *a correlated strategy* $\alpha \in \Delta(S)$ *recommended by a mediator is called a correlated equilibrium if*

$$u_i(\alpha) \geq \sum_{(s_i, s_{-i}) \in S} \alpha(s_i, s_{-i}) \ u_i(\delta_i(s_i), s_{-i}) \ \forall \delta_i : S_i \to S_i \ \forall i \in N. \tag{25.1}$$

Note that when a correlated equilibrium is recommended, every player finds it a best response to obey the recommendation of the mediator. Thus a correlated equilibrium is any correlated strategy for the players which could be self-enforcingly implemented with the help of a mediator who can make non-binding recommendations to each player.

Computing Correlated Equilibria

It can be shown that the inequalities (25.1) are equivalent to the following set of inequalities.

$$\sum_{s_{-i} \in S_{-i}} \alpha(s)[u_i(s_i, s_{-i}) - u_i(s'_i, s_{-i})] \geq 0 \quad \forall s_i \in S_i; \; \forall s'_i \in S_i; \; \forall i \in N. \quad (25.2)$$

The equivalence can be shown by fixing s_i and unfolding the original inequalities (left as an exercise). Equation (25.2) asserts that no player i could expect to increase his expected payoff by using some disobedient action s'_i when the mediator recommends s_i. The constraints (25.2) are called *strategic incentive constraints*. They are the constraints to be satisfied by a mediator's correlated strategy for ensuring that all players could rationally obey the recommendations. It can also be noted that

$$\alpha(s) \geq 0, \; \forall s \in S$$
$$\sum_{s \in S} \alpha(s) = 1$$

Note. It can be shown that the set of all payoff allocations under correlated equilibria in a finite game is a *compact and convex* set. Recall that the set of all payoff allocations under correlated strategies as well as the set of payoff allocations under individually rational correlated strategies are also compact and convex.

Let us look at the following linear program:

$$\max \sum_{i \in N} u_i(\alpha)$$

subject to

$$\sum_{s_{-i} \in S_{-i}} \alpha(s) \left[u_i(s_i, s_{-i}) - u_i(s'_i, s_{-i}) \right] \geq 0 \quad \forall i \in N \; \forall s_i \in S_i \; \forall s'_i \in S_i$$

$$\alpha(s) \geq 0 \; \forall s \in S$$
$$\sum_{s \in S} \alpha(s) = 1$$

Any feasible solution of this linear program will give a correlated equilibrium. An optimal solution of this linear program will give a correlated equilibrium that maximizes the social welfare.

Example 25.9 (Computation of correlated equilibria). Consider the game shown in Figure 25.5. The linear program here is:

maximize $6\,\alpha(x_1, x_2) + 0\,\alpha(x_1, y_2) + 8\,\alpha(y_1, x_2) + 6\,\alpha(y_1, y_2)$ subject to

$$(5-4)\,\alpha\,(x_1, x_2) + (0-1)\,\alpha\,(x_1, y_2) \geq 0$$
$$(4-5)\,\alpha\,(y_1, x_2) + (1-0)\,\alpha\,(y_1, y_2) \geq 0$$
$$(1-0)\,\alpha\,(x_1, x_2) + (4-5)\,\alpha\,(y_1, x_2) \geq 0$$
$$(0-1)\,\alpha\,(x_1, y_2) + (5-4)\,\alpha\,(y_1, y_2) \geq 0$$
$$\alpha\,(x_1, x_2) + \,\alpha\,(x_1, y_2) + \alpha\,(y_1, x_2) + \alpha\,(y_1, y_2) = 1$$

This yields the solution

$$\alpha\,(x_1, x_2) = \frac{1}{3};\ \alpha\,(y_1, x_2) = \frac{1}{3};\ \alpha\,(y_1, y_2) = \frac{1}{3};\ \alpha(x_1, y_2) = 0$$

This shows that the above correlated strategy yields the maximum total payoff to the two players. The above also shows that the sum of expected payoffs cannot exceed $6\frac{2}{3}$ under non-binding mediated communication scenario.

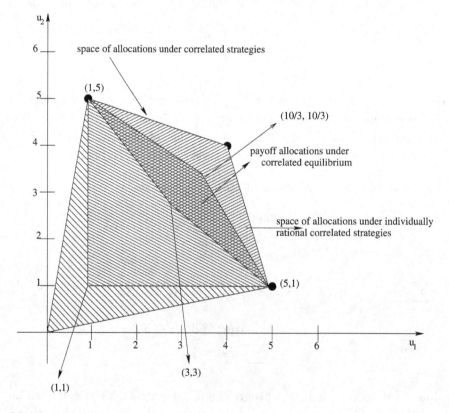

Fig. 25.6: Payoff allocation vectors under correlated strategies and correlated equilibria

Figure 25.6 shows the sets of all payoff allocations for this example under correlated strategies (convex hull with corner points $(0,0),(1,5),(5,1),(4,4)$), under individually rational correlated strategies (convex hull with corner points $(1,1),(1,5),(5,1),(4,4)$) , and under correlated equilibria (convex hull with corner points $(1,5),(5,1),(3,3),(\frac{10}{3},\frac{10}{3})$). $\square$

We can now ask the following question: Can we select a small number of (perhaps a single) desirable or best outcomes among the above sets. For two player games, this issue was settled by the Nash bargaining theorem which we discuss in the next chapter. For multi-player games (including two player games), a variety of solution concepts have been suggested: The core, Shapley value, bargaining sets, nucleolus, etc. We will be studying these in the other following chapters.

25.5 Summary and References

The key learnings from this chapter include the following.

- Games with contracts and games with communication provide different ways of modeling cooperation among players. Contracts and communication transform games with less desirable equilibria to games with more desirable equilibria. Correlated strategies provide the framework for defining games with contracts and games with communication.

- Given a coalition of players, a correlated strategy of the players is a probability distribution on the space of strategy profiles of these players. A correlated strategy captures cooperation among the players in that coalition. A correlated strategy also enables to express the fact that the choice of pure strategies by players may be correlated since they might be observing the same or similar random events in deciding which pure strategies to play.

- A correlated strategy of the grand coalition is said to be individually rational if the expected payoff for each player under this correlated strategy is at least the security value or minmax value of the player. An individually rational correlated strategy induces a Nash equilibrium in the contract signing game.

- A correlated equilibrium is a correlated strategy of the grand coalition which leads to all players self-enforcingly obeying the recommendations of a mediator who implements the correlated strategy.

- The set of all correlated equilibria could be computed as feasible solutions of a linear program. Using this linear program, we can also compute correlated equilibria that maximize social welfare.

- The following sets of payoff allocations are convex and closed. (1) Set of all payoff allocations under correlated strategies (2) Set of all payoff allocations under individually rational correlated strategies which is the same as the set of allocations under Nash equilibria of contract signing games (3) Set of all payoff allocations under correlated equilibria.

The material discussed in this chapter draws upon mainly from the book by Myerson [1]. The concept of correlated equilibrium was first introduced by Robert Aumann [2]. There are many recent papers on efficient algorithms for computing correlated equilibria. The reader is referred to the book by Chalkiadakis, Elkind, and Wooldridge [3]. For an excellent detailed treatment of correlated strategies and correlated equilibria, we refer the reader to the books by Peleg and Sudholter [4] and Maschler, Solan, and Zamir [5].

References

[1]   Roger B. Myerson. *Game Theory: Analysis of Conflict*. Harvard University Press, Cambridge, Massachusetts, USA, 1997.

[2]   Robert J. Aumann. "Subjectivity and correlation in randomized strategies". In: *Journal of Mathematical Economics* **1** (1974), pp. 67–95.

[3]   Georgios Chalkiadakis, Edith Elkind, and Michael Wooldridge. *Computational Aspects of Cooperative Game Theory*. Morgan & Claypool, 2011.

[4]   B. Peleg and P. Sudholter. *Introduction to the Theory of Cooperative Games*. Kluwer Academic, Boston, USA, 2003.

[5]   Michael Maschler, Eilon Solan, and Shmuel Zamir. *Game Theory*. Cambridge University Press, 2013.

25.6   Exercises

(1) Given a strategic form game and a mixed strategy profile σ, find a correlated strategy α such that $u_i(\alpha) = u_i(\sigma) \ \forall i \in N$.

(2) Suppose $(\sigma_1^*, \ldots, \sigma_n^*)$ is a mixed strategy Nash equilibrium of a strategic form game $\Gamma = \langle N, (S_i), (u_i) \rangle$. Define a correlated strategy induced by the above equilibrium:

$$\alpha(s_1, \ldots, s_n) = \sigma_1^*(s_1) \ldots \sigma_n^*(s_n); \ \ \forall s_i \in S_i \ \forall i = 1, \ldots, n.$$

Show that such a correlated strategy is a correlated equilibrium.

(3) If α is a correlated equilibrium of a strategic form game, show that $u_i(\alpha)$ is equal to the maxmin value of i for each $i = 1, \ldots, n$.

(4) If α is a correlated equilibrium of a matrix game, show that $u_1(\alpha)$ is equal to the value in mixed strategies of the game.

(5) Give a simple example of a strategic form game such that the space of all payoff profiles achievable under mixed strategy profiles is the same as the space of all payoff profiles achievable under correlated strategies.

(6) Give a simple example of a strategic form game such that the space of all payoff profiles achievable under mixed strategy profiles is a strict subset of the space of all payoff profiles achievable under correlated strategies.

(7) Given a strategic form game, define the minmax value under correlated strategies

as:

$$v_i = \min_{\tau_{N-i} \in \Delta(S_{N-i})} \max_{s_i \in S_i} u_i(s_i, \tau_{N-i})$$

Show, using a two player zero-sum game interpretation of the above game, that the value v_i also satisfies

$$v_i = \max_{\tau_i \in \Delta(S_i)} \min_{s_{N-i} \in S_{N-i}} u_i(\tau_i, s_{N-i})$$

where

$$u_i(\tau_i, s_{N-i}) = \sum_{s_i \in S_i} \tau_i(s_i) u_i(s_i, s_{N-i})$$

(8) Given a finite strategic form game, show that the following sets are closed and convex.

- The space of all payoff allocations achievable under correlated strategies
- The space of all payoff allocations achievable under individually rational correlated strategies
- The space of all payoff allocations achievable under correlated equilibria

(9) Show the equivalence of the set of inequalities presented in equation (25.2) and the set of inequalities presented in equation (25.1).

(10) Compute all correlated equilibria of

1	2	
	x_2	y_2
x_1	2, 2	0, 6
y_1	6, 0	1, 1

1	2	
	x_2	y_2
x_1	2, 2	0, 0
y_1	0, 0	1, 1

(11) Consider the following two player game:

	A	B
A	5, 5	1, 1
B	1, 1	3, 3

For this game,

- compute the set of all payoff utility pairs possible (a) under correlated strategies (b) under individually rational correlated strategies.
- compute all correlated equilibria that maximize the sum of utilities of the two players.

(12) Consider the following two player game:

	A	B
A	4, 1	0, 0
B	3, 3	1, 4

For the above game, compute:

- the space of all payoff allocations under mixed strategy profiles
- the space of all payoff allocations under mixed strategy Nash equilibria
- the space of all payoff allocations under correlated strategies
- the space of all payoff allocations under individually rational correlated strategies
- the space of all payoff allocations under correlated equilibria

(13) Suppose $\sigma^* = (\sigma_1^*, \ldots, \sigma_n^*)$ is a mixed strategy Nash equilibrium of a strategic form game. Consider the correlated strategy $\alpha_{\sigma^*} \in \Delta(S)$ defined by

$$\alpha_{\sigma^*}(s_1, \ldots, s_n) = \sigma_1^*(s_1) \times \cdots \times \sigma_n^*(s_n).$$

Show that the above correlated strategy is a correlated equilibrium.

(14) **Programming Assignment.** Computing correlated equilibria of a finite strategic form game is an important computational problem. We have shown that these can be computed as feasible solutions of a linear program. Design and develop a program to compute correlated equilibria and welfare maximizing correlated equilibria. Also, compute the spaces of allocations under correlated strategies, under individually rational correlated strategies, and under correlated equilibria.

Chapter 26

The Two Person Bargaining Problem

The Nash bargaining theory, based on the brilliant work of John Nash, represents one of the earliest and most influential results in cooperative game theory. Given two rational and intelligent players and a set of feasible allocations from among which a unique allocation is to be chosen, the Nash bargaining theory proposes an elegant axiomatic approach to solve the problem. This chapter sets up the problem, presents the axioms of Nash bargaining theory, and provides a proof of the Nash bargaining result.

26.1 Nash Program

Cooperation refers to coalitions of two or more players acting together with a specific common purpose in mind. Since rationality and intelligence are two fundamental assumptions in game theory, any cooperation between players must take into account the objective of maximizing their own individual payoffs. As we have seen in the previous chapter, the notion of cooperation which is closely tied with the notion of correlated strategies can be developed without abandoning the basic tenets underlying non-cooperative game theory. This has been emphasized by John Nash himself [1, 2]. According to Nash, cooperative actions can be considered as the culmination of a certain process of bargaining among the cooperating players and consequently, cooperation between players can be studied using core concepts of non-cooperative game theory. In this bargaining process, we can expect each player to behave according to some bargaining strategy that satisfies the original utility maximization criterion as in standard non-cooperative game theory.

The ingenious idea of Nash is to define a *cooperative transformation* that will transform a strategic form game into another strategic form game that has an extended strategy space for each player. The extended strategy set for a player has all the strategies of the original game and also additional strategies that capture bargaining with the other players to jointly plan cooperative strategies. This is on the lines of what we have studied in the previous chapter on games with contracts and games with communication. We will illustrate this with the standard example of the prisoner's dilemma problem which provides a classic example for illustrating the benefits of cooperation.

	NC	C
NC	$-2, -2$	$-10, -1$
C	$-1, -10$	$-5, -5$

Clearly, the rationality of the players suggests the equilibrium (C, C) which is obviously not an optimal option for the players. The two players here have a strong incentive to bargain with each other or sign a contract to transform this game into one which has equilibria that are better for both the players. The concept of a *Nash program* for cooperative game theory is to define cooperative solution concepts such that a cooperative solution for any given game is a Nash equilibrium of some co-operative transformation of the original non-cooperative game. The notion of Nash program was introduced by Nash in his classic paper [2]. If we carefully describe all the possibilities that are feasible when the players bargain or sign contracts with each other, we may end up with a game that has numerous equilibria. This means the Nash program may not lead to a unique cooperative solution. This means that we should have a sound theory of cooperative equilibrium selection. This is what the Nash bargaining theory offers in an axiomatic and rigorous, but in a highly intuitive way.

26.2   The Two Person Bargaining Problem

According to Nash, the term *bargaining* refers to a situation in which

- two individuals have the possibility of concluding a mutually beneficial agreement
- there is a conflict of interest about which agreement to conclude
- no agreement may be imposed on any player without that player's approval.

The following assumptions are implicit in Nash's formulation: when two players negotiate or an impartial mediator arbitrates, the payoff allocations that the two players ultimately get should depend only on:

- the payoffs they would expect if the negotiation or arbitration were to fail to reach a settlement, and
- the set of payoff allocations that are jointly feasible for the two players in the process of negotiation or arbitration.

The two person bargaining problem has been applied in many important contexts including:

- *Management labor arbitration* where the management negotiates contracts with the labor union
- *International relations*, where two nations or two groups of nations work out agreements on issues such as nuclear disarmament, military cooperation, anti-terrorist strategy, bilateral emission control initiatives, etc.

- *Duopoly market games* where two major competing companies work out adjustments on their production to mutually maximize their profits
- *Bilateral trade situations* where a buyer and seller engage in bargaining over the trade
- *Supply chain contracts* where a buyer and a supplier work out a mutually beneficial contract that facilitates a long-term relationship
- *Negotiation protocols* in multiagent systems
- *Property settlement disputes* between corporations or individuals

The Bargaining Problem

The two person bargaining problem consists of a pair (F, v) where F is called the feasible set and v is called the disagreement point.

- F, the feasible set of allocations, is a closed, convex subset of $\mathbb{R}^2$.
- The disagreement point $v = (v_1, v_2) \in \mathbb{R}^2$ represents the disagreement payoff allocation for the two players. It is also called the *status-quo point* or the *default point* or *de facto point*. This gives the payoffs for the two players in the event that the negotiations fail. It may be noted that v is invariably chosen to belong to the feasible set F.
- The set $F \cap \{(x_1, x_2) \in \mathbb{R}^2 : x_1 \geq v_1; x_2 \geq v_2\}$ is assumed to be non-empty and bounded.

Rationale Behind the Assumptions

- Convexity of F: This has the following rationale. It is reasonable for the two players to agree to correlated strategies. Consequently, if the utility allocations $x = (x_1, x_2)$ and $y = (y_1, y_2)$ are feasible and $0 \leq \lambda \leq 1$, then the expected utility allocation $\lambda x + (1 - \lambda)y$ can be achieved by planning to implement a correlated strategy which assigns probability λ to $x = (x_1, x_2)$ and probability $(1 - \lambda)$ to $y = (y_1, y_2)$.
- Closedness of F: This means any convergent sequence in F will converge to a point that belongs to F. It would be strange if we have a sequence of allocations belonging to F and the limiting allocation does not belong to F. In fact, without this assumption, it may happen that there may not exist a solution to the bargaining problem since the limit of a sequence may not be in F. Closedness of F is therefore a natural topological requirement.
- The third assumption is the set $F \cap \{(x_1, x_2) \in \mathbb{R}^2 : x_1 \geq v_1, x_2 \geq v_2\}$ is non-empty and bounded. This assumption implies that (a) there exists some feasible allocation that is at least as good as the disagreement point for both players, however (b) unbounded gains over the disagreement point are not possible. Both these requirements are clearly reasonable.

Connection to Two Player Non-Cooperative Games

Suppose $\Gamma = \langle \{1,2\}, S_1, S_2, u_1, u_2 \rangle$ is a two person strategic form game. If the strategies of the players can be regulated by binding contracts, then one possibility for the feasible set F is the set of all allocations under correlated strategies:

$$F = \{(u_1(\alpha), u_2(\alpha)) : \alpha \in \Delta(S_1 \times S_2)\} \quad \text{where}$$

$$u_i(\alpha) = \sum_{s \in S} \alpha(s) u_i(s)$$

We could also choose the set of allocations under individually rational correlated strategies (recall that the payoffs for players under individually rational correlated strategies will be at least the respective minmax values). If the players' strategies cannot be regulated by binding contracts then a possibility for F would be the set of all allocations under correlated equilibria:

$$F = \{(u_1(\alpha), u_2(\alpha)) : \alpha \text{ is a correlated equilibrium of } \Gamma\}$$

There are several possibilities for the disagreement point v. The first possibility is to let v_i be the minmax value for player i.

$$v_1 = \min_{\sigma_2 \in \Delta(S_2)} \max_{\sigma_1 \in \Delta(S_1)} u_1(\sigma_1, \sigma_2)$$

$$v_2 = \min_{\sigma_1 \in \Delta(S_1)} \max_{\sigma_2 \in \Delta(S_2)} u_2(\sigma_1, \sigma_2)$$

The above choice is quite reasonable and scientific because the minmax value for a player is the minimum guaranteed payoff to the player even in a strictly competitive setting where the other player always tries to hurt this player the most.

A second possibility is to choose some focal Nash equilibrium (σ_1^*, σ_2^*) of Γ and let

$$v_1 = u_1(\sigma_1^*, \sigma_2^*); \quad v_2 = u_2(\sigma_1^*, \sigma_2^*)$$

A focal Nash equilibrium is one which becomes a natural choice for the players due to some external factors prevailing at the time of allocation.

A third possibility is to derive $v = (v_1, v_2)$ from some *rational threats*. The theory of rational threats has been proposed using rationality-based arguments and the reader is referred to the book by Myerson [3] for more details.

A sound theory of negotiation or arbitration must allow us to identify, given any bargaining problem (F, v), a unique allocation vector in $\mathbb{R}^2$ that would be selected as a result of negotiation or arbitration. Let us denote this unique allocation by $f(F, v)$. Thus the bargaining problem involves finding an appropriate solution function $f(.)$ from the set of all two-person bargaining problems into $\mathbb{R}^2$, which is the set of payoff allocations.

26.3 The Nash Axioms

John Nash used a brilliant axiomatic approach to solve this problem. He first came up with a list of properties an ideal bargaining solution function is expected to satisfy and then proved that there exists a unique solution that satisfies all of these properties. The following are the five axioms of Nash:

(1) Strong Efficiency
(2) Individual Rationality
(3) Scale Covariance
(4) Independence of Irrelevant Alternatives (IIA)
(5) Symmetry

Let us use the notation $f(F, v) = (f_1(F, v), f_2(F, v))$ to denote the Nash bargaining solution for the bargaining problem (F, v).

Axiom 1: Strong Efficiency

Given a feasible set F, we say an allocation $x = (x_1, x_2) \in F$ is *strongly Pareto efficient* or simply *strongly efficient* iff there exists no other point $y = (y_1, y_2) \in F$ such that $y_1 \geq x_1$; $y_2 \geq x_2$ with strict inequality satisfied for at least one player. An allocation $x = (x_1, x_2) \in F$ is *weakly Pareto efficient* or *weakly efficient* iff there exists no other point $y = (y_1, y_2) \in F$ such that $y_1 > x_1$; $y_2 > x_2$.

The strong efficiency axiom asserts that the solution to any two person bargaining problem should be feasible and strongly Pareto efficient. Formally, $f(F, v) \in F$ and there does not exist any $x = (x_1, x_2) \in F$ such that $x_1 \geq f_1(F, v)$; $x_2 \geq f_2(F, v)$ with $x_i > f_i(F, v)$ for at least some $i \in \{1, 2\}$. This implies that there should be no other feasible allocation that is better than the solution for one player and not worse than the solution for the other player.

Axiom 2: Individual Rationality

This axiom states that $f(F, v) \geq v$ which implies that $f_1(F, v) \geq v_1$; $f_2(F, v) \geq v_2$. This means, neither player should get less in the bargaining solution than he/she could get in disagreement. Figure 26.1 illustrates Axioms 1 and 2.

Axiom 3: Scale Covariance

This axiom is stated as follows. For any numbers $\lambda_1, \lambda_2, \mu_1, \mu_2$ with $\lambda_1 > 0$, $\lambda_2 > 0$, define the set $G = \{(\lambda_1 x_1 + \mu_1, \lambda_2 x_2 + \mu_2 : (x_1, x_2) \in F\}$ and the point $w = (\lambda_1 v_1 + \mu_1, \lambda_2 v_2 + \mu_2)$. Then the solution $f(G, w)$ for the problem (G, w) is given by

$$f(G, w) = (\lambda_1 f_1(F, v) + \mu_1, \lambda_2 f_2(F, v) + \mu_2)$$

In the above, the bargaining problem (G, w) can be derived from (F, v) by applying an affine utility transformations which will not affect relevant properties of the utility

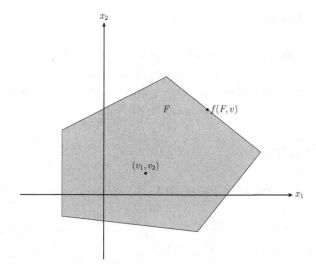

Fig. 26.1: Illustrating strong efficiency and individual rationality

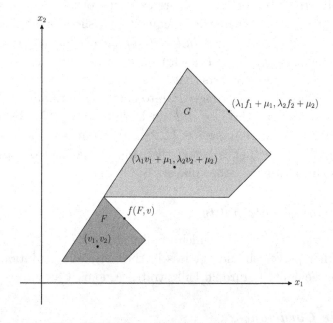

Fig. 26.2: Illustration of scale covariance

functions. The axiom implies that the solution of (G, w) can be derived from that of (F, v) by the same transformation. Figure 26.2 illustrates this axiom.

Axiom 4: Independence of Irrelevant Alternatives

This axiom states that, for any closed convex set G,

$$G \subseteq F \text{ and } f(F, v) \in G \Longrightarrow f(G, v) = f(F, v)$$

The axiom asserts that eliminating feasible alternatives (other than the disagreement point) that would not have been chosen should not affect the solution. The eliminated alternatives are referred to as irrelevant alternatives. This axiom is illustrated in Figure 26.3. If a mediator or referee were to select a solution by maximizing some aggregate measure of social gain, that is,

$$f(F, v) = \max_{x \in F} M(x, v)$$

where $M(x, v)$ is a measure of social gain by choosing x instead of v, then Axiom 4 can be shown to be always satisfied.

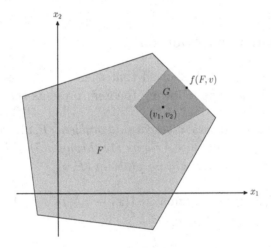

Fig. 26.3: Independence of irrelevant alternatives

Axiom 5: Symmetry

This axiom asserts that if the positions of players 1 and 2 are completely symmetric in the bargaining problem, then the solution should also treat them symmetrically. Formally,

$$v_1 = v_2 \text{ and } \{(x_2, x_1) : (x_1, x_2) \in F\} = F \Longrightarrow f_1(F, v) = f_2(F, v)$$

This axiom is illustrated in Figure 26.4.

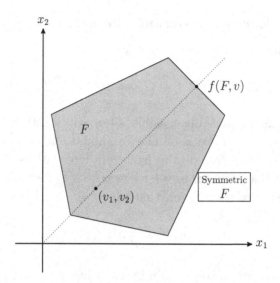

Fig. 26.4: Illustration of symmetry

26.4 The Nash Bargaining Solution

Using ingenious arguments, Nash showed that there exists a unique solution that
satisfies all the five axioms. The following theorem presents the solution.

Theorem 26.1. *Given a two person bargaining problem (F, v), there exists a unique
solution function $f(.,.)$ that satisfies Axioms (1) through (5). The solution function
satisfies, for every two person bargaining problem (F, v),*

$$f(F, v) \in \underset{\substack{(x_1, x_2) \in F \\ x_1 \geq v_1; x_2 \geq v_2}}{\operatorname{argmax}} \left((x_1 - v_1)(x_2 - v_2)\right)$$

An Illustrative Example

Figure 26.5 shows a closed convex set F which is actually the convex hull enclosing
the points $(4, 0)$, $(1, 1)$, and $(0, 4)$. Suppose F is the feasible set and $(1, 1)$ is the
default point. It can be shown that the Nash bargaining solution is $(2, 2)$. This
illustrates Pareto efficiency, individual rationality, and symmetry. We shall define a
new feasible space G obtained by the following scaling: $\lambda_1 = \lambda_2 = \frac{1}{2}$; $\mu_1 = \mu_2 = 1$.
Consider the bargaining problem (G, w) with $w = (\frac{3}{2}, \frac{3}{2})$ that is obtained using
$w = (\lambda_1 v_1 + \mu_1, \ \lambda_2 v_2 + \mu_2)$. Using scale covariance, the Nash bargaining solution
becomes $(2, 2)$. If H is the feasible space obtained using $\lambda_1 = \lambda_2 = \frac{1}{2}$; $\mu_1 = \mu_2 = 0$,
then the problem $(H, (\frac{1}{2}, \frac{1}{2}))$ illustrates another instance of scale covariance.

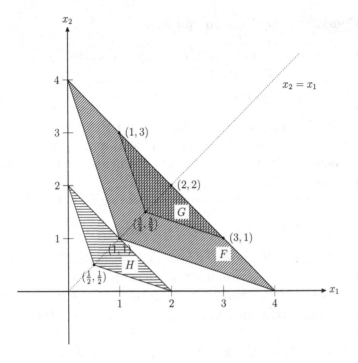

Fig. 26.5: An example to illustrate Nash axioms

26.5 Proof of the Nash Bargaining Theorem

First we prove the theorem for a special class of two person bargaining problems called *essential* bargaining problems and subsequently, we generalize this to the entire class of problems. A two person bargaining problem (F, v) is said to be *essential* if there exists at least one allocation $y \in F$ that is strictly better for both the players than the disagreement allocation v, that is, $y_1 > v_1$ and $y_2 > v_2$.

Proof for Essential Bargaining Problems

We are given an essential two person bargaining problem (F, v). Clearly, there exists some $y = (y_1, y_2) \in F$ such that $y_1 > v_1$ and $y_2 > v_2$.

Recall the definition of a quasiconcave function from Chapter 10: A function $f : S \to \mathbb{R}$ where S is non-empty and convex is said to be quasiconcave if

$$f(\lambda x + (1 - \lambda)y) \geq \min(f(x), f(y)) \ \forall x, y \in S \ \forall \lambda \in [0, 1]$$

f is strictly quasiconcave if

$$f(\lambda x + (1 - \lambda)y) > \min(f(x), f(y)) \ \forall x, y \in S \ x \neq y \ \forall \lambda \in (0, 1)$$

It is known that a strictly quasiconcave function will have a unique optimal solution (maximum). Consider the optimization problem:

$$\max_{\substack{(x_1, x_2) \in F \\ x_1 \geq v_1; x_2 \geq v_2}} \left((x_1 - v_1)(x_2 - v_2) \right)$$

where $(v_1, v_2) \in F$. The function $(x_1 - v_1)(x_2 - v_2)$ is strictly quasiconcave (since we are dealing with an essential bargaining problem) and therefore it has a unique maximizer. Therefore the above optimization problem has a unique optimal solution. Call this solution as (x_1^*, x_2^*).

Let $F \subset \mathbb{R}^2$ be convex and closed. Suppose $v = (v_1, v_2) \in F$ and

$$F \cap \{(x_1, x_2) \in \mathbb{R}^2 : x_1 \geq v_1; x_2 \geq v_2\}$$

is non-empty and bounded. Suppose the function $f(F, v)$ satisfies the five axioms (1) strong efficiency (2) individual rationality (3) scale covariance (4) independence of irrelevant alternatives, and (5) symmetry. Then the Nash bargaining theorem states that $f(F, v) = (x_1^*, x_2^*)$ which happens to be the unique solution of optimization problem above.

The proof of the Nash bargaining theorem proceeds in two parts. In Part 1, we show that the optimal solution (x_1^*, x_2^*) of the optimization problem above satisfies all the five axioms. In Part 2, we show that if $f(F, v)$ satisfies all the five axioms, then $f(F, v) = (x_1^*, x_2^*)$. We use the following notation for the objective function in the rest of this proof:

$$N(x_1, x_2) = (x_1 - v_1)(x_2 - v_2)$$

The objective function is appropriately called the *Nash Product*.

Proof of Part 1

We have to show that the optimal solution (x_1^*, x_2^*) of the optimization problem above satisfies all the five axioms. We do this sequentially.

Strong Efficiency

We have to show that there does not exist $(\hat{x}_1, \hat{x}_2) \in F$ such that $\hat{x}_1 \geq x_1^*$ and $\hat{x}_2 \geq x_2^*$ with at least one inequality strict. Suppose such a $(\hat{x}_1, \hat{x}_2)$ exists. Since there exists a $(y_1, y_2) \in F$ such that $y_1 > v_1$ and $y_2 > v_2$, the maximum value of the Nash product in the optimization problem is strictly greater than zero. Since the objective function $N(x_1, x_2)$ is increasing in x_1 and x_2, we have

$$N(\hat{x}_1, \hat{x}_2) > N(x_1^*, x_2^*)$$

which is not possible since $N(x_1^*, x_2^*)$ is the maximum possible value of $N(x_1, x_2)$ in the optimization problem.

Individual Rationality

This is immediately satisfied, being one of the constraints in the optimization problem.

Scale Covariance

For $\lambda_1 > 0, \lambda_2 > 0, \mu_1, \mu_2$, define

$$G = \{\lambda_1 x_1 + \mu_1, \lambda_2 x_2 + \mu_2) : (x_1, x_2) \in F\}$$

Consider the problem

$$\max_{(y_1, y_2) \in G} (y_1 - (\lambda_1 v_1 + \mu_1))(y_2 - (\lambda_2 v_2 + \mu_2))$$

This can be written using $y_1 = \lambda_1 x_1 + \mu_1$ and $y_2 = \lambda_2 x_2 + \mu_2$ as

$$\max_{(x_1, x_2) \in G} (\lambda_1 x_1 + \mu_1 - (\lambda_1 v_1 + \mu_1))(\lambda_2 x_2 + \mu_2 - (\lambda_2 v_2 + \mu_2))$$

The above problem is the same as

$$\max_{(x_1, x_2) \in G} \lambda_1 \lambda_2 (x_1 - v_1)(x_2 - v_2)$$

which attains maximum at (x_1^*, x_2^*). Therefore the problem

$$\max_{(y_1, y_2) \in G} (y_1 - (\lambda_1 v_1 + \mu_1)) (y_2 - (\lambda_2 v_2 + \mu_2))$$

attains maximum at $(\lambda_1 x_1^* + \mu_1, \lambda_2 x_2^* + \mu_2)$.

Independence of Irrelevant Alternatives

We are given $G \subseteq F$ with G closed and convex. Let (x_1^*, x_2^*) be optimal to (F, v) and let (y_1^*, y_2^*) be optimal to (G, v). It is also given that $(x_1^*, x_2^*) \in G$.

- Since (x_1^*, x_2^*) is optimal to F which is a superset of G, we have

$$N(x_1^*, x_2^*) \geq N(y_1^*, y_2^*)$$

- Since (y_1^*, y_2^*) is optimal to G and $(x_1^*, x_2^*) \in G$, we have

$$N(y_1^*, y_2^*) \geq N(x_1^*, x_2^*)$$

Therefore we have

$$N(x_1^*, x_2^*) = N(y_1^*, y_2^*)$$

Since the optimal solution is unique, we then immediately obtain

$$(x_1^*, x_2^*) = (y_1^*, y_2^*)$$

Symmetry

Suppose we have $\{(x_2, x_1) : (x_1, x_2) \in F\} = F$ and $v_1 = v_2$. Since $v_1 = v_2$, we can use v_1 and v_2 interchangeably. We can therefore say that (x_1^*, x_2^*) maximizes $(x_1 - v_2)(x_2 - v_1)$. Since the optimal solution is unique, we should have $(x_1^*, x_2^*) = (x_2^*, x_1^*)$ which immediately yields $x_1^* = x_2^*$.

Proof of Part 2

We are given that $f(F, v)$ is a bargaining solution that satisfies all the five axioms. We have to show that $f(F, v)$ is the same as (x_1^*, x_2^*) which is the unique solution of the optimization problem:

$$\max \quad ((x_1 - v_1)(x_2 - v_2))$$
$$(x_1, x_2) \in F$$
$$x_1 \geq v_1; x_2 \geq v_2$$

We have that $x_1^* > v_1$ and $x_2^* > v_2$. Consider the following transformation

$$L(x_1, x_2) = (\lambda_1 x_1 + \mu_1, \lambda_2 x_2 + \mu_2)$$

where

$$\lambda_1 = \frac{1}{x_1^* - v_1}; \quad \lambda_2 = \frac{1}{x_2^* - v_2}; \quad \mu_1 = \frac{-v_1}{x_1^* - v_1}; \quad \mu_2 = \frac{-v_2}{x_2^* - v_2}$$

In other words, we have

$$L(x_1, x_2) = \Big(\frac{x_1 - v_1}{x_1^* - v_1}, \; \frac{x_2 - v_2}{x_2^* - v_2}\Big)$$

Note that $L(v_1, v_2) = (0, 0)$ and $L(x_1^*, x_2^*) = (1, 1)$. Defining

$$G = \{L(x_1, x_2) : (x_1, x_2) \in F\},$$

we have thus transformed the problem $(F, (v_1, v_2))$ to the problem $(G, (0, 0))$. In fact, since $L(x_1^*, x_2^*) = (1, 1)$, it is known that the transformed problem $(G, (0, 0))$ has its solution at $(1, 1)$. See Figure 26.6. Also observe that the objective function of the transformed problem is $(x_1 - 0)(x_2 - 0) = x_1 x_2$.

It can be shown that

$$x_1 + x_2 \leq 2 \; \forall (x_1, x_2) \in G$$

To show this, we assume that $x_1 + x_2 > 2$ and we can arrive at a contradiction. We leave this as an exercise.

G is bounded and we can always find a rectangle H which is symmetric about the line $x_1 = x_2$ such that $G \subseteq H$ and H is also convex and bounded. Further choose H such that the point $(1, 1) \in G$ is on the boundary of H.

Strong efficiency and symmetry imply that

$$f(H, (0, 0)) = (1, 1)$$

We can now use independence of irrelevant alternatives to get

$$f(G, (0, 0)) = (1, 1)$$

We know G is obtained through scaling. Now use scale covariance to get

$$f(G, (0, 0)) = L(f(F, v))$$

This implies

$$L(f(F, v)) = (1, 1)$$

Since we know that $L(x_1^*, x_2^*) = (1, 1)$, we finally obtain

$$f(F, v) = (x_1^*, \; x_2^*)$$

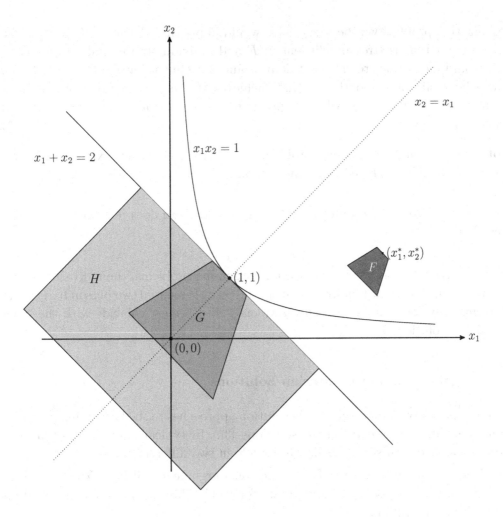

Fig. 26.6: Diagram showing F, G, H for proving the Nash bargaining theorem

Proof for Inessential Bargaining Problems

Consider the case when the problem (F, v) is inessential, that is, there does not exist any $(y_1, y_2) \in F$ such that $y_1 > v_1$; $y_2 > v_2$. Since F is convex, the above implies that there exists at least one player i such that

$$y_1 \geq v_1 \text{ and } y_2 \geq v_2 \Longrightarrow y_i = v_i \ \forall \, (y_1, y_2) \in F$$

The reason is if we could find $(y_1, y_2), (z_1, z_2) \in F$ such that $(y_1, y_2) \geq (z_1, z_2), y_1 > v_1, z_2 > v_2$, then $\frac{1}{2}(y_1, y_2) + \frac{1}{2}(z_1, z_2)$ would be a point in F that is strictly better than (v_1, v_2) for both the players. In the rest of the discussion, let us assume without loss of generality that

$$y_1 \geq v_1 \text{ and } y_2 \geq v_2 \Longrightarrow y_1 = v_1 \ \forall \, (y_1, y_2) \in F$$

Suppose x^* is an allocation in F that is best for the player 2 subject to the constraint $x_1 = v_1$ (with this constraint, the maximum value of the Nash product in the optimization problem will be zero). This would imply that the vector (x_1^*, x_2^*) is the unique point that is strongly efficient in F and individually rational relative to v. This would mean that, to satisfy Axioms 1 and 2, we must have $f(F, v) = (x_1^*, x_2^*)$. It can be easily observed that (x_1^*, x_2^*) achieves the maximum value of the Nash product $(x_1 - v_1)(x_2 - v_2)$ which happens to be zero for all individually rational allocations. ∎

Note. For essential bargaining problems, the strong efficiency axiom can be replaced by the following weak efficiency axiom:

Axiom 1′. (Weak Efficiency). $f(F, v) \in F$ and there does not exist any $y \in F$ such that

$$y > f(F, v).$$

Also, it is trivial to see that for essential bargaining problems, the individual rationality assumption is not required. Thus in the case of essential two person bargaining problems, any solution that satisfies Axioms $1', 3, 4, 5$ must coincide with the Nash bargaining solution.

26.6   Egalitarian and Utilitarian Solutions

We now discuss two other well known solution approaches to the bargaining problem, namely egalitarian and utilitarian solutions [3]. In typical bargaining situations, interpersonal comparisons of utility are made in two different ways.

- *Principle of Equal Gains*: Here a person's argument will be: "You should do this for me because I am doing more for you." This leads to what is called an egalitarian solution.
- *Principle of the Greatest Good*: The argument here goes as follows: "You should do this for me because it helps me more than it hurts you." This leads to the so called utilitarian solution.

For a two-person bargaining problem (F, v), the egalitarian solution is the unique point $(x_1, x_2) \in F$ that is weakly efficient in F and satisfies the equal gains condition:

$$x_1 - v_1 = x_2 - v_2$$

Recall that $(x_1, x_2) \in F$ is said to be weakly efficient if there does not exist any $(y_1, y_2) \in F$ such that $y_1 > x_1$ and $y_2 > x_2$.

A utilitarian solution is any solution function that selects, for every two person bargaining problem (F, v), an allocation $(x_1, x_2) \in F$ such that

$$x_1 + x_2 = \max_{(y_1, y_2) \in F} (y_1 + y_2)$$

If agents in negotiation or arbitration are guided by the equal gains principle, the natural outcome is the egalitarian solution. If it is guided by the principle of greatest good, a natural outcome is a utilitarian solution.

It can be shown that the egalitarian and the utilitarian solutions violate the axiom of scale covariance.

λ-Egalitarian Solution

Consider a two person bargaining problem (F, v). Given numbers $\lambda_1, \lambda_2, \mu_1, \mu_2$, with $\lambda_1 > 0$, $\lambda_2 > 0$, let

$$L(y) = (\lambda_1 y_1 + \mu_1, \lambda_2 y_2 + \mu_2) \text{ for } y \in \mathbb{R}^2$$

Given the problem (F, v), define

$$L(F) = \{L(y) : y \in F\}$$

Then the egalitarian solution of $(L(F), L(v))$ is $L(x)$, where x is the unique weakly efficient point in F such that

$$\lambda_1(x_1 - v_1) = \lambda_2(x_2 - v_2)$$

This is called the λ-egalitarian solution of (F, v). If $\lambda = (1, 1)$, this is called the simple egalitarian solution. The egalitarian solution does not satisfy scale covariance because the λ-egalitarian solution is generally different from the simple egalitarian solution.

λ-Utilitarian Solution

A utilitarian solution of $(L(F), L(v))$ is a point $L(z)$ where $z = (z_1, z_2)$ is a point in F such that

$$\lambda_1 z_1 + \lambda_2 z_2 = \max_{(y_1, y_2) \in F} (\lambda_1 y_1 + \lambda_2 y_2)$$

The solution point z is called a λ-utilitarian solution of (F, v). Utilitarian solutions do not satisfy scale covariance because a λ-utilitarian solution is generally not a simple utilitarian solution.

Relationship to the Nash Bargaining Solution

Note that the equal gains principle suggests a family of egalitarian solutions and the greatest good principle suggests a family of utilitarian solutions. These solutions correspond to application of these principles when the payoffs are compared in a λ-weighted utility scale.

As λ_1 increases and λ_2 decreases, the λ-egalitarian solutions will present us with an individually rational, weakly efficient frontier moving in the direction of decreasing payoff to player 1. Also as λ_1 increases and λ_2 decreases, the λ-utilitarian solutions will present us with an entire weakly efficient frontier, moving in the direction of increasing payoff to player 1.

It turns out that for an essential two person bargaining problem (F, v), there exists a vector $\lambda = (\lambda_1, \lambda_2)$ such that $\lambda > (0, 0)$ and the λ-egalitarian solution of

(F, v) is also a λ-utilitarian solution of (F, v). λ_1 and λ_2 that satisfy this property are called *natural scale factors*.

Remarkably, the allocation in F that is both λ-egalitarian and λ-utilitarian in terms of the natural scale factors is the Nash bargaining solution. Thus the Nash bargaining solution can be viewed as a natural synthesis of the equal gains and greatest good principles. The following proposition formalizes this fact.

Proposition 26.1. *Let (F, v) be an essential two person bargaining problem. Suppose x is an allocation vector such that $x^* \in F$ and $x^* \geq v$. Then x^* is the Nash-bargaining solution for (F, v) iff there exist strictly positive numbers λ_1 and λ_2 such that*

$$\lambda_1 x_1^* - \lambda_1 v_1 = \lambda_2 x_2^* - \lambda_2 v_2; \quad \text{and}$$

$$\lambda_1 x_1^* + \lambda_2 x_2^* = \max_{y \in F} (\lambda_1 y_1 + \lambda_2 y_2)$$

The reader is referred to the book by Myerson [3] for a proof of this result.

26.7   Summary and References

We summarize the main results of this chapter below.

- The two person bargaining problem $(F, (v_1, v_2))$ involves finding a satisfactory allocation of payoffs to two players, given a closed, convex set F of possible payoff allocations and a disagreement allocation (v_1, v_2) (that will be enforced in the event of disagreement). It is also assumed that unbounded gains over the disagreement allocation are not allowed.

- John Nash solved this problem using an axiomatic approach that mandates five axioms to be satisfied by any solution: (1) Pareto efficiency (2) individual rationality (3) scale covariance (4) independence of irrelevant alternatives (5) symmetry. Nash showed that there exists exactly one solution that satisfies all the five properties and it is the unique solution of the simple constrained optimization problem:

$$\max_{\substack{(x_1, x_2) \in F \\ x_1 \geq v_1; x_2 \geq v_2}} ((x_1 - v_1)(x_2 - v_2))$$

- There are several other approaches for solving the two person bargaining problem. Two of these were discussed: (a) egalitarian approach and (b) utilitarian approach. The solutions produced by these two approaches would be the same and in fact coincide with the Nash bargaining solution, for a particular natural choice of scale factors.

The original discussion of the Nash bargaining problem and its solution is of course found in the classic paper of Nash [1]. The discussion and approach presented in this chapter closely follows that of Myerson [3]. There are two books that deal with the bargaining problem quite extensively. The book by Muthoo [4] deals exclusively with the bargaining problem. The book by Osborne and Rubinstein [5] discusses bargaining theory extensively and presents rigorous applications to market situations of different kinds. The book by Maschler, Solan, and Zamir [6] is a rich source of material for the Nash bargaining problem. The book by Straffin [7] provides two real-world applications of the two person bargaining problem: (1) management - labor union negotiations, and (2) duopoly Model of two competing companies trying to maximize their revenues. The concept of Nash program is discussed by Nash [2].

The Nash bargaining solution does not generalize to the case of three or more players. We bring out this fact in the next chapter and start studying other solution concepts in cooperative game theory.

References

[1]   John F. Nash Jr. "The bargaining problem". In: *Econometrica* **18** (1950), pp. 155–162.

[2]   John F. Nash Jr. "Two person cooperative games". In: *Econometrica* **21** (1953), pp. 128–140.

[3]   Roger B. Myerson. *Game Theory: Analysis of Conflict*. Harvard University Press, Cambridge, Massachusetts, USA, 1997.

[4]   Abhinay Muthoo. *Bargaining Theory with Applications*. Cambridge University Press, 1999.

[5]   Martin J. Osborne and Ariel Rubinstein. *Bargaining and Markets*. Academic Press, 1990.

[6]   Michael Maschler, Eilon Solan, and Shmuel Zamir. *Game Theory*. Cambridge University Press, 2013.

[7]   Philip D. Straffin Jr. *Game Theory and Strategy*. The Mathematical Association of America, 1993.

26.8   Exercises

(1) With reference to the axiom on independence of irrelevant alternatives, show the following property: Given a Nash bargaining problem (F, v), if an arbitrator were to select a solution by maximizing some aggregate measure of social gain, that is,

$$f(F, v) = \max_{x \in F} M(x, v)$$

where $M(x, v)$ is a measure of social gain by choosing x instead of v, then Axiom 4 can be shown to be always satisfied.

(2) Suppose F is the convex hull enclosing the points $A = (1, 8)$; $B = (6, 7)$; $C = (8, 6)$; $D = (9, 5)$; $E = (10, 3)$; $F = (11, -1)$; and $G = (-1, -1)$. Suppose the default point (status quo point) is $(2, 1)$. Compute the Nash bargaining solution for this situation. Draw a picture and that will be helpful.

(3) In the above problem, how will the Nash bargaining solution change when you choose each of the points A, B, C, D, E, F, G as the default point?

(4) Provide an example of a two player bargaining problem which has the same Nash bargaining solution irrespective of the default point chosen.

(5) In the proof of Part 2 of the Nash bargaining theorem, show the following result:

$$x_1 + x_2 \leq 2 \quad \forall (x_1, x_2) \in G$$

Hint: Assume that $x_1 + x_2 > 2$ and arrive at a contradiction.

(6) Consider the following two player game:

	A	B
A	5, 5	2, 2
B	2, 2	3, 3

For this game,

- Compute the set of all payoff utility pairs possible (a) under correlated strategies (b) under individually rational correlated strategies.
- What would be the Nash bargaining solution in cases (a) and (b) assuming the minmax values as the disagreement points?

Chapter 27

Coalitional Games with Transferable Utility

In the previous chapter, we have studied the two person bargaining problem where we have explored the effect of cooperation between two players. In this chapter, we introduce multi-player coalitional games. In particular, we discuss *transferable utility (TU) games*, also called characteristic form games. We present several examples of these games to bring out the use of TU games in capturing cooperative interactions among rational, intelligent players.

27.1 Multi-Person Cooperative Games

Let $N = \{1, \ldots, n\}$, as usual, be the set of players. We have already seen the Nash bargaining solution for a two player game. It would be interesting to see what this solution would look like for an n-player game with $n > 2$. Let F be the set of feasible allocations that the players can get if they all work together. Let us assume that F is a closed convex subset of $\mathbb{R}^n$. Suppose $(v_1, \ldots, v_n)$ is the disagreement payoff allocation or default payoff allocation the players would expect to get if they do not cooperate. Also assume that the set $\{(y_1, \ldots, y_n) \in F : y_i \geq v_i \ \forall i \in N\}$ is non-empty and bounded. The pair $(F, (v_1, \ldots, v_n))$ is then called an *n-person bargaining problem*. The bargaining problem $(F, (v_1, \ldots, v_n))$ is said to be *essential* if there exists $y \in F$ such that $y_i > v_i \ \forall i \in N$.

Suppose $(F, (v_1, \ldots, v_n))$ is essential. Then its Nash bargaining solution can be defined to be the unique strongly efficient allocation vector that maximizes the product $(x_1 - v_1) \ldots (x_n - v_n)$ over all vectors $x \in F$ such that $x_i \geq v_i \ \forall i \in N$. However, this Nash bargaining solution may ignore the possibility of cooperation among proper subsets of the players as shown in some of the examples below. Consequently for $n > 2$, the Nash bargaining solution may not give a satisfactory solution. So we have to look for more appropriate solution concepts.

Divide the Dollar Problem

Example 27.1 (Divide the Dollar Game - Version 1). In this problem, $N = \{1, 2, 3\}$. The players wish to divide a total wealth of 300 (to be regarded as a real number) among themselves. Each player can propose a payoff such that no player's payoff is negative and the sum of all the payoffs does not exceed 300. The strategy sets can therefore be defined as follows:

$$S_1 = S_2 = S_3 = \left\{ (x_1, x_2, x_3) \in \mathbb{R}^3 : x_1 + x_2 + x_3 \leq 300; \ x_1 \geq 0; \ x_2 \geq 0, \ x_3 \geq 0 \right\}$$

Assume that the players will get a zero payoff unless all three players propose the same allocation. That is, for $i = 1, 2, 3$,

$$u_i(s_1, s_2, s_3) = x_i \text{ if } s_1 = s_2 = s_3 = (x_1, x_2, x_3)$$
$$= 0 \text{ otherwise}$$

Note that the players can achieve any allocation in which their payoffs are non-negative and sum to ≤ 300. The minimum guaranteed wealth is 0 for each player. The above game can therefore be described as a three person bargaining problem (F, v) where:

$$F = \left\{ (x_1, x_2, x_3) \in \mathbb{R}^3 : x_1 + x_2 + x_3 \leq 300, x_1 \geq 0; \ x_2 \geq 0, \ x_3 \geq 0 \right\}$$
$$v = (v_1, v_2, v_3) = (0, 0, 0)$$

The Nash bargaining solution for this problem is $x = (100, 100, 100)$, which is clearly a reasonable outcome for this situation. □

Example 27.2 (Divide the Dollar Game - Version 2).

This is a variant of Version 1 with the difference that players get a zero payoff unless players 1 and 2 propose the same allocation in which case the allocation proposed by players 1 and 2 is enforced. That is, for $i = 1, 2, 3$,

$$u_i(s_1, s_2, s_3) = x_i \text{ if } s_1 = s_2 = (x_1, x_2, x_3)$$
$$= 0 \text{ otherwise}$$

The same bargaining problem (F, v) as in Version 1 would describe the situation here and hence the Nash bargaining solution for this problem also is $x = (100, 100, 100)$. This solution looks unsatisfactory because players 1 and 2 together determine the payoff allocation and player 3 is not involved in the decision. So, we would expect players 1 and 2 to divide the payoff equally between them, leading to the allocation $(150, 150, 0)$. Another viewpoint which supports this argument is as follows. Suppose 1 and 2 ignore 3 and engage in a two person cooperative game. The resulting two person game would have the Nash bargaining solution that divides 300 equally between 1 and 2.

Having noted the above, there are a few reasons for arguing in favor of the solution $(100, 100, 100)$ as well.

- The players are required to choose their proposals simultaneously and both $(100, 100, 100)$ and $(150, 150, 0)$ are Nash equilibria for the players since unilateral deviation by any player will make all their utilities equal to zero.
- If player 3 has any influence, then player 3, being rational, would clearly try to influence players 1 and 2 to go for the equilibrium $(100, 100, 100)$.

However, there is one central assumption based on which the outcome $(100, 100, 100)$ loses credibility and cannot be justified. This is the *effective negotiation* assumption, which is a natural assumption to make, as articulated by Myerson in his book [1]. □

Myerson [1] defines effective negotiation as follows and asserts that effective negotiation is the key assumption that distinguishes cooperative game theory from non-cooperative game theory.

Definition 27.1 (Effective Negotiation). *The members of a coalition of players are said to* negotiate effectively *and are said to form an* effective coalition *if the players, on realizing that there is a feasible change in their strategies that would benefit them all, would all agree to actually make such a change unless such a change contradicts some agreements that some members of the coalition might have made with other players outside this coalition, in the context of some other equally effective coalition.*

The n-person Nash bargaining solution would be relevant if the only coalition that can negotiate effectively is the *grand coalition* that includes the whole of N. If other coalitions also can negotiate effectively, then the Nash bargaining solution is no longer relevant. This is because it ignores all information about the power of multi-player coalitions other than the grand coalition N. In Version 1 of the divide-the-dollar game, no coalition that is smaller than $\{1, 2, 3\}$ can guarantee more than 0 to its members. In Version 2, the coalition $\{1, 2\}$ could guarantee its members any payoff allocation that they could get in the coalition $\{1, 2, 3\}$.

Example 27.3 (Divide the Dollar Game - Version 3). This is a variant of Version 2 with the difference that players get a zero payoff unless player 1 and player 2 propose the same allocation or player 1 and player 3 propose the same allocation, in which case the players would get what is proposed. That is, for $i = 1, 2, 3$,

$$u_i(s_1, s_2, s_3) = x_i \text{ if } s_1 = s_2 = (x_1, x_2, x_3) \text{ or } s_1 = s_3 = (x_1, x_2, x_3)$$
$$= 0 \text{ otherwise}$$

The bargaining problem (F, v) as in Versions 1 and 2 would describe the situation here and hence the Nash bargaining solution for this problem also is $x = (100, 100, 100)$. Much like in the case of Version 2, this solution also is unsatisfactory since players 1 and 2 together or players 1 and 3 together determine the payoff allocation. Player 1 is necessarily involved in both the above situations. So, we would expect the players to divide the payoff in a way that players 2 and 3 get the same payoff but this payoff should be less than the payoff that player 1 would get (since player 1 has to necessarily agree for a non-zero allocation). This leads to uncountably infinite number of possibilities, such as (120, 90, 90), (150, 75, 75), (200, 50, 50), (280, 10, 10), etc. One can even suggest an allocation (300, 0, 0) on the ground that player 1 is indispensable for a non-zero allocation. $\square$

Example 27.4 (Divide the Dollar - Version 4 - Majority Voting Game). In this version, the players get a zero payoff unless there is some pair of players $\{1, 2\}$, $\{2, 3\}$, or $\{1, 3\}$ who propose the same allocation, in which case they get this allocation. That is,

$$u_i(s_1, s_2, s_3) = x_i \text{ if } s_j = s_k = (x_1, x_2, x_3) \text{ for some } j \neq k$$
$$= 0 \text{ otherwise}$$

Here again, the Nash bargaining solution is $(100, 100, 100)$. This solution is clearly justified for this version because of symmetry and equal bargaining power of the players. Observe that this allocation is a Nash equilibrium. If we assume that every coalition can negotiate effectively, the analysis becomes quite interesting as seen below (citeMYERSON97).

- If players 1 and 2 negotiate effectively in the coalition $\{1, 2\}$, they can agree to the allocation $(150, 150, 0)$ which is attractive for both of them. Observe that this allocation is clearly a Nash equilibrium.

- If $(150, 150, 0)$ is the expected outcome, then player 3 would be eager to persuade player 1 or player 2 to form an effective coalition with him. For example, player 3 would be willing to negotiate an agreement with player 2 to both propose $(0, 225, 75)$ or, for example, $(0, 200, 100)$. This allocation is also a Nash equilibrium.

- If $(0, 225, 75)$ is the expected outcome in the absence of further negotiations, then player 1 would be willing to negotiate an agreement with player 3 to propose an allocation that is better for both of them, say, $(100, 0, 200)$. This allocation is again a Nash equilibrium.

- It turns out that in any equilibrium of this game, there is always at least one pair of players who would both do strictly better by jointly agreeing to change their strategies together and move to another equilibrium.

The above sequence of coalitional negotiations can go on endlessly. There are two possible ways in which the negotiations could conclude. The first possibility is the following. Let us say that a player, having negotiated an agreement as part of a coalition, cannot subsequently negotiate a different agreement with another coalition, that does not contain all the members of the first coalition. For example, if the grand coalition $\{1, 2, 3\}$ has negotiated the agreement $(100, 100, 100)$ before any two player coalition could negotiate separately, then no two player coalition can veto this outcome. Another example would be, if players 1 and 2 first negotiated an agreement $(150, 150, 0)$, then player 3 would be unable to increase this payoff by negotiating with player 1 or player 2 separately. It is clear that the order in which coalitions can negotiate will crucially determine the outcome of the game. The advantage lies with coalitions that get to negotiate earlier.

The second possibility is as follows. Suppose the negotiated agreements are only tentative and non-binding. Thus a player who negotiates in a sequential manner in various coalitions can nullify his earlier agreements and reach a different agreement with a coalition that negotiates later. Here the order in which negotiations are made and nullified will have a bearing on the final outcome. For example, let us say the order of negotiations is $\{1, 2\}$, $\{2, 3\}$, $\{1, 3\}$ and $\{1, 2, 3\}$. Here any agreement by $\{1, 2\}$ and $\{2, 3\}$ in that order to pay non-zero amount to player 2 can be overturned by the coalition $\{1, 3\}$ which might agree on $(150, 0, 150)$. Player 2 may not be able to make them agree to anything when the turn of coalition $\{1, 2, 3\}$ arises. As another example, assume that player 1 believes that, any negotiated agreement with player 2, would be overturned by player 3. Player 1 may first suggest $(100, 100, 100)$ and stick to it and refuse to agree for $(150, 150, 0)$. This he would do to prevent any possibility of his getting zero payoff. It is clear that coalitions that get to negotiate later hold the advantage in this scheme. □

In real-world scenarios where different coalitions could form, the number of ways in which negotiations could be conducted is mind-boggling and a systematic analysis of all scenarios may not be feasible. There are as many as $2^n - 1$ such coalitions possible and therefore there is a need for a theory of cooperative games that can provide us with a clear sense of what to expect as a result of the balance of power among various coalitions. Such an order-independent theory will be extremely useful but will pose challenges in interpretation because ordering is often natural and important [1].

27.2 Transferable Utility Games (TU Games)

The assumption of *transferable utility* (TU) makes cooperative games easier to analyze and makes the analysis more tractable. The TU assumption implies that there is a commodity called money that the players can freely transfer among themselves such that the payoff of any player increases by one unit for every unit of money that he gets. With the assumption of transferable utility in place, the cooperative possibilities of a game can be described by a *characteristic function* $v : 2^N \to \mathbb{R}$, that assigns a number $v(C)$ to every coalition $C \subseteq N$. $v(\emptyset)$ is always taken to be zero. $v(C)$ is called the *worth* or *value* of the coalition C and it captures the total amount of transferable utility that the members of C could earn without any help from the players outside of C.

Definition 27.2 (TU Game). *A cooperative game with transferable utility is defined as the pair (N, v) where $N = \{1, \ldots, n\}$ is a set of players and $v : 2^N \to \mathbb{R}$ is a characteristic function, with $v(\emptyset) = 0$. We call such a game also as a game in coalition form, or game in characteristic form, or coalitional game, or TU game.*

Note. Under the assumption of transferable utility, specifying a single number for each coalition is enough to describe what allocations of utility can be achieved by the members of the coalition.

Non-Transferable Utility (NTU) Games

Games without transferable utility (also called NTU coalitional games or games in NTU coalitional form) are defined as follows.

Definition 27.3 (NTU Game). *An NTU coalitional game is a pair (N, V) where N is a set of players N and $V(\cdot)$ is a mapping with domain 2^N such that, for any coalition $C \subset N$,*

- *$V(C)$ is a non-empty closed and convex subset of $\mathbb{R}^{|C|}$, and*
- *The set $\{x : x \in V(C) \text{ and } x_i \geq v_i \ \forall i \in C\}$ is a bounded subset of $\mathbb{R}^{|C|}$, where*

$$v_i = \max\{y_i : y \in V(\{i\})\} < \infty \ \forall i \in N.$$

In the above definition, $V(C)$ is the set of expected payoff allocations that the members of coalition C could guarantee for themselves if they act cooperatively. An NTU game is a generalization of a TU game. In the remainder of the discussion, we will consider only TU games.

Examples of TU Games

Example 27.5 (Divide the Dollar Games). The Divide the Dollar - Version 1 game discussed in Example 27.1 has the following characteristic function.

$$v(\{1,2,3\}) = 300$$
$$v(\{1,2\}) = v(\{1,3\}) = v(\{2,3\}) = 0$$
$$v(\{1\}) = v(\{2\}) = v(\{3\}) = 0$$

Version 2 of the game (Example 27.2) has the characteristic function:

$$v(\{1,2,3\}) = v(\{1,2\}) = 300$$
$$v(\{2,3\}) = v(\{1,3\}) = 0$$
$$v(\{1\}) = v(\{2\}) = v(\{3\}) = 0$$

Version 3 of the game (Example 27.3) has the characteristic function:

$$v(\{1,2,3\}) = v(\{1,2\}) = v(\{1,3\}) = 300$$
$$v(\{1\}) = v(\{2\}) = v(\{3\}) = v(\{2,3\}) = 0$$

Version 4 of the game (majority voting game) (Example 27.4) has the characteristic form:

$$v(\{1,2,3\}) = v(\{1,2\}) = v(\{2,3\}) = v(\{1,3\}) = 300$$
$$v(\{1\}) = v(\{2\}) = v(\{3\}) = 0$$

□

Note. In the sequel, we will follow a slight abuse of notation while referring to the argument of the $v(\cdot)$ function: we shall drop the braces and commas while representing sets; for example, instead of $v(\{2,3\})$, we will simply write $v(23)$, etc., whenever there is no confusion.

Example 27.6 (A Voting Game). This example is taken from [2]. Consider that the Parliament of a certain Nation has four political parties 1, 2, 3, 4 with 45, 25, 15, 12 members respectively. To pass any bill, at least 51 votes are required. This situation could be modeled as a TU game with $N = \{1,2,3,4\}$ and

$$v(1) = v(2) = v(3) = v(4) = 0$$

$$v(12) = v(13) = v(14) = v(123) = v(124) = v(134) = v(234) = v(1234) = 1$$

$$v(23) = v(24) = v(34) = 0$$

□

Example 27.7 (Minimum Spanning Tree Game). Suppose multiple users are to be connected to a shared resource (for example, a power plant, a synchrotron, a radio telescope, a computational cluster, a logistics hub, a centralized drainage system, etc.). In order to utilize this resource, a user should either be directly connected to the facility or be connected to some other connected user. Figure 27.1(a) provides a picture of a typical network of customers consisting of three players $1, 2, 3$ and a central shared facility F. We provide several typical examples of such a network below.

- Players $1, 2, 3$ could correspond to three different industrial units and the facility F could be a power plant from which the units draw their power. The edges in the graph correspond to high capacity power lines and the weights on the edges correspond to the cost of power distribution.
- Players $1, 2, 3$ could correspond to three different city corporations and F could correspond to a drainage system. The edges represent the drainage connections between the pairs of locations and the edge weights correspond to the cost of maintaining and using the connections.
- Players $1, 2, 3$ could correspond to pick up points in a logistics network and F could be a logistics hub. The edges correspond to the roads in the network and the edge weights correspond to the distances.

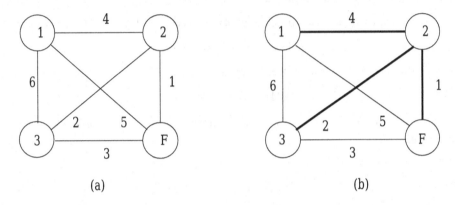

(a)   (b)

Fig. 27.1: A network of users connected to a central facility F

Suppose each player gets a benefit of 10 units when he gets connected to F directly or indirectly. Note that, given a coalition $C \subseteq \{1, 2, 3\}$, the minimum cost incurred by the members of coalition C to get connected to F is given by the sum of edge weights in a minimal spanning tree involving F and the members of C. For example, suppose $C = \{2, 3\}$. Then the minimum cost corresponding to C would be given by the sum of costs of edges in a minimal spanning tree involving the vertices $2, 3, F$. Such a minimal spanning tree consists of the edges $(2, F)$ and $(2, 3)$ and therefore has total cost 3. If $C = \{1, 2, 3\}$, then, the minimum cost would be the sum of edges of a minimal spanning tree involving the vertices $1, 2, 3, F$, which can be seen to be 7. Figure 27.1(b) depicts the minimal spanning tree involving $1, 2, 3, F$ through the thick edges.

We can in a natural way, define the worth of each coalition as the total benefit that accrues to the members of the coalition minus the minimum cost incurred in providing connectivity from all members of the coalition to F. For example, $v(23)$ would be $20 - 3$ since 20 is the total benefit that accrues to players 2 and 3 and the cost of the minimal spanning tree involving the nodes $2, 3, F$ is 3 units. We can now model the above situation as a TU game with characteristic function given by

$$v(\emptyset) = 0; \ v(1) = 10 - 5 = 5; \ v(2) = 10 - 1 = 9; \ v(3) = 10 - 3 = 7$$

$$v(12) = 20 - 5 = 15; \ v(13) = 20 - 8 = 12; \ v(23) = 20 - 3 = 17; v(123) = 30 - 7 = 23.$$

Such a game formulation would be useful in determining how the costs and profits could be shared by the players involved.   □

Example 27.8 (A Logistics Game). Figure 27.2 shows a logistics network that provides connectivity between two important cities S and T. There are five logistics hubs A, B, C, D, E which are intermediate points from S to T. Transportation is provided by service providers 1, 2, 3, 4. Each edge in the network is labeled by two quantities namely the service provider and the cost of service. For example, the label $3, 15$ on the directed edge from A to B means that service provider 3 provides the logistics service from A to B at a cost of 15 units. Assume that movement from S to T fetches a revenue of 100 units. The objective is to choose an optimal path from S to T that maximizes the profit obtained while moving from S to T. We can formulate this as a cooperative game with $N = \{1, 2, 3, 4\}$ and with characteristic function

$$v(1) = v(2) = v(3) = v(4) = 0$$

$$v(12) = v(13) = v(14) = v(23) = v(24) = v(34) = v(234) = v(123) = 0$$

$$v(134) = 100 - 60 = 40$$

$$v(124) = 100 - 55 = 45$$

$$v(1234) = 100 - 35 = 65$$

A game such as above would be valuable in determining profit sharing protocols among the logistics providers.   □

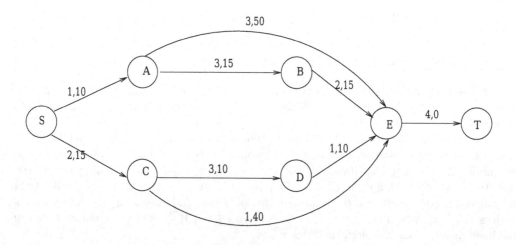

Fig. 27.2: A logistics network

Transforming Strategic Form Games to TU Games

If we have a strategic form game model of interactions among players and we wish to model cooperation among these players, there are several natural ways of defining the characteristic function of a TU game. Three of the more common representations are: (1) Minimax representation, (2) Defensive equilibrium representation, and (3) Rational threats representation. For more details on these, we refer the reader to the book by Myerson [1] and the book by Maschler, Solan, and Zamir [3].

Imputations

Definition 27.4 (Imputation). *Given a TU game (N, v), an imputation is an allocation $x = (x_1, \ldots, x_n) \in \mathbb{R}^n$ that satisfies*

- *Individual Rationality : $x_i \geq v(\{i\})$ $\forall i \in N$*
- *Collective Rationality : $\sum_{i \in N} x_i = v(N)$*

An imputation keeps all individual players happy and also distributes the total value of the grand coalition among the players (Pareto efficiency).

Definition 27.5 (Domination of Imputation). *An imputation $x = (x_1, \ldots, x_n)$ of a TU game (N, v) is said to dominate an imputation $y = (y_1, \ldots, y_n)$ if there exists a coalition C such that*

$$\sum_{i \in C} x_i \leq v(C); \text{ and } x_i > y_i \ \forall i \in C$$

Example 27.9 (Imputations and Domination). We make several observations concerning the notion of domination. Consider the majority voting game.

(1) The allocations $(150, 150, 0)$ and $(100, 0, 200)$ are both imputations while the allocations $(0, 0, 0)$, $(100, 50, 50)$ are not imputations. The imputation $(150, 150, 0)$ dominates the imputation $(100, 0, 200)$ since the coalition $\{1, 2\}$ is such that $150 > 100$ and $150 > 0$.

(2) Given two imputations x and y, it is possible that neither dominates the other. An immediate example would be the majority voting game where the imputation $x = (150, 150, 0)$ neither dominates nor is dominated by the imputation $y = (0, 150, 150)$.

(3) The relation of domination is not transitive and cycles of domination are possible. Again an immediate example would be majority voting game where imputation $(0, 180, 120)$ dominates imputation $(150, 150, 0)$ which dominates imputation $(90, 0, 210)$ which in turn dominates $(0, 180, 120)$.

$\square$

27.3 TU Games with Special Structure

In this section, we define several special classes of TU games.

Monotonic Games

A monotonic TU game is one in which as we add players to a coalition, the worth of the coalition does not decrease.

Definition 27.6 (Monotonic Game). *A TU game (N, v) is called monotonic if*

$$v(C) \leq v(D) \ \forall C \subseteq D \subseteq N.$$

Example 27.10. It can be verified that both the minimum spanning tree game (Example 27.7) and the logistics game (Example 27.8) are monotonic. In fact, all the examples we have discussed so far in this chapter are monotonic. A simple example of a non-monotonic game would be (N, v) with $N = \{1, 2\}$ and $v(1) = 10$; $v(2) = 20$; $v(12) = 15$. $\quad\square$

Superadditive Games

Superadditive games are TU games where the value of union of any two disjoint coalitions is at least as much as the sum of values of the individual coalitions, that is, two disjoint coalitions, on coming together, produce a non-negative additional value beyond the sum of the individual values.

Definition 27.7 (Superadditive Game). *A TU game (N, v) is said to be superadditive if*

$$v(C \cup D) \geq v(C) + v(D) \ \forall \, C, D \subseteq N \ \text{such that} \ C \cap D = \phi$$

Example 27.11. The majority voting game with $N = \{1, 2, 3\}$ and v given by $v(1) = v(2) = v(3) = 0$ and $v(12) = v(13) = v(23) = v(123) = 300$ is a superadditive game. The minimum spanning tree game discussed in Example 27.7 is also a superadditive game. $\quad\square$

Example 27.12 (A Non-Superadditive Game). The following three player game is not superadditive.

$$v(1) = 10; \ v(2) = 15; \ v(3) = 20; \ v(12) = 20; \ v(13) = 30; \ v(23) = 35; \ v(123) = 40$$

$\square$

Note. Note that a monotonic game need not be superadditive and a superadditive game need not be monotonic. It would be instructive to construct examples of games in all the four cases: (a) monotonic as well as superadditive (b) monotonic but not superadditive (c) non-monotonic but superadditive (d) neither monotonic nor superadditive.

Essential and Inessential Games

Definition 27.8 (Essential Superadditive Game). *A superadditive game (N, v) is said to be inessential if*

$$\sum_{i \in N} v(i) = v(N)$$

and essential otherwise.

If (N, v) is inessential then,

$$\sum_{i \in C} v(i) = v(C) \quad \forall\, C \subseteq N$$

Therefore $(v(1), v(2), \ldots, v(n))$ is the only possible imputation for an inessential game. On the other hand, there are infinitely many imputations possible for an essential game.

Strategic Equivalence of TU Games

Definition 27.9. Two TU games (N, v) and (N, w) are said to be strategically equivalent if there exist constants $c_1, c_2, \ldots, c_n$ and $b > 0$ such that

$$w(C) = b(v(C) + \sum_{i \in C} c_i) \quad \forall\, C \subseteq N$$

Intuitively, strategic equivalence means that the "dynamics" among the players would be identical in the two games.

An important result concerning strategic equivalence is that any superadditive, essential n-person characteristic form game G is strategically equivalent to a unique game with

$$N = \{1, 2, \ldots, n\}$$

$$v(1) = v(2) = \cdots = v(n) = 0; \quad v(N) = 1$$

$$0 \le v(C) \le 1 \quad \forall\, C \subseteq N$$

This unique game is called the *0-1 normalization* of the original game.

Triangular Representation for Three Person Superadditive Games

The imputations in any three person game with $v(1) = v(2) = v(3) = 0$ and $v(N) = 1$ can be represented using an interesting triangular representation. This representation uses the following property: Suppose P is any point in an equilateral triangle with height h. Then the sum of the perpendicular distances from P to the three sides of the triangle is equal to h (see Figure 27.3).

Example 27.13. If we consider the majority voting game with $v(1) = v(2) = v(3) = 0; v(12) = v(13) = v(23) = v(123) = 1$ then any point $\rho = (x_1, x_2, x_3)$ inside the triangle represents an imputation because $x_1 \ge 0;\ x_1 \ge 0;\ x_2 \ge 0;\ x_3 \ge 0;\ x_1 + x_2 + x_3 = 1$. Figure 27.4 depicts several representative imputations. $\qquad \square$

Example 27.14 (Bargaining in Majority Voting Game). Consider the majority voting game where we have $N = \{1, 2, 3\}$ and $v(1) = v(2) = v(3) = 0; v(12) = v(13) = v(23) = v(123) = 300$. Suppose we start with an allocation $(150, 150, 0)$ which indicates

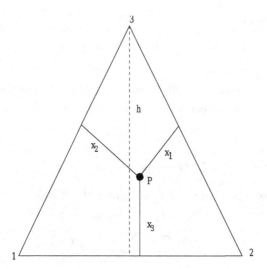

Fig. 27.3: An equilateral triangle, $x_1 + x_2 + x_3 = h$

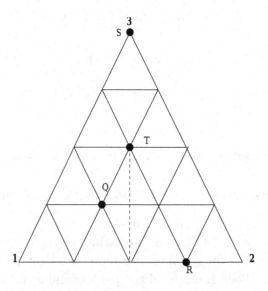

Fig. 27.4: $Q = (\frac{1}{2}, \frac{1}{4}, \frac{1}{4})$; $R = (\frac{1}{4}, \frac{3}{4}, 0)$; $S = (0, 0, 1)$; $T = (\frac{1}{4}, \frac{1}{4}, \frac{1}{2})$ are imputations

a coalition between players 1 and 2. Player 3 can entice player 1 by proposing an allocation such as (180, 0, 120). Player 2 can now propose an allocation such as (0,120,180) and draw player 3 out of the coalition with player 1. In this particular game, bargaining can go on endlessly without any allocation being agreed upon. A graphical representation of this endless negotiation is presented in Figure 27.5.   □

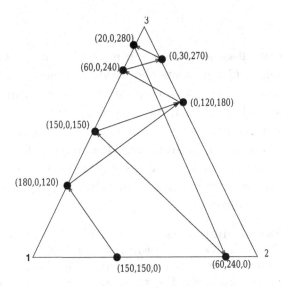

Fig. 27.5: Chain of unending negotiations in majority voting game

Convex Games

Convex games are those TU games where the marginal contribution of any player to a coalition rises as more players join the coalition. That is, players have an incentive to join larger coalitions than smaller coalitions. Formally convex games are defined as follows.

Definition 27.10 (Convex Game). *A TU game is said to be convex if*

$$v(C \cup D) + v(C \cap D) \geq v(C) + v(D) \; \forall C, D \subseteq N.$$

Note. In the above definition, suppose C and D are disjoint. Then we obtain

$$v(C \cup D) \geq v(C) + v(D) \; \forall \, C, D \subseteq N \text{ with } C \cap D = \emptyset$$

The above is precisely the definition of superadditivity. Thus every convex game is superadditive. The converse need not be true.

In the following propositions, we provide two equivalent definitions for convex games. The proof of these propositions is left as an exercise.

Proposition 27.1. *A TU game (N, v) is convex iff*

$$v(C \cup \{i\}) - v(C) \leq v(D \cup \{i\}) - v(D) \; \forall C \subseteq D \subseteq N \; \forall i \in N \setminus D.$$

Proposition 27.2. *A TU game (N, v) is convex iff*

$$v(C \cup E) - v(C) \leq v(D \cup E) - v(D) \; \forall C \subseteq D \subseteq N \; \forall E \subseteq N \setminus D.$$

27.4 Cost Games

The TU games we have discussed so far are referred to as *profit games* since the worth $v(C)$ of a coalition C represents the total (maximum) value that could be earned together by the members of the coalition without any help from other players (not belonging to the coalition C). If on the other hand, the worth of a coalition C represents the minimum total price the members of the coalition have to pay if the coalition were to form, then the resulting TU game is called a *cost game*. Cost games are complementary to profit games as illustrated in the following example. Often, cost games may be more natural to the given setting than profit games as shown in the following example.

Example 27.15 (Cost Game). Consider the minimum spanning tree game we discussed in Example 27.7. Let us define the worth of each coalition as the minimum cost incurred by the members of coalition C to get connected to F. Recall that, given a coalition $C \subseteq \{1, 2, 3\}$, the minimum cost incurred by the members of coalition C to get connected to F is given by the sum of edge weights in a minimal spanning tree involving F and the members of C. The characteristic function of the cost game in this situation is:

$$v(\emptyset) = 0;\ v(1) = 5;\ v(2) = 1;\ v(3) = 3$$

$$v(12) = 5;\ v(13) = 8;\ v(23) = 3; v(123) = 7.$$

Such a game formulation would be useful in determining how the costs could be shared by the players involved.   □

27.5 Summary and References

The following are the salient aspects of this chapter.

- A natural extension of the Nash bargaining solution will not work for cooperative games containing three or more players since Nash bargaining only takes into account negotiations among all players in the grand coalition. This is illustrated clearly by the different versions of the divide the dollar problem.
- Coalition formation and negotiation among players in a cooperative game could involve intricate analysis since the negotiations might proceed endlessly and players may always find it in their benefit to leave a coalition and join a new coalition. Cooperative game theory provides a set of solution concepts to suggest outcomes that represent an acceptable and scientific end result of these complex negotiations.
- A transferable utility (TU) game or characteristic form game represents a cooperative game through a characteristic function $v : 2^N \to \mathbb{R}$ that associates a value or worth to each coalition of players. The worth of a coalition is the total utility the players of the coalition will be able to earn by themselves. Once a characteristic function is defined, the rest of the analysis can follow.

- A key issue in TU games is to derive the characteristic function $v(\cdot)$ to faithfully reflect the effect of cooperation among different subsets of players. Often, the physics of the underlying problem will naturally suggest a way of computing the characteristic function for different coalitions.

- An imputation in a TU game (N, v) is an allocation of payoffs to the players such that the sum of all payoffs is equal to $v(N)$ and the payoff for each player $i \in N$ is at least $v(\{i\})$.

- Superadditive games are TU games where the value of union of any pair of disjoint coalitions is no less than the sum of the values of the individual coalitions. Three person superadditive games can often be represented using a convenient triangular representation.

- Convex games are those in which a player's marginal contribution to any coalition is less than or equal to his marginal contribution to any superset of the coalition. Intuitively, marginal contribution of a player monotonically increases when more players join that coalition. Convex games are superadditive but not vice-versa.

- Cost games are TU games in which the the worth of a coalition is measured by the minimum cost incurred by the players rather than the maximum profit they can make by themselves. The TU games that are usually studied are called profit games and cost games are complementary to them.

The material in this chapter is mostly based on the books by Myerson [1] and Straffin [4]. The recent book by Maschler, Solan, and Zamir [3] is another valuable reference. The next three chapters deal with different solution concepts for TU games.

References

[1] Roger B. Myerson. *Game Theory: Analysis of Conflict.* Harvard University Press, Cambridge, Massachusetts, USA, 1997.

[2] Yoam Shoham and Kevin Leyton-Brown. *Multiagent Systems: Algorithmic, Game-Theoretic, and Logical Foundations.* Cambridge University Press, New York, USA, 2009, 2009.

[3] Michael Maschler, Eilon Solan, and Shmuel Zamir. *Game Theory.* Cambridge University Press, 2013.

[4] Philip D. Straffin Jr. *Game Theory and Strategy.* The Mathematical Association of America, 1993.

27.6   Exercises

(1) Provide an example of a a TU game in which every imputation is such that it is dominated by some other imputation.

(2) Construct examples of TU games for the following situations:

- Monotonic and superadditive

- Monotonic but not superadditive
- Superadditive but not monotonic
- Neither superadditive nor monotonic

(3) Show that the following game (called communication satellite game) is superadditive. Is it convex? (Source: [3]).

$$v(1) = 3; \ v(2) = 2; \ v(3) = 1; \ v(12) = 8; \ v(13) = 6.5; \ v(23) = 8.2; \ v(123) = 11.2$$

(4) Consider a TU game (N, v) where $N = \{1, 2, 3\}$ and

$$v(1) = v(2) = 1; \ v(3) = 2; \ v(12) = v(23) = v(13) = 4; \ v(123) = 5.$$

Is this game superadditive? Is it convex? (Source: [3]).

(5) Give an example of a TU game that is superadditive but not convex.

(6) Show that the 0-1 normalization of any three person constant sum game (that is, a TU game where, for every coalition $C \subseteq N$, $v(C) + v(N \setminus C)$ is a constant) is the three person majority voting game. (Source: [4]).

(7) Given two TU games (N, v) and (N, w), and a number $\lambda \in [0, 1]$, define a convex combination of the games as the game (N, z) where

$$z(C) = \lambda v(C) + (1 - \lambda)w(C) \ \forall C \subseteq N.$$

If (N, v) and (N, w) are convex, then would (N, z) also be convex? Prove your result.

(8) Prove Proposition 27.1: A TU game (N, v) is convex if and only if

$$v(C \cup \{i\}) - v(C) \le v(D \cup \{i\}) - v(D) \ \forall C \subseteq D \subseteq N; \ \forall i \in N \setminus D.$$

(9) Prove Proposition 27.2: A TU game (N, v) is convex if and only if

$$v(C \cup E) - v(C) \le v(D \cup E) - v(D) \ \forall C \subseteq D \subseteq N \ \forall E \subseteq N \setminus D.$$

Chapter 28

The Core of Coalitional Games

Given a transferable utility game (N, v), there are two key questions that are of fundamental interest: (1) Which coalition(s) will form? (2) How should a coalition divide its value among its members? An answer to the second question has a bearing on the answer for the first question. In this chapter, we start studying the answers to these questions using the notion of *the core*, a central notion in cooperative game theory. We discuss the significance of the core of a TU game with several illustrative examples and present several key results concerning this solution concept.

28.1 The Core: Definition and Examples

The core is a set solution concept, that is, it is a set of payoff allocations each of which could be a possible solution to the given TU game Let $N = \{1, \ldots, n\}$ be a set of players and let (N, v) be a TU game. A payoff allocation $x = (x_1, \ldots, x_n)$ is any vector in $\mathbb{R}^n$. x_i is the utility payoff to player i, $i \in N$. We first define the notions of feasible allocation, individually rational allocation, coalitionally rational allocation, and collectively rational allocation.

Definition 28.1 (Feasible Allocation). *An allocation $x = (x_1, \ldots, x_n) \in \mathbb{R}^n$ is said to be feasible for a coalition C if*

$$\sum_{i \in C} x_i \leq v(C)$$

If an allocation x is feasible for C, the players in C can achieve their respective allocations in x by dividing among themselves the worth $v(C)$ that they would be able to earn by cooperating together.

Definition 28.2 (Rational Allocations). *A payoff allocation $x = (x_1, \ldots, x_n)$ is said to be individually rational if*

$$x_i \geq v(\{i\}) \ \forall i \in N$$

It is said to be collectively rational if

$$\sum_{i \in N} x_i = v(N)$$

It is said to be coalitionally rational if

$$\sum_{i \in C} x_i \geq v(C) \quad \forall C \subseteq N$$

Note that coalitional rationality implies individual rationality. We have, in the previous chapter, defined the notion of an *imputation*. It can be seen that an imputation is a payoff allocation that is individually rational and collectively rational. Collective rationality is the same as (Pareto) efficiency.

Definition 28.3 (The Core). *The core of a TU game* (N, v), *denoted by* $\mathbb{C}(N, v)$, *is the set of all payoff allocations that are coalitionally rational and collectively rational.*

$$\mathbb{C}(N, v) = \left\{ (x_1, \ldots, x_n) \in \mathbb{R}^n : \sum_{i=1}^{n} x_i = v(N); \quad \sum_{i \in C} x_i \geq v(C) \quad \forall C \subseteq N \right\}$$

In other words, the core is the set of all imputations that are coalitionally rational.

Definition 28.4 (Blocking). *We say a coalition* C *can* improve on *an allocation* $x = (x_1, \ldots, x_n) \in \mathbb{R}^n$ *if*

$$v(C) > \sum_{i \in C} x_i$$

We also say that the coalition C blocks *allocation* x.

The above definition implies that C can improve upon x iff there exists some allocation y such that y is feasible for C and every player in C can get strictly higher payoff in y than in x (that is $y_i > x_i \; \forall i \in C$).

Definition 28.5 (The Core: An Alternative Definition). *The core of* (N, v) *is the set of allocations* x *such that* x *is feasible for* N *and no coalition* $C \subseteq N$ *can improve upon it.*

We can make the following observations on the concept of the core.

Note. If an allocation x that is feasible for N is not in the core, then there would exist some coalition C such that the players in C could all do strictly better than in x by cooperating together and dividing the worth $v(C)$ among themselves.

Note. If an allocation x belongs to the core, then it implies that for each player, a unilateral deviation will not make the player strictly better off. This means x is a Nash equilibrium of an underlying contract signing game.

Note. The core is an appealing solution concept in the light of the assumption that all coalitions can negotiate effectively. Each allocation in the core could be viewed as resulting out of effective negotiations.

Note. The core of a TU game can be empty. If the core is empty, then we are unable to draw any conclusions about the game. At the same time, if the core consists of a large number of elements, then also, we have difficulty in preferring any particular allocation in the core.

Note. The core of a TU game can be shown to be convex and compact. Convexity and compactness are two desirable properties satisfied by the core. For a proof of this result, the reader is referred to the book by Maschler, Solan, and Zamir [1].

The Core: Some Examples

Example 28.1 (Divide the Dollar Game). For the Divide the Dollar game (Version 1), $\mathbb{C}(N, v)$ is given by.

$$\{(x_1, x_2, x_3) \in \mathbb{R}^3 : x_1 + x_2 + x_3 = 300, x_1 \geq 0, x_2 \geq 0, x_3 \geq 0\}$$

The core treats the three players symmetrically and includes all individually rational, Pareto efficient allocations. In Version 2 of the game (where players 1 and 2 by themselves can earn 300 without the involvement of player 3), the core will be

$$\{(x_1, x_2, x_3) \in \mathbb{R}^3 : x_1 + x_2 = 300, x_1 \geq 0, x_2 \geq 0, x_3 = 0\}$$

If players 1 and 2 can earn 300 together without player 3 or players 1 and 3 can earn 300 together without player 2 (Version 3 of the game), it can be seen that the core consists of just a single element, namely $(300, 0, 0)$.

    If the players get a nonzero allocation whenever any two players suggest the same allocation (Version 4 of the game - three person majority game), it can be seen that the core is empty. The following two insights provide a rationale for the emptiness of the core in this case. First, when any player i obtains a positive payoff in a feasible allocation, the other two players must get less than 300 which they would be able to gain by themselves. Second, regardless of what the final allocation is, there is always a coalition that could gain if that coalition gets one final opportunity to negotiate effectively against this allocation. $\square$

Example 28.2 (A Three Player TU Game). This example is taken from [2]. Here, $N = \{1, 2, 3\}$ and $v(1) = v(2) = v(3) = 0; v(12) = 0.25; v(13) = 0.5; v(23) = 0.75; v(123) = 1$. Note that $(x_1, x_2, x_3) \in \mathbb{C}(N, v)$ iff

$$x_1 \geq 0; \ x_2 \geq 0; \ x_3 \geq 0$$

$$x_1 + x_2 \geq 0.25; \ x_1 + x_3 \geq 0.5; \ x_2 + x_3 \geq 0.75;$$

$$x_1 + x_2 + x_3 = 1$$

This would mean $x_1 \leq 0.25$; $x_2 \leq 0.5$; $x_3 \leq 0.75$. The core is depicted in Figure 28.1 and happens to be a trapezoid with vertices at $(0, 0.25, 0.75), (0, 0.5, 0.5), (0.25, 0, 0.75)$, and $(0.25, 0.5, 0.25)$. $\square$

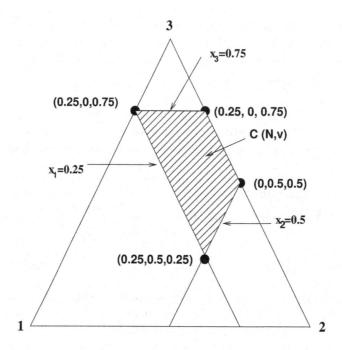

Fig. 28.1: Core of the game in Example 28.2 is a trapezoid

Example 28.3 (House Allocation). This example is originally from the book by von Neumann and Morgenstern [3]. Player 1 has a house which she values at Rs 1 million and wishes to sell the house. There are two potential buyers, player 2 and player 3 who have a valuation of Rs 2 million each and who also have with them Rs 2 million each. Suppose player 1 sells the house to player 2 at a price p million where $1 \leq p \leq 2$. Then the utility of player 1 is p million; utility of player 2 is $(2 - p) + 2 = 4 - p$ million; and the utility of player 3 is 2 million. A similar situation arises if player 1 sells house to player 3 at a price p million, where $1 \leq p \leq 2$. We thus get the characteristic form of the game as:

$$v(1) = 1; \ v(2) = 2; \ v(3) = 2; \ v(12) = v(13) = v(23) = 4; \ v(123) = 6$$

An allocation $(x_1, x_2, x_3) \in \mathbb{C}(N, v)$ iff

$$x_1 \geq 1; \ x_2 \geq 2; \ x_3 \geq 2; \ x_1 + x_2 \geq 4; \ x_2 + x_3 \geq 4; \ x_1 + x_3 \geq 4; \ x_1 + x_2 + x_3 = 6.$$

The only allocation that satisfies the above equations is $(2, 2, 2)$ which is the lone element in the core. This corresponds to player 1 selling her house at the maximum possible price of Rs. 2 million. □

Example 28.4 (Core of MST Profit Game). Consider the minimum spanning tree game with $N = \{1, 2, 3\}$, discussed in Example 27.7:

$$v(1) = 5; \ v(2) = 9; \ v(3) = 7; \ v(12) = 15; \ v(13) = 12; \ v(23) = 17; \ v(123) = 23$$

The equations defining the core are given by

$$x_1 \geq 5; \ x_2 \geq 9; \ x_3 \geq 7 \ x_1 + x_2 \geq 15; \ x_1 + x_3 \geq 12; \ x_2 + x_3 \geq 13; \ x_1 + x_2 + x_3 = 23.$$

The above equations imply that the core is given by the set

$$\{(x_1, x_2, x_3) : \ 5 \leq x_1 \leq 6; \ 9 \leq x_2 \leq 11; \ 7 \leq x_3 \leq 8; x_1 + x_2 + x_3 = 23\}$$

Clearly this is an uncountably infinite set. Note that the core allocation for player 2 is the highest as expected; the core allocation for player 1 is the least which is again according to intuition. □

Example 28.5 (A Glove Market). This example shows that core may be non-empty in some pathological cases. First we consider a simple case and then generalize it. Let there be 5 suppliers of gloves. Of these the first two players can each supply one left glove and the other three players can supply one right glove each. Suppose $N_L = \{1, 2\}$ is the set of left glove suppliers and $N_R = \{3, 4, 5\}$ the set of right glove suppliers. Suppose the worth of each coalition is the number of matched pairs that it can assemble. For example, if $C = \{1, 3\}$, the worth of C is 1, whereas if $C = \{3, 4\}$, the worth of C is 0. In general, given $C \subseteq N$,

$$v(C) = \min\{|C \cap N_L|, \ |C \cap N_R|\}$$

The core of this game can be seen to be the singleton $\{(1, 1, 0, 0, 0)\}$.

On the other hand, if $N_L = \{1, 2, 3\}$ and $N_R = \{4, 5\}$, the core of the game would be the singleton $\{(0, 0, 0, 1, 1)\}$. If the cardinalities of the two sets N_L and N_R are equal, then the core takes a different form altogether. For example, if $N_L = \{1, 2\}$ and $N_R = \{3, 4\}$, the core of the game would contain many elements including $(\frac{1}{2}, \frac{1}{2}, \frac{1}{2}, \frac{1}{2})$.

We will now generalize the example to $n = 2,000,001$. Of these, $1,000,000$ players can each supply one left glove and the other $1,000,001$ players can each supply one right glove. The core of this game consists of the unique allocation x such that

$$x_i = 1 \text{ if } i \in N_L$$
$$= 0 \text{ if } i \in N_R$$

The reason for this is:

$$\sum_{i \in N_L} x_i + \sum_{j \in N_R \setminus \{k\}} x_j \geq 1,000,000 \quad \forall k \in N_R$$

Suppose that some right glove supplier has some positive payoff in a feasible allocation. Then the total payoff to the other $2,000,000$ players must be less than $1,000,000$, which they could improve by making $1,000,000$ matched pairs among themselves, without this distinguished right glove supplier. An economic interpretation of the example is as follows. Since right gloves are in excess supply, they have a market price of 0. If we add just two more left glove suppliers, the unique core allocation would switch to

$$x_i = 0 \text{ if } i \in N_L$$
$$= 1 \text{ if } i \in N_R$$

in which every left glove supplier gets zero payoff while every right glove supplier gets payoff 1. It would be interesting to see what the core would be if there are $1,000,000$ left glove suppliers and $1,000,000$ right glove suppliers.   □

Epsilon Core

The instability displayed by the core for large games (such as the glove market example) can be somewhat overcome using the notion of ε-core or ε-approximate core. Given any number $\varepsilon \geq 0$, an allocation x is in the ε-core of the coalitional game (N, v) iff

$$\sum_{i \in N} x_i = v(N)$$

$$\sum_{i \in C} x_i \geq v(C) - \varepsilon |C| \ \ \forall C \subseteq N$$

If x is in the ε-core, then no coalition C would be able to guarantee all its members ε more than what they get in x.

Example 28.6 (Epsilon Core of Glove Market). For the glove market example, an allocation x is in the ε-core iff

$$\min\{x_i : i \in N_L\} + \min\{x_j : j \in N_R\} \geq 1 - 2\varepsilon$$

This means the worst-off left glove supplier and the worst-off right glove supplier together must get at least $1 - 2\varepsilon$. With $1,000,000$ left glove suppliers and $1,000,001$ right glove suppliers, if $\varepsilon > 0.0000005$, then for any number λ such that $0 \leq \lambda \leq 1$, the allocation x such that

$$x_i = 1 - \lambda \ \ \forall i \in N_L; \quad x_i = \frac{\lambda}{1.000001} \ \ \forall i \in N_R$$

is in the ε-core of the above glove market game.   □

28.2 Characterization of Games with Non-Empty Core

The classic, independent findings of Shapley and Bondereva provide a characterization of games with non-empty core, using linear programming [4, 5]. To understand this characterization, we first look into the following linear program (LP), given a TU game (N, v).

$$\text{minimize } x_1 + x_2 + \ldots + x_n \text{ subject to}$$
$$\sum_{i \in C} x_i \geq v(C) \ \forall C \subseteq Ni; \ (x_1, \ldots, x_n) \in \mathbb{R}^n.$$

The above LP determines the least amount of transferable utility which is necessary for an allocation so that no coalition can improve upon it. Note that this LP definitely has a solution if it is feasible. This is because all the inequalities are of the *greater than or equal to* type and also because of the structure of the inequalities. Let $(x_1^*, x_2^*, \ldots, x_n^*)$ be an optimal solution of this LP. Then we know

$$\sum_{i \in C} x_i^* \geq v(C) \quad \forall C \subseteq N$$

In particular, $x_1^* + \ldots + x_n^* \geq v(N)$. There are two possibilities:

(1) $x_1^* + \ldots + x_n^* = v(N)$. In this case, all solutions of this LP will constitute the core $\mathbb{C}(N, v)$. In fact, the core will consist precisely of the solutions of this LP.
(2) $x_1^* + \ldots + x_n^* > v(N)$. In this case, it is clear that the $\mathbb{C}(N, v)$ is empty.

Example 28.7 (Divide the Dollar Game). Recall Version 4 of the divide the dollar game (majority voting game) where $N = \{1, 2, 3\}$ and $v(1) = v(2) = v(3) = 0; v(12) = v(23) = v(13) = v(123) = 300$. The linear program would be:

$$\begin{aligned} \text{minimize} \quad & x_1 + x_2 + x_3 \\ \text{subject to} \quad & x_1, x_2, x_3 \geq 0 \\ & x_1 + x_2 \geq 300 \\ & x_2 + x_3 \geq 300 \\ & x_1 + x_3 \geq 300 \\ & x_1 + x_2 + x_3 \geq 300 \\ & x_1, x_2, x_3 \in \mathbb{R} \end{aligned}$$

The unique optimal solution of this LP is:

$$x_1^* = x_2^* = x_3^* = 150$$

Since $x_1^* + x_2^* + x_3^* = 450 > 300 = v(\{1, 2, 3\})$, the core is empty.

Now consider Version 3 of the Divide the Dollar game. Recall for this game that $N = \{1, 2, 3\}$ and $v(1) = v(2) = v(3) = v(23) = 0; v(12) = v(13) = v(123) = 300$. The LP here is:

$$\begin{aligned} \text{minimize} \quad & x_1 + x_2 + x_3 \\ \text{subject to} \quad & x_1, x_2, x_3 \geq 0 \\ & x_1 + x_2 \geq 300 \\ & x_1 + x_3 \geq 300 \\ & x_2 + x_3 \geq 0 \\ & x_1 + x_2 + x_3 \geq 300 \end{aligned}$$

The unique optimal solution here is:

$$x_1^* = 300; \quad x_2^* = x_3^* = 0$$

The optimal value is 300. Since $x_1^* + x_2^* + x_3^* = v(N)$, the core consists of a single element $(300, 0, 0)$. $\qquad \square$

Example 28.8 (Duals of the Linear Programs for Divide the Dollar). Let us first examine the dual of the LP for the majority voting game. The objective function of the dual LP is:

$$\alpha(1)[v(1)]+\alpha(2)[v(2)]+\alpha(3)[v(3)]+\alpha(12)[v(12)]+\alpha(23)[v(23)]+\alpha(13)[v(13)]+\alpha(123)[v(123)]$$

The dual LP for the majority voting game will be:

$$
\begin{aligned}
\text{maximize} \quad & 300[\alpha(12) + \alpha(23) + \alpha(13) + \alpha(123)] \\
\text{subject to} \quad & \alpha(1) + \alpha(12) + \alpha(13) + \alpha(123) = 1 \\
& \alpha(2) + \alpha(12) + \alpha(23) + \alpha(123) = 1 \\
& \alpha(3) + \alpha(13) + \alpha(23) + \alpha(123) = 1 \\
& \alpha(1) \geq 0; \ \alpha(2) \geq 0; \ \ldots; \ \alpha(123) \geq 0
\end{aligned}
$$

An optimal solution of this dual LP is given by:

$$
\begin{aligned}
\alpha(12) = \alpha(13) = \alpha(23) &= \frac{1}{2} \\
\alpha(1) = \alpha(2) = \alpha(3) = \alpha(123) &= 0
\end{aligned}
$$

Here the core is empty. Now we examine the dual of the LP for Version 3 of the game. The dual LP is:

$$
\begin{aligned}
\text{maximize} \quad & 300[\alpha(12) + \alpha(13) + \alpha(123)] \\
\text{subject to} \quad & \alpha(1) + \alpha(12) + \alpha(13) + \alpha(123) = 1 \\
& \alpha(2) + \alpha(12) + \alpha(23) + \alpha(123) = 1 \\
& \alpha(3) + \alpha(13) + \alpha(23) + \alpha(123) = 1 \\
& \alpha(1) \geq 0; \ \alpha(2) \geq 0; \ \ldots; \ \alpha(123) \geq 0
\end{aligned}
$$

The optimal value of the dual is again, clearly, 300. The optimal solution is $\alpha(12) = \alpha(13) = \frac{1}{2}$ with all other $\alpha(\cdot)$ values zero. $\qquad\square$

Shapley - Bondereva Characterization

In general, the primal LP is:

$$\text{minimize} \ \sum_{i \in N} x_i \ \ \text{subject to}$$

$$\sum_{i \in C} x_i \geq v(C) \ \forall C \subseteq N \quad x_i \in \mathbb{R} \ \forall i \in N.$$

The dual LP is given by:

$$\text{maximize} \ \sum_{C \subseteq N} \alpha(C)v(C) \ \ \text{subject to}$$

$$\sum_{C \supseteq \{i\}} \alpha(C) = 1 \ \forall i \in N; \quad \alpha(C) \geq 0 \ \forall C \subseteq N.$$

Let us apply the *strong duality theorem* here. Recall: if the primal (dual) has an optimal solution, then the dual (primal) has an optimal solution and the optimal values are the same. It is easy to see that an optimal solution exists for the above primal. Hence by applying the strong duality theorem, given a TU game (N, v), there exists an allocation $x^* \in \mathbb{R}^n$ and a vector $\alpha^*(C)_{C \subseteq N}$ such that

$$\sum_{i \in C} x_i^* \geq v(C)$$

$$\alpha^*(C) \geq 0 \quad \forall C \subseteq N$$

$$\sum_{C \supseteq \{i\}} \alpha^*(C) = 1 \quad \forall i \in N$$

This is illustrated by both Example 28.7 and Example 28.8 presented above. Let us now impose the following condition:

$$\sum_{C \supseteq \{i\}} \alpha(C) = 1 \quad \forall i \subseteq N \implies \sum_{C \subseteq N} \alpha(C)v(C) \leq v(N)$$

That is, feasibility of the dual implies that the value of the objective function of the dual is $\leq v(N)$. We know that the optimal value of the primal $\geq v(N)$. Since the LP has a solution, the optimal solution therefore will have value $v(N)$. This ensures that the core is non-empty. This means we have a necessary and sufficient condition for the non-emptiness of the core. This necessary and sufficient condition is called *balancedness*.

Definition 28.6 (Balanced TU Games). *A TU game (N, v) is said to be balanced if*

$$\sum_{C \supseteq \{i\}} \alpha(C) = 1 \quad \forall i \in N \implies \sum_{C \subseteq N} \alpha(C)v(C) \leq v(N)$$

We are now in a position to state the important theorem that we have just now proved.

Theorem 28.1. *The core of a TU game (N, v) is non-empty iff the game (N, v) is balanced.*

The components of any optimal solution $(x_1^*, x_2^*, \ldots, x_n^*)$ of the above optimization problem are called *balanced aspirations* of the players. The phrase is appropriate since

$$\sum_{i \in C} x_i^* \geq v(C) \quad \forall C \subseteq N$$

The aspirations are balanced by the fact that $(x_1 + x_2 + \ldots + x_n)$ is minimized.

28.3   The Core of Convex Games

Recall from Chapter 27 that a TU game (N, v) is said to be convex if for every $i \in N$, the marginal contribution of player i to larger coalitions is larger. Interestingly, the core of any convex game is non-empty. The following result on convex games exhibits an allocation that surely belongs to the core of the game.

Proposition 28.1. *Given a convex game* (N, v), *the allocation* $x = (x_1, \ldots, x_n)$ *defined by*

$$x_1 = v(\{1\})$$
$$x_2 = v(\{1, 2\}) - v(\{1\})$$
$$\ldots$$
$$x_n = v(\{1, 2, \ldots, n\}) - v(\{1, 2, \ldots, n-1\})$$

belongs to the core of the game. That is, $x \in \mathbb{C}(N, v)$.

Proof: It can be easily verified for the allocation $x = (x_1, \ldots, x_n)$ defined above, that $x_1 + \ldots + x_n = v(N)$ and therefore X is collectively rational. It remains to be shown that x is coalitionally rational. That is, we have to show that

$$\sum_{i \in E} x_i \geq v(E); \ \ \forall E \subseteq N.$$

Note that $N = \{1, 2, \ldots, n\}$. Suppose E is any coalition of players in N. We can write $E = \{i_1, i_2, \ldots, i_k\}$ for some $k \leq n$. We can assume without loss of generality that $i_1 < i_2 < \cdots < i_k$. This will enable us to observe that

$$\{i_1, i_2, \ldots, i_{j-1}\} \subseteq \{1, 2, \ldots, i_j - 1\}; \ \ \forall j \in \{1, 2, \ldots, k\}.$$

At this point, recall proposition 27.1 which states that a TU game (N, v) is convex iff

$$v(C \cup \{i\}) - v(C) \leq v(D \cup \{i\}) - v(D) \ \forall C \subseteq D \subseteq N \ \forall i \in N \setminus D.$$

Choosing $C = \{i_1, i_2, \ldots, i_{j-1}\}$; $D = \{1, 2, \ldots, i_j - 1\}$; and $i = i_j \in N \setminus D$, we immediately obtain

$$v(\{i_1, i_2, \ldots, i_j\}) - v(\{i_1, i_2, \ldots, i_{j-1}\}) \leq v(\{1, 2, \ldots, i_j\}) - v(\{1, 2, \ldots, i_j - 1\}).$$

Using the above, we next observe that

$$x_{i_1} = (v(\{1, 2, \ldots, i_1\}) - v(\{1, 2, \ldots, i_1 - 1\})) \geq (v(\{i_1\}) - v(\emptyset)),$$

$$x_{i_2} = (v(\{1, 2, \ldots, i_2\}) - v(\{1, 2, \ldots, i_2 - 1\})) \geq (v(\{i_1, i_2\}) - v(\{i_1\})),$$

and so on until

$$x_{i_k} = (v(\{1, 2, \ldots, i_k\}) - v(\{1, 2, \ldots, i_k - 1\})) \geq (v(\{i_1, i_2, \ldots, i_k\}) - v(\{i_1, i_2, \ldots, i_k - 1\})).$$

Summing the above k inequalities and simplifying, we obtain

$$x_{i_1} + x_{i_2} + \cdots + x_{i_k} \geq v(\{i_1, i_2, \ldots, i_k\}) = v(E).$$

The above is clearly true for any $E \subseteq N$, thus proving coalitional rationality.   ■

The above proposition immediately leads to the following result which shows that any allocation obtained through a permutation of the set N will also work. We first define some notation. Let $\Pi(N)$ denote the set of all permutations of $N = \{1, 2, \ldots, n\}$. Suppose $\pi \in \Pi(N)$ is any permutation. Let $P(\pi, i)$ denote the set of players who are predecessors of i in the permutation π. That is

$$P(\pi, i) = \{j \in N : \pi(j) < \pi(i)\}.$$

Define the marginal contribution of player i to his predecessors in π by

$$m(P, i) = v(P(\pi, i) \cup \{i\}) - v(P(\pi, i)).$$

Proposition 28.2. *Suppose (N, v) is a convex game and $\pi \in \Pi(N)$ is any permutation. Then the allocation $y^\pi = (m(\pi, 1), m(\pi, 2), \ldots, m(\pi, n))$ belongs to the core of (N, v). That is, $y^\pi \in \mathbb{C}(N, v)$.*

We will be using the above proposition in the next chapter to prove that the Shapley value of any convex game belongs to the core of the game.

28.4   The Core of Cost Games

We have seen in Chapter 27 that TU games where the worth of a coalition is given by the total minimum cost incurred by the players in the coalition are called cost games. When we work with cost games, the definition of the Core will involve $\leq$ instead of $\geq$:

$$\mathbb{C}(N, v) = \left\{ (x_1, \ldots, x_n) \in \mathbb{R}^n : \sum_{i \in C} x_i \leq v(C) \ \forall C \subseteq N; \ \sum_{i \in N} x_i = v(N) \right\}.$$

Example 28.9 (Core of MST cost game). Consider the cost game with $N = \{1, 2, 3\}$ corresponding to the minimum spanning tree game:

$$v(1) = 5; \ v(2) = 1; \ v(3) = 3; \ v(12) = 5; \ v(13) = 8; \ v(23) = 3; \ v(123) = 7$$

The equations defining the core are given by

$$x_1 \leq 5; \ x_2 \leq 1; \ x_3 \leq 3 \ x_1 + x_2 \leq 5; \ x_1 + x_3 \leq 8; \ x_2 + x_3 \leq 7; \ x_1 + x_2 + x_3 = 7.$$

The above equations imply that the core is given by the set

$$\{(x_1, x_2, x_3) : \ 4 \leq x_1 \leq 5; \ -1 \leq x_2 \leq 1; \ 2 \leq x_3 \leq 3; x_1 + x_2 + x_3 = 7\}$$

Note that the core allocation for player 2 could even be negative, meaning player 2 can actually receive money. It would be interesting to compare this with the core of the MST profit game (example 28.4).   □

28.5   Summary and References

We summarize here the important concepts discussed in this chapter.

- Given a characteristic form game or TU game (N, v), the core of the game consists of all allocations that are coalitionally rational and collectively rational. Given an allocation $x = (x_1, \ldots, x_n)$ in the core, no coalition C of players will be able to block x because the worth of the coalition, $v(C)$, is less than or equal to the sum of the allocations in x of players of C. The elements of the core can be interpreted as Nash equilibria of an appropriate, underlying contract signing game.

- The core of a TU game can be empty, may be a countable set, or may even be an uncountable set. A game with empty core (majority voting game being an immediate example) implies that negotiations among players may be never ending. The core of a TU game will always be convex and compact.

- If the core consists of a large number of elements, the difficulty would be how to select a particular best element from the core. Other solution concepts in cooperative game theory could be useful here.

- Shapley and Bondereva have provided a characterization of TU games with non-empty core. They have independently proved, using LP duality, that a TU game has non-empty core if and only if it is balanced.

- An appropriate linear programming formulation can be used to determine whether or not a given TU game has non-empty core. The linear program can be used to compute the elements of the core.

- In order to compute the core of a cost game, we need to reverse the inequalities in the core equations from $\geq$ to $\leq$.

- The core of a convex game is non-empty.

The discussion presented in this chapter follows that of Myerson [6] and Straffin [2]. The foundations for the results on the core have been laid in the classic papers by Gerard Debreu and Herbert Scarf [7] and Herbert Scarf [8]. The balancedness characterization of the core is by Bondereva [4] and Shapley [5]. For an excellent detailed treatment of the core and key results concerning the core, we refer the reader to the books by Peleg and Sudholter [9] and Maschler, Solan, and Zamir [1]. In the next chapter, we discuss the Shapley value.

References

[1]   Michael Maschler, Eilon Solan, and Shmuel Zamir. *Game Theory*. Cambridge University Press, 2013.

[2]   Philip D. Straffin Jr. *Game Theory and Strategy*. The Mathematical Association of America, 1993.

[3]   John von Neumann and Oskar Morgenstern. *Theory of Games and Economic Behavior*. Princeton University Press, 1944.

[4] O.N. Bondereva. "Some applications of linear programming methods to the theory of cooperative games". In: *(In Russian)* (1963).

[5] Lloyd S. Shapley. "On balanced sets and the core". In: *Naval Research Logistics Quarterly* **14** (1967), pp. 435–460.

[6] Roger B. Myerson. *Game Theory: Analysis of Conflict.* Harvard University Press, Cambridge, Massachusetts, USA, 1997.

[7] Gerard Debreu and Herbert Scarf. "A limit theorem on the core of an economy". In: *International Economic Review* **4** (1963), pp. 235–246.

[8] Herbert E. Scarf. "The core of an *n*-person game". In: *Econometrica* **35** (1967), pp. 50–69.

[9] B. Peleg and P. Sudholter. *Introduction to the Theory of Cooperative Games.* Kluwer Academic, Boston, USA, 2003.

28.6 Exercises

(1) A constant sum TU game (N, v) is one in which

$$v(C) + v(N \setminus C) = c$$

where c is some constant. Show that the core of any essential, constant sum game is empty. (Source: [2]).

(2) Consider the glove market example. What will be the core of this game if there are $1,000,000$ left glove suppliers and $1,000,000$ right glove suppliers?

(3) Consider the following variant of the real estate example. Player 1 has a value of Rs. 1 million; player 2 has value of Rs. 2 million; and player 3 has a value of Rs. 3 million for the house. Player 2 has Rs. 3 million cash, so also player 3. Formulate an appropriate TU game and compute the core. (Source: [2]).

(4) Consider a three person superadditive game with $v(1) = v(2) = v(3) = 0; v(12) = a; v(13) = b; v(23) = c; v(123) = d$ where $0 \leq a, b, c \leq d$. Compute the core for this game. When is the core non-empty for this game? (Source: [2]).

(5) Find the core of the *communication satellites game* defined as follows:

$$v(1) = v(2) = v(3) = 0$$

$$v(12) = 5.2; \quad v(13) = 2.5; \quad v(23) = 3; \quad v(123) = 5.2$$

(Source: [2]).

(6) Consider a TU game (N, v) where $N = \{1, 2, 3\}$ and

$$v(1) = v(2) = 1; \quad v(3) = 2; \quad v(12) = V(23) = v(13) = 4; \quad v(123) = 5.$$

What is the core of this game? (Source: [1]).

(7) Compute the core of the logistics game discussed in Chapter 27. Recall that $N = \{1, 2, 3, 4\}$ and the characteristic function is

$$v(1) = v(2) = v(3) = v(4) = 0$$

$$v(12) = v(13) = v(14) = v(23) = v(24) = v(34) = v(234) = v(123) = 0$$

$$v(134) = 40; \quad v(124) = 45; \quad v(1234) = 65$$

(8) Consider a game with five players where player 1 is called a big player and the others are called small players. The big player with one or more small players can earn a worth of 1. The four small players together can also earn 1. Let

$$N = \{1, 2, 3, 4, 5\}$$
$$v(C) = 1 \text{ if } 1 \in C \text{ and } |C| \geq 2$$
$$= 1 \text{ if } |C| \geq 4$$
$$= 0 \text{ otherwise}$$

Compute the core for this game. (Source: [1]).

(9) Let us consider a version of divide the dollar problem with 4 players and total worth equal to 400. Suppose that any coalition with three or more players will be able to achieve the total worth. Also, a coalition with two players will be able to achieve the total worth only if player 1 is a part of the two player coalition. Set up a characteristic function for this TU game and compute the core.

(10) Consider another version of divide the dollar problem with 4 players and total worth equal to 400. Any coalition containing at least two players and having player 1 would be able to achieve the total wealth of 400. Similarly, any coalition containing at least three players and containing player 2 also would be able to achieve the total wealth of 400. Set up a characteristic form game for this situation and compute the core.

(11) It has been stated that the core of a TU game is convex and compact. Prove this result.

(12) A market game is a TU game that consists of a set B of buyers and a set S of sellers such that $N = B \cup S$ and $B \cap S = \emptyset$, and

$$v(C) = \min(|C \cap B|, |C \cap S|); \; \forall C \subseteq N.$$

Compute the core of a market game. (Source: [1]).

(13) Consider a TU game with $N = \{1, 2, 3, 4\}$ and $v(C) = 0$ for all coalitions C of cardinality 1 or cardinality 3; $v(C) = 30$ for all coalitions C of cardinality 2; and $v(C) = 50$ for all coalitions C of cardinality 4. Compute the core of this game. (Source: [1]).

(14) **Programming Assignment**. Design a program that, given a TU game, would formulate an appropriate LP and tell us whether the core of the game is empty or non-empty finite or non-empty infinite. In case the core is non-empty and finite, the program should output the elements of the core.

Chapter 29

The Shapley Value

The Shapley value is a popular solution concept in cooperative game theory that provides a unique allocation to a set of players in a coalitional game. Like the Nash bargaining solution, the Shapley value is based on a set of axioms that determine the allocations to different players based on the axioms. The Shapley value faithfully captures the marginal contributions of the players in deciding the allocations. It has found widespread applications in a variety of engineering applications. In this chapter, we present the Shapley axioms and prove the existence and uniqueness of the Shapley value. We present several illustrative examples and also prove key results.

Given a coalitional game, the core may be empty or may be very large or even uncountably infinite. These certainly cause difficulties in getting sharp predictions for the game. The *Shapley value* is a solution concept which is motivated by the need to have a solution concept that would predict a unique expected payoff allocation for every given coalitional game. The Shapley value concept was proposed using an axiomatic approach by Shapley in 1953, as a part of his doctoral dissertation at the Princeton University. Given a game in coalitional form (N, v), we denote the Shapley value by $\phi(N, v) = (\phi_1(N, v), \ldots, \phi_n(N, v))$ where $\phi_i(N, v)$ is the expected payoff to player i. When there is no confusion, we use $\phi(v)$ instead of $\phi(N, v)$, $\phi_i(v)$ instead of $\phi_i(N, v)$, etc. Also, note that $v \in \mathbb{R}^{2^n - 1}$, where we have omitted $v(\emptyset)$ which is obviously equal to 0.

The Shapley value tries to capture how coalitional competitive forces influence the possible outcomes of a game. It describes a reasonable or fair way of dividing the gains from cooperation given the strategic realities captured by the characteristic function. It crucially uses the marginal contributions of players as a guiding factor.

Note. In this chapter, as we have done in some earlier chapters, we shall (by slight abuse of notation) denote sets $\{1\}$, $\{2\}$, $\{3\}$, $\{1, 2\}$, $\{1, 2, 3\}$ simply by 1, 2, 3, 12, 123, respectively. This is purely for the sake of convenience.

**Lloyd Shapley** can be considered as one of the most influential game theorists of all time. In particular, he is the most important contributor to cooperative game theory. He has made numerous pioneering contributions which have started new areas in game theory. He is a co-recipient with Alvin Roth of the Nobel Prize in Economic Sciences for the year 2012. Many concepts, lemmas and theorems have been named after him. These include, first and foremost, the Shapley value, a popular solution concept in cooperative game theory.

Shapley's pioneering contributions include: (1) Bondareva - Shapley theorem (see previous chapter) which provides a necessary and sufficient condition for the non-emptiness of the core of a coalitional game and which also implies that convex games have non-empty cores (2) Gale - Shapley algorithm [1] which provides the first and perhaps the most used solution to the stable marriage problem (3) Aumann - Shapley pricing that pioneered the pricing of products and services that share resources (4) Shapley - Folkmann lemma which settled the question of convexity of addition of sets (5) Shapley-Shubik power index [2] for determining voting power. Moreover, stochastic games were first proposed by Shapley as early as 1953 [3]. Potential games which are extensively used by researchers these days were proposed by Monderer and Shapley in 1996 [4]. His joint work with Maschler and Peleg on the kernel and the nucleolus is quite path breaking and so is his work with Robert Aumann on non-atomic games and on long-term competition.

Shapley was born in 1923 in Cambridge, Massachusetts and he was a genius in mathematics from an early age. He joined Harvard university for his undergraduate studies and got his A.B. Degree in 1948. During 1943 - 45, he worked for the American Military and as a Sargeant in Army Corps in 1943, he brilliantly broke the Soviet weather code and was decorated with a Bronze star at the age of 20. He started working with Albert Tucker at the Princeton University in 1949 and got his Ph.D. in 1953. The work on what is now called the Shapley value was carried out during this period. The title of his doctoral dissertation was *Additive and Nonadditive Set Functions*. John Nash and Shapley were contemporaries working with the celebrated Albert Tucker. From 1954 to 1981, Shapley spent 27 years at the Rand Corporation as research mathematician and produced many path breaking results. Since 1981, he has been at the University of California, Los Angeles, working in the Department of Economics as well as the Department of Mathematics.

29.1 The Shapley Axioms

Let (N, v) be a game in coalitional form. Let π be a permutation on the set N. Let $(N, \pi v)$ be the coalitional game with the permuted value function given by

$$\pi v(\{\pi(i) : i \in C\}) = v(C), \ \forall \, C \subseteq N$$

This means that the role of any player $i \in N$, in the game (N, v) is essentially the same as the role of player $\pi(i)$ in $(N, \pi v)$.

Example 29.1. Suppose $N = \{1, 2, 3\}$. Consider the permutation π on N defined by $\pi(1) = 3; \pi(2) = 1; \pi(3) = 2$. Then the game $(N, \pi v)$ will be the following: $\pi v(1) = v(2)$; $\pi v(2) = v(3)$; $\pi v(3) = v(1)$; $\pi v(12) = v(23)$; $\pi v(23) = v(13)$; $\pi v(13) = v(12)$; $\pi v(123) = v(123)$. $\qquad\qquad\square$

Shapley proposed three axioms to describe the desirable properties that we would expect a good solution concept to satisfy: (1) Axiom 1 : Symmetry; (2) Axiom 2 : Linearity; (3) Axiom 3 : Carrier.

Axiom 1: Symmetry

For any $v \in \mathbb{R}^{2^n - 1}$, any permutation π on N, and any player $i \in N$, the symmetry axiom states that

$$\phi_{\pi(i)}(\pi v) = \phi_i(v)$$

Informally, the Shapley value of a player relabeled by a permutation, under the permuted value function is the same as the Shapley value of the original player under the original value function. This axiom implies that only the role of a player in the game should matter. The labels or specific names used in N are irrelevant.

Axiom 2: Linearity

Let (N, v) and (N, w) be any two coalitional games. Suppose $p \in [0, 1]$. Define a new coalitional game $(N, \ pv + (1 - p)w)$ as follows.

$$(pv + (1 - p)w)(C) = pv(C) + (1 - p)w(C) \ \ \forall C \subseteq N$$

Axiom 2 states that, given any two coalitional games (N, v) and (N, w), any number $p \in [0, 1]$, and any player $i \in N$,

$$\phi_i(pv + (1 - p)w) = p\phi_i(v) + (1 - p)\phi_i(w)$$

In other words, the Shapley value of a player for a convex combination of coalitional games is the convex combination of Shapley values of the player in the individual games. This axiom asserts that the expected payoff to each player is the same before resolution of uncertainty and after resolution of uncertainty.

Axiom 3: Carrier

Definition 29.1 (Carrier). *A coalition D is said to be a* carrier *of a coalitional game (N, v) if*

$$v(C \cap D) = v(C) \ \ \forall C \subseteq N$$

If D is a carrier and $i \notin D$, then

$$v(\{i\}) = v(\{i\} \cap D) = v(\phi) = 0$$

If D is a carrier of (N, v), all players $j \in N \setminus D$ are called *dummies* in (N, v) because their entry into any coalition cannot change the worth of the coalition. Also, for any $C \subseteq N$ and $i \notin D$,

$$v(C \cup \{i\}) = v((C \cup \{i\}) \cap D) = v(C \cap D) = v(C)$$

Intuitively, D includes all influential players (it might also include non-influential players but it will not exclude any influential player). If D is a carrier and $i \in N$, then for any $C \subseteq N$,

$$v(C) = v(C \cap D) = v(C \cap (D \cup \{i\}))$$

Hence, $D \cup \{i\}$ for any $i \in N$ is also a carrier. In fact, the set N is always a carrier. This means that $v(D) = v(N)$. This can also be seen from

$$v(D) = v(D \cap N) = v(N)$$

It is however possible that no proper subset of N is a carrier.

The *Carrier Axiom* (Axiom 3) states that, for any $v \in \mathbb{R}^{2^n - 1}$ and any coalition D that is a carrier of (N, v),

$$\sum_{i \in D} \phi_i(v) = v(D) = v(N)$$

The carrier axiom immediately implies that

$$\phi_i(v) = 0 \ \forall \ i \notin D$$

$$\sum_{i \in N} \phi_i(v) = v(N)$$

This axiom asserts that the players in a carrier set should divide their joint worth (which is equal to the worth of the grand coalition) among themselves. This means the dummies are allocated nothing. The above expression also illustrates a key fact that the Shapley value always divides the worth of the grand coalition among the players of the game. This means that Shapley value implicitly assumes the formation of the grand coalition (however some of these players may be dummy players who do not get anything allocated).

Note. Throughout the rest of this chapter, we will denote, for the sake of convenience, the set $N \setminus \{i\}$ by the notation $N - i$.

29.2   Shapley's Theorem and Examples

With the above three axioms in place, we are now in a position to state the celebrated result due to Shapley [5].

Theorem 29.1. *There is exactly one mapping $\phi : \mathbb{R}^{2^n - 1} \to \mathbb{R}^n$ that satisfies Axiom 1, Axiom 2, and Axiom 3. This mapping satisfies:* $\forall i \in N, \ \forall v \in \mathbb{R}^{2^n - 1}$,

$$\phi_i(v) = \sum_{C \subseteq N - i} \frac{|C|! \ (n - |C| - 1)!}{n!} \ \{v(C \cup \{i\}) - v(C)\}$$

The term $\frac{|C|! \ (n-|C|-1)!}{n!}$ can be interpreted as the probability that in any permutation, the members of C are ahead of a distinguished player i. The term $v(C \cup \{i\}) - v(C)$ gives the marginal contribution of player i to the worth of the coalition C. Thus the above formula for $\phi_i(v)$ gives the expected contribution of player i to the worth of any coalition.

Suppose there is a collection of n resources and each resource is useful in its own way towards executing a certain service. Suppose $v(N)$ is the total value that this collection of resources would create if all the resources are deployed for the accomplishment of the service. Let us focus on a certain resource, say resource i. Now, this resource will make a marginal contribution to every subset C of $N - i$ when it is included to the set C. We can choose the set C in $(|C|! \ |n-|C|-1|!)$ ways and when this is divided by $n!$, we obtain the probability of choosing a particular subset C. Thus the Shapley value of resource i is the average marginal contribution that resource i will make to any arbitrary coalition of resources that is a subset of $N - i$.

Alternatively, imagine that there is committee room where an important discussion is in progress and only one person can enter the committee room at a time. Suppose the committee room currently consists of individuals belonging to a certain coalition C with the rest of the individuals outside the committee room. An individual $i \notin C$ entering the committee room will contribute in a certain way to the ongoing discussion in the committee room. The contribution of i will pretty much depend on how influential, powerful, and articulate the individual i is. If the committee room is equally likely to have any coalition that is a subset of $N - i$, then the average contribution i would make to any arbitrary such coalition would be the Shapley value of i.

Example 29.2 (Divide the Dollar Game). First, let us consider Version 3 (Example 27.3). Recall that $N = \{1, 2, 3\}$; $v(1) = v(2) = v(3) = v(23) = 0$; $v(12) = v(13) = v(123) = 300$. The Shapley value expression for $\phi_1(v)$ would be:

$$\phi_1(v) = \frac{2}{6}(v(1) - v(\emptyset)) + \frac{1}{6}(v(12) - v(2)) + \frac{1}{6}(v(13) - v(3)) + \frac{2}{6}(v(123) - v(23))$$

Similarly,

$$\phi_2(v) = \frac{2}{6}(v(2) - v(\emptyset)) + \frac{1}{6}(v(12) - v(1)) + \frac{1}{6}(v(23) - v(3)) + \frac{2}{6}(v(123) - v(13))$$

$$\phi_3(v) = \frac{2}{6}(v(3) - v(\emptyset)) + \frac{1}{6}(v(13) - v(1)) + \frac{1}{6}(v(23) - v(2)) + \frac{2}{6}(v(123) - v(12))$$

It can be easily seen that

$$\phi_1(v) = 200; \quad \phi_2(v) = 50; \quad \phi_3(v) = 50$$

Also, it can be easily verified from the above expressions that

$$\phi_1(v) + \phi_2(v) + \phi_3(v) = v(123)$$

It can also be verified easily that $\phi = (100, 100, 100)$ for Version 1 (Example 27.1) and Version 4 (Example 27.4) of the game, while $\phi = (150, 150, 0)$ for Version 2 (Example 27.2) of the game. $\qquad\square$

Example 29.3 (Minimum Spanning Tree Game). Consider the minimum spanning tree game considered in Example 27.7. Recall that $N = \{1, 2, 3\}$ and

$$v(\emptyset) = 0; \ v(1) = 5; \ v(2) = 9; \ v(3) = 7$$

$$v(12) = 15; \ v(13) = 12; \ v(23) = 17; v(123) = 23.$$

Following the expressions in the previous example, it can be shown that

$$\phi_1(v) = 5.5; \quad \phi_2(v) = 10; \quad \phi_3(v) = 7.5$$

Notice that the payoff allocation to player 2 is the highest which is clearly justified. Also, it is logical that player 1 gets the least allocation while player 3's allocation is greater than that of player 1. Also, note that this allocation belongs to the core of the game. $\qquad\square$

Example 29.4 (Glove Market). Consider the glove market game (Example 28.4) with $2,000,001$ players, having one $1,00,000$ left glove suppliers and $1,000,001$ right glove suppliers. We have seen that the core of this game is a singleton. Here, the Shapley value of any right-glove supplier is the probability that he would find in any coalition more left glove suppliers than right-glove suppliers. Here the Shapley value for each right-glove supplier is 0.499557 and for each left glove supplier is 0.500443. Note that the Shapley value is able to capture the effect of coalitional forces better than the core. Also note that the Shapley value does not belong to the core. $\qquad\square$

Example 29.5 (Apex Game). In this game, there are five players: $N = \{1, 2, 3, 4, 5\}$. Player 1 is called the big player and the other players are called small players. The big player with one or more small players can earn a worth of 1. The four small players together can also earn 1.

$$v(C) = 1 \text{ if } 1 \in C \text{ and } |C| \geq 2$$
$$= 1 \text{ if } |C| \geq 4$$
$$= 0 \text{ otherwise}$$

The Shapley value is

$$\phi(v) = \left(\frac{3}{5}, \frac{1}{10}, \frac{1}{10}, \frac{1}{10}, \frac{1}{10}\right)$$

Note that the core of this game is empty. $\qquad\square$

Example 29.6 (A Logistics Game). Figure 29.1 shows a logistics network that provides connectivity between two important cities S and T. There are five hubs A, B, C, D, E which are intermediate points from S to T. The transportation is provided by service

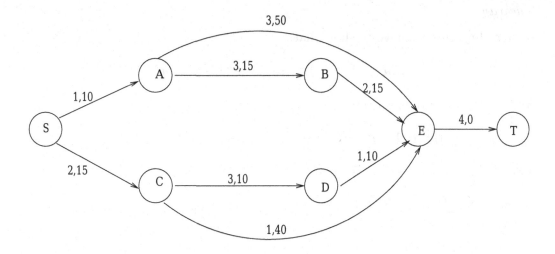

Fig. 29.1: A logistics network

providers 1, 2, 3, 4. We have already seen this example in Chapter 27, where we formulated this as a TU game with $N = \{1, 2, 3, 4\}$ and with characteristic function

$$v(1) = v(2) = v(3) = v(4) = 0$$

$$v(12) = v(13) = v(14) = v(23) = v(24) = v(34) = v(234) = v(123) = 0$$

$$v(134) = 40; \quad v(124) = 45; \quad v(1234) = 65$$

It can be shown that the Shapley values here are given by $\phi(v) = (20, 20, 5, 20)$. This can be shown to belong to the core of this game. □

29.3   Proof of the Shapley Theorem

The proof proceeds in two parts. In Part 1, we show that the formula for $\phi_i(v)$ satisfies all the three axioms. In Part 2, we show that there exists a unique mapping ϕ that satisfies all the three axioms.

Proof of Part 1

Symmetry

Observe that in the formula for $\phi_i(v)$, what only matters about a coalition is whether it contains i and the number of players it contains. Thus relabeling does not affect the value in any way. This observation clearly shows that symmetry (Axiom 1) is satisfied.

Linearity

To show linearity, we have to show that

$$\phi_i(pv + (1-p)w) = p\phi_i(v) + (1-p)\phi_i(w)$$

We have, by definition, for any $p \in [0,1]$,

$$(pv + (1-p)w)(C) = pv(C) + (1-p)w(C) \; \forall C \subseteq N \tag{29.1}$$

Note that $\phi_i(pv + (1-p)w)$ is equal to

$$\sum_{C \subseteq N-i} \frac{|C|! \; (n - |C| - 1)!}{n!} \; ((pv + (1-p)w)(C \cup \{i\}) - (pv + (1-p)w)(C))$$

By expanding this and applying equation (29.1), linearity can be established.

Carrier Axiom

Suppose D is a carrier of (N, v). Then, we know that

$$v(C \cap D) = v(C) \; \forall C \subseteq N$$

We have also seen that

$$v(\{i\}) = 0 \;\; \forall \; i \in N \setminus D \;\; \text{and} \;\; v(D) = v(N)$$

If we take a look at the formula for the Shapley value, it is very clear that

$$\phi_i(v) = 0 \; \forall i \in N \setminus D$$

since

$$v(C \cup \{i\}) = v((C \cup \{i\}) \cap D) = v(C \cap D) = v(C)$$

We have to show for all carriers D that

$$\sum_{i \in D} \phi_i(v) = v(D)$$

Substituting the formula for $\phi_i(v)$ from the Shapley theorem and simplifying, we can show that

$$\sum_{i \in N} \phi_i(v) = v(N)$$

Since D is a carrier, we have $v(D) = v(N)$, hence the carrier axiom follows.

Proof of Part 2

Here we show that there exists a unique mapping ϕ that satisfies the three axioms. First we prove that the mapping ϕ is a linear transformation by making the following observations.

- Let (N, z) be the coalitional game that assigns worth zero to every coalition, that is, $z(C) = 0 \ \forall C \subseteq N$. Then Axiom 3 (carrier axiom) implies that

$$\phi_i(z) = 0 \ \forall i \in N \tag{29.2}$$

- From Axiom 2, we have

$$\phi_i(pv + (1-p)w) = p\phi_i(v) + (1-p)\phi_i(w)$$

Choosing $w = z$ in the above, we get

$$\phi_i(pv) = p\phi_i(v) \ \forall i \in N \tag{29.3}$$

Equations (29.2) and (29.3) together with the linearity axiom imply that ϕ is a linear transformation.

Suppose $L(N)$ denotes the set of all non-empty subsets of N. Clearly, $|L(N)| = 2^n - 1$ and hence $\mathbb{R}^{|L(N)|}$ is a $(2^n - 1)$-dimensional vector space. Let $D \subseteq N$ be any coalition. Define for D, a coalitional game (N, w_D):

$$w_D(C) = 1 \ \text{if } D \subseteq C$$
$$= 0 \ \text{otherwise}$$

This implies that a coalition C has worth 1 in w_D if it contains all the players in D and has worth zero otherwise. The game (N, w_D) is called the simple D-carrier game. To get a feel for this game, we discuss a simple example before resuming the proof.

Example 29.7 (D-carrier game). Let $N = \{1, 2, 3\}$. Let w_1, w_2, w_3, w_{12}, w_{13}, w_{23}, and w_{123} be the characteristic functions of the D-carrier games corresponding to the coalitions $\{1\}, \{2\}, \{3\}, \{1, 2\}, \{1, 3\}, \{2, 3\}, \{1, 2, 3\}$, respectively. For instance, w_{12} would be:

$$w_{12}(1) = 0; w_{12}(2) = 0; w_{12}(3) = 0; w_{12}(12) = 1; w_{12}(13) = 0; w_{12}(23) = 0; w_{12}(123) = 1$$

We can write all the w values as follows. Note that each one is a 7-tuple.

$$w_1 = (1, 0, 0, 1, 1, 0, 1)$$
$$w_2 = (0, 1, 0, 1, 0, 1, 1)$$
$$w_3 = (0, 0, 1, 0, 1, 1, 1)$$
$$w_{12} = (0, 0, 0, 1, 0, 0, 1)$$
$$w_{13} = (0, 0, 0, 0, 1, 0, 1)$$
$$w_{23} = (0, 0, 0, 0, 0, 1, 1)$$
$$w_{123} = (0, 0, 0, 0, 0, 0, 1)$$

We will be showing subsequently that these seven vectors is a basis of $\mathbb{R}^7$. $\qquad\square$

Continuing the proof of Part 2, note that D is a carrier of (N, w_D) since

$$w_D(C) = w_D(C \cap D) \ \forall C \subseteq N$$

In fact, $D \cup \{j\}$ is also a carrier $\forall j \in N$. Also

$$w_D(N) = 1 \text{ since } D \subseteq N$$

$$w_D(D) = 1 \text{ since } D \subseteq D$$

Application of the carrier axiom leads to the following

$$\sum_{i \in D} \phi_i(w_D) = 1 = w_D(D) = w_D(N) \text{ and}$$

$$\phi_j(w_D) = 0 \ \forall j \notin D$$

The above holds because both D and $D \cup \{j\}$ are carriers of w_D.

Now, by the symmetry axiom, all players in D should get the same payoff. This is because the players in D all contribute equally to the characteristic function w_D. There is no way to distinguish them in any manner, so relabeling can be freely done. This implies:

$$\phi_i(w_D) = \frac{1}{|D|} \ \forall i \in D$$

$$\phi_j(w_D) = 0 \ \forall j \notin D$$

For each coalition $D \subseteq N$, there is a game (N, w_D) and therefore we have $2^n - 1$ such games. Each game is represented by a characteristic function which is a vector of $2^n - 1$ elements. Thus we have $2^n - 1$ vectors each of size $2^n - 1$. We now show that these are linearly independent in the space $\mathbb{R}^{2^n - 1}$. To show linear independence, we have to show that

$$\sum_{D \in L(N)} \lambda_D w_D = (0, 0, \ldots, 0) \implies \lambda_D = 0 \ \forall D \in L(N)$$

Suppose not. Now,

$$\sum_{D \in L(N)} \lambda_D w_D = (0, 0, \ldots, 0) \implies \sum_{D \in L(N)} \lambda_D w_D(C) = 0 \ \forall C \subseteq N$$

Let $C \subseteq N$ be any coalition of minimal size such that $\lambda_C \neq 0$. Based on the observation that D is either a subset of C or not, we can write:

$$\sum_{D \subseteq C} \lambda_D w_D(C) + \sum_{D \subsetneq C} \lambda_D w_D(C) = 0 \implies \sum_{D \in L(N)} \lambda_D w_D(C) = 0 \ \forall C \subseteq N$$

We know that $w_D(C) = 1 \ \forall D \subseteq C$ and $w_D(C) = 0$ otherwise (that is, if D is not a subset of C). Therefore, the above implication leads to

$$\sum_{D \subseteq C} \lambda_D = 0$$

Since C is a subset of minimal size for which $\lambda_C \neq 0$, we have that $\lambda_D = 0$ for all subsets $D \subset C$. Thus the above sum is equal to λ_C. This means $\lambda_C = 0$. This is a contradiction! Thus the set $\{w_D : D \in L(N)\}$ is a basis of the space $\mathbb{R}^{2^n - 1}$. Since a linear transformation is completely determined by what it does on a basis of the vector space, the mapping ϕ is unique. ∎

29.4 Alternative Formulae for Shapley Value

We now describe several alternative ways of developing the Shapley value. Each of these will provide an interesting interpretation for this solution concept.

Approach 1

Given a TU game (N, v), the Shapley value can be written as :

$$\phi_i(v) = \sum_{C \subseteq N-i} \frac{|C|!(n - |C| - 1)!}{n!} \{v(N \setminus C) - v(C)\}$$

This is because the coefficients of $\{v(N \setminus C) - v(C)\}$ and $\{v(C \cup \{i\}) - v(C)$ in the above expression are the same. The above expression shows that the value of each player depends only on the difference between the worths of the complementary coalitions. For each pair of complementary coalitions C and $N \setminus C$, the values of players in $N \setminus C$ increase as $v(N \setminus C) - v(C)$ increase while the values of players in C increase as $v(C) - v(N \setminus C)$ increases.

Approach 2

Another formula for Shapley value is:

$$\phi_i(v) = \sum_{\substack{C \subseteq N \\ i \in C}} \frac{(|C| - 1)!(n - |C|)!}{n!} \{v(N) - v(N \setminus \{i\})\}$$

It is to be noted that

$$\frac{(|C| - 1)!(n - |C|)!}{n!}$$

is the probability that in a random permutation, the coalition C arises as the union of $\{i\}$ with all the predecessors of i.

Approach 3

Let $C \subseteq N$ and $i \notin C$. The marginal contribution of i to C, denoted by $m(C, i)$, is given by:

$$m(C, i) = v(C \cup \{i\}) - v(C)$$

Given any permutation $\pi \in \Pi(N)$, the set of predecessors $P(\pi, i)$ of i in the permutation π is given by:

$$P(\pi, i) = \{j : \pi(j) < \pi(i)\}$$

We have seen that $\phi_i(v)$ is the average marginal contribution of i to any coalition of N assuming all orderings are equally likely. Another way of interpreting this is that

$\phi_i(v)$ is the average marginal contribution of i to the set of his predecessors where the average taken over all permutations equally likely. We therefore get

$$\phi_i(v) = \frac{1}{n!} \sum_{\pi \in \Pi(N)} m(P(\pi, i), i); \ \forall i \in N. \tag{29.4}$$

Similarly, if

$$S(\pi, i) = \{j : \pi(i) < \pi(j)\}$$

denotes the set of all players who are successors of i in the permutation π, we also get

$$\phi_i(v) = \frac{1}{n!} \sum_{\pi \in \Pi(N)} m(S(\pi, i), i); \ \forall i \in N. \tag{29.5}$$

One can verify that (29.4) and (29.5) independently satisfy the expression for the Shapley value.

29.5 Shapley Value of Convex Games

In Chapter 27, we have already defined convex games. In Chapter 28, we have also shown that the core of any convex game is non-empty. We now show that the Shapley value of a convex game belongs to the core of the game. Note in general that the Shapley value need not be a member of the core even if the core is non-empty.

Theorem 29.2. *Let (N, v) be a convex game. Then $\phi(v) \in \mathbb{C}(N, v)$.*

Proof: Let $\Pi(N)$ as usual denote the collection of all permutation of the set N. Suppose $\pi \in \Pi(N)$ is any permutation. Define the allocation $y^\pi \in \mathbb{R}^n$ as follows.

$$y^\pi = (m(\pi, 1), m(\pi, 2), \ldots, m(\pi, n)).$$

We have seen in Chapter 28 (Proposition 28.2) that

$$y^\pi \in \mathbb{C}(N, v) \ \forall \pi \in \Pi(N).$$

Furthermore, we have already seen that

$$\phi_i(v) = \frac{1}{n!} \sum_{\pi \in \Pi(N)} m(P(\pi, i), i)$$

Thus $\phi(v)$ is a convex combination of all vectors y^π; $\pi \in \Pi(N)$. Since the core $\mathbb{C}(N, v)$ is a convex set, it follows immediately that $\phi(v) \in \mathbb{C}(N, v)$. ∎

The above result is a useful one. If we are able to model a physical situation as a convex game, then the Shapley value has the added characteristic that it is also a stable allocation since it belongs to the core. Thus for convex games, the Shapley value provides an excellent solution concept.

Example 29.8 (Shapley value of MST profit game). Consider the MST profit game with $N = \{1, 2, 3\}$ corresponding to the minimum spanning tree game discussed in Example 27.7:

$$v(1) = 5; \ v(2) = 9; \ v(3) = 7; \ v(12) = 15; \ v(13) = 12; \ v(23) = 17; \ v(123) = 23$$

This is a convex game and we have shown that the core is given by

$$\{(x_1, x_2, x_3) : \ 5 \le x_1 \le 6; \ 9 \le x_2 \le 11; \ 7 \le x_3 \le 8; x_1 + x_2 + x_3 = 23\}$$

The Shapley value can be shown to be given by $(5.5, 10, 7.5)$ which clearly belongs to the core. It is logical to see that player 2 gets the highest allocation and player 1 gets the lowest allocation in the Shapley value. □

29.6 Shapley - Shubik Power Index

The Shapley - Shubik power index is an apt solution concept used in the context of a decision making process to determine the power of each player in the process. A decision making process involving a set of players $N = \{1, \ldots, n\}$ can be modeled as a simple, monotonic TU game. Recall that a TU game (N, v) is monotonic if

$$v(C) \le v(D) \ \ \forall C \subseteq D \subseteq N.$$

The game (N, v) is said to be a *simple game* if $v(C)$ is either 0 or 1 for any coalition $C \subseteq N$. The Shapley - Shubik power index of a simple, monotonic TU game is simply the Shapley value of the game. Given a player $i \in N$, define the set

$$Q_i(N, v) = \{C \subseteq N : v(C \cup \{i\}) = 1 \ \text{and} \ v(C) = 0\}$$

That is, $Q_i(N, v)$ consists of all coalitions such that the coalition changes over from a losing coalition to a winning coalition when player i is inducted into the coalition. It can be shown that the Shapley value of simple monotonic games (and hence the Shapley - Shubik power index) is given by

$$\phi_i(v) = \sum_{C \in Q_i(N, v)} \frac{|C|!(n - |C| - 1)!}{n!}$$

Example 29.9 (Shapley - Shubik Power Index). Consider the following three player simple TU game which can be easily shown to be monotonic:

$$v(1) = 1; \ v(2) = v(3) = 0; \ v(12) = v(13) = v(23) = v(123) = 1.$$

Note for this game that

$$Q_1(N, v) = \{\emptyset, \{2\}, \{3\}\}; \ Q_2(N, v) = \{\{3\}\}; \ Q_3(N, v) = \{\{2\}\}$$

Applying the formula above, we get the Shapley - Shubik power index as $(\frac{2}{3}, \frac{1}{6}, \frac{1}{6})$. This is in fact the Shapley value of the given game. Note that players 2 and 3 have the same index due to symmetry. Player 1 is four times as powerful as player 2 or player 3. □

29.7 Banzhaf Index

Like the Shapley - Shubik power index, the Banzhaf index (often called the Banzhaf power index) also measures the power of a player in a coalitional game. Suppose (N, v) is a TU game and recall the expression for computing the Shapley value (Equation 29.4):

$$\phi_i(N, v) = \frac{1}{n!} \sum_{\pi \in \Pi(N)} v(P(\pi, i) \cup \{i\}) - v(P(\pi, i)) \ \forall i \in N$$

In the above expression, the average is taken over all permutations which are assumed to be equally likely. On the other hand, consider the following expression

$$\psi_i(N, v) = \frac{1}{2^{n-1}} \sum_{C \subseteq N-i} (v(C \cup \{i\}) - v(C)) \ \forall i \in N$$

In the above expression, the average is taken over all coalitions assuming that all coalitions are equally likely. The index $\psi_i(N, v)$ is called the *Banzhaf Index* of player i. This signifies the average marginal contribution of the player i to any coalition under the assumption that all coalitions are equally likely. The following example shows that Banzhaf index is not the same as the Shapley value.

Example 29.10 (Banzhaf Index). Consider the so called *unanimity game* which is any TU game (N, v) such that $v(N) = 1$ and $v(C) = 0 \ \forall C \subset N$. The Shapley value for this game turns out to be

$$\phi_i(N, v) = \frac{1}{n} \ \forall i \in N$$

The Banzhaf index for this game can be shown to be

$$\psi_i(N, v) = \frac{1}{2^{n-1}} \ \forall i \in N$$

Note from the above that the sum of Banzhaf indices for all the players is not equal to $v(N) = 1$. Therefore the Banzhaf does not satisfy Pareto optimality which the Shapley value satisfies. In fact, except Pareto optimality, Banzhaf index satisfies all other axiomatic properties of the Shapley value. $\qquad\square$

Several variants of the Banzhaf power index have been proposed in the literature. The paper by Dubey and Shapley [6] may be consulted for more details.

29.8 Summary and References

The Shapley value of a TU game is a unique allocation vector that satisfies three properties axiomatized by Shapley, namely (1) symmetry (2) linearity and (3) the carrier property.

- The Shapley value (in superadditive games) distributes the value of the grand coalition among the players in a way that reflects the marginal contribution of each node to the game on an average. In this sense, Shapley value captures a fair distribution of total value among individual players. However, the Shapley value implicitly assumes that the grand coalition forms. The carrier property ensures that dummy players get a zero allocation while the other players get non-zero allocations.

- There are many alternate formulations of Shapley value and the chapter has presented several different formulations.

- The Shapley value may or may not belong to the core (if the core is non-empty). This means that the Shapley value, though a fair allocation, may not be a sustainable allocation unlike any allocation that belongs to the core.

- The core of a convex game is non-empty and moreover, the Shapley value of a convex game always belongs to the core.

- The Shapley-Shubik power index is defined for simple, monotonic games that represent a decision making process. This index is obtained by computing the Shapley value of the game. This index captures the power of different players in the decision making process and can be computed efficiently due to the special structure of games to which it is applicable.

- The Banzhaf index is defined as the average marginal contribution of the player i to any coalition under the assumption that all coalitions are equally likely. The Shapley value computation assumes that all permutations are equally likely while the Banzhaf index assumes that all coalitions are equally likely. The Banzhaf index does not satisfy Pareto optimality but satisfies all other axiomatic properties of the Shapley value.

The material discussed in this chapter draws upon mainly from the book by Myerson [7]. The recent book by Maschler, Solan, and Zamir [8] is an excellent source for further reading. The volume edited by Roth [9] embodies a comprehensive account of Shapley value and extensions until 1988.

Computation of Shapley value is a hard problem and clearly it has exponential time complexity. The book by Chalkiadakis, Elkind, and Wooldridge [10] has pointers to several references on this important topic. In special cases such as convex games (where the Shapley value is in fact the center of gravity of the core), the computation is somewhat easier.

The Shapley value is extremely useful in practical applications. Two such applications are efficient methods for clustering [11] and determining most influential nodes in social networks [12].

The Shapley-Shubik power index was introduced in [2] and the Banzhaf index is discussed in [13]. For more details about the Banzhaf index, the paper by Dubey and Shapley [6] can be consulted.

References

[1]   D. Gale and L. S. Shapley. "College admissions and the stability of marriage". In: *The American Mathematical Monthly* **69**(1) (1962), pp. 9–15.

[2]   Lloyd S. Shapley and Martin Shubik. "A method for evaluating the distribution of power in a committee system". In: *American Political Science Review* **48** (1954), pp. 787–792.

[3]   Lloyd S. Shapley. "Stochastic games". In: *Proceedings of the National Academy of Sciences* **39**(10) (1953), pp. 1095–1100.

[4]   D. Monderer and L. S. Shapley. "Potential games". In: *Games and Economic Behavior* **14** (1996), pp. 124–143.

[5]   Lloyd S. Shapley. "A value for n-person games". In: *Contributions to the Theory of Games.* Ed. by Robert Kuhn and Albert Tucker. Princeton University Press, 1953, pp. 307–317.

[6]   Pradeep Dubey and Lloyd S. Shapley. "Mathematical properties of the Banzhaf power index". In: *Mathematics of Operations Research* **4**(2) (1979), pp. 99–131.

[7]   Roger B. Myerson. *Game Theory: Analysis of Conflict.* Harvard University Press, Cambridge, Massachusetts, USA, 1997.

[8]   Michael Maschler, Eilon Solan, and Shmuel Zamir. *Game Theory.* Cambridge University Press, 2013.

[9]   Alvin E. Roth (Editor). *The Shapley Value: Essays in Honor of Lloyd S. Shapley.* Cambridge University Press, Cambridge, UK, 1988.

[10] Georgios Chalkiadakis, Edith Elkind, and Michael Wooldridge. *Computational Aspects of Cooperative Game Theory.* Morgan & Claypool, 2011.

[11] Vikas K. Garg, Y. Narahari, and M. Narasimha Murty. "Novel biobjective clustering (BiGC) based on cooperative game theory". In: *IEEE Transactions on Knowledge and Data Engineering* **25**(5) (2013), pp. 1070–1082.

[12] Ramasuri Narayanam and Y. Narahari. "A Shapley value approach to discovering influential nodes in social networks". In: *IEEE Transactions on Automation Science and Engineering* **8**(1) (2011), pp. 130–147.

[13] John Banzhaf. "Weighted voting does not work: A mathematical analysis". In: *Rutgers Law Review* **19** (1965), pp. 317–343.

29.9   Exercises

(1) Show using the expression for Shapley value that the sum of Shapley values of all players will be equal to the value of the grand coalition.

(2) Suppose (N, v) is a TU game and we define a unique imputation as follows.

$$\xi_i(N, v) = v(\{i\}) \ \forall i \in N.$$

Which of the Shapley axioms does the above satisfy and which of the Shapley axioms does it violate?

(3) Suppose (N, v) is a TU game and we define a unique imputation as follows.

$$\xi_i(N, v) = v(\{1, \ldots, i-1, i\}) - v(\{1, \ldots, i-1\}) \ \forall i \in N.$$

Which of the Shapley axioms does the above satisfy and which of the Shapley axioms does it violate.

(4) Consider a three person superadditive game with $v(1) = v(2) = v(3) = 0; v(12) = a; v(13) = b; v(23) = c; v(123) = d$ where $0 \leq a, b, c \leq d$. Compute the Shapley value for this game.

(5) Consider the following characteristic form game with three players. $v(1) = v(2) = v(3) = 0; v(12) = a; v(13) = b; v(23) = c; v(123) = 1$. Assume that $0 \leq a, b, c \leq 1$.

    (a) Find the conditions under which the core is non-empty.

    (b) Compute the Shapley value.

    (c) Assuming the core is non-empty, does the Shapley value belong to the core? Under what conditions will the Shapley value belong to the core of this game.

(6) Let us consider a version of divide the dollar problem with 4 players and total worth equal to 400. Suppose that any coalition with three or more players will be able to achieve the total worth. Also, a coalition with two players will be able to achieve the total worth only if player 1 is a part of the two player coalition. Set up a characteristic function for this TU game and compute the Shapley value.

(7) There are four players $\{1, 2, 3, 4\}$ who are interested in a wealth of 400 (real number). Any coalition containing at least two players and having player 1 would be able to achieve the total wealth of 400. Similarly, any coalition containing at least three players and containing player 2 also would be able to achieve the total wealth of 400. Set up a characteristic form game for this situation and compute the Shapley value.

(8) Give simple examples of two player games where

    • The core is empty and Nash Bargaining Solution (NBS) = Shapley Value (SV)

    • The core is empty and NBS is not the same as SV

    • The core is non-empty and NBS = SV

    • The core is non-empty and NBS is not the same as SV

(9) Give simple examples of TU games where

    • The core is non-empty and the Shapley value belongs to the core

    • The core is non-empty and the Shapley value does not belong to the core

(10) A TU game (N, v) is said to be additive if

$$v(C) = \sum_{i \in C} v(\{i\}) \ \forall C \subseteq N.$$

Determine the Shapley value of such a game in closed form.

(11) Given a TU game (N, v), define the dual game (N, w) by

$$w(C) = v(N) - v(N \setminus C) \ \forall C \subseteq N.$$

Show that the dual of the dual game is the original game (primal game) itself. Also show that the Shapley values of the primal game and the dual game are identical.

(12) Consider the following three player simple TU game which can be easily shown to be monotonic:

$$v(1) = v(2) = v(3) = v(23) = 0; \; v(12) = v(13) = v(123) = 1.$$

In fact, the above game is modeled on the lines of version 3 of the divide the dollar game. Determine the Shapley-Shubik power index of this game.

(13) Consider a TU game with four players where

$$v(12) = V(13) = v(123) = v(134) = v(124) = v(234) = v(1234) = 1.$$

The characteristic function takes zero value for the rest of the coalitions. Is this game monotonic? If yes, compute the Shapley - Shubik power index for this game.

(14) Is the voting game discussed in Chapter 27 (Example 27.6) monotonic? If yes, compute the Shapley - Shubik power index for this game.

(15) Is the apex game monotonic? If yes, compute the Shapley - Shubik power index for this game.

(16) **Programming Assignment**. Undertake a survey of computational methods available for Shapley value computation. Implement efficient algorithms for computing Shapley value.

(17) **Programming Assignment**. Design and implement a program for finding out if a given TU game is a convex game. Implement efficient algorithms to compute Shapley value of convex games.

Chapter 30

Other Solution Concepts in Cooperative Game Theory

Thus far, we have studied two key solution concepts (the core and the Shapley value) in cooperative games. The core is a set solution concept while the Shapley value is a single point solution concept. Many other solution concepts have been proposed and studied in cooperative game theory. In this chapter, we briefly study five other concepts: (1) Stable Sets; (2) Bargaining Sets; (3) Kernel; (4) Nucleolus; and (5) Gately Point. The first three are set solution concepts while the last two are single point solution concepts.

30.1 Stable Sets

We first present several definitions before introducing the concept of stable sets.

Definition 30.1 (Excess). *Given a TU game (N, v), a coalition C, and an allocation $x = (x_1, \ldots, x_n)$, the excess of C at x is defined as*

$$e(C, x) = v(C) - \sum_{i \in C} x_i$$

The excess $e(C, x)$ is the *net transferable utility* that coalition C would be left with after allocating x_i to player i for each $i \in C$. If $e(C, x) \geq 0$, the implication is that the coalition, on its own, would be able to achieve its share of the allocation x. The excess of a coalition C in relation to an allocation x is a measure of unhappiness of C with the allocation.

Example 30.1 (Version 3 of Divide the Dollar). Recall this game with $N = \{1, 2, 3\}$ and $v(1) = v(2) = v(3) = v(23) = 0$; $v(12) = v(13) = v(123) = 300$. Consider allocation $x = (100, 100, 100)$. Then we have

$$e(1, x) = -100; \; e(2, x) = -100; \; e(3, x) = -100$$
$$e(23, x) = -200; \; e(12, x) = 100; \; e(13, x) = 100; \; e(123, x) = 0.$$

Suppose $y = (200, 50, 50)$ then

$$e(1, y) = -200$$
$$e(2, y) = e(3, y) = -50$$
$$e(23, y) = -100$$
$$e(13, y) = e(12, y) = 50$$
$$e(123, y) = 0$$

If $z = (300, 0, 0)$, we have $e(1, z) = -300$; $e(2, z) = e(3, z) = 0$, $e(23, z) = e(12, z) = e(13, z) = 0$ and $e(123, z) = 0$. □

We now recall, from Chapter 27, the definition of domination of an imputation by another imputation and rephrase the definitions in terms of *excess*.

Definition 30.2 (Domination). *An imputation* $x = (x_1, \ldots, x_n)$ *is said to dominate another imputation* $y = (y_1, \ldots, y_n)$ *if there is some coalition* $C \subseteq N$ *such that*

(1) $e(C, x) \geq 0$
(2) $x_i > y_i \ \forall i \in C$

Definition 30.3 (Undominated Imputation). *An imputation* $x = (x_1, \ldots, x_n)$ *is said to be* undominated *if no other imputation dominates it.*

One can immediately note that the core of a TU game is simply the collection of all undominated imputations.

Definition 30.4 (Internal Stability). *Given a TU game* (N, v), *a set of imputations* Z *is said to be* internally stable *if*

$$\forall x, y \in Z, \ \forall C \subseteq N, \ x_i > y_i \ \forall i \in C \implies e(C, x) < 0$$

This means no imputation in Z is dominated by any other imputation in Z. Internal stability implies that if an imputation y belonging to Z is proposed, then no coalition C can block this since a strictly better, feasible allocation does not exist in Z for the players in C.

Definition 30.5 (External Stability). *Given a TU game* (N, v), *a set of imputations* Z *is said to be* externally stable *if every imputation not in* Z *is dominated by some imputation in* Z.

External stability can be described as follows: For all imputations y of (N, v), $y \notin Z$, there exists an $x \in Z$ such that there is at least one coalition $C \subseteq N$ for which

$$x_i > y_i \ \forall i \in C \implies e(C, x) \geq 0$$

External stability implies that if an imputation y not belonging to Z is proposed, then there is at least one coalition C of players that could block the adoption of

y by insisting on getting their share of some strictly better allocation in Z that is feasible for them.

Stable Sets

This is a solution concept that was first studied by von Neumann and Morgenstern in 1944. A *stable set* is also called a von Neumann - Morgenstern solution.

Definition 30.6 (Stable Set). *A stable set of a TU game (N, v) is a set of imputations Z satisfying internal stability as well as external stability.*

Example 30.2 (Majority Voting Game). Recall this game with $N = \{1, 2, 3\}$ and characteristic function given by

$$v(1) = v(2) = v(3) = 0; \; v(12) = v(23) = v(13) = v(123) = 300.$$

One possible stable set here is $Z = \{(150, 150, 0), (150, 0, 150), (0, 150, 150)\}$. The set of imputations for this example is given by

$$\left\{ (x_1, x_2, x_3) \in \mathbb{R}^3 : x_1 \geq 0; x_2 \geq 0; x_3 \geq 0; x_1 + x_2 + x_3 = 300 \right\}$$

To get a feel for the definition of a stable set, let us try out different test cases.

- Suppose the imputation $(300, 0, 0) \notin Z$ is suggested. Now, the imputation $(0, 150, 150) \in Z$ is such that the coalition $\{2, 3\}$ will block $(300, 0, 0)$.
- Let us explore the imputation $x = (100, 100, 100) \notin Z$. The imputation $(150, 150, 0) \in Z$ is such that the coalition $\{1, 2\}$ will block x. If we consider imputation $(150, 0, 150) \in Z$, then the coalition $\{1, 3\}$ will block x. The imputation $(0, 150, 150) \in Z$ is such that the coalition $\{2, 3\}$ will block x.

On the other hand, we observe that $(150, 150, 0) \in Z$ is not dominated by either $(150, 0, 150)$ or $(0, 150, 150)$. □

Given a TU game, a stable set may or may not exist. The problem of existence of a stable set was open for a long time until William Lucas finally constructed, in 1968, a 10 person game for which there was no stable set. This counterexample was gleefully welcomed by many frustrated researchers working on this open problem. Stable sets can offer valuable insights into coalitional dynamics, however the limitations arise because

- there may be many stable sets
- there may not be any stable set
- they may have a quite complex structure.

30.2 Bargaining Set

This solution concept was introduced by Aumann and Maschler [1] in 1964. The intuition behind this solution concept is as follows. When players debate among themselves about a proposed division of total worth, there may be unsatisfied players who might object to the proposal. These objections could lead to certain counter objections by some other players. An objection that does not lead to any counter objection will become a justified objection. The bargaining set consists of all imputations where each imputation is such that no player has any justified objection against any other player. We shall first formalize the notion of an objection and a counter objection.

Definition 30.7 (Objection). *An objection by a player i against another player j and a payoff allocation x is a pair (y, C) where y is another payoff allocation and C is a coalition such that*

$$i \in C$$
$$j \notin C$$
$$e(C, y) = 0$$
$$y_k > x_k \ \forall k \in C$$

Example 30.3 (Majority Voting Game). Recall again the three person majority voting game. Let $i = 1, j = 2$, and $x = (50, 100, 150)$. An objection by player 1 against player 2 and the payoff allocation x is a pair (y, C) where

$$y = (125, 0, 175)$$
$$C = \{1, 3\}$$

Note that $i \in C$; $j \notin C$; $e(C, y) = 0$; $y_1 > x_1$ and $y_3 > x_3$.   □

Definition 30.8 (Counterobjection). *Given a player i's objection (y, C) against player j and a payoff allocation x, a counterobjection by player j is any pair (z, D) where z is another payoff allocation and D is a coalition such that*

$$j \in D$$
$$i \notin D$$
$$C \cap D \neq \phi$$
$$e(D, z) = 0$$
$$z_k \geq x_k \ \forall k \in D$$
$$z_k \geq y_k \ \forall k \in C \cap D$$

Example 30.4 (Majority Voting Game). For the objection described in Example 30.3, a counter objection by player 2 would be the pair (z, D) where

$$z = (0, 125, 175); \ D = \{2, 3\}; \ C \cap D = \{3\}; \ e(D, z) = 0;$$

$$z_2 \geq x_2; \ z_3 \geq x_3; \ z_3 \geq y_3$$

The above example motivates the definition of a bargaining set.   □

Before we define a bargaining set, we introduce some additional notation. Let (N, v) be a TU game and suppose Q is a partition of N. We define

$$I(Q) = \left\{ x \in \mathbb{R}^n : x_i \geq v(\{i\}) \; \forall i \in N, \; \sum_{i \in C} x_i = v(C) \; \forall C \in Q \right\}$$

One can immediately note that if $Q = \{N\}$, that is the partition consisting of only one part namely the entire set N, then $I(Q)$ is exactly the set of all imputations of (N, v).

Definition 30.9 (Bargaining Set). *Given a TU game (N, v) and a partition Q of N, a bargaining set is a collection of payoff allocations $x \in \mathbb{R}^n$ such that*

(1) $x \in I(Q)$

(2) For any coalition D in Q and for any two players $i, j \in D$, there exists a counterobjection to any objection by i against j and x.

Example 30.5 (Apex Game). Recall the apex game that we have studied earlier:

$$N = \{1, 2, 3, 4, 5\}$$
$$v(C) = 1 \text{ if } 1 \in C \text{ and } |C| \geq 2$$
$$= 1 \text{ if } |C| \geq 4$$
$$= 0 \text{ otherwise}$$

We have seen that the core and the Shapley value are given by

$$\text{Core } (N, v) = \emptyset; \quad \phi(N, v) = \left(\frac{6}{10}, \frac{1}{10}, \frac{1}{10}, \frac{1}{10}, \frac{1}{10} \right)$$

Consider the partition $Q = \{N\}$. With respect to this partition, the bargaining set can be shown to be

$$\left\{ (1 - 4\lambda, \lambda, \lambda, \lambda, \lambda) : \frac{1}{13} \leq \lambda \leq \frac{1}{7} \right\}$$

An immediate observation we make is that the Shapley value of this game belongs to this bargaining set. There are three representative situations here that we need to look at so as to confirm that the above is the bargaining set.

- *Situation 1:* Assume that the small players do not all get the same payoff. In this case, suppose small player i gets strictly less than small player j. Then player i would have an objection in collaboration with the big player 1 that player j would not be able to counter.
- *Situation 2:* Suppose all the small players manage to get a payoff greater than $\frac{1}{7}$. Then player 1 would have, for example, an objection $\left(\left(\frac{3}{7}, \frac{4}{7}, 0, 0, 0 \right), \{1, 2\} \right)$ for which player 3 or player 4 or player 5 would not be able to counter.
- *Situation 3:* If all the small players get an amount less than $\frac{1}{13}$, then player 1 would get greater than $\frac{9}{13}$. Then each of the small players can immediately object. For example, player 2 could have an objection $\left(\left(0, \frac{1}{13}, \frac{4}{13}, \frac{4}{13}, \frac{4}{13} \right), \{2, 3, 4, 5\} \right)$ which player 1 would not be able to counter.

Coalition structure (partition)	Bargaining Set
$\{\{1\}, \{2\}, \{3\}\}$	$\{(0, 0, 0)\}$
$\{\{1, 2\}, \{3\}\}$	$\{(20, 40, 0)\}$
$\{\{1, 3\}, \{2\}\}$	$\{(20, 0, 60)\}$
$\{\{1\}, \{2, 3\}\}$	$\{(0, 40, 60)\}$
$\{\{1, 2, 3\}\}$	$\{(15, 35, 55)\}$

Table 30.1: Bargaining sets for different partitions

For the above apex game, if $Q = \{\{1, 2\}, \{3\}, \{4\}, \{5\}\}$ then the set

$$\left\{ (1 - \alpha, \alpha, 0, 0, 0) : \frac{1}{4} \leq \alpha \leq \frac{1}{2} \right\}$$

would be the bargaining set.   □

Example 30.6. This example is taken from [2]. Consider a three player game with $N = \{1, 2, 3\}$ and characteristic function:

$$v(1) = v(2) = v(3) = 0; \quad v(12) = 60; \quad v(13) = 80; \quad v(23) = 100; \quad v(123) = 105$$

It can be shown that the core is empty here. The Shapley values can be shown to be

$$\phi_1(N, v) = 25; \quad \phi_2(N, v) = 35; \quad \phi_3(N, v) = 45$$

Consider the situation facing players 2 and 3 if they decide to form a coalition, leaving out player 1. The two players 2 and 3 will have to share 100 units and if they do admit player 1 into their coalition, they will have to share 105 units among three players. In the latter case, players 2 and 3 may actually end up getting less than what they would have possibly got if only two of them formed a coalition. In addition to this, there is also time and effort spent in extra negotiation, so players 2 and 3 may desist from inviting player 1 to join their coalition. This leads to the partition $\{\{1\}, \{2, 3\}\}$. It can be shown that $(0, 40, 60)$ is the only stable allocation for this partition. In fact, for each of the five possible coalition structures, there is exactly one allocation in the bargaining set, as shown in Table 30.1.

If the value of the grand coalition changes to 135 instead of 105, then the bargaining set for the partition $\{\{1, 2, 3\}\}$ will be exactly equal to the core:

$$\left\{ (x_1, x_2, x_3) \in \mathbb{R}^3 : x_1 \geq 0; \ x_2 \geq 0; \ x_3 \geq 0; x_1 \leq 35; \ x_2 \leq 55; x_3 \leq 75; \ x_1 + x_2 + x_3 = 135 \right\}$$

The bargaining sets for other coalition structures will remain the same as before.   □

Some Observations on the Bargaining Set

- The core is a (possibly empty) subset of the bargaining set of (N, v) relative to the partition $Q = \{N\}$.

- Given a partition Q, if $I(Q)$ is non-empty, then the bargaining set relative to Q is non-empty.
- Recall that a TU game (N, v) is said to be superadditive if for all coalitions $C, D \subseteq N$,

$$C \cap D = \emptyset \implies v(C \cup D) \geq v(C) + v(D)$$

If the game (N, v) is superadditive, then for any partition Q, the set $I(Q)$ is non-empty and hence the bargaining set with respect to Q is also non-empty.
- The Shapley value need not belong to the bargaining set corresponding to any given partition. Thus the allocations suggested by a bargaining set need not be fair in the sense of Shapley value.

30.3 Kernel

This solution concept was proposed by Davis and Maschler [3]. The kernel of a TU game (N, v) is defined with respect to a partition Q of N (like the bargaining set). In fact, like the bargaining set, the kernel is also a subset of $I(Q)$. The intuition behind the kernel is that if two players i and j belong to the same coalition in Q, then the highest excess that i can make in a coalition without j should be the same as the highest excess that j can make in a coalition without i. While defining the kernel, we focus on the maximum excess a player would be able to make.

Definition 30.10 (Kernel). *Given a TU game (N, v) and a partition Q of N, the kernel is a set of allocations $x \in \mathbb{R}^n$ such that*

(1) $x \in I(Q)$
(2) For every coalition $C \in Q$ and every pair of players $i, j \in C$,

$$\max_{\substack{D \subseteq N-j \\ i \in D}} e(D, x) = \max_{\substack{E \subseteq N-i \\ j \in E}} e(E, x)$$

Example 30.7 (A Four Person Game). Consider the following four person game:

$$N = \{1, 2, 3, 4\}$$

$$Q = \{\{1, 2\}, \{3, 4\}\}$$

$$i = 1; \quad j = 2$$

$$I(Q) = \{(x_1, x_2, x_3, x_4) : x_1 \geq 0; x_2 \geq 0; x_3 \geq 0; x_4 \geq 0; x_1 + x_2 = v(12); \ x_3 + x_4 = v(34)\}$$

The kernel of (N, v), with respect to Q will be the set of all allocations (x_1, x_2, x_3, x_4) from $I(Q)$ satisfying:

$$\max_{\substack{D \subseteq \{1,3,4\} \\ 1 \in D}} e(D, x) = \max_{\substack{E \subseteq \{2,3,4\} \\ 2 \in E}} e(E, x)$$

$$\max_{\substack{D \subseteq \{1,2,3\} \\ 3 \in D}} e(D, x) = \max_{\substack{E \subseteq \{1,2,4\} \\ 4 \in E}} e(E, x).$$

$\square$

Example 30.8 (Apex Game). For the five player apex game considered earlier, the kernel with the partition $\{\{1,2,3,4,5\}\}$ is $\{(\frac{3}{7},\frac{1}{7},\frac{1}{7},\frac{1}{7},\frac{1}{7},)\}$ where as with the partition $\{\{1,2\},\{3\},\{4\},\{5\}\}$ the kernel is $\{(\frac{1}{2},\frac{1}{2},0,0,0)\}$. □

30.4 Nucleolus

The Shapley value of a TU game is a solution concept that is primarily based on a certain notion of fairness in allocation. The nucleolus which is also a unique allocation, like the Shapley value, is primarily based on bargaining considerations. This solution concept was proposed by David Schmeidler (1970) [4].

Recall that the excess of a coalition C with respect to an allocation x is a measure of unhappiness of C with allocation x. Let us say we find an imputation that minimizes the largest among all excesses $e(C,x)$. This means the chosen imputation makes the most unhappy coalition as little unhappy as possible. The nucleolus is based on this idea and minimizes not only the level of unhappiness of the most unhappy coalition but also the levels of unhappiness of the second most unhappy coalition, third most unhappy coalition, etc.

Example 30.9. Consider a three player game [2] with $N = \{1,2,3\}$ and characteristic function defined by

$$v(1) = v(2) = v(3) = 0$$

$$v(12) = 60; \ v(13) = 80; \ v(23) = 100$$

$$v(123) = 105$$

Given an allocation $x = (20, 35, 50)$, the excess values for the coalitions are as follows.

$$e(1,x) = -20; \ e(2,x) = -35; \ e(3,x) = -50$$

$$e(12,x) = 5; \ e(13,x) = 10; \ e(23,x) = 15$$

$$e(123,x) = 0$$

In the above, the largest excess is $e(23,x) = 15$. Let us try to reduce this by trying the allocation $y = (15, 35, 55)$ (say). Now we notice that

$$e(12,y) = 10; \ e(13,y) = 10; \ e(23,y) = 10$$

If we try to lower this any further, it would raise at least one other excess beyond 10. Thus the allocation y achieves the lowest excess for any coalition. In general, there may be multiple imputations which minimize the second largest excess to obtain a subset of the above set of imputations. Next, we minimize the third largest excess, fourth largest excess, etc. until, as shown in [4], we end up with a unique imputation. This unique imputation is called the *nucleolus*. □

Defining Nucleolus

Consider any allocation $x = (x_1, \ldots, x_n)$ and let $e_k(x)$ be the kth largest excess generated by any coalition with allocation x. This means the cardinalities of the stated sets satisfy:

$$|\{C \subseteq N : e(C, x) \geq e_k(x)\}| \geq k$$

$$|\{C \subseteq N : e(C, x) > e_k(x)\}| < k$$

Now, x belongs to the core $\mathbb{C}(N, v)$ implies $e_1(x) \leq 0$. Suppose we denote by $J(k)$ the set of all imputations that minimize e_k where e_k is the kth largest excess and by $I(N, v)$ the set of all imputations of (N, v). Then

$$J(1) = \underset{x \in I(N,v)}{\arg\min} \ e_1(x)$$

If the core is non-empty, then $J(1) \subseteq \mathbb{C}(N, v)$. We can define $J(2), J(3), \ldots, J(2^{|N|} - 1)$ as follows.

$$J(k) = \underset{x \in J(k-1)}{\arg\min} \ e_k(x) \quad \text{for} \ k = 2, 3, \ldots, 2^{|N|} - 1$$

It was shown by Schmeidler [4] that the set $J(2^{|N|} - 1)$ is a singleton and this point is called the nucleolus of the TU game (N, v).

Note that when the core is non-empty, for any imputations in the core, all the excesses are zero or negative. For finding the nucleolus, we choose the imputation in the core which makes the least negative excess as negative as possible. Geometrically, the nucleolus is a point in the core whose distance from the closest wall of the core is as large as possible. Intuitively, the nucleolus is a point in the core that is as far inside the core as possible. We note a few other aspects about this solution concept. For details, the reader is referred to [2].

- The nucleolus always exists and is unique.
- If the core is non-empty, the nucleolus belongs to the core.
- The nucleolus always belongs to the bargaining set for the grand coalition. Also, it always belongs to the kernel.
- The nucleolus is not necessarily equal to the Shapley value.
- The nucleolus can be computed by solving a series of linear programs.

30.5 The Gately Point

This solution concept was proposed by Dermot Gately (1974) [5]. Like the nucleolus, this is also based on the bargaining ability of the players. Suppose we have a TU game (N, v) with $N = \{1, 2, \ldots, n\}$. Let us focus on player i. If player i breaks away from the grand coalition, it might result in a loss (or gain) for the players. Suppose

$x = (x_1, \ldots, x_n)$ is the original allocation for the grand coalition. Then the loss to the player i due to breakup is $x_i - v(\{i\})$. The joint loss to the rest of the players is

$$\sum_{j \neq i} x_j - v(N \setminus \{i\})$$

The disruption caused by player i breaking away can be measured in terms of so called *propensity to disrupt* which is defined as

$$d_i(x) = \frac{\sum_{j \neq i} x_j - v(N \setminus \{i\})}{x_i - v(\{i\})}$$

The Gately point is defined as an imputation that minimizes the maximum propensity to disrupt. It can be shown that minimizing the maximum propensity to disrupt can be achieved by making the propensities to disrupt of all the players equal.

Example 30.10. Consider a three player game with $N = \{1, 2, 3\}$ and

$$v(1) = v(2) = v(3) = 0$$

$$v(12) = 4; \ v(13) = 0; \ v(23) = 3$$

$$v(123) = 6$$

With respect to the allocation $x = (2, 3, 1)$, the propensities to disrupt are given by

$$d_1(x) = \frac{1}{2}; \ d_2(x) = 1; \ d_3(x) = 1$$

If we try to equalize the propensities to disrupt, we end up with the allocation $y = (\frac{18}{11}, \frac{36}{11}, \frac{12}{11})$ which yields

$$d_1(y) = d_2(y) = d_3(y) = \frac{5}{6}$$

The above allocation y turns out to be the Gately point.   □

We now state a few observations about Gately point.

- Gately point does not necessarily belong to the core if the core is non-empty.
- The concept of Gately point can be extended by considering propensities to disrupt of coalitions rather than individual players. The resulting solution concept is called *disruptive nucleolus* which has been shown to belong to the core if the core is non-empty.

30.6 Summary and References

Cooperative game theory is replete with a variety of solution concepts. In this chapter, we have studied five different solution concepts. These concepts are based on the following notions:

- *Imputation*: An imputation of a TU game is an allocation $x = (x_1, \ldots, x_n)$ such that the sum of the x_i's is the same as the value $v(N)$ of the grand coalition, with each x_i no less than $v(\{i\})$.

- *Excess*: The excess of a coalition C with respect to an allocation x is the difference $(v(C) - \sum_{i \in C} x_i)$. This could be described as the level of unhappiness of the coalition C.
- *Domination*: An imputation $x = (x_1, \ldots, x_n)$ is said to dominate another imputation $y = (y_1, \ldots, y_n)$ if there exists a coalition C such that the excess of C wrt x is non-negative and every x_i is strictly greater than y_i for all $i \in C$.

The solution concepts studied in this chapter include:

(1) *Stable Sets*: A stable set of a TU game is a set of allocations (in fact, imputations) Z satisfying internal stability as well as external stability. Internal stability means that no imputation in Z is dominated by any other imputation in Z. External stability means that every imputation not in Z is dominated by some imputation in Z.

(2) *Bargaining Set*: A bargaining set with respect to a partition of the set of players is a set of imputations where each imputation is such that no player will object to the imputation since it will attract a counter objection from another player.

(3) *Kernel*: Given a partition Q of the set of players N, the kernel contains payoff allocations such that if players i and j belong to the same coalition in Q, the highest excess that player i can make in a coalition without j is the same as the highest excess that player j can make in a coalition without i.

(4) *Nucleolus*: The nucleolus always belongs to the kernel and is a unique imputation that minimizes the level of unhappiness of the most unhappy coalition, the second most unhappy coalition, etc.

(5) *Gately Point*: This is an imputation that minimizes the maximum tendency of players to break away from the grand coalition.

The choice of which solution concept to use in a given situation depends on what is being studied. The computation of the solution concepts is in general hard except in special cases.

This chapter has relied extensively on the textbooks of Myerson [6], Straffin [2], and Maschler, Solan, and Zamir [7]. These references may be looked into for more details. The book by Straffin [2] discusses illustrative case studies on all the above solution concepts. The original references for the solution concepts discussed here are: stable sets [8], bargaining sets [1], kernel [3], nucleolus [4], and Gately point [5].

Computation of the solution concepts discussed in this chapter is an important issue. The book by Chalkiadakis, Elkind, and Wooldridge [9] has a detailed discussion on this important topic.

References

[1]   R. Aumann and M. Maschler. "The bargaining set for cooperative games". In: *Advances in Game Theory*. Princeton University Press, 1964, pp. 443–476.

[2] Philip D. Straffin Jr. *Game Theory and Strategy*. The Mathematical Association of America, 1993.

[3] M. Davis and M. Maschler. "The kernel of a cooperative game". In: *Naval Research Logistics Quarterly* **12** (1965), pp. 223–259.

[4] David Schmeidler. "The nucleolus of a characteristic function game". In: *SIAM Journal on Applied Mathematics* **17** (1969), pp. 1163–1170.

[5] Dermot Gately. "Sharing the gains from regional cooperation: A game theoretic application to planning investment in electric power". In: *International Economic Review* **15** (1974), pp. 195–208.

[6] Roger B. Myerson. *Game Theory: Analysis of Conflict*. Harvard University Press, Cambridge, Massachusetts, USA, 1997.

[7] Michael Maschler, Eilon Solan, and Shmuel Zamir. *Game Theory*. Cambridge University Press, 2013.

[8] John von Neumann and Oskar Morgenstern. *Theory of Games and Economic Behavior*. Princeton University Press, 1944.

[9] Georgios Chalkiadakis, Edith Elkind, and Michael Wooldridge. *Computational Aspects of Cooperative Game Theory*. Morgan & Claypool, 2011.

30.7 Exercises

(1) For the majority voting game (Example 30.2), compute any other stable sets if it has any.

(2) Prove that the kernel of the apex game having five players with the partition $\{\{1,2,3,4,5\}\}$ is $\{(\frac{3}{7},\frac{1}{7},\frac{1}{7},\frac{1}{7},\frac{1}{7})\}$ while with respect to the partition $\{\{1,2\},\{3\},\{4\},\{5\}\}$, the kernel is $\{(\frac{1}{2},\frac{1}{2},0,0,0)\}$. What will be the kernel with respect to the partition $\{\{1\},\{2,3,4,5\}\}$?

(3) Show that the nucleolus of the apex game with five players is $(\frac{3}{7},\frac{1}{7},\frac{1}{7},\frac{1}{7},\frac{1}{7})$.

(4) Consider a three person superadditive game with $v(1) = v(2) = v(3) = 0; v(12) = a; v(13) = b; v(23) = c; v(123) = d$ where $0 \le a,b,c \le d$. Compute the nucleolus and Gately point for this game.

(5) For the following three player game, compute the core, Shapley value, kernel, nucleolus, and Gately point.

$$v(1) = v(2) = v(3) = 0$$

$$v(12) = 4; \quad v(13) = 0; \quad v(23) = 3; \quad v(123) = 6$$

(6) **Programming Assignment**. Study the computational issues involved in computing the solution concepts discussed. It will be an interesting project to implement efficient computational algorithms for determining the solution concepts.

Chapter 31

Stable Matching

The Sveriges Riksbank Prize in Economic Sciences, in Memory of Alfred Nobel, for the year 2012 was awarded to Lloyd S. Shapley and Alvin E. Roth. The prize is in recognition of their pioneering contributions to theory of stable allocations and the practice of matching market design. The theory of matching and matching algorithms involves use of concepts in equal measure from non-cooperative game theory, cooperative game theory, and mechanism design. In this chapter, we describe matching algorithms and bring out their connection to game theory.

31.1 The Matching Problem

One of the common problems encountered in real life is that of matching, which is the process of allocating one set of resources or individuals to another set of resources or individuals. Common examples include matching buyers to sellers in a market; matching resources to tasks; allocating home seekers to houses; matching new doctors to hospitals; matching students to schools; matching job-seeking engineers to companies; matching advertisers to sponsored slots on a search engine page, etc. There are also examples with deep societal impact such as matching kidneys or human organs to needy patients. The matching has to be accomplished in a way that the preferences that the individuals may have, are honored, and the social welfare (measured in a reasonable way) is maximized. On the face of it, the problem looks deceptively simple, however, when the number of individuals/resources involved is large and in addition, certain inevitable, practical constraints have to be satisfied, the problem becomes complex and finding even feasible solutions (let alone optimal solutions) could be hard.

A key requirement of any solution to the matching problem is *stability*. Informally, a solution is stable if the solution cannot be improved upon, through a reallocation or further trading. Shapley and Roth have brilliantly pioneered the research and practice of the matching problem in complementary ways: In the 1960s, Shapley investigated the deep questions underlying the theory of matching and came up with an extremely elegant theory for solving the problem while Roth, in the 1980s, discovered a creative opportunity for exploiting the abstract theory of Shapley to practical problems and came up with masterly implementations to several practical problems waiting for better solutions. In the 1990s and beyond, several non-trivial extensions to the matching theory were proposed by Roth and other researchers to take into account practical issues such as strategic manipulation by the users of the matching market. Matching theory and matching markets currently constitute a lively and active area of research not only in economics but also in computer science, Internet advertising, and social computing.

Alvin Elliot Roth was born on December 19, 1951. His first degree was in operations research at the Columbia University. He completed his M.S. in 1973 and Ph.D. in 1974 both in Stanford University again in operations research. During 1975-82, he taught at the University of Illinois and he next taught at the University of Pittsburgh during 1982-98. In 1998, he joined the Harvard University where he is currently Gund Professor of Economics and Business Administration Emeritus in the Harvard Business School. Since 2013, he is Craig and Susan McCaw Professor of Economics at Stanford University.

Roth is a recipient of numerous honors including Alfred P. Sloan Fellowship, Guggenheim Fellowship, Fellowship of the American Academy of Arts and Sciences, and membership of the National Bureau of Economic Research and the Econometric Society. Besides matching markets [1], Roth has made pioneering contributions to game theory and experimental economics. One of his important contributions was to characterize the Shapley value as a risk-neutral utility function on the space of cooperative games. Roth has made influential contributions to experimental economics which are well explained in the scientific background document compiled by the Nobel Prize committee [2]. Roth's work essentially shows that the explanatory and predictive power of game theory can be enhanced with carefully and skilfully designed economic and laboratory experiments.

31.2   Matching Algorithms

In this section, we mainly discuss the college admissions problem for which Gale and Shapley [3] designed their famous algorithm.

The College Admissions Problem

Consider that there are m colleges to which a population of n students would like to get admitted (typically, $n \geq m$). Each college has a certain upper bound or quota on the number of students who could be offered admission to that college. Each college also has a strict ranking (also called preference order) of students. Likewise, each student has a strict ranking of colleges. The problem is to determine an allocation of students to colleges, according to one or more well defined criteria (such as stability, optimality, incentive compatibility, etc.). We use the words allocation, assignment, and matching synonymously.

An Example of College Admissions

Suppose there are five students, call them $1, 2, 3, 4, 5$ and two colleges A, B. Suppose the preferences of the students are as follows.

$$1 : B \succ A; \quad 2 : A \succ B; \quad 3 : A \succ B; \quad 4 : B \succ A; \quad 5 : B \succ A;$$

Let the preferences of the colleges be the following.

$$A : 1 \succ 2 \succ 3 \succ 4 \succ 5; \quad B : 1 \succ 5 \succ 4 \succ 3 \succ 2$$

Assume that each college can take up to 3 students. An allocation would be represented by a set of pairs such as

$$\alpha_1 = \{(1, A), (2, B), (3, A), (4, B), (5, A)\}$$

Another allocation would be:

$$\alpha_2 = \{(1, B), (2, A), (3, A), (4, B), (5, B)\}$$

Yet another allocation would be:

$$\alpha_3 = \{(1, A), (2, A), (3, A), (4, B), (5, B)\}$$

Stability, Optimality, and Incentive Compatibility

We now discuss three important properties to be satisfied by a matching algorithm for college admissions: stability, optimality, and incentive compatibility.

Definition 31.1 (Stable Allocation). *An allocation is said to be* unstable *if it contains the pairs $(1, A)$ and $(2, B)$ even though 1 prefers B to A and B prefers 1 to 2 (where $1, 2$ are representative students and A, B are representative colleges). An allocation that is not unstable is said to be stable.*

Note in the above definition that if we allocate 1 to B, then both 1 and B are strictly better off. In the language of cooperative game theory, the two element coalition $\{1, B\}$ *blocks* the allocation in question. A stable allocation cannot be blocked by any coalition of size 2. The set of all stable allocations is the *core* of an underlying allocation game. The allocation game here is actually a non-transferable utility (NTU) game.

We would be interested in a stable allocation in which all students as well as all colleges are as well off under it as under any other stable allocation. That is, we seek a stable allocation such that every student (college) is matched to a college (student) that is at least as much preferred as any college (student) to which the student (college) is matched in any other stable allocation. This leads to the following definition.

Definition 31.2 (Optimal Allocation). *A stable allocation is said to be* student optimal *if every student is at least as well off under it as under any other stable allocation. A stable allocation is said to be* college optimal *if every college is at least as well off under it as under any other stable allocation.*

A student optimal allocation need not be college optimal and vice-versa. Also, it can be shown that a student (college) optimal allocation, if one exists, is unique.

Definition 31.3 (Incentive Compatible Allocation). *A stable allocation is said to be* incentive compatible for students *(colleges) if it is a best response for every student (college) to report his/her true ranking of colleges (students).*

Recall that the stronger version of incentive compatibility which is dominant strategy incentive compatibility (DSIC) in this context would mean that reporting truth is a best response regardless of what is reported by the other students (other colleges).

The Marriage Problem

The marriage problem is a special case of the college admissions problem where the number of students is equal to the number of colleges (that is $n = m$). For the sake of simplicity, we will study this problem and it turns out that many results can be generalized in a natural way to the college admissions problem. In the rest of the section, we assume that there are n students and n colleges and each student has to be matched to a college; each college can only be matched to at most one student. We shall use the numbers $1, 2, \ldots$ to denote students and the upper case letters $A, B, \ldots$ to denote colleges.

Example 31.1 (A Marriage Problem). This example is a relabeled version of the example presented by Gale and Shapley [3]. Consider three students $1, 2, 3$ and three colleges A, B, C with the following preferences.

$$1 : A \succ B \succ C; \quad 2 : B \succ C \succ A; \quad 3 : C \succ A \succ B$$

$$A : 2 \succ 3 \succ 1; \quad B : 3 \succ 1 \succ 2; \quad C : 1 \succ 2 \succ 3$$

For this situation, there are clearly six matchings or allocations. These are given by

$$\{(1, A), (2, B), (3, C)\}, \{(1, A), (2, C), (3, B)\}, \{(1, B), (2, A), (3, C)\}$$

$$\{(1, B), (2, C), (3, A)\}, \{(1, C), (2, A), (3, B)\}, \{(1, C), (2, B), (3, A)\}$$

Of these six matchings, the following can be seen to be stable:

$$\{(1, A), (2, B), (3, C)\}, \{(1, B), (2, C), (3, A)\}, \{(1, C), (2, A), (3, B)\}$$

The allocation $\{(1, A), (2, B), (3, C)\}$ can be verified to be student optimal while the allocation $\{(1, C), (2, A), (3, B)\}$ can be seen to be college optimal. The allocation

$\{(1, C), (2, B), (3, A)\}$ is neither student optimal nor college optimal. The following allocations are unstable:

$$\{(1, A), (2, C), (3, B)\}, \{(1, B), (2, A), (3, C)\}, \{(1, C), (2, B), (3, A)\}$$

To see why the allocation $\{(1, A), (2, C), (3, B)\}$ is unstable, notice that the coalition $\{3, A\}$ blocks this allocation: (a) $(3, A)$ is better than $(3, B)$ for student 3 since student 3 prefers A to B. (b) $(3, A)$ is better than $(1, A)$ for college A since college A prefers student 3 to student 1. □

Deferred Acceptance Algorithm for the Marriage Problem

We are now in a position to describe the algorithm proposed by Gale and Shapley [3] for the marriage problem. This is called the *deferred acceptance* algorithm for reasons that will become clear soon. There are two versions of this algorithm:

(1) Students-proposing version
(2) Colleges-proposing version

We shall describe the students-proposing version. The algorithm proceeds iteratively in stages.

(1) In stage 1, each student proposes to her most favored college. It is possible that some colleges may not receive any proposals; other colleges receive one or more proposals. Each college receiving two or more proposals rejects all but the most favored student. This most favored student is put in a queue (admission is deferred in the hope of getting a more favored student in a later round).
(2) In stage 2, each rejected candidate proposes to her next most favored college. Again, each college receiving two or more proposals (including any in its queue) rejects all but the most favored student. The selection of the most favored student by a college takes into account the student who might be in its queue.
(3) Stages 3, 4, etc., proceed in a manner identical to stage 2.

The algorithm terminates when every college has received a proposal. The colleges-proposing version is identical to that of the students-proposing version, except that the roles of students and colleges are reversed.

Example 31.2 (Deferred Acceptance Algorithm). This example is a relabeled version of the example presented in [2]. Consider four students and four colleges with the following preferences.

$$1 : A \succ B \succ C \succ D; \quad 2 : A \succ C \succ B \succ D$$

$$3 : A \succ B \succ D \succ C; \quad 4 : C \succ D \succ B \succ A$$

$$A : 4 \succ 3 \succ 2 \succ 1; \quad B : 4 \succ 1 \succ 3 \succ 2$$

$$C : 1 \succ 2 \succ 4 \succ 3; \quad D : 2 \succ 1 \succ 4 \succ 3$$

Suppose students propose. Then in stage 1, students $1, 2, 3$ propose to college A since this college is most favored by all of them while student 4 proposes to college C and college C puts student 4 in queue. College A rejects students $1, 2$ and puts student 3 in queue. In stage 2, the rejected students $1, 2$ propose to the next favored colleges B, C, respectively. Now, college C has one fresh proposal from student 2 and also has student 4 in queue. C now rejects student 4 and puts student 2 in queue. Also, college B places student 1 in its queue. Thereafter, in stage 3, student 4 proposes to college D. Now colleges A, B, C, and D all have one proposal each and the algorithm terminates with the allocation $\{(1, B), (2, C), (3, A), (4, D)\}$. This can be verified to be a student optimal allocation.

In the colleges-proposing version, it is easy to see that the algorithm returns the allocation $\{(1, C), (2, D), (3, A), (4, B)\}$. This can be verified to be a college optimal allocation.

Suppose the students and colleges are strategic and may not report their preferences truthfully. As an illustrative example, suppose student 4 is strategic while all other students and all the colleges are truthful. Assume that student 4 misreports her preferences as $C \succ D \succ A \succ B$ instead of her actual preferences $C \succ D \succ B \succ A$. If we now apply the colleges-proposing deferred acceptance algorithm with only the preferences of student 4 changed, then we end up with the allocation $\{(1, B), (2, C), (3, A), (4, D)\}$ which is very different from $\{(1, C), (2, D), (3, A), (4, B)\}$ that was obtained with a truthful report from student 4. In fact, this one report has turned a college optimal allocation into a student optimal allocation! This shows that the colleges-proposing version of the Gale-Shapley algorithm is not incentive compatible to the students. However, it has been shown that the colleges-proposing version is dominant strategy incentive compatible for colleges. Similarly, the students-proposing version is DSIC for students but is not incentive compatible for colleges. □

Key Properties of the Deferred Acceptance Algorithm

We now state, without proof, several attractive properties of the deferred acceptance algorithm.

- In the students-proposing (colleges-proposing) version, no student (college) proposes to the same college (student) more than once.
- Each version of the algorithm results in a unique stable allocation. The students-proposing (colleges-proposing) version results in a student (college) optimal allocation. The original paper by Gale and Shapley [3] can be consulted for an elegant proof of optimality of allocation.
- The maximum number of stages before the termination of the algorithm is $n^2 - 2n + 2$. Thus the Gale-Shapley algorithm has worst case quadratic time complexity.
- The students-proposing (colleges-proposing) algorithm is DSIC for students (colleges) but is not incentive compatible for colleges (students).
- The algorithm can be generalized in a natural way to the college admissions problem.
- Shapley and Shubik [4] have shown that the core of the assignment game (the

non-transferable utility game underlying the college admissions problem) is non-empty. This result guarantees the existence of a stable allocation in a fairly general setting.

House Allocation Problem

The deferred acceptance algorithm was a path breaking effort in the area of two sided matching problems, where the players on either side have preferences over the players on the other side. There is another important class of problems called the *house allocation* problems. In this class of problems, we have a set of players who exchange indivisible objects without any side payments. The players have preferences over objects and also own certain objects. An example situation is provided by a set of home seekers who are in search of houses for rent and have individual preferences for houses. The houses on the other hand do not have any preferences over the individuals seeking houses. Shapley and Scarf [5], in a landmark paper, designed an algorithm (based on an earlier idea from Richard Gale) called the *top trading cycle algorithm* for obtaining a stable allocation for this class of problems. This algorithm and its variants have been applied in a wide variety of problems including the kidney exchange problem.

31.3 Matching Markets

The deferred acceptance algorithm and the top trading cycle algorithm are two key algorithms for matching which have been extensively studied and modified for practical applications. A rich variety of other algorithms have been devised for matching problems of various kinds and concurrently, deep analytical studies have been carried out to establish theoretical properties (for example, stability, optimality, and incentive compatibility) of these algorithms. Lloyd Shapley who laid the foundations of cooperative game theory in the 1950s and 1960s has, in collaboration with leading game theorists, used this theory to resolve several central questions that arise in matching [1].

Alvin Roth, in the 1980s, discovered that Shapley's theory can be applied to analyze existing markets, for example the National Residents Matching Program (NRMP), a clearing house for matching new doctors with hospitals in the USA. Through a series of empirical studies and laboratory experiments, Roth and his collaborators were able to establish that stability is the most critical requirement for the success and sustainability of any matching market. In the process of this research, Roth and his team of co-researchers were able to redesign and improve the performance of many existing practical matching markets. In the 1990s, new theoretical advances, using tools including game theory, were made by Roth and colleagues in order to take care of possible strategic manipulations by the rational users of the market. Practical implementations were extended to New York schools and

Boston schools for matching students to schools. The crowning glory was achieved when the implementations were successfully applied, in the 1990s and 2000s, to the matching of organ donors to organ recipients, in particular the kidney exchange program [2].

31.4 Summary and References

In this chapter, we have only looked at some essential but elementary aspects of matching algorithms for non-strategic agents. The topic involves use of non-cooperative game theory, cooperative game theory, and mechanism design. Our exposition has covered the following aspects.

- We have touched upon the college admissions problem, the marriage problem, and the house allocation problem. In the college admissions problems, there are m colleges and n students (typically $n \geq m$) and both colleges and students have preferences. The marriage problem is a special case of the college admissions problem with $n = m$. In the house allocation problem, players on only one side have preferences.
- We have discussed the celebrated Gale-Shapley algorithm for the college admissions problems and brought out some interesting properties satisfied by this algorithm.

The award of the Sveriges Riksbank Prize in Economic Sciences in Memory of Alfred Nobel for 2012 has certainly catapulted interest in matching theory and matching markets. The scientific background document hosted at the Nobel Prize website [2] is a rich source of information on matching theory and matching markets. The book by Roth and Sotomayor [1] is an authentic source of all key results until 1990. The paper by Gale and Shapley [3] which contains the deferred acceptance algorithm is a must read.

References

[1]   A.E. Roth and M. Sotomayor. *Two Sided Matching: A Study in Game Theoretic Modeling and Analysis*. Econometric Society Monograph Series, Cambridge University Press, 1990.

[2]   The Economic Sciences Prize Committee. *Stable matching: Theory, Evidence, and Practical Design - The Sveriges Riksbank Prize in Economic Sciences in Memory of Alfred Nobel 2012: Scientific Background*. Tech. rep. The Nobel Foundation, Stockholm, Sweden, 2012.

[3]   D. Gale and L. S. Shapley. "College admissions and the stability of marriage". In: *The American Mathematical Monthly* **69**(1) (1962), pp. 9–15.

[4]   Lloyd S. Shapley and Martin Shubik. "The Assignment Game I: The Core". In: *International Journal of Game Theory* **1**(1) (1971), pp. 111–130.

[5]   Lloyd S. Shapley and Herbert Scarf. "On cores and indivisibility". In: *Journal of Mathematical Economics* **1** (1974), pp. 23–37.

31.5 Exercises

(1) Show for the college admissions problem that a student optimal (college optimal) allocation, if one exists, must be unique.

(2) Investigate the stability, optimality, and incentive compatibility of the allocations $\alpha_1, \alpha_2, \alpha_3$ given in the example of college admissions problem.

(3) Show in Example 31.1 of three students and three colleges (marriage problem) that the allocations $\{(1, A), (2, B), (3, C)\}$, $\{(1, B), (2, C), (3, A)\}$, and $\{(1, C), (2, A), (3, B)\}$ are stable while the allocations $\{(1, B), (2, A), (3, C)\}$ and $\{(1, C), (2, B), (3, A)\}$ are unstable.

(4) Apply the deferred acceptance algorithm to the above example (both the students-proposing as well as the colleges-proposing versions).

(5) Apply the deferred acceptance algorithm to the case when student 4 misreports in the four students, four colleges example.

(6) Show that the maximum number of stages in the deferred acceptance algorithm is $n^2 - 2n + 2$ where n is the number of students (also the number of colleges). (Hint: Look at the worst case scenario).

(7) Consider four students $1, 2, 3, 4$ and four colleges A, B, C, D with the following preferences.

$$1 : A \succ B \succ C \succ D; \quad 2 : A \succ B \succ C \succ D;$$

$$3 : B \succ C \succ A \succ D; \quad 4 : C \succ A \succ B \succ D$$

$$A : 3 \succ 4 \succ 1 \succ 2; \quad B : 4 \succ 1 \succ 2 \succ 3$$

$$C : 1 \succ 2 \succ 3 \succ 4; \quad D : 4 \succ 3 \succ 1 \succ 2$$

Apply the Gale-Shapley algorithm to the above problem. What do you observe?

(8) How do you generalize the Gale-Shapley algorithm for the marriage problem to the college admissions problem?

(9) **Programming Assignment**. It would be interesting to implement classic algorithms such as the Gale-Shapley algorithm, top trading cycle algorithm, and a host of other matching algorithms available in the literature.

Chapter 32

Epilogue

In this chapter, we recall the key learnings in this book and the key concepts and results we have covered in this book. We also list several important topics that we have not been able to cover in the book. We provide pointers to the literature for deeper inquiry.

Game theory helps us analyze the equilibrium behavior of interacting decision making agents while mechanism design enables us to design games in which strategic agents will exhibit a desirable equilibrium behavior. This book has attempted to offer a self-sufficient treatment of game theory and mechanism design.

32.1 Intent of the Book

After a thorough reading of this book, the reader is expected to be in a position to apply game theory and mechanism design in a principled and mature way to solve relevant problems in computer science, communications, networks, electrical engineering, management science, microeconomics, and industrial engineering. The following are certain use-cases that demonstrate the utility of this book to different types of audience.

- The book could be used as a textbook or a reference book by faculty members for undergraduate level and master's level courses on game theory. The book will have utility as a supplementary resource for a graduate level course on game theory.
- Students of computer science and engineering will be able to make forays into topical areas such as algorithmic game theory, algorithmic mechanism design, computational social choice, auctions and market design, electronic commerce, Internet monetization, and mechanism design for multiagent systems.
- Students of computer science, electronics, and electrical engineering would be able to explore research areas like network protocol design, dynamic resource allocation in networks, design of multiagent smart grid networks, and network science.
- Industrial engineering or management science students would be in a position

to undertake research in supply chain network design, logistics engineering, auctions in e-commerce, dynamic pricing in e-business, etc.

- Inter-disciplinary researchers in important areas such as cyberphysical systems, intelligent transportation, multiagent coordination (such as in multi-robot systems), public policy, green supply chains, service science, social network analysis, and the like would find this book useful in formulating and solving interesting current problems.

By melding game theory and mechanism design with optimization, machine learning, and algorithms, an entire canvas of contemporary problems (including inter-disciplinary problems) will open up for exploration and intelligent solutions.

The purpose of this book is served if a reader, after a thorough study of this book, has clarity of understanding of scientific notions in game theory and mechanism design and ability to answer certain fundamental questions while applying game theory and mechanism design to problem solving.

32.2   To Probe Further

In a book with a specific focus and intent such as this one, it is impossible to provide a comprehensive coverage of a vast area like game theory. Further, the coverage of topics covered varies widely in detail and depth of treatment. There are therefore many important aspects of game theory and mechanism design that we have left out completely or have covered only at a cursory level. These include:

- Algorithmic game theory (notions such as price of anarchy, price of stability, algorithms for computing equilibria, complexity of computing equilibria, network routing games, etc.)
- Network formation games
- Extensive form games (with perfect information, with imperfect information), subgame perfect equilibrium, etc.
- Notions such as behavioral strategies and solution concepts such as perfect equilibrium, sequential equilibrium, etc.
- Approximate notions for analysis or design such as ε-Nash equilibrium, ε-core, ε-incentive compatibility, etc.
- Stackelberg games
- Repeated games
- Dynamic games
- Learning in games
- Evolutionary games
- Stochastic games
- Potential games
- Non-transferable utility games
- Dynamic mechanisms

- Online mechanisms
- Mechanisms without money
- Voting mechanisms and computational voting theory
- Computational social choice
- Graphical games
- Security games
- ...

Fortunately, many fine textbooks are available which cover the above topics. First we refer the readers to the recent, extremely comprehensive book by Maschler, Solan, and Zamir [1]. The following books provide excellent sources for different subsets of the above topics: Easley and Kleinberg [2]; Goyal [3]; Jackson [4]; Mas-Colell, Whinston, and Green [5]; Myerson [6]; Narahari, Garg, Narayanam, and Prakash [7]; Nisan, Roughgarden, Tardos, and Vazirani [8]; Osborne [9]; Shoham and Leyton-Brown [10]; and Straffin [11]. A superb collection of classic papers in game theory brought out in 1997 [12] is a delightful source of archival papers in game theory and is a must read for interested readers.

Current Research Trends

As already stated, game theory and mechanism design have moved to the centerstage of numerous applications enabled by the recent technological advances. The gamut of applications includes auctions, electronic marketplaces, matching markets, procurement markets, service marketplaces, design of network protocols, social network monetization, crowdsourcing, human computation platforms, multiagent systems, resource allocation in smart grids, securing critical infrastructure, carbon footprint optimization, etc. Naturally there is an explosion of literature in these topics. In addition to the classical journals in economics and game theory disciplines, there are now many publication fora where applied game theory and mechanism design papers are published aplenty.

There are several conferences, some of them recently launched, which report the applications of game theory and mechanism design. These include: ACM Conference on Electronic Commerce (ACM EC) (recently rechristened as ACM Conference on Economics and Computation), International Conference on Web and Internet Economics (WINE), International Conference on Autonomous Agents and Multi-Agent Systems (AAMAS), International Conference on the World Wide Web (WWW), International Joint Conference on Artificial Intelligence (IJCAI), International Conference of the American Association of Artificial Intelligence (AAAI), Conference on Uncertainty in Artificial Intelligence (UAI), etc. Occasionally, conferences such as the IEEE Conference on Foundations of Computer Science (FOCS), ACM Symposium on Theory of Computing (STOC), ACM-SIAM Symposium on Discrete Algorithms (SODA), ACM Conference on Communications (SIGCOMM), ACM Principles of Distributed Computing (PODC), International Conference on

Machine Learning (ICML), and International Conference on Neural Information Processing Systems (NIPS) also publish relevant work. These venues constitute a valuable source to look up the current art in the area. Archival results appear in the journals, which have been listed as part of the references in the book. The blog *Turing's Invisible Hand: Computation, Economics, and Game Theory* (http://agtb.wordpress.com/) is a rich source of scholarly updates on game theory related events and articles.

32.3   Conclusion

It is pertinent to ask the question: what if we do not use game theoretic analysis or mechanism design? In the introduction (Chapter 1) and elsewhere in this book, we have alluded to many current and future problems in which the transactions are determined by the actions of self-interested agents. In these problems, the agents cannot be assumed to obey the prescribed algorithm – they would rather follow their individual interests. If the designer of modern Internet-based / network-based / multiagent systems wishes to ensure that the interests of the agents are best served by honest behavior, then game theoretic analysis and mechanism design principles hold the key to the success of these systems. Because of this reason, game theory and mechanism design are now an integral part of many lively areas of research in engineering. On the one hand, the rich theory offered by them has significantly impacted many practical applications in engineering and on the other, challenging problems in engineering have given rise to new theoretical questions in game theory and mechanism design. Modern applications call for a variety of mathematical tools and techniques to be deployed; game theory and mechanism design, in conjunction with machine learning, statistics, algorithms, and optimization, promise to provide the mathematical fulcrum for next generation applications.

The book has presented and provided what we believe is the essential paraphernalia required in game theory and mechanism design. In closing, we sincerely hope that the book will provide the readers with a gateway into the exciting modern disciplines where game theory and mechanism design have a natural role to play.

References

[1]   Michael Maschler, Eilon Solan, and Shmuel Zamir. *Game Theory*. Cambridge University Press, 2013.
[2]   David Easley and Jon Kleinberg. *Networks, Crowds, and Markets: Reasoning About a Highly Connected World*. Cambridge University Press, 2010.
[3]   Sanjeev Goyal. *Connections: An Introduction to the Economics of Networks*. Princeton University Press, Princeton, NJ, USA, 2007.
[4]   Mathew O. Jackson. *Social and Economic Networks*. Princeton University Press, Princeton, NJ, USA, 2007.

[5]   Andreu Mas-Colell, Michael D. Whinston, and Jerry R. Green. *Microeconomic Theory*. Oxford University Press, 1995.

[6]   Roger B. Myerson. *Game Theory: Analysis of Conflict*. Harvard University Press, Cambridge, Massachusetts, USA, 1997.

[7]   Y. Narahari, Dinesh Garg, Ramasuri Narayanam, and Hastagiri Prakash. *Game Theoretic Problems in Network Economics and Mechanism Design Solutions*. Springer, London, 2009.

[8]   Noam Nisan, Tim Roughgarden, Eva Tardos, and Vijay Vazirani (Editors). *Algorithmic Game Theory*. Cambridge University Press, 2007.

[9]   Martin J. Osborne. *An Introduction to Game Theory*. The MIT Press, 2003.

[10] Yoam Shoham and Kevin Leyton-Brown. *Multiagent Systems: Algorithmic, Game-Theoretic, and Logical Foundations*. Cambridge University Press, New York, USA, 2009, 2009.

[11] Philip D. Straffin Jr. *Game Theory and Strategy*. The Mathematical Association of America, 1993.

[12] Harold W. Kuhn (Editor). *Classics in Game Theory*. Princeton University Press, 1997.

Chapter 33

Mathematical Preliminaries

In this appendix, we provide essential definitions and key results which are used at various points in the book. We also provide a list of sources where more details and proofs may be looked up. The topics covered include: probability, linear algebra, linear programming, mathematical analysis, and computational complexity. We have only presented key definitions and results here and for rigorous technical details, the reader is urged to look up the references provided at the end.

33.1 Probability Theory

A probability model is a triple $(\Omega, \mathbb{F}, \mathbb{P})$ where

- Ω is a set of outcomes of an experiment and is called the sample space.
- $\mathbb{F} \subseteq 2^{\Omega}$ satisfies closure under complement and countable union of sets, and contains Ω; $\mathbb{F}$ is called a σ-algebra over Ω and the elements of $\mathbb{F}$ are called events.
- $\mathbb{P} : \mathbb{F} \longrightarrow [0, 1]$ is a probability mapping that satisfies

  (a) $\mathbb{P}(\emptyset) = 0 \leq \mathbb{P}(A) \leq \mathbb{P}(\Omega) = 1, \forall A \in \mathbb{F}$

  (b) (Countable Additivity): Given a countably infinite number of disjoint subsets A_i $(i = 1, 2, \ldots)$ of Ω,

$$\mathbb{P}(A_1 \cup A_2 \cup \ldots) = \mathbb{P}(A_1) + \mathbb{P}(A_2) + \ldots$$

The above two properties are also called axioms of probability. A random variable X is a mapping $X : \Omega \longrightarrow \mathbb{R}$ such that the probability $\mathbb{P}\{X \leq x\}$ $\forall x \in \mathbb{R}$ is well defined and can be computed.

The cumulative distribution function (CDF) of a random variable X is a mapping $F_X : \mathbb{R} \longrightarrow [0, 1]$ defined by

$$F_X(x) = \mathbb{P}\{X \leq x\}$$

The CDF is monotone non-decreasing and right continuous and satisfies

$$\lim_{x \to -\infty} F_X(x) = 0$$

$$\lim_{x \to \infty} F_X(x) = 1$$

A random variable where range is countable is called a discrete random variable while, a random variable whose CDF is continuous is called a continuous random variable. Clearly the range of a continuous random variable is uncountably infinite.

If X is a discrete random variable with range $\{1, 2, \ldots\}$ we define its probability mass function as

$$\mathbb{P}\{X = i\} \text{ for } i = 1, 2, \ldots$$

It can be shown easily that $\sum_i \mathbb{P}\{X = i\} = 1$. If X is a continuous random variable, we define its probability density function, if it exists, as

$$f_X(x) = \frac{dF_X(x)}{dx}; \; \forall x \in \text{range}(X)$$

It is a simple matter to show that

$$\int_{-\infty}^{\infty} f_X(x) dx = 1$$

Two events E and F are said to be mutually exclusive if $E \cap F = \emptyset$ which means

$$\mathbb{P}(E \cup F) = \mathbb{P}(E) + \mathbb{P}(F)$$

The events E and F are called independent if the probability of occurrence of E does not depend on the occurrence of F. It can be shown that independence of events E and F is equivalent to:

$$\mathbb{P}(E \cap F) = \mathbb{P}(E)\mathbb{P}(F)$$

If $E_1, E_2, \ldots, E_n$ are mutually disjoint events such that $E_1 \cup E_2 \cdots \cup E_n = \Omega$ and $\mathbb{P}(E_i) > 0 \; \forall i$, then for any event $F \in \mathbb{F}$, we can write

$$\mathbb{P}(F) = \sum_{i=1}^{n} \mathbb{P}(F|E_i)\mathbb{P}(E_i)$$

The Bayes Rule is an important result on conditional probabilities which states that for any two events $E, F \in \mathbb{F}$ such that $\mathbb{P}(E) > 0$ and $\mathbb{P}(F) > 0$,

$$\mathbb{P}(E|F) = \frac{\mathbb{P}(F|E)\mathbb{P}(E)}{\mathbb{P}(F)}$$

$\mathbb{P}(E)$ is called the prior; $\mathbb{P}(E|F)$ is called the posterior; $\mathbb{P}(F|E)\mathbb{P}(E)$ represents the support F provides to E.

An immediate extension of Bayes' rule is when the sets $E_1, E_2, \ldots, E_n$ are mutually exclusive such that $\cup_{i=1}^{n} E_i = \Omega$ and $\mathbb{P}(E_i) > 0 \; \forall i$. In such a case, we have for $i = 1, \ldots, n$,

$$\mathbb{P}(E_i|F) = \frac{\mathbb{P}(F|E_i)\mathbb{P}(E_i)}{\sum_{i=1}^{n} \mathbb{P}(F|E_i)\mathbb{P}(E_i)}$$

Suppose we have a random vector $X_1, \ldots, X_n$. Define the random variable X as:

$$\mathbb{P}\{X = (s_1, \ldots, s_n)\} = \mathbb{P}\{X_1 = s_1; \ldots; X_n = s_n\}$$

This is called a joint probability distribution. If $X_1, \ldots, X_n$ are mutually independent, then $\forall (s_1, \ldots, s_n)$, we will have:

$$\mathbb{P}\{X = (s_1, \ldots, s_n)\} = \mathbb{P}\{X_1 = s_1\} \ldots \mathbb{P}\{X_n = s_n\}$$

The probabilities $\mathbb{P}\{X_i = s_i\}$ are called the marginal probabilities. Also, given that $X_1, \ldots, X_n$ are mutually independent random variables, we can define the following joint distributions with the probability mass functions:

- $\mathbb{P}\{X_1 = x_1\}\mathbb{P}\{X_2 = x_2\}$
- $\mathbb{P}\{X_1 = x_1\}\mathbb{P}\{X_2 = x_2\}\mathbb{P}\{X_3 = x_3\}$
- $\ldots$
- $\mathbb{P}\{X_1 = x_1\} \ldots \mathbb{P}\{X_n = x_n\}$

33.2 Linear Algebra

We present here a few key concepts in linear algebra. For the sake of brevity, we avoid defining a vector space here. The books [1, 2] must be consulted for more details.

Suppose $V = \{v_1, v_2, \ldots\}$ is a set of vectors and I is the index set $\{1, 2, \ldots\}$ for V. We say a vector x can be expressed as a linear combination of vectors in V if there are real numbers λ_i $(i \in I)$ such that not all λ_i are zero and

$$x = \sum_{i \in I} \lambda_i v_i$$

The set of all vectors that can be expressed as a linear combination of vectors in V is called the span of V and denoted by $\mathrm{span}(V)$.

Linear Independence and Linear Dependence

A finite set of vectors $V = \{v_1, v_2, \ldots, v_n\}$ is said to be linearly dependent if there exist $\lambda_i (i \in I)$, not all zero, such that

$$\sum_{i \in I} \lambda_i v_i = 0.$$

A finite set of vectors $V = \{v_1, v_2, \ldots, v_n\}$ is said to be linearly independent if they are not linearly dependent.

Example 33.1. The set $\{(1, 0, 0), (0, 1, 0), (0, 0, 1)\}$ is linearly independent. The set $\{(5, 0, 0), (0, 1, 0), (0, 0, 10)\}$ is linearly independent. The set $\{(1, 0, 0), (0, 1, 0), (1, 1, 0)\}$ is linearly dependent. The set $\{(1, 0, 0), (0, 1, 0), (5, 6, 0)\}$ is also linearly dependent. $\square$

Rank

The rank of a set of vectors V is the cardinality of a largest subset of linearly independent vectors in V.

Basis

Let V be a set of vectors and B a finite linearly independent subset of V. The set B is said to be a maximal linearly independent set if

$$B \cup \{x\} \text{ is linearly dependent } \forall x \in V \setminus B$$

A basis of V is a maximal linearly independent subset of V. It can be shown that every vector space $V \subseteq \mathbb{R}^n$ has a basis and if B is a basis of V, then $\text{span}(V) = \text{span}(B)$. Moreover if B and B' are two bases of V, then $|B| = |B'| = \text{rank}(V)$. The cardinality of the set B is called the dimension of V.

33.3 Linear Programming and Duality

A linear program (LP) consists of

- a set of variables $x_1, x_2, \ldots, x_n \in \mathbb{R}$,
- a linear objective function

$$\sum_{i=1}^{n} c_i x_i$$

  where $c_1, c_2, \ldots, c_n \in \mathbb{R}$ are known real numbers (called weights), and
- a set of linear constraints that weighted sums of variables must satisfy.

A linear program in canonical form is described by

$$\begin{aligned} \text{minimize} \quad & cx \\ \text{subject to} \quad & Ax \geq b \\ & x \geq 0 \end{aligned}$$

where

$$c = [c_1 \ldots c_n]; \quad x = [x_1 \ldots x_n]^T; \quad A = [a_{ij}]_{m \times n}; \quad b = [b_1 \ldots b_m]^T.$$

A linear program in standard form is described by

$$\begin{aligned} \text{minimize} \quad & cx \\ \text{subject to} \quad & Ax = b \\ & x \geq 0 \end{aligned}$$

The following is a typical maximization version of a linear program:

$$\begin{aligned} \text{maximize} \quad & cx \\ \text{subject to} \quad & Ax \leq b \\ & x \geq 0 \end{aligned}$$

A linear programming problem without an objective function is called a feasibility problem. A vector $x = (x_1 \ldots x_n)^T$ which satisfies the constraints is called a feasible solution. A feasible solution x that optimizes (minimizes or maximizes as the case may be) the objective function is called an optimal solution and is usually denoted by the vector $x^* = (x_1^*, \ldots, x_n^*)^T$.

The set of all feasible solutions of a linear program corresponds to a convex polyhedron in n-dimensional space. The constraints which are linear correspond to hyperplanes in the n-dimensional space.

As a consequence of the objective function being linear, any local optimum in the feasible space is also a global optimum. Furthermore, at least one optimal solution will exist at a vertex of the polyhedron.

The well known simplex algorithm for solving linear programs works as follows. The algorithm starts from a vertex and proceeds to neighboring vertices, each time improving the value of the objective function ("decreasing" in the case of minimization and "increasing" in the case of maximization) until an optimum is found. The worst case time complexity of the simplex algorithm is exponential in the number of variables and constraints.

Interior point methods solve linear programs by exploring the interior region of the polyhedron rather than vertices. Interior point methods with worst case polynomial time complexity have also been developed.

Duality in Linear Programs

Example 33.2. First we consider an example of an LP in canonical form:

$$\text{minimize } 6x_1 + 8x_2 - 10x_3$$
$$\text{subject to } 3x_1 + x_2 - x_3 \geq 4$$
$$5x_1 + 2x_2 - 7x_3 \geq 7$$
$$x_1, x_2, x_3 \geq 0$$

The dual of this LP is given by

$$\text{maximize } 4w_1 + 7w_2$$
$$\text{subject to } 3w_1 + 5w_2 \leq 6$$
$$w_1 + 2w_2 \leq 8$$
$$-w_1 - 7w_2 \leq -10$$
$$w_1, w_2 \geq 0$$

We now generalize this example in the following discussion. □

Given

$$c = [c_1 \ldots c_n]; \quad x = [x_1 \cdots x_n]^T$$
$$A = [a_{ij}]_{m \times n}; \quad b = [b_1 \cdots b_m]^T$$
$$w = [w_1 \cdots w_m]$$

the primal LP in canonical form is:

$$\text{minimize } cx$$
$$\text{subject to } Ax \geq b$$
$$x \geq 0.$$

The dual of the above primal is given by

$$\text{maximize } wb$$
$$\text{subject to } wA \leq c$$
$$w \geq 0.$$

A primal LP in standard form is

$$\text{minimize } cx$$
$$\text{subject to } Ax = b$$
$$x \geq 0.$$

The dual of the above primal is:

$$\text{maximize } wb$$
$$\text{subject to } wA \leq c$$
$$w \quad \text{unrestricted}$$

The above forms appear in the maxminimization and minmaximization problems in matrix games (Chapter 9). It is a simple matter to show that the dual of the dual of a (primal) problem is the original (primal) problem itself. We now state a few important results concerning duality, which are relevant to our requirements.

Weak Duality Theorem

If the primal is a maximization problem, then the value of any feasible primal solution is less than or equal to the value of any feasible dual solution. If the primal is a minimization problem, then the value of any feasible primal solution is greater than or equal to the value of any feasible dual solution.

Strong Duality Theorem

Given a primal and its dual, if one of them has an optimal solution then the other also has an optimal solution and the values of the optimal solutions are the same. Note that this is the key result which is used in proving the minimax theorem.

Fundamental Theorem of Duality

Given a primal and its dual, exactly one of the following statements is true.

(1) Both possess optimal solution (say x^* and w^*) with $cx^* = w^*b$.
(2) One problem has unbounded objective value in which case the other must be infeasible.
(3) Both problems are infeasible.

33.4 Mathematical Analysis

Metric Space

A metric space (V, d) consists of a set V and a mapping $d : V \times V \to \mathbb{R}$ such that $\forall x, y, z \in V$, the following holds.

(1) $d(x, y) \geq 0$
(2) $d(x, y) = 0$ iff $x = y$
(3) $d(x, y) = d(y, x)$
(4) $d(x, z) \leq d(x, y) + d(y, z)$

The mapping d is called a *metric* or *distance* function. It may be noted that the first condition above follows from the other three.

Open Ball

Given a metric space (V, d), an open ball of radius $r > 0$ and center $x \in V$, is the set $B(x, r) = \{y \in V : d(x, y) < r\}$.

Open Set

An open set X in a metric space (V, d) is a subset of V such that we can find, at each $x \in X$, an open ball that is contained in X.

Bounded Set

A subset X of a metric space (V, d) is said to be bounded if X is completely contained in some open ball, around 0, with a finite radius.

Closed Set

A subset X of a metric space V is said to be a closed set iff every convergent sequence in X converges to a point which lies in X. That is, for all sequences $\{x_k\}$ in X such that $x_k \to x$ for some $x \in V$, it will happen that $x \in X$. It may be noted that a set X is closed iff the complement set $X^c = V \setminus X$ is an open set.

Compact Set

Given a subset X of a metric space (V, d), X is said to be compact if every sequence of points in X has a convergent subsequence. A key result is that if the metric space V is $\mathbb{R}^n$ (under the Euclidean metric), then a subset X is compact iff it is closed and bounded.

Example 33.3 (Compact Sets). The closed interval $[0, 1]$ is compact. None of the sets $[0, \infty)$, $(0, 1)$, $(0, 1]$, $[0, 1)$, $(-\infty, \infty)$ is compact. Observe that the sets $[0, \infty)$ and $(-\infty, \infty)$ are closed but not bounded. Any finite subset of $\mathbb{R}$ is compact. $\square$

A Useful Result

Let $X \subset \mathbb{R}^n$ and let $f : X \to \mathbb{R}^k$ be a continuous function. Then the image of a compact set under f is also compact.

Weierstrass Theorem

Let $X \subset \mathbb{R}^n$ and let $f : X \to \mathbb{R}$ be a continuous function. If X is compact, then f has and attains a maximum and a minimum in X.

Convexity

Convex Combination

Given $x_1, \ldots, x_m \in \mathbb{R}^n$, a point $y \in \mathbb{R}^n$ is called a convex combination of $x_1, \ldots, x_m$ if there exist numbers $\lambda_1, \ldots, \lambda_m \in \mathbb{R}$ such that

(1) $\lambda_i \geq 0, \quad i = 1, \ldots, m$
(2) $\sum_{i=1}^{m} \lambda_i = 1$
(3) $y = \sum_{i=1}^{m} \lambda_i x_i$

Convex Set

A set $X \subset \mathbb{R}^n$ is said to be convex if the convex combination of any two points in X is also in X. The above definition immediately implies that a finite set with two or more elements cannot be convex. Intuitively, the set X is convex if the straight line segment joining any two points in X is completely contained in X.

Example 33.4 (Convex Sets). A singleton set is always convex. The intervals $(0, 1)$, $(0, 1]$, $[0, 1)$, $[0, 1]$ are all convex. The set $X = \{x \in \mathbb{R}^2 : ||x|| < 1\}$ is convex. The set $X = \{x \in \mathbb{R}^2 : ||x|| = 1\}$ is not convex. □

Concave and Convex Functions

Let $X \subset \mathbb{R}^n$ be a convex set. A function $f : X \to \mathbb{R}$ is said to be concave iff $\forall x, y \in X$ and $\forall \lambda \in (0, 1)$,

$$f[\lambda x + (1 - \lambda)y] \geq \lambda f(x) + (1 - \lambda)f(y)$$

f is said to be convex iff $\forall x, y \in X$ and $\forall \lambda \in (0, 1)$

$$f[\lambda x + (1 - \lambda)y] \leq \lambda f(x) + (1 - \lambda)f(y)$$

An alternative definition for convex and concave functions is as follows. If $X \subset \mathbb{R}^n$ is a convex set and $f : X \to \mathbb{R}$ is a function, define

$$\text{sub } f = \{(x, y) : x \in X, y \in \mathbb{R}, f(x) \geq y\}$$
$$\text{epi } f = \{(x, y) : x \in X, y \in \mathbb{R}, f(x) \leq y\}$$

f is *concave* if sub f is *convex* ; f is *convex* if epi f is *convex*.

Example 33.5 (Convex and concave sets). The function $f_1(x) = x^3, x \in \mathbb{R}$ is neither convex nor concave. The function $f_2(x) = ax + b, x \in \mathbb{R}^n$ and $a, b \in \mathbb{R}$ is both convex and concave. The function $f_3 : \mathbb{R}^+ \to \mathbb{R}$ defined by $f_3(x) = x^\alpha$ where $\mathbb{R}^+$ is the set of all positive real numbers is concave for $0 < \alpha < 1$ and convex for $\alpha > 1$. If $\alpha = 1$, then f_3 is both concave and convex. $\square$

Some Results on Convexity

Suppose $X \subset \mathbb{R}^n$ is a convex set. Then:

(1) A function $f : X \to \mathbb{R}$ is concave iff the function $-f$ is convex.
(2) Let $f : X \to \mathbb{R}$ be concave or convex. If X is an open set, then f is continuous on X. If X is not an open set, then f is continuous on the interior of X.

Quasi-Concavity and Quasi-Convexity

Let $X \subset \mathbb{R}^n$ be a convex set and let $f : X \to \mathbb{R}$ be a function. The *upper contour set* of f at $a \in \mathbb{R}$ is defined as

$$U_f(a) = \{x \in X : f(x) \geq a\}$$

The *lower contour set* of f at $a \in \mathbb{R}$ is defined as

$$L_f(a) = \{x \in X : f(x) \leq a\}$$

A function $f : X \to \mathbb{R}$ is said to be *quasi-concave* if $U_f(a)$ is convex for all $a \in \mathbb{R}$ and is said to be *quasi-convex* if $L_f(a)$ is convex for all $a \in \mathbb{R}$.

Alternatively, $f : X \to \mathbb{R}$ is *quasi-concave* on X iff $\forall \, x, y \in X$ and $\forall \, \lambda \in (0, 1)$,

$$f[\lambda x + (1 - \lambda)y] \geq \min(f(x), f(y))$$

and *quasi-convex* on X iff $\forall x, y \in X$ and $\forall \lambda \in (0, 1)$,

$$f[\lambda x + (1 - \lambda)y] \leq \max(f(x), f(y))$$

It can be immediately noted that every convex (concave) function is quasi-convex (quasi-concave).

Example 33.6 (Quasi-concave and Quasi-convex sets). The function $f(x) = x^3$ on $\mathbb{R}$ is quasi-convex and also quasi-concave on $\mathbb{R}$. But it is neither convex nor concave on $\mathbb{R}$. Note that the upper contour set and also the lower contour set are both convex and hence the function is both quasi-convex and quasi-concave. Also, for every pair of points x_1 and x_2, the values of the function for points between x_1 and x_2 lie between $\min(f(x_1), f(x_2))$ and $\max(f(x_1), f(x_2))$ and therefore the function is both quasi-convex and quasi-concave. Any non-decreasing function $f : \mathbb{R} \to \mathbb{R}$ is quasi-convex and quasi-concave. But it need not be convex and need not be concave. $\square$

33.5   Computational Complexity Classes

$\mathbb{P}, \mathbb{NP},$ *and* $\mathbb{NPC}$

The notion of $\mathbb{NP}$-completeness is studied in the framework of decision problems. Most problems we are typically interested in are optimization problems. In order to apply the theory of $\mathbb{NP}$-completeness, we have to recast optimization problems as decision problems.

Example 33.7. Consider the problem SPATH that finds, given an unweighted, undirected graph $G = (V, E)$ and two vertices $u, v \in V$, a shortest path between u and v. An instance of SPATH consists of a particular graph and two vertices of that graph. A given instance may have no solution, exactly one solution, or multiple solutions. A decision problem PATH related to optimization problem SPATH will be : given a graph $G = (V, E)$ and two vertices $u, v \in V$, and a non-negative integer k, does there exist a path between u and v of length at most k? The decision problem PATH is one way of transforming the original optimization problem into a decision problem. $\square$

If an optimization problem is easy, then its related decision problem is easy as well. Similarly, if there is evidence that a decision problem is hard, then its related optimization problem is hard.

The classes $\mathbb{P}$ *and* $\mathbb{NP}$

The complexity of an algorithm is said to be polynomially bounded if its worst case complexity is bounded by a polynomial function of the input size. The common reference model used here is a deterministic Turing machine. $\mathbb{P}$ is the set of all problems which are solvable in polynomial time on a deterministic Turing machine.

$\mathbb{NP}$ represents the class of decision problems which can be solved in polynomial time by a non-deterministic Turing machine. A non-deterministic Turing machine makes the right guesses on every move and races towards the solution much faster than a deterministic Turing model. An equivalent definition of $\mathbb{NP}$ is : $\mathbb{NP}$ is the set of all decision problems whose solutions can be verified in polynomial time. More specifically, given a candidate solution to the problem (call it certificate), one can verify in polynomial time (on a deterministic Turing machine) whether the answer to the decision problem is YES or NO.

Clearly, $\mathbb{P} \subseteq \mathbb{NP}$. However it is unknown whether $\mathbb{NP} = \mathbb{P}$. This is currently the most celebrated open problem in computer science.

Reducibility of Problems

Suppose we have an algorithm for solving a problem Y. We are given a problem X and assume that there is a function T that takes an input x for X and produces $T(x)$ which is an input for Y, such that the correct answer for X on x is YES if and only if the correct answer for Y on $T(x)$ is YES. Then by using T and the algorithm for Y, we have an algorithm for X. If the function T can be computed in polynomially bounded time (on a deterministic Turing machine), we say X is polynomially reducible to Y and we write

$$X \leq_P Y$$

If $X \leq_P Y$, the implication is that Y is at least as hard to solve as X. That is, X is no harder to solve than Y. Clearly

$$X \leq_P Y \text{ and } Y \in \mathbb{P} \Longrightarrow X \in \mathbb{P}$$

NP-*hard and* NP-*complete Problems*

A decision problem Y is said to be NP-hard if $X \leq_P Y, \ \forall X \in \mathbb{NP}$. An NP-hard problem Y is said to be NP-complete if $Y \in \mathbb{NP}$. The set of all NP-complete problems is denoted by $\mathbb{NPC}$.

Note. Informally, an NP-hard problem is a problem that is at least as hard as any problem in NP. If, in addition, the problem belongs to NP, it would be called NP-complete.

Note. In order to show that a decision problem Y is NP-complete, it is enough we find a decision problem $X \in \mathbb{NPC}$ such that $X \leq_P Y$ and $Y \in \mathbb{NP}$.

Note. If it turns out that any single problem in $\mathbb{NPC}$ is in $\mathbb{P}$, then $\mathbb{NP} = \mathbb{P}$.

Note. An alternative way of characterizing $\mathbb{NPC}$ is that it is the set of all decision problems $Y \in \mathbb{NP}$ such that $X \leq_P Y$ where X is any NP-complete problem.

A List of NP-*complete Problems*

Here is a list of popular problems whose decision versions are NP-complete.

(1) 3-SAT (Boolean satisfiability problem with three variables)
(2) Knapsack problem
(3) Traveling salesman problem
(4) Vertex cover problem
(5) Graph coloring problem
(6) Steiner tree problem
(7) Weighted set packing problem
(8) Weighted set covering problem

33.6 Summary and References

In this appendix, we have provided key definitions and results from probability theory, linear algebra, linear programming, mathematical analysis, and computational complexity. While these definitions and results serve as a ready reference, the reader is urged to look up numerous scholarly textbooks which are available in the area. We only mention a few sample texts here:

- Probability [3]
- Linear Algebra [1, 2]
- Linear Programming [4]
- Mathematical Analysis [5]
- Computational Complexity [6, 7]

The books by Vohra [8], Sundaram [9], and by Mas-Colell, Whinston, and Green [10] are excellent references as well for many of the mathematical preliminaries.

References

[1]   Kenneth M. Hoffman and Ray Kunze. *Linear Algebra*. Prentice Hall, Second Edition, 1971.
[2]   Gilbert Strang. *Introduction to Linear Algebra*. Wellesley-Cambridge Publishers, Fourth Edition, 2009.
[3]   Sheldon M. Ross. *A First Course in Probability*. Pearson, Eighth Edition, 2010.
[4]   Vasek Chvatal. *Linear Programming*. W.H. Freeman & Company, 1983.
[5]   Walter Rudin. *Principles of Mathematical Analysis*. McGraw-Hill International Edition, Third Edition, 1976.
[6]   Michael R. Garey and David S. Johnson. *Computers and Intractability: A Guide to the Theory of NP-Completeness*. W. H. Freeman and Company, 1979.
[7]   Thomas H. Cormen, Charles E. Leiserson, Ronald L. Rivest, and Clifford Stein. *Introduction to Algorithms*. The MIT Press and McGraw-Hill, Third Edition, 2009.
[8]   Rakesh Vohra. *Advanced Mathematical Economics*. Cambridge University Press, 2009.
[9]   Rangarajan K. Sundaram. *A First Course in Optimization Theory*. Cambridge University Press, 1996.
[10]   Andreu Mas-Colell, Michael D. Whinston, and Jerry R. Green. *Microeconomic Theory*. Oxford University Press, 1995.

Index

Printed in the United States
By Bookmasters